second edition

ACCOUNTING INFORMATION SYSTEMS
Theory and Practice

Robert A. Leitch
University of South Carolina

K. Roscoe Davis
University of Georgia

Prentice Hall, Englewood Cliffs, New Jersey 07632

Library of Congress Cataloging-in-Publication Data

Leitch, Robert A.
    Accounting information systems : theory and practice / Robert A.
Leitch, K. Roscoe Davis. -- 2nd ed.
        p.   cm.
    Includes bibliographical references and index.
    ISBN 0-13-006032-1
    1. Accounting--Data processing.   I. Davis, K. Roscoe
II. Title.
HF5679.L38   1992
657'.0285--dc20

                                                          91-25982
                                                              CIP

Editorial/production supervision
  and interior design: Shelly Kupperman
Cover design: Wanda Lubelska Design
Prepress buyer: Trudy Pisciotti
Manufacturing buyer: Bob Anderson
Acquisitions editor: Joseph Heider
Acquisitions assistant: Linda Albelli
Copy editor: Sandy Di Somma

©1992, 1983 by Prentice Hall, Inc.
A Simon & Schuster Company
Englewood Cliffs, New Jersey 07632

Printed in the United States of America
10 9 8 7 6 5 4 3 2 1

ISBN   0-13-006032-1

Prentice Hall International (UK) Limited, *London*
Prentice Hall of Australia Pry. Limited, *Sydney*
Prentice Hall Canada Inc., *Toronto*
Prentice Hall Hispanoamericana, S.A., *Mexico*
Prentice Hall of India Private Limited, *New Delhi*
Prentice Hall of Japan, Inc., *Tokyo*
Simon & Schuster Asia Pte. Ltd., *Singapore*
Editors Prentice Hall do Brasil, Ltda., *Rio de Janiero*

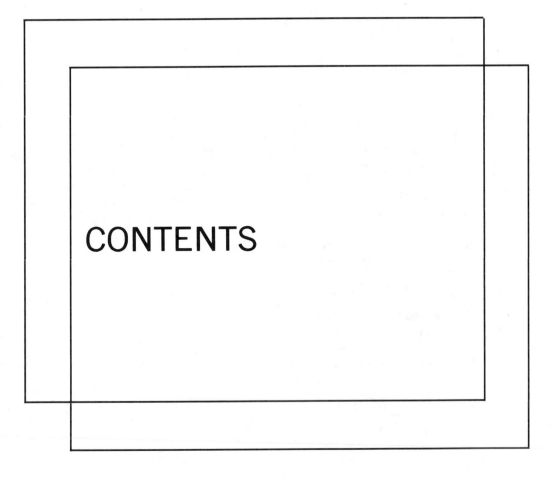

CONTENTS

9   FILE MANAGEMENT ACCOUNTING SYSTEMS   233

10   DATABASE ACCOUNTING INFORMATION SYSTEMS   254

13 STRUCTURED SYSTEMS ANALYSIS AND DESIGN CONCEPTS: DESIGN AND IMPLEMENTATION   379

14 PRODUCTION AND INVENTORY SYSTEMS   426

15   MARKETING SYSTEMS AND THE REVENUE CYCLE   472

16   FINANCIAL INFORMATION SYSTEMS   519

17   DECISION SUPPORT SYSTEMS   551

20   COMPUTER AUDITING   684

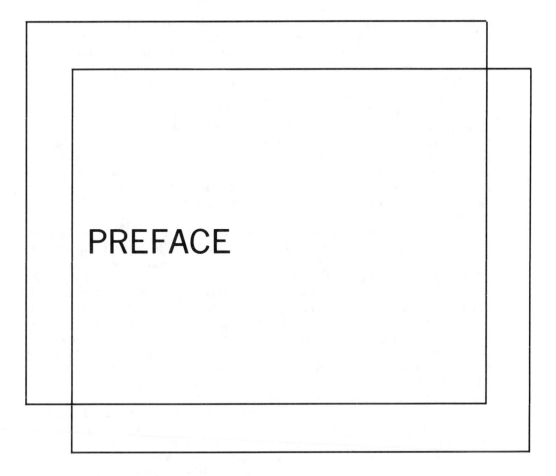

PREFACE

Accounting information systems support the transaction processing, reporting, and decision-making systems of most organizations. To support these management systems and their requirements effectively, an accountant must be able to integrate data processing elements with managerial activities within the decision-making and organizational framework of the organization.

This text provides a conceptual framework for integrating all the elements required to support accounting information systems. These are: hardware, software, database, controls, procedures, and personnel. The framework builds on the premise that the elements should be organized to support the transaction processing, reporting, and decision-making requirements of the organization. This framework is well-founded in management information systems design theory, and it is the focal point of all the discussion in the text.

The objective of this text is to expose students to the elements that constitute an accounting system and the theory upon which a system should be designed and organized. The material is also written for the education of current or future practitioners who will deal with challenging systems design and operation problems of clients or their own organizations.

The text encompasses six major areas: (1) a theoretical framework for accounting systems; (2) procedures for systems analysis and design that are founded on organizational and behavioral concepts; (3) accounting and management information requirements that follow from transaction processing, reporting, and decision-making needs; (4) information technology and database concepts; (5) a broad spectrum of accounting systems applications; and (6) internal control structure and EDP auditing. The text covers the entire range of accounting systems from small, ledgerless bookkeeping systems to complex decision support systems used by large international corporations. This coverage includes marketing, production, financial, and personnel accounting systems. Moreover, microcomputer as well as mainframe computer networks are illustrated.

The sequence followed in the text begins with a discussion of the importance and the use of accounting information. This is followed by an outline of general systems theory and a framework for the development of an effective and efficient accounting information system. This general framework is followed by several chapters on systems elements and information technology (Chapters 3 to 10). It is important that accountants have an understanding of the organizational concepts, behavioral factors, decision-making processes, and communication theory prior to initiating any systems analysis, design, and implementation activities. Moreover, it is important that they understand the value of information to the organization in today's competitive environment. These concepts are reviewed in Chapters 3 and 4. It is also important that a student have a basic understanding of information technology, including microcomputer developments such as local area networks (Chapters 5 and 6). Chapter 7 is designed to introduce students to various modes of data processing as well as the communication hardware and networks involved in distributed processing. Accountants must also have a working knowledge of flowcharting and documentation concepts. These topics are covered in detail in Chapter 8. File management and database system form the basis for more and more accounting information systems, thus, it is essential that accounting students have an understanding of these systems (Chapters 9 and 10).

Since one of the major roles of accountants is the evaluation of accounting systems, this text gives considerable emphasis to an accounting and information systems control structure. In addition to the detailed discussion of control structure in Chapter 11, the risks associated with various transaction processing cycles and database systems are emphasized throughout the text. The control structure discussion is founded on SAS 55.

Structured systems analysis and design procedures are used to integrate the theoretical and technical material in the text. Chapters 12 and 13 set forth a structured set of procedures for the analysis, design, and implementation of accounting systems. The philosophy upon which these chapters are built is that a well-conceived, designed, and implemented system will go a long way toward achieving the control that management and accountants desire for an organization.

An application section is presented in the final section of the book. The objective is to integrate the theoretical, organizational, decision-making, technical, and design concepts of previous chapters. The emphasis here is on the characteristics of systems that are required to meet the various transaction processing, reporting, and decision-making needs of management. Examples are used to demonstrate the achievement of these objectives. Manual, batch, on-line, database, and distributed processing accounting systems, are all illustrated.

Many of the illustrations and cases used in this section have been abstracted from actual business situations. They include microcomputer as well as mainframe examples. Chapters 14 and 15 concentrate on logistical and marketing systems and their respective processing cycles. Contemporary JIT logistics systems as well as microcomputer sales order-entry systems are illustrated for special emphasis. Financial management systems are discussed in Chapter 16. The financial accounting aspects of accounts receivable, accounts payable, payroll, inventory, general ledger, and facilities management transaction processing systems are emphasized in Chapter 16. A complete financial accounting system for a microcomputer is provided in an appendix to Chapter 19 for small businesses to illustrate financial information requirements. Decision support systems with a special emphasis on budgeting, financial planning, and modeling systems that are used for managerial and strategic decision making are described in Chapter 17. Newer developments in artificial intelligence which are designed to help management make decisions are also reviewed here. Large and complex distributed processing accounting systems that rely on electronic data interchange and integrate a number of functional areas are illustrated in Chapter 18. Chapter 19 focuses on systems that are required to satisfy the special needs of small businesses. All of these applications chapters emphasize the effective use of an accounting system to meet the information needs of management with respect to transaction processing, reporting, and decision making. Finally, an introduction to key aspects of EDP auditing is presented in Chapter 20.

In summary, some of the special features of this text are:

1. A theoretical framework for systems development.
2. A structured approach to systems analysis and design.
3. An emphasis on the control structure set forth in SAS 55.
4. A chapter on data flow diagrams and system flowcharting.
5. A chapter on organizational and behavioral theory related to systems design.
6. A chapter on decision-making and communication concepts that are essential to an effective accounting information system.
7. A substantive review of systems hardware and software including microcomputers and networks.
8. Two chapters on file management and database systems.
9. A complete discussion of small entrepreneurial accounting systems with a microcomputer illustration.

10. A chapter of decision support systems with an emphasis on financial planning systems.
11. A detailed discussion of large complex distributed processing accounting systems.
12. Cases and examples based on actual experience.
13. Many cases that require the student to integrate knowledge from several chapters, such as flowcharting, system design, control structure, database, and software concepts.
14. Many CPA and CMA questions.
15. Several cases requiring the use of common microcomputer software to give the students hands-on experience in the development and use of accounting information systems.

This text is designed for either a one-semester or a one-quarter junior, senior, or introductory graduate level course. With the addition of outside readings and extensive EDP or system design projects, the text can easily be used for a two-semester or two-quarter course sequence in accounting systems.

This text assumes that students have had a basic course in computers or computer programming. An elementary understanding of computer processing is assumed; Chapters 5, 6, and 7 are designed for an update and review. If a student has no prior background, a supplement may be used to develop the computer basics. The text also assumes that students have had some accounting course work so that they have a very basic understanding of the various transaction processing accounting cycles.

The text is flexible enough that the instructor can select subsets of chapters, depending on the background of the students, the material to be introduced, the level at which the course is to be taught, and the credit hours to be assigned. For example, if the course follows an in-depth course in computers, Chapters 5, 6, 7, and 8 may be used only for review. If it follows an auditing course in which internal control is stressed, Chapter 11 may be reviewed lightly. If it precedes an auditing course the control chapter and the EDP audit chapter serve as excellent introductions to these aspects of auditing. On the other hand, if the instructor is pressed for time, Chapter 4, the technology chapters, and a few of the application chapters may be either skipped or treated lightly.

Moreover, the sequence may be altered. For example, the flowcharting chapter may be taught at an earlier point in time, and the chapter on small business may follow either Chapter 13 or 16 if the students need the background earlier in the semester for a project. In addition some like to delay Chapter 4 and use it as an introduction to Chapter 17 on decision support systems.

In summary, the core of the text is contained in Chapters 1, 2, 3, 8, 9, 10, 11, 12, 13, 14, 15, 16, and 17. The other chapters build upon and support this basic framework.

The overall objective of the text is to develop a sound framework for the analysis, design, and review of accounting information systems. Based on this framework, the objective is then to show the student how to analyze, design, and implement accounting information systems that satisfy the transaction processing, reporting, and decision-making requirements of management. In addition, the objective is to provide accounting students with a better understanding of accounting systems and their related controls and to enable them to more effectively audit accounting systems.

Robert A. Leitch
K. Roscoe Davis

INFORMATION PROCESSING: AN OVERVIEW

INTRODUCTION

Accounting information systems have undergone significant changes during the last several years due to rapid changes in the business and government environment and in the technology of computer systems. As a result, the roles of the controller and the public accountant have greatly expanded in terms of information processing, information utilization, information system design, and information system review. Today accountants have at their disposal data processing power that was considered a farfetched dream several years ago. This is true whether the accountant's role is in auditing; providing information to decision makers through managerial accounting systems; providing financial statements to investors and other interested parties; or in designing systems which enable management to engage in a variety of transaction processing, reporting, and decision-making activities.

Several major developments have led to these changing roles. First, there have been many major advances in computer technology. The first bulky, slow-speed electromechanical computers of the 1940s and 1950s have been replaced with large, high-speed electronic computers that provide billions of bits of storage with rapid access and execution times. Even small desk-top microcomputers today have far more capacity for processing information than these early computers. This growth in computer technology has resulted in expanded capabilities in information processing. Payroll, accounts receivable, and accounts payable processing applications were novel ideas in the mid-1950s; today they are routine. Today large, complex integrated and/or distributed systems support a whole array of managerial decision-making, reporting, and transaction processing activities.

Recent innovations in computer chip technology have led this increase in power and corresponding reduction in cost of processing capability. Large-scale integrated chips have led to the cost reduction of microcomputers and their explosive growth. These advances in chip technology have enabled many more users to gain access to the power of the computer because these advances have led to much more user friendly software for accounting and decision-making activities.

The advent of large fast supercomputers has led the way for sophisticated decision support systems for corporate planning and for the development of artificial intelligence systems for accounting activities such as auditing and accounting system development.

The explosive growth of microcomputers has placed the power of the computer and its wealth of easy-to-use personal productivity software in the hands of virtually every manager and accountant in the country. This software includes spreadsheets for analysis, graphics for presentation, word processing for reporting and presentation, communication for coordination of activities, and databases for the management of information. Due to their low cost virtually every small business can now make effective use of microcomputers and their easy-to-use personal productivity, communication, and accounting software. Accountants must now audit these systems, help clients design and make effective use of these small systems, and use microcomputers to audit systems and to generate managerial information.

In addition significant technological advances and cost reductions in storage have enabled management to store and access vast amounts of information for decision making.

Advances in communications equipment and software have enabled managers in widely distributed locations to communicate effectively. Furthermore, the development of local area networks have enabled those in one location to share hardware resources such as laser printers and file servers, to share software such as accounting packages, to share common data such as accounting records, and to communicate with fellow employees via electronic mail.

Software has become more user friendly, enabling many employees to access information and in some cases to develop their own application programs. Database management systems have enabled managers and accountants to access and use vast amounts of data more easily. Moreover, recent developments in database technology have made these tasks even easier. These new developments in software database, technology, and storage have enabled accounting information systems to be more integrated and to use common databases.

Because of these developments, the computer can now be used more effectively to support complex and unstructured types of decisions via decision support systems. Moreover, the advent of many of these technological break-throughs, particularly in the software and database areas, has led to the rapid growth of end-user systems. A manager, using these systems, can more easily interact with the organization's data and in some cases even design their own application programs for their decision-making needs.

On the negative side, these developments have led to a significant increase in the complexity of accounting information systems. Thus, even though they are generally easier to use, they are often more difficult to design and to audit. To counter this increase in complexity new approaches in systems analysis and design procedures have been developed to facilitate the efficient design and effective implementation of these new accounting information systems. Moreover, new concepts of internal control have evolved to deal with these complexities.

The contrast between the traditional accounting information system and those systems which are evolving from the advances in technology cited here, and the need to deal with a much more complex organizational environment, is shown in Figure 1-1. Under the traditional system, the accounting system constituted the only formal aspect of a firm's information system. Only financial data were collected, classified, stored, and processed. The financial reporting component of the information system was transaction oriented and consisted mostly of historical records and financial reports. Information generated for planning and control activities was generally developed from a separate set of data on management activities. Management information outside the quantitative realm was often generated and transmitted via informal channels to various users.

Due primarily to the development of sophisticated computer hardware and to developments in information processing technology, this simple system has evolved into large, complex integrated database accounting information systems like that illustrated in Figure 1-1. All managerial levels in organizations can now access transaction data stored in the system via report generators. The transaction data now includes much more data on production, marketing, financial, and personnel activities. Often the data is analyzed using complex decision-making models which integrate data from many sources. These systems can even be further complicated by the wide dispersion of these activities in a distributed system spread over many states. Under the traditional system, the accountant was primarily a provider of information; under the complex integrated systems, the accountant is a user, provider, and designer of the information system. Many accounting systems today are integrated or at least interface with most other formal information systems via the data collection, processing, and reporting process as well as in the storage of information in a common database.

To understand contemporary accounting information systems, an introduction to basic systems concepts is important. It needs to be emphasized that accounting information is a key resource which often has strategic significance. Given this basis we can define accounting information and the role of accountants in the analysis, design, use, and audit of accounting information systems. A general definition of information systems and a look at some historic developments that have supported the development of information are also necessary. The relationship of these developments to accounting systems and the typical transaction processing cycle also needs to be identified.

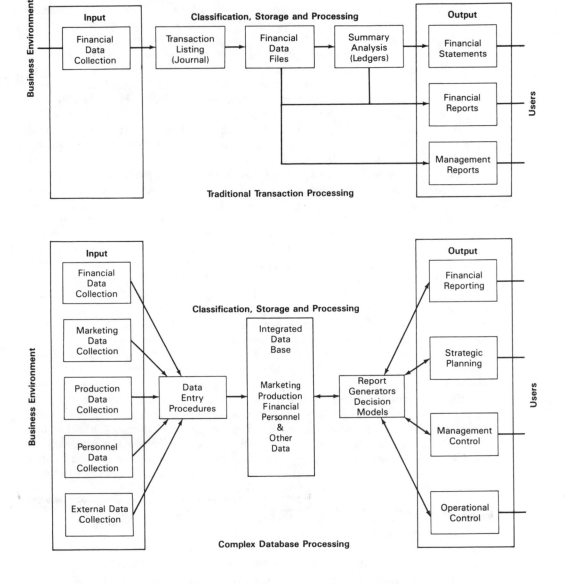

FIGURE 1-1 Traditional transaction processing vs. complex database accounting information system.
Source: Adapted from an article appearing in *Cost and Management,* by Thomas Lin and William Harper, November/December 1981 edition, by permission of the Society of Management Accountants of Canada.

In general this text is designed to prepare the accounting student to use, manage, and design accounting information systems in today's organizational environment using the latest in hardware, software, and systems technology and theory.

MANAGEMENT USE OF ACCOUNTING INFORMATION

Management uses accounting information for decision making, planning, and control activities as well as for transaction processing activities related to the production of its goods and services. These activities involve transaction processing, decision making, reporting, and the incorporation of information into its product or service.

Transaction Processing

In almost any organization, day-to-day ongoing transactions, involving the purchase of supplies, the production of goods and services, the distribution and storage of finished products, and the sale of these goods and services, must be recorded for good control of an organization. Sales must be recorded, cash receipts posted, costs allocated to goods as they are produced, and employees paid for their services. These are but a sample of the numerous transactions necessary for the operation of any organization. Data associated with these activities constitute the basis of much of the data used in the accounting information system which provides useful information to management.

Decision-Making, Planning, and Control Activities

Planning precedes any activity whether it is strategic, managerial or operational. Objectives are determined, actions are set forth via the decision-making process, and resources necessary to implement the actions selected to accomplish the objectives are acquired. Control activities include both control of action through the planning, establishment of a budget, and the setting of standards or other performance criteria, and the feedback which compares the results of the action with the anticipated or planned outcome.

Many reports and other forms of information dissemination are used in this planning and control process. These include

1. *Routine or scheduled plans and reports* which communicate plans and expectations to management, as well as report the results of management's action.
2. *Inquiries* which enable management to access accounting data in a non-routine way as they need information that may not be routinely reported.
3. *Exception reports* which set forth only those deviations from planned results, so that management can concentrate on problems or opportunities.
4. *Predictive reports* which forecast the future of some activity.

Product and Service Use of Information

In addition to the traditional use of accounting information for transaction processing, planning, and control activities, information may also be used as an integral component of an organization's product or service. For example, a pharmacy may offer detailed records of transactions to customers for tax and insurance preparation.

STRATEGIC USE OF INFORMATION

Recently, the computational power of the computer has increased to the extent that information can be used as a strategic resource like technology, personnel, capital or fixed assets. Due to new technology available to managers, information can be used in many ways heretofore not considered. It can be used to process more information more rapidly to allow managers access to more information than they dreamed of several years ago. This new technology has enabled managers to analyze problems in much more sophisticated ways for more enlightened decision making.

According to Ives and Learmonth,[1] information from a contemporary marketing and production system can even alter the competitive balance in customer services, supplier relations, and product development. For example, it can be used to provide a unique service such as daily delivery of parts to an organization using a just-in-time manufacturing (JIT) system. It can be used to communicate directly with suppliers on the quality and quantity of components needed for manufacturing so that just the right amount of components arrive at the factory for manufacturing operations. It can be used to query and survey customers on their desires for product modifications. It can be used to target specific customers for promotional efforts for new product introductions, based on information kept on each of the organization's existing customers in an accounts receivable or customer file. As another example, the use of automatic teller machines (ATMs) in banking has increased entry barriers as a result of the cost of the equipment. ATM systems and the information they can generate have provided added service for users and have redefined the nature of customer service for the banking industry. In general, accounting information systems can offer information to help customers better manage their affairs. Using such tactics, an organization can gain a competitive edge as well as remain competitive,[2] that is, survive.

INFORMATION AS A RESOURCE

In general, we are now entering a new organizational era. *Information-based organizations* will become more and more prevalent in society according to Peter Drucker.[3] In the past, managers were faced with the time-consuming analysis of data in order to arrive at a decision, or they relied on periodic reports to help guide their analysis of problems and their decision making. Today, managers can access a wealth of data from their desk when they need it. The simple use of a wide variety of microcomputer programs has enabled managers to assess many

---

[1] Blake Ives and Gerard P. Learmonth, "The Information System as a Competitive Weapon," *Communications of the ACM*, December 1984.

[2] See Ives and Learmonth, "The Information System as a Competitive Weapon," pp. 1193–1201; F. Warren McFarland, "Information Technology Changes in the Way We Compete," *Harvard Business Review*, May–June 1984, pp. 98–103; James I. Cash and Been R. Konsynski, "IS Redraws Competitive Boundaries," *Harvard Business Review*, March–April 1985; and Michael E. Porter and Victor E. Millar, "How Information Gives You Competitive Advantage," *Harvard Business Review*, July–August 1985, pp. 149–160.

[3] Peter E. Drucker, "The Coming of the New Organization," *Harvard Business Review*, January–February 1988, pp. 45–53.

alternatives, based on this data, very quickly and arrive at a more informed decision. According to Drucker, this is just the beginning of a new trend where business will be run more and more by specialists who rely on information to manage the operations of the organization.

As a result, information has become a valuable organizational resource like equipment, financial capital, and personnel. It must be carefully acquired, managed, and utilized like all other valuable assets. To be effective the information obtained from the organizations' accounting information system must support the information needs of management. Management needs information for day-to-day transaction processing, for decision making, and for reporting. In addition, in today's information society, management can use information to enhance their organizations' competitive position. In summary, the accounting information system must meet management's needs to be of value to management; otherwise, it is like any other obsolete asset and should be replaced.

ACCOUNTING AND INFORMATION

Accounting Information

Based on the use of accounting information, an *accounting information system* may be defined as follows:

> That portion of the information system concerned with the measurement, analysis, and prediction of income, wealth, and other economic events of the organization and its subunits and entities.[4]

A narrow, more traditional definition would include only financial and transaction information, as shown in Figure 1–2. Regardless of the definition we adopt, it should be clear that the boundaries of the traditional accounting system have been expanded to include not only monetary items but all significant economic events that may be quantified and used for transaction processing, decision making, reporting, and adding value to the product or resource.

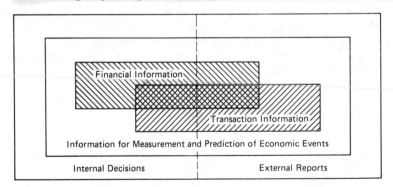

FIGURE 1-2 Accounting system for internal and external decisions and reports.

---

[4] "Report of the Committee on Accounting and Information Systems," *The Accounting Review Supplement,* 1971, pp. 289 and 290.

The Role of the Accountant

The role of the accountant has expanded due to the more pervasive impact of accounting information in all areas of business and due to the complexity and vast amount of information that can now be accessed for decision making. This changing role stems primarily from the technological breakthroughs mentioned earlier in this chapter. Traditionally accountants have been involved in

1. The attest function
2. Maintaining records on economic performance
3. The management, planning, and control function
4. Financial management
5. Designing and managing information systems
6. Supporting management decision making with timely and relevant information

In the past, emphasis has been on the first three, which embody auditing and financial and managerial accounting. Today, much more emphasis is placed on the latter three. Accountants have begun to use sophisticated financial planning models and large databases to assist in an organization's financial planning activities. Accounting firms now derive a large portion of their income from systems design and consulting activities. Accountants in general must be active in the design process to ensure adherence to effective internal controls and adherence to the needs of users of accounting information. They also serve clients with a wide variety of financial service activities. Finally accountants have become important users of information systems in providing management with decision-making information. In general, an accountant's role in the use and the analysis and design of information systems has been expanded and has become more complex as the information revolution moves forward.

Thus, knowledge and understanding of the basics of computer technology, information systems, systems analysis and design, and control and accounting information requirements of various functions have become essential to the professional accountant. These concepts are stressed in this text. Moreover, it is important for the professional accountant to understand the organizational aspects of the environment, the decision-making needs of management, and the behavior of all parties involved to effectively render advice in the design, implementation, and operation of accounting information systems.

DEFINITION OF INFORMATION SYSTEMS AND INFORMATION PROCESSING

General Definition

In this text, *information processing* and *information systems* will be used interchangeably. These terms have a much broader connotation than *management information systems* (MIS) in that information is used for more than routine decisions supported by regular periodic reports. A wide range of users now access information as they need it for a wide variety of uses as shown in Figure 1–1. Another reason that would justify use of the term *information processing* or *information system* (IS) is that neither term implies a computer-based system. It is quite possible for some organizations with low-volume, minimal complexity and slow-time requirements to develop viable manual information systems. A term is needed that also encompasses these systems. Many simple systems used in small business are discussed in Chapter 19.

All organizations have some form of information system regardless of whether it is merely a manual accounting system consisting of a set of filing cabinets and a chart of accounts in a ledger or a sophisticated on-line interactive database management system that provides accounting information as well as information for a wide range of managerial decision making. The latter system, however, is a more viable information system; not because it is a computer system, but simply because it has the means by which data pertaining to organizational needs can be recorded, stored, processed, retrieved, and communicated in a form required by individuals within and by constituents outside the firm.

Finally, an information system is analogous to a manufacturing process that takes raw material and converts it into a product that either is utilized by a consumer or becomes the input to another manufacturing process. An information system converts raw data, via data processing, into management reports or reports for external users. It can also provide selected data as input to decision models or other systems which further process the data to support management decision making. In general, an information system adds value to raw data by making it useful for transaction processing needs, reporting, decision making, or adding information value to goods and services.

Historical Perspective

Information systems existed prior to the development of the computer. Information technology, as stated earlier, made possible sophisticated, integrated, as well as distributed, information systems that can process vast amounts of information. Several other factors and developments in addition to computer technology have influenced and contributed to the growth of the field. Specifically, four concepts that have emerged over the past two decades have had a bearing on the evolution of information systems: (1) internal and external information requirements; (2) technological developments in both software and hardware in data processing; (3) the idea that activities and operations within a firm can be viewed as a system (i.e., the "systems approach"); and (4) the development of the scientific approach to management, which involves the development of decision science (mathematical) models to support decision making.

INFORMATION REQUIREMENTS.   Managing a firm, regardless of whether it is a small single proprietorship or a large corporation, can be enhanced by effective use of information. Effective information systems that support the management activities of the firm can be developed. However, before we can develop a system to support the firm's activities, we must first define and identify the firm's information needs.

Most organizations have two global information needs: (1) internal information requirements (transaction processing, managerial decision making, and control), and (2) external reporting requirements (transaction processing and financial reporting). Both factors have an impact on the structure and development of information systems.

The rise of large corporations in the early 1900s created the need for larger and more complex systems than those simple and sometimes informal information systems used to provide internal information. Information systems in the early 1900s concentrated on simple cost accounting and budget reporting, which often proved inadequate in decision making. As firms continued to expand in the 1930s and 1940s, more detailed cost reporting resulted. Full cost, direct cost, marginal cost, replacement cost, and opportunity cost information began to appear. Moreover, sophisticated systems for product costing also began to evolve. Detailed cost and product costing reports increased the volume of data handled and information generated.

Formalized internal reporting systems then emerged. These systems were built on the idea of responsibility and profitability accounting in which each manager receives reports covering his or her area of responsibility. Variances from planned performance were identified. Lower-level reports were summarized for upper-level management, and problem areas and causes were summarized. Obviously the larger the corporation, the larger the volume of data handled, and the greater the need to employ decision support techniques such as capital budgeting, cost-volume-profit analysis, resource allocation procedures, inventory control procedures, cash flow analysis, and sales analysis.

In the large corporation, managerial control problems became more complex, programming and budgeting and planning became necessary, and decision models or management science models became more applicable. Management's response was to develop decision support systems which often used corporate planning models. Recently, network and database systems have emerged where managers can interact with large databases (often spread over a wide area) in an "end-user" mode to access data for decision making. The advent of minicomputers and microcomputers has helped even small companies to better satisfy these information requirements.

Like internal reporting, the growth in external reporting requirements has had an impact on information systems and accounting systems. The most obvious external reporting requirement is that of periodic financial statements, which report the status of the firm and are made available, often on a quarterly basis, to every stockholder. Interest groups other than stockholders also affected external reporting requirements. In the preindustrial 1800s, only a limited amount of external reporting was needed. Corporate enterprises have now grown to the point that suppliers, customers, labor unions, financial institutions, and a variety of governmental agencies require information on the status of different aspects of the business. Moreover, the SEC, FASB, AICPA, IRS, ICC, etc., all have issued pronouncements of various kinds for external reporting.

Finally, the rise of multinational enterprises has hastened the need to develop wide area communication networks. This has led to rapid developments in electronic data interchange (EDI). All of these requirements have a bearing on the structure of an accounting information system.

COMPUTER TECHNOLOGY.   As we indicated earlier, information system (IS) does not necessarily imply the use of computer-based systems. But we can hardly argue that current information systems could exist without the support of computer technology. Close to fifty years have elapsed since the emergence of the first commercial computer in 1947. However, the development of sophisticated computer-based information systems has occurred within the past twenty-five years. Early information systems were primarily transaction-based systems which were developed principally to handle day-to-day operations and to provide record-keeping functions for large organizations. The development of cost-effective decision support systems, such as those discussed in Chapter 17, to support top-level decision-making activities, did not occur until the early 1970s, even though cost-effective systems were used to support middle-and lower-level management in the 1960s. Moreover, until the advent of microcomputers, small organizations could not afford the benefits of computer processing and decision support technology.

The reason for the time gap in the development of sophisticated information systems was the delayed development of computer software and the reduction of the cost of computer power indicated earlier in the chapter (that is, the cost of chips). A basic computer system consists of *hardware* (physical elements such as input/output units, peripheral storage devices, and the central processing unit) and *software* (languages and stored programs that control and/or provide operating flexibility). Hardware and software developments did not occur simultaneously.

In the last several years hardware has evolved at a rapid pace, as indicated earlier in this chapter. Much of this was due to the development of new high-speed microchips, supercomputers, telecommunication advances, and high-capacity storage systems. Software developments, however, have usually lagged behind hardware developments because increased computational power and storage capabilities are generally necessary for more sophisticated and user friendly software.

Lately, however, software has begun to keep pace with hardware developments. Numerous software vendors have emerged to market sophisticated operating systems; complex database management systems; effective and easy-to-use database software; easy-to-use fourth-generation programming languages for easier software development; telecommunication software for widely disbursed operations as well as local areas; personnel productivity software such as word processing and spreadsheets, statistical and other number-crunching packages; a whole host of sophisticated, integrated accounting and financial planning packages; and even artificial intelligence packages. Moreover, new developments in what are called end-user systems even enable managers to develop their own application software on short notice for special decision-making needs. This capability has been spurred on by the development of new fourth-generation languages which make it much easier to interact with complex systems and their databases. Many of these even run on microcomputers.

THE SYSTEMS APPROACH.   Another factor that has affected the evolution of information processing is the emergence of the "systems approach." The systems approach is a way of structuring and coordinating the activities and operations within an organization. A fundamental precept of the systems approach is the interrelationship of the parts, or subsystems, of the organization. The systems approach begins with a set of organizational objectives and focuses on the design of the information system as a whole. If the system is designed properly, the effectiveness of its components considered collectively will be greater than the sum of the effectiveness of each component considered separately. The result is a more efficient system. The most widely accepted development in the systems approach to accounting information development is called the structural approach to analysis and design; we use this approach as the basis for the text. Other systems development procedures are currently being used to expedite the development process. These also take a systems approach and will be discussed in this text.

In the past, organizations have fallen short of optimal effectiveness because they have failed to coordinate the different functions within the organization. The sales function, for example, was sometimes performed without regard to the production activity; production quite often was not coordinated with financial or personnel planning. To compound coordination problems, manual accounting systems have traditionally concentrated only on periodic, historic information of financial statements and not on forward-looking planning and control information for management decision making. It is important to coordinate both the financial reporting and the managerial planning and control information systems for the organization's system to run smoothly. With the advent of good database management systems and related software, this coordination effort has become much more feasible.

DEVELOPMENT OF MANAGEMENT SCIENCES AND APPLIED STATISTICS.   The size and the complexity of organizations have changed significantly over the past two decades. To remain competitive it has become increasingly important for organizations to manage their resources as efficiently as feasible, and this has led to the development of the field of management sciences and applied statistics. *Management science* (often referred to as *operations research* or *decision sciences*) is the application of the scientific method to management problems. Management science is rooted in the use of mathematical models to identify and study solution alternatives. *Applied statistics* is the application of statistical methods to data and management decision making and analysis.

Managers of organizations are often faced with decisions that deal with the future course or direction of their organization. Managers are often confronted with decisions ranging from basic routine operating decisions to highly complex decisions that involve millions of dollars. Applied statistical methods such as linear regression have been used to analyze past relationships among key decision variables and to forecast expected results. Management sciences can be used to determine the best or most satisfactory course of action from those available to management. Management science and applied statistical methods are used extensively in inventory management, distribution, production scheduling, plant location, cost analysis, and cost allocations, as well as in financial planning and investment analysis.

Obviously the application of mathematical and statistical models can never provide the basis for all decisions, and many information needs of an organization can be met by establishing a well-designed database that will provide timely reports or on-line response to management inquiries. But applied statistics and management science are important developments relative to information processing because they can provide procedures for analyzing and studying problems. When we move beyond simple transaction processing in information systems, the models and algorithms of applied statistics and management science play an important role in the design of management information systems and decision support systems.

General Characteristics of Information Systems

Most information systems have characteristics in common with those shown in Figure 1–3. Data are first collected from various sources, input into the system, processed, generally stored in some form pending its use, retrieved and further processed into information output and transmitted to various users for their transaction processing, reporting, and decision-making needs. Generally, *input, processing,* and *output* processing steps involve several functions. Transaction data are captured and entered into the system at the source of the transaction and external data are entered from various sources outside the organization. These data are then classified and stored in a database or a set of files for further processing. Processing then continues as information is needed for reports and management inquiry. Data are then sorted, summarized, and analyzed using

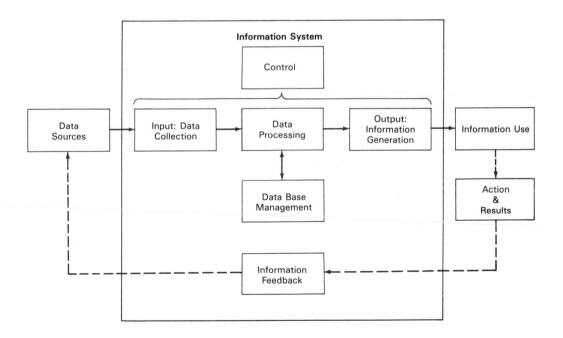

FIGURE 1-3 Characteristics common to all information systems.

many of the methods noted earlier to provide useful information to management. The output of information may consist of routine reports developed by the information systems analysts and programming staff, on-the-spot inquiries using report generators which are part of the database management system, and end-user-developed reports. There is a control system to regulate the flow and quality of this process and its stored data. Generally there is a feedback loop where results of various actions taken, based on the information, are fed back into the information system for future use. The overall process takes raw data and adds value to it by processing it so that it becomes a valuable resource for managers to use. In general *data* are transformed into useful *information* via data processing procedures.

Information systems supply information to external constituents, to managers (decision makers), or to the decision models employed as an aid in the decision-making process. A distinction between the "formal" and the "informal" systems should be made. A *formal system* has a prescribed set of rules and procedures for gathering and analyzing data and for disseminating information. An *informal system* involves highly ad hoc information that is not generated routinely; such systems tend to develop noticeably within the organization where the formal system fails to satisfy management needs. Informal systems are common in small organizations, although this is rapidly changing due to the advances in good microcomputer software for small businesses.

Generalized Accounting Cycle

The characteristics and components typical of transaction processing accounting information systems are illustrated in Figure 1–4 for an on-line interactive integrated system which uses a common database. Data are collected on financial transactions; keyed into the system; posted and organized in a database for further processing; stored in a form that can be used by many different types of users; and retrieved for managerial reports, financial statements, and management inquiry for a variety of decision-making needs. The results of these decisions and their corresponding actions are then captured as part of the feedback process and cycled through the system. All transaction processing accounting information cycles follow this general sequence of steps. Examples of these systems which are designed for various management accounting, financial accounting, decision support, and general management requirements are outlined in the application chapters: Chapter 14 on logistical systems; Chapter 15 on marketing systems; Chapter 16 on financial accounting systems; Chapter 17 on decision support and planning and control systems; Chapter 18 on large corporate distributed systems; and Chapter 19 on small entrepreneurial accounting information systems.

Data Sources

Many sources of data are used in generating information. Some are *internal* and are generated by the daily activities of the organization as it produces its goods and services and interacts with vendors and customers. This is generally referred

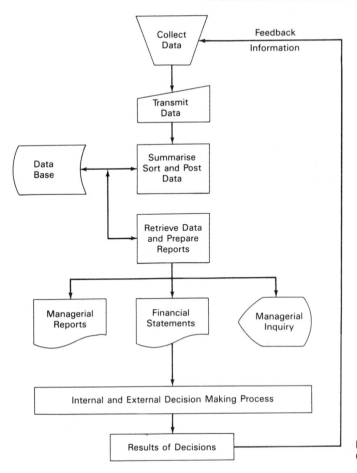

FIGURE 1-4
General accounting cycle.

to as *transaction information* even though it is usually just raw transition data. A transaction processing system like that generalized in Figure 1-4 is very important to most organizations' information system because it provides essential data about current and past activities of the organization. Many older systems concentrated solely on this aspect of the information system and developed their accounting system first. Other data is *external* and is gathered via various industry, market, and economic studies and services which the particular organization may subscribe. As an example, it may be generated by querying customers as is the case with much market research data. Data may be *historic* and reflect past transaction or economic data or it may result from some sort of analysis of this data in the form of a prediction, such as an economic *projection* of interest rates and other economic indicators.

In the previous discussions, the terms *data* and *information* were used to describe information systems and processing. These terms relate to two distinct concepts. *Data* are raw facts, such as transaction details from sales invoices which are input into the system as indicated in Figures 1-3 and 1-4. *Information,* on the other hand, is communicated knowledge that is sufficiently relevant, timely, and accurate for the users purpose. To generate information, data is usually transformed as shown in Figure 1-3. One must carefully examine the definition of information, however. Information does not result simply because data is transformed and stored. Consider what will result if we take raw data, store these data, and simply output these data. The output will probably not be in a form that is useful, because the decision maker may be swamped by huge amounts of data on computer printouts. This is sometimes called "information overload." It only confuses the prospective users.

First, information must be sent, received, recognized, and accepted by the individual to whom it was directed. Second, the information usually results from performing a series or group of operations which add value to the raw data. These include classifying, sorting, summarizing, analyzing, or modeling input data as illustrated in Figure 1-3. Finally, the information must be presented (reported) in such a form that it can be used by the recipient. The importance of presentation and its contribution to the value of information is emphasized in Chapter 17 which discusses decision support systems in detail.

To demonstrate these aspects of information consider a manager who receives a report that is outdated by two months, recognizes that the report is outdated, and discards it. This is not useful information because it is no longer relevant or timely, even though data was analyzed and presented to the user. To have value, information must meet the needs of users for reporting, transaction processing, and decision making; the mere transmittal of relevant and timely facts is not the creation of information.

SUMMARY

Before addressing the question of how an information requirement is analyzed and how an accounting information system is designed and developed, we must have a firm understanding of the components and concepts on which a system is built. Some of these basic concepts have been presented in this chapter. First the impact of a variety of historical and contemporary developments in information requirements, technology, the systems concept, and the scientific approach to management was reviewed in light of their impact on accounting information systems. This impact has been substantial and has changed forever the role of an accountant in an organization and greatly expanded the role of public accountants and the types of client engagements they can expect in the future. Second we presented a broad definition of accounting information which is consistent with the expanding responsibility of the professional accountant in providing management with information for decision making, reporting, and transaction processing. Third the general characteristics of information systems were discussed as well as the way they apply to the accounting cycle. We differentiated between *data* and *information,* noting that the processing of data adds value only if the resulting information is useful.

SELECTED REFERENCES

ABRAMSON, DAVID H., "The Future of Accounting: Scenarios for 1996," *Journal of Accountancy*, October 1986, pp. 120–24.

AMERICAN ACCOUNTING ASSOCIATION COMMITTEE ON CONTEMPORARY APPROACHES TO TEACHING ACCOUNTING INFORMATION SYSTEMS "1986–1987 Report," *The Journal of Information Systems*, Spring 1987, pp. 127–56.

AMERICAN ACCOUNTING ASSOCIATION COMMITTEE ON INFORMATION SYSTEMS "Accounting and Information Systems," *Accounting Review, Supplement*, vol. 46, 1971.

ARTHUR ANDERSON & CO., *Trends in Information Technology: 1986, Chicago, Ill.:* Arthur Anderson & Co., 1986.

BEDFORD, NORTON M. and WILLIAM G. SHENKIR, "Reorienting Accounting Education," *Journal of Accountancy*, August 1987, pp. 84–91.

CASH, JAMES I. and BENN R. KONSYNSKI, "IS Redraws Competitive Boundaries," *Harvard Business Review*, March–April, 1985, pp. 134–142.

DAVIS, KEAGLE W., "The Information Systems Auditor of the 1980s," *Management Accounting*, 43 (March 1981), pp. 40–47.

DRUCKER, PETER F., "The Coming of the New Organization,"*Harvard Business Review*, January–February, 1988, pp. 45–53.

LIN, W. THOMAS, and WILLIAM K. HARPER, "A Decision Oriented Management Accounting Information System," *Cost and Management*, November–December 1981.

MCFARLAND, F. WARREN, "Information Technology Changes the Way You Compete," *Harvard Business Review*, May–June 1984, pp. 98–103.

PORTER, MICHAEL E., and VICTOR E. MILLAR, "How Information Gives You Competitive Advantage," *Harvard Business Review*, July–August 1985, pp. 150–160.

ROUSSEY, ROBERT S., "The CPA in the Information Age: Today and Tomorrow," *Journal of Accountancy*, October 1986, pp. 94–107.

SIMON, HERBERT A. *The New Science of Management Decision*, rev. ed. Englewood Cliffs, N.J.: Prentice Hall, 1977.

STOCKS, KEVIN D., and LYNN J. MCKELL, "Accounting Education and Management Advisory Services," *The Journal of Information Systems*, Fall 1987, pp. 65–76.

STOCKS, KEVIN D., and MARSHALL B. ROMNEY, "The Supply and Demand for IS/MAS Graduates," *The Journal of Information Systems*, Spring 1987, pp. 83–100.

REVIEW QUESTIONS

1. What major developments have led to the expanded role of the accountant?

2. Define the term *accounting information system.*

3. In what ways has the advance of chip technology led the way for other technological developments which have impacted the ability of accountants to do their job and the complexity of that job?

4. How can an accounting system be used to add value to data so that accounting information is an important economic resource?

5. How has the advent of the microcomputer influenced small business accounting systems and as a result public accounting practice?

6. Data base systems and easier-to-use software have greatly enhanced the use of computer systems for management and accountants. What is the negative side of these advances in technology? Discuss how accountants have countered these negative aspects.

7. What is the sequence of input, processing

and output steps in a transaction processing cycle?

8. Define the term *information systems.* Give an example.

9. What four major factors have had an impact on the evolution of contemporary accounting information systems? Elaborate on each with respect to managerial or financial accounting information systems.

10. In what areas are public accounting firms typically involved with their clients in terms of accounting systems?

11. Discuss how recent database management systems have aided in the development of accounting information systems.

12. Differentiate between *data* and *information.*

13. How has database storage technology impacted the type of information available for management decision making?

14. Name several uses of accounting information.

CASES

1-1 Tavil Corporation has been manufacturing high-quality wood furniture for over fifty years. Tavil's five product lines are Mediterranean, Modern, Colonial, Victorian, and the recently introduced Country. Business has been very good for Tavil recently.

Part of the reason for Tavil's recent success has been the ability of Sally Grant, chief executive officer. Grant has assembled a first-rate top management team that has now been together for the past four years. All major decisions are made by this centralized top management team after thorough study and review. Many members of top management were not expecting Grant's suggestion, at a regular staff meeting, that management should consider dropping the Victorian line—Tavil's oldest furniture line.

Grant indicated that Victorian sales had dropped in total and as a percentage of Tavil's total sales during the last three years. This conclusion was supported by the following schedule that shows sales percentage by line for the last three years.

Table C1-1 Product-Line Sales Percentage

	MEDITER-RANEAN	MODERN	COLONIAL	VICTORIAN	COUNTRY	TOTAL
1989	31%	26%	21%	20%	2%	100%
1990	28	28	21	14	9	100
1991	24	26	23	10	17	100

Sam Mills, vice-president of sales, commented that the data did not reflect important regional differences in the market. Victorian total sales of $413,000 in 1989 were almost entirely in New England and New York. In fact, Victorian sales constituted over half of all Tavil sales in some of these locations. He indicated that more Victorian could be sold if production could produce it. He believes that he will lose at least two top salespeople in New England to competitors if the Victorian line is dropped.

However, Mills also conceded that many sales have been lost in other sales regions due to the long lead time on the Country line. In fact, sales of Colonial were dangerously ahead of supply.

Bob James, vice-president of production, pointed out that production of all lines was possible in existing facilities. However, he also identified several problems with the Victorian line's quality. Quality had traditionally been Tavil's greatest asset. The major problem was that highly skilled craftsmen were just not available in the labor market anymore, making it difficult to support increased production. Also several of Tavil's craftsmen would need special training on their new production assignments if the Victorian line were eliminated. James also indicated that margins on the Victorian line have dwindled due to the relatively high labor-intensity on the Victorian line and the high union wages of the skilled craftsmen. Dropping the Victorian line would also cause $80,000 worth of fabric in inventory to become totally obsolete.

Grant asked Jack Turner, chief financial officer, to collect and assimilate the necessary data to aid in the evaluation of whether to keep or drop the Victorian line. As she closed the staff meeting, she stated, "Eventually we might consider expansion, but currently we must consider our present markets and resources."

REQUIRED: Discuss the type and nature of information that Jack Turner should provide to the rest of Tavil Corporation's top management to assist in the decision to keep or drop the Victorian line. As part of your discussion, give specific examples of information that Turner should prepare and present.
(CMA (Certified/Management/Accountant) adapted.)

1-2 An electronics firm has decided to expand overseas to manufacture several of its components. Management needs to monitor these worldwide operations closely.

REQUIRED: What recent developments in information technology will enable management to accomplish this monitoring activity more closely?

1-3 Maxway Discount Merchandise started out as a small retailer in Texas and has grown very fast since the early 1970s . Maxway now has 100 stores throughout the Southwest. When they first computerized their accounting information system, they developed batch processing systems for accounts receivable, accounts payable, payroll, inventory, and the general ledger. They operated this system using a centrally located mainframe computer and cash registers tied to tape drives with modems and

printers in each location. The general operating procedure was for sales and inventory transactions to be stored at each location on the tape and transferred to the main office via the modem after the close of business that day. All processing was done at the home office in Ft. Worth, and management information was sent back to the store to be printed before the opening of the store the next day.

REQUIRED: Discuss how the recent changes in technology can help Maxway do a better job in managing its business through improvements in its accounting information system.

1-4 How can the new data processing technological advances help management communicate, share information, and make better decisions in a (1) smaller organization; and (2) a global enterprise?

1-5 Stewart and Miller, CPAs have been serving clients in a small town south of Pittsburgh for twenty years. Their clients have begun to ask their advice about acquisition of microsystems to assist them in managing their firms and keeping their records. Stewart and Miller have not been able to render this service because of the firm's lack of computer expertise, and they have lost several clients to a new CPA firm in town. Moreover, for those clients who have converted their accounting systems to EDP, Stewart and Miller have felt very uneasy trying to audit the new system. The partners of this new firm have strong background in accounting systems and are quite knowledgeable about microsystems. They even use their own microcomputer for write-up work and tax planning.

REQUIRED: As Ron Miller's close friend and controller for one of Ron's clients, what action would you suggest that he and Bob Stewart take with regard to this ominous trend in adverse client relations?

1-6 As controller of a glass company, you have been under a lot of pressure to improve your budget process because of several serious inventory problems. Production never seems to produce the correct style demanded by marketing. Stockouts of one line of glass and an over-supply of another line of glass are common. You use a straightforward budget process. Sales forecasts are made monthly, and production is instructed to produce to meet these forecasts. Production is then scheduled, and sufficient materials are ordered to comply with the needs of marketing. A manual system of reports is used to implement this system, but it is apparent that a quicker, more flexible system is now needed to accommodate changes in a very competitive retail market. The problem is that you are comfortable with your current batch processing accounting system, which uses card tabulating equipment and magnetic tapes, and the manual budget reporting system. Moveover, you do not understand the new on-line system your boss is urging you to consider. Your friend, a CPA, has suggested that you take a few professional development courses that cover information systems, systems approach to management, general ledger systems, and decision support and planning systems.

REQUIRED: Should you follow her advice? Why?

1-7 Overweight Trucking Company, located in central Ohio, has just purchased a small computer system to schedule its trucks more efficiently. Included in the package it purchased were programs to schedule its truck routes. These programs, designed for a trucking company with one freight terminal, were thoroughly tested and have been used extensively in the trucking industry. Overweight, however, has had difficulty in operating the system.

REQUIRED: Why do you think such a problem has arisen, given that the new system is a proven one?

1-8 The Scarf Toy Manufacturing Company has a responsibility accounting system. Managers receive reports on operation which aggregate details of shop operations for each plant. Plant operations are further aggregated in the report received by the vice-president of manufacturing. These reports show the budgeted and actual operating results for the current month and the year to date. These, along with inventory status reports, provide the major source of production information for planning. Management can look at the variances and determine whether manufacturing operations are under control. If the variances are large, management takes appropriate action: changing the manufacturing plans.

The company's profits have been decreasing, and management has requested similar aggregate sales data from marketing. It feels that this added information will suffice for its decision-making needs. It has asked your advice as the company's CPA.

REQUIRED: Do you agree? Why? Do you foresee any needs that will not be met by this information? If so, what additional information do you suggest that management provide with its accounting system?

1-9 The Block Baking Company produces a variety of bread and other baked goods. Block Baking has a perpetual inventory system, which gives inventory on hand at the end of each day. This information is used to schedule the next day's production. Management tries to produce what is in short supply so that it will not incur any stockouts that will send customers elsewhere. This goal has not been achieved, however. Sales are lost, management is considering increasing its overall inventory so that there will be enough stock. The president, however, has rejected this because of the company's policy of shipping only fresh bread. Large stocks will increase the probability of stale bread being delivered to customers, and fresh products are important in the company's market area. You have been called in to help management resolve this problem.

REQUIRED: Write a brief assessment of the problem and outline your suggestions for expanding the system to resolve the company's dilemma.

1-10 Greentree Garden Supply is considering the installation of a new sales order inventory system to tabulate sales statistics and to properly account for their large inventory of garden supplies.

REQUIRED:

1. As their CPA, outline the general infor-

mation processing steps required to accumulate the necessary sales data and to generate reports on sales.

2. Explain how they can use computer technology to enhance their competitive edge by providing better management reports and by providing some customer service.

2

ACCOUNTING INFORMATION SYSTEM CONCEPTS AND DIMENSIONS

INTRODUCTION

In this chapter, the dimensions of information processing are presented in an overall framework which can be used to design accounting and information systems that effectively satisfy management needs. The systems concept is reviewed. The dimensions include all the elements of data processing, various levels of managerial activity, and the organizational functions used to carry out the objectives of the organization. It's important that the total system be considered in the development of accounting and information systems in order to coordinate all the activities included in an organization's production of goods or delivery of services. Several types of accounting information systems are briefly discussed that can be used to support different aspects of the management system. Finally a systematic procedure for analyzing information requirements and designing an effective system is presented.

GENERAL SYSTEMS MODEL

Definition of Systems

As we indicated briefly in Chapter 1, the systems approach is a philosophy or perception of a structure that seeks to coordinate, in an efficient manner, the activities or operations of an organization. In an elementary sense, a system is a group of elements, such as the functional areas of marketing, production, and finance, which make up a larger unit such as a business enterprise. Systems are developed to accomplish certain objectives. Specifically an organization is a system of integrated activities that includes decision-making activities which must be coordinated for the organization to accomplish its objectives. For example, marketing, finance, and production must cooperate in order to deliver goods and services to customers. Management must develop the *management system* to accomplish its mission. The *information system,* including the subset defined as accounting information, must support this management system to enable it to carry out its objectives. The information system's objective is to provide information of sufficient quality and quantity to allow the management system to function effectively.

DIMENSIONS OF ACCOUNTING INFORMATION PROCESSING

Accounting information has been defined in Chapter 1, along with the historical and contemporary developments that influenced accounting systems and the generation of valuable accounting information from raw data. A framework that integrates these concepts into an effective system which can deliver the information needed by the organization to process transactions, support decision-making needs, and supply all users and interested third parties with the necessary reports has not been described. Before we can do this, we need to examine the different *dimensions* of information processing. Three dimensions exist in any information system: (1) data processing (elements); (2) managerial activities; and (3) organizational functions.

Data Processing (Elements)

The first dimension of information processing is the physical components of a system. If we were to ask to view an information system, we would probably be shown the physical components, or the *data processing elements,* of the system. These components would include (1) hardware; (2) data storage equipment; (3) software; and (4) operating procedures. A fifth element that would be necessary to make the system operational would be personnel.

The *hardware* for a system consists principally of what in global items is referred to as "the computer" and includes the central processing unit, input/output devices, storage devices, communication network and equipment, and data preparation equipment. *Data storage equipment* includes storage media such as magnetic tapes, disks, drums, bubble memory and floppy disks, and the devices (drives) necessary to use the media for data storage.

Software is divided into three major areas: (1) general operating software; (2) application software; and (3) in many cases file management and database management software. General operating software consists of software programs provided by the computer manufacturer or a software vendor that guides the general operations of the computer; this software is often called the operating system or the database management system. Application software can be classified as either generalized or specialized. Generalized application software includes general accounting packages for common needs, such as inventory, accounts receivable, accounts payable, payroll, cost accounting, and general ledger and general analysis applications such as budget planning, PERT analysis, and statistical analysis packages. Software is typically available from software vendors, the computer manufacturers and other vendors. Specialized application software consists of programs written specifically for individual applications. File management software and database management software is used to bridge the gap between these applications and data. This software will be discussed more in Chapter 9 and Chapter 10.

A *file* or *database* consists of data stored on storage devices. (File structures and database models and their accounting implications will be examined in chapters 9 and 10.)

Procedures are viewed as physical elements of an information system because they appear in physical form, such as instruction booklets and manuals. In general, two types of operating procedures are necessary: (1) instructions for system users (these include general operating, data preparation, information access and user instructions); and (2) instructions for computer center personnel who will be involved in running the system. In addition there are a variety of control procedures which help ensure the integrity of data and the accuracy of accounting information. *Personnel* necessary for an information system include: (1) computer operators, who handle the physical aspects of running the system; (2) systems analysts and programmers, who developed the systems; (3) data preparation personnel, who prepare data to be input; and (4) system users. Some current systems even enable end users to develop their own applications.

Managerial Activities

The second dimension of information processing concerns the managerial activities associated with different levels in an organization. These activities influence information processing because the information required for their support differs from each managerial level in the organization. We can gain an understanding of the different requirements by examining each of these activities. It should be recognized, however, that these activities have subdimensions such as (1) the degree to which decision-making activities are programmable or nonprogrammable; (2) the degree to which decision activities require internal or external information; and (3) the frequency with which the information should be updated. We will examine each of these subdimensions separately.

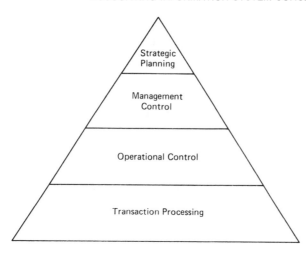

FIGURE 2-1
The managerial activity dimension
of information processing.

Activity Levels

First we must define *managerial activity levels*. The different decision-making activities can best be amplified by using the classical framework developed by Robert Anthony[1] and shown in top portion of Figure 2-1. Anthony identifies three categories of activities and argues that the decision-making activities differ significantly enough among these categories to warrant the development of different views of an information system. Ideally, all these perspectives can be supported by the same information system, but this is not always the case.

STRATEGIC PLANNING.   The first category or activity level is *strategic planning,* which Anthony defines as follows:

> *Strategic planning* is the process of deciding on objectives of the organization, on changes in the objectives, on the resources used to obtain these objectives, and on the policies that are to govern the acquisition, use, and disposition of these resources.[2]

In strategic planning the decision maker is involved with three key issues: (1) the development of organization objectives; (2) the selection of a strategy to achieve these objectives; and (3) the allocation of resources required to attain the objectives. Decisions at this level tend to be made over a long period of time and involve the commitment of substantial resources.

MANAGERIAL CONTROL.   The second category is management control, which Anthony defines as follows:

---

[1] Robert N. Anthony, *Planning and Control Systems: A Conceptual Framework for Analysis* (Boston: Division of Research, Harvard University Graduate School of Business Administration, 1965).
[2] Ibid., p. 24.

Management control . . . is the process by which managers assure that resources are obtained and used effectively and efficiently in the accomplishment of the organization's objective.[3]

In this category the decision maker is involved with monitoring the use of financial, physical, and human resources within the organization. Both the efficient use of resources on hand and the plans for future resource usage are important. Historically most of the decision-making activity at this level is financial related to technological capabilities of resources, or related to employee issues. A typical problem at the managerial control level is determining the reason for a variance between budgeted and actual costs. More recently, decision making has considered market and resource environments. For example, a JIT (just in time) inventory and manufacturing system must consider both the supply of materials and the distribution system of the finished goods.

OPERATIONAL CONTROL.   Anthony's third category of managerial activity is operational control, which he defines as follows:

Operational control . . . is the process of assuring that specific tasks are carried out effectively and efficiently.[4]

Operational activities are those activities involved in the day-to-day operations of the organization, An example of an operational activity is recognizing the need to reorder an inventory item, preparing appropriate documents, and following up to see that the item is purchased. Another example would be the stoppage of production in order to fix a problem whenever a product fails a quality control test. The key distinction between operational control activities and management control activities is that operational control is *task centered*, whereas management control is more *decision centered*. In the operational control area tasks, goals, and resources have been delineated by management control activity and the foreman or department manager must make efficient and effective use of these resources to produce and to deliver a quality product or service.

TRANSACTION PROCESSING.   To complete the activity level analysis we should include a fourth activity, *transaction processing*. This activity is generally not included in the traditional decision-making activity dimension (Anthony, for example, excludes this in this review) because it does not involve management decision-making tasks or events. Transaction processing involves the handling of the organization's daily business transactions, such as payroll, accounts receivable, accounts payable, sales, updating of expense ledgers, and changes in inventories. It supports a wide variety of clerical transactions. Transaction processing is an important building block in information systems because it furnishes the system database with much of the data required for decision making, planning, and control.

---

[3] Ibid., p. 27.
[4] Ibid., p. 67.

PROGRAMMED AND NONPROGRAMMED DECISIONS. Managerial activities may involve either *programmed* and *nonprogrammed* decisions. Systems built to support programmed, or structured, decision making will differ significantly from those for nonprogrammed, or unstructured, decision making. The former are often referred to as *management information systems* (MIS) and the latter are often referred to as *decision support systems* (DSS). Both will be discussed later in the chapter. A structured problem is one in which all three phases of decision making are structured. Briefly stated, the three phases of decision making are:

1. determining the problem
2. finding alternative systems
3. choosing the best alternative

An unstructured problem is one in which none of the phases is structured. Semistructured problems are those in which one of the phases is unstructured. For handling structured problems, decision models or algorithms are most applicable. Such models are particularly applicable for identifying solution alternatives and selecting the best solution. The fact that a problem is structured, however, does not imply that it is associated with any particular managerial level. An EOQ (economic order quantity) model is an example of a decision model that is applicable to the operational control problem of inventory control. The strategic planning problem of production facility location can easily be handled with a decision model. In general though structured decision making is linked more with operational control and managerial control activities, whereas unstructured decision making is linked more with strategic planning. This seems logical because the information requirements for strategic planning are broad and encompassing, but the requirements for operational and managerial control are more detailed, well defined, and narrow.

Other activities of the structured and nonstructured relationship to the managerial activities (strategic planning, management control, and operation control) are shown in Figure 2-2. Note that transaction processing is not mentioned in the above discussion; it is a data/information handling activity. Its interface with the decision models, however, is critical to any information processing system.

Organizational Functions

The third dimension of information processing is that of organization. Historically many organizations, particularly larger corporations, are structured and organized in terms of functional activities such as marketing, production, personnel, accounting, and finance. For many this is a reasonable basis for organizing and developing an information system. In designing or viewing an information system from the organizational perspective, we are not restricted to these functional groupings. Many other structures may be far superior and enable management to more effectively organize to compete in today's dynamic and changing

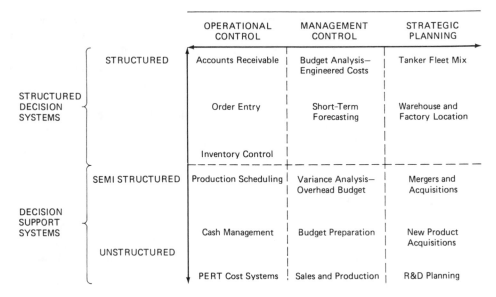

FIGURE 2-2   Structured/unstructured problems associated with different managerial activities.
Source: G. Anthony Gorry and Michael S. Scott Morton, "A Framework for Management Information Systems," *Sloan Management Review* (Fall 1971), p. 59.

markets.[5] Whatever the structure, the organizational arrangement will dictate the structure of the accounting information system.

Each organizational unit, however defined, is viewed as a subsystem having all the elements needed to perform all processing related to its function. Each functional subsystem is assumed to have the personnel, hardware, software, database, and procedures to support its operation. These processing facilities could be provided by a centralized organizational unit within the firm or by a decentralized units throughout the firm. There will be some programs (software), as well as database and decision models, common to several or all functions or subunits, such as divisions, as explained in Chapter 3. Financial and managerial accounting systems can use common databases, for example. Thus a combination of centralized and decentralized organizational units may be appropriate. In addition to the link between the functional units and the facilities, there is a link with managerial activities. Each function can be viewed in terms of the information required to support operational control, management control, strategic planning, and transaction processing.

Figure 2-3 illustrates the functional dimension of information processing. We identify four basic subunits within the functional dimension: (1) finance; (2) marketing; (3) production (logistics); and (4) personnel. Other possible subunits are detailed in Chapter 3. (Chapters 14 to 19 include detailed descriptions of each of the basic functional subunits and its information requirements. These chapters examine the relationships between each function and the other dimensions of information processing.

---

[5] See Michael E. Porter, *Competitive Advantage*, New York: Free Press, 1985 for a discussion of these issues.

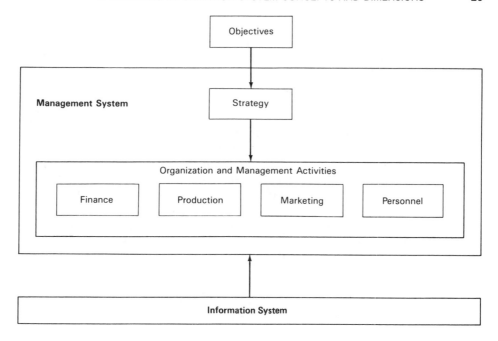

FIGURE 2-3   Management system and information system.

INFORMATION AND MANAGEMENT SYSTEM

An information system must be designed to support the decision-making, transaction processing, and reporting needs of management and any third party which may need feedback information on the organization's activities. These activities are a function of the organization's objectives, the strategy needed to accomplish these objectives, and the organization needed to implement the strategy as shown in Figure 2-3. Management typically sets the organization's objectives, determines a strategy to accomplish the objectives, and organizes its resources to carry out its strategy. The combination of the strategy and the organization used to implement the strategy is called the *management system*. Different objectives and strategies will lead to different organizations and still different information systems. In general, the information system is designed to assist management in its various activities by providing timely, accurate, clear, and relevant information so that it can manage the physical activities of the organization as well as make managerial and strategic decisions. When we combine the management system with the information system and the physical activities of the organization we have the complete *organizational system.*

Management systems and information systems have characteristics in common:

1. Both management systems and information systems can be analyzed, designed, and managed by the general principles of systems design.

2. Both are ongoing processes. They are dynamic rather than static, and their dynamic nature must be planned for in the design and development process. (This concept is reviewed briefly in this chapter and discussed at length in chapters 12 and 13.)

3. The elements of each are operationally linked, but the information system must be designed to complement the management system, not the reverse. The management system should be designed to achieve the objectives of the organization most effectively; the information system should be designed to complement the management system.

4. Both the management system and the information system have outputs. Output of the information system, however, is an input to the management system. It aids in the transaction processing and decision-making activities of the organization.

5. Finally, an accounting subsystem is at the center of both systems, and, as a result, controllers and CPAs need to understand the structure of the management system and the supporting information system.

In summary all the major elements (components) of the information system must be organized to support the management system. As noted earlier, these elements include hardware, software, data, personnel, and procedures.

Major Components

In general, an organizational system consists of a physical system, management system, and information system. Operational, management, and strategic control activities comprise the *management system.* The physical system transforms various input resources such as personnel, financial capital, raw materials or components, equipment, and information into goods and services output. As is the case with an information system, the three major components of a *physical system* consist of *input, transformation process, and output* as shown in Figure 2-4. The physical system is monitored and controlled by an *operational control system* which makes various decisions regarding the input, transformation process, and the nature of the output. Data is received from these three physical stages, analyzed, and transmitted to those responsible for operation of each of these stages.

An organization also has an *information system* it uses to represent the activities and states of the physical system, monitor the business and economic environment, and provide information to its management system. This includes *feedback* information used by managers to manage the flow of resources in the physical system. Feedback measures the output (such as the number of units or the costs per unit for material, labor, and overhead) of the system and conveys this information to the decision maker via a feedback loop. It is often used to compare actual results with expected results (such as standard costs) and presented to management in terms of exception reports. In more advanced systems, managers may even obtain information on the physical system from an on-line system which shows the current status of the transformation process, the input, or the output. An example might be a production report showing the stage of completion of each of the orders which have been placed in production and the

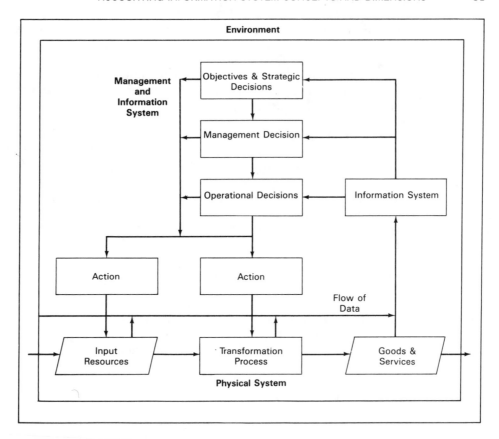

FIGURE 2-4 Organization system (physical, management, and information).

costs applied to these products through this stage. This information flow is illustrated in Figure 2-4.

Moreover, *managerial and strategic* decision-making activities use information to plan, coordinate, and acquire the resources to accomplish the organization's objectives. Furthermore, information systems do not exist in a vacuum; they function in an *environment*. They gather market information, provide information to customers, and supply third parties with financial information. In this manner, accounting information systems support the strategic, managerial, operational, and transaction processing activities of an organization.

INFORMATION REQUIREMENTS TO SUPPORT ACTIVITY LEVELS. Transaction processing does not specifically involve decision making. It simply includes the collecting, sorting, editing, and processing of daily transaction data. The other managerial activities do involve decision making and because the activities differ by level, the information required to support them differs. Likewise, data requirements for each activity differ. The accountant, as a user, provider, designer, and reviewer of information, needs to be cognizant of these differences. They affect the transaction processing activities required and the characteristics of the accounting information system he or she will play a major part in designing, controlling, and auditing. Operational control, for example, implies a high frequency of data collection. Decision making at the operational level is based on very detailed information generated within the organization. Data, as well as information that supports operational control, must be up to date, accurate, and precise.

In strategic planning, the frequency of data collection is low, and quite often the data are obtained from external sources. In general, the data, and thus the information employed, cover a long time frame and in many instances do not have to be current. Managers at the strategic level have a greater need for summary or aggregate information than for the detailed information employed at the managerial and operational levels. This does not imply that simple aggregation of managerial or operational data will satisfy strategic planning and the other managerial levels, because the characteristics are vastly different as shown in Figure 2-5.

Information requirements for managerial control decisions fall between strategic planning and operational control requirements. The level of detail and other characteristics included in managerial control information is greater than that required for strategic planning but less than that required in operational control, where weekly or daily updates are often required. Figure 2-5 lists the data/information characteristics involved in supporting the three decision activity levels.

System vs. Component Approach

According to general systems theory, when the subsystems are considered collectively as an *integrated system*, the system's effectiveness is greater than the sum of the effectiveness of each subsystem considered separately. In the past, many organizations have fallen short in the development of an effective information system because they failed to relate all components. Such failures can be attributed to a narrow view often taken by specialists such as accountants, engineers, and marketing people. There is a tendency in any organization for each individual to concentrate on the different aspects of his or her specialty without relating it to the other activities in the organization.

FIGURE 2-5 Information requirements required to support management activities.

CHARACTERISTICS DATA AND INFORMATION	STRATEGIC CONTROL	MANAGERIAL CONTROL	OPERATIONAL CONTROL	TRANSACTION PROCESSING
Time Horizon	Long and Futuristic		Short (Daily)	Instantaneous
Frequency of Use	Infrequent		Frequent	Continuous
Accuracy Level	Not Critical	⟶	Very Critical	Very Critical
Source	Mostly External		Mostly Internal	Mostly Internal
Level of Detail	Summarized		Very Detailed	Complete Detail
Breadth of Information	Broad		Narrow	Very Narrow

If each of the separate subsystems (components) of the physical process in Figure 2-4 (input, transformation, and output) are considered separately, as would be the case if marketing did not communicate with the production (transformation) process, excessive inventory would build up, because there would be a strong likelihood that production would not be producing the right product mix for sale in the market place. Likewise if production did not communicate with procurement and procurement ordered the wrong components for production, production might grind to a halt for lack of parts. Thus, for the physical system to operate efficiently and effectively, it must operate as an integrated system with all of its components linked together. This means that its activities need to be coordinated through an effective management system which is supported by an information system consisting of transaction data, managerial reports and access to data for decisions. Even very simple, traditional accounting systems can be utilized effectively to provide this support through the transaction, recording, budgeting, planning, and reporting processes. It is not necessary that all the components of an integrated system be located in one place. They may be distributed over a wide area in a *distributed system.* These systems are discussed in Chapter 7.

The *component approach* on the other hand, focuses the summation of the individual parts rather than on an interrelated whole. Component objectives are not necessarily linked and the complete system is defined as the collection of separate components. In such a situation each component may go its separate way and not achieve a common objective. The basic difference between an integrated and a component approach is the linkages between the subsystems.

Sometimes an organization is too large to rigidly apply the integrated systems concept to the entire firm. In these situations, boundaries are drawn around subsystems (components) and interfaces are developed to enhance the coordination between the subsystems. There is usually a cost associated with the resulting suboptimization from this decoupling of the various components or subsystems. However, this must be compared to the cost of a completely integrated system for a large organization. Such an integrated (tightly coupled) system can be very expensive.

TYPES OF INFORMATION SYSTEMS

Several different types of information are required to accommodate the different needs of management for decision making, reporting, and transaction processing. These needs as noted earlier are also dependent on the level of managerial activity. The general classification of each system, is described next along with an accounting example. Their original relation to each level of activity is shown in Figure 2-6.

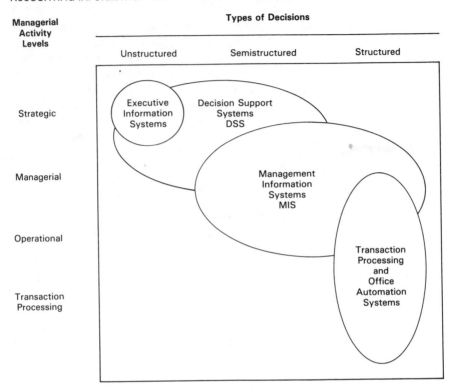

FIGURE 2-6 Information systems needed for types of decision-making and managerial activity.

Transaction Processing System

Transaction processing systems are the most detailed. They record the day-to-day economic activities and events of the organization such as a sale, the receipt of merchandise, the issuance of a purchase order, and the purchase of equipment. This system is the organization's interface with its environment. Moreover, it forms the basis for much of the information used in the various level of managerial control and activity. It is primarily used to support the operational activities of the organization.

Office Automation System

An office automation system is a relatively new type of system. It is designed to more effectively and efficiently do many of the clerical activities of the organization. It consists of word processing, filing or posting information in a data file or in an accounting system. It includes reproduction, facsimile and data transmission, and electronic mail. Often microcomputers with communication networks are used to accomplish these tasks. Often information is down loaded from other types of systems to be further processed by an office automation system.

Management Information Systems

Management information systems provide the routine information for managerial activities such as planning, controlling, and decision making. Often this information is based on transaction processing data and presented to management in the form of routine periodic reports which summarize the ongoing activities of the organization. Some examples would include sales analysis reports by various territories and products as well as production variance analysis by manufacturing locations. Most MIS systems support routine, structured managerial decisions. Budgeting activities generally fall into this classification of information system.

Decision Support Systems

Decision support systems are designed to support unstructured managerial and strategic decisions. They are often based on the data generated by the transaction processing system and the reports provided by the MIS system, as well as external economic and business indicators. They often enable managers to access and analyze data in ways particular to each individual manager. In general they allow the manager to interact in a user friendly way with the data stored in the computer system.

Managers can use decision support systems to analyze data using planning models and to access that information quickly. In general, they are used to support managerial and strategic activities of the organization. An example would include a model of the organization's financial plan. Managers could quickly alter some assumptions and decisions in the plan in order to assess the impact of a competitor's actions on their profit or to assess the impact of a new product line on the resources available to other lines of business.

Executive Information System

Executive information systems are designed to support the very top levels of management in the organization with their strategic decision-making needs. They are less analytical and model oriented than decision support systems. They tend to present summarized, externally generated or projected information in graphical forms which are usable to top management for setting policy or devising strategies to implement the organizations objectives.

Examples would include the generation of market information related to potential customers for a new product or the projected productivity and quality increases of a new manufacturing technique. These tend not to use as much accounting data as the other types of information systems. They do, however, use some accounting data to form the basis for many of the planning models used by top management. All of these systems process data into information that is usable by management to help them achieve the objectives of the organization.

AN INFORMATION SYSTEM FRAMEWORK

In this chapter we identified three dimensions of information system used to support the management system: (1) the management activity; (2) the organization and management system; and (3) the data processing, or elements. Rather than being viewed separately, these dimensions should be synthesized into a framework, particularly if we take a systems view of an information system. What is needed is a conceptual framework that will allow us to examine and evaluate the interaction of these dimensions.

An understanding of this conceptual framework of an information system can be developed by examining each dimension. First each functional unit (finance, marketing, production, personnel) can be subdivided into activities ranging from transaction processing to strategic planning. The degree of activity in each component (subdivision or subsystem) will vary with the function. Marketing and finance, for example, would obviously have more activity at the strategic level; accounting would have a high degree of activity at the transaction processing level; while production and logistics management would have the highest degree of activity at the operational and managerial control levels. If an organization were organized along product lines, each product would likewise require different degrees of management activity.

The impact of functional-managerial activity subsystems on the information system is through the demand for (1) timely, accurate and relevant information; (2) common information (accessible as a database); (3) common software and hardware; (4) specialized software and hardware; (5) common decision support systems; and (6) unique decision support systems. This impact is represented by the matrix in Figure 2-7. All of these demands may not occur within every firm; it depends on the size and nature of the business. Some firms may have even more demands.

To gain an understanding of how such demands occur, we can examine the framework further. Each functional unit will probably have unique data files that are used only by that functional area or product division. In fact, some individual applications within some functional units will have unique data files not required by other applications in functional areas. Pricing analysis within the managerial control and strategic planning areas of marketing is an example of an application requiring a unique data file. There will also be files that need to be accessed by more than one functional or divisional unit or application. Those are usually organized into a general database. The management of the database generally requires special software called *file management* or *database management systems software.*

In addition to common and specialized files, common and specialized software may be required to support the functional and divisional units within the firm. If one of the subunits of a functional area is involved with a special problem, then special applications software must be written for that subunit. A plant layout decision, to be made by a division manager, is an example of a problem that may require special applications software. Many common software packages and decision support models (such corporate planning models) can also be used by all subunits within the functional areas as well as across the areas. Software

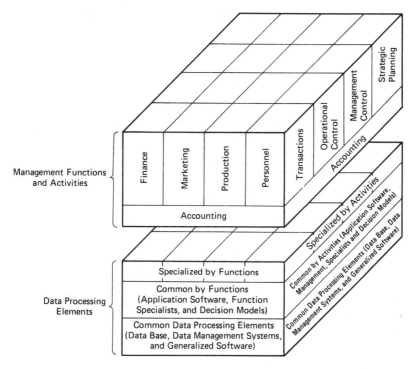

FIGURE 2-7 Conceptual framework of an information system.

that spans the functional and divisional areas forms the *decision model base* for the decision support system, as discussed later. If we examine information demands from the viewpoint of activity levels rather than functional units, we find demands comparable to those by function. Both unique and common files as well as specialized software, common software, and decision support models will probably be required. Each of these needs is depicted in Figure 2-7.

It is very important that this total framework be considered in the analysis and design of an information system in order for all the dimensions to comprise an effective system to support management's objectives.

A SYSTEMATIC PROCEDURE FOR SYSTEM DESIGN AND DEVELOPMENT

Information System Life Cycle

In the dynamic environment of today's society, objectives, strategies, and organizations change. Their information systems change also. Management must be constantly aware of new and varying information needs and the potential of increased information usage due to improvements in technology. As a result, accounting and information systems change. This change must be well managed and requires specific procedures for implementing the analysis of new information needs such as those for the various levels of management. The design of systems to satisfy these needs and the implementation of these systems will be reviewed in detail later in this text. This whole process must be well planned as is the case with the acquisition of any key resource of the organization. This process is often called the systems development life cycle. Information needs are analyzed and systems are planned; new systems are designed or old ones are modified to meet these needs; the most appropriate design is selected and implemented; and the new or modified system is operated and monitored until it falls short of meeting the requirements of management. Then the whole process starts over again as shown in Figure 2-8, which captures the basic steps.

In a *structured analysis* and *design* framework shown in Figure 2-8, the problem is first defined. A feasibility study is then undertaken to determine the existence of a feasible solution. A detailed analysis of what must be done to solve the problem is then undertaken. Following this, the general design of the accounting and information system is undertaken to determine in general how the problem should be solved; or, stated from a different perspective, what alternatives are feasible for providing the management system with the information it needs? This is the beginning of the physical design. Next, the most appropriate alternative is selected and designed in detail. In some cases, specifications are spelled out for the purchase of various elements of the information system. Next, the design is implemented via the acquisition, development, installation, and personnel training. For example, in some cases software will need to be written, in other cases it will be purchased from a software vendor. In summary implementation involves the (1) ordering and installation of hardware and software; (2) programming and testing; (3) systems testing and conversion from the old to the new system. Finally, the system will be monitored for continued compliance with management needs and maintained for efficient operation. When it fails to meet the needs of the management system the cycle is started all over again. Hence it is often called the system life cycle.

AICPA Phases to Systems Development

The AICPA EDP Applications Systems Task Force, in its Management Advisory Services guidelines, denotes several phases[6] to systems analysis and design which parallel the structured approach to systems development. They are defined as:

Phase I—Requirements Definition and Alternative Approaches
Phase II—General Design
Phase III—Detailed Design
Phase IV—Program Specification and Implementation Planning
Phase V—Program Development and Testing
Phase VI—System Testing
Phase VII—Final Testing and Conversion
Phase VIII—Implementation
Phase IX—Review

---

[6] See AICPA, *Guidelines for Development and Implementation of Computer-Based Application Systems,* AICPA Management Advisory Services Guideline Series Number 4 (New York: American Institute of Certified Public Accountants, copyright 1976) for the objectives of these phases.

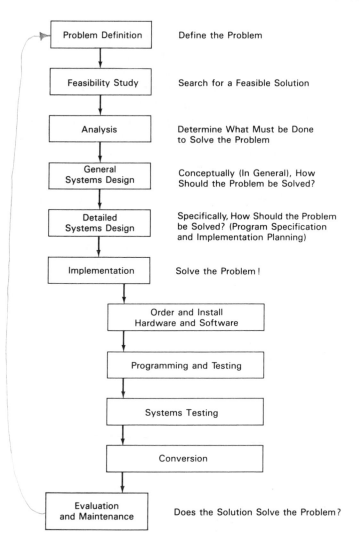

Problem Definition	Define the Problem
Feasibility Study	Search for a Feasible Solution
Analysis	Determine What Must be Done to Solve the Problem
General Systems Design	Conceptually (In General), How Should the Problem be Solved?
Detailed Systems Design	Specifically, How Should the Problem be Solved? (Program Specification and Implementation Planning)
Implementation	Solve the Problem!
Order and Install Hardware and Software	
Programming and Testing	
Systems Testing	
Conversion	
Evaluation and Maintenance	Does the Solution Solve the Problem?

FIGURE 2-8   System life cycle.

SUMMARY

An accounting information system that transforms raw data into usable information has several dimensions. These consist first of data processing elements: hardware, data storage, software, procedures, and personnel. The second key dimension consists of managerial and transaction processing activities. These include strategic planning, managerial and operational control as well as transaction processing. Decisions at these levels may be structured, semistructured or dimension consists of managerial and transaction processing activities. These include strategic planning, managerial and operational control as well as transaction processing. Decisions at these levels may be structured, semistructured or unstructured. The third dimension is the organization and its corresponding management system which the accounting information must support.

The general systems model of an organization and the information system with all its components is designed to help management carry out its objectives in its ultimate delivery of its products and services to customers and to monitor this activity and to make decisions on future activities. In theory, a systems approach coordinates and integrates all the managerial activities and organization and data processing elements into a framework that can better accomplish management's objectives than an uncoordinated component approach. Thus it is very important that all the dimensions of the framework be considered in designing an information system to support a management system. Several types of systems have evolved to help accomplish this. They are: (1) transaction processing; (2) office automation; (3) management information; (4) decision support; and (5) executive information systems. To satisfy the needs of management at the various level of activity, accounting information systems need to be well designed. A structured system analysis and design procedure is presented which, if followed, will greatly contribute to the systematic design of accounting systems that consider all the dimensions of the information systems framework. Such an approach is needed to satisfy the requirements of management.

SELECTED REFERENCES

ACKKOFF, RUSSELL L., "Management Misinformation Systems," *Management Science,* 14 (December 1967), B147–56.

AMERICAN INSTITUTE OF CERTIFIED PUBLIC ACCOUNTANTS, *Guidelines for Development and Implementation of Computer-Based Application Systems,* Management Advisory Services Guideline Series Number 4 (1976).

CASH, JAMES I., and BENN R. KONSYNSKI, IS redraws competitive boundaries," *Harvard Business Review,* March–April, 1985, pp. 134–142.

DIETZ, DEVON D., and JOHN D. KEANE, "Integrating Distributed Processing within a Control Environment," *Management Accounting,* 62 (November 1980), 43–47.

DRUCKER, PETER F., The Coming of the New Organization, *Harvard Business Review,* January-February, 1988, pp. 45–53.

GODFREY, JAMES J., and THOMAS R. PRINCE, "The Accounting Model from an Information System," *Accounting Review,* January 1971, pp. 75–89.

GORRY, G. ANTHONY, and MICHAEL S. SCOTT MORTON, "A Framework for Management Information Systems," *Sloan Management Review,* Fall 1974, pp. 55–70.

MCFARLAND, F. WARREN, "Information technology changes the way you compete," *Harvard Business Review,* May-June, 1984, pp. 98–103.

PORTER, MICHAEL E., and VICTOR E. MILLAR, "How information gives you competitive advantage," *Harvard Business Review,* July-August, 1985, pp. 150–160.

REVIEW QUESTIONS

1. Define the term *system* as it relates to a firm.

2. Differentiate between an *information system* and a *management system.* Identify factors that are common to both.

3. Differentiate between a *systems approach* and a *component approach* in formulating an information system. What factors should be considered in employing a systems approach?

4. Identify data processing elements that might be common between production and marketing.

5. Explain the basic differences between a *decision support system* and *management information systems.*

6. What are three dimensions of information processing?

7. What is the classification of management activities useful in structuring an information system?

8. What elements are associated with the data processing dimension of information processing?

9. Explain Anthony's framework of decision-making activities. How does this framework relate to information processing? What are its accounting implications?

10. What role does the "systems life cycle" play in information processing? How is it related to systems analysis and systems design?

11. How does the information system relate to the physical system used to produce goods or deliver services?

12. Describe each of the types of information systems.

13. Will aggregation of transaction data be sufficient for strategic decision-making information needs? Why or why not? How does your answer influence accounting systems such as those used in planning and control for a manufacturing division?

CASES

2-1 Curtis Company operates in a five-county industrial area near Cleveland, Ohio. The company employs a manual system for all its record keeping except payroll; the payroll is processed by a local service bureau. Other applications have not been computerized because they could not be cost justified.

The company's sales have grown at an increasing rate over the past five years. With this substantial growth rate, a computer-based system seemed more practical. Consequently, Curtis engaged the management consulting department of its public accounting firm to conduct a feasibility study for converting its record-keeping systems to a computer-based system. The accounting firm reported that a computer-based system would improve the company's record-keeping system and still provide material cost savings.

Therefore, Curtis decided to develop a computer-based system for its records. Curtis hired a person with experience in systems development as manager of systems and data processing. His responsibilities are to oversee the entire systems operation, with special emphasis on the development of the new system.

REQUIRED: Describe the major steps that will be undertaken to develop and implement Curtis Company's new computer-based system.
(CMA adapted.)

2-2 Arment Company has sales that range from $25 million to $30 million; has one manufacturing plant; and employs seven hundred people, including fifteen national account salespeople and eighty traveling sales representatives. The home office and plant are in Philadelphia; the product is distributed east of the Mississippi River. The product is a line of pumps and related fittings used at construction sites, in homes, and in processing plants. The company has total assets equal to 80 percent of sales. Its capitalization consists of the following: current liabilities, 30 percent; long-term debt, 15 percent; and shareholders' equity, 55 percent. In the past two years sales have increased 7 percent annually; income after tax has amounted to 5 percent of sales.

REQUIRED: List the strategic planning decisions that must be made or confirmed during the preparation of the annual profit plan or budget.
(CMA adapted.)

2-3 Classify the following decisions as operational, managerial, or strategic. Also classify them as structured or unstructured.

1. Ordering inventory by using the EOQ model
2. Locating a retail outlet for a large fast-food company
3. Terminating an R&D project that does not seem fruitful
4. Planning the construction of a large office building
5. Adding a second shift
6. Promoting a plant manager to vice-president
7. Adding a new product
8. Merging with a raw material vendor
9. Repairing a lathe
10. Inspecting finished goods by using an electronic tester
11. Selecting a vendor from a catalog

2-4 Johnson Typewriter, Inc., an old-line manufacturer of electric typewriters, was one of the leaders in the typewriter industry. Commercial and retail sales topped $475 million in 1991. This was up $55 million from 1990 and exceeded 1989 sales by $75 million. Profits, on the other hand, slid from a record high of $45 million in 1989 to a loss of $95 million in 1991. This disastrous profit picture was even more perplexing because a new management team took over the reins of Johnson Typewriter in 1983 and they quickly merged with AWP (Automatic Word Processing) to apply state-of-the-art microprocessing to commercial typewriters. To compound Johnson Typewriter's troubles, the external auditors are the subject of litiga-

tion for rendering a clean opinion on what has been described as materially false and misleading financial statements for 1990 and 1991. As a result, the management team which led Johnson Typewriter into their problems has been replaced by long-time Johnson employees headed by Mr. Reed, who was vice-president of research and development. Mr. Reed promptly engaged the services of another public accounting firm to assist him in his analysis of the current situation.

Upon their joint examination of the operating and financial activities of business, they found that the condition was far worse than their wildest fears.

1. Johnson's debt, most of which was short term, had risen drastically. It was nearly equal to the company's equity. Cash reserves were nearly depleted. All of this was necessary according to the previous management team in order to enter the age of microprocessing technology. They said, "It was an investment in the future."

2. Some of the commercial sales contracts were misclassified and as a result of reclassification to the typewriter division the Automatic Word Processing division showed an adjusted loss of nearly $90 million. This misclassification was due to the absence of simple controls over sales contract classification.

3. A further examination of the financial statements revealed that several of the adjustments made to the financial statements in 1991, which precipitated the heavy loss, should have been recognized in 1990 and 1989. The accounting system again failed to classify these according to generally accepted accounting principles.

4. Assets were misstated in almost every division. Receivables and inventories were consistently overstated in value. Far too much reliance was placed on a perpetual inventory system which lacked adequate controls.

5. Inefficiencies were present throughout the organization.

   a. In accounting, billing was accomplished using an old overloaded system. The result was that customers received multiple statements, received statements prior to delivery of the typewriter or word processor, and sometimes never received invoices for delivered equipment.

b. In the inventory management system, parts were often not on hand for production or service. This resulted in poor service and the return of many pieces of equipment and the loss of many labor hours.

c. In the distribution of units to commercial distributors and retailers, orders or requisitions for certain popular models would go unheeded and alternative models were frequently shipped as they were produced. The result was the loss of several unhappy distributors and retailers.

d. In production, insufficient arrangements were made with suppliers of microchips. Orders were often placed two months in advance and not delivered to the appropriate plant until three months had lapsed. The result was that manufacturing often had to "make do."

e. A careful investigation yielded the striking revelation that AWP was selected for merger not because of its R&D technology but because of beneficial tax implications. It was discovered after review that other potential word processing companies with much more advanced microprocessing technology were not even considered for a merger.

REQUIRED: From the results of this joint investigation, what information system failures do you recognize? What management decisions were not supported by an effective accounting information system? Classify these decisions as operating, managerial, and strategic.

2-5 Inner City Bus Company had difficulty in scheduling its drivers, buses, and maintenance operations, particularly in snowy weather. To help resolve this problem, Inner City purchased a minicomputer and scheduling software. Furthermore, radio receivers were installed in each bus so that the routes could be altered by a dispatcher as he or she keyed in route delays due to the weather. Drivers could immediately be informed of route alterations.

REQUIRED:

1. Considering the life cycle concept, can you foresee any difficulties Inner City may face due to their purchase and implementation procedures?

2. Can this scheduling system be altered to effect better matching of data and information requirements?

3. Are the communication channels sufficient to alter bus schedules?

2-6 Lakeland Chemical is a middle-sized chemical processing firm with several major products and distribution and sales organizations throughout the upper Midwest. Lakeland had been experiencing coordination problems in marketing, distribution, and production. Each product had its own manager, who was responsible for production, distribution, and sales. Each region also had its own sales and distribution manager. Each manager was paid a substantial bonus on meeting budgeted production or sales. The firm had only one processing facility for all products. In the late 1960s it centralized all computer operations for efficiency and control reasons. The system has been upgraded several times in the past fifteen years. The manager of the processing facility was attempting to comply with the requests of the sales personnel by rescheduling production, working overtime, expediting materials, and even contracting some processing. Top management is worried. Company profits have been falling even though sales have been excellent.

REQUIRED: Is there a system problem that, if resolved, can alleviate some coordination and decision-making difficulties and improve profits? If so, what is it and what is your suggestion, as the company's CPA, on an alternative system and why?

2-7 Your firm has been asked to design a system for strategic planning for May's, a regional department store. Specifically, May's needs help with planning store locations and the type of merchandise to carry in each store. May's management tried to summarize credit sales by location in the metropolitan area and sales at each of its locations. It felt that the aggregated information, aggregated by simply totaling transaction data, was not *sufficient for marketing* and called upon your firm for assistance.

REQUIRED: Why wasn't management satisfied with the simple aggregation of data? Characterize the nature of the two decisions involved here.

2-8 Minnesota Pump, a manufacturer of industrial pumps for a wide variety of uses ranging from waste treatment to natural gas, has three manufacturing plants. These plants specialize in different types of pumps. Minnesota's sales and distribution function is organized by metropolitan area and is concentrated in the upper Midwest. Its finance function is centralized and located in St. Paul. Each plant and sales district has its own data processing system to support functional decision-making, reporting, and transaction processing needs.

The manufacturing plants are operated as cost centers. Managers are evaluated on how well they meet their production schedule and control their costs. The production schedule is set by the home office.

Sales and distribution districts are contribution centers. Managers are evaluated on their budgeted contribution to the overall profit of the firm. Moreover, they forecast sales that are aggregated by the home office and used as the basis for production planning. Each sales district has its own warehouse to serve customer needs because service is the key to success in the industrial pump business.

The finance function's role is to make sure that all capital requests yield a reasonable return on investment. The company has the final word on all capital requests that originate from the plants or sales offices.

Minnesota Pump has had considerable difficulty in getting its management to work together. Coordination is often difficult and none of the managers seem to take action to maximize long-run returns on equity, which is the company's overall goal.

REQUIRED: What kind of management and information system does Minnesota Pump have? Will this management system, along with its supporting system, lead to dysfunctional consequences with regard to achievement of the company's overall goal? Why? Briefly, as Minnesota Pump's CPA, could you render any advice and, if so, what would it be?

2-9 Old Way Publishers collect sales data on text sales by university, book, and author. They use these data along with typical text life cycles where sales are slow at first, accelerate, peak out, and finally slow due to used books. They use this to determine the timing of revisions. This information seems fine but management is unhappy because the company is often slow to come out with revisions when major new theories or events occur in the political, business, or scientific environment.

REQUIRED: Does their current information system used to schedule revisions satisfy their needs? If not, what improvements would you suggest and why?

2-10 Baker and Bennett Financial Planners are in the business of helping individuals as well as small businesses with their financial planning. They are experts in tax law, investment strategy, and budgeting, and their practice reflects this expertise. They decided a new computer system, so Bennett purchased a Megacomp-2000-AT-XL from Village Micro Mart. Moreover, the sales staff at Village Micro Mart suggested that Bennett could make excellent use of Megatax and Compuplan, two "state-of-the-art" software packages designed to run on the Megacomp-2000-AT-XL. Upon arriving at the office, Baker wanted to see how it worked and wanted Bennett to explain how it would improve their efficiency and effectiveness in financial and tax planning. Neither Baker nor Bennett had any computer experience. After several unsuccessful attempts to demonstrate the "user friendly" system, Bennett called Village Micro Mart and wanted to return the hardware and software.

Village Micro Mart said all sales of Megacomp were final because the company was going out of business.

REQUIRED:

1. What step-by-step approach should Baker and Bennett have taken to resolve their

"problem" and to avoid this problem? Why should they take such an approach?

2. For each step, what key questions should have been asked to avoid such a disaster?

2-11 Hang Ten Windsurfers manufactures and distributes windsurfers all along the east coast. They can't seem to coordinate their marketing and production efforts. Every time marketing has a promotion in a certain part of the country, production either can't deliver the products or distribution has excess stock in another part of the country. Moreover, they keep missing market shifts in terms of demand and style. In addition, they have had several production stoppages due to insufficient stock at the manufacturing plant.

REQUIRED: In terms of their management and information system what are their problems? How can they be reduced in the future?

3

ORGANIZATIONAL AND BEHAVIORAL PRINCIPLES

OVERVIEW

The systems approach to any management or accounting system is based on the interrelationships of the activities, the functions, and the information processing elements of an organization. These interrelationships involve the firm's objectives, strategy, organization structure, and technology and the behavior of individuals in the organization. All of these require system choices. Many organizations have failed to make consistent decisions regarding these choices. These organizations and their associated, supporting accounting information systems have fallen short of their potential because they have failed to coordinate these activities, functions, and data processing dimensions with the major variables of their management system. Moreover, they have failed to motivate the individuals who are to implement the system.

The management system consists of the strategy and the organization structure including various managerial activities and functions and their interrelationships. Ideally, the management system should be organized (structured) to achieve, through individual behavior, the objectives of the organization as whole. These activities are generally characterized as strategic planning, management control, operational control, and transaction processing. To accomplish the firm's objectives, management must develop business strategy and must plan, organize, staff, coordinate, direct, and control these activities. This strategy and plan must be implemented through human interaction. In Chapters 1 and 2 we noted that it is imperative that the information system be designed to support this management system, not the reverse. Thus, both the design and implementation of an accounting information system and its subsequent operation are functions of the overall strategy and the decision-making activities of the firm; of the organization structure of the firm; and of the behavioral patterns of the individuals involved in the design, implementation, reporting, transaction processing, and decision-making activities of the firm. All of these components make up the *organizational and social environment* of the management system and the supporting information system.

The objective of this chapter will be to provide the accountant, as information system user and designer, with a better appreciation of the impact of organizational and behavioral factors on an information system and vice versa. This is important because the accounting system is an integral part of every organization. A fundamental understanding of why accounting systems evolve and how to better develop them requires an understanding about organizations and the behavior of those who use and operate the system. For example, why are some organizations profit centers while others are nonprofit centers? The accounting systems in each instance are likely to be quite different.

In this chapter we will consider the theory and the key variables with respect to the organizational structure of the firm; organization of the accounting and information systems department or departments; and behavioral issues, including the problem of employee resistance to change. We will see that accounting information systems play a key role in the management and control of organizations via agency relationships. We will see that various organization systems are contingent on the needs of management to process information and to make decisions. We will see that technology clearly influences these causal relationships. In summary we will also see that an information system, and its accounting subsystem, is contingent on the organization and its business strategy.

Organizational Theory

An organization can be thought of as legal entity which consists of sets of contracts or agreements between a number of different parties. These agreements specify the rules of the game within the organization as well as between the organization and external parties such as owners, suppliers, and customers. Internal contracts (agreements) are often referred to as *hierarchies;* external contracts (agreements) are often referred to as *markets.* This is because the first is generally part of the organizational structure and standard operating procedures, and the latter deals with third parties in the market place. In accounting, the team *agency theory* is frequently used to describe these contractual relationships. In agency theory, as shown in Figure 3-1, one or more persons—the principal(s)—engage another person or persons—agent(s)—to perform some service on their

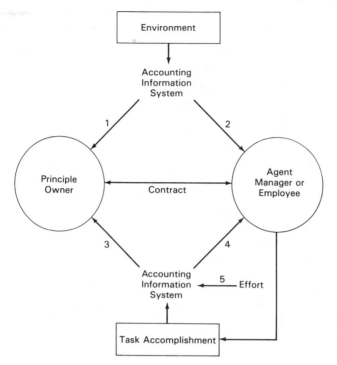

FIGURE 3-1
Accounting system and
principal–agent relationships.

behalf.[1] For example, owners engage the service of a manager to operate their store; the employment agreement between owners and manager constitutes the contract. The fundamental challenge for management is to structure these contracts and their resulting organization structure and management system in order to achieve the objectives of the organization. To complicate the problem it is generally assumed that both the agent and the principal operate in their own self-interest and that they both operate in an uncertain environment. This involves setting organizational strategy and developing an information system to support the resulting organization.

An accounting system must be developed to reduce the uncertainty about the environment for both the principal and the agent. For example, a good fore-

---

[1] For a discussion of the impact of agency theory on organizations and their information systems, see Stanley Baiman, "Agency Research in Managerial Accounting: A Survey," *Journal of Accounting Literature* 1 (1982), 154–213; Michael C. Jensen, "Organizational Theory and Methodology," *The Accounting Review*, LVIII, no. 2 (April 1983), 319–337; Michael C. Jensen, and W. H. Meckling, "Theory of the Firm: Managerial Behavior, Agency Costs and Ownership Structure," *Journal of Financial Economics*, 1976, pp. 305–360; Barry H. Spicer, and Van Ballew, "Management Accounting Systems and the Economics of Internal Control," *Accounting Organizations and Society* 8, no. 1 (1983), 73–96; and P. Tiessen and J. H. Waterhouse, "Towards a Descriptive Theory of Management Accounting," *Accounting, Organizations and Society*, 8 (1983), 251–267.

casting system based on economic indicators will help both management and employees develop better plans for the future. An accounting system must be developed to obtain better feedback information on the accomplishment of the tasks required and the effort put forth to accomplish these tasks so that the employee (agent) does not have an advantage because the manager (owner) does not know whether the employee (agent) has lived up to his or her end of the agreement. For example, an effective standard cost system which isolates variances by responsibility center will help in determining the accomplishment and perhaps the comparative effort to control costs of an employee or departmental manager.

These accounting systems are not costless and they are not perfect. In other words, management or the owners (principals) must conduct cost benefit analysis on the system and recognize that there will always be some asymmetry (one party will have more information) in the amount of information, either about the environment or the accomplishment of the task or the effort expended to accomplish the task. For example, a salesperson may know more about the market than their manager, and as a result "pad" the sales quotas (set low quotas) so that they will always be easily met and he or she will always receive a bonus. One way to reduce some of this asymmetry is to offer incentives to the employee (agent) not to be opportunistic and take advantage of their unique knowledge, but to work in the best interests of the welfare of the owner or manager (principal). This is done using an *internal labor contract* (agreement) which includes incentives and reward structures to encourage cooperation in sharing information and in efforts to accomplish the goals of the organization. These labor contracts constitute an organizational hierarchy and they replace the need to negotiate new contracts for ongoing routine work of the organization when the negotiation cost would be too high and repetitive. In effect, these labor agreements become the standard operating policies of the organization. An example might be some form of salary plus profit sharing system for employees rather than hiring external personnel to do the work. The accounting system and its performance measures are part of these contracts. For example, cost and variance information may be used to measure a production foreman's performance.

The form of these contracts between all the principals and agents within the organization will vary greatly given the objectives of the organization and its strategy for implementing these objectives. According to *contingency theory* [2] there is no one best organization structure and the structure is contingent upon the objectives and the strategy of the organization. If the organization consists of the summation of all the contracts between all the parties of the organization, as noted above, then the organization structure will parallel or be contingent upon the nature of these contracts.

As an illustration of these concepts, consider two general contractors. Both build commercial and residential buildings. One decides that its best strategy is

---

[2] For a current discussion of contingency theory, see Robert H. Chenhall, and Deigan Morris, "The Impact of Structure, Environment and Interdependence on the Perceived Usefulness of Management Accounting Systems," *The Accounting Review, LXI, no. 1, (January 1986)*, 16–35; D.C. Hayes, "The Contingency Theory of Managerial Accounting," *The Accounting Review*, 1977, pp. 22–39; and Spicer and Ballew, "Management Accounting Systems and the Economics of Internal Control" *Accounting Organizations and Society*, Pergamon Press PLC, 8, no. 1, 1983.

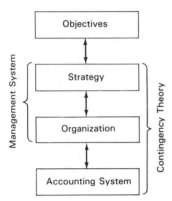

FIGURE 3-2
Contingency theory.

to employ subcontractors for all of its projects. This contractor has only a skeleton organization consisting of few supervisors and office staff and engineers. It must ask for bids for each project and negotiate separate contracts for each project with each subcontractor, such as the electrician, the framers, and the masons. This contractor needs an accounting system which can handle the payables for each of these on percentage-of-completion basis and an effective planning system for evaluating bids. The other contractor decides that these transaction costs are too high and too laden with uncertainty and so he employs his own crews rather than hiring subcontractors. Thus this contractor has a much larger organization with various departments for each type of activity and these departments are organized around different projects. They enter into labor contracts with their employees in this instance. For example, they agree to pay so much an hour for skilled tradespersons and laborers and a salary for the supervisors. This contractor needs an entirely different accounting system to set standards for each project, to set salaries and wages, and to evaluate the performance of their employees. This suggests a job-cost system based on history of performance on similar jobs. Since the second contractor has control of the entire operation, the firm probably needs an inventory and accounts payable system to account for all the supplies used on the projects.

In this example, the nature of the organization is very much dependent upon the business strategy chosen to implement the objectives of the organization. The accounting system which must support the organization is contingent upon the organization which is a function of the business strategy. As result it is imperative that accountants and systems designers understand the nature of the business, the business strategy, and the resulting organization structure and process in order to develop an effective accounting system to support management decision-making and reporting and transaction processing requirements. This ordering of objectives and their relationships to strategy, organization and accounting information system is illustrated in Figure 3-2.

ORGANIZATIONAL STRUCTURE

Structure and Process

It is important that accountants understand the structure and processes of the organization so they can design systems that are responsive to management information needs. Business strategy and patterns of authority, responsibility, and decision processes related to the imbedded contractual agreements which comprise the organization will dictate the flow of information. These contracts, along with reward criteria and management policy, will lead to certain types of organization structure. *Structure* is generally defined as how the organization gets work done via hierarchical labor contracts (agreements) consisting of lines of authority, assignment of decision-making responsibility, and communication channels through which inquiries, reports, and transaction documents flow. With larger, more mature (in terms of more formalized organizational hierarchies) systems, and with longer time frames (rate of technological change and strategic decision making), this understanding is much easier to achieve because the organization tends to be fairly stable. For example, a large well-established automotive manufacturer will have a relatively stable structure compared to those in the rapidly changing computer software industry.

It is not enough to know the structure of the organization; the transaction and decision-making processes must also be understood because they are also important facets of the organizational hierarchy. *Process* refers to the processing of transactions and reports and the methods of decision making used at all levels of activity and in each functional area to achieve the contractual agreements between the managers and employees or owners and managers. This may not be readily apparent from formal organization charts and descriptions. This information must be obtained to understand the organizational and social environment of a firm so that needed information can be provided on a timely basis to the various parties which comprise the organization. Input such as organization charts, labor contracts containing descriptions of duties, the flow of documents, charts of accounts, and personal conversations with employees should help the systems designer or accountant gain insight into the organization structure and processes. For example, what is the nature of the decision process involved in the preparation of a bid for a new audit engagement for a CPA firm.

Criteria for Assessing Structure and Process

Organizations may take many forms or structures to comply with the nature of the organizational hierarchy and strategic plans. According to contingency theory, not all structures are equally effective. An organization must continually evaluate it's strategic plans, the uncertainty related to these plans, and the information requirements of management needed to deal with the implementation of these plans.[3] These structures can be assessed in terms of management ability to process transactions, report on these transactions, and make decisions to meet the objectives of the organization given the nature of the contractual arrange-

---

[3] For a complete discussion, see Jay R. Galbraith, *Organizational Design: An Information Processing Point of View* (Reading, Mass.: Addison-Wesley, 1974); and Paul R. Lawrence and Jay W. Lorsch, *Developing Organizations: Diagnosis and Action* (Reading, Mass.: Addison-Wesley, 1969).

PROCESS CRITERIA	OBJECTIVES	OUTCOME
1. Steady-state efficiency 2. Operating responsiveness 3. Management responsiveness 4. Strategic responsiveness 5. Structural responsiveness	1. Maximize near-term performance 2. Long-term growth 3. Protection from catastrophic risk	Maximization of return on resources employed by organization

FIGURE 3-3   Process criteria, objectives, and outcome.

ments of the organization, as outlined in Figure 3-3.

Steady-state efficiency, as noted in Figure 3-3, refers to the organization's economies of scale, optimization procedures, and synergistic aspects. In other words, steady-state efficiency represents smooth operation that functions at maximum efficiency within its hierarchical structure. *Operating responsiveness* refers to the organization's responsiveness to market and operating challenges. *Management responsiveness* refers to the organization's responsiveness to the reallocation of its resources to accomplish its strategic objectives. *Strategic responsiveness* refers to the organization's ability to change its objectives and policies when environmental changes occur in products, technology, markets, and society. In other words, the organization is responsive at the strategic level. *Structural responsiveness* refers to the organization's ability to design new organizational hierarchical structures and processes to meet new challenges and problems as they arise and cause changes in the contractual relationships within and outside the organization. In general, the more uncertain the environment and the tasks of the organization, the greater the responsiveness needed at all levels of management activity. This need is often critical to an organizations success in todays dynamic and global markets.

These five criteria, which follow from Anthony's[4] decision-making activities, can be used to assess the organization's transaction and decision-making processes and the related structure and set of contracts used to carry out its objectives.

Basic Framework

VERTICAL AND HORIZONTAL HIERARCHY. An organization can be structured *vertically* along hierarchical lines of authority and responsibility with the president at the top, vice-president in charge of various functions, and managers reporting to the vice-presidents. Supervisory personnel then report to these managers. This is the most common form of an organization. On the other hand, an organization can be structured around *horizontal* departmentalization. This departmentalization may be by function, location, process, or product. For example, a team of engineers assigned to a certain research project, as in an automotive corporation, is an example of organization around product lines.

---

[4] These were presented in chapter 2. See Robert N. Anthony, *Planning and Control Systems: A Framework for Analysis* (Boston: Harvard Business School, 1965).

CENTRALIZED FUNCTIONAL FORM. One of the more common ways for an organization to structure itself to process information and make decisions to meet its objectives is through centralization and vertical differentiation following traditional functional lines. This type of structure lends itself well to an organization that wants its decision making to be highly centralized. Recent advances in computer technology and telecommunications have made this centralization easier to achieve.

Each vice-president or manager is responsible, by virtue of his or her labor contract (agreement), for specific part of the organization. This has the advantage of steady-state efficiency in terms of economy of scale and specialization. Moreover, communication and decision-making networks and their related accounting systems used to monitor performance and compliance with these contracts are relatively straightforward. For example, in Figure 3-4, part A, all sales activities are the province of the vice-president of marketing, who can employ specialists for assistance. Each regional manager, who reports to the vice-president, can do the same. Throughout the organization each manager is concerned with only one function and can therefore do better job of supervision, especially in such technical areas as engineering and manufacturing. Interfaces with other parts of the organization can be achieved using a centralized information system.

Functional organizations can effectively be used to control an organization if its product is fairly homogeneous. Cost centers can effectively be used for planning and control, and needed coordination of activities can be achieved at the executive level, which is the only level with company wide perspective. This type of organization has disadvantages. The centralized functional form suffers from low strategic and structural responsiveness because top management is often overloaded with operating problems, swamped with too much operating data, and has little time for managerial and strategic decision making. There is also an absence of coordination, except via a large, complex, centralized computer processing system, between various functions, such as marketing and production, to ensure smooth flow of product at a profit. As a result, there is little support for corporate strategy founded upon product lines or projects. To compound this problem, management cannot easily evaluate profitability and return on investment for divisions, products, or projects. In summary, management has a very difficult time monitoring and controlling the activities of organization with diverse product lines.

DECENTRALIZED DIVISIONAL FORM. If a firm wants its organization to be more responsive to opportunities for profit and return on investment for each division or product line, it may structure its organizational hierarchy along division lines or product lines, as shown in part B of Figure 3-4. Note that this figure is only schematic; the divisional forms may be used through several levels before a functional form is used. Also, this structural form and its resulting process has good steady-state efficiency and operating responsiveness due to its hierarchical relationships.

This type of organization is more flexible because new products and/or divisions can be added, changed, or deleted more easily. Moreover, there is much more product and dimensional autonomy resulting in more localized planning, control and decision making. Thus strategic and structural responsiveness

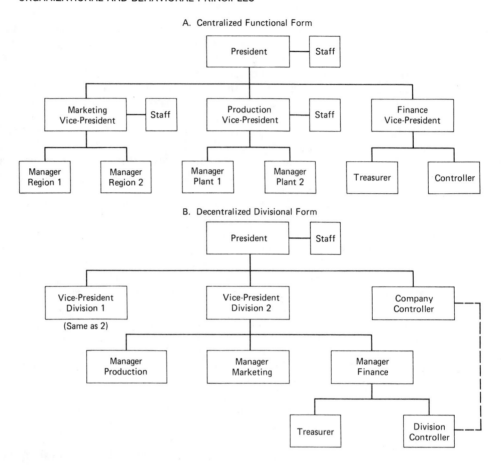

FIGURE 3-4 Hierarchical organization structure.

is better than that for the centralized structure because coordination of activities is done at the divisional level. Profit and investment planning, responsibility, and control activities constitute an important component of labor contracts and the resulting organizational hierarchy. This type of structure can also be effective in training managers to deal with problems from the perspective of the organization as whole.

The decentralized divisional organization form also has disadvantages. The degree of specialization existing in the centralized form will generally not exist in this structural form. Divisions and product lines will necessarily vie for scarce company resources that will have to be allocated, resulting in competition instead of cooperation. Therefore, this type of organization is generally characterized by decentralized decision-making activities. Microcomputers have, moreover, given even small divisions the ability to have their own computing operations. This is called distributed processing. Part of the processing and even some of the data is distributed to each division, rather than processing and storing data at a centralized location.

RESPONSIBILITY AND PROFITABILITY ACCOUNTING SYSTEMS.   To aid in the planning and controlling of management activities in both of these hierarchical organization forms, responsibility accounting systems may be used by management. Such systems would help management obtain feedback on employees' or managers' (agents) efforts and accomplishments and relate this feedback to their agreed-upon contractual arrangements. In responsibility, or profitability, accounting systems, each manager or vice-president is responsible for all of those costs, revenue, and investments that are under that person's control. Control is defined as significant influence (delegated authority) over the expenditure or revenue item. As part of the overall organizational contract (set of agreements) all plans, programs, budgets, and reports follow these lines of responsibility. For example, consider the divisional form for small company. Plant supervisors are responsible for labor, overtime premiums, materials, tools and supplies, setup and rework costs, and maintenance. They each report to the plant manager, who is responsible for all the operations of the plant assembly, and finishing, as well as plant overhead operations such as engineering and accounting. The plant managers, along with the sales manager, reports to the divisional Vice president, who is responsible for all the operations of the division and its' resulting profitability. In turn, the president is responsible for two different divisions. Table 3-1 illustrates a typical performance report used by management to assess performance (compliance with contract) for such a system. Note that each supervisor and manager is only held responsible for controllable costs. In this case, performance evaluations at the managerial level are based on the difference between the actual and budgeted costs (the variance). The division vice president is responsible for divisional profit. Investment in the division is sometimes included in the performance report to assess the division vice presidents profit performance relative to the division investment.

Adaptive Framework

PROJECT MANAGEMENT.   If a firm's strategy requires project management with a specific beginning and end, such as the construction of a building or the manufacture of a specific number of aircraft of certain type, it may be useful to combine both the divisional and the centralized hierarchical structures. Functional resources can then be assigned to specific projects for their duration. Upon completion of the project, these resources (personnel, financial, manufacturing facilities, constructions equipment, etc.) are returned to pool for use on another project. Each time this happens, a different contract (agreement) is reached with the managers (principals) and employees (agents) involved in terms of project expectations, completion criteria, and information. Such a structure is generally called project management structure. As can be seen in part A of Figure 3-5, the organization structure has permanent functions such as marketing, production, and finance; and flexible project groups that are drawn from the permanent functional areas and assigned to specific projects for their duration. Project managers must integrate all the functions in order to accom-

Table 3-1 Responsibility Accounting System

	AMOUNT		VARIANCE F(U)	
	Current Month	Year to Date	Current Month	Year to Date
President				
Division A Net Income	$30,000	$50,000	$700	($300)
Division B Net Income	$25,000	$55,000	($500)	$500
Home Office Expenses	$5,000	$10,000	$200	($400)
Corporate Net Income	$50,000	$95,000	$400	($200)
Division A Vice President				
Sales Revenue	$120,000	$240,000	$500	($600)
Expenses				
Sales	$15,000	$32,000	$100	$200
Overhead	$15,000	$30,000	($200)	($400)
Plant 1	$24,000	$44,000	($200)	$100
Plant 2	$36,000	$84,000	$500	$400
Total Expenses	$90,000	$190,000	$200	$300
Net Income	$30,000	$50,000	$700	($300)
Plant 1 Manager				
Overhead	$3,000	$5,000	$0	$0
Finishing Dept.	$11,500	$21,500	$200	$200
Assembly Dept	$9,500	$17,500	($400)	($100)
Total Controllable Costs	$24,000	$44,000	($200)	$100
Assembly Dept. Supervisor				
Labor	$3,000	$6,000	($200)	$100
Materials	$5,000	$9,500	$100	$0
Supplies	$500	$700	($100)	($100)
Setup & Rework	$300	$500	$0	$100
Maintenance	$700	$800	($200)	($200)
Total Controllable Costs	$9,500	$17,500	($400)	($100)

plish their mission or objectives and they are evaluated on this basis. As a result, such an organization has much greater managerial, strategic, and structural responsiveness than the previously discussed structures. This type of organization is also quite useful in companies where technology, markets, and products are rapidly changing and responsive, strategic decision making is essential to the company's success. As can be seen, this type of organization relies less on formal organizational hierarchies and more on market forces than previously discussed organizational structures. Project management organizations will have more complex transaction processing and decision-making networks.

MATRIX STRUCTURE. In matrix structure each member is responsible both to the project manager (or, as illustrated in part B of Figure 3-5, the partner in charge of specific engagement) and to functional manager. This state of dual responsibility and authority is much more permanent in a matrix organization than in a project management form, even though projects begin and end. In fact, a particular individual may even be working on more than one project, such as an audit engagement, at one time.

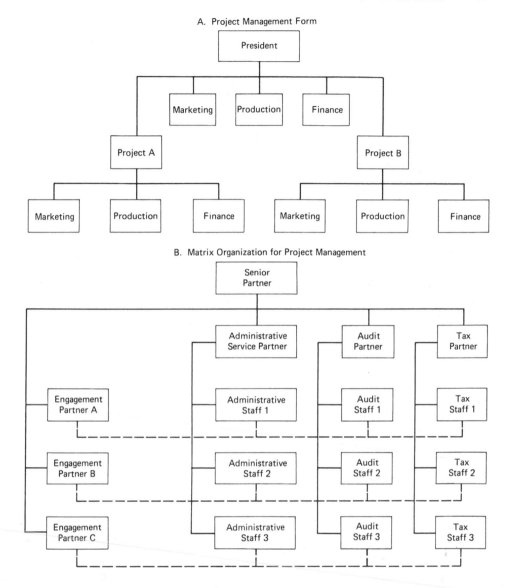

FIGURE 3-5 Adaptive organizational structures.

Such an organization has good strategic and structural responsiveness but very poor steady-state efficiency because of the complex nature or the employment contracts. Economies of scale and technical efficiency are hampered by dual responsibilities and competition for resources. With matrix structure, a very high degree of integration is required. This integration will be reflected in a very complex decision and transaction flow process. This organizational hierarchy will have not only formal lines of responsibility, as in the division structure, but also will have technical lines of responsibility for the functional areas, as in the functional form. Employment labor contracts will reflect these arrangements, and processes will follow these agreements.

INNOVATION STRUCTURE.   Hybrids of these structures can be used effectively. For example, the centralized or divisional form, which maximizes steadystate efficiency, can be used for current business, and the matrix structure can be used for innovative products and projects. Moreover, some organizations (as suggested in the earlier illustration involving two contractors with different business strategies), instead of building an internal organizational hierarchy, will rely almost entirely on the market and contracts with others (subcontractors) to achieve their objectives.

Decision and Transaction Flow Network

From Figure 3-2, we see management must organize to carry out activities within particular business strategy. Management must in turn develop an accounting system to plan and control these activities. Several structural and processing hierarchies have been proposed to help achieve this goal and to reduce uncertainty and asymmetry in the accounting information system in order to enhance cooperation between owners, managers, and employees. Responsibility accounting system is one such structural and processing hierarchy for structuring the organization, controlling its operations, and providing information for decision making. As we noted in our discussion of divisional organization structures, revenue and investment responsibilities may be part of the various contracts between the parties involved in order to evaluate the performance of managers, employees, or divisions on a return-on-investment basis.

Other methods (hierarchies) have been proposed. One frequently used method where there are multiple and often nonquantifiable organizational goals is management by objectives. The managers set personal objectives with the guidance and counsel of their superiors and are evaluated on the accomplishment of these objectives. Another method combines planning, programming, and budgeting systems into an integrated control system known as PPBS. This system is primarily used in large organizations, especially those that are program or project oriented, such as construction or aerospace.

Regardless of the organization's hierarchical or market structure and the method of planning, control, and reporting used, the information system, and specifically the accounting system, must be designed to support the organization's transaction processing, reporting, and decision-making networks and the people who operate these networks. (More will be said about design, development, and implementation of information systems in Chapters 12 and 13.)

Data Structure

To provide effective information for the organization, the information system, file management system, or database must be structured around the organizations hierarchical and market framework. For example, if matrix structure is used, the database must permit efficient updating, summary, and retrieval of information for projects as well as for functional areas. This is to help project and functional managers make decisions and control their operations to achieve the firm's objectives. Strategy which calls for such adaptive structures may require a database that is application independent so that both data and application can easily be changed. This type of database structure will be described in Chapter 10.

INFORMATION SYSTEMS STRUCTURE

These systems link the functional and decision-making activities and the data processing elements of the organization in order to provide management with information. The information systems literature indicates that numerous types of systems exist to support the variety of organizations just noted. Most information systems can be classified as a centralized or distributed system. These can be either integrated or take a component approach. In a component approach every segment of the organization has its own separate system. Both of these approaches along with their hardware, network configurations, and communication equipment are discussed in Chapter 7.

Centralized Systems

As we have noted in earlier chapters in our conceptual examination of an information system, both specialized and common data files as well as specialized and common software needs can exist in an information system. The fact that specialized data, software, and other needs exist, however, does not prevent the structuring of totally integrated information systems. Those specialized parts of the total system will simply have limited usage. A centralized information system is designed so that all the processing and data of an organization are centralized.

Distributed Systems

Another approach is to distribute subsystems throughout the organization and link the subsystems via a communication network. This latter process is the distributed systems approach. While the centralized system utilizes the central data processing facility with a common database, the distributed system is built by aggregating a group of small, separate information systems each with its own database. An argument often used to support adopting the distributed systems approach is that localized information systems can bettter serve the subunits of the organization because they are customized to meet the particular needs of each subunit. In addition, these separate subsystems are easier to modify to meet changing divisional needs.

A distributed system in most instances will require a much more elaborate communication network. This is one of the disadvantages of distributed system. If it is assumed that every subsystem is tied to every other subsystem and to the centralized operation, then N (N-1)/12 channels are required. For example, if we have an organization with five subsystems (users) plus the central operations, then fifteen communications channels are required. Large distributed systems can become very complex. In recent years, highly efficient and economical telecommunications equipment has been developed to ease the cost associated with this complexity. In addition, the development of economical microcomputers has enhanced the cost effectiveness of the distributed systems approach. By using a distributed system, costs are also reduced because some of the processing burden is removed from the centralized facility, which means that smaller, more economical, computers can be employed. Distributed systems are discussed in much more detail in Chapter 7 on system structures.

Integrated Systems

As noted, either the centralized or the distributed systems can be integrated via common databases or extensive telecommunication networks. This has the advantage of maximizing the coordination of all the activities of the organization because all activities of the organization are linked together. These integrated systems may be tightly coupled, representing total integration, or loosely coupled. The problem with total integration or a total system, as it has been historically called, is that the organizational commitment to such a system and the cooperation among the units is enormous. This problem can be mitigated to some degree by using a distributed processing and database system where the various systems are linked but not as tightly coupled.

Summary

The advantages and disadvantages of the distributed systems approach are summarized in Chapter 7. In general, centralized and distributed systems are two different approaches to structuring an information system. A centralized system matches the needs of centralized operations with limited degree of distribution; whereas the distributed system better matches the needs of decentralized operation with limited degree of centralization.

If top management wants strong centralized organization with limited flexibility at lower levels in the organization, then the information system should be centralized to every degree possible. On the other hand, if the organization is relatively diverse with significantly different operations, a centralized system is probably inappropriate. For example, a commercial airlines organization is likely to need an centralized system because most operations, such as scheduling and maintenance, revolve around passenger activity and the organization is very centralized. On the other hand, a large aerospace organization is more amenable to the distributed systems approach because the organization probably has diverse functions and operations that are relatively independent. In some situations top management should probably not even try to integrate via either type of system. It may be better to have independent systems for each component.

ORGANIZATION OF ACCOUNTING AND MIS DEPARTMENT

MIS Location Issues

The location of the information systems department within the organization is the subject of great deal of controversy. The fact that the information emanating from this department is the lifeblood of the organizations decision making and transaction processing network gives the manager or the vice-president of this department considerable influence over the decision-making activities at all levels within the organization.[5]

The emerging consensus is that the information systems department should be headed by a chief information officer (CIO) with responsibilities for the acquisition of information resources, the storage of data, monitoring the use of the system, and the development of new or modified applications. The CIO may have several different titles such as manager or vice-president of information systems. He or she should report to the highest level manager or the president. This location tends to ensure a more division wide or company wide perspective for information processing and communication and better coordination of information resources.

This is in contrast to another common location in the controller's department or under the vice-president of finance. The problem with this latter location is that financial information tends to dominate the system and coordination of the organization information resources become unwieldy when there is no CIO to set policies. Most computerized information systems probably started in this location because financial transaction information was the first to be incorporated into the computer system. If on the other hand the controller's role is expanded as it should be to include all information (not only financial), many of these problems will be mitigated; both locations, in effect, will be similar in organizational behavior, and the controller will function as the CIO for the organization. In this text we assume that this expanded role of the controller includes all information, recognizing that this is not always the case.

Controllership and Treasurership Functions

One of the cardinal principles of any organization hierarchy is the separation of the duties of the custody of assets and the recording of transactions pertaining to these assets. This separation of duties is key to effective internal control. Based on this organizational independence premise, the Financial Executives Institute (FEI) has proposed that controllership and treasurership functions be separated, as shown in Figure 3-6. The treasurership is basically a custodial function, and the controllership is basically an information and reporting function. Note that according to the FEI, systems procedures and information processing, if located in the financial area, are controller functions.

The controller is thus charged with two types of activities. One can be categorized as day-to-day accounting activities and the other as planning and control activities. These must be separated, or the latter will never be accomplished because day-to-day problems will dominate the schedule. Thus it is further suggested that the controller's department be organized so that the day-to-day activities are grouped together under the chief accountant or assistant controller (see Figure 3-7). Using this type of organization, there is also an assistant controller for planning and control. Moreover, there are managers for economic analysis, tax planning, and special projects. As with information systems, it is of-

---

[5] See Martin L. Bariff and Jay R. Galbraith, "Intraorganizational Power Considerations for Designing Information Systems," *Accounting, Organizations and Society*, 3, no. 1 (1978), 15–27. Copyright 1978, Pergamon Press, Ltd.

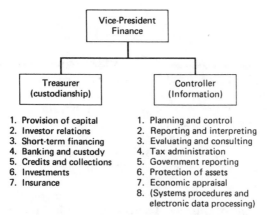

FIGURE 3-6 Controllership and treasurership functions defined by Financial Executives Institute.
Source: Adapted from Financial Executives Institute with permission, New York, N.Y.

ten recommended that the internal audit department report to the highest level within the firm as shown in Figure 3-7.

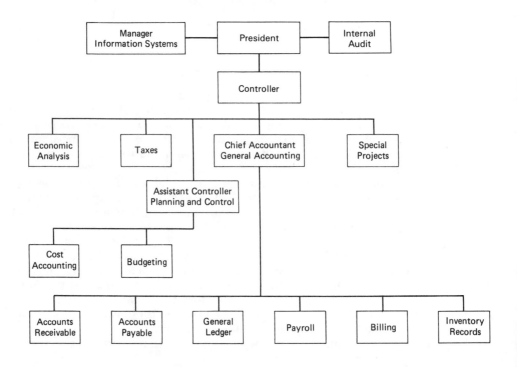

FIGURE 3-7 Organization of controller's department.

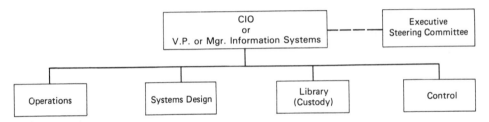

FIGURE 3-8 Organization of information systems department.

Organization of Information Systems Department

Regardless of the location of the information systems department within the firm, certain functions must be kept separate, as shown in Figure 3-8. The actual operation of the computer system (running the computer programs) must be separate from system design and programming. To guarantee the security of the firm's assets and the reliability of information, these two functions must never be combined. The manager of systems analysis and design is responsible for the development of all the system projects within the firm. These projects should be coordinated by the executive or the CIO responsible for the management information system in conjunction with the directives given by the information systems steering committee of top management personnel responsible for overseeing the information systems of the organization. The CIO is generally the chairman of this committee. Moreover, the development and implementation of these projects should follow a well-conceived plan such as the structured approach to systems analysis and design presented in Chapters 12 and 13. For larger organizations, each systems project will have a manager. The manager of systems analysis and design is also responsible for the programming, testing, and maintenance of the system. Personnel in the systems analysis and design section, because of their knowledge of the system and their technical expertise, must not have access to the system other than in very controlled situation that involves systems analysis and design tasks.

Custody of data in the form of tapes and disks must be separate from both of these functions for the same reason that the treasurership and controllership functions must be separate. Generally there is a tape or disk library with a librarian. In database systems similar control is established using system software to restrict access to data. Finally, input, output, database and processing flows must all be controlled by a manager. All of these report to the CIO, vice-president of information or manager of information systems. These functions may exist at each level in an organization if computer operations are distributed along divisional or functional lines.

Management of Information Systems

All projects and changes in hardware, software, and applications ought to conform to a long-range master plan. The chief information officer (or equivalent person) is responsible for implementation of this plan. For example, each project must conform to this plan during the early phases of systems development and implementation. To assist in this planning process, an information system should have an executive systems steering committee to help set broad policies and plans for the firms information system. The leader of this committee must be the senior executive who is responsible for the firm's information system. This is the CIO. Members should include the manager of information systems, the controller, and the senior managers from major users within the organization. This committee can also review major projects, changes, purchases, application systems, exceptions to internal control procedures, and hiring of key personnel. A further benefit of such a committee is that it involves top management in the firm's information and accounting activities. Without top management support and steering committee directing information systems management and planning, no system can be successful.

In addition to these organization and planning activities, it is also necessary to price information and data processing services. There should be an equitable allocation of resources, costs for these services, and motivation to provide service to users so that users can fully utilize the resources of the information or accounting department. The center can also be either a profit or cost center. Its information pricing structure will have a great impact on its utilization.

BEHAVIORAL CONCEPTS

Basic Motivation Concepts

As indicated earlier in this chapter, an organization is a coalition held together by set of contracts (agreements) between individuals working toward a set of goals. The job of management, and, in turn, of the information system that supports management, is to obtain congruence of these individual goals and the objectives of the entire organization. (Congruence means that all parties work together toward common goal; they do not pursue separate objectives and go in different directions.) This is achieved through set of contracts between principals (owners or managers) and agents who work for the principals. It may never be achieved completely in practice, but management should attempt to obtain a reasonably high degree of cooperation. The establishment of effective agreements between the parties involved requires reasonable understanding of human behavior and motivation in an organizational setting on the part of management and the systems designer and the accountant, who assists management in the development and implementation of information systems.

Motivation is a function of many factors. It is the task of the systems designer or accountant to work with these various factors to motivate individuals or groups of individuals to achieve the overall goals of the organization through the hierarchy of the organization. **Based on a composite of the prevailing literature [6], the performance of individuals and groups is combination of (1) aptitude;**

---

[6] This discussion is based in part on John P. Campbell and Robert D. Pritchard, "Motivation Theory in Industrial and Organizational Psychology," in *Handbook of Industrial and Organizational Psychology*, ed. Marvin D. Dunnette (Chicago Rand McNally; 1976), pp. 63–130. See also Brownell, Peter and Morris McInnes, "Budgetary Participation, Motivation, and Managerial Performance," *The Accounting Review*, LXI, no. 4 (October 1986), 587–598; and E. E. Lawler and J. L. Suttle, "Expectancy Theory and Job Behavior," *Organizatiional Behavior and Human Performance*, 9 (1973), 482–503 for a discussion of these issues.

(2) skill level; (3) understanding of the task; (4) choice to expend effort; (5) degree of effort to expended; (6) persistance; and (7) facilitating and inhibiting conditions not under the individual's control. In addition, the presence of unique information that no one else has, such as more accurate cost estimates, (information asymmetry) can also affect individual motivation and performance. For example, if management cannot monitor the results of an employee's efforts, he or she may elect not to work very hard.

To further compound the motivation problem, organizations are dynamic. Every management decision or absence of decision, change in the social environment or organizational hierarchy, or impact of the external factors (including system changes) will have an effect on one or more of the factors just summarized. The effect will be different for each individual and can lead to either functional and dysfunctional motivational consequences with respect to overall goals of the organization. Functional consequences enhance the goal congruence and cooperation, and dysfunctional consequences distract from goal congruence and cooperation.

Motivational theories can be classified as *process* theories, which attempt to define the major processes and variables leading to choice and effort; or they can be classified as *content* theories, which attempt to identify the variables that influence behavior, such as needs, rewards, and punishment. The information aspects of agency theory noted earlier affect both of these because the information system affects the process (information) and the content (evaluation). The dominant cognitive process theory of motivation is Vroom's *expectancy valence (Expectancy Theory)* model,[7] which states that motivation is function of (1) the expectancy (likelihood or probability) that effort will result in attaining some outcome; and (2) the valence (payoff) from the outcome. *Valence* is defined as the perceived value of outcomes stemming from the action. From the accountant's or the systems designer's perspective, this means that individual motivation to comply with organization policies is a function of the individual's expectations and perceptions of the future consequences of his or her actions and the probability that individual actions will succeed and the value attached to success. Others have extended this theory to emphasize the feedback loops of past experiences, and how they alter perceptions of probability of success, and perceptions of values. Recently, agency theory has added the nature of the feedback information, probabilities, and perceptions of values. For example, if all previous system changes were successful in terms of the individual's ability to adapt, that individual would perceive the probability of success of the next system change to be high. This would probably lead to a greater degree of functional behavior on the part of the individual within the organization.

Content theories are, to large extent, founded on several theories of individual need and performance outcomes and the way in which they influence behavior. Maslow ranks these needs starting with basic physiological needs and ending with self-actualization or self-fulfillment. The hierarchical rank is as follows: (1) physiological needs (hunger, thirst, etc.); (2) safety needs (protection from injury); (3) social needs (love, friendship, affection, etc.); (4) esteem needs (self-respect); and (5) self-actualization needs (achieve fulfillment).[8] Basic, lower-level

---

[7] See Campbell and Pritchard, pp. 74–75 for a more complete discussion.
[8] See Abraham H. Maslow, *Motivation and Personality* (New York: Harper & Row, 1970).

needs must be satisfied to some degree before higher-level needs will motivate the individual.

On the other hand, Herzberg concentrates on extrinsic and intrinsic performance factors related to the workplace environment. His job satisfaction and work motivators are classified as extrinsic and intrinsic factors. Extrinsic factors stem from organizational content: (1) pay (salary increase); (2) technical supervision (competent supervisor); (3) human relations (quality of supervision); (4) company policy and administration; (5) working conditions (safety/physical surroundings; and (6) job security. Intrinsic factors or motivators are related to person's job: (1) achievement (success and personal worth); (2) recognition (praise); (3) responsibility (status); and (4) advancement (status).[9] Many of these comprise working contracts between managers and employees.

The first group, the extrinsic factors, are the rewards and needs related to the job environment and are sometimes called "hygiene" factors. These are the "motivators." Absence of these may cause dissatisfaction and probably a greater degree of dysfunctional activities. The second group, the intrinsic factors, describe the individual's relation to the job. The presence of these will motivate people toward their individual goals. In the development, implementation, and operation of an information system, the accountant must be cognizant of the need to satisfy the variables that influence an individual's behavior and be aware of the fact that the variables involved are ordered. Moreover, the nature of the information system and its content will have a bearing on this behavior. Without satisfactory interpersonal relationships, there is little reason to worry about the higher-order needs.

In terms of information systems design success, an overview of the higher-order factors that most influence human behavior is presented in Figure 3-9. All of these will influence the information system and the organizational hierarchy. These in turn impact human behavior. Of these, job social structure is perhaps the most important single factor according to Herzberg. Change in the social structure via system change affects key factors such as interpersonal relationships and decision making responsibilities which can lead to behavioral problems. These higher order needs may be reinforced either positively or negatively by top management support, clear communication of objectives, past experience, job complexity, an individual's aptitude, and the external factors noted by Herzberg. Although this summary is not all inclusive, it does present the key variables of which an accountant or systems analyst must be aware in the development and implementation of a system.

In addition to these factors that influence human behavior, leadership styles which comprise part of the organizational hierarchy must be considered. At the extreme, leadership styles can be characterized as authoritarian and participative. They will have an impact on the design procedures as well as the operation of any information system. The latter is more likely to set a better psychological climate for systems change than the former because employees will be more part of the change. Some advocate a very broad decision-making base which includes workers as well as managerial personnel. This in turn requires a very broad base of participation in system design and change. A better "psycho-

---

[9] See Frederick Herzberg, *Work and the Nature of Man* (Cleveland: World Publishing Co., 1966).

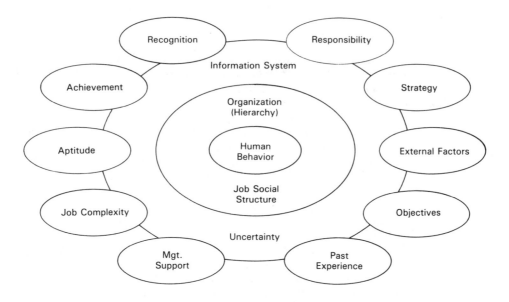

FIGURE 3-9 Major factors influencing organization structure and human behavior.

logical climate" through participation, however, may or may not result in more efficient system because some employees are better motivated by authoritarian leadership.

Levels of Management

The impact of these behavioral factors varies at different levels of management within an organization.[10] Moreover, the actions of different levels of management and the way they structure their contractual agreements and labor contracts with lower levels of employees through organization hierarchy will directly influence the psychological climate for the organization and thus the success of the information system.

One of the major contributing factors having bearing on successful information system implementation is the way each of the levels deals functionally or dysfunctionally with an inherent *resistance to change.* Much of this resistance comes from the hierarchical organizational structures and processes management creates in the process of designing, implementing, and using an information system. Employees are reluctant to change these labor contracts. Resistance may take many forms: persistent reduction in output, increase in the number of "quits" and requests for transfer, chronic quarrels, sullen hostility, wildcat or

---

[10] The framework for some of the discussion of top management, middle management, and nonsupervisory personnel characteristics which follows is summarized in James B. Bower, Robert E. Schlosser, and Maurice S. Newman, *Computer-Oriented Accounting Information Systems,* (Cincinnati, Ohio: South-Western, 1985), p. 367.

slow-down strikes, and of course, the expression of a lot of pseudological reasons why the change will not work.[11]

It is necessary for each of these levels to deal with these problems, and it is suggested that the key to the problem is to understand the true nature of the resistance. Actually, what employees resist is usually not technical change per se, but social change—the change in their human relationships which are expressed in terms of their formal and informal contracts (agreements) that generally accompany technical change.[12]

The need for stable social structure (expressed as an organizational hierarchy of agreements) is very important, as was suggested earlier in this chapter in the discussion of content theory. Employees will resist any change that threatens to disrupt this hierarchical structure, which supports many of their needs, such as love, friendship, affection, self-respect, self-fulfillment, achievement, recognition, responsibility and advancement.

TOP MANAGEMENT.   A summary of major research on the impact of organization structure and human behavior suggests that some variables that play a key role in the success of any information system and its accounting subsystem are controllable. Other variables are either partially controllable or uncontrollable. Top management controls many of these variables. The effective participation of the senior executives, decision makers, controller, and systems personnel on a steering committee for systems development, implementation, and ongoing operations is controllable by management and necessary for systems success.[13]

The assignment of responsible executive personnel to the steering committee is essential. Success can be enhanced by devoting organizational resources such as time and money to the project. Furthermore, success can be facilitated by top management's providing a positive behavioral climate for implementation of the project. To reduce uncertainty, the objective of the new system must be clearly communicated to all personnel involved. Any new agreements which result from change in principal (manager) and agent (employee) relationships must be carefully worked out in advance. Support and communication of objectives are necessary prerequisites for good psychological climate. Other factors that top management can influence to help achieve a more positive climate include concern for employees, use of employee input and participation in systems planning, training and placement programs to retain displaced employees, encouragement of teamwork with regard to systems design, and assignment of reliable people to the development and implementation of the project. It is also important that management set a good pattern over the years for change, for past experience will greatly affect employee attitudes and cooperation (as outlined in the earlier review of process motivational theory). All changes should be well organized, well supported, and effectively communicated to the entire organization. All of this is easier to accomplish with more mature and larger organiza-

---

[11] Reprinted by permission of the *Harvard Business Review.* Excerpt from "How to Deal with Resistance to Change" by Paul R. Lawrence (January–February 1969). Copyright 1969 by the President and Fellows of Harvard College; all rights reserved.

[12] Ibid.

[13] Philip Ein-Dor and Eli Segev, "Organizational Context and the Success of Management Information Systems," *Management Science,* June 1978, pp. 1064–77.

tions, which have a reasonably long time frame for change. If these variables are positive, the system will be more successful.

Other variables such as the size, structure (in many cases), and time frame (rate of change in the decision-making activities and information processing technology) of the organization and external pressures are generally uncontrollable. These variables must be considered, however, for they do influence the success of any accounting or information system. *Success* is defined as the final implementation of an information system that supports the strategic, managerial, operational, and transaction processing needs of the management system.

MIDDLE MANAGEMENT.   Middle management cooperation is necessary for the successful design and implementation of a system. These managers are the ultimate users of most of the information generated by the system in making their managerial and operating decisions and in preparing their reports. Moreover, they are the providers of much of the information and have the opportunity to make opportunistic gains by keeping some information private (resulting in some asymmetric information). They must be involved and consulted during all of the information systems analysis and design phases noted in earlier chapters. A tremendous amount of work involving long hours is required of these middle managers in the testing, conversion, and implementation phases. They are the people who ultimately make the system work. Their acceptance and cooperation is a must if the system is to function as designed.

The reason middle managers often resist change so much is that changes can alter organizational hierarchies and thus their job social structure, including the status quo (established hierarchy of labor contracts) in terms of responsibility, reporting, decision making, and, most important, their interpersonal relationships. Their jobs may actually be eliminated because more advanced information systems can reduce the need for several middle managerial layers in an organization and enable those who remain to increase their span of control. The net effect may be a need for fewer middle managers. Also, middle level managers often fail to recognize the need for any change because they have narrow or technical perspective of the organization. Communication of objectives from top management is crucial in overcoming this perception. Middle level managers need to understand the reason for any change and the forthcoming benefits (valence), and they must be assured that they will be capable of performing any new duties and making any new decisions under the new system (expectancy of success). Above all, their sense of status and personal worth must be maintained. Their reluctance to accept a new system is often magnified, as suggested in the expectation theory, by any bad prior experience with systems that did not deliver and by lack of top management consideration for their situation. On the positive side, these managers are capable of working toward long-term objectives and capable of allowing a reasonable time period for the system to demonstrate its worth.

NONSUPERVISORY PERSONNEL.   For nonsupervisory personnel, the positive trait of patience exhibited by middle management does not exist. These individuals can best be characterized as employees with short-range goals and group orientation. They also must be kept well informed and, to the extent possible, reassured that they will be treated with equity, will be trained if necessary, and above all, will not be out of work. Changes to their job social structure and its related organizational hierarchy must be made carefully because of their strong group orientation. This can be a problem because increased automation (in information systems as well as production) usually leads to more rigid job structure due to increased coordination with other aspects of the organization. These employees may feel "driven" in their job by the computer time schedule.

The manager (principal) and employee (agent) contracts, at this level are often union contracts that must be renegotiated to implement any change, such as in the way accounting systems measure performance. Obviously market forces have a bearing on these negotiations and on employee's willingness to cooperate. They may go elsewhere to work or demand contracts like that of a competitor.

Impact of Information Systems on Business Organizations

The impact of the advent of computer processing on business organizations, their structure, their mode of decision making, their flow of transactions, and their employees' behavior has been profound for all functions at all levels of activity. This was discussed at length in earlier chapters.[14] Historically, if one were to analyze the essential characteristics of the decision-making and transaction process—which can be classified as reliability, speed, accuracy, and intelligence—one would expect the greatest impact on reliability, speed, and accuracy, areas in which the computer clearly has superiority. The historical evidence does suggest that the greatest impact is in the area where the computer has the edge in reliability, speed, and accuracy—that is, in the routine tasks that can be programmed, and in which measurement is relatively straightforward and volumes are large. Database and communication technolgy also brings the manager closer to their physical system, customers and vendors; thereby reducing the need for as many middle managers who previously analyzed and reported this information. With the new developments in microcomputers, these criteria will apply to smaller units in an organization and to smaller organizations.

With improved modeling and database technology, this impact will have a bearing on what the computer can do better than people and, in turn, on the organization. The result most likely will give the computer more of an edge in well structured complex tasks where expert systems and artificial intelligence can be used to assist in management decision making.

SUMMARY

The accountant and the systems designer must consider several variables in the analysis, design, and implementation of information systems. These variables consist of the objectives and strategy of the organization, the decisions related to the accomplishment of these objectives, the organization structure and its associated set of employment contracts (agreements) and organizational hierarchy,

---

[14] See also Arthur Anderson & Co., *Trends in Information Technology: 1986* for an excellent overview of IS trends and their organizational impact.

the people who operate within this structure and who process transactions and made decisions, and the technology used for information processing and decision making. Organizations can be structured in many ways, and the information and accounting systems must adapt to and support the management system structure. Special care must be given to the structure of the information system and the accounting organization. An understanding of the behavioral and motivational factors is key to the successful analysis, design, and ultimate implementation of an information system. Moreover the motivation and behavior are functions of the information system and its resulting organizational hierarchy. Of these, the key factors seem to be the employee's job social structure and related employment contracts, higher order needs, and perception of the probability of system success and its resulting value to the individual. Top management control of the key behavioral variables will greatly influence the system success or failure. Finally, the greatest impact of systems changes resulting from improvements in technology has been wherever data processing has been superior in terms of reliability, speed, accuracy and in dealing with well structured complex tasks. In varying degrees, these changes have influenced the information system and structure of the firm at all levels.

SELECTED REFERENCES

ANTHONY, ROBERT N., *Planning and Control Systems, Framework for Analysis*, Boston, Harvard Business School, 1965.

ARTHUR ANDERSEN & CO., *Trends in Information Technology;* 1986. Chicago, Ill.: Arthur Andersen & Co., 1986, p. 43.

BAIMAN, STANLEY, "Agency Research in Managerial Accounting, Survey," *Journal of Accounting Literature*, vol. 1, 1982, pp. 154–213.

BARIFF, MARTIN L., and JAY R. GALBRAITH, "Intraorganizational Power Considerations for Designing Information Systems," *Accounting Organizations and Society, Vol 3,* (1978), 15–27.

BOWER, JAMES B., ROBERT E. SCHLOSSER, and MAURICE S. NEWMAN, *Computer Oriented Accounting Information Systems*, Cincinnati, Ohio, South Western, 1985.

BROWNELL, PETER, and MORRIS MCINNES, "Budgetary Participation, Motivation, and Managerial Performance," *The Accounting Review*, Vol. LXI, No. 4, October 1986, pp. 587–598.

CAMPBELL, JOHN P., and ROBERT D. PRITCHARD, "Motivation Theory in Industrial and Organizational Psychology," in *Handbook of Industrial and Organizational Psychology*, ed. M. V. Dunnette, Chicago: Rand McNally, 1976, pp. 63–130.

CASH, JAMES I., and BENN R. KONSYNSKI, "IS redraws competitive boundaries," *Harvard Business Review*, March-April, 1985, pp. 134–142.

CHENHALL, ROBERT H., and MORRIS DEIGAN, "The Impact of Structure, Environment and Interdependence on the Perceived Usefulness of Management Accounting Systems," *The Accounting Review*, LXI, no. 1 (January 1986), pp. 16–35.

CYERT, RICHARD M., and JAMES G. MARCH, *Behavioral Theory of the Firm*, Englewood Cliffs, N.J.; Prentice Hall, 1963.

EIN DOR, PHILIP, and ELI SEGEV, "Organizational Context and the Success of Management Information Systems," *Management Science*, June 1978, pp. 1064–77.

GALBRAITH, JAY R., *Organizational Design, An Information Processing Point of View*. Reading, Mass.; Addison-Wesley, 1974.

HAYES, D. C., "The Contingency Theory of Managerial Accounting," *The Accounting Review*, 1977, pp. 22–39.

HERZBERG, FREDERICK, *Work and the Nature of Man.* New York: World, 1966.

IVES, BLAKE, and GERARD P. LEARMONTH, "The Information System as a Competitive Weapon," *Communications of the ACM*, December, 1984, vol. 27, no. 12, pp. 1193–1201.

JENSEN, MICHAEL C., "Organizational Theory and Methodology," *The Accounting Review*, LVIII, no. 2 (April 1983), pp. 319–337.

JENSEN, MICHAEL C., and W. H. MECKLING, "Theory of the Firm, Managerial Behavior, Agency Costs and Ownership Structure," *Journal of Financial Economics*, 1976, pp. 305–360.

KEEN, PETER G. W., "Information Systems and Organizational Change," *Communications of the ACM*, January, 1981, vol. 24, no. 1, pp. 24–33.

LAWLER, E. E., and J. L. SUTTLE, "Expectancy Theory and Job Behavior," *Organizational Behavior and Human Performance*, (1973), pp. 482–503.

LAWRENCE, PAUL R., "How to Deal with Resistance to Change," *Harvard Business Review*, January–February 1969, p. 176.

LAWRENCE, PAUL R., and JAY W. LORSCH, *Developing Organizations, Diagnosis and Action*, Reading, Mass.: Addison-Wesley, 1969.

MARCH, JAMES G., and HERBERT A. SIMON, *Organizations*, New York: John Wiley, 1958.

MASLOW, ABRAHAM H., *Motivation and Personality*, New York: Harper & Row, Pub., 1970.

McFARLAND, F. WARREN, "Information technology changes the way you compete," *Harvard Business Review*, May–June, 1984, pp. 98–103.

MERCHANT, KEN, and JEAN FRANCOIS MANZONI, "Achievability of Budget Targets in Profit Centers, Field Study," *The Accounting Review*, July 1989, pp. 539–58.

OUCHI, WILLIAM G., *Theory Z, How American Business Can Meet the Japanese Challenge*, Reading, Mass.: Addison-Wesley, 1981.

PORTER, MICHAEL E., and VICTOR E. MILLAR, "How information gives you competitive advantage," *Harvard Business Review*, July–August, 1985, pp. 150–160.

SIMON, HERBERT A., "Information Technologies and Organizations," *The Acocunting Review*, July 1990, pp. 658–67.

SPICER, BARRY H., and VAN BALLEW, "Management Accounting Systems and the Economics of Internal Control," *Accounting Organizations and Society*, 8, no. 1 (1983).

TIESSEN, P., and J. H. WATERHOUSE, "Towards Descriptive Theory of Management Accounting," *Accounting, Organizations and Society*, vol. 8, 1983, pp. 251–267.

ULLRICH, ROBERT A., and GEORGE F. WIELAND, *Organization Theory and Design*, Homewood, Ill.: Richard D. Irwin, 1980.

WALTON, RICHARD E., *Up and Running*, Cambridge, Mass.: Harvard Business School Press, 1990.

WEBER, RON, *EDP Auditing*, 2nd ed. New York: McGraw-Hill, 1988.

REVIEW QUESTIONS

1. What is the theory which describes the agreements between various parties within hierarchies and markets?

2. Explain the role of an accounting information system in small firm with a manager who runs the organization, and an absentee owner.

3. How can the labor contract and an accounting information system encourage employees to cooperate and to rearrange their personnel priorities so that they are congruent with the objectives of the organization?

4. Is business strategy important in the design of an acounting information system?

5. What is the basic concept of contingency theory and how does it impact accounting information systems?

6. Explain the difference between structure and process. What are the criteria for assessing the effectiveness and efficiency of these concepts?

7. Contrast the advantages and disadvantages of the centralized functional form and the decentralized divisional form of organizational structure.

8. Contrast the matrix form and the centralized functional form of organizational structure with respect to the five process criteria.

9. Why must agreements between managers and employees be reconstituted each time a new project or engagement is undertaken by a project organization?

10. What is the role of the chief information officer in an organization? What are the problems associated with locating the MIS department in the controller's office?

11. Describe the traditional controllership and treasurership functions.

12. How should an information systems department be organized and why?

13. What is the steering committee and who should be on the committee?

14. What variables have bearing on job performance? How does this affect the accounting information system?

15. Contrast Vroom's expectancy valence process theory and Maslow's need content theory of motivation.

16. Contrast the impact that various levels of management have on systems change.

17. What is the key issue in nonsupervisory employee resistance to change?

18. Why is it important for a company to establish a good track record in dealing with employees when systems change?

19. How can an accounting system reduce asymmetric information (where one party, such as owner or employee knows more about the environment or effort, for example, than the other) and thus contribute to congruent employee and owner goals?

20. How can the accounting system be used to monitor employee effort and accomplishment? Is this important from an agency theory perspective?

CASES

3-1 The B & B Company manufactures and sells chemicals for agricultural and industrial use. The company has grown significantly over the last ten years but has made few changes in its information gathering and reporting system. Some of the managers have expressed concern that the system is essentially the same as it was when the firm was only half its present size. Others believe that much of the information from the system is not relevant and that more appropriate and timely information should be available.

Dora Hepple, chief accountant, has observed that the actual monthly cost data for most production processes are compared with the actual costs of the same processes for the previous year. Any variance not explained by price changes requires an explanation by the

individual in charge of the cost center. She believes that this information is inadequate for good cost control.

George Vector, one of the production supervisors, contends that the system is adequate because it allows for explanation of discrepancies. The current year's costs seldom vary from the previous year's costs (as adjusted for price changes). This indicates that costs are under control.

Vern Hopp, general manager of the Fine Chemical Division, is upset with the current system. He has to request the same information each month regarding recurring operations. This is a problem that he believes should be addressed.

Walter Metts, president, has appointed a committee to review the system. The charge to this System Review Task Force is to determine if the information needs of the internal management of the firm are being met by the existing system. Specific modifications in the existing system or implementation of a new system will be considered only if management's needs are not being met. William Afton, assistant to the president, has been put in charge of the task force.

Shortly after the committee was appointed, Afton overheard one of the cost accountants say, "I've been doing it this way for fifteen years, and now Afton and his committee will try to eliminate my job." Another person replied, "That's the way it looks. John and Brownie in general accounting also think that their positions are going to be eliminated or at least changed significantly." Over the next few days, Afton overheard a middle management person talking about the task force saying, "That's all this company thinks about—maximizing its profits—not the employees." He also overheard a production manager in the Mixing Department say that he believed the system was in need of revision because the most meaningful information he received came from Brad Cummings, a salesperson. He stated, "After they have the monthly sales meeting, Brad stops by the office and indicates what the sales plans and targets are for the next few months. This sure helps me in planning my mixing schedules."

Afton is aware that two problems of paramount importance to be addressed by his System Review Task Force are (1) to determine management's information needs for cost control and decision-making purposes; and (2) to meet the behavioral needs of the company and its employees.

REQUIRED:
1. Discuss the behavioral implications of having an accounting information system that does not appear to meet the needs of management.
2. Identify and explain the specific problems B & B Company appears to have with regard to the perception of B & B's employees concerning:
   a. the accounting information system.
   b. the firm.
3. Assume that the initial review of the Sys-

tem Review Task Force indicates that a new accounting information system should be designed and implemented.
   a. Identify specific behavioral factors that B & B's management should address in the design and implementation of a new system.
   b. For each behavioral factor identified, discuss how B & B's management can address the behavioral factor.
   (Adapted from CMA examination)

3-2 The Jerment Company is a growing manufacturer of modular office furniture. The company has been experiencing internal problems due to their failure to keep pace with the rapid growth of their segment of the industry. The company began as a small, one-plant operation, but has since expanded into four adjacent states. Now there are seven branch offices in addition to the home office, with each branch having a sales force and a manufacturing plant.

The condensed organization chart presented in Figure C3-1 shows six functional departments at the home office level—finance, marketing, administrative services, research and development, manufacturing, and personnel. Each of the seven branch offices has a branch manager of sales and a branch manager of manufacturing, each of whom reports to the home office's vice-president of marketing and vice-president of manufacturing, respectively. Services for the other four functional areas are carried out at the home office.

Every manufacturing plant produces the complete Jerment product line. The twelve product lines are somewhat complementary. There is very little, if any, brand awareness in this segment of the office furniture industry. Some of the sales force find certain products more difficult to sell and, thus, do not push them in their sales calls.

The home office management has insisted over the years that control be maintained at the home office. However, there has been increasing conflict between the home office and the branches. Branch managers insist they need more flexibility and autonomy to deal with differing local environments. Home office management believes a change in autonomy would damage its efforts to keep up with industry growth. Branch managers believe that the

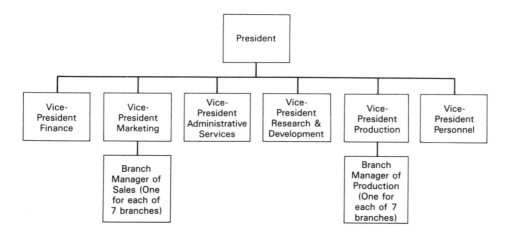

FIGURE C3-1   Jerment Company.

home office is reluctant to modernize and streamline the company. The branch managers' attempts to make some autonomous decisions have conflicted with home office directives. This has led to ambiguous communications and delays in parts shipments to the plants.

REQUIRED:

1. Jerment Company currently employs an organization structure that is departmentalized by function.

   a. Discuss why Jerment Company probably selected this type of departmentalization when it started operations.

   b. Explain the behavioral consequences of a functional type of organization structure.

2. Identify two alternative methods of departmentalizing a company's organization structure and for each alternative method.

   a. Explain why a company would select the type of organization structure.

   b. Discuss the strengths and weaknesses of the types of organization structure. (Adapted from CMA examination)

3-3   Foodway is a regional supermarket chain with two hundred stores in five states, and warehouse and distribution operations in each of these states. Each state has a manager for retail warehouse and distribution operations. Although each state manager purchases from a different set of wholesalers, the operations are virtually identical from state to state. Currently each state has its own computer system for scheduling distribution, inventory reorder, purchasing, sales analysis, and transaction processing. Foodway is considering centralizing its operations.

REQUIRED:

1. Comment briefly on the pros and cons of such centralization.

2. One of the managers has just attended a conference where the attributes of microcomputers were discussed. Especially interesting was their ability to link up with larger central processing units. Comment briefly on the impact of recent technological developments and Foodway's centralization.

3-4   John Knight founded the Newworld Co. over thirty years ago. Although he has relied heavily upon advice from other members of management, he has made all of the important decisions for the company. Newworld has been successful, experiencing steady growth in its early years and very rapid growth in recent years. During this period of rapid growth Knight has experienced difficulty in keeping up with the many decisions that needed to be made. He feels that he is losing control of the company's progress.

Regular discussions regarding his concern have been held with George Armet, the company executive vice-president. As a result of these discussions, Armet has studied possible alternative organizational structures to the present highly centralized functional organization.

In a carefully prepared proposal he recommends that the company reorganize according to its two product lines because the technology and marketing methods are quite different. The plastic products require different manufacturing skills and equipment from the brass products. The change could be easily accomplished because the products are manufactured in different plants. The marketing effort is also segregated along product lines within the sales function. The number of executive positions would not change, although the duties of the positions would change. There would no longer be the need for a vice-president for manufacturing or a vice-president for sales. Those positions would be replaced with a vice-president for each of the two product lines. Armet acknowledges that there may be personnel problems at the top management level because the current vice-presidents may not be competent to manage within the new structure.

The proposal also contained the recommendation that some of the decision-making power, long held by John Knight, be transferred to the new vice-presidents. Armet argued that this would be good for the company. They would be more aware of the problems and solution alternatives of their respective product lines because they are closer to the operations. Fewer decisions will be required of each person than now are required of John Knight; this would reduce the time between problem recognition and implementation of the solution. Armet further argued that distributing the decision-making power would improve the creativity and spirit of company management.

Knight is intrigued by the proposal and the prospect that it would make the company more manageable. However, the proposal did not spell out clearly which decisions should be

transferred and which should remain with the president. He requested Armet prepare a supplemental memorandum specifying the decisions to be delegated to the vice-presidents.

The memorandum presented the recommended decision areas, explaining in each case how the new vice-persidents would be closer to the situation and thereby be able to make prompt, sound decisions. The following list summarizes Armet's recommendations:

1. Sales
   a. Price policy
   b. Promotional strategy
   c. Credit policy
2. Operations
   a. Manufacturing procedures
   b. Labor negotiations
3. Development of existing product lines
4. Capital investment decision—up to amounts not exceeding the division "depreciation flow" plus 25 percent of its after-tax income (excluding ventures into new fields).

The corporate management would be responsible for overall corporate development. Also, they would allocate the remaining available cash flow for dividends, for investment projects above the limited prescribed, and for investment into new ventures.

REQUIRED:
Does the company have the characteristics needed for decentralized profit centers? Briefly explain your answer.
(Adapted from CMA examination)

3-5 Why each of the following may be an inappropriate reporting practice for RD Microchip?

1. Providing detailed daily production reports to the president.
2. Providing complete listings of the status of all production jobs and inventory items to the production vice president.
3. Providing the last period's income statement and balance sheet to the sales manager when she requests information to plan the sales activities for next year.
4. Providing information concerning todays

employee productivity to the production foreman next week.

5. Providing to the respective production foreman responsibility reports that include allocations of plant depreciation and other overhead costs.

6. Provide the production supervisor with information on next years sales forecast.

3-6 Your accounting firm has been asked to design and install new microprocessing cash registers in the thirty store locations of Shells, Inc., a regional department store on the Florida east coast specializing in sportswear, beach supplies, and souvenirs. Management wants these cash registers to control its inventory of numerous small items, which are spread over thirty locations. These new registers will gather data on a cassette tape, which can be transferred at the end of each day to the home store in Sea Oats Beach.

The last time Shells tried to implement a new system, it turned out to be a nightmare for the store managers, and the reports generated were useless in managing their respective stores. Moreover, the clerks had trouble using the system, and they had no interest in the corporation's inventory problems.

REQUIRED: Do you expect any motivation problems with the new system even though *no* employees will be laid off, the system is in fact easy to operate, the reports are purported to be useful to store managers, and very little training is needed by clerks and management who use the system? If so, why, in terms of motivation theory?

3-7 Greengrass Company is an established manufacturer and wholesaler of a broad line of lawn fertilizer and yard maintenance products. The company has annual sales of approximately $100 million and has been a wholly owned subsidiary of a large conglomerate, KSU Corporation, for the past five years. Prior to that, it was an independent corporation whose stock was controlled by the founding and managing family.

A. B. Cardwell, son of the founder, is currently the president of the company, but he is scheduled to retire soon. His niece, Bonnie Cardwell, is currently executive vice-president

and has been heir apparent to the presidency ever since A. B. Cardwell became president.

Greengrass had maintained a pattern of increasing profits for many years. During the past three years, however, profits have decreased significantly. Management has attributed this to reduced demand caused by cool, wet summers in the company's primary marketing area coupled with intense competition.

After a week-long KSU corporate planning meeting, A. B. Cardwell called a staff meeting to discuss plans for the next marketing season. At the close of the meeting, he announced that the KSU board had named William Thoma president of Greengrass Company. Cardwell explained that KSU management was concerned about the subsidiary's slumping profits and had decided to assume a greater degree of control over Greengrass operations. Thoma's appointment was the first step in this direction. In addition, a new system of financial reporting to KSU management is to be installed.

Mr. Thoma's reputation was well known by the entire staff. He had been executive vice-president of two other KSU-owned companies during the previous three years. In both cases, the companies had records of declining profits prior to his appointment. A significant management reorganization occurred in each of those companies within twelve months after his appointment. In each case, some members of senior management were given early retirement or released, depending on their age. Their replacements usually came from other KSU companies with which Thoma had been associated. Although earnings did increase following the reorganizations, the entire personality of the companies changed.

REQUIRED: As Greengrass's auditor, write a memo explaining the potential need for additional audit work on the new financial reporting system due to your expectations regarding the quality of the financial information which will be generated by the new system. This report should focus on the enthusiasm given the development and implementation of the new system. Specifically, do you expect the current management to be motivated to support the new system?
(Adapted from the CMA examination)

3-8 Gulf and Northern, a wood product corporation with forests, lumbering operations, and paper mills throughout the Northwest and Southeast, has been experiencing astronomical travel costs between its widely scattered field and plant offices, divisional offices, and corporate offices. It has decided to install a system of video communications equipment at each location so that managers, engineers, accountants, and many of the others who regularly travel can substitute conference calls using video equipment for these person-to-person meetings. It also intends to have the capability to transmit documents so that all parties to the video conference can talk about the same set of figures and documents.

REQUIRED: Top management personnel expected praise from their subordinates when they first mentioned this system, but received skepticism from potential users. Why?

3-9 The Reddon Company manufactures and sells plastic products. The company management believes a successful firm should have formally stated objectives. Financial and output goals have been established for all departments, and they are evaluated against those goals. In addition, the company aggressively seeks new products to support its goal of growth.

Last month Cupot, Inc., offered to sell its design and preliminary engineering studies for a plastic sewing machine housing to Reddon. Cupot management had concluded that the product was too remote from its normal product lines and, equally important, would require manufacturing expertise not possessed by Cupot.

Reddon management asked the marketing department to research the sales potential of the housing. The product development department, a department of the product division, studied the production problems of the product. Both departments concluded that it was feasible to add the housing to the company's product line. However, each observed that problems could be encountered because this was a new market for Reddon and that a modification of current manufacturing techniques and processes would be required. In spite of these warnings, Reddon management purchased the idea from Cupot and authorized the project.

Management concluded that the marketing and manufacturing requirements were of sufficient complexity to require a project team for the product. This was a new management technique for Reddon. George Aldon, an experienced sales manager with a strong manufacturing background, was chosen to head the project team. He was selected to head the team because he had been with the company for many years, and was well known and well liked by most people in the company. This was important because the project team had no resources of its own and would have to rely on regular departments to get the work completed.

Aldon was permitted to select one person each from the sales, manufacturing, and financial management departments to make a four-person project team. The project team was charged with the planning coordination and successful introduction of the housing. The three selected team members were responsible for developing the schedule of services needed, serving as liaison with their former areas, and evaluating the work done by the regular departments. All members of the team would return to their departments when the team completed its task of guiding the new product through its first year of sales.

The project team developed a schedule of events and activities leading to the introduction of this new product in one year. Included in the schedule were timetables for the development of a sales program, the modification of the manufacturing facilities, and the sample production run. Financial requirements and budget revision schedules were also prepared.

The product was not ready for introduction in one year as planned. The sales program was not yet completed, nor were the manufacturing modifications complete. The departments had worked on the project whenever time was available in the regular work schedules. The department heads stated that they were unable to do more because no adjustment in the available resources had been made. Although the project team had prepared a financial requirement schedule, it was not ready when the company budget was adopted. Consequently, the financial requirements were not incorporated in the budget.

George Aldon was disappointed that the team was unable to meet the planned introduction date. This was the first assignment he had failed to complete successfully. He attributed the lack of success to the departmental managers who regularly failed to meet the deadline in the original timetables. The other members of the project team worked hard but, in his opinion, were not forceful enough when dealing with their former departments.

REQUIRED:

1. Describe the potential advantages of the project approach to the development of a new product.
2. Using the information presented in the problem, describe the likely circumstances that caused the project to be late. (Adapted from CMA examination)

3-10 CSI&F Inc. is a successful Midwest corporation that had more than $200 million in sales in 1991. Carl Sedlitsky, president and majority stockholder of CSI&F Inc., started Carl's Scrap Iron Company shortly after World War II to take advantage of the surplus scrap iron that he knew would be available. The company thrived during the late 1940s. In 1950 Sedlitsky bought a cast iron foundry from a customer because he needed an outlet for the surplus iron his company was accumulating.

Sedlitsky incorporated his business after purchasing the cast iron foundry. As part of the transaction, the name of the company was changed to Carl's Scrap Iron and Foundry Incorporated; this was later shortened to the present name—CSI&F Inc. Carl's grandson Robert now runs the business.

CSI&F Inc. continued its acquisition activities during the next forty years, so that the corporation now has twenty-two separate divisions consisting of three malleable iron foundries, four speciality heat-treating plants, five finishing and fabricating plants, and the scrap iron yards.

Robert Sedlitsky has been known as a fair employer. The company's compensation and fringe benefit plans have been excellent and include a profit-sharing plan instituted in 1987. Mutual respect and personal contact with each management employee were standard when the company was small. Unfortunately, Sedlitsky

had to cut back on personal contacts in the 1980s as CSI&F continued to expand.

Sedlitsky still maintains personal contact with all division managers and their immediate assistants through quarterly meetings. The meetings are used to review the divisions' results and are held on three days during each quarter. This rarely allows sufficient time for all divisions managers to make their oral presentations and to discuss various problems with corporate management. Sedlitsky has the five to seven division managers who are unable to complete their reviews stay over for an additional meeting the following day, or he follows up by telephone in the next few days.

The quarterly meetings not only provide personal contact with the division manager but also provide an opportunity for clarification of monthly written reports. Because CSI&F Inc. has grown in a somewhat haphazard fashion, the accounting system for each of the divisions is different. Consequently the division managers' written reports lack comparability, thus making it difficult for Sedlitsky to digest and integrate the information in a reasonable period of time. In addition, Sedlitsky has been unable to devote the time necessary to analyze the written reports.

In an attempt to alleviate the reporting problems and the lack of comparability in reports, Sedlitsky's executive financial vice-president has drafted a plan that would establish a common accounting and reporting system for those divisions with similar activities. This plan also proposes that the number of divisions be reduced to six—malleable iron, cast iron, finishing and fabricating, specialty heat treating, and scrap iron. Six of the current division managers will head the six new divisions. The remaining sixteen managers will be reassigned and will be responsible for the operations that were formerly administered by the twenty-two division managers. However, the sixteen managers will now report to their respective new division managers rather than to the president. Thus the plan would change Sedlitsky's span of control.

REQUIRED:

1. Discuss the effect the new accounting and reporting system and reduced number of division managers as proposed by the

executive financial vice-president should have on Robert Sedlitsky's ability to manage CSI&F Inc. effectively.

2. Discuss how the executive financial vice-president's proposal to reduce the number of divisions is likely to affect the behavior of the two groups of CSI&F's division managers—the six who will head the six new divisions and the remaining sixteen who now will report to the six new division managers.

(Adapted from the CMA examination)

3-11 Roadway Engineering specializes in the analysis, design, and supervision of interstate highway construction in and around large metropolitan areas. It has engineers, accountants, financial advisers, draftsmen, and urban planning specialists located in major cities throughout the United States. Each location is a profit center and the manager is responsible for all activities at the locations. Because of the nature of government contracts, however, the company has experienced wide fluctuations in the performance of these managers. Due to several large contracts, business is sometimes so good that employees must work overtime to complete these contracts. The company must even subcontract much of the work locally to get it done on time. On the other hand, other locations are hurting; engineers are just sitting around waiting for a new contract. Roadway is reluctant to let these experienced personnel go because next month they may be needed again.

REQUIRED: As an information systems expert, where might you begin to advise Roadway on possible solutions to these problems? Write a brief memo explaining any organizational changes Roadway should consider and the possible functional and dysfunctional consequences of these changes.

3-12 Chesapeake Lighting manufactures a line of lighting products and markets them via dealers in thirty-five states. All decisions are made centrally in Bay City. Manufacturing plants and dealers send their cost and sales statistics to Bay City for consolidation and comparison with various budgets. All manufacturing plants report to a vice-president of manufacturing, and all dealers report to a vice-president of marketing and distribution.

Top management has been complaining for a long time that dealers are not selling the higher margin items. Manufacturing plants have production runs that are too long. These reduce costs but result in many shortages and lost orders at the dealer level.

Management of Chesapeake Lighting has asked you, the company's accountant, to suggest a budget system to motivate the managers to make decisions more consistent with the firm's objective of profit maximization.

REQUIRED: In general terms, write a brief memo outlining your suggestions for a budget system and any accompanying organizational charges and your rationale.

3-13 A nationwide survey was conducted recently by an independent research center among professional engineers employed in industrial, academic, and governmental, and other not-for-profit organizations. The survey concerned the "wants" of the engineers. The results of the survey are listed next. The order of the items does not indicate the degreee of importance; the importance varied with the type of activities and type of organization in which the engineer was associated.

1. Freedom to publish and discuss work with other professional engineers
2. Association with, and intellectual stimulation from, high-caliber colleagues
3. A technically trained management
4. Freedom in solving problems and managing own work (within specified limits)
5. An organization with a reputation for engineering advancement
6. Adequate facilities, resources, and assistance from technicians
7. Opportunity for advancement in salary and status along either the management route or the technical route
8. Competitive salaries and benefits
9. Job security based on achievements
10. A community providing schools, colleges, libraries, other cultural opportunities, and good transportation
11. Treatment as professionals

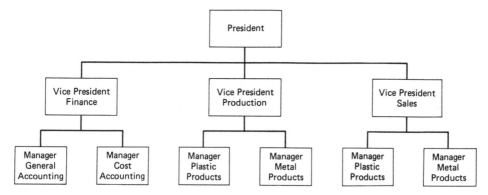

FIGURE C3-2 Current organizational structure.

12. Opportunity to continue formal education while employed
13. Variety and challenge in work
14. Opportunity to see ideas put to use

REQUIRED:

1. Identify and discuss the specific needs of people that are described in motivational theories.
2. Relate each of the specific wants identified in the survey to the specific needs described in motivational theories.
(Adapted from the CMA examination)

3-14 Although some physiological functions take place without motivation, nearly all conscious behavior is motivated by some need or desire. In recent years, psychologists, sociologists, and others have been placing increased emphasis on the importance of human motivation both in general terms and in terms of business organizations.

Some observers of employee motivation have developed theories that have identified specific types or classes of needs, and they have categorized these needs into levels or priorities. By identifying and classifying its employees' needs, the company hopes to take actions that will improve its employees' motivation and job performance.

REQUIRED:

1. Identify and explain the various types of needs that motivate employees.
2. Place each of the identified needs in a

hierarchy ranging from lower-level needs to higher-level needs.

3. Explain how an employee's job can satisfy the needs in each major level of the hierarchy.
(Adapted from the CMA examination.)

3-15 The Hopper Company is considering a reorganization. The company's current organizational structure is represented by the chart shown in Figure C3-2.

The company recently hired a new vice-president for metal products. This vice-president has an extensive background in sales, which complements the production background of the vice-president for plastic products. The new vice-president for metal products believes that Hopper Company would be more effective if it were reorganized according to the organizational structure shown in Figure C3-3.

REQUIRED:

1. Identify the two types of organizational structure depicted by the two charts.
2. Compare the two organizational structures by discussing the advantages and disadvantages of each using the criteria suggested in the chapter.
3. Which structure would be more conducive to profitability objectives and responsibility? Why?
4. Which structure would be more likely to overload the president's office with data for decision making? Why?
(CMA adapted)

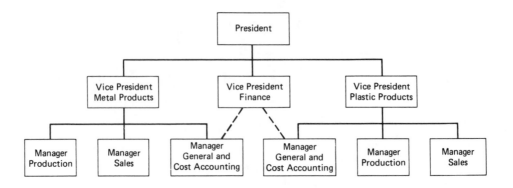

FIGURE C3-3   Proposed organizational structure.

3-16   Contronics, Inc. is a large electronics-component manufacturer in Fort Wayne, Indiana. It has grown substantially during the past four years. As the company has expanded its operations, the duties and responsibilities of the accounting department have increased. Both the size of the controller's staff and the number of the department's responsibility centers have also increased.

Each responsibility center manager reports directly to William Smart, the company controller. An organization structure in which all subordinates report directly to a single supervisor is referred to as a flat organization. The organization chart in Figure C3-4 represents the controllership function of Contronics Inc.

Each manager of a responsibility center supervises a moderate-sized staff and is responsible for undertaking the tasks assigned to the position to accomplish the designated objectives of the individual responsibility center. The managers depend on William Smart for direction in coordinating their separate activities.

REQUIRED: Redraw the organization chart of the controllership function to reflect sound organizational standards; add one or more staff units that should facilitate the communication process of Contronics's controllership function.
(CMA adapted)

3-17   Bluestone Foundry and Metal Products Company of Youghiogheny City, Pennsylvania, produces small tools for craftsmen for various industries and for wide distribution throughout the nation under various house brands used by discount department stores. Bluestone, at another plant, produces high-quality roller and ball bearings for industrial use. Recently it has added a metal products division that markets metal casting to a wide variety of industries ranging from toys to aerospace. Many of its products require state-of-the-art chemical and metallurgical technology and the best in industrial engineering know-how so that they can be manufactured to rigid specifications. Bluestone has therefore employed a large staff of engineers in research and development. Currently Bluestone is organized as shown in the organization chart in Figure C3-5. Four vice-presidents report to the president. Since the company places considerable emphasis on marketing its products and on customer service, three marketing managers report to the vice-president of marketing. Plant managers report to these marketing managers to achieve effective coordination of production and marketing for each product. The rest of the organization is shown in Figure C3-6.

Bluestone has used a local CPA in Youghiogheny City for twenty years, but due to its growth and the acquisition of the metal

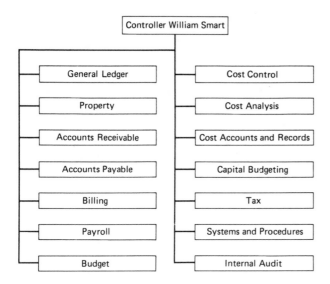

FIGURE C3-4   Controller's department.

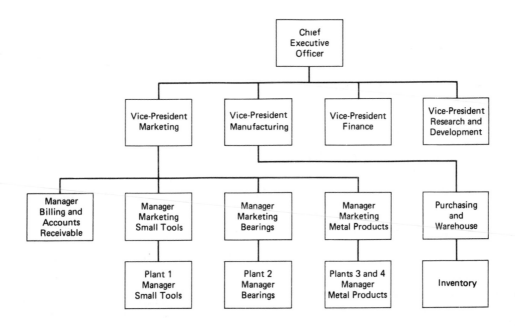

FIGURE C3-5   Bluestone Foundry and Metal Products.

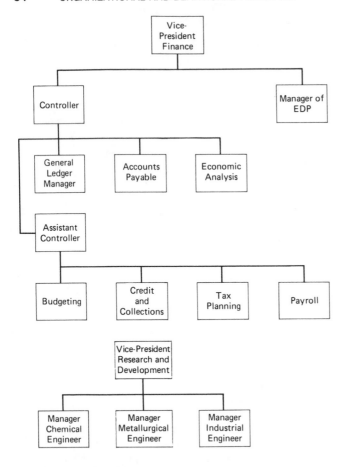

FIGURE C3-6   Bluestone Foundry and Metal Products.

products division, it has asked your firm to conduct the annual audit and give advice on modernizing its information system, which is strictly a transaction-based financial and cost accounting system. Bluestone does use a standard cost system and a flexible budget, and the standards are set by the industrial engineering staff.

REQUIRED: As part of your report, the company would like you to prepare a brief outline giving your suggestions on the following issues:

1.   Any organization structural changes you consider necessary and why. Draw the new organization charts involved.

2.   The inability of Bluestone's R&D department to deal with its various assignments.

3.   The coordination of manufacturing, purchasing, and inventory with respect to the contribution of each product to profit.

4.   The location of the information systems unit.

5.   Behavioral implications of any structural and information changes you propose at

   a.   The vice-president's level

   b.   The manager's and supervisor's level

   c.   The lower levels

6. How Bluestone should deal with these potential changes.

3-18 Huron Company has just been acquired by ANX Industries, a competitor of Huron. There will be some shifting of personnel as a consequence of the acquisition. For instance, Huron's controller is being transferred to ANX's corporate staff; Helen Kane, Huron's assistant controller, will assume the controllership position for Huron. Some accounting personnel will be transferred to Huron from ANX, but ANX wants to retain a large core of Huron's qualified accounting personnel at Huron's offices. Kane has been directed to recommend the employees she wishes to retain.

Kane has not yet decided whether to retain Robert Perrin who has worked in Huron's Cost Accounting Department since receiving his undergraduate degree four years ago. She believes Perrin to be technically competent but lacking in motivation. Kane has decided to meet with Perrin. Since she has been with Huron for only two years, she prepared for her meeting by reviewing Perrin's annual employee evaluations in his personnel file. The evaluations did not disclose any major problems with Perrin. The evaluations indicated that his technical skills were very good but that he was weak in communication skills. The evaluations for the last two years seemed to indicate that Perrin had an attitude problem. As a consequence, Perrin has not been promoted, nor has he achieved the level of performance originally expected.

During the meeting, Perrin said he had confidence in his ability to handle increased responsibility, but he believed that the controller did not support him and would not promote him. Kane informed Perrin of the controller's scheduled transfer. She also explained that some Huron employees would have to be dismissed immediately due to the acquisition while others would be selected for retention. If an employee selected for retention did not wish to remain with Huron, the employee would be eligible for a bonus equal to 30 percent of annual gross salary to remain with Huron for six months in order to integrate Huron's accounting system with ANX's. At the conclusion of the meeting, Kane told Perrin that she would recommend him for retention because she believed he had the qualifications to advance and

to make a worthwhile contribution to Huron. She also indicated that he would have two weeks in which to make his decision regarding continued employment at Huron.

REQUIRED:

1. Expectancy theory is an accepted model of motivation and involves two factors—valence and expectancy. Explain expectancy theory, including a definition of each of these two factors.

2. Identify and explain which of the factors in expectancy theory is more controllable by management.

3. On the basis of the information presented and applying expectancy theory, explain whether Robert Perrin would be motivated to remain with Huron Company.

4. Robert Perrin's productivity would be increased by increasing his motivation. Explain how else Huron Company could increase Perrin's productivity.
   (CMA adapted)

3-19 U.S. Swimming and Diving Supply Company needs a new budgeting system to control its sales, distribution, and manufacturing operations. The old owners were involved in the daily operations of each of these areas, but the new owners need to hire three managers to oversee these three different activities. Moreover, they need to appont a company president to oversee the entire operation on their behalf.

REQUIRED:

1. What arrangements can the new owners make to ensure that the new managers comply with the objectives of the organization?

2. How can the accounting system, specifically the budgeting system, be used to assist in meeting these objectives?

3-20 Mr. Lewis has been padding the budget for several years. He will understate sales revenue and overstate costs and as a result he always shows a positive variance for profit. This has worked well because the general manager of the division doesn't really have sufficient information to get a good assessment of the real revenue potential and what the costs should be in their line of business. As a result, Mr. Lewis has enjoyed the good life, he takes long vacations and plays golf three times a week. Moreover, his list of perks include club memberships and a company car.

The general manager has reason to believe that these activities are excessive and that she is not getting the true picture of what Mr. Lewis is capable of doing with the organization's resources.

REQUIRED:

1. What is the cause of this problem?
2. From an accounting system perspective, what can be done to remedy the problem? Why?

4

DECISION-MAKING, INFORMATION, AND COMMUNICATION CONCEPTS

OVERVIEW

Management must select courses of action consistent with its objectives in an uncertain, complex, and dynamic environment. As noted in Chapter 2, the management system designed to implement these operational, managerial, and stragetic decisions must be supported by an effective and efficient information system. The accounting system is a major subsystem of such a decision support or information system. In many cases the accounting system is the dominant subsystem; in some cases it is the only component of the system. The combined management and information systems are used to plan and control the firm's operations. Finally this planning and control process relies on an effective communication network.

The information system is a key asset and it must support the organization's decision-making activities. Moreover, it is often valuable as a competitive weapon. As noted in Chapter 3, these decision-making activities are the third major component of the social and decision-making environment in which the information or accounting system must operate. The other two major components discussed in Chapter 3 are the organization structure and human behavior. Thus it is vital that accountants and system designers understand the decision-making process, for the decision network will ultimately be the basis for system design. In this chapter, a conceptual framework for decision making will be developed for use in understanding and specifying various decision activities. Decision-making systems will be classified based on this framework, to assist the designer in assessing the key parameters of new and old systems. Measurement and communication concepts will be related to this framework. The key mathematical and behavioral features of decision theory and information value will be reviewed relative to this framework in two modules in this chapter. Particular attention will be given to the value of accounting information in shaping an organization's competitive strategy.

CONCEPTUAL FRAMEWORK FOR DECISION MAKING

From earlier chapters we see that the organizational system consists of the physical, management, and information system. In the physical system input resources are transformed into goods and services. The management system and the information system—through managerial decision, actions, and feedback on the feedback on the nature of the input, transformation, and output process—directs, controls, and reports on these physical activities. The accounting information system needs to provide management with the needed information to set strategy, make managerial and other decisions. All this is done in the organization's business and economic environment.

DECISION-MAKING SYSTEMS

Decision-Making Process

Management decision making is carried on in an uncertain, complex, and dynamic environment. This environment includes constraints related to the business, economic, and political environment. Moreover as illustrated the decision-making process[1] takes place given the business strategy of the organization, the resources as its disposal, and the organizational and behavioral constraints of the organization. First, as shown in Figure 4-1, the problem or opportunity must be defined. This is not easy to do and an effective intelligence-gathering system must be in place in order to enable management to do this effectively. Next, data must be gathered related to the problem or opportunity. The accounting information system is especially useful here in providing a wealth of financial information related to the problem. These data sources consist of relevant objects, activities, and results of prior actions and they are necessary to provide information about potential courses of action. For example, in the budget process the sources may represent such objects as historical costs, sales, inventory, and assets. These data sources are observed, selected, filtered, classified, and measured using a code or scale that will be helpful for decision-making purposes. This must be done in such a way that management is able to use this data, which

---

[1] Herbert A. Simon, *Administrative Behavior*, 3rd ed., (New York; Free Press a division of Macmillan, Inc., 1976), pp. 67, 97, 232–34. Copyright 1947, 1957, 1976.

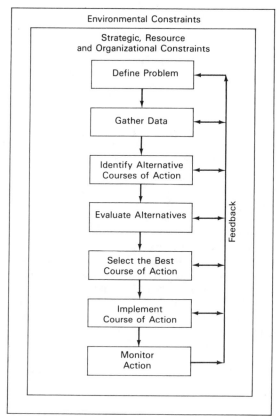

Porter's Model.

FIGURE 4-1
Decision-making process.

is often stored, to identify all the alternative strategies or courses of action that may be used to resolve the problem or exercise the opportunity.

Next, these alternatives need to be evaluated in terms of the consequences that would follow upon the adoption of each strategy, given the criteria set forth by management. Functional relationships and behavioral patterns are useful in describing these alternatives to management. Predictions and inferences may be generated using regression and cost-volume-profit analysis, for example, to illustrate the consequences of each action. In the budget process this may be represented by forecasts, flexible budgets, and other plans regarding future courses of action. In capital budgeting, revenue and cost forecasts for several alternative courses of action may constitute such predictions.

This part of the process is followed by an analysis of alternatives and the selection of the most appropriate, best, or in some cases optimal solution based on the selection criteria and goals of the organization. To accomplish this, clear objectives must be set and translated into criteria for selection of a course of action. For example, in the budget process management may select the set of plans that maximizes profit, maximizes market share, minimizes costs, yields a satisfactory profit with little risk, yields the maximum return on investments, yields the largest net present value, and so on. Next management must implement the course of action selected. Finally management must monitor the results of the action selected via the accounting information system. This process incorporates a feedback mechanism, that corrects the decision-making process when needed and communicates the results of the action, which may influence subsequent mechanism decisions.

Sometimes the decision maker has complete knowledge of the relevant alternatives and the outcomes resulting from management action for each alternative. Such a decision process is insulated from the unknown influences of the environment. Moreover, the decision maker has a model that will permit an ordering of alternatives in accordance with the firm's objectives. In such cases we have a *closed system*. Closed systems are more likely to be found in cases in which an information system encompasses most or all of the decision-making steps shown in Figure 4-1. More-automated systems will fit this pattern, in which there is a lack of unknown environmental influences.

On the other hand, if the decision process in Figure 4-1 is heavily influenced by an unpredictable environment, the decision maker has knowledge of neither all the alternatives nor the consequences of management action for each alternative. As a result, the model used must be applied to an incomplete set of alternatives for which the outcomes are not certain. Moreover, the model may not be capable of dealing with uncertainty, nor with the complexity of the many environmental variables bearing on the decision. Such a system is an *open decision system*. In cases such as this, the decision is clearly influenced by the environment and, to further complicate the situation, the environment may even be influenced by the decision.[2] In open systems, the decision-making process will be left up to the individual decision maker to a greater degree. Fewer steps will be formally incorporated into the information system, and more of the steps will be part of the management system used by the organization.

Types of Decision-Making Systems

Within the social and decision-making environment (organization, human behavior, and decision making) described in Chapter 3, the accountant or system designer must implement an information system that will ultimately reduce the uncertainty of the consequences of various actions which impact the physical system of the organization. Moreover, this must be done so that the incremental value of the information exceeds the incremental cost. In designing the accounting information, the accountant must decide where the formal information system stops and the management system (human information processing) begins in the decision-making process. This is called the *point of articulation* between the information and the management decision-making system. In this text, decision-making processes are classified[3] based on this interface between the manage-

---

[2] For an excellent review of this last issue, see J. Forrester, *Industrial Dynamics* (Boston: MIT Press, 1961). See *A Business Users Guide to STELLA*, High Performance Systems, Inc., Lyme NH, 1987.

[3] R. O. Mason, "Basic Concepts for Designing Management Information Systems," AIS Research Paper No. 8, October 1969.

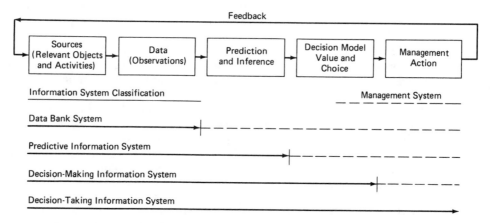

FIGURE 4-2 Information and management system framework for decision making.
Source: Adapted with permission from Richard O. Mason, "Basic Concepts fof Designing Management Information Systems".

ment (decision) system and the information system. This interface classification is shown in Figure 4-2 and can be used to define the level of support that the information system gives to management in the decision-making process.

DATA BANK SYSTEMS   A data bank information system is structured to collect, classify, and store data by applying the lowest common denominator that will suffice for a variety of uses. The interface between the information system and the management system is between gathering of data and predictions used to identify alternatives. It becomes the function of management to request the data needed, make predictions and inferences from these data for various alternatives, and select and follow what seems to be the best course of action. Many of these requests will be routine and will constitute a set of management reports. Most traditional accounting systems found in practice will probably fall into this class. The objective of the information system is simply to support management decision making with a timely supply of reliable data. A sales analysis report which shows total sales by product and by region would be an example of output from such a system. This is all that can be done in many open systems. The data bank system has two main deficiencies: (1) irrelevant data that do not relate to any decision are often collected; and (2) data manipulation and calculations are left to the manager (decision maker). As a result, the manager is often offered more detailed data than can possibly be organized for an effective and efficient evaluation of alternative courses of action. Information overload often exists with these systems.

PREDICTIVE INFORMATION SYSTEMS. In a predictive information system the manager asks "what if" questions to evaluate the various alternatives. The information system is based on a set of assumptions about the behavior of the relevant objects and activities of the firm and the environment. The system predicts a set of expected results (perhaps even probability distributions) for various alternative courses of action deemed relevant by the decision maker. This type of system supports managers by focusing on the relevant information for particular decisions, thus reducing the information overload.

In general, such a system would take the sales analysis information above, develop trends and other relationships, incorporate economic data and prepare a forecast of future sales. Financial planning and budget simulation models are excellent examples of this type of system. Most of these financial planning models are founded on simple financial and cost accounting relationships and transactions, which can be expressed as systems of equations, as will be demonstrated in Chapter 17. The manager may give the information system the current financial position of the firm, a sales forecast, a set of revenue and cost transaction assumptions, and a set of collection and inventory policies or assumptions. A pro forma income statement, balance sheet, and statement of changes in financial position, as well as information such as return on investment and earnings per share, can be generated by the system given these assumptions. The impact of these alternative assumptions and actions on the financial statement is thus inferred by the system. No attempt is made by the system to evelute the predicted results or, in the example cited, the pro forma set of financial statements. The manager must do the evaluation and ultimate selection of a course of action. Thus the interface (level of support) between the information system and the management system is schematically located between the evaluation and prediction phase and the selection process in Figure 4-2.

This type of system works well when the volume of data is large, interrelationships among the data items are complicated, and the interrelationships are predictable or, in the case of financial statements, follow a general set of rules, such as generally accepted accounting principles. As in budgeting, many alternatives can be assessed by the decision maker. Many "what if" questions can also be asked, such as: What is the impact on sales of a price decrease of 10 percent, which according to market research will yield a 5 percent increase in sales? When using such a system, a management must be cognizant of all underlying assumptions, to ensure that they coincide with the manager's best assessment of reality and with corporate policies. Because of the advantages offered by such systems in terms of reducing masses of data to commonly used accounting reports familiar to managers, it is strongly suggested that more traditional accounting systems move in this direction. Managers will be able to make better, more informed decisions. Many of the popular spreadsheet packages for microcomputers are particularly useful in assisting management in evaluating various alternatives using predictions and inferences based on various criteria.

DECISION-MAKING INFORMATION SYSTEMS.   When relevant data can be collected, and sufficient structural and behavioral relationships exist among data elements and the environment so that the outcomes can be predicted for a set of alternatives, it is sometimes feasible to incorporate the organization's set of values and choice criteria into the information system and actually let the information system select the best alternative. Such a system is called a decision-making information system. Management merely asks which action is best, and the information system responds using a programmed decision model that selects the best alternative based on the organization's goals. Considering again the sales example, if the objective of the firm is to maximize the volume of sales, subject to an acceptable profit and other organizational constraints, a planning model may be used to select the most appropriate course of action. Another example would be a mathematical model used to allocate scarce resources, such as labor, to competing jobs to maximize contribution to profit. Generally such systems use operations research, management science, and mathematical or statistical models to sort through the various alternatives to select the "best" course of action for management. In such a system, therefore, the locus of the interface between the information system and management system is between the decision model and management action. Management must then take action to maximize sales volume for example.

AUTOMATIC DECISION-MAKING INFORMATION SYSTEMS. Sometimes, usually in a closed system, the information system can be designed not only to collect data, draw inferences from the data, and select the best course of action, but also to implement the selected action. A good example of this type of decision-taking information system is a just-in-time (JIT) purchase and inventory system. Data consist of the status of inventory items, lead times, and production schedules. Inferences are drawn from usage rates, lead time, and production schedules. At the appropriate time action is taken in the form of automatic issuance of a purchase order by the information system. This action may be done using electronic data interchange (EDI) to communicate directly between the company and its vendors computers to ensure that the right amount of inventory arrives as it is needed. Most information systems of this type operate in limited environments, such as the inventory control system in the example just given. Clearly, for such a system to operate without management's interaction, management must have complete confidence in the model and the assumptions upon which it is founded.

Many organizations, including public accounting firms, are now attempting to move as far as possible along this continuum of information systems toward a system which will actually implement the decision. They are using expert systems to take advantage of the best knowledge they have in the organization to automate various steps in the process, from the definition of the problem through the use of judgment in evaluation of alternatives, to the selection and ultimate implementation of the best course of action. These methods are discussed more completely later in the text.

In summary, the interface between the information and the management system (decision maker) can take place at any juncture in the decision process shown in Figure 4-2. This level of decision-making support is a function of the firm's social and decision-making environment. The accountant and the system designer must be aware of the factors influencing this interface in the decision process so that he or she will be able to assess the decision network of the organization in order to design an effective system. This awareness is critical, for the decision network and the level of support to be rendered by the information system are the basis for system design and implementation.

INFORMATION AND COMMUNICATION
CONCEPTS—OVERVIEW

As organizations grow and become more geographically disbursed, it is important that good communication be established between management and the various plants, sales offices, and headquarters around the country and even in many cases around the world. As discussed throughout this text, distributed databases and distributed processing systems are becoming the norm for many companies. Moreover, electronic data interchange, electronic mail, wide area networks, and local area networks are becoming routine. The use of these communication networks to control operations and to report the results to management depends on accurate measurement of operations and an effective communication system. Measurement and communication concepts are thus important to the accountant as he or she manages the information of the organization and assists in the design of accounting information systems.

Measurement

The collecting, sorting, and storing of data (noted in Figure 4-2 between the sources and the data in the decision-making process) require the classifying, coding, and assigning of numbers to events, objects, and even other measurements by using a set of rules. Effective forms, data input procedures, and reports are essential in this data-capturing process. There is probably no such thing, in practice, as a perfect representation of the various events and activities observed. As a result, surrogates must often be used for measurement of economic events and activities in decision-making models. The effective assignment of appropriate surrogates presents a difficult problem for the accountant. Timeliness, reliability, objectivity, and relevance must all be weighed and balanced in the selection of a surrogate.

Nominal, ordinal, interval, and ratio scales can be used as units of measurement. On a nominal scale, events are only classified. An example of a nominal classification is that of an inventory item as an asset. An ordinal scale, which expresses position in a series (such as one item being more valuable than another), or an interval scale, which expresses magnitudes of differences, can also be used. A ratio scale, such as the number of units, enables the manager to use numerical manipulation, such as addition or multiplication. Regardless of the measurement or scale used to encode the relevant economic events and activities for decision making, the generation of useful data must follow the process outlined in Figure 4-3. Events, objects, and possibly other measurements, such as competitors' financial statements, are selected, observed, and filtered. Next they are classified using the assignment of classification codes, such as chart-of-account numbers. An appropriate scale, generally a ratio scale such as dollars or units, is used to assign a number to the observation. Once this measurement process has been completed, the measurements are recorded via an appropriately designed form, or input via a computer terminal and transmitted to the database for future reference by the information system or management.

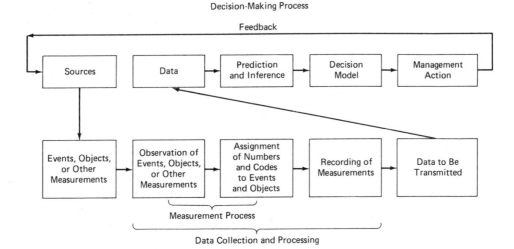

FIGURE 4-3 Basic measurement concepts for designing management information systems.
Source: Adapted with permission from American Accounting Association Committee on Information Systems, "Accounting and Information Systems." *The Accounting Review Supplement,* vol. XLVI (1971), and R. O. Mason, "Basic Concepts for Designing Management Information Systems".

Communication

An accountant should be aware of the basic communication concepts related to the decision-making process in order to render advice to management on the design and use of communication networks. Shannon and Weaver[4] state that there are three types of problems associated with communication:

1. The technical problem—"How accurately can the symbols of communication be transmitted?"
2. The semantic problem—"How precisely do the transmitted symbols carry the desired meaning?"
3. The effectiveness problem—"How effectively does the received meaning affect conduct in the desired way?"

The first problem is primarily a *transmission problem,* and it exists at each juncture in the decision-making process. Data, including results of predictions, decision models, or management actions, must be encoded on forms or via a computer monitor, then transmitted and finally decoded to provide a signal for the next step in the decision process. This signal can be a simple output report or an electronic signal used by the next stage in the decision-process. This transmission may be part of either the information system or the management sys-

---

[4] C. E. Shannon and W. Weaver, *The Mathematical Theory of Communication* (Urbana: University of Illinois Press, 1949), with permission.

tem. Statistical communication theory[5] has shed some light on procedures for converting data into messages that may be transmitted, characteristics of transmission channels, and eventual conversion into usable signals.

It is important that the accountant be aware of the encoding, transmission, and decoding problems associated with the amount of information actually conveyed. Generally great care is exercised via internal control procedures to enhance the accuracy of this process. Only the information conveyed can be used in decision making. Aggregation of data for more efficient communication, information losses associated with this aggregation, and the presence of noise in the system are also important to the accountant as he or she seeks to design effective input documents, data files, and output reports for the accounting system.

Noise is basically interference. It can occur at either the input or output interface with the information system or it can occur as electrical interference during the transmission of data. Input/output noise follows from (1) conflicting signals or meaning from like data; or (2) different data causing a similar signal (message) due to coding, transmission, and decoding processes.

The *semantic problems* as well as the *effectiveness problem* are, to a large extent, behavioral problems. They result in misunderstandings and misperceptions. As a result, the accountant should continually be aware of the individual's role in collecting, processing, and transmitting, and receiving data in the communication process. The individual receives signals, makes observations from these signals based on individual perceptions, and processes and filters these observations according to a personal set of biases. The individual then takes action or sends signals based on these filtered signals. Because of this role, it is important that the system designer understand the impact of signal (message) differences on perceptions, filtering methods, and the ultimate actions of the individuals who make the decisions in a firm. Expertise in communication, semantics, social psychology, sociometrics, learning theory, and psychology may be needed to resolve some of the problems associated with this process. The strategy by which individuals reach a decision is also important in understanding the behavioral process. The accountant and the system designer are challenged to design a system with its related manual forms, input screens, and output reports that is usable by a wide range of employees with different ways of solving problems. This user interface will be explored more in the chapter on decision support systems.

Form, Screen, and Reported Design

From the theoretical communication concepts above it is apparent that manual forms, input and output screens (computer display) used in on-line systems, and reports be carefully designed to effectively measure the activities of the organization and to communicate these to decision makers and those who need to process daily transaction in the organization.

---

[5] Statistical measures of entropy, or disorder, have been useful to a limited degree in assessing the amount of information transmitted through the system and the loss of information due to aggregation in the coding process. For a full discussion of statistical communication theory in the accounting literature, see Baruch Lev, *Financial Statement Analysis: A New Approach* (Englewood Cliffs, N.J.: Prentice Hall, 1974); and H. Theil, "On the Use of Information Theory Concepts in the Analysis of Financial Statements," *Management Science*, May 1969.

Input forms and computer screens must be easy to use and must collect the necessary information as efficiently and effectively as feasible. They must contain identification such as company name, division, type of input, dates, and times. They must also contain a provision for the user to identify themselves either in the form of a signature or in the case of computer input, a password. The input format must correspond to the transaction in order for clerical personnel to easily follow the form or the screen. If a computer screen is used, appropriate blanks can be highlighted and edited to lead the user through the input process and to immediately reject any erroneous transactions. Moreover, forms must be prenumbered for control of the documents and both forms and screens should contain as much preprinted material or display as much information as possible to reduce the amount of input on the user's part. For example, turnaround documents can be used with part numbers, departments, employee numbers, customer account numbers and amount due, and can be used where the user only fills in a limited amount of information, such as number of parts used or amount remitted. This will greatly reduce input errors. Output and reports must contain only relevant information for processing the transaction or making the decision. If this is not the case, information overload will occur and the reports or the display on the monitor will not be very effective in helping management make a decision. Again it should be in a convient format, with appropriate identification and dates. Often it should contain comparative information to help put the information in perspective for the user. It should also be consistent from department to department to avoid conflicting signals. More will be said about representation of information in Chapter 17, Decision Support Systems.

VALUE OF ACCOUNTING INFORMATION

Relevance, Timing, and Accuracy

Accounting information is an important business asset whose acquisition, like that of other resources, constitutes a problem of economic choice. One can obtain insight into the value of information by considering some of the key precepts of decision theory. First, decisions basically follow the process outlined in Figure 4-1. Second, organizational decision making involves a search process and a learning process. Third, the models used by management range from rational optimization to satisficing models which search for a satisfactory solution. Finally, the search process and models used are tempered by the structure of the problem and the decision-making style of management. These are examined in more detail in modules A and B of this chapter. Very briefly, information has value if it has the potential to impact a decision. In addition, accounting information can be used very effectively to enhance an organization's competitive position in the market. Finally the value (benefit) of the information must be greater than its cost.

Technically, the signal (report or other information) from the accounting system has *value* only if it is *relevant* and only if it *may* result in a management (or other) user of the information taking course of action other than the one that would be taken if the information were not present. For example, variance information has value if it may result in the selection of a supplier which would ship better quality components; or financial statements may have value if they may lead to different investment decisions. Relevance can also be defined as the set of information that has the greatest future predictive ability.

Sensitivity analysis is useful in assessing the possible impact of an information system on a decision. To assess this impact, one can alter the assumptions and the parameters of the problem to see whether information from the system can alter a decision; it may be that no matter what information is received, the decision will not change. The system may have no value in this case, because the decision cannot be affected by the accounting information received from the system.

In addition to relevance, information must be as *timely* and *accurate* as possible without incurring excessive costs, otherwise it will reach users too late to affect decisions and users will not have confidence in it for those decisions.

The sequence of events relating cost to value to relevance to potential courses of action must be considered in the design and implementation of any information system; this sequence is outlined in theory in Module B of this chapter. In addition, decision tables and payoff matrices can help the accountant or system designer gain insight into the economic parameters affecting the value of an information system. These are illustrated in the Module B.

Competitive Value of Accounting Information

In the past, the major competitive weapons used by organizations were physical and related to the nature of the product. With the decrease in cost in computers and the increase in computer processing power available to organizations, we can expect information generated by accounting systems to be used more and more to add value to a product and thus be used as an aggressive competitive weapon.[6] Accounting information and their related systems, such as detailed billing systems, can change the nature of an industry; create tremendous competitive advantage, such as in the area of electronic funds transfer systems, for those who take advantage of its potential; and spawn new business for many organizations such as CPA firms who specialize in developing new systems which deliver more information to their client's management.

Often the potential of using information aggressively is great; but the cost of not using it can be catastrophic. In other words survival of an organization may depend on its use of information to add value to their product or service to compete.

CHANGING INDUSTRY STRUCTURE. According to Porter,[7] there are five major competitive forces in an industry. These include: rivalry among existing competitors, threat of new entrants into the market, pressure from substitute products, bargaining power of suppliers, and bargaining power of customers.

[6] See B. Ives and G.P. Learmonth, "Information as a Competitive Weapon," *Communications of ACM*, December 1984; and Michael E. Porter, *Competitive Advantage* (New York: Free Press, 1985) for a complete discussion. The list below is founded on these two references.

[7] See Michael E. Porter, *Competitive Advantage* (New York: Free Press, 1985) for a complete discussion of competitive forces.

Accounting information can alter each of these five major components in a significant way.

For example, automated order processing, production scheduling, and billing systems have made placing orders more efficient, thus increasing the rivalry among competitors. Once one firm has such a system, others need it to compete effectively and to process orders in a timely manner.

As another example, some banks have provided their customers with ready access to account information and automated checking using their home computer. The programs to run these systems are expensive and complex and pose a tremendous entry barrier for new entrants into the banking business in the metropolitan areas where these systems exist.

Even the smallest of organizations can have computerized vendor files on microcomputer systems that make it easer to find the most reasonable price and delivery schedule and thus reduce their overall operating costs. In addition, computerized customer lists have made it easier for the small business to target customers with promotional material and to customize products.

In general, the competitive boundaries have been increased via information to include the entire interorganizational system, including the supplier, the organization itself, the distribution channels, and the customer.[8] This can be done via electronic data interchange.

CREATING COMPETITIVE ADVANTAGE. A competitive advantage can be created via cost reduction or product differentiation. For example, costs can be reduced via an information system which informs vendors when supplies are needed so that they are shipped and arrive just in time for their utilization in the production process. This results in substantial reduction of inventory and obsolescence because only those parts and components actually needed for current production are in the supply channel.

Another way to create a competitive advantage is for an organization to tie its information system to its customers via electronic data interchange.[9] An organization can link its distribution system to the customers manufacturing system so that just the right amount of parts arrive at just the right time for production. Such an arrangement can make it very expensive for a customer to switch vendors. Often competitive advantages are not permanent; so as technology changes and opportunities present themselves, organizations need to continue to seek such advantages.

SPAWNING NEW BUSINESS. Finally, an organization can utilize the power of the computer and the information it can produce to create a new business or a spin off of its existing business. For example, the use of automated cash registers and the automated checkout lanes at grocery stores have enabled these organizations to provide advertisers with rapid feedback on the impact of their promotional efforts.

Information technology can also add value through support activities such as product development, using computer aided design in order to develop prod-

---

[8] See James I. Cash and Benn R. Konsynski, "IS Redraws Competitive Boundaries," *Harvard Business Review*, March-April 1985, pp. 134–142.

[9] See Blake Ives and Gerard P. Learmonth, "The Information System as a Competitive Weapon," *Communications of the ACM*, December 1984, pp. 1193–1201.

Support Activities

Infrastructure	Planning Models				
Human Resource Management	Automated Personnel Scheduling				
Technology Development	Computer Aided Design				
Procurement	On-Line (Immediate Data Access) Parts Procurement				
Examples	Automated Warehouses	Flexible Manufacturing	Automated Order Processing	Remote Terminals for Salespersons	Computer Scheduling of Repair Trucks
Primary Activities →	Input Resources & Logistics	Transformation Process & Operations	Output Goods & Services	Distribution Marketing & Sales	Service

FIGURE 4-4   Information technology and the value chain.
Source: Michael E. Porter, and Victor E. Millan, *An exhibit from* "How Information Gives You Competitive Advantage", (July/August 1985). Copyright © 1985 by the President and Fellows of Harvard College, all rights reserved. Reprinted by permission of Harvard Business Review.

ucts which are easier to manufacture, require fewer parts, cost less in general, and result in greater quality. In summary, information can add value through the primary activities of converting input into goods and services and the efficient delivery of these to customers. Figure 4-4 outlines several examples of this, such as remote sales terminals for sales personnel to enhance the sales effort.

SUMMARY

Accounting information is a valuable asset for an organization. It is useful for decision making and for competing in the market. The decision-making process, whether it involves a decision regarding the need to resolve a problem or take advantage of an apparent opportunity, or involves the actual selection of a course of action, is comprised of the sequence of steps outlined in Figure 4-1: (1) defining the problem; (2) gathering and measuring data; (3) identification of alternatives; (4) evaluation of alternatives based on a criterion; (5) selecting the best alternative; (6) implementation; and (7) monitoring the results. The information system may automate this process, as described in Figures 4-1 and 4-2 or it may only begin the process by offering management a set of data from which to make decisions. The management system will complete the process starting where computerized support stops. This interface will be a function of many social and decision-making environmental factors, such as the nature of the decision, the behavior of the firm, and the style of its management. In order to effectively design a system to support management needs, the accountant must understand this process and, most important, the interface between the information system and the management system. As pointed out in Chapter 2, the objective of the accounting information is to support management's decision-making, reporting, and transaction processing requirements.

The decision-making process outlined in the chapter is not simple. Many complex factors influence the process. Objects and activities must be measured and these must be encoded, transmitted, and decoded into signals that are significant and relevant to the decision maker. This is an imprecise and complex task that often involves many sets of behavioral assumptions. Measurement and communication concepts can be quite useful in understanding this part of the process.

The accountant must also understand that information ultimately only has value if it has the potential either to alter courses of action via the decision process or to add value to an organization's product or service. Decision theory (outlined in Module A) can give the accountant or system designer important guidelines in system design. An understanding of the decision-making practice in organizations where individual goals must be reconciled with corporate goals, an understanding of decision models, and an appreciation of the basic economic issues (Module B) regarding the value and potential value of information systems are all important to anyone who must design an effective, efficient, and cost-justified system that managers can use. Finally, recognizing that most of the key variables in business systems can be cast as control and communication variables is important. The science of cybernetics, which deals with such variables, may be helpful in systems design.

In summary, the accountant or systems designer must understand the value of information and social and decision-making environment in which the system must function.

MODULE A

DECISION-MAKING THEORY—OVERVIEW

The decision model is dependent on the accounting information system which provides signals to the model. In addition, the selection of the type of information system required is influenced by type of decisions made by management and other users of accounting information. In this module, we review some of the traditional concepts of decision theory. Mathematical and statistical decision models for the more structured information systems will also be reviewed briefly. The value of information and information economics issues will be discussed Module B.

There are various decision-making theories: some are descriptive in nature, some are behavioral models, and others are founded on organizational theory. They all relate in various ways to the decision-making process. Because these theories indicate how decisions are made by individuals and organizations, they are important in the design and implementation of accounting information systems because information systems are used to support all the levels of managerial activities.

Decision-Making Process

The decision-making process according to Simon[10] consists of several stages, like those outlined in Figure 4-1, which also shows strategic resources and environmental constraints, the flow of feedback and control information, and the basic decision-making process. First, the problem must be determined through an intelligence system. Second, alternatives must be determined to deal with the problem or in many cases to take advantage of a competitive opportunity. Third, one of the alternatives must be selected or chosen to be implemented. This requires a selection process and criteria. Finally, the decision will be implemented. Throughout this whole process, the decision maker needs to access the necessary accounting information to make a decision on the problem or competitive opportunity, the alternatives to consider, the selection criteria, the evaluation of the alternatives, the implementation process and feedback information on compliance with the organizational objectives.

Descriptive Theory

Cyert and March,[11] in an effort to describe organizational decision making while developing a behavioral theory of the firm, outline four major decision-making concepts: (1) quasi resolution of conflict; (2) uncertainty avoidance; (3) problematic search; and (4) organizational learning.

First, they recognize that any organization is a coalition of individuals (or segments of the organization), each with different goals and each with some influence to alter the organizational objectives (see Chapter 3). These different objectives must be resolved (1) by allowing subsystems (or individuals) to pursue their own goals (local rationality); (2) by permitting subsystems (or individuals) to make their own decisions within specified limits (acceptable-level decision rules); and (3) by resolving conflicts sequentially so that they are not handled at the same time and each decision is based on the prior decisions (sequential attention to goals). These strategies constitute quasi-resolution of conflict and are important to the design of management systems and supporting accounting information systems.

Second, uncertainty is avoided as much as possible by shortening the time horizons of the decision-making process. This is accomplished via faster turnaround or feedback of information related to the consequences of action. Also management may enter into long-term arrangements (linkages) with third parties, such as suppliers or customers, to avoid uncertainty by reducing the risk of changes in supplier relations or customer demand.

The third step, is the problematic search for a solution to the problem. This search is started with the statement of the problem itself and its obvious symptoms. If a solution to the problem is not found in the location of its origin, the search is shifted to other parts of the organization structure in an attempt to find a solution. In other words, there is a definite sequence to the process of

---

[10] H.A. Simon, *The New Science of Management Decision*, revised edition (Prentice Hall, Englewood Cliffs, N.J.). See also H.A. Simon, "Information Technologies and Organizations," *The Accounting Review*, July 1990, pp. 658–67 for a discussion of the impact of technology on organizations.

[11] The descriptive theory of decision making presented here is based largely on Richard M. Cyert and James G. March, *A Behavioral Theory of the Firm* (Englewood Cliffs, N.J.: Prentice Hall, copyright 1963). Used with permission.

searching for a solution to a problem and to the selection of the best way to take advantage of an opportunity. Again this search process has important implications for the type of accounting information required to support management decision making.

Finally, organizations adapt their behavior over time. Goals and procedures are modified as environmental conditions change. Cyert and March refer to this process as organizational learning. The decision maker's style can be heuristic and follow a logical process founded on experience with similar problems, common sense, and emotion. The style can be systematic and analytic and follow a sequential (often mathematical) set of problem-solving steps generally based on a search procedure for underlying cause-and-effect relationships. The system designer or the accountant must be aware of these various cognitive styles involved when designing an accounting information system that will support a management system.

In addition, a systems designer or an accountant must consider the degree of structure in each particular type of decision. Some decisions are very structured where all three phases of decision making are structured. These phases include defining the problem, determining alternative solutions, and selecting the best alternative. Unstructured decisions are those where none of the three phases are readily determinable. Semistructured decisions are those where some of the phases are easily determined. This structure will in part dictate the nature of the decision model and search process that can be used.

Decision Models and Search Process

Many different decision-making models are used in practice. These models basically describe the objectives or selection criteria used by the decision maker, the characteristics of alternatives to be considered, the search process for the best alternative, and implementation procedures. They are both mathematical and behavioral in nature and as a result, more than one model may be used in any given circumstance. They range in structure from very rational optimization models, to models which search for a satisfactory solution, to no model at all. Indeed, some are heuristic and result from experience, emotion, common sense, business intuition, and past trial and error and, in general, the expertise of the decision maker.

Contemporary search literature classifies search procedures as compensatory and noncompensatory.[12] Compensatory procedures consider all the alternatives and their dimensions (factors which may be important in the decision) to come to a conclusion. A discounted cash flow model of all the cash flows for each alternative would be an example. Mathematical programming models can handle many more and diverse dimensions. The problem with this search procedure is that weights can not always easily be assigned either mathematically or as manager views all of the alternatives and assigns weights mentally. This happens when the number of alternatives or dimensions are large. When this happens a noncompensatory search process may be necessary. In such a process the decision maker will either prioritize certain aspects or eliminate some alternatives

---

[12] See E R, Iselin, "The Effects of Information Diversity on Decision Quality in a Structured Decision Task," *Accounting Organizations and Society*, 13 1988, pp. 147-64; Tversky, A., "Elimination by Aspects: A Theory of Choice," *Psychological Review*, vol 79, 1972, pp. 281-99.

because some of the dimensions are clearly not acceptable. This will reduce the size of the problem and make it more meaningful. This process is important to the designer of information systems because information may need to be presented in such a way as to facilitate comparisons to enable the decision maker to eliminate many of the alternatives by their various dimensions (aspects).

RATIONAL OPTIMIZATION MODEL.   The rational decision-making model assumes that the decision maker has a set goal; a criteria for ranking or evaluating this goal; a weighting or an ordering procedure if there happens to be multiple objectives; and a finite set of alternatives, each with known outcomes. This would be a compensitory model. The decision process is generally more complex than this, however. There are often multiple goals to consider, as indicated in the descriptive theory discussion. Not all alternatives are known and it is unlikely that they can all be considered at once in an optimization model. Most likely the search process is sequential, as noted in the descriptive theory. Also the selection criteria are difficult to define in many cases. However, in some very structured situations, primarily in manufacturing, rational optimization models based in part on typical cost accounting data can be used effectively.

These models can mathematically choose the best solution given a certain set of input data and assumptions. In some mathematical procedures, the input may be in the form of probability distributions. These models may relate outcomes to various actions and they may even model the essential characteristics of bargaining. They may even model sequential decisions.

The output criteria for selecting among alternatives cannot always be expressed as an expected value or the maximum contribution to profit because there are various degrees of risk associated with each outcome. In this case, utility and indifference curves can be used in conjunction with several of these mathematical models. Moreover, statistical inference can be used for sampling, correlation analysis, testing hypotheses, and determining probability distributions for both input into the models and output from some of the models.

The accountant or system designer must understand the essential nature of the model (not necessarily the mathematical manipulation or derivation), the necessary assumptions, and the character of the input and information requirements. Design of an effective and efficient information system to support a management decision-making system is impossible without this knowledge. Often, outside advice should be sought to gain the necessary understanding of this aspect of the management decision network.

SATISFICING AND BOUNDED RATIONALITY.   To overcome some of the difficulty and the limitations using the rational optimization approaches, some[13] argue that individuals and organizations really searched for the most satisfactory solution using a sequential process. All alternatives were not considered in this process and only one goal is considered at one time. In other words, they solved one problem based on one objective in a satisfactory way then move on to the next problem, goal, or competitive opportunity. This search process in noncompensitory. These sequential bounds on the search process and the satisfactory rather than optimal selection criteria led to the terms *bounded rationality* and *satisficing.*

---

[13] See J.C. March, and H. A. Simon, *Organizations*, Harper and Row, NY. NY. 1958 and Simon, *New Science of Management Decision*. For a discussion of satisficing and bounded rationality.

INCREMENTAL MODEL. Other individuals and organizations do not set forth a selection criteria and a set of alternatives. These decision makers adopt an incremental decision-making process and select that alternative which appears to be only marginally different than the current mode of operation.[14] They just muddle through. This leads to an evolutionary sequence of small changes in the organizations activities.

In summary, it is important that systems designers need to carefully consider the decision-making process and the information required by its search process in designing an accounting information system.

MODULE B

THE VALUE OF INFORMATION

Information, like any resource, has value. This is particularly true when one considers the effect on managerial decision making.[15] To illustrate this, we make use of decision tables. Consider two alternative management actions in a simple breakeven context. Both alternatives have a selling price of $5 per unit. Alternative A_1 has a variable cost of $4 per unit and a total fixed cost of $500,000. Alternative A_2 has a variable cost of only $3 per unit and a total fixed cost of $1,200,000. In the former case, the unit combination is $1 per unit, and in the latter case it is $2 per unit; the breakeven points are 500,000 and 600,000 units, respectively. Clearly, higher sales will favor A_2 and lower sales will favor A_1. The problem is that higher sales of 1,000,000 units and lower sales of 600,000 units are equally probable as far as management is concerned. Each alternative contribution to profit is analyzed in Table M4-1. Given this example, there are *two questions* facing management:

1. Should more information be bought? (Should the firm pay for an information system that will give management a better feel for the level of sales?)
2. Which action will maximize contribution to profit? (Other situations could require management to minimize costs, maximize sales, or optimize other objective criteria.)

To decide what action is preferable given *only* the information in Table M4-2, management uses the following procedure:

1. The expected value of each action is calculated by multiplying the contribution to profit for each alternative possible for each event by the probability of the event's occurrence. For example, the expected value of alternative A_1 is the contribution to profit for A_1 for the high sales condition

---

[14] See C.E. Lindbloom, "The Science of Muddling Through," *Public Administration Review*, vol. 19 (1959), 79–88.

[15] With permission this illustration is based in part on "Report of the Committee on Managerial Decision Models," *The Accounting Review Supplement*, vol. XLIV (1969).

Table M4-1 Decision Table: Contribution to Profit Analysis—Cost-Volume-Profit Analysis of Alternatives

	EVENTS	
	High Sales	Low Sales
ACTION	Resulting Contribution to Profit	
A$_1$	$500,000[a]	$100,000
A$_2$	800,000	0

[a]Sample calculation:
Unit contribution=$5/unit−$4/unit=$1/unit
Total contribution=1,000,000 units×$1/unit= $1,000,000
Less fixed costs   (500,000)

Expected Total contribution to *profit* $ 500,000

Management Activities Summary

Management Actions:

Alternative A$_1$
   Selling price $5/unit, variable costs $4/unit, and fixed costs $500,000
   Unit contribution $1/unit, and breakeven 500,000 units

Alternative A$_2$
   Selling price $5/unit, variable cost $3/unit, and fixed cost $1,200,000
Unit contribution $2/unit, and breakeven 600,000 units

[1] With permission this illustration is based in part on "Report of the Committee on Managerial Decision Models," *The Accounting Review Supplement*, vol. XLIV (1969).

($500,000) times the probability of high sales (.5), plus the contribution to profit for the low sales condition ($100,000), times the probability of low sales (.5). The expected value of alternative A$_1$ is therefore $300,000.

2. Because management wishes to maximize contribution, alternative A$_2$ (higher fixed costs and lower variable costs) is selected. This alternative yields the higher expected contribution to profit.

To answer the first question about the potential value of added information, we must analyze how the added information will affect the decision process, the costs associated with the added information, and the information system needed to provide it to management. The value of the information is related to its ability to reduce the uncertainty surrounding the choice of courses of action. Such an analysis should proceed by first considering the value of *perfect information*. In the case of perfect information, the information system will give the decision maker perfect foresight upon receipt of the signal from the system. This perfect foresight eliminates the possibility of making a wrong choice. The signal in the example just considered is whether there will be high or low sales.

Table M4-2   Decision Table: Expected Values for Contribution to Profit for Alternatives A_1 and A_2 Given No Information

	EVENTS		EXPECTED VALUE OF CONTRIBUTION[a]
	High Sales 1,000,000 units	*Low Sales* 600,000 units	
Probability	.5	.5	
ACTION	CONTRIBUTION TO PROFIT		
A_1	$500,000	$100,000	$300,000
A_2	800,000	0	400,000

[a] Expected value $A_1 = E(A_1) = \$500,000(.5) + \$100,000(.5) = \$300,000$
Expected value $A_2 = E(A_2) = \$800,000(.5) + 0(.5) = \$400,000$

This signal cannot be known prior to its receipt and the probability of high or low sales, in this case a 50 percent chance of each sales event, will not change. *After* the decision maker receives the information, the course of action yielding the highest contribution will be chosen. The procedure for determining the value of this "perfect" information or "forecast" is as follows:

1. Select the action that will yield the highest contribution to profit for each possible forecast. Specifically, if the new information indicates low sales, alternative A_1 is preferable because it will yield a $100,000 contribution whereas A_2 will yield 0. Likewise, if high sales are forecast, A_2 is preferable, as indicated in Table M4-2.

2. Calculate the expected value of each action choice, since it is *not* known in advance which perfect forecast will come out of the information system. For each forecast, this is accomplished by multiplying the contribution of the action that would have been chosen given a particular forecast by the information system, as shown in Table M4-3.

3. Add the expected values of each action to get a total expected value for the perfect information. The total expected value for perfect information in this example, shown in Table M4-3, is $450,000.

4. Finally, the value of the perfect information provided by the forecast is calculated by subtracting the expected value of the action taken with no information, from Table M4-2, from the expected value of the perfect information calculated in step 3. In this example, we calculate the value of the perfect information to be $450,000 − $400,000 = $50,000, where $450,000 is the expected value of perfect information from Table M4-3 and $400,000 is the expected value from Table M4-2 for the best choice, A_2, which could be made without any information.

Table M4-3 Decision Table: Perfect Information—Expected Values for Contribution to Profit for Alternatives A_1 and A_2 Given Perfect Information

	EVENTS		EXPECTED VALUE OF CONTRIBUTION[a]
	1,000,000 units	*600,000 units*	
Probability	.5	.5	
ACTION	CONTRIBUTION TO PROFIT		
A_1		$100,000	$ 50,000
A_2	$800,000		400,000
Total expected value of perfect information			$450,000

[a] $E(A_1)=.5(0)+.5(\$100,000)=\$50,000$
$E(A_2)=.5(\$800,000)+.5(0)=\$400,000$

Any system costing more than the value of perfect information, which eliminates the possibility of making a wrong decision can be rejected immediately as costing more than it can possibly benefit the firm.

Most information is not perfect but is *imperfect information.* Consider an information system that *may* yield a more optimistic forecast for high sales, a forecast of a stable sales level, or a more pessimistic forecast for low sales. The information is relevant in the sense that the probabilities associated with potential outcomes (events) are altered, given the information provided by the system. For example, assume that an 80 percent conditional probability is now associated with high sales given an optimistic forecast, and a 20 percent conditional probability for low sales.

Calculation of the value of the imperfect information proceeds as follows:

1. The *revised expected values* of each action are calculated as was done in Table M4-3 for the decision given no information. This is done for each possible outcome from the system and for each action. In this example, one outcome, the stable sales forecast, has the value that was calculated with no information. Only the expected values for the optimistic and pessimistic forecasts are calculated.

2. As before, the action with the greatest expected value is selected for each alternative. For the optimistic, same, and pessimistic forecasts, the actions chosen in this example are A_2, A_2, and A_1, respectively, as shown in tables M4-2 and M4-4. For example, if an optimistic forecast is obtained from the information system, alternative A_2 should be chosen because it yields the greatest expected contribution to profit ($640,000). The $640,000 is calculated as before: .8 ($8,000,000) + .2 (0) = $640,000.

3. Management must next estimate the probability of each type of forecast or report. This is necessary to assess the expected value of the imperfect information. For example, assume that in this case management estimated the probabilities of pessimistic, same, and optimistic forecasts as .4, .2, and .4, respectively.

Table M4-4 Decision Table: Imperfect Information—Expected Values of Contribution to Profit for Alternatives A_1 and A_2 Given Optimistic and Pessimistic Imperfect Information

	EVENTS		EXPECTED VALUE OF CONTRIBUTION
	High Sales *1,000,000 Units*	*Low Sales* *600,000 Units*	
Optimistic probability	.8	.2	
ACTION	CONTRIBUTION TO PROFIT		
A_1	$500,000	$100,000	$420,000
A_2	800,000	0	640,000
Pessimistic probability	.2	.8	
ACTION	CONTRIBUTION TO PROFIT		
A_1	$500,000	$100,000	$180,000
A_2	800,000	0	160,000

4. Next the expected value of contribution to profit for the alternative that would be chosen for each type of forecast is weighted by its respective probability, as shown in Table M4-5. The calculation is .4 ($640,000) + .2 ($400,000) + .4 ($180,000) = $408,000. In other words, a system that would generate this information has a total value with respect to contribution to profit of $408,000. Finally, the expected value of the imperfect information, as shown in Table M4-5, is compared with the expected value of the action chosen given no information, as shown in Table M4-2. The value of the imperfect information is the amount of the expected value of the imperfect information less the expected value of the action given no information. In this example, that value is $408,000 − $400,000 = $8,000. In other words, the value of the new system is $8,000 given this set of reports or forecasts with their estimated probabilities of occurrence, sales levels, and alternative actions.

If the system yielding the imperfect information costs less than $8,000, it should be implemented. Otherwise its costs exceed its benefits and it should not be implemented. Note that the value of the system is totally dependent upon the potential alternative actions, the cost behavior patterns of these alternatives, the reports generated by the system, and the probabilities and conditional probabilities associated with these reports. This will always be the case, and the accountant or systems designer must always be cognizant of these factors when considering the economic value of an information system.

Table M4-5   Decision Table: Expected Value of Imperfect Information—Predictions from New Information System

	PESSIMISTIC	SAME	OPTIMISTIC	EXPECTED VALUE OF CONTRIBUTION
PROBABILITY	.4	.2	.4	
ACTION	CONTRIBUTION TO PROFIT FOR OPTIMAL COURSE OF ACTION FOR EACH PREDICTION			
A_1	$180,000			$ 72,000
A_2		$400,000	$640,000	$336,00
Total expected value of imperfect information				$408,000

SELECTED REFERENCES

AMERICAN ACCOUNTING ASSOCIATION COMMITTEE ON INFORMATION SYSTEMS, "Accounting and Information Systems," *Accounting Review Supplement*, vol. XLVI, 1971.

CASH, JAMES I., and BENN R. KONSYNSKI, "IS Redraws Competitive Boundaries," *Harvard Business Review*, March–April 1985, pp. 134–42.

CYERT, RICHARD M., and JAMES G. MARCH, *A Behavioral Theory of the Firm*, Englewood Cliffs, N.J.: Prentice Hall, 1967.

DEMSKI, JOEL S., *Information Analysis*. Reading, Mass.: Addison-Wesley, 1972 and 1980.

DRUCKER, PETER F., "The Coming of the New Organization," *Harvard Business Review*, January-February, 1988, pp. 45-53.

IJIRI, Y., *The Foundations of Accounting Measurement*. Englewood Cliffs, N.J.: Prentice Hall, 1967.

IVES, BLAKE, and GERARD P. LEARMONTH, "The Information System as a Competitive Weapon," *Communications of the ACM*, December, 1984, vol. 27, No. 12, pp. 1193-1201.

KAPLAN, ROBERT S., and ANTHONY A. ATKINSON, *Advanced Mangement Accounting*, 2nd ed. Englewood Cliffs, N.J.: Prentice Hall, 1989.

KEEN, PETER G. W., "Information Systems and Organizational Change," *Communications of the ACM*, January, 1981, vol 24, No 1., pp 24-33.

LEV, BARUCH, *Financial Statement Analysis: A New Approach*. Englewood Cliffs, N.J.: Prentice Hall, 1974.

LIBBY, ROBERT, *Accounting and Human Information Processing: Theory and Applications*. Englewood Cliffs, N.J.: Prentice Hall, 1981.

LOBO, GERALD, and MICHAEL MOHER, eds., *Information Economics and Accounting Research*. Ann Arbor: University of Michigan, 1980.

MASON, R.O., "Basic Concepts for Designing Management Information Systems." *AIS Research Paper No. 8*, October 1969.

MCFARLAND, F. WARREN, "Information Technology Changes the Way You Compete," *Harvard Business Review*, May-June, 1984, pp. 98-103.

MOCK, THEODORE J., and HUGH D. GROVE, *Measurement, Accounting, and Organizational Information*, New York: John Wiley, 1979.

PORTER, MICHAEL E., *Competitive Advantage*, New York: Free Press, 1985.

PORTER, MICHAEL E. and VICTOR E MILLAR, "How Information Gives You Competitive Advantage," *Harvard Business Review*, July-August, 1985, pp. 150-160.

SHANNON, C. E., and W. WEAVER, *The Mathematical Theory of Communication.* Urbana, Ill.: University of Illinois Press, 1964.

SIMON, HERBERT A., *Administrative Behavior*, 3rd ed. New York: Free Press, 1976.

SIMON, HERBERT A., "Information Technologies and Organizations," *The Accounting Review*, July 1990, pp. 658–67.

THEIL, H., "On the Use of Information Theory Concepts in the Analysis of Financial Statements," *Management Service*, May 1969.

WAGNER, G. R., "The Future of Corporate Planning and Modeling Software Systems." Paper presented at the Corporate Planning Models Conference at Duke University, 1981.

REVIEW QUESTIONS

1. Contrast an *open* and a *closed* system.

2. When are *predictive information systems* useful? What must be true of the environment and what are the assumptions?

3. What must be quantifiable for a *decision-making information system?*

4. What are the essential steps in the measurement process and why is knowledge of these steps important in the design of an accounting system?

5. Contrast transmission, semantic, and effectiveness problems of communication.

6. What are the major steps in a decision-making process? What role can accounting information play in each of these steps?

7. Cite some accounting examples of a predictive information system.

8. List several considerations that are important in good data input form designs.

9. When does information have value from a decision-making perspective? Can it add value to a product or service? How?

10. How do the concepts of quasi-resolution of conflict, uncertainty avoidance, problemistic search, and organizational learning have an influence of an accountant in the design of an accounting system? (See Module A.)

11. Contrast *heuristic* and *analytic* decision-making styles and their influence on an accounting systems. (See Module A.) Which one is likely to be compensatory and non compensatory?

CASES

4-1 Marine Products, a manufacturer of supplies for the Gulf fishing industry, has a large manufacturing plant near New Orleans and sales offices in many of the port cities along the Gulf of Mexico. The production vice-president, on the advice of top management, plans production runs for a wide variety of fishing gear and other marine supplies. The marketing vice-president conducts all the promotion, distribution, and sales activities. The marketing manager prepare a sales forecast by product line and presents it to top management. Management then adds its input and informs the production vice-president on production requirements. This is done once a year at budget time and has apparently worked well for several years.

As their auditor, however, you have noticed a large increase in inventory, an increase in stockouts. You are aware of an increase in competition from overseas suppliers and of many improvements in technology in the fishing industry.

They have asked your firm to render some assistance with their inventory problems. Specifically, they think that a new computer with on-line access to records will help keep costs down. Marketing personnel will know

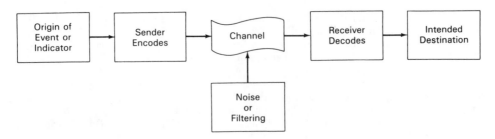

FIGURE C4-1   The communication process.

what is available and thus be able to push items which are overstocked and know when items are in short supply.

REQUIRED: Is this the problem? In your opinion, what is the problem and what would be the objective of your system analysis engagement?

4-2 The communication process is depicted in contemporary literature by the model presented in Figure C4-1. To be successful, the message must arrive at the intended destination in a form that depicts the true nature and impact of the event or incident that caused the message to be sent.

Management accountants are an important part of the communication process. Their responsibilities require reports in both oral and written form.

REQUIRED: For each of the six cells depicted in the communications model discuss the role of the accountant in ensuring accurate, clear and effective transmission of information. (Adapted from CPA examination.)

4-3 Wright Manufacturing Company employs a computer-based data processing system for maintaining all company records. The present system was developed in stages over the past five years and has been fully operational for the past two years.

When the system was being designed, all department heads were asked to specify the types of information and reports they would need for planning and controlling operations. Moreover, they were asked to specify the as-

sumptions and decision criteria for some of the information. The systems department attempted to meet the specifications of each department head. Company management specified that certain other reports be prepared for department heads. During the five years of systems development and operation, there have been several changes in the department head positions because of attrition and promotions. The new department heads often made requests for additional reports according to their needs. The systems department complied with all of these requests. Reports were discontinued only upon request by a department head, and then only if it was not a standard report required by top management. As a result, few reports were actually discontinued and the data processing system was generating a large quantity of reports each reporting period.

Company management became concerned about the quantity of information that was being produced by the system. The internal audit department was asked to evaluate the effectiveness of the reports generated by the system. The audit staff determined early in the study that more information was being generated by the data processing system that could be used effectively. They noted the following reaction to this information overload:

1.   Many department heads would not act on certain reports during periods of peak activity. The department head let these reports accumulate until he or she had sufficient time to analyze the data.

2.   Some department heads had so many reports that they could not filter out the relevant information for timely decision making.

3. Frequently, reports were ignored because department heads did not agree with the assumptions underlying the analysis of the data.

4. Department heads would often develop the information they needed from alternative, independent sources, rather than utilizing the reports generated by the data processing system. This was often easier than trying to search among the reports for the needed data.

REQUIRED: From the decision process outlined in the text, outline the problems associated with the new system. From the discussion of the types of information systems briefly note how you would suggest that the company remedy these problems.
(Adapted from the CMA examination.)

4-4 Fargo Creek Chemical Company, a vertically integrated chemical processing company, specializes in agricultural chemicals such as pesticides and fertilizer. The company is organized functionally into a manufacturing division, a distribution and warehouse division, and a marketing division. The corporate budget is usually prepared by first working with a sales forecast. Then the distribution of resources is made, based on these forecasts. From this distribution, inventory decisions are made. These budgets are finally forwarded to the manufacturing division, which produces the company's chemical products from natural gas and petroleum products. This system of manually prepared budgets has worked well for years.

The high cost of gas and petroleum products, however, recently caused Fargo Creek's corporate management to question the profitability of some of its products. The marketing manager was asked to work with the manufacturing manager in developing a new budget based on an assessment of each product's contribution to the company. After a week of discussion, these managers both submitted a letter of resignation. Each stated that it was not possible to work with the other and that they needed more support for their decision making.

REQUIRED: Why did these problems never occur before? Given your answer to this question, should Fargo Creek try to coordinate its activity? As its accountant, corporate management has asked for your assistance in reconciling this sticky budgeting problem. What brief comments would you have for management from an organizational and behavioral point of view, as well as from a decision-making perspective? (From your previous visits to Fargo Creek, you would have classified its information system as a data bank system.)

4-5 Smith, Davis, and Davis Brokers, Inc., has recently installed a new security analysis system that calculates how each security price moves relative to a market index and even calculates "optimal" portfolios for clients with particular risk-and-return preferences. The system also displays coded reports pertaining to a company's earnings, product acquisitions, financial activities, management decisions, asset acquisitions, and so on. It is very efficient and quickly gives feedback to individual brokers while they are advising their clients.

Many of the brokers really like the new system; however, others miss the older, more detailed reports that formed the basis of their "hunches," which they claim have had a major impact on their success as brokers. Moreover, some of the clients don't like the new system's analytic approach and don't trust the models.

REQUIRED (MODULE A): From a behavioral and a decision-making perspective, what have the systems designers and analysts overlooked, if anything?

4-6 The management of Cabin Creek Chemical Company recently had considerable difficulty in sorting through the large volume of computer output while trying to schedule manufacturing processes. Cabin Creek has had a series of problems such as insufficient raw materials, lost sales due to late deliveries, and idle plant facilities over the past few years. These problems have prompted management to ask for some assistance in allocating manufacturing resources.

Currently, management receives information on:

Sales forecasts

Inventory (raw chemical stock, in-process chemicals, and manufactured products)

Machine and plant capabilities

Labor resources

Maintenance schedules

REQUIRED: Can you advise management on any changes it should consider in its information and decision support system and why these changes should be made?

4-7 Fresno Valley Frozen Foods' management has had considerable difficulty in planning its operations (sales, distribution, and manufacturing) each year due to the large volume of detailed data on supplies of produce and marketing and distribution requirements. The relationships between the supply and marketing data have become too complex for Fresno Valley's management to comprehend. Fresno Valley currently has what could be classified as a data bank system.

REQUIRED: What level of decision support would you recommend that it consider? Why? What assumptions are necessary for this level of support?

4-8 The management of ABC Retailers is constantly faced with decisions regarding sales promotions. ABC's management is considering an information system that would generate market information and would cost approximately $30,000 per market survey, and it is trying to assess the value of the information generated by this system. A "typical" sales promotion decision for ABC's business involves the following information, which is now obtainable by the company. With promotion there is a 40 percent chance of no sales increase. The sales increase will result in a $500,000 contribution to profit and fixed costs. The promotion expenditure is $300,000 and is considered a fixed cost. Without promotion there is a 0 percent chance of a sales increase and a 100 percent chance of no sales increase. Adoption of the new information system would add the following information:

1. The expected results of a survey may be positive or negative. If positive, the results are expected to show a 90 percent chance of a sales increase with promotions. If negative, results are expected to show a 30 percent chance of a sales increase with promotions. There will therefore be a 10 percent and a 70 percent respective chance of no increase in sales for the two possible survey results.

2. The probability of a positive survey is 50 percent, and the probability of a negative survey is 50 percent.

REQUIRED (MODULE B): ABC's management has asked you, its accountant, to assist in the analysis and comment on the following:

1. Should ABC Retailers use sales promotions, given no information other than what it currently has for a typical case?

2. What is the maximum amount ABC should pay for the additional information generated by the new system in the typical case?

3. Given positive or negative survey results, what action should it take in each case for the typical solution noted here?

4. Should ABC adopt the market survey information system?

4-9 Ohio Valley and Citizens National Bank has twenty branch offices in addition to the home office in River City. Management receives daily transaction summaries from all the branches. Ohio Valley's management is proud of the system that generates this information. These summaries include not only the withdrawals, deposits, transfers, loans, and other typical bank transactions, but also many ratios, statistical analyses, and even profit-and-loss statements for each branch.

One day, however, a power outage in River City prevented the EDP Department from receiving the ratio, statistical, and financial analysis information at the home office. Much to its surprise, the EDP Department never received a phone call asking for the missing information. This was particularly discouraging to the EDP manager. The transaction summary information that was forwarded was exactly the same as the information generated by a previous manual system and consisted of a three-page summary for each branch and totals for the entire bank. The new automated system had been designed to ensure that the home office would receive this information daily.

REQUIRED: Should Ohio Valley and Citizens National Bank be proud of this new system? Do you have any suggestions for improving the system, given that many banking decisions are rather routine and assumptions are easily specified?

4-10 Seventy-Six Frozen Seafood Wholesalers needed a system to control its inventory. Carrying costs were extremely high because frozen-food lockers were expensive to build and operate, especially given the high cost of energy. As a result, management asked your firm to help it establish a simple automatic EOQ (economic order quantity) system so that it would know when to order and how much to order. Your firm complied with this request. As manager of the project, you found the average usage rates and average lead times for each item in stock, calculated the cost of processing an order and storing the frozen seafood item, and established an optimal reorder point and quantity for each item. You also added a small buffer stock for each item in case more than an average usage rate was encountered during the period between the reorder point and ultimate delivery of the item. You presented this plan to the management of Seventy-Six Frozen Seafood. In summary, your plan suggested great reductions in the current stock of many items. Management balked at implementing this automatic reorder point system. Management felt that with so little stock, the company would constantly stock out because of the great uncertainty in demand and delivery schedules from the docks.

REQUIRED:

1. How would you convince management to try the system?

2. Could it be that the managers are correct and you have overlooked some aspects of the problem?

3. What must be true of this type of automatic system to be implemented successfully?

4-11 King's Mountain Quarries, Inc., a large extractor of rock, aggregate, gravel, sand, and other rock products used in the construction industry, has several quarries throughout northern Georgia, western North Carolina, and eastern Tennessee. The firm uses an annual budget to communicate its plans to quarry managers. Monthly budgets detail the amount and type of aggregate quarry managers should extract, process, stockpile, and deliver. Managers are rewarded on how well they meet their budgets. They are, however, expected to react to special orders as they arrive so that the company will not lose any lucrative contracts. Quarry managers are expected to maintain their equipment, train their subordinates, and find new quarry locations within their geographic area. On the other hand, they are expected to keep costs to a minimum.

Corporate management, after a few years of operating under this budget system, has discovered several types of managerial behavior leading to the following typical results:

Manager A—meets budget, but equipment is in disrepair

Manager B—meets budget, but no new rock locations were found

Manager C—costs exceeded budget, but equipment is in good repair

Manager D—costs exceeded budget, but three new quarry locations were found

Manager E—costs are less than budget, but equipment is in disrepair and no new gravel pits were found

Managers C and D—resigned due to low salary and bonus

Corporate management was distraught because C and D were the two finest managers it had.

REQUIRED: What led to these problems in terms of the desire to communicate objectives via the budget information system?

4-12 Heathwood British Clothes has retail outlets in many of the largest malls in the U.S. and Canada. They collect information on sales, by store, for the purpose of forecasting demand for new woolen goods. The data collected consists of sales by merchandise class (type of product such as sweater, skirt and coat); by outlet identification; by customer number for analyzing data by customer characteristics; and by data for accurate seasonal determination. This data is then summarized by state and used to forecast demand for new merchandise.

Production planning personnel welcome this data but have trouble determining style, color and sizes. They usually adjust last year's distribution by informed feedback they get from sales managers who note the styles they usually need to mark down at the end of the season.

REQUIRED: In the communication of the sales data through channels to those production managers who use it to make decisions, what communication problems exist? Is the data collected appropriate? If not, what would you add?

4-13 Mead Tire Company recently started to use its sales history file to notify customers when they should consider an oil change and a new set of tires. They simply analyzed the year of car, the mileage (the last time in), and the work done to project these needs. They then used their customer database for the name and address of the customer. Furthermore, at the end of the year, they sent out an analysis of the work done for the year to commercial customers who needed it for tax purposes. As a result, they increased their repeat customers.

REQUIRED: How has Mead Tire used its accounting information to enhance its competitive edge?

5

INFORMATION TECHNOLOGY

INTRODUCTION

In Chapters 1 and 2 we identified three dimensions of information processing: (1) systems elements; (2) managerial activities; and (3) organizational functions. We also noted that in designing an information system, these dimensions should be synthesized into a conceptual framework. In this chapter we will examine the systems dimension of the framework. Recall that the *elements* of the system dimension consist of (1) hardware; (2) software; (3) database; (4) procedures; and (5) personnel. Basic concepts relating to personnel were discussed in Chapter 3. Decision-making and data processing activities (procedures) were discussed in Chapter 4 and will be further discussed in the application chapters. Database concepts are covered in Chapters 9 and 10. This chapter will focus on hardware and software concepts. Chapters 6 and 7 will focus more on microcomputers and distributed network concepts. Specifically, in this chapter we will examine the basic physical components that make up a computer system (the central processing unit, input/output devices, and storage devices) and the computer programs that are employed in data processing. These have historically been called electronic data processing EDP; today they are often referred to as *information technology* (IT).

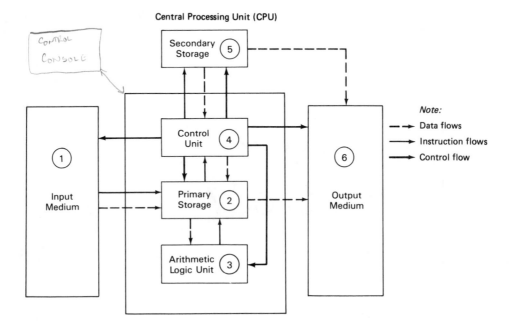

FIGURE 5-1 Basic computer components.

HARDWARE COMPONENTS

Central Processing Unit

The central processing unit (CPU) is the focal point of an computer system. It controls the entire data processing (hardware) system and performs arithmetic and logical operations on data. The CPU includes a *control section,* an *arithmetic-logic unit,* and a *high-speed storage unit* (primary storage). To better understand the structure and function of the CPU as well as the overall computer, we can view the "computer" in terms of the basic functions shown in Figure 5-1. The six basic components are: (1) an input medium or device; (2) primary storage; (3) an arithmetic-logic unit; (4) a control unit; (5) secondary storage devices; and (6) an output medium or device.

The flows of data, application instructions, and controls are also shown in Figure 5-1. These interact with the basic components as discussed next.

INPUT MEDIUM. Data, as well as the instructions for handling data, are input to the computer and are made available to the CPU via an input device such as a terminal or a magnetic disk.

PRIMARY STORAGE. Data and instructions received from input devices are transferred to the main (primary) storage section of the CPU. Instructions from the control section and results from the arithmetic-logic section of the CPU also reside in primary storage. When a software program is executed (run), this transfer to primary storage occurs in conjunction with the arithmetic-logic and control units.

In general, the internal primary memory can be either read-only memory (ROM) or random access memory (RAM). ROM is nonvolatile (it is permanent and does not disappear when the power is turned off), and it cannot be changed. It is used to provide the computer with basic operating instructions such as character set storage, and visual display printer instructions. In some microcomputers, ROM even contains the basic components of the operating system. RAM, on the other hand, is the portion of the memory used by the application programs to hold instructions, data, and, in some cases, the operating system. It is generally volatile and will be lost when power is turned off.[1]

Primary storage is structured so that each storage location has a unique address. Thus, to store or access data or instructions, a specific storage address is employed. Data are stored in a computer in a binary form, commonly called a *bit.* The smallest addressable location in primary storage, however, is not a single binary digit (bit). It is a *byte.* This is because a series of binary digits are required to store a decimal number or an alphabetic character in binary form. A byte is made up of either six, eight or more bits (plus an additional parity or check bit) depending upon the design of the computer. Within the byte structure, each byte of primary storage is addressable and the number of addressable bytes determines the *size* of primary memory. Therefore, RAM is generally discussed in terms of kilobytes, megabytes or gigabytes; which refer to approximately 1 thousand, 1 million or 1 billion bytes of memory. For example, a computer with 4M memory (where *M* is the metric notation for millions) has 4 million bytes of addressable main storage in the CPU. Many microcomputers today have several megabytes of memory. Chips containing more than a megabyte are becoming available and will vastly increase the memory of these systems. Large mainframe computers have billions of bytes of memory.

ARITHMETIC-LOGIC UNIT.   All computational processing in the computer (the manipulation of data in accordance with given instructions) occurs in the arithmetic-logic unit. The computational operations include addition, subtraction, multiplication, division, and logic operations such as comparing the magnitude of numbers. This occurs at an incredible speed. The speed at which a computer executes an instruction is called the *clock speed.* This *execution time,* as it is sometimes called, is the time interval required to execute an instruction in the arithmetic-logic unit. An instruction is obtained from primary storage and transferred to the arithmetic-logic unit (access time). Here it is decoded according to its operation code, which specifies the address of the data to be operated upon. The decoded instruction is then executed using the data specified in the instruction. For microcomputers, the clock speed is measured in megahertz which means millions (mega) of cycles (execution) per second (hertz). For large mainframe computers it is much faster.

CONTROL UNIT.   The focal point of the CPU is the control unit. The input devices, primary storage, secondary storage, arithmetic-logic unit, and output

---

[1] Some RAM cards in microcomputers are nonvolatile and will continue to store data when computer is off, providing it still has battery power.

devices all interact to perform a data processing task such as the updating of an inventory file. The control section's role is to coordinate all the components of the computer. Specifically, the control section (1) indicates to the input medium when data are needed by primary storage and the type and quantity of data needed; (2) indicates where the data entering primary storage (from the input medium) are to be stored; (3) informs the arithmetic-logic section when a computational operation is required, the type operation required, where the associated data are to be found, and where to store the results; (d) "flags" the appropriate secondary storage device indicating where the data are to be found and what data to access; and (5) indicates the specific output medium for displaying results, such as a printer for an inventory report. *Access time* refers to the time it takes the control section to locate and retrieve data and instructions for processing. Access time is measured in microseconds or, for faster computers, in nanoseconds.[2]

Thus the speed of the CPU is measured by two factors: (1) access time; and (2) execution time. In developing computer systems, access time and execution time are considered jointly because the *total* cycle time (access time and execution time) is what actually determines the speed of the CPU.

The key cost factor of the CPU is primary storage, or memory. Magnetic cores (very tiny doughnut-shaped ferrite rings that can be magnetized in either a clockwise or counterclockwise direction) were the predominant form of primary storage throughout the 1960s and early 1970s. Semiconductor memory chips (which are structured by taking a tiny chip of silicon and inscribing a number of miniature circuits, each of which may be "conducting" or "not conducting") first appeared in 1971. Memory chips are smaller and faster than magnetic core memory and are the dominant primary storage devices today, although newer memory technology is on the horizon.

As technology changes, large-scale integration circuits will see increasing use. All of these devices vary in size, speed, and cost. In general, decreases in primary memory size and increase in performance (speed) correspond to increases in cost.

SECONDARY STORAGE.   Because primary storage is expensive relative to other storage devices, and because it is not necessary that all data at all times reside in primary storage, secondary storage devices (such as magnetic tapes and disks) were developed. Characteristics about these will be detailed later. Generally, the amount of secondary storage can be easily increased as needed, whereas primary storage is relatively fixed in size and hard to increase.

OUTPUT MEDIUM.   Results from the data processed in the CPU are output (reported or stored) in some form. Several output media and devices (such as printers, plotters, CRT terminals, monitors for microcomputers, and microfilm) may be used. This will be detailed later.

When comparing one computer system with another, factors such as size, speed, and cost are often considered. When manufacturers state the size of their computer, it is the size of the primary storage section of the CPU to which they

---

[2] A *microsecond* is one–one-millionth of a second, or .000001 seconds. A *nanosecond* is one–thousand-millionth of a second, or .000000001 seconds.

refer. The maximum size of a program and the associated data available for processing at any one time is mainly determined by the size of primary storage. The size of primary storage has a large bearing on the computer's capability to process the program. Since speed is also important, management must often make cost trade-offs between access time and execution time. Therefore, in determining the cost per bit of data (stored and processed), we must consider both size and speed.

Input/Output Devices

As we indicated in the preceding discussion of the CPU and in Figure 5-1, input and output devices are also integral hardware components. A number of input and output mediums and devices can be used to input data and to obtain information form the computerized accounting system. Figure 5-2 illustrates the various types of input and output devices found in a computer system. In the figure, magnetic tape, direct-access devices, and special-purpose devices are shown as both input and output devices. These devices can also serve as secondary storage devices, which will be discussed later in this chapter. Typically, input and output devices are classified as either slow speed or high speed. Card readers, various keying devices, and printers are slow-speed devices. Magnetic tape units and direct-access devices (disk drives, drum storage units, data-cells) are high-speed devices. These devices may also be classified as either off line or those which are required for on-line processing where the user is interacting with the computer and the data.

CARD READERS AND PUNCHES. In the 1960s and 1970s, most computer systems were primarily card input systems. Most of their processing was done off line in a "batch mode." Card-reading devices feed a single card at a time through a mechanism that converts the data on the card into electronic form. Card-reading speeds vary but a typical card reader operates at a speed of 500 cards per minute. The processing of data onto and from cards is referred to as a *unit-record concept,* in which all data relating to a transaction are recorded on a single document, the punched card.[3] Output, if stored on cards, is recorded via a card-punching device. Card processing systems are becoming increasingly rare today, but accountants may find them in client offices which use old systems.

MAGNETIC TAPE. Magnetic tape is an effective input/output medium for off-line "batch" processing systems. It is still the choice for many high-speed and large-volume batch processing systems because its data density (the number of characters which can be stored per inch) and its transfer rate (speed of copying data to and from the CPU) is high. Data are recorded on magnetic tape as magnetized dots (called bits). Therefore, the data can be retained indefinitely if desired, or can be erased automatically and the tape reused.

---

[3] Although the commercial use of punched cards only dates back to the mid-1950s, the punched-card code utilized in most card-reading devices, was invented in the 1880s by Herman Hollerith, a U.S. Census Bureau statistician. Hollerith later founded the Tabulating Machine Company, which after several mergers changed its name to International Business Machines Corporation in 1924.

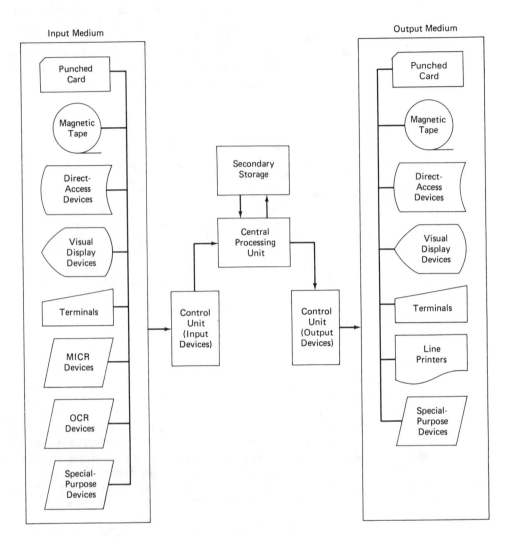

FIGURE 5-2 Input and output devices employed in a computer system.

Data on magnetic tapes are read into or output (written) from the CPU by means of a magnetic tape drive. Data are read or written as the tape moves, at a constant speed, past a read/write head. Operating speeds of existing tape drive units range from 60,000 to 1,250,000 characters per second. In many cases, tapes may be in the form of cartridges or cassettes; these do not have the same capacity as the tapes mentioned in the last paragraph.

Original (source) data can be recorded directly onto magnetic tape (without using) the computer via a key-to-tape device. To create a record of transactions, tapes may also be a byproduct of other transaction processing activities.

They are also used to back up critical data or programs. In addition, they may be used as a medium for the transfer of data from one processing step to another.

DIRECT-ACCESS DEVICES.   Direct-access devices are primarily used as secondary storage devices rather than input or output devices. However, as we noted, direct-access disks or diskettes can be used in conjunction with other input and output equipment, such as key-to-disk, to form "data preparation systems." Often a minicomputer or a microcomputer is used to control direct-access data input. Like tape, these disks can be erased and written over as new data is entered.

A disk drive, which is the actual direct-access device for reading and writing data to the disk, has a high transfer rate. It may also be a microprocessor. Other direct-access devices, such as drums, data cells, and large magnetic core storage devices, can also be used as input/output devices; however, as we noted earlier, these are primarily viewed as storage devices.

VIDEO DISPLAY, TERMINAL, AND COMPUTER MONITORS.   These are widely used in mainframe, minicomputer, and microcomputer systems. Some times the terminals are called CRT (cathode ray displays) or VDT (video display terminals). They are used to display output from the computer or to enter data into the computer system via an attached keyboard. Often they are located at sites that are some distance from the computer and they are connected via a communication network such as those discussed in Chapters 6 and 7. These are often called remote terminals. Some times they are connected to a printer and constitute a remote job entry (and output) site, frequently called RJE.

Input is entered by means of an alphanumeric *keyboard*. The input is buffered and immediately displayed on the screen. Before data are forwarded to the CPU, they can be corrected, erased entirely, or reentered. This capability is very useful for internal control. Output information can also be displayed on the screen. If a printer is attached to the system, the output on the screen can be directed to the printer.

KEYBOARDS AND MOUSE.   To aid in effective terminal input, there are numerous keyboards with numeric, alphabetic, and function keys designed to ease data input and to control the processing of the data. Moreover, there are several devices, such as the mouse commonly found on personal computers, which enable the operator to simply point and click to make data input and control easier.[4]

MAGNETIC-INK CHARACTER RECOGNITION (MICR) DEVICE.   Data can be represented by magnetic-ink characters and symbols that are readable by both the computer and by human beings; the technology is referred to as MICR. The primary application of MICR has been in the banking industry where check number, account numbers, bank identification numbers, and the amount of the check are recorded with magnetic-ink characters.

---

[4] Other devices include a track ball, sketch pad, joy stick, light pen, and a touch screen.

FIGURE 5-3
Universal product code.

OPTICAL CHARACTER RECOGNITION (OCR) DEVICE. Data can also be recorded on and read from paper documents by means of optically readable characters. The most common of these readers is the holographic device used in the local supermarket that reads the universal product code (UPC) on merchandise. (Point-of-sale systems that use this equipment are discussed in Chapter 15.) An example of the Universal Product Code is shown in Figure 5-3. Hand-held light pens are also used to read codes such as the Universal Product Code.

Another familiar, optical readable character is a pencil mark, used on multiple-choice tests. Optical characters, however, are not limited to simply line codes or dots. Many OCR devices can handle the letters of the alphabet, the ten decimal digits, and several other special characters. Some common applications of OCR devices include the reading of utility billings, insurance premium notices, product codes, and sales invoices. Reading speeds of OCR devices range from 500 to thousands of characters per second.

MAGNETIC STRIPS. Magnetic strips are often printed on cards such as credit cards. These can be inserted into a modem which can be used at a retail establishment to record a credit sale and check a customer's credit.

FAX MACHINES AND SCANNERS. In addition to the optical scanners designed for the input of structured characters, there are optical scanners which can be used to input graphics and pictures. There are facsimile machines which can read and transmit pictures of anything over telephone lines to a receiving FAX machine or computer. Computers can transmit directly via these FAX machines from remote locations.

PRINTERS AND PLOTTERS. Several types of printers exist for outputting data from a computer system. Printers have an advantage over monitors or video display terminals is that they produce "hard copy" which is useful for reference, audit trails, and reports. The speeds of these devices vary from hundreds of characters per second for dot matrix printers (which use a multiple-pin print head), to many pages per minute for laser printers. Generally speaking, laser printers are much faster than dot matrix printers. In addition, there are ink-jet printers which produce output quality between that of dot matrix and laser printers, at speeds comparable to dot matrix printers. All three of these are used extensively for personal computers and individual work stations. In addition, the large electromechanical line printers which can produce a line with up to 132 characters at once, have speeds of thousands of lines per minute. Many of these printers are capable of printing in color.

Microfilm devices, which use a photographic reduction process, can print a great deal of information on microfilm or microfiche. The output speeds of these devices range from about 10,000 to 50,000 lines per minute.

There are many plotters on the market for both microcomputers and individual work stations, as well as for large mainframe computer systems. These are effective for graphic presentations.

VOICE RECOGNITION INPUT AND OUTPUT. Some more advanced systems can even receive voice input and respond to user requests with voice output. For example, a mail order department of a retail store may automatically dial your number and tell you that your order is in stock.

Secondary Storage Devices

The most common types of secondary storage devices available for use in data processing systems are (1) magnetic tapes; (2) magnetic disks; and (3) optical disks. Magnetic tape, in addition to being considered an input medium, is also highly utilized secondary storage device. For operating purposes, secondary storage devices are categorized as either *sequential access* or *direct access* (random access). A sequential-access storage device is one in which any single record stored on the medium can be accessed only after all other preceding records have been read or processed. If a file is created on a sequential device, all records in the file are maintained in sequential order, utilizing a name or number field common within each record. This process will be discussed in detail in Chapter 9. Magnetic tape is a sequential-access storage medium. Using direct-access storage devices, any single record stored on the medium can be accessed directly without reading or processing other records. Magnetic disk, drum, data cells, optical disk and other mass storage are all direct-access storage devices.

MAGNETIC TAPE. A reel of tape is typically one-half inch in width and comes in lengths up to 2,400 feet. Magnetic tape is structured in row or in tracks and columns (frames). The rows are referred to as *channels* or *tracks* and tapes are available in 7-track or 9-track structures as well as very high density 18-track cartridges. Tapes have a check (parity) bit to check the parity of the dots stored on the tape. If one of the dots is in error or changed accidentally, the parity will not agree with the combination of dots and an error message will indicate that there is a problem with the data. The majority of tapes in use today are 9-track, because two numeric characters, each using four bits, can be recorded in a single 9-track column, enabling more data to be stored on a 9-track tape.

The storage capacity of a magnetic tape depends upon the density of the tape and the manner in which records are stored. The density of magnetic tape is represented by the number of characters recorded per inch, or *bytes* per inch if we are referring to the manner in which characters are represented in the CPU. The most common tape densities are 800 and 1,600 characters per inch, although tapes with higher densities exist.

Use of a high-density tape does not necessarily mean that a large quantity of data can be stored on a small segment of tape unless an efficient record storage (blocking) procedure is employed. Each *physical* record that is written on or read from a tape is separated by a blank segment of tape (usually ½″ or ¾″), referred to as an *interblock gap* (IBG). The tape drive used in reading or writing information stops and starts at each IBG. That half of the IBG preceding a record allows the tape unit to reach its operating speed before reading or writing. The first half of the IBG following a record allows time for the tape unit to decelerate after a read or write operation. The tape must be moving at its designated operating speed before it can be read from or be written on; when the end of a record is reached, the unit must be stopped. The IBG allows for both procedures to occur.

If an 800-character-per-inch density tape is employed with a half-inch IBG, and 80-character records are to be stored on the tape, then 83.33 percent of the tape storage area as well as 83.33 percent of the processing time will be consumed in processing the IBG. This occurs because each 80-character record requires 0.10 inches of tape (80/800), and the IBG requires 0.50 inches of tape. In each 0.60-inch segment of tape, 0.10/0.60 (16.66 percent) of the length is used to store the record, and 0.50/0.60 (83.33 percent) of the length is consumed by the IBG.

To avoid this waste in storage and time, records can be grouped into a tape block. By grouping or blocking a number of records, most interblock gaps can be eliminated. Each block of record is preceded by an IBG. The number of records contained in a block is referred to as the *blocking factor*. For example, if five records were grouped into a block, the blocking factor would be 5. Using the example, with a blocking factor of 5, each block of records would contain 400 characters; therefore, in each inch of tape 50 percent of the area (400/800) is utilized for storage and 50 percent (½ inch) of the area is consumed by the IBG. Storage space and access time are thus improved with blocking. By employing a large blocking factor, a large amount of data can be stored on a magnetic tape. A single reel of tape can hold up to 50 million characters or more for higher density tapes. Figure 5-4 illustrates the concepts of *blocked* and *unblocked* records.

When records are blocked, each single record in the block is referred to as a *logical record;* the complete block is referred to as a *physical record.* When the input/output device processes records, it handles physical records or the complete block of logical records. The CPU, however, processes one logical record at a time. Therefore, when a block of records is read from or written to tape, adequate storage space must be available in main memory to store the entire block. Fortunately, the operating system software in the CPU controls the reading and writing of blocked records. It accepts single records from CPU processing and holds them in buffer storage until a block has been accumulated; or conversely, it can deblock a block of input records and likewise store them so that single records are made available to the CPU as needed. Because of this, the size of blocks are limited by the amount of buffer storage in the CPU which can be used for an input/output buffer.

The major advantage of magnetic tape is that very large volumes of data can be stored in a sequential manner to be processed efficiently (in the same se-

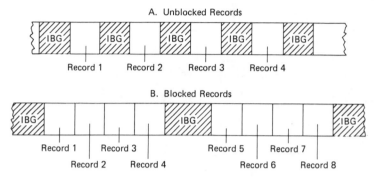

FIGURE 5-4 Blocked and unblocked records.

quence) in a batch mode. Another major advantage is that it is relatively inexpensive compared to a random access medium.

Obviously the disadvantage of magnetic tape is that it is a sequential medium. Thus, access to a particular record is obtained only after all preceding records have been read. If rapid direct access to specific records is required, magnetic tape is not the appropriate storage medium. Moreover, they are awkward to use for database systems which require access to data on multiple files (tapes) at the same time. In summary, tapes play an important role as a "backup storage" medium and are unchallenged for low-cost, high-capacity applications requiring only sequential access.

MAGNETIC DISK.   Magnetic disk storage, unlike tape storage, allows data to be read or written directly to a specific location without the need to read all the records in preceding storage locations. Access to specific information is immediate.

There are many different sizes of magnetic disks. Stacks of 14-inch disks are used for large mainframe systems; 9-inch, 8-inch, 5¼-inch, and 3½-inch hard disks are used for minicomputers. In addition, there are 5¼-inch and 3½-inch floppy disks used on microcomputers. Most of these are double sided and some have a very high density. Basically, a magnetic disk is a thin circular disk, similar to a phonograph record, coated on both sides with a magnetic recording material. Data are stored on the disk using the same general principle employed with magnetic tapes. Characters are formed by grouping a series of magnetized or nonmagnetized bits. Characters and bytes are grouped together to form words, and groupings of words form records. Physically, the disk is structured in a series of concentric circles called *tracks*. Records are grouped together and stored in the tracks. Tracks for floppy disks are further divided into *sectors*. These features are shown Figure 5-5.

In most mainframe disk storage units, several disks are stacked on a vertical shaft. Space is left between each disk to allow for the reading or writing of data on both the upper and lower surfaces of the disk. Data are accessed or written by a read/write head that can move to any location on the surface of the disk. Most of these larger disk units have one read/write head for each disk re-

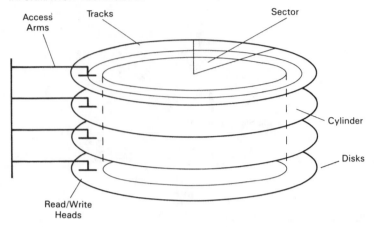

FIGURE 5-5 Disk drive mechanism.

cording surface. The stacked set of disks, referred to as a disk pack, is usually removable from most disk drive systems. Data stored on a magnetic disk are accessible through a surface number (side), track number (sector if applicable), and record number. Any record on any disk surface can be accessed directly, since the surface, track, and record numbers provide a unique address for each record. As with magnetic tape, physical records on disk may be separated by interrecord gaps. To conserve storage space, it is customary to block records, using the same general procedure employed with tapes.

The capacity of a disk pack depends upon the number of bytes per track (or bits per inch of track); the number of tracks per inch of surface; and the number of surfaces. Utilization of the capacity will obviously depend on how records are blocked. A disk pack with ten recording surfaces, for example, each with 200 accessible tracks with 3,625 bytes per track, will provide storage for up to 7.25 million characters of data. A disk system consisting of eight on-line drives, each utilizing a disk pack with twenty recording surfaces having 200 tracks per surface and 7,294 bytes per track, will provide storage for more than 200 million bytes of data. On the other hand, for a microcomputer, a double-sided 3 ½ floppy disk typically stores 800K, 1.44M, or more.

Costs, access time, and reading speeds (transfer rate) of disk storage units vary widely, in much the same manner that the capacity of these units varies. The average access time for most hard disk systems ranges from 10 to 100 milliseconds. The average access time for floppy disks is much slower and averages in the range of 60 to 600 milliseconds. Also the transfer rate for floppy disks is usually from 30,000 to 150,000 characters per second, whereas it ranges from 200,000 to 2 million characters per second for hard disks. Sometimes a segment of RAM (the computer's random assess primary storage) is partitioned to act like a disk. This is called a RAM disk and because everything is stored in RAM, these possess extremely fast access and transfer rates.

The advantages of using the magnetic disk or diskette rather than magnetic tape as a storage device are: (1) data can be organized and stored sequentially and processed like a magnetic tape, even though direct-access capabilities exist; (2) transactions can be processed as they occur, i.e. no batching or sorting of transactions is necessary; and (3) files can be structured and stored in a manner that permits transactions to be processed against multiple files simultaneously. The disadvantage of the magnetic disk is the cost of storage; in terms of cost per character stored, magnetic disk storage is more expensive than magnetic tape. An additional disadvantage of using an on-line disk system is that it is often difficult to clearly discern an *audit trail*. Due to the on-line nature of the processing, when updating a file on magnetic disk a record is read, updated, and written back to the same location and the original contents are destroyed. Also, if no provision is made for recording transactions and detecting errors, errors may go undetected and file reconstruction becomes impossible.

OPTICAL DISKS CD-ROM AND WORM.   Data may also be stored on CD-ROM disks which can be read optically via laser. The technology for CD-ROMs is similar to that used in audio CDs. The storage capacity of these is enormous and 550 megabytes or a gigabyte are common. In addition, the cost is very low for the volume that can be stored and the access speed is very fast. One can read many of these disks, however, and thus they are excellent for reference material like part numbers and description of parts. A WORM (write-once-read-mostly) drive, however, uses the same reading technology but it permits one to write once on the disk. These, likewise, hold huge amounts of data and are excellent for the storage of records to be referenced for historical purposes, such as sales history for customers. Today, there are even some new optical drives which are erasable and can be used over and over in the same way as a hard or floppy magnetic disk. Data is stored on CD-ROM and WORM disks using tiny pits which are burned into a thin coating on the disk.

DATA-CELL DEVICES AND MASS-STORAGE DEVICES.   In designing and structuring an information processing system, speed is not always the key criterion. A number of systems exist in which the need is to store large data files and backup files, and because the files are seldom used or do not require rapid access, a low-cost, medium-to-slow direct-access device is desirable. Devices that meet this need are generally referred to as mass-storage devices. Data cells and mass storage systems exist that can handle very large volumes but have slower access times.

SELECTION OF SECONDARY STORAGE FOR ACCOUNTING SYSTEMS.   From the preceding overview of magnetic tapes, magnetic disks and drums, optical storage devices, and data cells and other direct-access storage devices, it should be obvious that price, capacity, and speed differences exist for each. In structuring an accounting information system, the type of device chosen will depend on trade-offs among these factors and the importance of these factors to the efficient and effective operation of the accounting system.

Additional Hardware Concepts

In Figure 5-2, we showed a variety of input and output devices that could be employed in a data processing (computer) system. In the figure we did not tie the devices directly to the CPU. *Control units* connect the CPU to the input and output devices. Control units are an integral part of a data processing system. *Channels, buffers,* and *preprocessors* are also important components.

COMMUNICATION CONTROL UNITS. Every input/output device and secondary storage device will have been or will be tied to a control unit. The control unit governs the activity of the device. In some cases the control unit is built into the devices; in other cases the unit is separate and may control several devices.

Several functions are performed by the control unit: (1) code conversion between the machine language of the CPU and the input/output or secondary storage device; (2) check validity of data; and (3) buffer data (which we examine shortly). Additionally, if several devices are controlled by a single unit, the unit must determine the priority of servicing of the devices. The unit must also generate and transmit the device number when servicing an input device or secondary storage unit or when routing data to a particular output device or storage unit.

CHANNELS. It may not have been obvious in the overview of input/output devices and secondary storage devices that the speeds of these units are slow relative to the speed of the CPU. Data can be transferred or processed at a very high rate of speed by the CPU, but some input/output devices are very slow. To avoid having the CPU sit idle while data are being input or output, channels are included in data processing systems to direct input/output operations in coordination with the CPU. Physically it is often contained within the housing of the CPU. Functionally, the channel operates much like a small computer.

The CPU operates in conjunction with, but independently of, the channel. When an input/output operation is to be performed, the CPU identifies the proper channel and issues a command (input or output) to the channel. The CPU then is free to perform processing on other programs. The channel operates on its own, working with several input/output control units simultaneously, maintaining communication with each. Just as the CPU is free to continue further processing once it has given an instruction to the channel, a channel is free to execute other commands once a control unit has been instructed as to what to do and which device to employ. Thus a channel is constantly juggling various input/output operations to make the most efficient use of time and to avoid tying up the CPU with input-output operations.

BUFFERING. The use of channels can improve the efficiency of the CPU. Maximum efficiency, however, will result only when *buffering,* or *overlapped processing,* is employed. In earlier computers, the read-compute-print cycle was performed in a serial fashion. Even though channels were able to reduce the total cycle time by increasing the speed at which data were input and output, the total time was the sum of the input time, processing time, and output time. With overlapped processing, the total time for handling a transaction is the time it takes to handle the longest operation (input, processing, or output). Figure 5-6 illustrates the difference between serial and overlapped processing.

With overlapped processing, buffering of the input (or output) into primary storage is required while the CPU is processing a previous transaction.

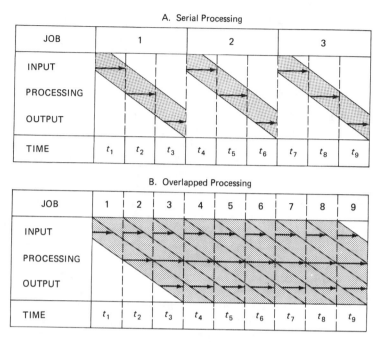

FIGURE 5-6 Serial vs. overlapped processing.

The term *buffering* is often used to refer to the overlapped processing concept. A buffer is a section of memory separate from internal memory that acts as temporary storage of input and output. The net result is an increase in throughput.

PREPROCESSING.   In addition, small computers are often present at terminals or microcomputers are used to control input/output devices and communications at remote job-entry stations or as part of individual personnel computer workstations. These are often used to perform some of the processing steps such as data editing and other control activities. This is called preprocessing.

SOFTWARE AND OPERATING SYSTEMS

Software is as essential a part of a computer system as hardware. The term *software* refers primarily to computer programs, although it encompasses program documentation, as well as the standards and techniques used in systems analysis and program development. A variety of software programs exist in most computer systems. These include job-control programs, supervisor routines, file maintenance programs, data base management systems, report generators, information retrieval routines, utility programs, library programs, language translators (such as Assembler, BASIC, FORTRAN, C, Pascal, and COBOL), specific user-written programs, and operating systems. In actuality, all these programs and routines are components of the operating system. Therefore, we will first examine the functions, types, and structure of an operating system and then examine each of the specific component programs. In the latter part of the section we will examine some advanced software concepts, such as multiprogramming, virtual storage, and multiprocessing.

Operating Systems: Functions, Types, Structure

An operating system (OS) is is an integrated set of programs used to manage the computer operations. The operating system permits the computer to manage itself. The operating system is responsible for scheduling jobs on a priority basis, handling the allocation of resources requested by users, and resolving conflicts that occur when multiple users request the same input/output device, storage device, or storage area. In addition, the operating system performs the accounting function for the computer; it keeps track of all resource usage.

A variety of software programs make up an operating system. Since all the programs are not utilized simultaneously, they are stored on a secondary storage unit called the *system residence device*. The programs are called into primary storage using the supervisor program located in primary storage. Figure 5-7 identifies the component programs of an operating system and depicts other areas and functions of the system residence device. A variety of operating systems are available for use with most computer systems, particularly with large computer systems. A computer system, however, will usually employ only a single operating system. The operating system used will depend upon the computer's purpose, design, and structure; for example, a PC will use an entirely different operating system than a large mainframe computer. The most basic type of operating system is a *batch system*, structured to process a multiple number of jobs in a predetermined priority sequence. On the other hand, an *on-line operating system* can respond to spontaneous requests for resources, such as inquiries entered from on-line terminals. A *multiprogramming operation system* can operate upon a multiple number of jobs concurrently. Some operating systems, particularly the more sophisticated, can handle *batch, on-line,* and *multiple tasks.* (Other types of operating systems are also discussed in the "Advanced Software Concepts" subsection of this chapter.)

Operating System Components

An *operating system* is an integrated collection of programs, each performing specific duties. In order to better understand the function of each program and how it interrelates and works in unison with the CPU, the programs are generally classified as control programs or processing programs.

Control programs control system operations and perform such tasks as scheduling jobs; handling interrupts caused by error conditions; locating, storing, and retrieving data; and communicating with the computer operator and programmers. In addition, the control programs supervise the execution of processing programs. The *initial program loader routine* (IPL routine), the *supervisor*, and the *job-control program* are control programs.

Processing programs facilitate efficient processing operations and are available to the computer user to simplify program preparation and execution. The major

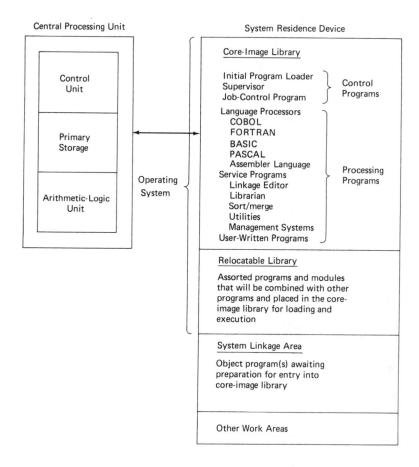

Central Processing Unit

System Residence Device

FIGURE 5-7 Operating system stored on system residence device.

processing programs contained in a typical operating system are *language transla-tors* (Assembler, FORTRAN, COBOL, Pascal, BASIC, C, and others) and *service programs* (linkage editor, librarian, sort/merge, and utilities). The functions of some of the control programs and processing programs are described in the following paragraphs. Their relationships are shown in Figure 5-8.

SUPERVISOR AND INITIAL PROGRAM LOADER (IPL). The initial program loader locates the supervisor on the residence device and loads it into primary storage. Control is then passed to the supervisor. The supervisor routine (monitor, kernel or executive) is the major control program and the major component of the operating system. It coordinates all the other activities and parts of the operating system. It calls the other programs as needed and loads them into primary storage. It remains in primary storage throughout all operations. The sup-

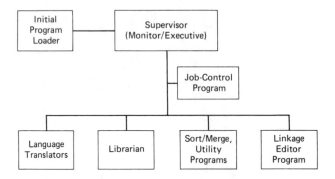

FIGURE 5-8 Components of an operating system.

ervisor also schedules input/output operations and allocates channels to various I/O devices.

JOB-CONTROL PROGRAMS. Since the supervisor is the control mechanism for the operating system, a means must exist on mainframe computers for communicating with it, particularly regarding jobs to be processed and resources required. A job-control language (JCL) serves as this link. Job-control statements are used to specify (1) the beginning of a user's job (program); (2) the utility, library, or management system routines that are required; and (3) the I/O devices required. A *job-control program* takes the job-control statements written by users and translates them into machine-language instructions that can be executed by the CPU.

UTILITY PROGRAMS. As the number of jobs handled by the computer system increases and as the number of data files within the system increases, sort/merge utilities are needed. Sort/merge programs are employed in organizing records in a file and in merging multiple files of sequence records into a single sequential file. Usually a sort/merge program is written as a set of generalized modules so that the program can be tailored for a variety of applications.

A number of utility programs such as sort/merge have been designed to perform data processing tasks common to many user jobs. Also, utility programs that transfer data from one medium to another, help in debugging, and provide diagnostics are common.

LIBRARIAN. The librarian is a set of service programs that performs the cataloging and management function associated with the libraries. These programs maintain, service, and organize all libraries, including those required by the operating system as well as user libraries. Librarians provide capabilities such as adding, deleting, and removing programs; listing the contents of different libraries; and repositioning programs in the library after deleting a program.

LINKAGE EDITOR. The linkage editor is a service program that is actively involved in the execution phase of processing a job. When a job (user program) has been input to the computer and translated to machine language, it is output in object program form on the residence device. The linkage editor will edit the object program and will pull together ("link") all library programs, utility programs, and management system programs that the job requires.

File Maintenance and Database Management Systems

These programs include file maintenance routines, database management systems, report generators, and other information retrieval routines. In general, a wide range of file activity demands will exist on a computer system. This is particularly true if the computer is used for transaction processing as well as supporting management decision making, as is the case in most large accounting systems. File maintenance capabilities and database management must exist for adding or deleting a record, depending upon the transaction and program requirements.

Application and End-user Programs

Application software includes those programs that actually process data into information, provide management with decision-making information or enable management to access data. Usually, most application software is written by information systems or vendor programmers. As the label implies, end-user programs are the application programs actually written by the user. These programs are usually written in a high-level computer language and translated into the machine language of the computer by a language translator. Many examples of these programs will be used throughout this text.

Programming Languages

A computer user employs a sequence of instructions to perform tasks such as those in the application programs above. These instructions can be written in different programming languages, depending upon the knowledge of the user and the availability of a language translator to convert the input language to the machine language of the computer. Thus, a programming language is a basic tool that a user employs in instructing the computer to perform tasks.

Four *levels* of computer languages exist on most computer systems: low-level (machine) languages; assembly languages; high-level (compiler) languages; and fourth-generation languages. Because each of these has advantages as well as disadvantages, and because each is employed in most computers, it is appropriate that we review them in detail.

MACHINE LANGUAGES.   Machine language is the only language the computer can execute directly. Since it can relate directly to the execution process, it is referred to as a low-level programming language. When machine language is used, the programmer must specify everything the computer needs to know to implement its particular job using a binary code (combinations of 0s and 1s) or a hexadecimal, octal, or some other equivalent, depending on the design of the computer. Regardless of the number system used, the process is complex and unique to each computer system rendering machine language extremely complex, tedious, time consuming, and limited, in its use.

ASSEMBLY LANGUAGES.   Because of the difficulty involved in using and in learning machine-language programming, other languages have been developed to reduce its complexity and tedious nature. One of these is assembly language, which is similar to machine language with some of the complexities of programming removed through the use of mnemonic symbols within the language. It is still referred to as a low-level language, and is often referred to as a symbolic language. For example, rather than employing the hexadecimal number that represents the STORE instruction, the assembly language would employ a symbol, such as STO. The programmer must still designate the operation to be performed and the storage locations to use. Therefore, assembly languages have some of the complexity of machine languages. Assembly languages are also similar to machine languages in that they are machine dependent; each assembly language is related to a specific machine and is not transferable.

HIGH-LEVEL PROGRAMMING LANGUAGES.   High-level languages are procedure- or problem-oriented languages. They are designed so that the user can focus on the problem or on the procedure for solving the problem, rather than on the computer operations that are the focus in machine and assembly languages. COBOL, FORTRAN, BASIC, PL/I, C, FORTH, and Pascal are examples of high-level languages.

The label *high-level* is used as the language designator because such languages are far removed from the hardware. These languages employ English-like terms and symbols and require much less programming effort than assembly and machine languages. Storage addressing is not required and fewer instructions are needed. While one assembly-language instruction is generally equivalent to one machine-language instruction, one high-level language statement can accomplish the same objective as several machine instructions. This is possible because the language translator for the high-level language carries the burden of generating the equivalent machine instructions. In contrast to assembly languages and machine languages, high-level languages are machine-independent. A program written in high-level language can therefore be used on many different computers, although some minor changes may be necessary because of differences in machine capabilities.

COMPILERS AND ASSEMBLERS.   As we noted earlier, before a program can be executed it must exist in machine-language form. Since assembly languages and high-level languages are not in machine language, they must be translated into machine instructions. The translator for an assembly language is called an *assembler* program. A high-level language translator is called a *compiler* program. Both assemblers and compilers are designed for specific computers, since differences exist in the design and structure of computers. Only one assembler is needed for a given computer, since each computer has a unique assembly language. In contrast, a compiler is required for each high-level language used on a given computer. A BASIC compiler will translate from BASIC to machine language; a COBOL compiler is required to translate from COBOL to machine language.

FOURTH-GENERATION LANGUAGES. Fourth-generation languages have moved the user even further from the programmer. These are nonprocedural (the user only defines the task and not the implementation instructions). There are application generators which enable the user to more easily develop software such as that required to develop an interactive monitor screen for data entry. There are also end-user tools which give the user a set of application rules that can be used for many programming tasks. Examples would be spreadsheet macros and database query languages.

ARTIFICIAL INTELLIGENCE AND NATURAL LANGUAGES. In addition, a great deal of work is currently being done to develop expert systems (ES) and to use artificial intelligence (AI) to assist management in problem solving. These approaches use natural languages to symbolically represent the thought process of experts in auditing, for example. That is, they trace their decision process so that less experienced auditors, for example, can use the experts' set of decision rules to solve a problem. The common languages used here are LISP (List Processor), Modula-2, and Prolog.

ADVANTAGES AND DISADVANTAGES OF LANGUAGES. The majority of application programs are written in high-level languages. End-user programs are generally written using fourth-generation languages. Both higher and lower levels of language have distinct advantages and disadvantages. For business data processing applications it is important that we be aware of these.

High-level languages are generally much easier to learn than assembly languages. Therefore it takes less time for the programmer to develop a program. Because the statements are English-like and fairly easy to interpret, they provide better documentation than assembly statements and make it easier to modify existing programs. Also, nonprocedural fourth-generation languages do not require the programmer to adhere to a well-defined set of rules (procedures). This helps make them easier to use.

Because high-level languages are machine-independent, programs do not become obsolete when a new computer is installed. In addition, machine independence allows programs to be shared with other users and general application programs to be purchased at low cost, since they are not written for a specific machine. One disadvantage of high-level languages, as compared with assembly languages, is that user-written programs are not efficient. Because there is a one-to-one correspondence between assembly-language instructions and machine-language instructions, a program written in assembly language can take full advantage of computer capabilities. A high-level language program will probably take longer to run and will require more core storage, since it must rely on the machine-language instruction generated by the compiler. The difference in computer run time can become significant if the program being run is used on a regular basis.

Another disadvantage of high-level languages is that significant quantities of computer time may be consumed in the compilation process, even though it is a one-time process. In contrast, the conversion of assembly-language programs to machine language will be likely to consume a relatively small amount of time. On some computer systems, particularly minicomputers, the size of the compiler may be a negative factor, since it requires much more storage space than the assembler.

Advanced Software Concepts

In our discussion of hardware we noted that though the CPU is designed to handle a large volume of data processing activities, it is often "I/O bound" because input/output (I/O) devices have limited capabilities (speeds). Communication control units, channels, and buffers are used to improve the interface between the CPU and input/output devices. In this section we will examine three software programs that can improve the operating efficiency of the CPU: *multiprogramming*, *virtual storage*, and *multiprocessing*.

MULTIPROGRAMMING. Although the CPU can process instructions very rapidly, it can operate on only one instruction at a time. In addition, the CPU cannot operate on data until the data are in primary storage. Since the speed of I/O operations is slower than the CPU processing speed, a significant amount of CPU time is wasted waiting on I/O operations. To help overcome this problem, multiprogramming allows several programs and their associated data to reside in primary storage at the same time. Under multiprogramming, the CPU executes only one instruction at a time, but it has flexibility in moving from one program to another, then another, and then back to the first program. Instructions from a program are executed until an instruction for an input or output device occurs. The I/O instruction passes control to a channel, thus freeing the CPU to rotate and begin processing instructions from another program. The CPU processes the second program until that program requires input or output, at which time the CPU rotates to another program or back to a previously partially executed program, and so on.

When more than one processing program is loaded into primary storage during multiprogramming, the programs must be held in separate areas. To accomplish this, primary storage is subdivided into areas called partitions. Each partition can handle one program. The size and structure of the partitions are determined by the type of operating system that the computer utilizes.

VIRTUAL STORAGE. Multiprogramming overcomes the problem of the CPU having to wait for an I/O operation. A limitation of multiprogramming, however, is that a partition must be large enough to hold an entire program and the entire program remains in the partition until it is fully executed. This results in inefficient use of main memory, particularly if a program contains a large sequence of instructions that is used infrequently and a small group of instructions that is used repeatedly. Since the size of main memory is limited, a procedure was necessary for handling the holding and execution of instructions for a program.

To overcome the necessity of having to hold an entire program in memory while it is executing, an extension of multiprogramming, called *virtual storage*, has been developed. The basic concept behind virtual storage is that only the portion of a program and data that are needed immediately must be held in primary storage; the remaining part of the program and any associated data can be held in an auxiliary storage device. The virtual storage technique gives the illusion that main memory is unlimited because only a portion of a program is in main memory at any point in time, and therefore more programs can reside in main memory simultaneously. A direct-access storage device, such as a magnetic disk unit, is used to establish a virtual storage system. The term *virtual storage* is given to the access storage, while *real storage* is the term used when referring to primary storage locations given addresses by the operating system. All instructions and data for a given program reside in virtual storage at all times. When data or instructions for a given portion of a program are needed in real storage, they are transferred from virtual storage to real storage. Two methods exist for storing and transferring data from virtual storage to real storage: (1) segmentation; and (2) paging.

In *segmentation* each program is broken into variable-size units referred to as segments. The segments could easily be defined as data, the main program, a subroutine of the program, and so on. Based on the size of the segments, the operating system allocates appropriate space in virtual storage. Since any segment in virtual storage must be readily available to be transferred to real storage, the addresses of all segments in virtual storage are kept in real storage in a segment table. Thus bringing a segment into real storage simply involves referencing the table and a transfer.

Paging is similar to segmentation except that all storage areas, both in main memory and in virtual memory, are of a standard fixed size called a page. The size of the page is determined by the characteristics of the given computer. Unlike segmentation, paging does not consider the logical subunits or portions of a program when storing the program. The programs are simply broken into equal-size pages. The transfer of a page of a program from virtual memory to real memory is similar to segmentation. An address for each program page in virtual memory is kept in a page table in real storage. A table reference and transfer are required to move a page of the program to real memory when the page is required during processing.

Fortunately the operating system handles all of the storage, development of tables, transfer of segments or pages, and other tasks associated with virtual storage operations. Virtual storage, however, has some basic limitations. First, an on-line auxiliary storage unit is required. Second, the operating system associated with virtual storage is highly sophisticated, requires a significant amount of storage in main memory, and is often rather expensive. Third, if a virtual storage system is not structured properly, a significant amount of time can be wasted in locating and exchanging program segments or pages.

MULTIPROCESSING.   Multiprocessing involves the use of two or more central processing units linked together to form a coordinated data processing operation. Multiprocessing is quite different from multiprogramming. Recall that multiprogramming involves the concurrent execution of instructions from two or more programs, all of which utilize one CPU controlled by a single operating system. In multiprocessing, more than one instruction can be executed simulta-

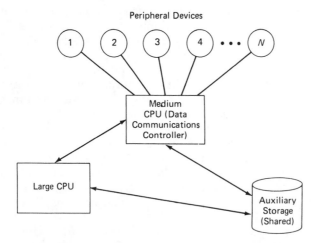

FIGURE 5-9 Multiprocessing system (medium-large, two-CPU arrangement).

neously because two or more CPUs are available. The CPUs can execute different instructions from the same program, or instructions from totally different programs.

One benefit that results from the multiprocessing structure is the "freeing up" of one CPU to primarily handle computational operations. One CPU handles such tasks as scheduling, editing data, and file maintenance while the second CPU is free to handle high-priority or complex processing, such as large mathematical calculations. One configuration used to provide this operating arrangement is a medium-size CPU, often a minicomputer, linked to a large CPU. Input/output operations and communications with peripheral devices are channeled through the medium-size CPU while the large CPU concentrates on computational processing. Figure 5-9 illustrates a medium-large, two-CPU multiprocessing system.

A multiprocessing system can also consist of two or more large CPUs, with each CPU having its own separate memory as well as a single shared memory. Figure 5-10 illustrates this type of configuration. In this figure, a medium CPU is used as a data communications controller and two large CPUs provide processing services. Under this arrangement, specific CPUs may be dedicated to specific tasks such as I/O processing, computational processing, or data management; or one CPU can handle on-line processing while another handles only batch processing. Some multiprocessing systems are also designed so that one or more of the CPUs is employed as a backup for the other CPUs. Obviously, multiprocessing systems of this nature are used by organizations with extremely large and complex information processing needs.

A multiprocessing system involves a great deal of hardware and software. A highly sophisticated operating system is needed if the CPUs and other resources are to be used effectively. The implementation of this type of system may also be very time consuming. The payoff from such systems is tremendous, however, particularly if the system is configured so that additional CPUs or storage can be

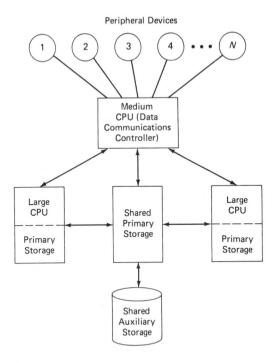

FIGURE 5-10 Multiprocessing system (multiple large-CPU arrangement).

added in the future as needed without reworking the entire system or having to adopt a totally new system.

SUMMARY

This chapter has focused on the hardware and software components of a computer system. In the hardware area we identified the elements that form the central processing unit (CPU), the unit that controls the entire computer. We discussed devices that are used as input/output units, including keying devices, terminals, monitors, magnetic tape drives, optical character recognition (OCR) devices and microcomputers. We also considered storage devices such as tape magnetic disk and CD-ROM. We also discussed devices that play an important role in the efficient operation of a computer system, particularly when a large number of peripheral devices are utilized in the system.

Our discussion of software included a coverage of the functions, types, and structure of operating systems. Specific topics examined included supervisors, initial program loader, job-control program, linkage editor, and librarian. A detailed coverage of programming languages was not provided, but we discussed the differences between machine languages, assembly languages, and compiler languages, along with their advantages and disadvantages. Some advanced software concepts were presented, such as multiprogramming, virtual storage, and multiprocessing. We noted that multiprogramming and virtual storage software can improve the efficiency and operation of a single computer system, whereas multiprocessing software is required when two or more CPUs are linked together. Examples were given to highlight the specific aspects of each software package.

SELECTED REFERENCES

ARTHUR ANDERSEN & CO., *Trends in Information Technology: 1986.* Chicago, Ill.: Arthur Andersen & Co., 1986.

MCKEOWN, PATRICK G., *Living with Computers,* San Diego: Harcourt, Brace, Jovanovich, 1988.

ROUSSEY, ROBERT, "The CPA in the Information Age: Today and Tomorrow," *Journal of Accountancy,* Oct 1986, pp. 90-105.

REVIEW QUESTIONS

1. Identify in a block diagram the basic components of a computer.

2. The central processing unit is generally considered to be made up of which of the following three parts?
   a. Control, arithmetic-logical, and storage
   b. Input, output, and processing
   c. Arithmetical, logical, and control
   d. Storage, processing, and output
   e. None of the above
      (Adapted from the CMA examination.)

3. What is the function of the following?
   a. Primary storage
   b. Arithmetic-logic unit
   c. Control unit
   d. Secondary storage

4. What factors are used to characterize or describe a central processing unit (CPU)?

5. What is the key cost factor associated with the purchasing of a CPU?

6. Which of the following best describes business and scientific computing needs for (1) input/output, and (2) computing speed?
   a. Business needs both and scientific needs neither.
   b. Business needs both and scientific only needs input/output.
   c. Business needs computing speed and scientific needs input/output.
   d. Business needs neither and scientific needs speed.
   e. Business needs input/output and scientific needs computing speed.
      (Adapted from the CMA examination.)

7. Which piece of data processing equipment *is not* considered to be an input/output device?
   a. CRT
   b. Magnetic tape
   c. Magnetic strip
   d. JCL
   e. Disk pack

8. Explain the difference between RAM and ROM.

9. Identify some of the more common input/output devices employed in a computer system.

10. Identify the characteristics of magnetic tape.

11. What are the characteristics of an MICR device? How is it used?

12. Describe how an OCR device is used.

13. Identify some of the more common secondary storage devices.

14. Explain the following concepts used in relationship to a magnetic tape:
    a. Density
    b. Logical record
    c. Physical record
    d. Blocking
    e. Interblock gap (IBG)
    f. Blocking factor

15. How is the size and the speed of a CPU measured?

16. Identify the structure of a magnetic disk. What is a disk pack?

17. Compare the capacity, access time, and average cost of a magnetic tape and a magnetic disk.

18. Which of the following is not a direct-access storage device (also called random access storage)?
    a. Disk
    b. Core
    c. Drum
    d. Data cell
    e. None of the above

19. What is the function of the control unit in a computer system?

20. A large bank is considering the implementation of a fast-response teller system. What type of peripheral equipment is normally associated with such fast-response computer systems?
    a. Magnetic tape
    b. Magnetic disk
    c. Magnetic core

    d. Punched cards
    (Adapted from the CMA examination.)

21. Explain the function of a channel.

22. Explain what is meant by "buffering."

23. What are the functions of an operating system?

24. Explain the term *system residence device.*

25. Differentiate between *control programs* and *processing programs.*

26. What components go together to make up an operating system?

27. Explain the function of each of the following:
    a. Initial program loader (IPL)
    b. Supervisor
    c. Job-control program (JCL)
    d. Sort/merge and utility programs

28. Distinguish between *access time* and *execution time.* What is the combination of these called?

29. What is the constraint on the number of records in a block that are stored on magnetic tape?

30. What are the basic differences between a machine-level, assembly, high-level, and fourth-generation languages? Which ones are easier for programmers and end users to use?

31. Define virtual storage. What are the two methods used to implement virtual storage?

32. What capabilities does multiprocessing offer?

33. What is multiprogramming and how is it different from multiprocessing?

CASES

5-1 For each of the following situations, identify the suitable input/output device or devices.

1. An electronics firm has decided to eliminate the use of time cards for recording the work/attendance times of its employees; instead, the company has adopted plastic badges that contain employee identification numbers. The badges have a magnetic strip that can be read by an input device tied to the company's computer system.

2. A building contractor wants to process its weekly payroll on the company's computer system, although the hours that employees work are recorded in pencil on time cards.

3. A metropolitan bank wants to employ a specialized means of inputting to the computer the large volume of checks it must process daily.

4. A television manufacturer wants to receive from its wholesalers orders that have been directly entered into its computer and transmitted to the manufacturer's shipping department.

5. A university wants to employ a specialized procedure to handle the registration forms used by students during the registration process. A semiautomated system is desired.

6. A public water works office wants to employ a procedure for handling the monthly water bills returned by customers with their checks.

7. A large retail clothing outlet wants to capture sales data so that each sales transaction can automatically be read, transmitted, and immediately completed via its central computer facility.

8. A stockbroker wants to provide stock prices to prospective customers by entering the appropriate request via a special telephone with a keyboard attachment.

9. A bank that has numerous branches wants to transmit data from its regional offices for rapid processing by the central computer at the central office.

10. A large wholesale organization wants to record the receipt and/or shipment of merchandise on documents that can be handled in batches by its computer system.

11. An oil company wants to record credit sales as they are made at its service stations.

5-2 Compare the two secondary storage devices according to the four criteria indicated:

	CRITERIA		
	ACCESS (Random/Sequential)	SPEED (Fast/Slow)	COST (Expensive/Cheap)	VOLUME (High/Low)
Magnetic tape				
Magnetic disk				

5-3 There is no universal I/O device nor storage device that can satisfy all applications. However, under certain circumstances a given I/O as well as a given storage device has advantages over other corresponding types of devices. Shown in columns 1 and 2 of the following table are two sets of devices:

	(1) DEVICE	(2) DEVICE
1	Printer	CRT terminal
2	Magnetic tape (storage)	Disk (storage)
3	CD-ROM	Floppy Disk

1. Under what circumstances would each item in column 1 have advantages over the corresponding item in column 2?

2. Under what circumstances would each item in column 2 have advantages over the corresponding item in column 1?

5-4 Following is a list of devices. Arrange the devices in describing order of I/O speed.

1. Magnetic tape drive
2. CRT terminal
3. Magnetic strip
4. Magnetic disk
5. Card punch
6. RAM
7. Magnetic drum
8. Optical scanner
9. Card reader

5-5 The First Bank of Athens has 50,000 savings accounts. All accounts are maintained on a single master file where each account consists of a record 200 characters in length.

1. Assume that the bank elected to store the master file of 50,000 records on a magnetic tape. Determine the number of inches of tape required to store the file using unblocked records, a 0.50-inch inter-block-gap size, and a tape density of 800 characters per inch.

2. Determine the inches of tape required to store the master file using a blocking factor of 5, a tape density of 800 characters per inch, and with the inter-block-gap of .05 inches.

3. Assuming that tapes were created under steps 1 and 2, which tape would take the least time to read? Why?

5-6 The Ben Davis Supply Company of Swanee, Georgia, employs key-to-disk equipment in its mail-order processing operation. They use 3 ½-inch 1.44K floppy disks to store data. Each order that is received may be made up of a number of different items. The company receives about two thousand orders per week; each order on the average contains six different items. Each item, on the average, contains 60 characters of information.

Equipment requirements and the associated costs are as follows:

1. Disks: $20 per box, 20 disks per box
2. Key-to-disks machines: monthly rental, $500 each
3. Key-to-disk verifiers: monthly rental, $500 each
4. Salary of equipment operators: $1,200 per month per person

All orders received are forwarded to the keying area for preparation. Upon completion of the keying operation, the order, along with the disk, is passed to a verification operation (essentially rekeying to check original keying). The company has found that, on the average, the error rate during keying is 15 percent; however, all errors are corrected once they have been sent back to keying (no verification is required on the corrected disks).

REQUIRED: For this operation:

1. Determine the number of key-to-disk personnel and verifiers required if it is assumed that exactly four weeks make up a month and an operator (regardless of whether keying or verifying is involved) works at a rate of 1,500 characters per hour.

2. Determine the monthly cost for the company.

5-7 Indicate whether a magnetic tape or a magnetic disk system would be more applicable for the following applications. Justify your choice in each case.

1. Airlines reservations
2. A clothing store inventory control system
3. A billing system for a doctor's office
4. State automobile registration of licenses

5-8 Given the following situations, specify a suitable storage medium and a suitable access medium (method). Justify your recommendations in each case.

1. A large hotel has a room reservation system that keeps track of the status of all rooms in a multibuilding complex. The system is maintained on a "room" master file. Each room in the hotel complex appears as a record on the master file. The system is such that each record must be updated and/or changed to reflect new occupants, food and phone charges, and checkout/departure of occupants. The system is linked to the billing process and is used to generate a customer's final bill. On the average, a room in the hotel has an 85 percent occupancy rate and each occupant stays two nights.

2. A large, earth-moving equipment company maintains 10,000 parts on an inventory system. Each item in inventory is identified with a unique record. Records are updated and/or deleted daily, depending on the sales activity. On the average, 600 orders are received daily; each order, on the average, contains six items. New parts or deletion of old parts occurs at a rate of twenty-five per day. The system is designed so that when a customer calls to place an order, an inquiry can be

made to determine the status of parts on hand. An inventory status report is generated at the end of each day. The report highlights, among other things, when parts on hand have declined to their reorder points.

3. The electric utility department in a major city maintains a master file of approximately 250,000 customers. Once a month the customers' electric meters are read to determine consumption. A card is prepared on each customer account to reflect the meter reading. All customer records in the master file are updated to reflect monthly usage. Bills are prepared and a master list, which reflects the customer's name, address, and amount billed, is generated.

5-9 The B & H Drug Company, Inc., owns a chain of stores throughout the Southwest. The store in Houston, Texas, has recently acquired a medium-sized computer and associated peripheral equipment. The configuration includes the following: (1) a CPU having 1,000,000 bytes of primary storage; (2) a key-to-tape device; (3) three magnetic tape drives for backup; (4) three magnetic disk drives; (5) a high-speed line printer; (6) ten key CRT display terminals.

REQUIRED:

1. Draw the configuration of equipment assuming that no overlapped processing capabilities exist.

2. Draw the configuration of equipment assuming that additional equipment is to be purchased (if necessary) so that overlapped processing exists.

5-10 The L & D Video Company is a manufacturer of video terminals as well as parts for maintaining terminals. The terminals are primarily used in commercial video equipment. The company produces eighty to ninety different varieties of terminals and markets them throughout the entire United States. The company has a work force of 150 employees and 6 managers. Sales revenues for Video were $9.2 million last year. The company foresees rapid growth in sales during the next five years.

Bob Lennox, owner of the company, is concerned about the current problems the company is experiencing as a result of rapid growth. For example, the number of sales orders has increased considerably and the company is having problems meeting promised delivery dates. When customers call to check on the status of their orders, it often is several hours before a response can be given. Materials and parts needed in the manufacturing area are frequently out of stock, and long delays occur in replenishing the critical items. Bad-debt expense has begun to increase at an alarming rate.

REQUIRED:

1. Identify a suitable computer hardware configuration that could be used to help improve the operation at Video.

2. Identify the software that would be required to support the hardware in part 1. Explain the purpose of each software item.

3. Identify some computer applications that might help Video handle its "growth problems."

5-11 The Bendix Company currently schedules its computer job stream so that one job has the full attention of the central processing unit (CPU) at a time. The company wants to increase the efficiency of its system.

REQUIRED:

1. One option available to the company is to apply the concept of multiprogramming. To accomplish this, the company should do which of the following?
   a. Obtain two CPUs in order to run two jobs simultaneously.
   b. Alter programs to perform more than one job in each program.
   c. Utilize an operating system feature that splits the CPUs attention to more than one job.
   d. Utilize a minicomputer associated with the main computer to run small jobs.
   e. Apply none of the concepts described above.

2. A second option would be to use multiprocessing. To do this the company should do which of the following?

a. Operate two independent computer systems.

b. Operate two CPUs sharing the same memory.

c. Operate two sets of on-line storage for access by different jobs.

d. Operate a minicomputer for preprocessing data before transmission to the main system.

e. Operate some system other than those described above.

5-12 Sobig Company is faced with a situation in which many of its programs are too large for the memory of its current computer. In attempting to solve this problem, Sobig could make use of the modular feature built into its system.

REQUIRED: To accomplish this the company should do which of the following?

1. Break programs into modules, thus permitting one module to be resident in memory at a time.

2. Use virtual storage, which allows the programs and data to be moved between primary and secondary storage and thus negates the memory-size constraint.

3. Be able to add modules of memory, thus expanding the size of the main memory.

4. Allocate sections of the system to each program to be processed.

5. Be able to switch to a larger computer in the same family, thus preventing the need to reprogram.

5-13 For each situation estimate the storage capacity needed.

1. A utility customer file with addresses for 2,000 customers. Each address consists of 100 characters of information.

   a. disk space on floppy 3 ½-inch disks

   b. inches of tape blocking records in blocks of 100 and 800 characters per inch and an IBG of ½ inch.

2. An auto parts dealer with an inventory of 5,000 parts with each part consisting of 200 characters of information. How much space should be allocated on a hard disk for this file?

5-14 Broadway and Hargrove CPA's use microcomputer tax packages to prepare tax returns, spreadsheets to analyze various financial options and word processing to write up results.

REQUIRED: How can they use multiple programming features of new PC and Macintosh operating systems to integrate these various activities to more effectively serve their clients?

5-15 Holland Freight uses three software packages to schedule its freight operations. One is very disk intensive in that it refers to routing, rate, and vehicle availability data on this disk frequently. Another simply loads its data into RAM and does its calculations. A third requires the use of virtual memory to operate.

REQUIRED: Which ones is more likely to require a hard disk and why?

6

MICROCOMPUTER AND LOCAL AREA NETWORK (LAN) PROCESSING TECHNOLOGY

INTRODUCTION

In the last several years microcomputers have been installed in most organizations. Most accountants, as well as their auditors, have one on their desk or they use one on a regular basis. The reasons for this have been numerous. Perhaps the most important is the tremendous reduction in cost for a typical microcomputer. One suitable for business may cost in the neighborhood of $1,000 to $5,000 depending on how it is configured. Adding to that, a few hundred for a printer and another few hundred for software, most organizations can now provide reasonable computational power for their employees. The driving force for this cost reduction has been the major advance in chip technology in the last several years. Chip technology alone is not the only reason for the popularity of microcomputers today, however. The other major factor has been the increase in reasonably priced, user friendly personal productivity and accounting software. The number of microcomputers now used in the home and in the schools has also led to their explosive growth because more and more individuals are accustomed to using them.

Engineers were able in the mid-1970s to produce the entire central processing unit (CPU) on a single silicon wafer or "chip" about a quarter-inch square. This "microchip CPU," referred to as a microprocessor, is about the size of a dime and costs very little to manufacture. A microprocessor is not a computer, but when it is coupled with memory chips and attached to input/output devices it becomes a microcomputer. Because of the generic nature of these components, many small companies (some are quite large now) can manufacture microcomputers. Many are IBM clones. A microcomputer is founded on a microprogramming process in which each machine instruction initiates a sequence of more elementary instructions (microinstructions). Using this microprogramming approach, the fixed conventional CPU control logic of a mainframe or minicomputer can be replaced with CPU control memory, which contains the basic microinstructions for the microcomputer's fundamental operations.

Personal computers can range in size from two- to ten-pound laptops with limited processing capability (used primarily for word processing, small spreadsheets, communication such as electronic mail, and the management of small databases) to large computers with substantial processing power that sit on the floor and are often used as a host for an office network of personal computers. This network is called a local area network.

HARDWARE

A microcomputer is actually the integration of five basic components mounted on or connected to the *motherboard* (the main circuit board) via slots or ports: (1) a processor (CPU); (2) random access memory (RAM); (3) preprogrammed read-only memory (ROM); (4) a clock; and (5) input/output peripheral devices. These are illustrated in Figure 6-1.

CPU

The motherboard contains a microprocessor chip. Like the processor of minis and mainframes, the microprocessor performs all data manipulation, program and decision-making logic, and arithmetic functions.

The hardware speed and size of personal computers has increased dramatically over the last several years and there is good reason to believe this trend will continue. The early 1970 PCs used microprocessors which operated on 8 bits of data at one time. Using a 16-bit data path to determine storage locations, these chips could only address 64K bytes of storage locations. Thus, these were generally called 64K personnel computers. In the 1980s this was improved using 16-bit microprocessors which enabled one to identify approximately 1 million storage locations. In general, microprocessor chips are identified first by the size of the data path, such as 16 bits, and then by the number of bits it can operate on at one time, such as 32 bits for the new 32-bit processors such as the Motorola 68000 series used in the Macintosh and the Intel 80286 PCs in the 1980s. Such a 16/32-bit chip permits a storage capacity of 16 megabytes. In the early 1990s, full 32/32-bit chips are being used in ever increasing numbers; these can address 4 million bytes of primary storage. These are used in the newer IBM mod-

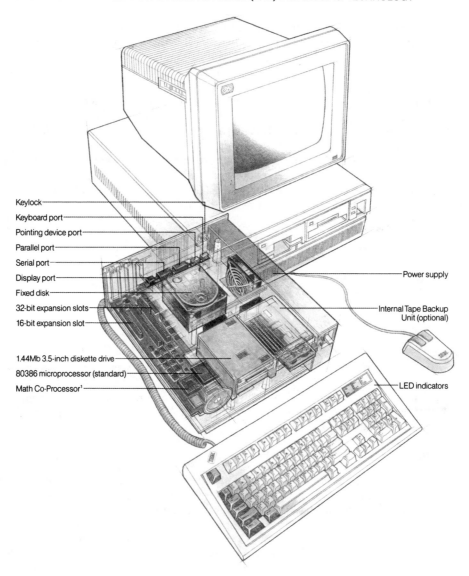

Keylock
Keyboard port
Pointing device port
Parallel port
Serial port
Display port
Fixed disk
32-bit expansion slots
16-bit expansion slot

1.44Mb 3.5-inch diskette drive
80386 microprocessor (standard)
Math Co-Processor[1]

Power supply
Internal Tape Backup Unit (optional)
LED indicators

FIGURE 6-1   Microcomputer components—IBM Personal System/2 Model 70 386.
Source: Courtesy of IBM Corporation.

els (such as those which use Intel 80386 processors) as well as new Macintoshs which use Motorola 68030 and 68040 processors. In summary, an 8-bit machine can handle only one 8-byte of data at one time where a 32-bit processor can handle 4 times 8-bytes of data at one time.

The electronic clock within the microcomputer is used to synchronize internal and external operations. The processor, when solving problems or handling data and instructions related to a problem, often subdivides individual problems into several component parts. The clock is the coordinating mechanism that brings together, at the proper time, each of the separate processing functions.

The speed of this clock governs the speed at which instructions are executed. Computers are described by this clock speed. Early chips operated at 6 MHz (6 million pulses per second), whereas today some operate in excess of 25 MHz). To further enhance this speed some chip manufacturers are experimenting with RISC (reduced instruction set computer) chips which execute several commonly used sets of instructions using one pulse rather than several clock pulses, as is the case with current chip architecture. This has the potential of increasing the speed of data processing even more. This speed is particularly useful in the processing of graphics.

The memory section of the micro is divided into two subsections. Random access memory (RAM) chips are available to handle primary storage and additional read-only memory (ROM) chips are generally used to permanently store preprogrammed data and operating instructions. Random access memory is the direct functional equivalent of the core memory that is used as primary storage in both mainframe and minicomputer systems. Unlike core memory, however, RAM is a semiconductor micromemory, or a "memory on a chip." This type of memory is small, fast, and economical and provides the bulk of the microcomputer's internal storage. The only limitation of RAM is that when the electrical power to the system is turned off, data stored in the memory are lost.

Read-only memory (ROM), or programmable read-only memory (PROM) as it is often called, has a permanent set of instructions that the microprocessor uses each time the system is operated. Since the functions performed by the processor are directly related to the ROM, the machine's characteristics can easily be altered by employing a different ROM. The read-only memory is a semiconductor micromemory. Unlike RAM memory, however, ROM memory does not lose the data or instructions when power is removed from the system, and ROM memory can only be read. Data or instructions cannot be written into the ROM during operation of the system; data and instructions are preprogrammed by the manufacturer. These are connected by a circuit called a *bus*.

In addition, the PC may be enhanced by the addition of cards installed in slots on the bus on the mother board. These cards may contain additional RAM, accelerator chips for increasing clock speed, modems for communication, hard disks for secondary storage purposes, and circuitry for emulating mainframe terminals. Figure 6-1 illustrates the typical layout of a motherboard for a personal computer.

Operating Systems

There are numerous operating systems for personal computers. It is important for the accountant to be aware of this when attempting to configure an accounting system using different personal computers. It is important that the PCs be able to communicate with each other and be compatible enough so that all the needs of management can be met. Sometimes only data need to be transferred and in other cases one PC may need to actually use data or applications which reside on the other PC's disk.

In the past, most operating systems were single-user and single-task operating systems. These were fine for applications where only one user uses one application at a time. The first commonly used generic operating system was CP/M (Control Program for Microcomputers); it was used extensively on 8-bit machines. Following this, the industry standard for the more powerful 16-bit machines became MS-DOS (Microsoft-disk operating system). Many of the most widely used personal productivity and accounting packages run on MS-DOS. Both of these are single-user, single-task command-driven operating systems. Command-driven systems require the user to learn and use commands such as COPY, DELETE, and FORMAT to use the computer. These operating systems are very efficient when the user uses the same programs quite often, such as an accountant who uses the same spreadsheet every day, or the secretary who uses the same word processor day in and day out to prepare reports and correspondence.

The other major PC single-task operating system is the original Macintosh operating system based on pull-down menus and icons. It provides users with a standardized, user friendly interface where the user can point and click the mouse to execute many of the necessary commands to operate the computer. Such a system is particularly useful for people who use the computer on an occasional basis, such as a manager who may use a wide variety of programs. The standard user friendly interface reduces the knowledge needed to operate each applications' basic functions because they are similar. More and more, the newer software is moving toward the easy-to-use graphic and menu-driven interface.

MULTIPLE PROGRAMS AND PROCESSING.   Some of the newer operating systems for personal computers enable the accountants to operate more than one program at one time, further enhancing their productivity. For example, a word processing program could be printing a report while the accountant is working with a spreadsheet on a budget problem. The successor to MS-DOS for the IBM and its clones is PS/2. It is a true multitasking system and when coupled with Microsoft Widows or other such products, provides a menu-driven interface similar to that of the Macintosh. UNIX, originally developed for minicomputers by AT&T, is a multiple-task as well as a multiple-user operating system that is also currently being touted as an effective general-purpose multiple-task operating system. The new Macintosh operating system can also run multiple applications concurrently. The accountant can expect many more advances in this area in the future as hardware and software vendors seek to make their systems and programs easier to use.

Communication

A microcomputer typically has a keyboard for input and some display device for output. A variety of keyboards exist, ranging from simple keyboard units to those which emulate the complex interactive 3270 type terminals used to communicate with mainframe computers. Visual output devices range from simple monochrome monitors to large full-color monitors for extensive use of graphics.

Many personal computers also offer a number of other interface options used to communicate with additional hard and floppy disk drives, modems, printers, plotters, FAX machines, mainframe computers, and local area networks.

Communication software packages also enable accountants to easily communicate with their office for mail and other key information, or to communicate with their clients to download information for auditing purposes, for example. Moreover, within an office setting, local area networks and communication with the mainframe have become commonplace. These will be discussed later.

Storage

A large variety of products are available for secondary storage. These include floppy disks which typically have a capacities (densities) ranging from 720K to 1.44M and typically come in 3 ½-inch or 5 ¼-inch sizes. Some of the drives can read a variety of densities and formats so that one may only need one floppy drive. In addition, many if not most desktop personal computers used in business have a hard drive ranging from twenty to over a hundred megabytes. These are used primarily for data files, the operating system, and the most widely used programs. In addition, the optical disks are becoming increasingly popular for reference data, and tape cassettes are widely used as backup media. A personal computer may have one or more of these secondary storage devices, depending on the users' needs.

User Interface

As discussed, microcomputers have become increasingly easy to use due in part to advances in user interfaces. Many PCs now have function keys that require only a single key to execute many of the commonly used commands needed to run a PC program. For example, function key F10 may be used to save a file and the shift key plus F10 may be used to retrieve a file from the disk. Many software programs offer key-stroke shortcuts for command implementation. Some of the improvement is the result of operating systems, such as Macintosh and Microsoft Windows, which seek to standardize the basic operations for a large subset of the software accountants or their clients use. They present the user with icons and pull-down or pop-up menus which require only the click of a mouse or a single key stroke to implement many of the software commands. Many other improvement have come as the result of more sophisticated menu-driven software where the user can easily find the correct command without memorizing it. Moreover, many systems have extensive help features to assist the user. Finally, many of the financial packages, including spreadsheets and accounting packages, have graphics features for the effective presentation of information.

PERSONAL PRODUCTIVITY AND END-USER SOFTWARE

To make effective use of the power of the personal computer, many vendors have developed a wide range of personal productivity programs that can aid the accountant in his or her everyday activities. These include word processing, spreadsheet packages, communication packages, electronic mail, database packages, and a host of other useful programs (an appointment calendar, for example) which can often run concurrently with the main program.

Word Processing

Word processing technology has been a tremendous boon to the preparation of reports and correspondence. For example, data from an audit can be quickly pasted into a client financial report. Conformation letters can be quickly generated from a client database and prepared using a mail merge program in the word processor. In addition, specific information can be easily inserted into standard reports for conformity with AICPA pronouncements and firm policies. Desktop publishing packages can even enable firms to publish many of the financial statements they prepare.

Spreadsheets

Spreadsheets can be easily prepared for financial planning and budgeting needs. They are easily modified to ask "what if" questions, to produce output in graphical form for presentations, and to export data to word processors for reports. Moreover, through the use of macros (programs written to automate the use of a spreadsheet) clerical personnel can perform many of these activities using the automated spreadsheet program.

Databases

Small databases enable organizations to maintain files on customers, vendors, inventory, and personnel. These may be an integral part of the microcomputer accounting system or may be used to manage the organization.

Communication Packages

Communication packages enable accountants to easily communicate with their office for mail and other key information, or to communicate with their clients to download information for auditing purposes. Moreover, in an office setting, local area networks and communication with the mainframe have become common place. These packages are essential for distributed processing systems where remote locations must communicate data and report to and from the main office or other remote locations. These will be discussed in more detail in the next chapter on distributed processing systems and telecommunications.

Graphics

Many of the small business accounting packages and spreadsheet packages, as well as some of the database packages, make use of presentation graphics to assist accountants and managers in displaying information. These are in addition to the many graphic design, drafting, and drawing packages. Often these can be "pasted" into word processing or desktop publishing packages for effective presentation. These are very helpful in the preparation of diagrams such as organization charts, sales forecasts, and systems flow charts.

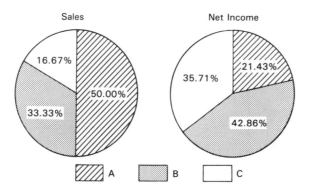

FIGURE 6-2 Combined graphical analysis and word processing.

Statistical

Many governmental and business decisions require the statistical analysis of data. Spreadsheets and database packages often provide the very basic statistics such as averages and trend lines. However, in many cases further analysis of the data is necessary. There are numerous statistical packages available for microcomputers that are relatively easy to use.

Summary

A large number of personal productivity software programs are available for accountants, managers, and their staff. These include: word processor, spreadsheet, database, communication, graphics, and statistical packages. Often they are integrated into one package and frequently the user can take the data from one and use it in another package. For example, the analysis of spreadsheet data can be displayed as a graph which is in turn "pasted" into a word processor or desktop publishing package in the preparation of an effective report for management use. This is illustrated in Figure 6-2. In summary, the low cost of these personal computers and their ever increasing computational power and ease of use have revolutionized the way accountants accomplish their day-to-day activities. Moreover, for the number of clients who now use the computer in part of their business—generally, the accounting system has vastly increased. Thus, the impact of personal computers on the accounting profession has been enormous.

ACCOUNTING SOFTWARE

Over the last several years, many accounting packages have been developed for use on personal computers. Several of these are illustrated in the application chapters of this text. In general, these packages enable even the smallest company to manage its inventory and purchasing operations, control its accounts receivable, grant credit to worthy customers, and generate its financial statements on a timely basis. Many other packages even help organizations manage personnel, aggregate costs for manufacturing operations, allocate costs to divisions, and prepare annual budgets. Still others have provisions for scheduling manufacturing and accounting for fixed assets. There are other packages with even more provisions for specific industry and service needs. For example, there are vertically integrated packages for the management and accounting needs of a doctor's office. Specialized systems such as this exist for virtually every line of business.

In addition to these productivity packages, many write-up programs, sampling programs, and other programs have been developed by various auditing firms and internal accounting staffs to automate the audit.

END-USER APPLICATIONS

Many of the application software packages used in microcomputers are easy to use and enable users such as managers and accountants to write their own applications. For example, a user can use a spreadsheet and its macro function to develop a financial planning model. As another example, an accountant can easily write a procedure to access a database to retrieve a special report on the status of a particular set of customer accounts. Even if this information is located on a mainframe computer, it is fairly easy to download the data and to use a microcomputer database, spreadsheet, or statistics package to analyze the data in order to supply management with information for decision making. Furthermore, with the communication software available, data can be accessed from remote locations. These software packages enable users to significantly shorten the lengthy process of systems development, which will be discussed later in this text. The potential problem is that this development can become uncontrolled if organizations do not specify very specific procedures for end-user development and control.

MINICOMPUTERS

With the increase in processing power of microcomputers, it is very difficult to define a minicomputer in terms of size other than to say that it is in the range between large mainframes and microcomputers. The internal structure is more like that of a mainframe because they are not designed around a microprocessor like microcomputers. In the early 1960s there was a need, particularly in the data processing and telecommunications areas, for an inexpensive programmable device to perform specific functions. Such a device needed only to provide computer logic; virtually no peripheral devices were needed. A process-oriented minicomputer emerged to fill this demand. Within a few years, however, the technology used within the mini was applied to the development of peripheral devices, and soon after stand-alone machines that could be used in a variety of commercial operations such as airlines reservations, car rentals, banking transactions, and inventory control became available. These early minicomputers had a 16-bit word length, weighed less than one hundred pounds, and required no special air conditioning or other support system. Many cost as much as $50,000 and had limited internal storage capacities.

More recently the reduction in the size and cost as well as an increase in processing capabilities of minis and their associated hardware have been beneficial to medium-size businesses and service facilities, such as sales offices and factories. Many microcomputer applications have been ported (converted) to minicomputers, and minicomputer manufacturers have been working closely with microcomputer manufacturers to develop a smooth interface between micros and minis. Moreover many have developed database management systems which can easily support multiuser accounting activities. As a result minicomputer systems have experienced a phenomenal growth, and mini systems are now available with more power and capabilities than some old mainframe computers. This resulted in an expansion of distributed processing systems for remote plants in other locations because they could now afford their own computer. In other words, the phenomenal growth of distributed processing networks and the communication networks which have developed around these networks was in a large part encouraged by the development of minicomputers.

With the increase in size and power of microcomputers and the development of multiuser systems and local area networks, however, the future of minicomputers is in doubt for many of the new microcomputers rival their processing power and data manipulation capabilities.

LOCAL AREA NETWORKS

Microcomputer hardware and software, such as that noted, earlier provide managers and accountants with data processing resources formerly provided by larger mainframe and minicomputer systems. Unlike these larger systems, microcomputer resources tend to be highly decentralized with little or no capability for sharing and coordinating accounting data transaction processing tasks. Consequently, microcomputers are employed primarily as stand-alone systems for personal productivity tasks such as those noted earlier. Their inability to communicate with other computer systems except via modems has severely limited their application and usefulness.

To overcome these deficiencies, an increasing number of firms are installing local area networks (LANs).[1] A LAN is a communication network that links microcomputers within a limited geographical area. A microcomputer attached to the LAN, commonly referred to as a workstation, is able to share hardware, software, and data with other microcomputers. This capability creates a data processing environment for the microcomputer similar to that of larger mini and mainframe computer systems.

---

[1] A large portion of this section on LANs follows the discussion in "Local Area Networks—Enhancing Microcomputer Productivity," by Robert Kee and Al Leitch, August 1989, reprinted with permission of *CPA Journal,* copyright 1989.

Technology

A LAN consists of two or more microcomputers, electrical cable, usually at least one network server, and an interface board for each microcomputer, as shown in Figure 6-3. The interface board is a printed circuit card installed in one of a microcomputer's expansion slots or it is part of the computer's motherboard. Electrical cable is connected to the interface card for communicating with other microcomputer servers and other peripheral devices attached to the network. Some LANs have larger computers with large disk drives which function as servers that share data and software with other workstations. These servers also manage other resources, such as letter-quality printers, digitizers, plotters, modems, and FAX machines. Some LANs also use bridges (devices that link LANs having similar protocol) and gateways (devices that link LANs having dissimilar protocol) to connect workstations to the firm's other computer systems and networks. Moreover, many LANs can be linked via a gateway to a large mainframe or minicomputer. With an appropriate gateway, microcomputers on the LAN can be used as terminals for the mainframe without an expensive individual terminal emulation board. Employing these interface devices, a workstation is able to communicate with or access hardware, software, and data on other microcomputers as well as on mainframe computer systems at the same location or at remote locations in a distributed network.

Network topology refers to the configuration used to physically link workstations and servers. In general, these configurations parallel those used in distributed networks that are featured in the next chapter. The three most commonly used topologies for LANs are the ring, the star, and the bus (as illustrated in Figure 6-3). A ring uses a closed loop, while a star uses a central hub as the communication pathway between network nodes. A bus, on the other hand, uses a central cable connected by shorter drop cables to link each workstation and server to the network.

Twisted-pair and coaxial ("coax") cable are the most popular electrical mediums used to physically connect workstations and servers. Twisted-pair cable consists of two wires twisted together (to reduce electrical interference), surrounded by an insulating material. Coaxial cable, on the other hand, consists of an inner and outer electrical conductor separated by an insulator which is further protected by an insulation shield. Fiber optic cable is significantly superior to both twisted-pair and coax in data carrying capacity, immunity from electrical interference, and transmission distance. These are increasingly expensive to install. But fiber optic and coax systems can accommodate more traffic than simple twisted-pair cables. Since it does not radiate a signal outside its cable, fiber optics is the most secure type of electrical medium currently available. The major disadvantages of fiber optics is its significantly higher cost and the skill required to install and implement. Figure 6-4 outlines some of the advantages of using different buses and cabling systems.

Network Protocol

Each workstation sends and receives data over a communication medium. Protocols are the methods used to manage the network's communication traffic. The two most commonly used protocols are carrier sense multiple access with colli-

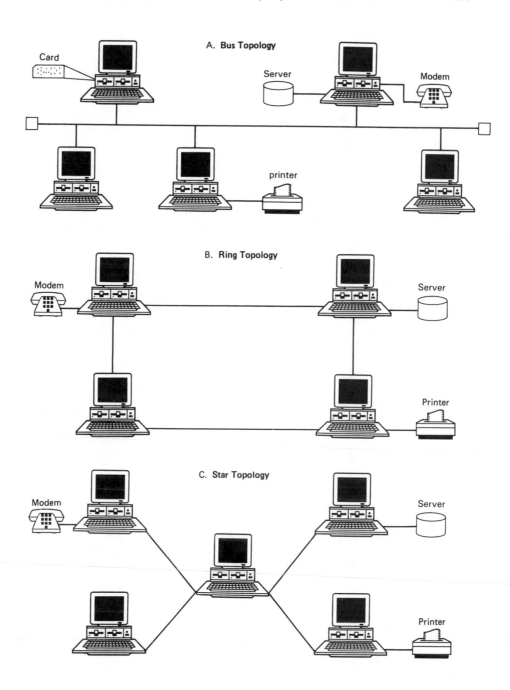

FIGURE 6-3   LAN topology.

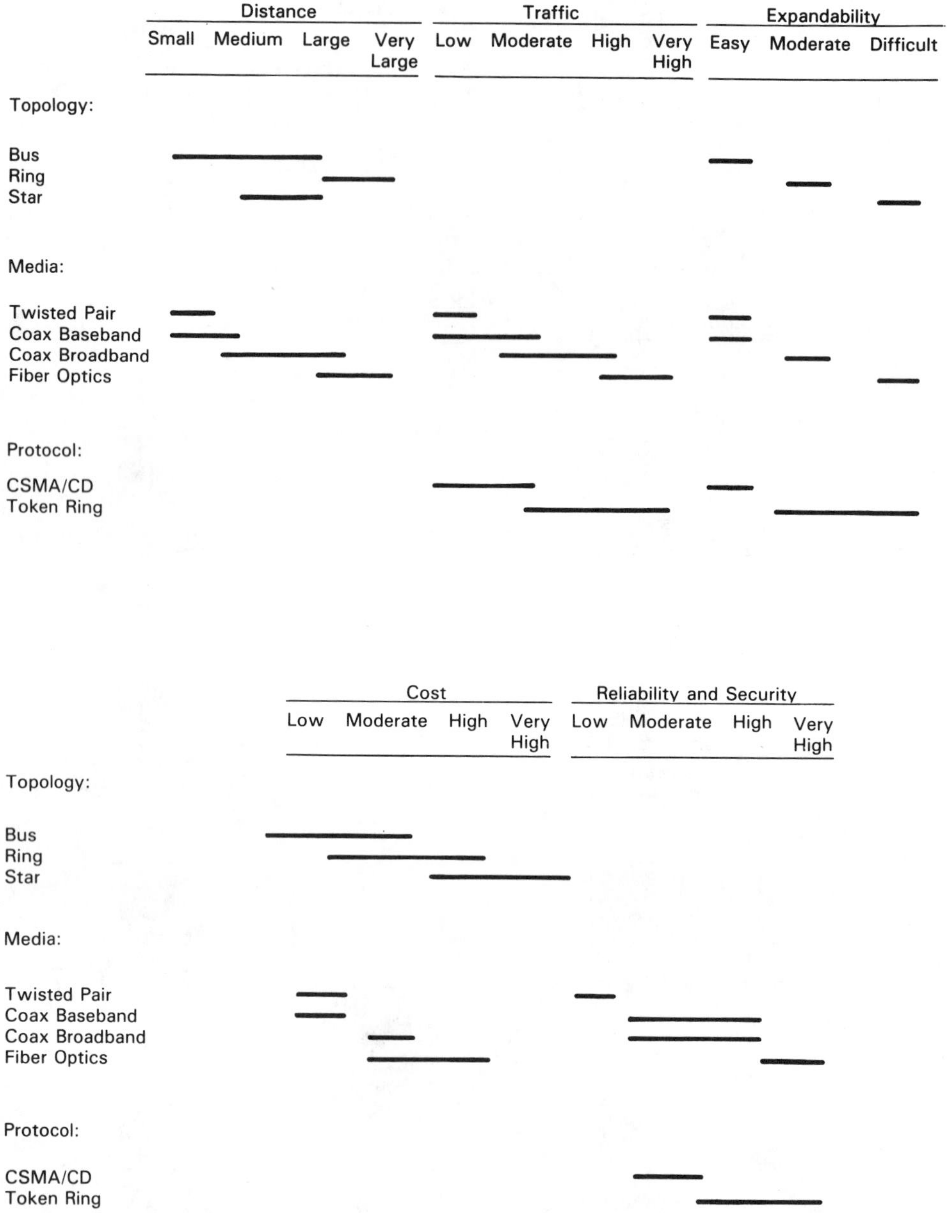

	Distance				Traffic				Expandability		
	Small	Medium	Large	Very Large	Low	Moderate	High	Very High	Easy	Moderate	Difficult
Topology:											
Bus	▬▬▬▬								▬		
Ring			▬▬							▬	
Star		▬▬									▬
Media:											
Twisted Pair	▬				▬				▬		
Coax Baseband	▬▬				▬▬				▬		
Coax Broadband		▬▬▬								▬	
Fiber Optics			▬				▬				▬
Protocol:											
CSMA/CD					▬▬				▬		
Token Ring						▬▬				▬	

	Cost				Reliability and Security			
	Low	Moderate	High	Very High	Low	Moderate	High	Very High
Topology:								
Bus	▬▬▬							
Ring		▬▬						
Star			▬▬					
Media:								
Twisted Pair	▬				▬			
Coax Baseband	▬					▬▬		
Coax Broadband		▬				▬▬		
Fiber Optics		▬▬						▬
Protocol:								
CSMA/CD						▬		
Token Ring							▬▬	

FIGURE 6-4 Advantages and disadvantages of network choices.

sion detection (CSMA/CD) and token passing. CSMA/CD requires workstations to monitor network communication and transmit only when the network is free. When two or more workstations transmit simultaneously, each workstation detects the signal collision, stops transmitting, waits a predetermined length of time, listens for a clear channel, and retransmits. Under light communication loads, CSMA/CD provides an efficient method of controlling network traffic as shown in Figure 6-4. However, as network communication increases its efficiency deteriorates, that is, more and more time is spent recovering from data collisions.

Token passing, on the other hand, sends a stream of data along with a token; a series of bits recognized by each workstation. Only the workstation with the token is permitted to transmit. Token passing effectively avoids the data collisions inherent in CSMA/CD and other protocols. Consequently, it is more efficient under heavy data communication loads.

The type of network communication software also depends on the various layers involved in protocol. The communication layers range from the application to the physical layer. From top (user's view) to bottom (physical hardware) they include application, presentation, session, transport, network data link, and physical layers. Many networks communicate at the data level, whereas others enable one to actually manipulate and use the applications on another computer using the presentation or the application level. Most software is at the low end but this situation is changing rapidly toward parallel processing using the same application. This is where two accounting clerks can manipulate and use the same data file at the same time. In other words, the level of communication and protocol used is in a state of flux and changing rapidly.

Hardware Sharing

One of the most tangible benefits of a LAN is the ability of workstations to share expensive peripheral devices such as hard disk, laser printers, modems, and FAX machines. This results in a higher utilization rate for peripheral devices and substantial cost savings. For large, more sophisticated networks with bridges, gateways, and multiuser software the savings can be even more dramatic.

Sharing Data and Communication

A major limitation of stand-alone microcomputer systems is their inability to share and cooperate in data processing tasks. For example, for several microcomputer users who are not on a network to access a database simultaneously, each user must have a copy of the data file(s). As users modify their files, different versions of the data are created which may lead to errors in the database and reports. Stand-alone microcomputers are similarly limited in their ability to exploit the productivity provided by large integrated software packages which may use a database system. For example, an integrated accounting package in a medium-size firm may require several microcomputers to process the daily volume of transactions. However, only one user can access the program and data files with a stand-alone system. As a result, larger and more integrated accounting data processing tasks have been delegated to multiusers mini and mainframe systems.

The communication capability of a LAN enables workstations to share data as well as hardware and software. Workstations are able to access data from a central database stored on the network's disk server. Record and file locking systems can prevent users from accessing a record currently being updated. These facilities permit multiple users to simultaneously access a database while maintaining data integrity. Equally important, it permits users to share and coordinate accounting transaction processing tasks necessary to implement large, integrated software packages. For example, with an integrated accounting package a LAN permits one clerk to record sales, another to record customer payments, while a third can answer customer requests for their account balance. Each of these clerks is able to work with the same set of programs and files. This capability permits microcomputer users to perform many of the data processing tasks normally delegated to larger mini and mainframe multiuser systems.

Electronic Mail and Office Automation

Electronic mail is a major, although frequently overlooked, benefit of a LAN. Most network vendors provide the ability to compose and send messages to another user or group of users on the LAN. This has the potential to greatly reduce telephone traffic. If LANs are linked to mini and mainframe computer systems, electronic mail is a potentially powerful means of integrating corporate-wide communication. With a modem on the LAN, managers away from the office can receive and send messages and files over the phone. Managers can interface with data, application programs, and office personnel to communicate and perform data processing tasks as if they were at the office.

A LAN provides the communication facilities via a shared getaway to the mainframe operating system for linking the firm's separate computer and data processing resources to form an integrated system. A LAN's operating system and communication medium provide the control and communication functions necessary to implement office automation.

Stand-Alone System

One of the most important advantages of a LAN is that workstations can operate independently of the network. Unlike a terminal on a mini or mainframe system, a workstation is still a computer system under the control of the user. Consequently, it can still be used as a stand-alone system for many personal productivity tasks.

Network Administration

A LAN, like any computer system, must be managed to achieve optimal results. The LAN administrator is responsible for managing the network, establishing security, and providing end users with support. Network management involves supervising the daily operations of the LAN, such as daily start up, monitoring the hardware and software to see that it is functioning properly, and periodically copying user files for backup purposes. The network management software is provided by many of the LAN vendors for monitoring the traffic over the network and preparing various statistics on the volume, origin, and destination of traffic to assist the administrator in his or her task.

Another major aspect of network administration involves establishing and maintaining network security. Security programs with password features enable the administrator to restrict network entry to authorized users and to limit their access to specific data files and application programs. The security programs maintain a log of each entry on the system and file access.

The final and perhaps the most important task of the network administrator is to serve as a resource person for system users. A capable administrator using an effective network manager is crucial to the daily operations of a LAN, ensuring that it fulfills the data processing role(s) for which it was designed.

LAN Summary

In general, a LAN can greatly expand the potential of microcomputers. Using a LAN they can provide some of the support found in mainframe or minicomputer systems. LANs enable microcomputers to share many data, software, and hardware resources. Accountants and managers can use integrated accounting systems in a multiuser environment. Each user can easily communicate with other users over the network. In addition each workstation may be used independently of the network as a stand-alone system. A LAN thus enables microcomputer users to exploit many of the advantages of both a multiuser and stand-alone system. This capability substantially enhances the microcomputer's usefulness for current transaction processing and accounting tasks as well as provides opportunities to exploit newer and much more powerful applications.

MICRO–MAINFRAME LINKS

Many of the distributed networks which will be discussed in the next chapter, as well as the local area networks cited in this chapter, require that microcomputers be linked to mainframe CPUs. This is necessary to interact with large databases, to communicate with others on a network, and to analyze data (even if it is stored locally) using sophisticated software, decision support models, and complex software necessary to support the more advanced executive information and expert systems of the future. The difficulty with this linkage is that one is dealing with two vastly different operating environments. The simple VDT terminals are relatively easy to use as input and output devices, even if modems are used for remote access, because they do not have any processing capability. Personal computers, however, do have this processing ability and as a result software and hardware is necessary to translate input and output from one operating system to another. In a one-to-one situation, an emulation package and a card can be inserted into the PC. In local area networks, an emulation controller can be used with a gateway to bridge this gap between operating systems. In these later cases an emulation card is not required for each PC.

SUMMARY

The advent of microcomputers, their power and speed, and their connectivity to other microcomputers as well as other types of computers have greatly expanded the computational power of many organizations. Small organizations can now use a computer for a variety of personnel productivity, accounting, and data management needs. Larger organizations can place PCs on the desk of many of their managers to help them access data and make more informed decisions. Moreover, all of these can be linked via local area networks and via wide area networks using telecommunications, as will be discussed in the next chapter. The result is that accountants and managers can now perform many information and data management tasks that they did not even dream were feasible just a few years ago.

SELECTED REFERENCES

ARTHUR ANDERSEN & CO., *Trends in Information Technology: 1986.* Chicago, Ill.: Arthur Andersen & Co., 1986.

DERFLER, FRANK J., JR., "Building Work Group Solutions," *PC Magazine,* November 29, 1988, pp. 92–112.

HEID, JIM, "MAC vs PC," *Macworld,* March 1991, pp. 120–129.

KEE, ROBERT, and AL LEITCH, "Local Area Networks–Enhancing Microcomputer Productivity" *The CPA Journal,* August 1989, pp. 16–23.

KOSIUR, DAVE, "Managing Networks," *Macworld,* February 1991, pp. 152–159.

MCKEOWN, PATRICK G., *Living with Computers,* 3rd ed. San Diego: Harcourt Brace Jovanovich Inc., 1991.

OVERBEY, JOHN T., JO ANN C. CARLAND, and JAMES W. CARLAND, "Impact of Microcomputers on Accounting Systems," *Journal of Systems Management,* June 1987, pp. 20–21.

RIZZO, JOHN, and JON ZILBER, "Networking the '90s," *MacUser,* January 1991, pp 92–97.

REVIEW QUESTIONS

1. What are the five basic components of a microcomputer?

2. What is meant by a 32-bit processor and how does this compare with a 16-bit processor?

3. What is the difference between RAM and ROM?

4. What have more recent operating systems enabled PC users to do to enhance their personal productivity?

5. What are minicomputers used for in today's organizations?

6. What is the advantage of the Macintosh and Microsoft Windows user interface?

7. Give some examples of personal productivity uses of PCs in an auditing firm. Give one example for each type of software and one which takes advantage of integrated software.

8. How is a minicomputer different from a microcomputer?

9. Cite several mainframe and minicomputer connectivity (data interchange) problems with microcomputers.

10. What does a LAN enable a firm A to do compared with firm B which only has stand-alone microcomputers?

11. Describe the three major topologies used in LANs.

12. Compare the three major cable types used to connect LANs.

13. Compare the CSMA/CD and the token passing protocol.

14. What is the role of a LAN administrator?

15. What is the advantage of a 25 megahertz, 32-bit processor compared with an 8 megahertz, 16-bit processor?

CASES

6-1 Golden Island Real Estate has had its customer-based accounts and database on a 286 PC for some time now. They are considering adding a graphics capacity to their listing database so they can show to customers pictures (in color) of their listings on the PC screen.

REQUIRED:

1. Explain why they may want to upgrade their computer to handle this graphics requirement. What new microprocessor would you recommend?

2. Why might a RISC chip based PC help with their graphics processing?

6-2 Lexington Manufacturing, a small company that manufactures low-energy lights, needs a microcomputer to schedule its production. For the process of scheduling production, it needs to know what is in stock and what sales orders it has to fill by certain dates. Moreover, they need information on the parts and manufacturing sequence of each light. They could model all this; but they are not math wizards. They would like to view the schedule, inventory, parts, manufacturing sequence, and sales order file at the same time and work with all of this information on the PC screen as they used to do when all this data was in hard copy (paper) form.

In addition, the sales people, as they work with these files, need to continue to update sales and inventory files. As lights are manufactured, factory personnel will need to input schedule and production transactions, such as material requisitions, and additions to work in process and finished goods.

REQUIRED: Assume that manufacturing, scheduling, sales, shop-flow supervisors, and clerical personnel all have PC terminals. Can you, as their accountant, suggest some key features their personal computer system should have to accomplish all these processing tools?

6-3 The training of new accounting and reservation personnel is very costly for Mid South Air a commuter airline serving several small towns in the Mississippi delta. They use PCs as terminals to process all accounting and reservation transactions. They have been keying in data using old DOS commands for several years and it has taken hours to train personnel to do this task accurately.

REQUIRED: As their accountant, suggest how some newer user interface (both hardware and software) can be used to cut this training cost.

6-4 The home office of Quality Rental located in Kansas City, is converting its old manual accounting, rental contract, and inventory system to a microcomputer system. All the clerical and managerial personnel will need to communicate with each other and share a common inventory of rental equipment. This inventory will need to be kept up to date as new contracts are prepared and equipment returned. Moreover, all rental fees need to be recorded as equipment is rented.

REQUIRED: Without the assistance of a systems analyst, suggest the nature of the PC hardware and software needed to configure a system that will enable management to accomplish these tasks.

6-5 Fred Manning, owner of Manning Construction Company, has been told that he can benefit from linking his accounting staff's microcomputer into a local area network. He was told this by a computer store salesperson and he is suspicious that he may be buying Florida swamp land.

REQUIRED: He has asked you, as his independent accountant, to list the potential benefits he may receive from a local area network.

7

SYSTEM STRUCTURES AND ASSOCIATED HARDWARE

In earlier chapters we discussed the three dimensions of information systems—(management activities, organizational functions, and data processing (elements)—and noted that these can be linked in a variety of ways. In this chapter we describe and discuss in some detail hardware and communication linkages for centralized and decentralized (distributed) processing systems. A number of firms still employ very centralized systems, but, because of the expanding technology of minicomputers and microprocessors, distributed processing has become a widely used structure in information systems. The objective of this chapter is to further examine these system structures. To provide a better understanding of these and other systems, we will trace the evolution of information systems from the basic, custodial transaction processing systems that existed prior to computers, up to and including distributed systems. In particular, we will examine some of the hardware used to support each of these systems.

Because batch processing and on-line processing are modes of operations that can be employed in a variety of system structures, including centralized as well as distributed processing systems, we will discuss these processing modes prior to examining the evolution of systems.

BATCH PROCESSING AND ON-LINE PROCESSING

The two general modes of operations that can exist, separately or jointly, in an information system, are *batch processing* and *on-line processing*. Under batch processing, similar transactions are accumulated into "batches" and processed periodically. In using on-line[1] processing, records are updated as transactions occur. In an on-line system, input/output (I/O) devices, data files, application software, and associated equipment are directly connected to the computer through networks or via telecommunications so that transactions can be transferred to and from the computer with a minimum of manual intervention.

Batch Processing

In batch processing, the data relating to the same type of transaction are first gathered into a batch and totaled. Then they are converted into a machine-readable form using a keying operation or some method of scanning. After they are edited, they are sorted into a logical order which matches the order of the master file to be updated if sequential files are used. They are then processed, in batches, against the master file in a processing run. The batch may then be sorted in another order and processed in another run to update another master file. Sometimes several runs will be needed to update the appropriate files. In a batch processed payroll system, all data relating to payroll checks (such as hours worked during the time period, vacation days taken, and routine hours worked) are accumulated before the processing of checks can be accomplished. For a batch processed payroll system, employee number or department number would probably be sequenced to control the batching of the input data.

In general, however, batch processing computer systems involve the same basic accounting cycles, reports, and files as manual systems. They tend to do more because they are automated and can process at a much greater speed than manual systems. They can also take advantage of computerized controls such as the comparison of control totals with the detail amounts in the batch, and can print out error messages when an edit check fails.

BATCH PROCESSING WITH SEQUENTIAL ACCESS FILES. Figure 7-1 illustrates the structure of a batch processing system with sequential files. In this type of system, the entire master file is read and written each time transactions are processed against it. This update activity requires sorting all input transactions into the same sequence that is found in the master file. The hardware, application software, and operating system within the CPU required for this processing procedure would be very elementary.

To better understand the structure of a sequential batch processing system, we will examine the detailed operation of a payroll system. A master file contains permanent employee information, such as the (1) name; (2) badge number; (3) address; (4) department; (5) number of exemptions; (6) miscellaneous deductions (such as insurance premiums or retirement contributions); (7) year-to-date pay; and (8) year-to-date withholdings. Transaction data in this case

---

[1] A version of the on-line mode may be classified as *real time*. This means that data are processed and handled so that the resulting information is retrieved in sufficient time to control the operating environment.

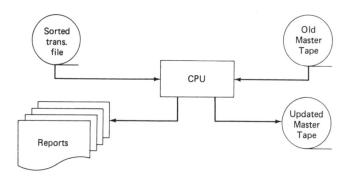

FIGURE 7-1 Batch processing sequential files.

would be on employee time records, which contain the (1) badge number; (2) hours worked; (3) overtime hours; (4) job classification (if variable); and (5) incentive bonus (if applicable). Using the transaction data and the master file, the payroll processing program performs three functions: (1) it checks the master file for the employee number and matches it with the employee number on the transaction card (recall that the input data are sorted prior to processing); (2) it generates employee payroll checks, as well as information for cost control and the general ledger; and (3) it updates the master file so that current records will be available for the next processing cycle.

There are many advantages of a batch processing system over an on-line system. First, sequential batch processing systems are relatively simple. Since the system is designed and operated around the traditional manual accounting process, it can easily be controlled and audited. Moreover, management can easily understand the system without a great deal of study of computer hardware or software. Generalized software programs are readily available from software vendors that are easy to modify for any business. This is particularly true for small firms using microcomputers. These systems are relatively inexpensive due to the simplicity of batch processing and the wide applicability of general software. They are very efficient for processing large batches (high volume) of transactions. They make effective use of batch controls. Finally, they are easier to audit due to their simplicity and it is easy to follow audit trails.

Though a number of advantages exist for batch processing systems with sequential files, there are also limitations and shortcomings compared with on-line systems. First, because a multiple number of processing runs involving several subsystems are needed to make up a total accounting information system, duplicate items of information exist on many files. A large amount of manual data handling is involved, and duplicate input data are often required because each processing program essentially operates independently of other programs. Second, records are out of date until the next batch is run. For example, an inventory item may be sold out due to a sales transaction and another sales representative may attempt to sell the same items because he or she does not know they are out of stock until the next batch of sales is processed. The time between processing runs is called a processing cycle. Data will not be updated until the next cycle which may be a day, a week or even a month away.

BATCH PROCESSING WITH RANDOM ACCESS FILES.   Batch processing is not limited to sequential access files. The basic batch processing system shown in Figure 7-1 can be modified by replacing the magnetic tape units with some type of random access storage device such as a magnetic disk.

There are several key advantages of random access batch processing compared to sequential batch processing: (1) on-line interrogation of the status of information is feasible; (2) application programs and files can be stored on the disk, thus eliminating the need for inputting the programs and files each time a different application is to be used (which is necessary under the basic batch processing system involving a sequence of runs); and (3) it is not necessary to sequence the input data, since any record in the mass-storage device is readily available regardless of the order in which records are input. Therefore extensive sorting of data is eliminated.

The key disadvantage is that an audit trail is more complex and as such may be difficult to maintain. When transaction data are processed, the master record is read (but not destroyed) from storage. The record is updated in the CPU, and the updated record is written back into mass storage. The writing of the updated record back into mass storage automatically eliminates the old record. Thus the audit trail is destroyed unless the mass storage is periodically dumped (copied) to another medium of storage and copies of all transaction data are preserved. The dumping of the mass-storage device provides information as to the status of records at specific points of time, and a chronological transaction log is kept to trace changes that have occurred between dumps. For example, the most recent balance for a given data item can be determined from a current dump, and the balance at the beginning of the period can be determined from the previous dump. The transaction log helps determine which transactions affect the new balance.

LOCAL AND REMOTE MODES OF BATCH PROCESSING.   Batch processing, regardless of whether it is accomplished with sequential or random files, can be structured to operate in two modes: (1) local batch; and (2) remote batch. In *local batch processing,* data are accumulated into batches within the firm and sent directly to the computer for processing. Reports and printed output documents are returned to the user within the firm. No data communication equipment is required, since the input data are processed on the firm's premises. In *remote batch processing,* a data communication system or a network is employed to transmit data that has been batched at remote locations. These remote locations are distant from the main computer installation.

SERVICE BUREAUS.   Sometimes an organization will contract with an outside organization to do some of its batch processing. It may send transactions in batch to a service bureau to process the data and generate needed reports. Many early payroll systems for smaller organizations used this mode of processing. The disadvantage of such an arrangement is that the organization loses control of its data processing operations. The advantage is that it can do some information processing without any investment or minimal expertise in information processing.

On-Line Processing

On-line processing is the processing of transactions and inquiries as they occur. Typical applications of on-line processing are airlines reservation systems, bank deposit and transfer accounting, hotel reservation systems, sales order entry, JIT inventory systems, hospital patient record systems, savings and loan accounting, and stock market information systems. Data stored in direct-access media are always kept current in order to reflect the status of the firm. All information is available at all times for immediate management use in an on-line system.[2] On-line storage devices are required for on-line systems. Also needed are input and output devices such as terminals; microcomputers which function as terminals in some cases; and point-of-sale (POS) scanners such as those found in supermarket checkout lines which can accommodate on-line input and output. Moreover, provisions must be made for files or databases to be maintained along with appropriate application software to be on line in order to handle data input and the random processing of a variety of transactions and requests for output.

Procedurally, an on-line system functions as shown in Figure 7-2. Data are first input immediately into the computer system (often source documents do not exist in a hard copy form). It is edited at the point at which it is input. Various procedures are used to edit the data. There are formatted screens where all the user does is fill in the blanks. Menus are often used to direct the user to the appropriate screen or course of action. Sometimes, an input sequence is dictated by a series of computer prompts to assist the user. In all cases, a set of edit routines is used to help ensure that the data is as accurate and as complete as possible. Exceptions are noted and corrected, in most cases immediately, before the computer will accept the transaction. Edited data is then used to directly update the files, as noted in the previous discussion of batch processing and random access files. A transaction log is generated. This log may be stored and sorted by transaction type to yield a record of various types of transactions such as cash receipts. Thus, if management wishes, it can generate various journals found in manual and batch systems.

On-line systems tend to differ significantly from manual and batch systems. The files and processing steps tend to be highly integrated. Integrated systems are those in which many of the accounting applications, report generation activities, and queries use common data files or a database and are closely linked. For example, a sales transaction will result in the immediate update of the sales file, the accounts receivable file, the inventory file, and the possible generation of a purchase order for more stock if inventory falls below a specified level. Often databases are used for integrated systems instead of separate files for each appli-

---

[2] *Time sharing* is a special-purpose form of on-line processing designed to serve the problem-solving, instead of transaction-handling, needs of users. Many users at different locations can be linked to one computer facility in a time-shared network. Under a time-sharing structure, remote terminals are used for developing and testing programs. Because it is interactive it is the preferred program development environment. It is also used for entering data and retrieving information from files. A large number of users are handled in the time-sharing mode by allocating and controlling the amount of CPU time available to each user. The operating system within the CPU allocates time so that each user is unaware that access to the CPU is being shared.

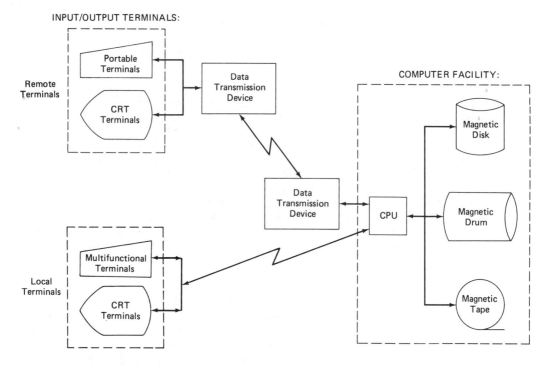

FIGURE 7-2 On-line systems.

cation. Moreover, output can be generated on demand by management. This is not the case in unintegrated, sequential batch processing systems. As a result, there are several significant advantages to on-line input and processing systems. First, information is always up to date for management use. Data is edited prior to entry into the system by referencing various records. Transcription errors are reduced because data are entered into the system directly, not first entered onto a form then keyed into the system. Further, redundant data is often reduced since files tend to be integrated into a database. The disadvantages are that on-line systems require more sophisticated hardware and software; this leads to an increase in complexity and cost. Exposure is often increased due to the number of terminals used in the system and controls need to be established to ensure the integrity of the files or the database. Audit trails tend to be more difficult to establish because of the on-line update procedure which erases historical data and replaces it with new data. Finally, data entry is relatively slow due to the random nature of transactions, the files which need to be accessed, the applications which need to be called, and the complex editing routines. This makes on-line procedures awkward to use in high-volume input and output situations such as the preparation of monthly statements for a large retail store.

A special class of on-line processing includes *real time processing*. Real time processing actually controls the activity. Examples would include the automatic granting of credit at the time of sale using on-line access to customer records to assess credit risk. Another example would be issuance of a purchase order when stock reaches a critical level based on information from an on-line inventory system.

In summary, sequential batch input and processing systems update single files sequentially and generally involve one application and file per run. On-line input and processing directly updates files. It often involves several applications. On-line processing requires random access storage. Batch systems are usually not integrated. On-line systems are often integrated in terms of data and applications. Combinations of these systems may be used, such batch processing of random files which enables management to use batch controls and input as well as on-line processing to output. These combinations of the two systems' use corresponding advantages. Moreover, it may be justified in some cases to use on-line input and batch processing and batch output. For example, a supermarket may collect its data as transactions occur at the checkout counter, but update its inventory and issue purchase orders for new merchandise in a batch mode once a day.

EVOLUTION OF ACCOUNTING SYSTEMS

This evolution, as pointed out in Chapter 1, has been led by many new developments in information technology. The overall result is that today accountants and managers have access to vast amounts of information to help with transaction processing, decision making, and even adding value to goods and services.

Traditional Manual Accounting Systems

Prior to the introduction of computers, information systems were concerned with providing historical summaries of a company's performance. The focus was on financial statement preparation. Little, if any, emphasis was placed on providing feedback and control information related to controlling day-to-day operations, let alone providing accounting information for managerial and strategic decision making. Traditional accounting information systems, therefore, were relatively simple, historically oriented, and founded on financial transactions. They typically consisted of a number of single subsystems such as accounts payable, accounts receivable, and the general ledger. There was no attempt to integrate files that might serve several functions or managerial activities. Each subsystem was treated as a separate entity.

Computerized Transaction Processing Systems

Computerized information systems began in 1950s with transaction processing systems. They were effective in keeping customer account information and inventory information and they were programmed to produce periodic reports to help operations management cope with the daily activities of the organization.

RESPONSIBILITY REPORTING SYSTEMS.   Manual and computerized transaction processing systems provided an overall historical picture of the firm and its operations; but they did little in terms of providing information to the managers responsible for activities at different levels within the firm. To overcome this deficiency, responsibility reporting systems emerged along with the introduction of computers. They were designed around a firm's organizational structure and designed to provide historical (often summarized) data at specified time intervals to the various managerial (responsibility) levels within the firm. Thus, they differed from the traditional financial accounting system in that they were based on budgets and lines of authority. In general, budgets were constructed from the top level of management to the lowest responsibility level in the firm. Every manager at every level participated in the preparation of the budget at his or her level of responsibility. Monthly reports of actual results were then compared with the budget using the responsibility reporting system. An example is provided in Chapter 3. A manager was held responsible for unfavorable deviations of actual costs or other goals from budgeted goals at his or her responsibility level. As a result, management accounting information began to be used on a widespread basis in many organizations. While the responsibility system concept predated the introduction of computers, computer technology made it feasible to pull together all the information which affected a particular responsibility center and compare the results of that center's operations with planned outcomes.

INTEGRATED TRANSACTION PROCESSING SYSTEMS. Early developments in transaction processing systems led to a piecemeal approach to the development and use of accounting systems because applications followed the organizational boundaries of the firm. Duplicate data and, in many cases, duplicate computer programs and subsystems existed. For example, marketing may have a customer file and the accounts receivable section of accounting may also have a customer file; and the two may not always agree. Most systems continued to be batch processing.

Recognizing this problem, those who design accounting information systems more recently have focused on linking the transaction processing activities of the firm by integrating the organization's major functions such as finance, marketing, and production. This has been made possible by the advent of the on-line input, storage, and processing capabilities of the newer, more powerful computers. The introduction of database models and technology has also helped to integrate the processing of transactions. For example, today a sale can be keyed into a terminal, the database is updated and as a result all accounts receivable, inventory, and sales data are immediately updated because they use a common set of data which resides in the database. More will be said about how databases operate later in this text.

In contrast, in a nonintegrated system, each application is separate, there is no common set of data, and attempts to link applications are minimal. Often data needs to be merged and sorted between applications if they are used by more than one application.

Management Information Systems (MIS)

BATCH SYSTEMS. In the 1960s, the speed and the power of the computer increased and this enabled managers to process more operational information and to use this information more effectively in the decision-making process. Many periodic reports were generated by these information systems to track the organization's operations and to provide management with summarized figures on these operations so that they could monitor their operations. As a result of the new developments in computer hardware as well as software, these reports went far beyond simple responsibility accounting reports.

As a result, management information systems (MIS) emerged. These resulted in a framework designed to provide decision-oriented information for management to use to plan, control, and evaluate the organization's activities. The focus of all systems prior to MIS was primarily to provide financial transaction information. A management information system, on the other hand, focuses on generation of reports and information that will assist management in all aspects of the organization, including the production and marketing of goods and services. Financial transactions and reports were generated by the system as a byproduct of management reports.

Figure 7-3 illustrates an integrated management information system. To specifically illustrate an integrated MIS framework, consider the receipt of a customer order. The order becomes part of an open order file that is used for preparing invoices and ultimately updating the accounts receivable file. Since the order will result in the production and shipment of a product, it has an impact on the raw material inventory file, production scheduling plans, labor scheduling routines, finished goods inventory file, shipping orders file, sales commission records, and market forecast routines. After processing of a number of incoming customer orders, the raw material inventory subsystem will probably trigger the issuance of a purchase order for raw materials. The raw material subsystem includes a routine decision-making program that will enable the computer to generate a purchase order using the reorder quantity, reorder point, and economic order quantity and mathematical model telling it when to act. The purchase order will also result in a credit to the accounts payable file.

The management information systems expanded the scope of the information provided to management to aid in operational and managerial decision making. However, the early versions of such systems are deficient in that they were batch oriented (refer to Figure 7-3). This was true even when random access devices were employed. Data thus had to be accumulated over time before processing occurred. This meant that information was not as current as it could be for decision making and operational control. This deficiency in management information systems was primarily due to the lack of equipment and software necessary to support on-line processing.

ON-LINE MANAGEMENT INFORMATION SYSTEMS.   While there is still widespread use of these batch systems for the reasons cited earlier in this chapter, the development of advanced hardware and software systems has led to on-line management accounting information systems. These emerged when on-line input/output and mass storage devices became readily available and when advanced software in the form of operating systems, multiprogramming, and multiprocessing were developed. Figure 7-4 illustrates an on-line integrated information system for a manufacturing firm.

On-line processing capabilities may even provide a control feedback mechanism to control operations. If this control is present the system is called a *real-time* on-line system. To clarify the real-time nature of the system, we will focus

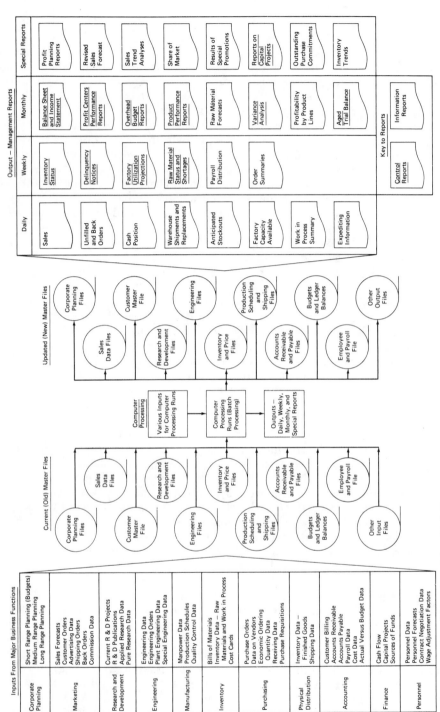

FIGURE 7-3 Integrated *management information system.*
Source: Robert J. Thierauf, *Distributed Processing Systems,* © 1978, pp. 18–19. Reprinted by permission of Prentice-Hall, Inc., Englewood Cliffs, N.J.

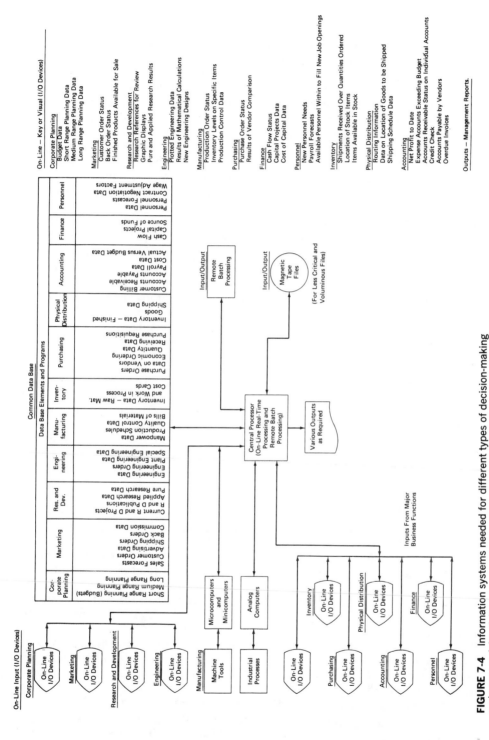

FIGURE 7-4 Information systems needed for different types of decision-making and managerial activity.

Source: Robert J. Thierauf, *Distributed Processing Systems*, © 1978, pp. 18–19. Reprinted by permission of Prentice Hall, Inc., Englewood Cliffs, New Jersey.

177

on the production area. We will assume that on-line terminals exist throughout the area and all variable manufacturing data are entered as they occur. The on-line database for this function, as well as those for related managerial activities, is always up to date. We will also assume that a scheduling subsystem is used to aid management in controlling the manufacturing area. At the beginning of each day the computerized scheduler simulates the activities in the manufacturing area and identifies work assignments and flow rates for all operations. When a breakdown or an unexpected bottleneck occurs in the area during the day, the information is fed back to the scheduler and to management. The scheduler computes new alternative work assignments and sends the information to the production manager for a decision. A report is also generated showing the impact on flow rates and shipping schedules, and the critical areas that require immediate attention. The system in essence provides a response that is fed back in sufficient time to control the daily manufacturing activities. Thus we have a real-time system.

All processing activities need not be on line; in many cases it is more economical to employ a batch processing approach. If the areas involved are widely dispersed geographically, then remote batch processing may be applicable, even if hardware may exist to support on-line processing. The cost of on-line processing, in general, is more than that of batch processing. If on-line is not required, batch processing may be the desired alternative, as noted earlier in this chapter.

DISTRIBUTED PROCESSING MIS.   Just as on-line processing was brought about by the development of hardware such as on-line CRT terminals and support software such as multiprogramming, distributed processing became economically feasible when low-cost minicomputers, microcomputers, terminals, and communications hardware and software became readily available. Organizational reasons for distributed systems were discussed in Chapter 3. A number of other factors, however, influenced the development of distributed accounting information systems. First, because integrated systems were historically built around one or more large centralized processing units, bottlenecks often occurred both in the input of data and in the feedback of output information. This weakness could be overcome to some extent by employing on-line capabilities. The costly random access devices and remote terminals employed in an on-line structure require large financial commitments at the initial development of the system. Many companies were unwilling or unable to commit such enormous amounts of capital and time. Second, in a centralized on-line MIS system, data security and vulnerability often become a problem. All data are forwarded to the central facility where without appropriate controls, many people have access to the data. In a large centralized MIS system operating in a heavily loaded multiprogramming and/or teleprocessing environment, line failures and teleprocessing problems are also a problem. More important, data were not controlled by users, who were often scattered in plants and offices throughout the country or world. These users wanted more autonomy and control over data.

Many of these problems were overcome by distributing data processing to remote sites where local managers would have control over their information processing. These remote sites would be linked to a central facility via communications systems.

Decision Support System (DSS)

While the development of MIS was an important step in providing managers with the information they need to make better operational decisions, managers were unable to ask questions of an MIS or to find solutions to many managerial and operational problems. The limitations of these systems were discussed in Chapter 4. For example, decision models were needed in evaluating trends, identifying favorable or unfavorable deviations in preestablished plans, and suggesting corrective action for areas that were out of control. Moreover, it was useful to present managers only with situations which needed attention, such as those which were exceptions to planned results. This type of activity is often called management by exception and systems were needed to support this method of management. To do this required the combination of the reporting function of MIS with graphics, the analytical and statistical problem-solving capabilities of management science, and a presentation mode that managers could easily use, because some part of the problems or solutions procedure was unstructured. In the 1970s and 1980s, the power of the computer increased to such an extent that complex mathematical models could now be used to process information, large amounts of data could be easily accessed, software could be made more user friendly, and the size of the computers was reduced so that managers could now have a computer sitting on their desk that was as powerful as the earlier computers in the 1960s. This has enabled managers to interact with data and generate the kind of information they need to make decisions and not to have to wait for a periodic report which may or may not give them the critical information they need to make a decision.

An information system which will do this is called a decision support system (DSS) because it supports decision makers at the managerial level with their tactical decisions rather than just providing MIS reports on past events. These tactical decisions tend not to be as well structured, often involve uncertainty, and require external data. These accounting-based decision support systems will be discussed in length in Chapter 17.

Executive Information System (EIS)

As personal computers became a commonplace occurrence in business, industry, and government in the middle 1980s, it became clear that while a DSS is very useful to managers who are comfortable with the computer, something else was needed for high-level executives. Many of these decision makers either did not have the time or the computer knowledge to work with a DSS. It was for them that executive information systems (EIS) began to be developed in the late 1980s. These systems tend to be less model oriented than DSS. An EIS frequently uses a personal computer interface that makes a heavy use of graphics and summary information based on a wealth of data, to display information for executives who make managerial and strategic decisions.

In addition to these information systems, two other systems are also becoming more important to accountants. These are strategic information systems

(SIS) and experts systems (ES). An SIS enables the organization to use strategic information for a competitive advantage, as suggested in earlier chapters. An ES provides staff as well as professional employees with the knowledge and expertise needed to do their jobs better. Expert systems are discussed in Chapter 17.

Office Information Systems

While the information systems just discussed were being developed, the office was also changing. Office automation evolved with the introduction of the personal computer in the early 1980s and with the expansion of the telephone industry. The PC and its related systems have been combined with network software and communications devices like the FAX machine to create an office information system capable of supporting and interfacing with the other information systems noted earlier.

DISTRIBUTED PROCESSING AND DATA NETWORKS

Distributed processing overcomes some of the limitations and deficiencies of centralized systems by organizing the data processing resources to support remote applications rather than organizing the system around the needs or constraints of a centralized computer site. In essence, distributed processing takes the computer to the job rather than the job to the computer. It means that individual processors, minicomputers, or microcomputers are located at sites remote from the central facility and that these machines handle the major processing operations that were originally handled at the central site. Moreover, management at the local and regional levels is responsible for processing and maintaining many of these applications. In general, local users have the autonomy and control the design. Thus, distributed processing overcomes some of the limitations and deficiencies of integrated centralized systems.

Characteristics of Distributed Processing Systems

The key characteristics that differentiate distributed systems from centralized accounting information systems are: (1) the employment of a *distributed database*; and (2) *local autonomy of data processing operations*. By employing a distributed database, some of the problems encountered with a large centralized database can be overcome. In a distributed database structure, the users' files are placed near the point at which the transactions occur, and therefore the users' data are always available. If data communication failures occur between the distributed site and the central facility, access to the local data is not lost. Likewise, by employing a distributed database, the volume and accuracy of data transmitted to the central site can be controlled. Distributed processing is based on the premise that remote systems with local databases can process and store much of the data that under a centralized framework would be sent to the main computer. Thus, under a distributed database structure, data are processed and stored locally, with only summary information being transmitted to the centralized database.

Partitioned vs. Duplicate Data

One of the arguments for a centralized integrated database is that redundant data are avoided. In a distributed database, a number of separate databases exist, and therefore duplication of data may occur. The challenge in this situation is to make sure that the duplicate sets of data are consistent. This can be accomplished with carefully orchestrated update procedures which make sure all copies are updated as transactions are processed.

Another way to accomplish this data management problem is to partition the data into those records or files that are germane to a particular site. However, provisions need to be made to access these files from other sites, when transactions involve those records. Again, distributed database systems are available to manage these partitioned databases. (Database management systems—DBMS—are examined in Chapters 9 and 10.)

An effective distributed database should have several important features. A user should be able to use data anywhere in the system without knowing where the data is located. A request should be able to be submitted from any site without any perceptual degradation in access or processing performance. A user should also be able to submit a request for data from another location which may use a different local DBMS and not be affected by this difference between DBMS location. The user should be unaware of differences in location, performance, or local DBMS. In other words, a distributed database should have location transparency, performance transparency, and local DBMS transparency.

Autonomy of Data Processing Operations

In a distributed processing structure, local and regional management have more control over hardware and operations, as well as over data processing applications. Transaction processing, management information systems, and to some extent decision support systems may not be dependent upon centralized processing facilities, particularly if a distributed database exists at the remote site. When user friendly processing equipment, such as microcomputers, are employed, source data can be collected and processed and summary management reports can all be generated by non-EDP personnel. In addition, unique or critical processing needs for managerial decision making and operational control can be handled quickly at the local level because program development on a small independent system is usually less demanding and more economical than developing all programs at a central site. In fact, some of the newer software permits end users to quickly develop their own applications and to readily generate their own reports. The development of unique applications at the local level not only ensures responsive service to divisional needs and provides more control to the responsible managers, but also minimizes the impact on central site resources. The central facility can therefore concentrate on programs and problems that have an impact on the entire distributed organization and improve the efficiency of the overall system. Local autonomy thus benefits both the distributed organization, such as a manufacturing or sales division, and the home office. In general, distributed processing systems have the advantages and disadvantages outlined in Figure 7-5.

ADVANTAGES	DISADVANTAGES

1. Local Control of Data and Data Processing
2. Faster Development Time
3. Local Autonomy
4. Reduced Risk of System Failure
5. Reduced Risk of Communication Problems
6. Reduced Cost and Complexity of Centralized
   Computer System
	1. Increased Cost at Remote Sites
	2. Increased Need for Data Processing
	   Personnel at Remote Site
	3. Data Partitioning and Duplication Problems
	4. Less Expertise for Systems Development
	5. Increased Network Costs
	6. Less Control over Data and Access to Data

FIGURE 7-5   Advantages and disadvantages of distributed data processing.

Distributed processing can take several forms. The most basic distributed processing system centers on the local processing of source data. Sometimes this is called *data-entry processing*. Fundamentally, this system consists of single or multiple data-entry units that are distributed throughout the organization at local or regional sites. The system is designed to capture business data at distributed field locations in an organization, as shown in Figure 7-6. Data are entered at the local level and processed by the local system, using a magnetic disk to temporarily hold data. Once the entries have been verified and errors have been corrected, the data are automatically transferred onto a disk and are then transferred in batch mode via a telecommunication device to the central computer facility.

One mode of operation in the data-entry processing arrangement consists of using the data-entry devices in an on line processing environment. This approach allows concurrent entry of source data while batch processing operations take place. Under this arrangement, the local processor must have a partitioned operating system that can handle batch processing communications or other "background processing" activities while simultaneously servicing data-entry devices. In employing this latter approach, it is not necessary to restrict input to local data-entry units while batch processing communications are being handled, which is the case for the more basic arrangement. The batch input data are stored on the magnetic disk medium until a predetermined time or until a specified volume of data is reached, at which point the batch data are transmitted to the central site. It should be noted that in Figure 7-6 a means is provided for on-line processing of source data via a telecommunication device to the central facility. This is an alternative mode of operation. In essence the diagram represents a hybrid form of a distributed batch and on-line system. In this distributed arrangement a database does not exist at the local level. The magnetic disk unit associated with the local processor is used for temporary storage of input data. All error-free data are transmitted to the central site.

Another form or level of distributed processing, which we label *local processing, data management and reporting*, builds upon the framework of data-entry processing by adding local processing of transactions and local preparation of management reports. This is made possible by providing the appropriate hardware and software at the local level to build and maintain a database and to handle local processing. The difference is shown in Figure 7-7. A local database, a local

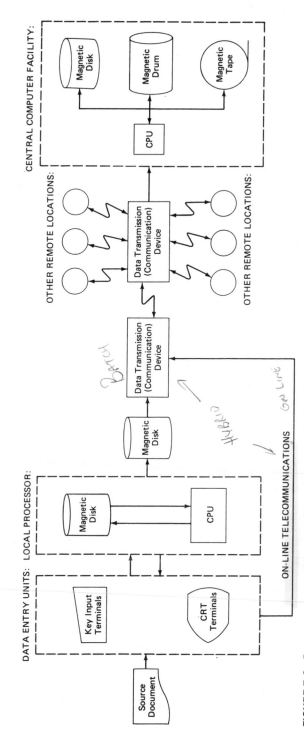

FIGURE 7-6 Data-entry processing arrangement of distributed processing.

183

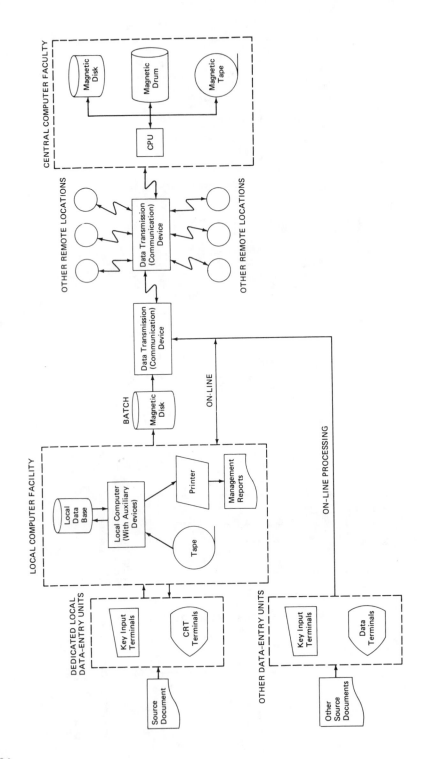

FIGURE 7-7 Local processing, data management, and reporting arrangement of distributed processing.

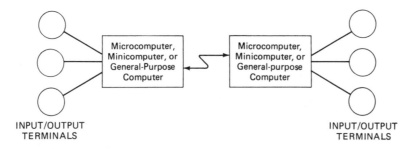

FIGURE 7-8   Point-to-point network.

computer that is capable of handling transactional processing of source input data, and other peripheral devices for input/output at the local level are added to the data-entry system. A means is also provided for on-line updating directly from terminals to the central computer via a communication device. Also a means is provided for the local computer to communicate in an on-line mode with the central computer. This system is capable of handling local operations and producing management information.

Network Structures

The systems just discussed focus on the processing and data management needs of the local plant or division (remote site). Network structures, on the other hand, focus on the communication needs across the firm and at the corporate level (central site). These latter needs arise from two sources: (1) some local operations may need data that are processed and/or stored at other local databases using a partitioning method; and (2) management as the corporate level is interested in how the firm is operating as a whole. Means should exist for accessing these data. Networks, structured by employing hardware such as communication control units and linking architecture, are thus needed to link remote processing centers and, in some cases, to link these with a centralized computer center. At least five basic network structures exist: (1) point-to-point network; (2) hierarchical or tree network; (3) star network; (4) loop or ring network; and (5) fully connected ring network. These parallel the topology used in local area networks discussed in the last chapter. We will examine each briefly.

POINT-TO-POINT NETWORK.   The point-to-point network, which consists of two or more microcomputers, minicomputers, or smaller mainframe computers linked together by a communication line, is the simplest form of a network (see Figure 7-8). In this arrangement each machine performs a specific, often complementary, function. For example, one can be devoted to data processing, while the other, which may be a special-purpose device, performs I/O control functions, including buffering and message switching.

HIERARCHICAL (TREE) AND STAR NETWORKS.   This network configuration complements the hierarchical structure of most firms in that a large or host computer provides the central processing function and dedicated small mainframes,

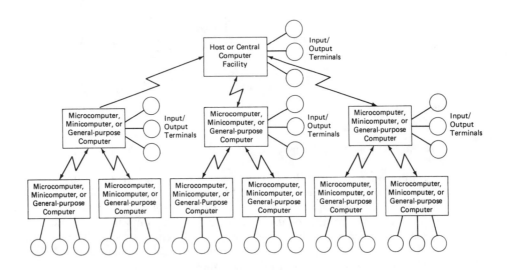

FIGURE 7-9 Hierarchical networks.

minicomputers, or microcomputers perform functional processing that is input to the next higher level in the organization. These distributed systems may use any combination of the arrangements as shown in Figures 7-6 and 7-7. In each case, in a hierarchical configuration, the communications that take place are between processors that exist on different levels. No communication link exists between machines at the same level. Figure 7-9 illustrates a hierarchical or tree network.

Structurally a star network is similar to a two-level hierarchy network with the host at the center. This is simply indicative of a heavier flow of communication existing between each smaller sublevel computer and the large central computer. Branch (remote) computers perform all local operations and communicate with the central site; the central computer controls the combined operations of the network and supplies centralized data as required by the branch units. A typical application of a star network is an airlines reservation and ticketing system.

RING NETWORK. A ring (loop) network is simply a group of mainframe, minicomputers, or microcomputers linked together to form a ring. Each computer is serially linked to the nearest adjacent computer via a communication line. If a unit needs data from a unit not linked directly to it, the request must be routed through all intermediate units. For this reason, a ring configuration is only used when the remote units are physically close together. Otherwise inquiry and data transfers become uneconomical.

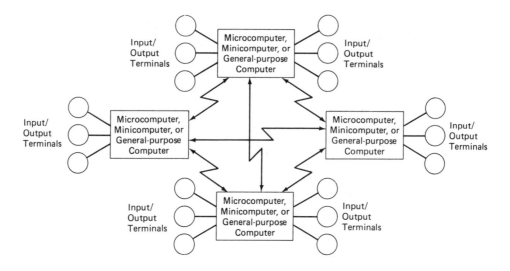

FIGURE 7-10   Ring networks.

The standard form of the ring network is very limited; because of this it is seldom employed in practice. The more commonly used form of a ring is the fully connected ring shown in Figure 7-10. Each mainframe, minicomputer, or microcomputer is cross-linked to every other unit. There is no central computer, and the cross-linking circumvents any breakdown in the flow of data or communications anywhere in the system. Obviously the cost of communication equipment for this configuration is much greater than that for other network structures. Some banking institutions utilize this form of network.

SUMMARY OF NETWORKS. The structure of most distributed processing systems will probably not conform strictly to any of the previously defined networks. They will be a variation of one of the structures, tailored for the specific firm or organization. We must always remember that the major objective of distributed processing is to organize data processing resources to support remote applications as well as to comply with the processing needs of the corporate office or central site. The *network architecture,* consisting of all the hardware and software that make up the system, must be designed to satisfy these needs. This architecture may differ depending on whether the structure is designed around a general-purpose mainframe computer, minicomputers, or microcomputer. Generally speaking, large mainframe host computers are often used in a hierarchy or star network which requires the processing power to be centralized. Minicomputers or large microcomputers are often found in ring networks where processing is more completely distributed.

The advantages and disadvantages of each type of network are listed in Figure 7-11. In general, there is no one dominant or best structure for a net-

NETWORK	ADVANTAGES	DISADVANTAGES
Point-to-Point	Simple High Reliability Short Distance Easy to Expand	Many Communication Lines Restricted to Short Distances

Hierarchical/Tree	Centralized Control of Data
	  and Processing
	High Communication Reliability
	Reduced Communication Costs
		Hard to Expand
		Expensive to Operate
		No Direct Communication between
		  Remote Sites

Ring	Direct Communication between
	  Adjacent Remote Sites
	All Processing and Data Distributed
	Maximum Local Autonomy
	Fewer Communication Lines
		Minimum Centralized Control
		No Centralized Host
		Decreased Reliability
		Messages Need to be Routed through
		  Adjacent Location

*Fully Connected
  Ring*
	Direct Communication
	  between All Remote Sites
	All Processing and Data Distributed
	Maximum Local Autonomy
	High Reliability
		Minimum Central Control
		High Communication Line Costs

FIGURE 7-11   Advantages and disadvantages of different networks.

work; each must be designed for the particular firm or organization involved. The following factors must be considered if the distributed network is to be effective:

1. Data must be edited as close as possible to the point of origin in order to detect and correct errors.
2. Processing requirements should be clustered to the degree necessary to make the purchase and operation of processing equipment cost effective.
3. Data should be moved from one place to another only when it is absolutely necessary.
4. The data flows upward within the network should include only data that are significant to the upper levels of the organization.
5. Computing power should be placed at each hierarchical level or remote site to the extent that it can be best used and cost justified.

In summary, the goal of a distributed network is to process as much information as possible to meet local transaction processing, operational, and managerial needs at the divisional level or the local site. The network and its architecture should be designed to accomplish this.

DISTRIBUTED SYSTEM HARDWARE: TELECOMMUNICATION EQUIPMENT

Up to this point in the chapter we have focused on the structure of systems (transaction processing, MIS, decision support, centralized and distributed processing systems) and have examined different modes of operation (batch versus on line). Little has been said about the telecommunication equipment and software that is necessary to support these systems or operations. In this section we examine these hardware elements, particularly those that relate to distributed processing networks, including: telecommunication equipment, control units, and terminals including minicomputers/microcomputers, and micro to mainframe links.

Telecommunications

Telecommunication (data communication) is the process of transmitting data from one location to another over communication channels such as telephone lines and microwaves. For example, when a distributed processing system is used and remote users access the central computer site, modems (message sending and receiving units), communication media, input/output terminals, and communication control units for controlling the flow of data are frequently required to transmit data.

COMMUNICATION MEDIA TRANSMISSION MODES. Communication media are the channels over which data is transferred from one site to another, such as from an overseas branch to a corporate office located in the host country. Telephone lines, coaxial cables, microwave links, and communication satellites are examples of communication media. These channels as a group cover the entire spectrum of data transfer capabilities including low, medium, and high transfer rates. The transfer rate or capability of a channel is determined by its *grade*, or *bandwidth*. Older telegraph lines were *narrow bandwidth* channels; they could only transfer data at a rate of 45 to 90 bits per second. Telephone lines, which are *voice-grade* level, offer a *broader bandwidth* and thus a greater transfer rate. The transmission rates of telephone lines often vary from 300 to 9,600 bits per second. Coaxial cables and microwaves provide *broad-band* channel capabilities, as do communication satellites, and other more advanced communication channels. Currently some leased-line services exist that provide data transmission rates in excess of 500,000 bits per second. In general, the broader the band the more rapid the transmission and the more sophisticated the equipment including the type of line and mode of communication.

There are several types of data transmission modes. Simplex transmits data in only one direction. Half duplex transmits data in two directions but not at the same time. Full duplex transmits data in both directions at once. An asynchronous mode may be used where each character is proceeded by a start bit and followed by a stop bit. A synchronous transmission mode may be used which enables one to transmit entire blocks of data continuously. Synchronized transmission requires that the sender and receiver be synchronized in order to communicate. Finally, in order to communicate over a channel there must be a set of rules for packaging data into packets or envelopes, as they are sometimes called. This set of rules is called the protocol. It often includes specifications for identification, message coding, mode of transmission, error (parity) checks, and procedures for identifying the start and stop of a packet.

MODEMS.   Special equipment is used in conjunction with a communication channel to send, code, amplify, and receive data; generally this is called a modem. Computers store data in *digital pulse* form. Electrical signals are transmitted in *wave* form. Consequently, when data from a computer are transmitted via a communication channel, they must first be converted from pulse form to wave form. This process of conversion is called *modulation. Demodulation* is the reverse process. Both conversion processes are performed by the modem. Often these modems are part of the computer hardware, such as a card in a personnel computer which may serve as a distributed processing terminal.

Communication Control Units

Communication control units are necessary to schedule and control the traffic resulting in multiple input and output devices in a computerized accounting system. The communication control units include: multiplexers, and concentrators, which are sometimes called communication channels; message switching devices; and communication processors. Some combination of these are usually essential for any distributed processing system. Communication control units and processors were noted briefly in Chapter 5.

MULTIPLEXER AND CONCENTRATOR.   When a number of low-speed units are connected on line to a CPU, each via a voice band (telephone) grade channel, communication can become very expensive, particularly if one or more of the terminals is outside the toll-free zone of the CPU. Since a voice-grade-level channel can transmit 9,600 bits per second, it would seem logical that more than one terminal can utilize a higher speed channel, particularly if data transmission from different terminals can be kept separate. This is precisely the *multiplexer's* function. It is placed between the CPU and the peripherals to poll data transmission from low-speed peripherals and combine it into high-speed input for the CPU. This arrangement is necessary in order to avoid having the CPU sit idle while waiting on the low-speed peripherals to interact with it. A *concentrator* enhances the task of the multiplexer. It controls access to the channels in the communication network by polling terminals enabling the communication channels to be used by several users or terminals. It monitors all channels to determine when the next channel will be come available for use. When another channel is free for transmission, the terminal polling process is once again repeated.

MESSAGE SWITCHER AND COMMUNICATION PROCESSOR.   *Message switching* devices are also located in some networks to control the flow of data through the networks. They enable several users or terminals to communicate with the CPU at the same time via multiple channels or via higher speed channels.

Typically a data communications system will contain a number of different types of terminals, along with a variety of peripherals (both local and remote), a number of modems, possibly a multiplexer or concentrator unit or both, and other electronic control devices. As long as the total number of electronic devices and the amount of data transmitted are maintained at certain levels, the operating system of the central computer can be programmed to handle message switching, error checking, directing of message queues and priorities, temporary storage and other duties associated with the throughput of data and information. However, if the number of terminals, peripheral devices, and other components and/or the volume of data transmission surpasses a certain level, a programmable *communications processor* (often called a front-end processor or preprocessor) can handle these tasks more economically than the central processor. A communication processor relieves the CPU of some of these communication burdens.

Terminals

The user interface with these networks is usually done via a terminal or a microcomputer. In Chapter 5 we identified and discussed a number of input/output terminal devices including key-to-tape/disk data entry devices, visual display terminal, magnetic-ink character recognition (MICR) device, optical character recognition (OCR) device, printers as well as personal computers. In this section we will extend this discussion by focusing on two general types of terminals.

First, a simple *"dumb" terminal* is a device connected to some form of computing capabilities. It simply provides a direct-access method to and from the computer. This type of terminal provides no error checking, editing, or storage capabilities other than a single line buffering of input character strings. The most versatile terminal of this type is commonly referred to as the CRT (cathode ray tube) or video display terminal (VDT). In general, these are used to simply interact with the computer in an interactive on-line mode or in a batch mode.

The other type of terminal is the so called *"intelligent" terminal.* These vary considerably in the functions they can perform for the user. At one end of the spectrum they can be designed to automatically perform such functions as data input, data output, editing. These are not user-programmable. The logic for the functions to be performed is usually preprogrammed through the internal read-only memory of the device, a task usually performed by the manufacturer. Organizations can often add data, such as product prices and product IDs, as well as unique data entry procedures and controls to these. Generally, only a limited number of specific functions can be performed by these relatively limited "intelligent" terminals. A point-of-sale (POS) terminal is an example of such a terminal. It performs the functions of a cash register and also captures sales data. The POS terminals have a keyboard for data entry as well as a character recognition reader for Universal Product Codes (UPC), a panel for displaying the price, a cash drawer, and a printer that generates a receipt. If the terminal is directly connected to a central computer, inventory and sales information can also be updated in an on-line mode.

Another such terminal is the device used to input data from remote sites via telephone lines to a central computer. A popular version of the terminal is that used in processing information relating to the credit status of credit-card customers. An access number (code) to the central computer is dialed by the sales clerk and the clerk inserts the customer's card. The customer's account is checked, and an approval number is displayed on the phone's video readout. A more sophisticated version of the terminal enters the sales transaction.

At the other end of the spectrum of intelligent terminals is the terminal that can be programmed, has storage and control functions, a set of instructions, and other components similar to a standard computer. Most of these employ a CRT and, in some cases, a reader/printer as input/output devices. In general, a high-end intelligent terminal must include, as a minimum, the following:

1. Self-contained storage (random access memory)
2. Stored program capabilities
3. A keyboard or some other form of human-oriented input device
4. A CRT or some other form of human-oriented output device
5. Ability to process, within the terminal, a user-written program
6. Ability to process on-line data communications from other intelligent terminals or from one or more computer sites.

Intelligent terminals such as these can serve a variety of functions, particularly if they are connected to other peripheral devices. By connecting a terminal to a communication data control unit, and then to a central computer through a communication channel, a remote job-entry (RJE) system is developed. By using a different set of peripherals and programs, a data-entry system such as a remote key-to-disk system can be created. By connecting the terminal to the proper set of I/O devices, a stand-alone computer for low-volume or special-purpose processing is created. In summary, some of these intelligent terminals are microcomputers in terms of functions they can perform; indeed microcomputers are actually used as these high-end intelligent terminals. Microcomputers were discussed at length in the last chapter.

Microcomputers as well as Intelligent terminals are extensively used in distributed processing networks, primarily for two reasons. First, the operation of the terminal is not dependent upon a central computer or any other terminal. If nonintelligent terminals are connected to the central processor and the processor breaks down, the terminals are not able to function and the entire system is inoperable. If microcomputers or intelligent terminals are employed in a network and the central computer or part of all of the data communication system breaks down, the microcomputers or terminals can still accept input transactions and can perform certain processing functions. Banks and retail stores have adopted intelligent terminals in many of their customer processing operations because of this key factor. Sales transactions in a store or account transactions in a bank can be recorded at the terminal and made ready for later transmission even when the central processor is off line. The second reason for using a network of microcomputers or intelligent terminals is that it can relieve the central processor workload. Due to the reduction in cost of microprocessors intelligent terminals as well as microcomputers have enabled distributed processing to become a reality for many organizations.

SUMMARY

In this chapter we have attempted to integrate some of the ideas and concepts discussed in previous chapters, particularly in regard to types of systems and the hardware that is required to support these different system structures. We traced the evolution of systems, which included (1) traditional accounting systems; (2) management information systems; and (3) distributed processing systems. These included on-line as well as batch processing modes. In addition, distributed processing systems and their networks were introduced along with the hardware and software necessary to support these networks.

SELECTED REFERENCES

BROWN, LARRY, "Defining Distributed Data Processing," *Cost and Management,* November–December, 1981.

DATE, C. J., *An Introduction to Database Systems.* Addison-Wesley, 5th ed. (1990).

DIETZ, DEVON D., and JOHN D. KEANE, "Integrating Distributed Processing Within a Central Environment," *Management Accounting,* vol. 62, November 1980.

LAUDON, KENNETH C., and JANE P. LAUDON, *Management Information Systems: A Contemporary Perspective.* New York: Macmillan, 1988.

MCKEOWN, PATRICK G., *Living with Computers.* San Diego: Harcourt Brace Jovanovich, 1988.

MISHKIN, HARRY, and DAN C. KNEER, "The Drive Toward DDP: A Management Perspective," *CMA Magazine* (January/February) 1987.

SIVULA, CHRIS, "Georgia-Pacific MRP II Test," *Datamation,* November 1989, pp. 95–101.

STONEBRAKER, MICHAEL, "The Distributed Database Decade," *Datamation,* September 1989, pp. 38–39.

REVIEW QUESTIONS

1. Differentiate between *batch processing with sequential access files* and *batch processing with random access files.* What are the advantages and disadvantages of each?

2. Explain the meaning of *remote batch* processing.

3. Identify some typical on-line processing applications and explain the concept of real-time processing.

4. Differentiate between batch and on-line processing.

5. Identify the system structures and information processing systems that have evolved over the past forty years.

6. What factors brought about the development of distributed processing systems?

7. Identify some of the key characteristics of a distributed processing system.

8. Explain the meaning of the terms *distributed database* and *autonomy of data processing operations.*

9. Identify several basic network structures used in distributed processing. Give an example of each.

10. Explain the term *bandwith (grade)* used in conjunction with a communication channel.

11. What role does a modem play in a data communication system?

12. What role does a communications processor play in a data communications system?

13. Differentiate between a *"dumb" terminal,* and an *"intelligent" terminal.*

14. What roles have minicomputers and microcomputers played in the development of distributed processing?

15. What is meant by a partitioned database? Why is it necessary to use such a database?

16. Explain the function of the communication control units.

CASES

7-1 Answer the following multiple choice questions.

1. The Alpha Corporation is preparing to computerize its personnel records using magnetic tape for its employee master file. In designing this system, the best choice for file organization would be
   a. Sequential
   b. Batch
   c. Random access
   d. On-line
      Give the justification for your answer.
   (Adapted from the CMA examination.)

2. The Petman Company is planning to acquire several "dumb" terminals to place in offices that are remotely located from the computer. What additional devices will the company need to acquire so that the terminals can operate properly?
   a. Key to disk devices for entering data
   b. Cathode ray tubes (CRTs) for displaying data
   c. Modems for translating electronic impulses
   d. Floppy disk units for storing data

3. Which of the following applications would be least likely to be done on an on-line basis?
   a. Airlines reservations
   b. Preparation of payroll checks
   c. A "dial-a-computer" stock market quotation system
   d. A computerized traffic light control system
   e. Computer monitoring of coronary care patients in a hospital

4. The meaning of the term *distributed data processing* is most closely associated with
   a. Computer networks
   b. Batch processing
   c. PERT networks
   d. Database management systems
   e. Centralization of corporate data banks

5. Direct-access storage devices are
   a. Basic to on-line operations
   b. Supplementary to on-line operations
   c. Harmful to on-line operations
   d. Incompatible with on-line operations
   e. None of the above

6. When a CPU is a great distance from user terminals, some form of communication system is required. Which of the following is *not* a component of a communication system?
   a. Modem
   b. Concentrator
   c. Multiprogramming
   d. Multiplexer
   e. Channel

7. The B & L Bookstore would like to purchase a terminal that could be used to capture sales data, generate receipts, and interface with a central inventory system. The type of terminal the store should consider is classified as
   a. An intelligent terminal
   b. A dumb terminal
   c. A microcomputer

8. A permanent set of instructions for a microcomputer is located in
   a. Secondary storage

b. Diskette

c. ROM memory

d. RAM memory

e. Arithmetic-logic unit

(Adapted from Robert J. Thierauf, *Distributed Processing Systems.* (Englewood Cliffs, N.J.: Prentice Hall, 1978), pp. 102, 105.)

7-2 Indicate whether a batch processing or an on-line processing system would be more appropriate for each of the following situations. Explain your answer.

1. Highly integrated operations that require close monitoring

2. Large volume of transactions that peak on a biweekly basis

3. Widely dispersed units within a corporation that require rapid transmittal of data and information

4. A small company that has a small volume of transactions but requires up-to-date and accurate records

5. A company that has a high volume of transactions but can tolerate a slow response time

6. Weekly inquiries relating to the status of certain items or products (i.e., a weekly status report on outstanding orders)

7. Managerial reports that need to be available on a demand basis

7-3 Given each of the following applications, indicate (1) whether a batch processing or an on-line processing operation is more applicable; (2) if batch processing is applicable, indicate whether sequential or random access files are needed and whether a local batch or a remote batch mode of operation is applicable; (3) if on-line processing is applicable, indicate whether an real-time operation is applicable. Explain your answer.

1. Monthly preparation of financial statements

2. A patient-care system in a large metropolitan hospital containing 600 beds

3. A payroll system used weekly or biweekly to produce employee checks and payroll records and statements

4. A system designed to keep track of "special orders" that have critical time schedules

5. Preparation of utility bills that are payable on a monthly basis

6. Access and maintenance of records at a credit bureau that processes 2,500 inquiries a week and maintains 350,000 records

7. A reservation system, used by a major airline, to determine and schedule seat occupancy

8. Preparation and generation of internal monthly responsibility reports

9. A system used to support the processing of orders received by mail for a "mail-order house" that stocks 2,500 different products

7-4 The controller of Kensler Company has been working with the Data Processing Department to revise part of the company's financial reporting system. A study is underway on how to develop and implement a data-entry and data-retention system for key computer files used by various departments responsible to the controller. The departments involved, and details on their processing-related activities, are as follows:

General Accounting

Daily processing of journal entries submitted by various departments

Weekly updating of file balances with subsystem data from areas such as payroll, accounts receivable, and accounts payable.

Sporadic requests for account balances during the month with increased activity at month-end

Accounts Receivable

Daily processing of receipts for payments on account

Daily processing of sales to customers

Daily checks to be sure that credit limit of $200,000 maximum per customer is not exceeded, and identification of orders in excess of $20,000 per customer

Daily requests for customer credit status regarding payments and account balances

Weekly reporting to general accounting file

Accounts Payable

Processing of payments to vendors three times a week

Weekly expense distribution reporting to general accounting file

Budget Planning and Control

Updating of flexible budgets on a monthly basis

Quarterly rebudgeting based on sales forecast and production schedule changes

Monthly inquiry requests for budget balances

The manager of Data Processing has explained the concepts of the following processing techniques to the controller's staff and the appropriate staff members of the departments affected:

Batch processing

On-line processing

Real-time processing

On-line inquiry

The manager of Data Processing has indicated to the controller that batch processing is the least expensive processing technique and that a rough estimate of the cost of each of the other techniques would be as follows:

TECHNIQUE	CAPS IN RELATION TO BATCH PROCESSING
On-line processing	1.5 times
Real-time processing	2.5 times
On-line inquiry	1.5 times

REQUIRED:

1. Define and discuss the major differences

between the input options of the following processing techniques:

a. Batch processing
b. On-line processing
c. Real-time processing

2. Identify and explain (1) the type of input technique; and (2) the type of file inquiry that probably should be employed by Kensler Company for each of the four departments responsible to the Controller:

General Accounting

Accounts Receivable

Budget Planning and Control

Assume that the volume of transactions is not a key variable in the decision.
(CMA adapted with permission)

7-5 For each of the following cases, indicate whether the described system is *batch processing, on-line processing,* or a *combination of both.*

REQUIRED: Sketch a pictorial configuration of the system. (Review system configurations in the text.)

1. A medical service bureau performs patient billing for numerous medical groups in a large city. Formerly, clients mailed their information to the bureau's data processing center where it was keyed and processed on the bureau's computer. However, third-party billing, such as Blue Shield, Medicare, and welfare, created bottlenecks as claims forms became more complex. As part of an expansion effort, the service bureau installed communicating processors as data-entry terminals at the offices of ten high-volume clients. For each of these clients the system allows efficient "fill-in-the-blanks" type of data entry. Formats appear on the CRT screen and prompt the user for all necessary information. As data are entered, the processor checks for mistakes, such as an operation date earlier than date of admission. Delays that used to occur in resolving such troublesome errors have now been completely eliminated.

Data recorded on diskettes are the validated source files. All billing data are accumulated, and at the end of the day, these files are communicated via high-speed communications to the central computer. The central system spools the files to magnetic tape that is in the proper format for final processing on the service bureau's computer. Billing is merely the first phase of a total medical system. Phase 2 is medical records, while Phase 3 involves diagnostics.

2. A major oil company maintains regional marketing centers which are responsible for order entry, invoicing, distribution, and sales analysis of the company's products. Previously, the manual system involved processing 400 orders per day. Invoices had to be typed and were then sent by manual teletypes to twenty distribution centers within each region. Complex tax codes and pricing and product information compounded the need for some system of local file maintenance, computation, and high-speed transmission.

After instituting a feasibility study, a key-to-diskette data-entry system was installed. It allows rapid data entry, and its diskettes provide unlimited storage, easy handling, and fast access to local files. After the operators key in the orders, the processor automatically verifies customer files and product codes. It also calculates price extensions and taxes, appends any special terms, and then stores the completed invoices on diskettes. In two hours of high-speed data transmission per day, all invoices are printed on remote receive-only printers. The complete invoice transaction file, in turn, is communicated to the corporate data center and is entered into the accounts receivable system on the host computer. At the regional level, the processors accumulate managerial sales analyses for summary reports that were previously unavailable at this level. In this sample application, regionally installed processors serve as "intelligent" data-entry systems for the central computer and act as transaction processing output systems for distributing a high volume of data to numerous field sites. (Adapted From Robert J. Thierauf, *Distributed Processing Systems.* (Englewood Cliffs, N.J. Prentice Hall 1978), pp. 102, 105.)

7-6 Each of the following cases represents a network structure of distributed processing (i.e., point-to-point, heirarchical, star, loop, or fully connected ring). Identify the type of network represented and sketch a pictorial configuration of the system.

1. In a large midwestern city, a motor freight carrier operated a central data processing center for the carrier's regional terminal centers in five large cities. Before the installation of the current distributed processing network, the payroll data had to be keyed in twice, once at the regional level and once at the headquarters level. Time slips had to be checked manually for accuracy of such data as drive time miles, stops, load weights, and route codes. To eliminate multiple-data entry, a microcomputer was placed in each regional center as well as in the central DP center. Currently payroll data are keyed daily into the regional processors for storage on diskettes; the daily files become the input for the weekly accumulations. The weekly data are then communicated to the central system and merged into a summary payroll file.

This multisite network system processes truckers' payroll at the regional level before transmitting the summary data to the central system. This system then stores the data on magnetic tape for further exception processing at the central processing center. Nothing is ever keyed more than once. Because the bottleneck at the central level has been eliminated, attention is given to generating detailed reports for management, such as weekly summary reports, driver performance, equipment optimization, route-loading comparisons, and overall productivity.

2. A medium-sized bank, after an exhaustive study of its entire DP operations, concluded that its current centralized DP operations are very expensive. At the hub of the current system is a large computer used for on-line processing by tellers in all of the bank's branch offices. When the

first system fails, processing is switched to a second computer of the same size for continuous on-line processing by bank tellers. It should be noted that the second computer system is regularly used for batch processing until the first computer fails.

Recognizing the need for lower processing costs and reliability of processing for on-line operations by bank tellers, the bank decided to restructure its DP operations. To achieve this, a software house, working in conjunction with the bank's systems analysts, decided to install a group of four minicomputers to service all banking operations handled by bank tellers. Each minicomputer services forty bank-teller terminals. Not only can tellers inquire about the status of bank balances, but they can also enter deposit items or deduct items in an on-line mode throughout the day. Thus several offices will be linked to one minicomputer. In turn, all minicomputers are linked together so that they can communicate directly with one another. This linking of all minicomputers is necessary in order to enable a teller to interrogate the database for a customer's account situated in a location other than that for the one being used. Likewise, all minicomputers are linked to the central banking office. This communication arrangement allows the main computer to post all cleared checks as well as debit and credit items against each account at the end of the banking day, that is, in the evening. During the day, however, the main computer is busy performing routine and special batch processing functions for the entire bank. Similarly, appropriate reports about bank operations are prepared daily and periodically to meet management needs.

3. A consumer products manufacturer found that its current DP system failed to produce timely management information. Based on this shortcoming and others, it decided to undergo a feasibility study which resulted in a decision to install a distributed processing system. The areas included were sales, research and development, and manufacturing. A communications network was designed to provide the mechanism for data communications between programs and devices on different systems and on computers running under different operating systems. All three functional areas were designed to run on a single network using minicomputers, including a general-purpose computer at central headquarters.

Sales offices that perform sales order processing are widely dispersed but need to access current inventory information and shipping data. Because individual telephone lines to a central computer are expensive, a communications network is used to reduce line costs. It contains terminal concentrators at local regional centers to send data over high-speed lines to the central system. These data are keyed in via a terminal or a microcomputer and temporarily stored on disk or tape for future communication. Processed sales information can be communicated back to the offices—to terminals or disk storage for later off-line printing, depending on the needs of the sales offices. However, at the highest level, weekly sales data (budget versus actual) are processed on Saturday and are available on Monday morning for evaluation by sales managers at the headquarters level. The ability of the distributed network, then, to provide timely sales reports gives the company "a handle" on where to focus its current sales efforts.

7-7 Quik-Shop Inc. owns and operates a number of twenty-four-hour convenience stores throughout the northeastern United States. The company is now using a second-generation batch-oriented computer system, at its main offices, to process accounting information and produce monthly reports. Currently the company produces monthly reports relating to (1) inventory status by store; and (2) sales statistics by product and store. The centralized data center also processes employee weekly payroll, processes purchases by vendors, prepares an accounts payable summary, and prepares vendor checks. Management at Quick-Shop believes that the existing computer system should be upgraded, possibly to an on-line system.

REQUIRED: As a systems consultant, you have been asked to prepare a report that highlights the advantages and disadvantages of different configurations of third- or fourth-generation equipment. Include in your report an examination of point-of-sale terminals as well as any other equipment that could be cost justified, based on the nature of the business.

7-8 Sketch an on-line integrated information system configuration that will support a large commercial bank operation. Assume that the bank uses magnetic-ink character recognition (MICR) equipment to process customer checks and deposit slips. Identify other types of terminals or equipment that would be required. In addition, indicate under what conditions it would be desirable to employ a distributed system rather than an integrated system.

7-9 Ohio Steel, a medium-sized steel firm that specializes in high-strength steel alloy manufacturing and sales to the automotive industry, has two mills on Lake Erie. Ohio Steel has an older medium-sized computer and an information system that is quite effective for scheduling production, financial planning, sales analysis, inventory control, and general accounting applications. It is a simple batch processing system. A complex system has not been necessary because daily updating of schedules and reports has been more than adequate, given that Ohio Steel has a few large customers in a reasonably stable market.

Ohio Steel's management has decided to diversify and is considering the purchase of a chain of fifty motels in the Midwest. You, the controller of the steel firm, are charged with the responsibility for providing management with the necessary information for decision making. You have been asked to report briefly on the changes in information requirements you would envision if the purchase takes place. You are also to discuss the cost implications of various alternative systems needed to cope with these possible changes.

REQUIRED: As part of this report comment on the merits of a centralized versus distributed system and the impact of recent technology on the feasibility of a distributed system.

8

DATA FLOW DIAGRAMS, SYSTEMS FLOWCHARTING, AND DOCUMENTATION

BASIC CONCEPTS

An accounting information system and information systems in general should be designed to support the management system of the organization. This is accomplished by processing transactions and providing information for the decision-making and reporting requirements of the business. The focus of these transaction processing, operational, managerial, and strategic activities should be to further the objectives of the organization. There are two basic ways accountants and systems analysts and designers use to describe this process. One is the data flow diagram for describing logically what is done in each step in the process; the other is the systems flow chart for describing how these activities are accomplished or expected to be done in physical terms. These follow the analysis and design concept outlined in Chapter 2 and described in detail in Chapters 12 and 13. The data flow diagram is used extensively in the analysis phase where the analyst concentrates on what the system must do to support the management system in logical terms. The system flow chart is used extensively in the design and implementation phase to describe how to do it in physical terms. Systems flowcharts are also used in the part of systems analysis where the current system is described and studied. Data flow diagrams are generally not used in the audit process because the system being audited is already designed.[1]

The essential characteristics of accounting and information systems can be described much more effectively by means of the standardized symbols of a data flow diagram or a systems flow chart than by using a narrative description. This is true for the following reasons:

1. The description is simpler and concentrates on the essential components that are relevant to the professional user.
2. A picture is always easier to use to communicate a message than an oral or written description.
3. A multitude of interrelationships can be communicated easily via a data flow diagram or a systems flowchart. A narrative can only be used to effectively describe a sequential relationship, whereas a diagram can more easily convey a variety of interactive relationships.

The more complex the accounting system, the more difficult it will be to describe these relationships. For the untrained user, often found in management, a narrative description may be an essential supplement to a data flow diagram or a systems flowchart.

DATA FLOW DIAGRAMS

A data flow diagram is a logical model of an accounting and information system. It describes what an accounting system must do to support the transaction processing, decision-making, and reporting requirements of management. As such, it is commonly used in the analysis phase of systems analysis and design. During this early phase, the analyst or the accountant collects a great deal of relatively unstructured information from charts of accounts, organization charts, job descriptions, file organization, and other sets of documentation. In addition, management indicates the attributes it would like to see in a new or revised system. These are in the form of objectives. The data flow diagram is used to summarize these attributes without reference to hardware, software, data structure, or file organization. The data flow diagram simply shows for each activity whether it's a transaction or decision-making activity, where the data comes from, where it goes, where it is stored, and what happens to it along the way.

Four basic symbols are used to represent these four attributes of the data flow diagram. They are illustrated in Figure 8-1. They are described as follows:

1. A square is used for a data *source* or *destination*. Often this is an external entity such as a customer or supplier. To avoid crossing, the same entity may

---

[1] Systems analysts are beginning to use data flow diagrams in design and implementation phases of system development. Also, Fitzgerald, EDPACS (October & November 1987), recommends that auditors use data flow diagrams.

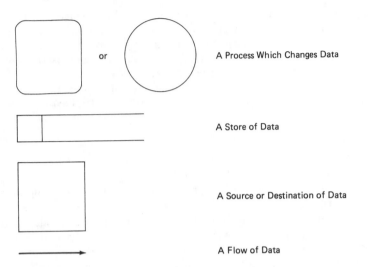

FIGURE 8-1   Data flow diagram symbols.

be represented more than once in the data flow diagram by using a slash or multiple slashes in the lower right-hand corner.

2. A rectangle with rounded corners is used for a *process* that transfers data or for what happens to data as they flow through the system. Some experts use circles instead of the rectangles. Each process will contain a description of the process. Often as is shown the information to identify the process will appear at the top of the rectangle, and the location of the process such as accounts receivable department will appear at the bottom. These added pieces of information are separated from the description of the process by horizontal lines.

3. An arrow is used to identify data flow. Ideally, each data flow will have a description of the data that flows along its path; this may not be necessary in simple flow diagrams where it is obvious. When a data store is accessed, the search argument may be added to this flow line for clarification if needed.

4. An open-ended rectangle is used to represent a data store or a repository of data. Often a box at the closed end will contain an identification. The same store can be shown more than once in the data flow diagram to avoid crossing flow lines.

Action verbs and object labels should be used to label data flow diagrams. For example, *update, read, prepare, compare,* and *edit* would be examples of the type of action verbs that could be used in describing a process. *Inventory, invoice, product name, product number, purchase order,* and *inquiry* are examples of objects.

Consider Buymore Corporation's[2] system for updating inventory files and issuing purchase orders. The data flow diagram for such a system is illustrated in Figure 8-2. The sources and destinations of data are the receiving department where goods are received, the stockroom where inventory is stored and issued to various production departments, miscellaneous adjustments and returns from various sources and vendors who supply the inventory. The three data stores are the purchase order records, the stock records, and the vendor information file. There are four different processing steps in their inventory and purchase order system. The nature of the information flowing along the data flow lines is illustrated in the figure. This diagram describes what is done and not how it accomplished. Often more detail is needed for each of these processing steps. When this is the case, the process is "exploded" and a more detailed data flow diagram of that process is developed. A complex system will have several levels of exploded data flow diagrams. An example is presented in Figure 8-3 for process 1 (post stock records) where three processing steps are needed: (1) the location of the record; (2) the creation of a new record if no record exists; and (3) the update of the record. These more detailed charts are very useful building blocks for future system design and programming.

The development of a data flow diagram generally starts with a very rough sketch of the logical process that is desired. Often a systems flowchart (which will be described next) of the current system is used as part of the input into this logical description. After several revisions and refinements, a data flow diagram such as that shown in Figure 8-2 is developed. This process is done for each level of data flow diagram, from the overall "high-level" logical description of what is to be done to the detailed "exploded" descriptions. At each level and at each stage of development, feedback from management is essential to make sure that the diagram adequately reflects what is done or their desires.

The data flow diagram has a variety of uses. First and foremost it is used in system analysis to describe in logical terms what a system is supposed to do. The logical model is used to organize information about the system. It is used to summarize information about the system through its high-level description. It is used to communicate with management the various aspects of the system and to make sure the analyst really understands the information requirements and relationships of the system in logical terms.

This model is used as the foundation for systems design and it is used as the basis for systems flowcharts which describe how to process and store data in a system. Finally, it is used effectively to explore with management various automation boundaries for alternative system designs.

The data flow diagram is an effective tool for describing, in logical terms, a system or proposed system prior to actual design. In summary, it is a conceptual "blueprint" of what must be done to solve the problem.

---

[2] AICPA, *Staff Level 1 Training Program—Systems Flowcharting* (New York: American Institute of Certified Public Accountants).

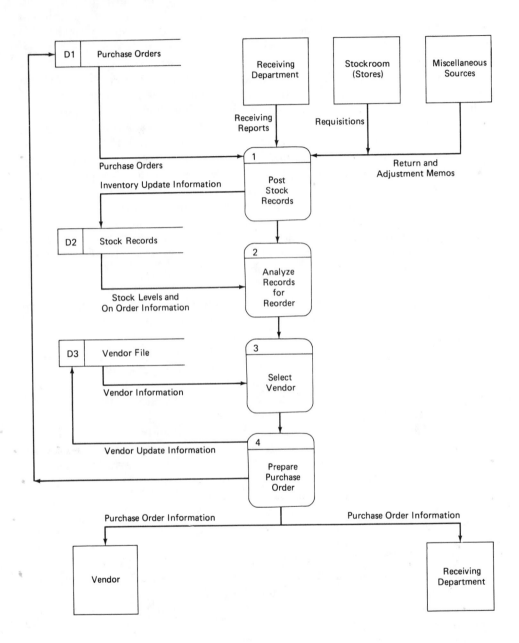

FIGURE 8-2 Data flow diagram, Buymore Corporation.

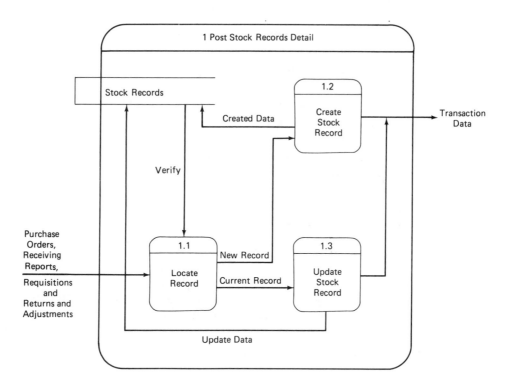

FIGURE 8-3   Exploded data flow diagram for posting stock records.

SYSTEM FLOWCHARTS

Systems flowcharting is an effective way to describe an information system to trained users, such as accountants and systems analysts. A systems flowchart is different from a data flow diagram because it describes how the system operates or will operate and not what must be done as in the case of the data flow diagram.

A systems flowchart is basically a communication document. It should therefore be organized with this purpose as its focus. The auditor, manager, accountant, or systems designer who prepares the flowchart should organize it around the relevant information he or she is trying to convey about the system, and all its relevant components, to current or future users. As outlined in Chapter 4, relevant information is a function of the decisions or reports of the users. This organization effort must consider the (1) flow of transactions; (2) interaction and characteristics of these flows; (3) decisions; (4) personnel or departments involved; (5) characteristics of processing steps; (6) nature of reports to be generated; (7) files and storage methods used; (8) input preparation procedures; (9) disposition of input; (10) automation boundaries; and (11) controls.

The following are some suggestions for the organization and focus of the systems flowchart:

1. The accounting transaction processing cycle may be the focus. These cycles are commonly referred to as
    a. Sales and collection cycle
    b. Payroll and personnel cycle
    c. Purchasing, production, inventory, and warehousing cycle
    d. Capital acquisition cycle
    e. Financial cycle

    These are probably the most common approaches used by auditors, due to the focus on the transaction processing cycle.

2. An organizational entity such as a store, plant, or department, may be the focus. All activities of the entity would be grouped together to focus on the activities of the entire entity. Often this is used to describe overall activities, and the cycle approach is used to give more detailed information about the system.

3. A decision, transaction, or report may be the focal point of the flowchart. An example of this for the inventory update and purchase order decision is given later in this chapter. This procedure is most useful in focusing on the transaction processing, reporting, and decision-making requirements of the information system. Moreover, it is valuable for an analysis of administrative controls.

4. A file or database may be the focal point of a flowchart used to communicate the level of interaction with the file or database. This will be useful in designing and analyzing a random access system databases and files where organization and retrieval requirements are important.

5. For manual systems, the flow of documents using a document flowchart (a version of a systems flowchart) is useful for tracing documents as they flow from department to department in the transaction cycle. This is most useful for an analysis of accounting controls for a manual system.

All systems flowcharts contain some elements of each of these items and can be used to describe and assess accounting and administrative controls. However, it is the organization of the document flows, processes, interaction of processes and information flows, personnel descriptions, report generation, files used, input preparation procedures, disposition of input, and controls that is critical to effective communication of the system to the users in the system flowchart. Therefore, care must be taken to arrange the presentation of the information.

The same organization concepts hold for data flow diagrams. Another important decision related to the focus of the flowchart is the level of detail presented. Some users require only a broad "high-level" overview of the system. (A block diagram consisting of rectangles used to represent each major processing step or activity is often used here.) Others need considerable detail. Generally, even in the latter case, a broad flowchart is still prepared to give the "big picture" of the information system. Then more detailed flowcharts are drawn to

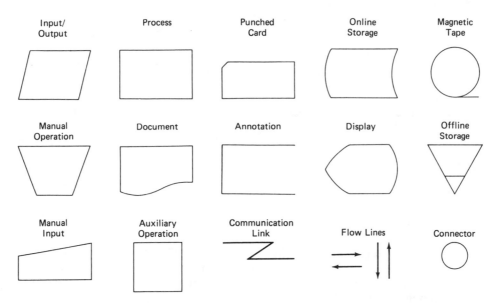

FIGURE 8-4   System flowchart symbols.

show various levels of detail, much in the same way that data flow diagrams are exploded.

SYSTEMS FLOWCHARTING TECHNIQUES

In 1966, the United States of America Standards Institute (USASI) adopted a standard set of systems flowchart symbols, as shown in Figure 8-4. A few modifications of the USASI symbols have been added in practice, as indicated in Figure 8-5, with a note describing their use. In this chapter we use only those symbols adopted by the USASI. Others, however, are used elsewhere in the text.

First, there are four general symbols. The *parallelogram* is used to represent input to and output from the system. Generally, however, specialized symbols are used for documents, cards, tapes, and random access files. The parallelogram is most frequently used to represent manual accounting records such as inventory, accounts receivable, accounts payable, and the general ledger. For every system, the flowchart should begin with an input and end with an output, and each input into the system must be shown as an output, that is, its final disposition must be shown.

The second basic symbol is the *rectangle,* which represents a processing operation or group of operations. Specialized symbols should be used for many processing operations. In practice the rectangle is most frequently used for operations performed by the computer (CPU) in data processing operations. A single rectangle may be used to represent many more detailed operations. Input/output symbols are always separated by one or more processing steps.

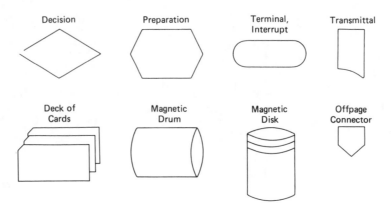

FIGURE 8-5 Other frequently used flowchart symbols.

The third major symbol is the *flow line*. The flowchart should flow from top to bottom[3] and left to right; if not, the lines should have an arrow indicating the direction of flow. Flow lines are always horizontal and vertical, and crossing lines should be avoided if possible.

A fourth basic symbol is the *annotation*. It is used to provide explanatory comments such as file contents, processing steps, and decisions to be made. Added information or reference to more detailed flowcharts also can be added by *striping*. The rectangle, for example, is divided into two sections where in the top section a code such as *C* representing cashier, or *106* representing a detailed flowchart, is noted to show *who* does the processing and *reference* to another more detailed flowchart, respectively. Sometimes references and identifications are noted at the top left or right outside the symbol. Whenever feasible, the accountant or system designer should use the more descriptive specialized flowchart symbols shown in Figure 8-4. There are four specialized symbols for different input and output media. The *document* symbol is used to represent paper documents such as invoices, checks, and reports. As we noted earlier, only the parallelogram, however, is used for basic accounting records, even though these can be defined as documents. In addition to this symbol, there are specialized symbols for *punched* or *mark-sense cards, magnetic disks,* and *magnetic tape.*

There are also three specialized input/output symbols representing input/ output devices rather than media. The *manual input* is used in computer systems to permit the operator to communicate with the computer while in operation using an on-line keyboard. Visual *display* devices, such as cathode ray tubes (CRTs), console printers, and graph plotters also require the use of a specialized symbol. In the case of microcomputers or other smart terminals where the user can interact with the host or mainframe system, this symbol can be used to represent both visual output as well as input from the same terminal. Finally, a *communication link* is used to represent communication between the computer system (CPU) and remote terminals and displays. This symbol may also be used to de-

---

[3] An interesting exception to this is the flow charting procedure suggested by Peat, Marwick, Mitchell & Co. in its *System Evaluation Approach: Documentation of Controls (SEADOC)* where the flow is from the bottom to the top to highlight the source of account balances.

scribe local area networks (LANs). As in flow lines, these communication links designate the flow of information with arrows.

The last two specialized input/output symbols represent storage. First, the *triangle* represents off-line storage, regardless of the medium. Such information is not under the control of the CPU. Striping is often used to locate a code at the bottom of the triangle to indicate the organization of the file. For example, the codes N and A may represent a numeric and an alphabetic life, respectively. The other storage symbol represents *on-line direct-access storage,* such as magnetic disk, diskettes drum, random access memory (RAM), and automatic microfilm systems. Several refinements of the *on-line storage* symbols are shown in Figure 8-5 and are frequently used in practice.

The remaining two specialized symbols are used for specific types of processing. The *square* represents auxiliary operations (off-line mechanical devices) not under the control of the CPU, such as a card sorter, reproducer, optical scanner, punched tape to magnetic tape converter, and mark-sense card punch, which reads cards and forms and records the data on electronic media. Many of these devices are still used in older systems. The *trapezoid* is used to represent any manual off-line operation, such as filing, inspecting, keypunching, posting, or reviewing. This symbol is used extensively in practice to describe manual systems.

Often there is no clear indication of which specialized symbol to use. The question may arise, for example, as to the proper representation of a particular file. The magnetic tape which represents the medium or the triangle which describes the off-line state of the file may be used. The accountant or systems designer must use that symbol which best characterizes the message he or she is trying to communicate with the flowchart.

The last symbol shown in Figure 8-4 is the *connector,* and it is used when several charts or pages are used to describe the flowchart (the *off-page-connector* symbol in Figure 8-5 is often used also). A reference number is inserted in the center of the circle, and the circle is inserted at the end of the flow line to connect the various aspects of the flowchart.

SYSTEM FLOWCHART ILLUSTRATIONS

Manual Illustration

Consider the Buymore Corporation again.[4] When they used a manual accounting system, they adopted the following specific procedures to update the inventory files and issue new purchase orders. The procedures are described in the company's Procedures Manual as follows:

Entries to stock inventory records are made from four sources:
1. Copies of issued purchase orders
2. New receipts of stock as indicated by copies of approved receiving reports
3. Store requisitions as approved by the storekeeper
4. Miscellaneous transactions such as returns and adjustments

---

[4] Adapted from AICPA, *Staff Level 1 Training Program—System Flowcharting* (New York: American Institute of Certified Public Accountants).

(1) The incoming documents are posted manually each day to the stock inventory records by a special group of clerks in the accounting department. After the posting is completed, the source documents are filed together by date of posting. The ledger cards are analyzed as each posting is made to determine if items on hand plus on order are below the reorder level.

(2) If a "below-minimum" condition exists, a purchase requisition is prepared and forwarded to the purchasing department.

(3) Vendors are selected from a master vendor file by employees in the purchasing department. A purchase order is prepared and mailed to the vendor. The master vendor file is updated when an order is placed. Four copies of the purchase order are prepared and routed as follows:

1. Original is sent to the vendor.
2. Copy, with purchase requisition attached, is filed in the purchasing department.
3. Copy is filed in the receiving department.
4. Copy is sent to the accounting department to adjust stock inventory records.

The system flowchart in Figure 8-6 describes what the manual system does. It corresponds to the data flow diagram (Figure 8-2) showing what must be done. The flow of transactions is clearly shown by noting the four input documents across the top of the figure, the processing steps with files accessed at the center, and the output at the bottom—that is, a top-to-bottom flow paralleling the sequence of processing steps is used. An annotation expands the description of the manual processing step, the descriptions in the symbols are brief, striping shows who or what department performs what task and how files are organized, and a feedback loop shows that the output of the last processing step becomes input to the first processing step, which is the posting of inventory records. A key on the chart explains the notation used in the symbols. Moreover, bidirectional flow lines are used to represent interaction (reference and updating of perpetual records, i.e., the stock record and vendor file) with records to simplify the flowchart.

Batch Processing

Consider again the same illustration with the same requirements as to what must be done illustrated in the data flow diagram in Figure 8-2. This time assume that Buymore Corporation has decided to automate by using a batch processing system consisting of a small mainframe or minicomputer with mark-sense card input and tape drives. This system consists of input documents, store ledger and vendor file, and processing.

INPUT DOCUMENTS.   Receiving reports and return and adjustment memoranda will be transferred from source documents to a transaction tape using a key to tape system before they enter the system. Stores requisitions will be origi-

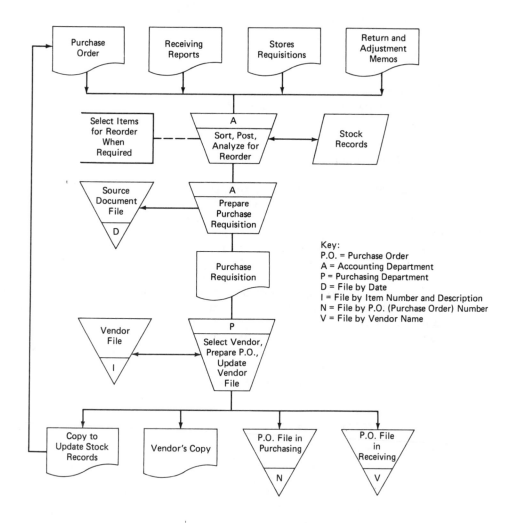

FIGURE 8-6 Manual system—typical small manual system.
Source: AICPA Staff Level I Training Program—Adapted.

nally prepared on mark-sense cards by the supervisors, and these cards will be read by an auxiliary machine operation. Purchase order information will be entered on the master file records as part of the processing. The system will use sequential batch processing, so all transaction tape and cards must be sorted into stock number order before they can be processed.

STORE LEDGER AND VENDOR FILE.   Store ledger and vendor files will be consolidated, and the information on them will be stored on magnetic tape in stock number order. Each record on the file will contain the following information arranged by fields:

1. Stock item number
2. Item description
3. Detail of current monthly transactions
4. Current balance on hand
5. Current balance on order
6. Total balance on hand and on order
7. Reorder point
8. Reorder quantity
9. Vendor's name and address

PROCESSING.   The master store ledger and vendor file will be updated by the transaction inputs, and a comparison check will be made between the balance on hand and on order and the reorder point. If a new purchase is required, a purchase order is prepared using the vendor's information and the reorder quantity from the master file. If no new order is required, processing of the transaction cards continues. Error messages are printed on the console printer if there is any miscoding of stock numbers on the transaction cards.

This batch processing system is shown in Figure 8-7. As in the manual illustration, the flow is from top to bottom. In this system, however, all tasks shown are performed in the IS department. Moreover, a father-son sequential updating process is used to update both the stock record and the vendor file at the same time. A new master is created, the old one is retained along with the transaction input cards, and an error listing is prepared. Furthermore, tape and card input into the update process is shown as output. Sometimes this output is not shown; it is assumed.

On-Line Interactive Processing

Consider again the same illustration. The Buymore Corporation decides to convert its records to a random access file, so that input is no longer required to be in sequential order by stock number. In addition, receiving information, returns and adjustments, and store requisitions are keyed into the system via terminals, some of which are at remote locations. Error messages will be displayed on a CRT, and three copies of the purchase order will be distributed and filed as before. A record of transactions will be retained on magnetic tape for future reference. Moreover, management now has access to the information on the master file via remote CRTs which have keyboard input. Key input is assumed with the CRT display; thus the key input symbol is redundant. As in the update process, this inquiry process generates a transaction tape. This on-line random access system is shown in Figure 8-8.

Document Flowchart

Since the objective of flowcharting is to describe the system, it is often advantageous to cast the basic elements of a flowchart in a different form. One of the more common alternatives stresses the flow of documents from one department to another. In Figure 8-9 we illustrate a *document flowchart* for the manual system

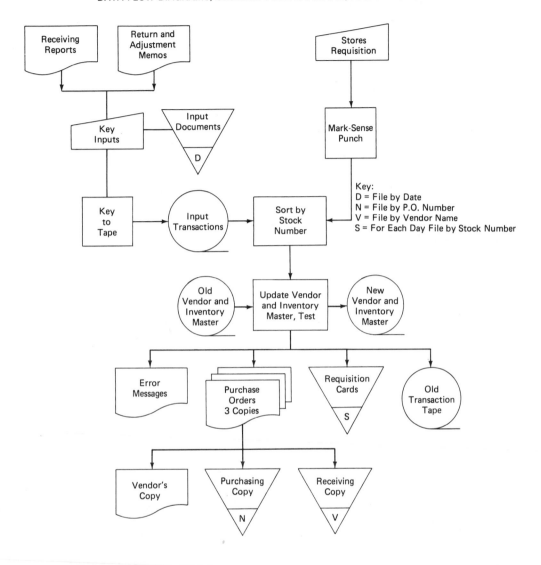

FIGURE 8-7 Batch processing.
Source: AICPA adapted.

in Figure 8-6. Across the top or down the side the various departments are noted, and the flow of each document is shown as it moves from its point of origin to its point of final disposition. Often just rectangles or squares are used to represent the documents; here we use the document symbol. In Figure 8-9 we also show the location of the files used in the system. An accountant or systems analyst generally adds the processing steps to this flowchart. With this last addition, the document flowchart will describe all the attributes of the system and

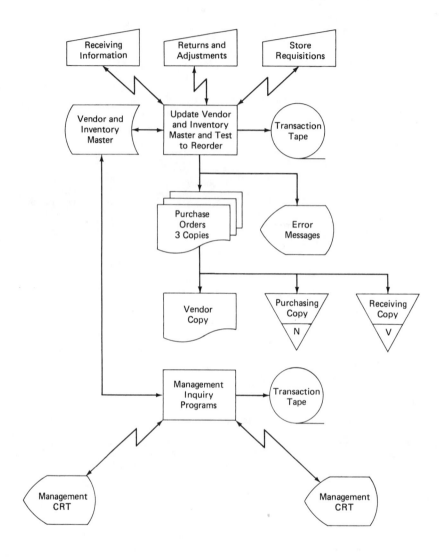

FIGURE 8-8   On-line processing.
Source: AICPA adapted.

how it operates like a systems flowchart. A good example of this combined system and document flowchart is shown in Figure 8-10, which describes a manual raw material purchase function.

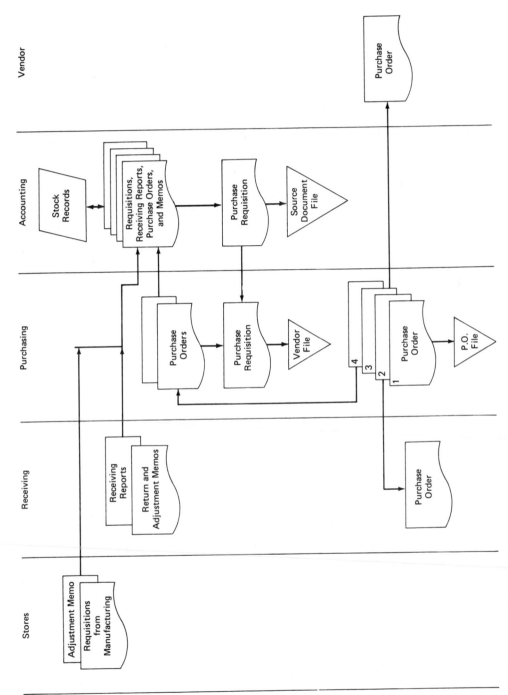

FIGURE 8-9 Document flowchart.

Source: AICPA Staff Level Training Program—Adapted.

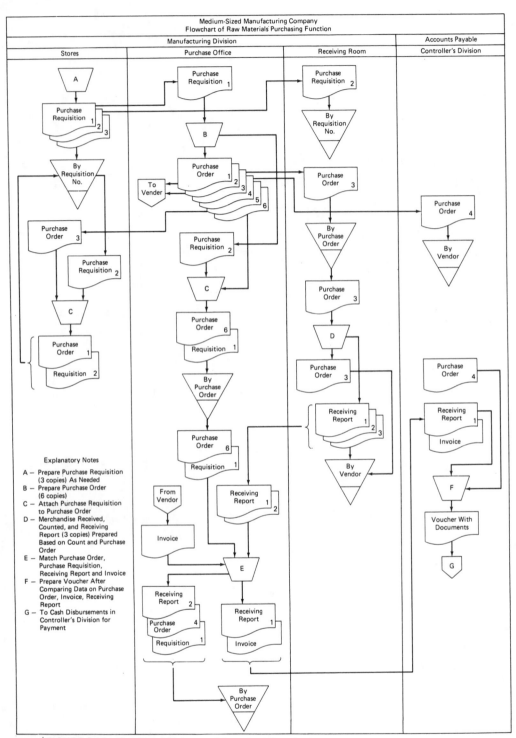

FIGURE 8-10 Combined system and document flowchart.

Source: AICPA adapted.

SYSTEMS FLOWCHART UTILIZATION

A systems flowchart or an amplified document flowchart that includes files and processing steps will be useful, if not absolutely necessary, for many reasons. First, it pictorially *describes a system* and shows how all the processing steps, controls, personnel or departments, decisions, documents, reports, files and databases, and processing equipment interrelate to form a system. This is almost impossible to do in a narrative description. This description is useful to auditors, accountants, and systems analysts and, to a limited degree, to management in helping to understand an *existing* or *proposed* system. Moreover, systems flowcharting is most useful in planning new accounting or information systems in which the accountant or systems analyst must integrate all the elements to support the management system effectively. Frequently it is prepared from data flow diagrams after it is determined how all the elements of the system are used to process information that is required in the data flow diagram which merely describes what must be done by the accounting system. A systems flowchart is also very useful in *documenting* a system. In brief form it describes the essential character of all the elements of the system and their interrelationships.

In addition to capturing the essence of the system as a whole, auditors, accountants, and systems analysts can use the systems flowchart to describe control, processing, and document flow *detail* for analysis and use by the company's employees as they process information.

In summary, in a series of flowcharts the organization of the system's elements, the movement of data, decisions, controls, processing functions, personnel, and audit trails can be shown for a variety of uses.

PREPARING DATA FLOW DIAGRAMS
AND SYSTEM FLOWCHARTS

The basic diagramming and charting guidelines can be outlined as follows:

1. Start with the focus of the data flow diagram or system flowchart.
2. Show input and output related to the focal point.
3. For the system flow chart show how input and output are prepared, filed, and distributed.
4. Show interface with other systems.
5. For system flowcharts show other relevant information using annotations, striping, and various codes. This may include departments, personnel, controls, interfaces, and references to other flowcharts.

Beyond guidelines such as these, an emphasis on communication of relevant information about the system (which is the purpose of the diagram or chart), and the use of standardized symbols and conventions, data flow diagram or flowchart preparation is much more of an art than a standardized procedure. No two auditors, controllers, managers, systems analysts, or systems designers will perceive the information needs or system the same way or in the same detail at every point. Thus all data flow diagrams and flowcharts will be different in terms of their emphasis, in much the same way that narrative description of an event or process will be different.

We have frequently referred to the fact that management is able to use data flow diagrams and system flowcharts. However, this is only true if management personnel have had some training. This is not always the case. In this latter situation, the narrative description of the system takes on a much more prominent role, and the data flow diagram or systems flowchart becomes supplementary information. A typical report to management describing a system may therefore adhere to the following general outline:

1. Description of business and decision-making environments
2. Narrative overview of decision or transaction processing cycles
3. For each decision or transaction processing cycle:
    a. A narrative outlining the system and detailing strengths and weaknesses found in the system
    b. Discussion of the consequences of these strengths and weaknesses
    c. Suggestions or recommendations for any problems found in the system
    d. Supporting systems flowchart showing recommendations
4. Summary suggestions and comments

In other words, less reliance is placed on the flowchart if management has not been trained to use system flowcharts effectively.

SYSTEMS DOCUMENTATION

Documentation is necessary for several reasons. First, it is useful for the *communication* of the essential elements, of an automated or manual data processing system, to many users who need to know how the system functions. It is the prime communication link between many parts of the organization and their respective systems. The users are managers, auditors, systems analysts, operators, clerks who prepare input, system designers, and programmers. Second, documentation sets forth *how the system should operate* through statements of policies and procedures, and as such serves as a benchmark for performance comparison by the company or by independent auditors. Third, documentation is very useful for *training* new employees in the operation of the system. Fourth, it is the *basis for future modification* of the system because the modification can affect all elements of the system, including hardware, software, personnel, and procedures. Fifth, it describes the logic used in computer programs. Sixth, documentation is useful for *ensuring* a high degree of *uniformity* and *consistency* within the system because it is a guideline for all the activities of the system. Finally, it *describes the organization* of the accounting or information system and shows how that system operates to meet the information requirements of the management system. Lack of documentation is a serious control weakness. The types of systems documentation that fill these needs are systems definition, program documentation, and operator instructions. We will examine each of these separately.

Systems Definition

The purpose of systems definition is to communicate to users of the information system how the system and all its elements are organized to accomplish the objective of supporting the management system. This purpose is accomplished through inclusion of the following elements of systems definition.

First, the documentation of each system and the modifications to the system must contain *basic descriptive data,* such as the name of the system, its purpose, the date of the documentation, the name of the analyst or designer, and the authorization and approval for modification or implementation.

Second, the *purpose of the system* must be summarized. This statement of purpose must include the transaction processing, operational, managerial, and strategic activities that require the information generated by the system. It must indicate how the information system proposes to satisfy these information requirements. Critical assumptions must also be included here.

Third, a *systems flowchart* should be included to document the information system. The flowchart should include all of the interrelated parts and interfaces, detailed processing procedures, data files, controls, and flows of data.

Fourth, a *narrative description* of the system should accompany the flowchart. This should not substitute for the flowchart. It should only complement the flowchart. An exception to this is noted earlier where management may not understand the flowchart.

Fifth, *input* into the system should be clearly specified. Responsibilities, procedures (including keying, batching, and control procedures), formats, and a complete description of each entry are necessary. Examples of input are the most useful way to clarify the form and content required. Descriptions of input for a general ledger subsystem would include, for example, the description of standard journal entries for recurring transactions, adjustments, and closing entries. Input for an on-line microcomputer general ledger system, for example, would include illustrations of input menus.

Sixth, as in the case of input, *output* must be clearly specified. Examples of output documents, reports, and on-line query menus are most useful in documenting output of a system.

Seventh, the organization, content, and actual layout of systems *files* and *database* must be specified. Actual examples of the record and file layouts are useful here. For database systems, the schema which describes the organization of the database data structure, and data dictionaries which describe the characteristics of the database, are essential. These will be described in detail in the next chapters. Moreover, backup and retention procedures must be described. The company's chart of accounts and coding structure, for example, should be specified as part of the description of the data files.

Eighth, a *description of hardware, software,* and *personnel* should be included. Both the specifications and the descriptions of the actual elements are useful for future evaluation or modification of the system.

Ninth, systems and programming *testing, conversion,* and *implementation procedures* are necessary to ensure that these activities are properly carried out for the system and all modifications. Therefore, all results of the tests for the initial installation and for each modification should be included with the system documentation. These results enable management, auditors, and systems analysts to know with reasonable assurance that the system is operating as it should.

Tenth, and perhaps of overriding importance, systems *analysis and design policies* and *procedures* must be spelled out. Adherence to these policies and procedures, such as the structured approach presented in this text, should be documented. Evidence of compliance with these procedures can go a long way toward ensuring that the information system supports the management system effectively, efficiently, and with a high degree of reliability.

Program Documentation

Programs must be described in detail so that the systems analysts and programmers can modify and change them. To a limited extent, the program documentation is used by auditors when they review the system.

First, as in systems documentation, each program and modification to a program must contain *essential data* such as the name of the program, a date, its purpose, preparer or programmer, authorization, and approval.

Second, each program must be described by a *program flowchart* detailing all input, logic, files, and output of the program. If the structured design approach is used, these need to be tied to the data flow diagrams or the hierarchical charts which describe what must be done.

Third, the flowchart must be accompanied by a *narrative description* to supplement the program flowchart. Decision tables and input/output matrices are useful for this description. Procedural specifications related to the program should be documented in the narrative description.

Fourth, as with systems documentation, *input, output,* and *files* must be fully specified using examples wherever feasible to enhance the description.

Fifth, *test procedures* and *results* should be included to ensure proper testing and give the user confidence in the program.

Sixth, a program *listing* should be included.

Seventh, *run procedures* exactly like those described in the next section should be included.

These documentation procedures should be followed even for end-user developed programs and reporting procedures. For example, microcomputer spreadsheet and database reports which are developed by management should be well documented for the reasons just given.

Operator Instructions

The operator of the system knows how files or data are organized, how programs actually work, and how the operating or database system operates. Thus, a special *run book,* or *book of operator instructions* is prepared so that he or she can operate the programs and procedures that constitute the system without detailed knowledge presented in other documentation. This is even true of small microcomputer systems.

First, as before, *descriptive data* such as the name of the program, data, preparer, authorization, and approval must be included.

Second, the *time schedules* for running the program and the data files (tapes, diskettes or disks) to be used are noted. Program, file, and disk labels are included in this description.

Third, *setup* procedures, including JCL (job-control language) instructions, *displays, start* procedures, *restart* procedures, *halt* procedures, *control* and *balancing* procedures, *output* distribution procedures, query, and *backup* procedures, are clearly spelled out. This generally means that sample form, report, and menu formats are included to aid in the description of each run.

The run book should be sufficient for the operator to do all that is necessary to run the program and no more. Many of the commercially available microcomputer accounting systems are excellent examples of these instructions with step-by-step operating procedures and accompanying input and output descriptions. Moreover, provisions are present in many of the software packages for microcomputer end-user systems to prevent operators from changing the program (spreadsheet or database for example). They can only fill in the blanks to enter or retrieve data with these programs. This is accomplished by locking the part of the program that the user should not have access to in the normal course of processing transactions.

Documentation Control and Summary

It is important that procedure manuals and general guidelines be set forth for each organization to ensure proper documentation. Moreover, control must be maintained over the documentation of systems. All documentation must be secure from unauthorized access, and sufficient backup must be retained to reconstruct all the records discussed earlier in this chapter. In addition, all modifications must be appropriately posted to both the main set of documentation records and the backup.

Good documentation, consisting of documentation of the system, the program or manual procedures used, and operator or clerical instructions, is very important. It not only affects the administrative and accounting control of the business but also gives auditors, managers, and analysts much-needed confidence in the information system. Good documentation is important for both those large complex systems designed using a formal structured approach and those small less formal systems such as spreadsheets or database report generators that are designed by end-users. Computer software can be used effectively to aid in maintaining good documentation. All the documentation can be retained in a wordprocessing file for easy modification as changes are made. For many micro systems the software itself provides much of the needed documentation via report format and data structure descriptions, for example.

If the system is well designed and properly documented, and if clerical, IS, and managerial personnel comply with the system as documented, the transactions will be processed, reports generated, and decisions made in accordance with managerial policy. Moreover, good documentation will aid in training users and operators of the system and in designing new systems or modifications of the present system. Good design is the cornerstone of effective and efficient accounting and administrative controls and can affect the information system's support of the management system.

SUMMARY

Data flow diagrams, system flowcharts, and documentation are essential for a well-designed information system that supports the management system of the company. Data flow diagrams show *what* the system must do to support the management system. Flowcharting is used to describe *how* the system operates. Flowcharts are used by a variety of users such as systems designers, auditors, the controller, and, to some extent, management. Documentation is the reference and set of instructions for future users, reviewers, and analysts of the system. Systems flowcharts are an integral part of documentation.

SELECTED REFERENCES

AICPA, *Staff Training Program—Level I System Flowcharting Seminar.*

ARENS, ALVIN A., AND JAMES K. LOEBBECKE. *Auditing: An Integrated Approach.* Englewood Cliffs, N.J.: Prentice Hall, 1980.

DAVIS, WILLIAM S., *Systems Analysis and Design: A Structured Approach.* Reading, Mass.: Addison-Wesley, 1983.

GOLEN, STEVEN AND JAMES WORTHINGTON, "Flowcharts and Graphics: Part I," *The CPA Journal*, March 1986.

MARSHALL, GEORGE R., *Systems Analysis and Design: Alternative Structured Approaches.* Englewood Cliffs, N.J.: Prentice Hall, 1986.

PEAT, MARWICK, MITCHELL & CO., "Systems Evaluation Approach: Documentation of Controls (SEADOC)," PPM & Co., 1980

PORTER, W. THOMAS, AND WILLIAM E. PERRY, *EDP Controls and Auditing.* 5th Ed. Kent Publishing Company, Boston, Mass, 1987.

WEBER, RON, *EDP Auditing: Conceptual Foundations and Practice.* 2nd. ed. New York: McGraw-Hill, 1988

REVIEW QUESTIONS

1. What flowchart symbol should be used for each of the following:
   a. CRT input
   b. key-to-disk
   c. video display
   d. computer processing
   e. a random access file
   f. magnetic tape
   g. connector
   h. a ledger
   i. sales journal
   j. paper source documents
   k. mechanical sorter
   l. diskette
   m. data card
   n. communication link
   o. on-line terminal

2. For what purposes is striping used?

3. What should be the focus of the flowchart?

4. What are the advantages of a document flowchart?

5. For what purpose are system flowcharts used?

6. Why is documentation necessary?

7. Of what does systems documentation consist?

8. What is a *run book* and how does it differ from *program documentation*?

9. What elements comprise a systems definition in a well-documented system?

10. Good program documentation should consist of what components?

CASES

8-1 (Data Flow Diagram and System Flowchart) Charting, Inc., a new audit client of yours, processes its sales and cash receipts documents in the following manner:

1. Cash receipts.   The mail is opened each morning by a mail clerk in the sales department. The mail clerk prepares a remittance advice (showing customer and amount paid) if one has not been received. The checks and remittance advices are then forwarded to the sales department supervisor, who reviews each check and forwards the checks and remittance advices to the accounting department supervisor.

The accounting department supervisor, who also functions as the credit manager, reviews all checks for payments of past-due accounts and then forwards the checks and remittance advices to the accounts receivable clerk, who arranges the advices in alphabetical order. The remittance advices are posted directly to the accounts receivable ledger cards. The checks are endorsed by stamp and totaled. The total is posted to the cash receipts journal. The remittance advices are filed chronologically.

After receiving the cash from the preceding day's cash sales, the accounts receivable clerk prepares the daily deposit slip in triplicate. The third copy of the deposit slip is filed by date, and the second copy and the original accompany the bank deposit.

2. Sales.   Salesclerks prepare the sales invoice in triplicate. The original and the second copy are presented to the cashier. The third copy is retained by the salesclerk in the sales book. When the sale is for cash, the customer pays the salesclerk, who presents the money to the cashier with the invoice copies.

A credit sale is approved by the cashier from an approved credit list after the salesclerk prepares the three-part invoice. After receiving the cash or approved invoice, the cashier validates the original copy of the sales invoice and gives it to the customer. At the end of each day the cashier recaps the sales and cash received and forwards the cash and the second copy of all sales invoices to the accounts receivable clerk.

The accounts receivable clerk balances the cash received with cash sales invoices and prepares a daily sales summary. The credit sales invoices are posted to the accounts receivable ledger, and then all invoices are sent to the inventory control clerk in the sales department for posting to the inventory control catalog. After posting, the inventory control clerk files all invoices numerically. The accounts receivable clerk posts the daily sales summary to the cash receipts journal and sales journal and files the sales summaries by date.

The cash from cash sales is combined with the cash received on account, and this constitutes the daily bank deposit.

3. Bank Deposits.   Monthly bank statements are reconciled promptly by the accounting department supervisor and filed by date.

REQUIRED:

1. Prepare a high-level data flow diagram of the basic sales and cash receipts functions and data stores of Charting, Inc.

2. Using a combined document systems flowchart, flowchart the sales and cash receipts functions for Charting, Inc., using good form. Show the segregation of duties.
   (AICPA adapted.)

8-2 You have been engaged to design a new order entry system for Peters Engine Company, a manufacturer of small, two-cycle engines for lawn mowers and outboard motors. During the analysis you reviewed their current order entry

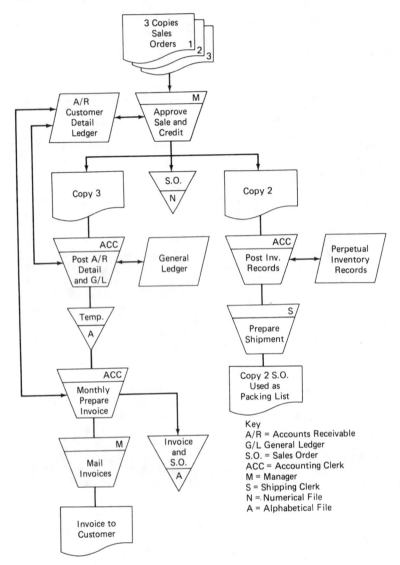

FIGURE C8-1   Peters Engine Company.

procedure. As part of this review you flow-charted their current order processing. This process is shown in Figure C8-1.

Before you begin to consider various design alternatives, you need to consider what process, data stores, and external entities are involved in this process. Moreover, it is imperative that you obtain a clear understanding of the logical process involved in processing sales orders.

REQUIRED: Prepare a data flow diagram for this system and explain how it is useful in the analysis phase of structured systems design.

8-3 (System Flowchart and Data Flow Diagram) Baxter Computer Mart sells computer hardware and software to customers through a mail and telephone order system. Sales orders are keyed into a CRT as they arrive via telephone or mail. Orders shipped the next day or they are back ordered. The following processing activities are performed:

1. Sales are recorded.

2. Invoices are sent to customers upon shipment of merchandise.

3. The accounts receivable file is updated.

4. Inventory is updated and replenished when stock is low.

5. Back orders are processed and shipped as stock is received.

6. Accounts receivable, back orders, and stock status reports are prepared for management for their use in responding to customer requests and inquiry. These reports are on line.

7. Summary sales statistics, aging schedules, and inventory status reports are prepared monthly for management decision making.

8. Purchase orders are prepared automatically for stock which is low. These are mailed after a listing of them is reviewed by the purchasing manager for items which are not longer in demand.

9. The accounts payable file is updated as merchandise and related invoices are received.

Baxter Computer Mart maintains the following files on a disk in a database:

1. Daily sales orders transaction file

2. Inventory

3. Back order list

4. Purchase order file

5. Accounts receivable file

6. Accounts payable file

7. Sales order file

REQUIRED: Prepare both a system flowchart and a data flow diagram for Baxter Computer Mart.

8-4 Well-managed organizations prepare, use, and maintain policy and procedure manuals covering all important functional areas. An accounting manual describes the accounting policies and procedures to be employed by an organization. However, because first-time development of an accounting manual may appear to be a formidable task, an organization may procrastinate in developing an accounting manual in spite of numerous long-term benefits.

REQUIRED:

1. Explain how systems documentation (accounting manual) benefits an organization.

2. Identify and discuss the content of such documentation
(CMA adapted.)

8-5 (Systems Flowchart) An on-line sales order entry system has an edit routine prior to master file updating and an inquiry provision to make sure sufficient stock is on hand prior to initiating the entry of the sales order. Orders are stored temporarily on a disk pending edit clearance. Sales personnel have access to the system via remote terminals in their field office. Once sufficient stock is deemed to be on hand, the order is cleared and the job-order master file is updated.

REQUIRED: Sketch a systems flowchart for the sales order entry system.
(CIA adapted.)

8-6 You have been assigned to review the documentation of accounting information system for your firm.

REQUIRED:

1. List the advantages of adequate documentation.

2. Indicate by each element in the list which manual it will be found in. Use a letter to indicate the following manuals:

A. System documentation
B. Run manual
C. Program Documentation

1. Purpose of system
2. Procedures needed to balance and reconcile data input/output
3. Record layouts
4. Data relationships
5. Data flow diagrams
6. Data formats
7. Instructions to show proper use of each report
8. Restart and recovery procedures
9. Instructions to ensure the proper completion of all input forms
10. System flowchart
11. Test results
12. Program flowchart
13. Time schedule for runs
14. Messages and programmed halts
15. Report distribution instructions
16. List of system controls

8-7 (Flowchart Symbols) You are reviewing audit work papers containing a narrative description of the Tenney Corporation's factory payroll system. A portion of that narrative follows:

Factory employees punch time clock cards each day when entering or leaving the shop. At the end of each week, the timekeeping department collects the time cards and prepares duplicate batch-control slips by department showing total hours and number of employees.

The time cards and original batch-control slips are sent to the payroll accounting section.

The second copies of the batch-control slips are filed by date. In the payroll accounting section, payroll transaction cards are keyed to a disk from the information of the timecards, and a batch total for each batch is keyed in for control purposes from the batch-control slip. The timecards and batch-control slips are then filed by batch for possible reference. Time data is stored by employee number within each batch. Each batch is edited by a computer program which checks the validity of the employee number against a master employee tape file and the total hours and number of employees against the batch total. A detail printout by batch and employee number is produced, which indicates batches that do not balance and invalid employee numbers. This printout is returned to payroll accounting to resolve all differences.

In searching for documentation, you found a flowchart of the payroll system that included all appropriate symbols but was only partially labeled. The portion of this flowchart described by the foregoing narrative is shown in Figure C8-2.

REQUIRED:

1. Number your answers 1 through 15. Next to the corresponding number of your answer, supply the appropriate labeling (document name, process description, or file order) application to each numbered symbol on the flowchart.

2. Flowcharts are one of the aids an auditor can use to determine and evaluate a client's internal control system. List the advantages of using flowcharts in this context.

(Adapted from the CPA examination.)

8-8 (Flowchart Symbols) The independent auditor must evaluate a client's system of internal control to determine the extent to which various auditing procedures must be employed. A client who uses a computer should provide the CPA with a flowchart of the information processing system so that the CPA can evaluate the control features in the system. Figure C8-3 shows a simplified flowchart, such as a client might provide. Unfortunately the client had only partially completed the flowchart when you requested it.

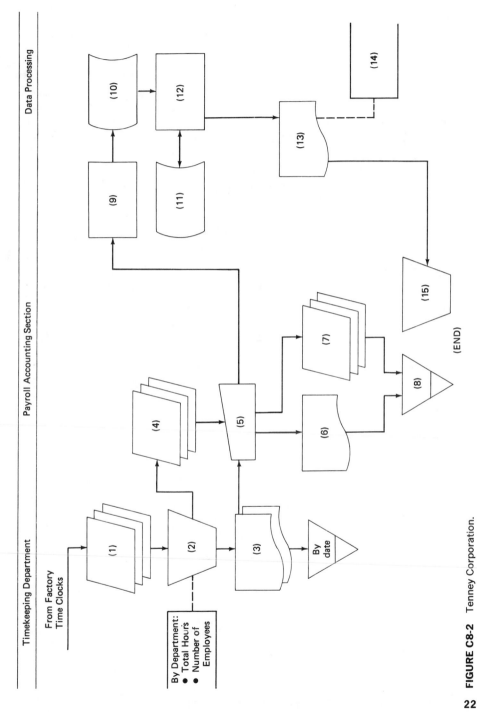

FIGURE C8-2 Tenney Corporation.

227

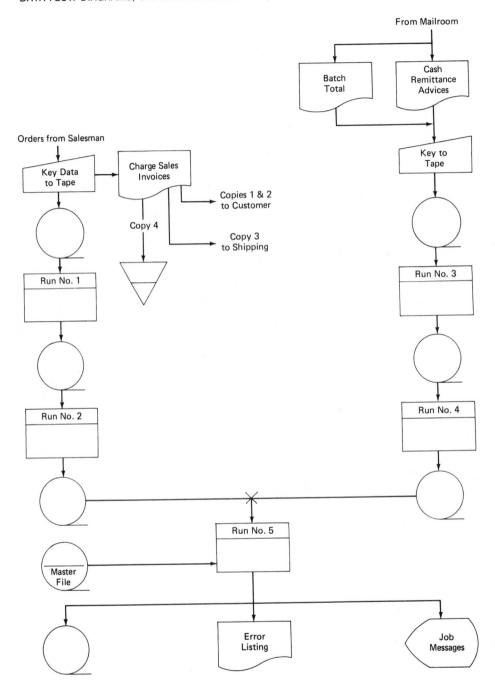

FIGURE C8-3 Simplified sample flowchart to be completed.

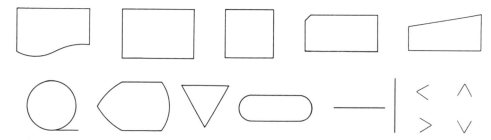

FIGURE C8-4   Flowchart symbols.

REQUIRED:

1. Complete the flowchart shown in Figure C8-3.

2. Describe what each item in the flowchart indicates. When complete, your description should provide an explanation of the processing of data involved. Your description should be in the following order:

   a. "Orders from salesperson" to "Run no. 5"

   b. "From mailroom" to "Run no. 5"

   c. "Run no. 5" through the remainder of the chart

3. Name each of the flowchart symbols shown in Figure C8-4 and describe what each represents.
   (Adapted from the CPA examination.)

8-9 (Documentation) The documentation of data processing applications is an important step in the design and implementation of any computer-based system. Documentation provides a complete record of data processing applications. However, documentation is a phase of systems development that is often neglected. While documentation can be tedious and time consuming, the lack of proper documentation can be very costly for an organization.

REQUIRED:

1. Identify and explain briefly the purposes that proper documentation can serve.

2. Discuss briefly the basic types of information that should be included in the documentation of a data processing application.

3. What policies should be established to regulate access to documentation data for purposes of information or modification for the following four groups of company employees?

   a. Computer operators

   b. Internal auditors

   c. Production planning analysts

   d. System analysts
      Adapted from the CMA examination.

8-10 (Data Flow Diagram and System Flowchart) Until recently, Consolidated Electric Company employed a batch processing system for recording the receipt of customer payments. The following narrative and attached flowchart (Figure C8-5) describe the procedures involved in this system.

The customer's payment and the remittance advice are received in the treasurer's office. These are optically scanned. The cash receipt is added to a control tape listing and is then filed for deposit later in the day. When the deposit slips are received from IS later in the day, the cash receipts are removed from the file and deposited with the original deposit slip. The second copy of the deposit slip and the control tape are compared for accuracy before the deposit is made and are then filed together. In the IS department, the remittance advices received from the treasurer's office are held until 2:00 P.M. daily. At that time the customer payments are processed to update the records on magnetic tape and to prepare a deposit slip in triplicate. During the update process, data are read from the master accounts receivable

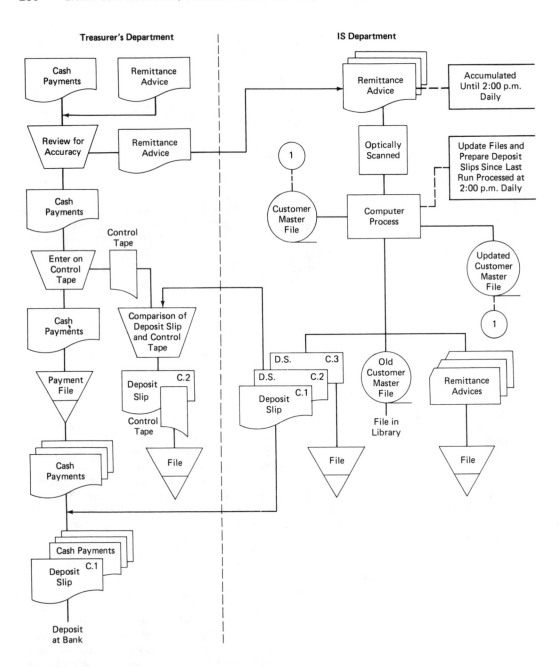

FIGURE C8-5 Consolidated Electric Company.

tape, processed, and then recorded on a new master tape. The original and a second copy of the deposit slip are forwarded to the treasurer's office. The old master tape (former accounts receivable file), the remittance advices (in customer number order), and the third copy of the deposit slip are stored and filed in a secure place. The updated accounts receivable master tape is maintained in the system for processing the next day.

The firm has revised and redesigned its computer system so that it has on-line capabilities. The new cash receipts procedures, described below, are designed to take advantage of the new system.

The customer's payment and remittance advice are received in the treasurer's office, as before. A cathode ray tube terminal is located in the treasurer's office to enter the cash receipts. An operator keys in the customer's number and payment from the remittance advice and check. The cash receipt is entered into the system once the operator has confirmed that the proper account and amount are displayed on the screen. The payment is then processed on-line against the accounts receivable file maintained on magnetic disk. The cash receipts are filed for deposit later in the day. The remittance advices are filed in the order in which they are processed; these punched cards will be kept until the next working day and then destroyed. The computer prints out a deposit slip in duplicate at 2:00 P.M. for all cash receipts since the last deposit. The deposit slips are forwarded to the treasurer's office. The cash receipts are removed from the file and deposited with the original deposit slip; the duplicate deposit slip is filed for further reference. At the close of business hours (5:00 P.M.) each day, the IS department prepares a record of the current day's cash receipts activity on a magnetic tape. This tape is then stored in a secure place in the event of a systems malfunction; after ten working days the tape is released for further use.

REQUIRED:

1. Prepare a data flow diagram of the logic of the cash-receipts procedure.
2. Prepare a system flowchart of the physical components of the cash-receipts procedure.
(Adapted from the CMA examination.)

8-11 (Systems Flowchart) A company uses sequential batch processing of invoices which are keyed on to a disk and tested by batch prior to processing. Hash, number of transactions, and dollar amount batch totals are used in the verification process. The original invoices are filed numerically. A transaction file is kept on all transactions prior to updating. Exception reports, which are used to reconcile batch totals, good transactions, and exceptions, are generated as a byproduct of updating the master file. The updated master file tape is used in further processing.

REQUIRED: Prepare a systems flowchart of this processing operation.

8-12 Aero Freight Corporation, an airline specializing in overnight delivery of freight throughout the continental United States, uses a microprocessor to schedule its thirty-one planes, which converge at a private airport near Oklahoma City, unload their freight, sort it, and fly it to various locations throughout the country. The airline grew rapidly over the years and employed very talented programming assistants who were trained in operations research to maximize throughput on the least number of aircraft at the lowest fuel cost.

One day Aero Freight's programmer (the top systems designer) left the company. Aero Freight operated without problems until it added a thirty-second plane to its fleet and the optimization program failed. No one could find the problem and fix it. Aero Freight therefore operated with thirty-one aircraft for six months until one of its analysts, who had some training in optimization models, discovered that one of the data fields in an obscure, little-used subroutine only had a dimension of 31 instead of 32.

REQUIRED: What could have prevented this problem from occurring in the first place? How?

8-13 Not too long ago, Cattleman's Supply of Kansas City merged with one of its competitors in the area, Big Ranch Supply, creating the entity now called Ranchers Supply. Both institutions had entrenched installations of personal computers with many users. In the organizational confusion that ensued, hundreds of employees were shuffled between retail outlets and offices in the region. PCs and software were similarly shifted about. Many dissatisfied employees left the newly created company and took their knowledge with them.

Ben Austin, who became Ranchers Supply manager of microcomputer-support services, after the merger said, "All of a sudden we had two of everything. We had two hardware vendors, two service contracts, and two departments for every function. We had to bring all this together into one cohesive, functioning microcomputer operation."

The biggest headache was yet to come. When the dust settled, department managers found that many of their PCs and applications had been separated from their original developers. As a result, department managers throughout the organization found themselves with important and valuable microcomputer applications that nobody knew how to use. "When things are going smoothly, and personnel changes are minimal, no one notices that there's no documentation," Mr. Austin said. "What really brought this problem to light was this merger. Division managers were faced with PC models for sales analysis and financial planning they couldn't use."

Many of these managers assigned new employees the task of unraveling the mysteries of these applications. "It was an extreme inconvenience," Mr. Austin said. "Good documentation would have helped considerably because spreadsheet models can attain stupefying levels of complexity. Some people had developed huge sales-analysis spreadsheets." Faced with this crisis Mr. Austin decided it was necessary to prevent the problem from happening again. "We established an in-house systems development course for PC software," said Mr. Austin. "It includes instruction on the fundamentals of systems analysis and design including procedures for good documentation. A manual accompanied this instruction." Mr. Austin emphasized that, "The information center microcomputer-support services alone could not handle the burden of documenting all PC applications and that end users must share the responsibility of good documentation."

REQUIRED:
1. What went wrong and caused the problems with microcomputers?
2. Why did the Ranchers Supply take the action noted above?
3. What burden is placed on the end user and how important is this task?

9

FILE MANAGEMENT ACCOUNTING SYSTEMS

INTRODUCTION

An organization's data resource is an extremely valuable asset and it must be managed carefully. In general, an organization may choose to organize this resource around applications and: (1) develop what constitutes a file-oriented system for these applications; or (2) develop a database approach where numerous applications would use a common database.

Data management systems are becoming increasingly important as a foundation for accounting information. Often transaction processing activities, which cut across functional areas in accounting, require a common database. Management often needs accounting information from a variety of sources pulled together to form a comprehensive view of a situation. These and many other accounting needs require the integration of varied data elements in order to process a transaction or to prepare a report. Contemporary file management and database systems provide management with the data integration facilities needed to accomplish this.

Data management systems may be classified as either single file management (often called file-oriented) systems and multiple file database systems. In

Single File Application Systems

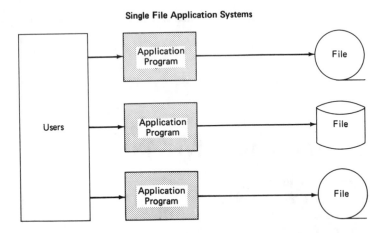

FIGURE 9-1   Single file application system vs. multiple file database system.

this chapter we focus on single file (or file-oriented) processing systems. We will examine data hierarchy concepts, consider accounting information classification requirements and data coding. Emphasis will be given to file organization and structure. Updating and file processing procedures will be reviewed for each of these structures. The weaknesses of the file-oriented approaches will be reviewed. In the next chapter, multiple file processing and database systems will be presented. Each chapter will review the key components, the structure of the data, and relevant advantages and disadvantages of each system.

Single file approaches to the management of accounting information have been used for many years. They tend to be used in the batch processing of transaction data and follow a procedure where transactions are processed with one file in run No. 1, then processed against another file in run No. 2, and so on. Often there exists a long series of these processing runs. What is unique is the processing data of one single file at a time and that each of these files is designed for that particular processing step, or, in a broader sense, a single application. Single file applications comprise a large number of accounting information systems in use today. These systems use flat files and they are relatively straightforward in design. They require less expensive hardware, simpler software, and less expertise to operate. For the most part they resemble, in appearance, a manual system and as such are fairly easy to understand. In many situations they are both effective and efficient. In a single file system, each application has its own file and generally there is little sharing of data among various applications. The application software (program) for a system built upon this file-oriented arrangement depends on the file structure; therefore, for example, if the format of the file changes, then the software also has to be changed. As a result applications and files are very *dependent* on each other. Figure 9-1 illustrates this data processing structure.

The single file approach to data processing is still used extensively in business even though database management systems are becoming more readily available and are often more desirable for organizing, storing, and accessing accounting data. The large investment in single file systems and their associated software, their simplicity, and the ease with which they handle batch processing requirements explains their continued widespread use in practice. In addition, there is a great deal of inertia to be overcome in shifting to a database approach. It is therefore important that we study the concepts associated with the file-oriented data management systems. Many of these concepts are also integral parts of database systems. The entire focus is different; single file systems are driven by the applications they serve where as database systems are founded on the overall needs of the organization for a common data set to be shared by all applications.

DATA HIERARCHY AND KEYS

Data Item (Element), Field, Record, and File

The smallest unit of data that has meaning to a user is a *data item (element)*. Data items are the basic building blocks of a data file or a database. These items are composed of characters which are technically called bytes. Each byte is, in turn, generally composed of 8 bits which are used to physically code the data[1] in the computer.

Keys

Data items are grouped together, depending on the needs of the user, to form *records* in a file-oriented system as shown by the rows in Figure 9-2. An application program usually reads and writes records. A user inquiry or an application program may access a single data item, a group of data items, and/or a record. Records that are grouped together are referred to as a *file*, such as the customer file shown in Figure 9-2. The grouping of data items into records, and records into files, does not mean that the items are necessarily physically grouped the same way, although the physical grouping does follow in many single file-oriented systems. In this last case, the data items in the record have the same physical and logical relationships.

A data item can have a *data value* as well as a *data label or field.* The data label is the name used to describe the particular piece of data; the data value is the actual content of the data item. In a payroll application, data items might appear with such labels or fields as EMPLOYEE NAME, SOCIAL SECURITY NUMBER, GROSS INCOME, STATE INCOME, TAX WITHHELD, FEDERAL INCOME TAX WITHHELD, and so forth. The actual data values for these may be: JOHN DOE; 421-32-6844,; $1,192.31; $29.47; and $291.87. For a marketing application, common data items would likely include SALESPERSON'S NAME, SALES TERRITORY, PRODUCT TYPE, NUMBER OF ORDERS, DOLLARS OF ORDERS, COMMISSION PAID, and so forth. Associated data values in this case could be: JOE JONES; MIDWEST; 10; 218; $7,814.00; and $843.21. In a large data file it would not be uncommon to have more than ten thousand data items.

---

[1] Chapter 5 has a complete discussion data.

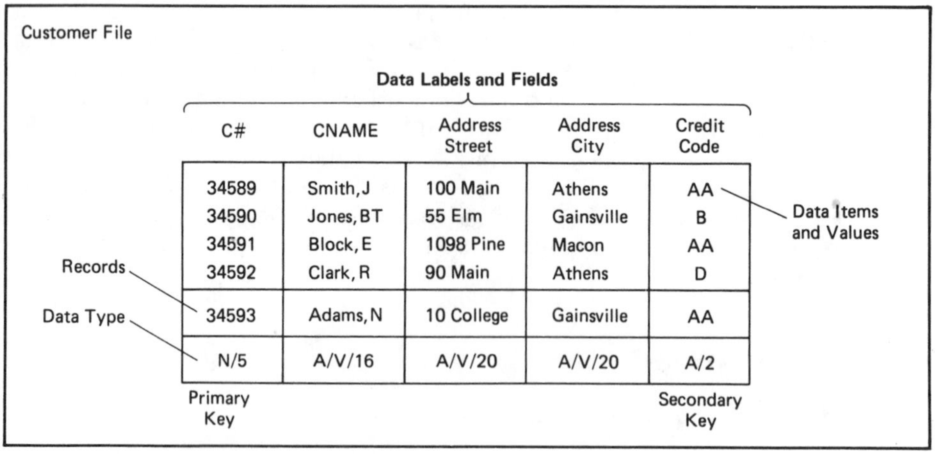

Customer File						

Data Labels and Fields

	C#	CNAME	Address Street	Address City	Credit Code	
	34589	Smith, J	100 Main	Athens	AA	Data Items and Values
	34590	Jones, BT	55 Elm	Gainsville	B	
	34591	Block, E	1098 Pine	Macon	AA	
Records	34592	Clark, R	90 Main	Athens	D	
Data Type	34593	Adams, N	10 College	Gainsville	AA	
	N/5	A/V/16	A/V/20	A/V/20	A/2	
	Primary Key				Secondary Key	

FIGURE 9-2 Data items, fields, records, and files.

Each data item in Figure 9-2 is a specific *data type*. The *data type* that a data item assumes depends upon the encoding scheme employed. Data may be represented in a variety of types (forms) such as the following: (1) alphanumeric; (2) numeric; fixed-point (integer) numeric; (3) numeric, floating-point (decimal) numbers; (4) binary; and (5) logical (true or false). Data items may be variable or fixed in length. Alphanumeric data items are usually variable in length, and numeric items are often fixed in length. In Figure 9-2, the values in the CUSTOMER NUMBER field are numeric and five digits in length (N/5). The CNAME field is alphanumeric, variable in length, up to sixteen characters, (A/V/16). The ADDRESS/STREET field is alphanumeric and variable with a maximum of 20 characters, (A/V/20). The CREDIT CODE field is alphanumeric with two characters, (A/2).

Two additional concepts are depicted in Figure 9-2; these are *primary key* and *secondary keys*. All records must have a primary key for data integrity. Because it is unique it prevents confusion as to what record the accounting application program desires to access or update and it can be used to access the record directly. C# (customer number) is the primary key for the customer record. Secondary keys may or may not be unique; a record can have one or more such keys. Secondary keys are used to access records selectively. For example, by using CREDIT CODE as 'the secondary key, we could selectively retrieve all records with an AA credit rating.

If a secondary key is not unique, the associated file is by definition partitioned into subsets. In Figure 9-2, CREDIT CODE partitions the file into a set of records with codes AA, B, and D. A *set*, therefore, is a group of records that have a common data value.

Data Classification and Coding

CLASSIFICATION.   Data must be organized into files such as those just illustrated, or into databases which will be illustrated in the next chapter. This organization is a function of the application programs which will use the files or the total set of information needs for a database. These needs will specify, for example, the nature of the data items, type of data, and level of detail required. As a result, data will need to be categorized to be stored in files or databases so that it can be used to generate information for transaction processing, reporting, or decision making. This data organization is called classification.

CODES.   Effective classification often requires the data to be coded in a specific way. In Figure 9-2, customer number and credit code are examples of data coding. Data codes serve two purposes: (1) they uniquely identify a record or identify a record as a member of a file; and (2) they are efficient for information transfer purposes, since they require few characters to convey a given amount of information. A number of different coding systems exist, such as *sequence codes, block codes, group codes,* and *mnemonic (association) codes.*

Sequence Codes.   Sequence coding systems employ consecutive numbers (or alphabetic characters) for identifying records, irrespective of the different data item values in the record. Thus a sequence code uniquely identifies a record, but the code indicates nothing further about the record. The customer number (C#) in Figure 9-2 is an example of such a code.

The major advantage of a sequence code is its simplicity. A new record can be added, for example, just by putting it at the end of the sequence and assigning it the next number in the sequence. But this advantage soon disappears when a significant number of records is deleted and added. Deleted records must have their codes reassigned to new records; otherwise gaps occur in the sequence and the code is no longer concise. Also the key has no intrinsic significance. Sequential files help in the establishment of an audit trail and help control for missing records because data can be easily located or missing data can easily be detected.

Block Codes.   Block codes assign blocks of numbers to the particular data items of a record. The primary data items on which records are to be categorized must be chosen and blocks of numbers assigned for each value of the data item. For example, if account numbers for customers are assigned on the basis of the discount allowed, a block code for customer records could be:

701	D. W. Brown	
702	R. K. Allen	5% discount
703	M. M. Moore	
801	S. Elvers	
802	D. D. Rathwell	$5\frac{3}{4}$% discount
803	L. Saunders	
901	M. Lather	$6\frac{1}{4}$% discount
902	L. F. Simmons	

Then all records with this value can be organized in sequence within the block where the first digit represents the block and subsequent digits represent a sequence within the block.

Block codes have the advantage that some information about the record is conveyed by the code. Also, it is relatively easy to add and delete from within each block. The disadvantage is in choosing the size of the block. If the block size is too small, an overflow will occur; if it is too large, wasted characters will occur and the code will no longer be concise. Charts of Account are good examples of block codes.

Chart of Accounts.   Coding and classification are basic to accounting systems, regardless of whether a file-oriented or a database system is employed. An *account* is simply a classification of information usually based on a block coding scheme. The basic double-entry accounting model contains four major accounts: assets, liabilities, revenues, and expenses. The last two comprise equity. But a chart of accounts contains more than aggregate information for these. Each of the major accounts is subdivided into numerous subclassification blocks. Assets are classified as current or noncurrent and are then further subdivided into cash, inventory, receivables, and so forth. Liabilities are subclassified as accounts payable, notes payable, bonds payable, and so forth. Revenues and expenses are subdivided into various revenue sources and categories of expenses, for example. Thus a chart of accounts is nothing more than a scheme for classifying the firm's accounting information in such a manner that the firm can respond to external financial reporting requirements. The classification is also useful for managerial reporting needs, even though it has several limitations in this regard which will be described in the database chapter.

Once the accounts have been selected, they must be grouped into a manageable framework. This can be accomplished using a block coding procedure by assigning each account a multidigit code in which each digit denotes a particular classification. Thus, as can be seen, items are blocks (nested) within blocks. Traditionally a three-digit code is employed, where each digit represents specific categories of information as follows:

```
X   X   X
|   |   |___ Detail account classification
|   |_____ Financial account classification
|_____ Major account classification
```

Major accounts are often classified 100 through 900 (in hundreds):

100	Assets
300	Liabilities
400	Stockholders' Equity
500	Sales
600	Cost of Sales
700	Expenses
800	Other Income
900	Summary Accounts

Within the major classifications, *financial subaccounts* are numbered 10 through 90 (in tens). An example of this subclassification block would be Inventory, with the code 120. The leftmost digit specifies the major account, Assets; the second digit, the subaccount Inventory.

Detailed account classifications are the transaction-level accounts into which data are posted. The subaccounts are generally numbered 1 through 9. An example that illustrates this level of classification or coding would be the bank checking account with code 111. The leftmost digit identifies the major account, Assets; the second digit identifies the financial account, Cash; and the rightmost digit identifies the specific cash account, Checking.

Although there are similarities among all charts of accounts, differences depending on the nature of the business. Accounting for an electronics firm is similar to, but also certainly different from, accounting for a textile firm. Uniform classification of accounts have been developed and published by trade associations and numerous other groups to encourage uniform accounting practice. Figure 9-3 illustrates a general chart of accounts.

Sometimes, as in the case of the chart of accounts, these blocks may be nested into a definite hierarchy according to type of accounts, the market location, or characteristics of the product. This may be done in order of importance. Such block codes are often called hierarchical.

Group Hierarchical Codes. In a group code there is a precise meaning for each component of the code. For example, a hierarchical code representing the

FIGURE 9-3 Chart of accounts (general).

CURRENT ASSETS (100–199)	OWNER'S EQUITY (400–499)
102 Petty cash	450 Capital stock
111 Cash in bank	460 Retained earnings
120 Inventory	
150 Supplies	REVENUES (500–599)
155 Prepaid rent	
	501 Sales—territory 1
PLANT AND EQUIPMENT (200–250)	502 Sales—Territory 2
201 Land	COST OF SALES (600–699)
220 Office equipment	
	610 Salaries
INTANGIBLE ASSETS (280–299)	630 Supplies
	640 Rent
285 Organization costs	
	EXPENSES (700–799)
LIABILITIES (300–399)	
	710 Overhead
310 Accounts payable	
330 Notes payable	SUMMARY ACCOUNTS (900–999)
	910 Income summary

cost item within a cost center within a department within a division of a company might appear as follows:

API	/	437	/	17	/	9113
Division		Department		Cost Center		Cost Item
No.		No.		No.		ID

Group codes can be very helpful to their users because each component of the code conveys information about the data item with which it is associated. There are some problems with using hierarchical codes. If a reorganization in the company occurs and cost center 17 is assigned to another department, then new codes will have to be assigned and the master file changed. This coding structure lends itself to financial reporting needs via responsibility centers. Sometimes the subclassification of a chart of accounts has a precise meaning and it may constitute a group code.

Mnemonic Codes.   Mnemonic codes can all be classified as association codes. With an associated code, the data item of a record is selected, and unique codes are assigned to each data item value. These convey information that is readily understandable. The codes may be alphabetic, numeric, or alphanumeric. The following is an example of an association code assigned to a pair of slacks in a textile plant: SLM3431DRCOT (where: SL = slack; M = male, 34 = 34″ waist size, 31 = 31″ leg inseam, DR = dress, and COT = cotton fabric). Although association codes convey a substantial amount of information about the associated record, they can become very long.

Often an organization will mix various coding schemes. A typical transaction coding structure might employ a seven-digit code, such as 27-111-01. The first two digits could represent a division, department, or profit center, with a sequential numbering scheme 10 through 99. These divisions may be: 10—Consumer Products Division, 20—Electronics Division, 27—Manufacturing Department in Electronics Division, 39—Marketing Department in Military Products Division.

The middle three digits could represent the chart-of-accounts block code. Finally, the last two digits could denote products or activities within different subunits. For example, the code 01 could refer to product 1, the code 02 could refer to product 2, and so forth. The whole code could be classified as group code where each component represents a certain characteristic of the transaction.

SINGLE FILE ORGANIZATION AND ACCESS

File organization is the method used to either physically store data on a tape or disk or the logical description of how it is organized. In the latter case, the file management system translates the logical (the user's view) into a physical organization which may differ from the logical. Often the logical organization is referred to as the file structure. File access, on the other hand, is the method used to access data from the storage medium.

The three basic file organizations (structures) are called sequential; random (direct); and indexed sequential, which represents a combination of the first two. The access method may be sequential or direct (sometimes called random). The direct procedure may use a linked list or an inverted list approach to effectively access data.

Many accounting records are organized as simple flat files, which consist of a series of records ordered sequentially on magnetic tape or disk, or randomly on a disk. A *sequential file* employs sequential organization and sequential access. An *indexed-sequential file* has a sequential organization; but uses direct access via an index structure. A *direct (random) access file* has records that are arranged randomly and employs a direct-access method to access data.

Sequential Files

Records in sequential files are organized in numerical or alphabetical order according to a primary key, like those shown in Figure 9-2. Often these files are referred to as lists. Given the key of a desired record, sequential reading of each record in the file occurs, beginning with the first, until the desired record is reached. For example, if a file had five records with the keys 1000, 1005, 2010, 2015, and 3000, and 2015 is the key for the desired record, four records would have to be read before locating the desired record.

As we noted in earlier chapters, sequential files are suitable for magnetic tape storage because, by design, such storage media facilitates sequential storage and sequential access. This type of file organization and search is excellent for large volumes of data processed in batch where a high proportion of the records are updated or referenced. A batch processing inventory system could make effective use of sequential files. All sales, returns, receipts, and purchase orders could be batched, sorted in the same sequence, and run against it once a day to update the inventory. Sequential access is not conducive to the timely retrieval of data on a random basis.

Indexed-Sequential Files

Assume that management needs to access, on occasion, a single inventory record. It would be very awkward to run the whole file to find a particular record. It may be better to "look up" its location in an index and go directly to it on a disk. In this file arrangement, the file is organized sequentially on a disk and records are accessed directly by referring to a table of disk addresses called an index, or directory. This index contains pointers which give the location, or address, of the record or records desired by the user or application program. This access method is called index-sequential-access method or ISAM. To locate a record stored in an index-sequential file requires several steps. First, the index must be accessed from storage, which is usually on the same disk as the indexed file. Second, the index must be searched to locate the key corresponding to the desired record. Third, the address corresponding to the key value is retrieved. Fourth, the record or record block is accessed during the disk address. Fifth, the block is then searched sequentially if appropriate.

Indexed-sequential files are a common type of direct access file and can be used in both sequential (batch) processing and on-line processing. For sequential processing, the indexed-sequential file is essentially treated as a sequential file. For on-line processing, the direct-access feature of the indexed-sequential file provides a viable access method that is faster than searching its entire file. An indexed-sequential method of storage and access works well as long as a large number of additions and deletions are not made.

Indexed-sequential files, however, have several disadvantages. First, they cannot use magnetic tape. Second, the indexes require added storage space and, in addition, they are a relatively inefficient direct-access method, since both the index and the address must be accessed. Third, because of the manner in which new records are added to an indexed-sequential file, a periodic maintenance procedure is required to physically reorder records. An indexed-sequential file does not permit records of the file to be reordered during an update run. Therefore, new records are put into an overflow area and "pointers" are used to link them to their respective places in the file. Periodically the file must be sorted in order to arrange all the records physically in the proper order.

Direct Access and Random Files

Suppose, the company decides to adapt an on-line inventory system where each record must be accessed as sales, receipt, and purchase transactions occur. This requires a high frequency of data access and no need for sequential processing. In this case, an efficient direct access is needed. Unlike the indexed-sequential access, which employs indexes, this method employs a record-access procedure that accesses the records directly in one step. Typically this is done using a formula that converts the primary key into a direct address. This formula often assigns records to these addresses randomly and is called *hashing*. The same formula and random assignment procedure is followed to locate the record when needed. This storage organization process is a significant disadvantage. Since random storage is employed, all available storage may not be employed, particularly when a formula method is employed to transform a primary key into a random assignment. Some record addresses may never be assigned. Hashing like this is often called randomizing.

Hashing may generate identical storage addresses for two or more record keys; when this occurs, the records that encounter occupied storage addresses are placed in an overflow area, with "pointers" linked to their position.

The advantage of using a direct access and random assignment of records approach to storage is that on-line queries can quickly and easily be processed. The disadvantage is that such an approach is not very efficient for large volumes of data where a large portion (high activity ratio) of the data items are processed in batch processing systems. Table 9-1 shows the relative advantages and disadvantages.

MULTIPLE-APPLICATION SINGLE FILE ACCESS

Single file systems may be accessed several ways. They may be accessed sequentially, they may be accessed directly, or they may be accessed using an index when they have an indexed-sequential file organization. All of these single file

CHARACTERISTIC	SEQUENTIAL	INDEXED SEQUENTIAL	RANDOM
Sequential Storage (Magnetic Tape)	+	+	−
On-Line Processing (Random Access)	−	/	+
Large Volumes (Batch Processing)	+	/	−
Batch Processing	+	+	−
Storage Efficency	+	−	−
Adding New Records	−	−	+
Fast Processing of Queries	−	/	+

Key + advantage, − disadvantage, and / neither an advantage or disadvantage.

TABLE 9-1   Advantages and disadvantages of file organizations.

access methods were discussed in conjunction with their respective file organization.

Often it is important to retrieve information selectively from a file that is organized in a way different from that needed by the application it was originally designed to support. For example, in Figure 9-2 assume the parts are numbered sequentially but it is often necessary to access part names alphabetically or to access vendor names for cash disbursement information. Single files may also be accessed by several applications. Often these files are sorted to comply with the sequential organization of each new application. This is very time consuming for large files. Using various linked lists or inverted lists for each application permits the multiple use of files without the need to sort the file for each use.

Linked List

A *linked list,* is nothing more than a group of records linked by pointers placed at the end of each record. To express the logical relationship of records used in an application, a separate set of pointers may be added for each application. Most linked lists have a *head* that points to the first item, and a *tail* (which may be a special data item or symbol) that indicates the last item in the list.

To illustrate the use of a linked list, assume that we have an array of records such as the customers in Figure 9-2, each of which has a data item that is used to identify the row number (link value) for the next record. Figure 9-4 illustrates the record array link-data-item relationship. In this example, assume Adams' record is the first record, with a *head* value of 5. The link number associated with Adams' record is 3; therefore Block's record is the second record. The pointer (link) for Block's record is 4; therefore Clark's record follows Block's re-

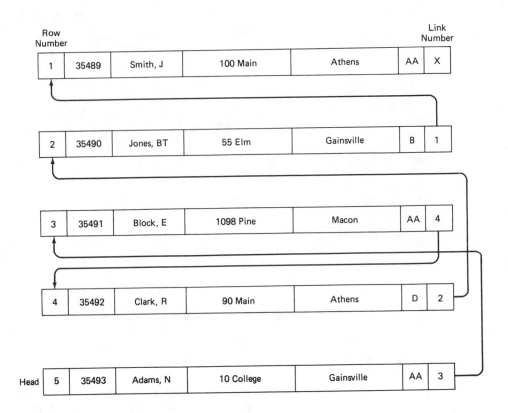

FIGURE 9-4 Linked list structure.

cord. Following the linking relationship through all records results in the following sequence of records: Adams, Block, Clark, Jones, and Smith.

Note that the order of the records in the linked list is not the same as the order in the array of records. Several benefits can result from this relationship. First, this means that records can be stored in any physical order and can be linked via a set of embedded pointers (as illustrated in Figure 9-4) to express their logical relationship. Second, records can easily be inserted into or deleted from a file without a vast reorganization of the file. We simply add the new record, change a pointer to refer to the new record in the sequence desired, and add the pointer in the new record to point to the next record in the logical sequence. Deleting a record by using a linked list would necessitate changing only one pointer. We would simply locate the record preceding the record to be deleted and change its associated pointer to the location of the record following the record to be deleted. The pointer of the "to be deleted" record is then blanked. Third, linked lists can easily be used to represent fairly complex data structures.

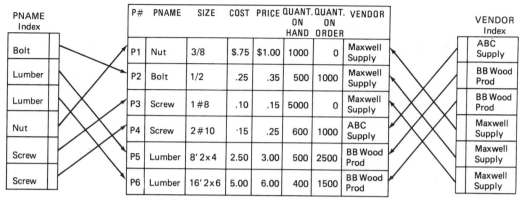

P#	PNAME	SIZE	COST	PRICE	QUANT. ON HAND	QUANT. ON ORDER	VENDOR
P1	Nut	3/8	$.75	$1.00	1000	0	Maxwell Supply
P2	Bolt	1/2	.25	.35	500	1000	Maxwell Supply
P3	Screw	1#8	.10	.15	5000	0	Maxwell Supply
P4	Screw	2#10	·15	.25	600	1000	ABC Supply
P5	Lumber	8' 2x4	2.50	3.00	500	2500	BB Wood Prod
P6	Lumber	16' 2x6	5.00	6.00	400	1500	BB Wood Prod

PNAME Index: Bolt, Lumber, Lumber, Nut, Screw, Screw

VENDOR Index: ABC Supply, BB Wood Prod, BB Wood Prod, Maxwell Supply, Maxwell Supply, Maxwell Supply

Indexing Inventory File on Part Name and Vendor Name

FIGURE 9-5   Indexing.

Thus working with linked lists in random access files is relatively easy, compared to actual physical lists which are common in many sequential files, when the data serves several needs. For example, an accounts receivable file may be organized via its customer account numbers using a hashing scheme on a hard disk. Pointers may be used to access this data in the order of past due accounts or by sales territories without the need to reorganize the records.

Indexing (Inverted Lists or Files)

Instead of using a set of pointers in a record to point to the next logical record for an application, a separate index file can be created to refer via pointers to the primary key to find the appropriate information for an application without reorganizing the file in order to satisfy a user request. This is shown in Figure 9-5. An index is merely a directory which contains pointers indicating the storage address of each record. Pointers are not placed in the record as in the case of the listing structure just discussed. These indexed files are often called *inverted lists*. A fully inverted list is one where each field has its own index so that records may be accessed using each field. Some popular microcomputer database programs make extensive use of this indexing feature.

PROCESSING MODES

There are basically two processing modes. These were discussed earlier in the text. They are batch and on-line. Batch processing is when transactions which are similar in nature, such as the day's sales or perhaps the day's receiving reports, are batched and then processed in a batch at a later time, such as at the end of the day. Any of the file organization structures may be used in this batch mode. In on-line processing, the user or the application interacts with the data file as each transaction occurs. For example, as a sale takes place, the sales file, the inventory file, and if applicable the accounts receivable file, are all opened and updated at the time the transaction is entered into the system. On-line processing, which places the computer in continual contact with transactions, requires on-line access to direct-access (sometimes called random access) files. These direct-access files may then be accessed using a set of pointers in a list, or an index, or directly. An example of this would be point-of-sale terminals in a large department store where each terminal is connected on line to the mainframe and sales transactions are posted as they occur. Real-time systems where the computer actually controls the nature of the transactions also require direct access using direct-access files.

WEAKNESS IN THE FILE-ORIENTED APPROACH

Early computerized accounting systems required a large number of files to support numerous applications. Each application had its own set of files or set of pointers or set of indices. Often files were sorted for different batch processing runs, sometimes creating another set of files. This occurred because each individual application focused on specific data needs rather than considering the overall information needs of the organization. Additional applications as they were added often resulted in the sorting and merging of existing files in order to create new files to satisfy the requirements of the new application. As a result, a tremendous number of application files emerged. Frequently there was little compatibility from file to file since each had been formatted to meet the needs of specific application programs. Also, similar programs and files usually existed because it was often more cost efficient to create a new program, as well as a new file, than to revise an old one.

Data Redundancy

As we noted earlier, single file-oriented systems are being widely used today. These systems, however, have some key weaknesses beyond the fact that many files are required to support most of them. One significant weakness is data redundancy. By data redundancy we mean that identical data are stored in two or more files; for example, an "employee file" would probably contain some of the same data as a "payroll file." Data editing, maintenance, and storage costs all increase as a result of redundancy. When data are updated, a separate program is required to revise each file so that they are consistent. If a data item is updated in some files but not in others, then the reports generated from the different files will not agree. Because of data redundancy, additional storage space is required; therefore, storage cost is greater.

Data Dependence

Another weakness of a file-oriented approach is that application programs are directly dependent upon the structure of the data file such as field and record content or even the sequence or index used to access the file. Since the business records related to an organization must be current, new data items must often be added and old data items deleted from associated files. These changes may not only result in a restructuring of the file and the method of accessing data in the file, but all the application programs that use the file must be changed. These changes or additions in data files are a major maintenance problem.

Lack of Compatibility and Flexibility

Most file-oriented systems are designed for predetermined sets of information requests and reports. The systems are not flexible enough to support management requests for unanticipated information, and reports for each new request may require a new program to be written by the MIS staff. This often involves considerable time and effort as well as the need for new data files derived from existing files. The net result of this lack of flexibility is that management often does not receive needed information on a timely basis.

Another problem, somewhat related to the changing of data within a file, is the lack of compatibility of existing application programs with changes in hardware such storage devices or software used to store the data. New technology often yields faster, larger, and less-expensive storage devices. But taking advantage of these changes requires the movement of records or files from the old device to the new one. If the new device has a slightly different storage structure than the old device, then all application programs that accessed the old device will have to be changed.

Lack of Data Integration

An additional weakness of a file-oriented processing approach is the lack of data integration and inability to handle unanticipated information requests. Data on different files can be related, as would be the case for an employee master file and a payroll master file. But, unless a specific application program is written to associate the data in the different files or unless an additional file is created containing combined information, the data will simply be used for the application for which they were built. This is a major problem because there are a number of benefits associated with integrated accounting software.

To illustrate the integration and flexibility problems, assume that a data file and program exist for employee information reporting, and that a data file and program exist for generating payroll checks and reports. Assume further that management would like to know the salary paid to each employee over thirty-five years of age who has been with the company more than seven years. To obtain this information, a new program must be written that will extract data from both the employee file and the payroll file or to merge this information into a third file. But a problem may exist in the extraction process since there is no guarantee the data files are compatible. If the two files exist in different formats, then one file must be converted to the other file's format before the new application program can be written. This process is likely to be time consuming and expensive. By the time the programming has been completed, the information may no longer be required or useful. For many years this has been a key problem in data processing.

SUMMARY

Single file accounting information systems have been used for many years. They tend to be used extensively today in simple straightforward batch processing situations. They may also serve on-line processing if they are stored on direct-access storage devices and accessed via index or direct-access methods. Furthermore, these single files may serve multiple uses or applications by using a linked list or an index for each application to direct the application program to the next logical record.

These single file systems require data to be classified so that it can be organized for effective access. Several codes may be used to aid in this classification. Sequence codes use a list of numbers; block codes organize data by categories; group codes add information content to the code itself; and mnemonic codes convey meaning as part of the code.

Files may be organized depending on their intended use (application) by several methods. These are: sequential, where data is used sequentially; direct access, where data must be accessed directly; and index-sequential, where blocks of data are accessed via an index which points to the disk address and then the block is sequentially searched.

These single files may be used by many applications by using a set of pointers to locate the records in the order they are needed by the application, or by using an index to locate the records needed by an application. A single file may have several sets of pointers or indices.

Sequential files are appropriate for batch processing of pending transactions and records that are in the same order. On-line processing requires the use of a direct-access scheme such as an index or straightforward direct access of the data.

In summary, single flat files are effective ways to store accounting data. They may be accessed in many ways to accommodate an accounting system's needs. However, they do have serious drawbacks in terms of data redundancy, data dependence, data incompatibility, and lack of data integration.

SELECTED REFERENCES

DATE, C. J., *An Introduction to Database Systems,* 5th ed., Reading, Mass.: Addison-Wesley, 1990.

EVERST, G. C., and R. WEBER, "A Relational Approach to Accounting Models," *The Accounting Review,* April 1977, pp. 340–359.

FARIN, JEFF, and AMOR NAZARIO, "DBMS Basics," *Infosystems,* June 1986.

MCCARTHY, W. E., "An Entity-Relationship View of Accounting Modeling," *The Accounting Review,* October 1979, pp. 667–686.

REVIEW QUESTIONS

1. Define the following terms:
   a. data item
   b. record
   c. file
   d. data value
   e. field
   f. primary key
   g. secondary key
   h. data type

2. Define the following codes:
   a. sequential
   b. block
   c. group
   d. mnemonic

3. Compare the three following file organizations and access methods:
   a. sequential
   b. index sequential
   c. direct access random files

4. Match the following according to their usefulness:

1. Batch processing of large department store sales   a. Direct Access

2. Airline reservations system   b. ISAM

3. Inventory system with occasional inquiries and batch updates   c. Sequential

5. Explain how a linked structure enables a single file to be used for a variety of applications.

6. Explain how an index (inverted list) can be used to use the same file for multiple applications.

7. Compare the approach used in indexing and that used in a linked list to enable one to use a file for many purposes.

8. For each of the coding schemes used in the chapter, give an example.

9. Identify some of the weaknesses of the file-oriented approach.

10. Why are file-oriented systems used extensively today.

CASES

9-1 Universal Floor Covering is a manufacturer and distributor of carpet and vinyl floor coverings. The home office is located in Charlotte, North Carolina. Carpet mills are located in Dalton, Georgia, and Greenville, South Carolina. A floor covering manufacturing plant is in High Point, North Carolina. Total sales last year were just over $250 million.

The company manufactures over 200 different varieties of carpet. The carpet is classified as being for commercial or residential purposes and is sold under five brand names with up to five lines under each brand. The lines indicate the different grades of quality; grades are measured by type of tuft and number of tufts per square inch. Each line of carpet can have up to fifteen different color styles.

Just under 200 varieties of vinyl floor covering are manufactured. The floor covering is also classified as being for commercial or residential use. There are four separate brand names (largely distinguished by the type of finish), up to eight different patterns for each brand, and up to eight color styles for each pattern.

Ten different grades of padding are manufactured. The padding is usually differentiated by intended use (commercial or residential) in addition to thickness and composition materials.

Universal serves over 2,000 regular wholesale customers. Retail showrooms are the primary customers. Many major corporations are direct buyers of Universal's products. Large construction companies have contracts with Universal to purchase carpet and floor covering at reduced rates for use in newly constructed homes and commercial buildings. In addition,

Universal produces a line of residential carpet for a large national retail chain. Sales to these customers range from $10,000 to $1,000,000 annually.

There is a company-owned retail outlet at each plant. The outlets carry overruns, seconds, and discontinued items. This is Universal's only retail sales function.

The company has divided the sales market into seven territories, with the majority of concentration on the East coast. The market segments are New England, New York, Mid-Atlantic, Carolinas, South, Midwest, and West. Each sales territory is divided into five to ten districts with a salesperson assigned to each district.

The current accounting system has been adequate for monitoring the sales by product. However, there are limitations to the system because specific information is sometimes not available. A detailed analysis of operations is necessary for planning and control purposes and would be valuable for decision-making purposes. The accounting systems department has been asked to design a sales analysis code. The code should permit Universal to prepare a sales analysis that would reflect the characteristics of the company's business.

REQUIRED:

1. Account coding systems are based upon various coding concepts. Briefly define and give an example of the following coding concepts:
   a. Sequence coding
   b. Block coding
   c. Group coding
2. Develop a coding system for Universal Floor Covering which would assign sales analysis codes to sales transactions. For each portion of the code,
   a. explain the meaning and purpose of the position.
   b. identify and justify the number of digits required.
   (CMA Adapted with permission)

9-2 The Trust Company of Denver has just converted its business loans processing systems to a file management system. Records will be stored randomly on a magnetic disk. Table C9-1 below shows the disk locations of these records. Linked lists will be formed from these records.

REQUIRED:

1. Prepare a matrix with five columns titled Loan Number Pointer, Amount Pointer, Name Pointer, Interest Rate Pointer, and Date Due Pointer. List the disk addresses above to the left of these columns. Then enter in the row under each of the five columns the pointers needed to create linked lists for retrieving values in the following sequences: (1) loan number, from lowest to highest; (2) amount, from lowest to highest; (3) name, alphabetically; (4) due date, chronologically. The pointers that form the loan number list would appear as follows:

Disk Address	Loan Number Pointer
7	5 +
5	9
9	3
3	* +

+ head record and * tail of list

TABLE C9-1

DISK ADDRESS	LOAN NUMBER	NAME	AMOUNT	INTEREST RATE (%)	DUE DATE
7	0010	Lawn Supply	$5,000	7	5/92
5	0015	Green Nursery	20,000	10	7/92
9	0020	B B Auto	10,000	8	2/92
3	0025	Ace Bakery	25,000	9	2/92

2. Explain how the linked lists can be employed in a file management system to provide an answer to the inquiry: What loan amounts are due in February 1992? (Adapted from SMAC)

9-3 For each of the following situations, specify the file arrangement method (sequential, direct or random, indexed-sequential) that best fits. Briefly justify your selection.

REQUIRED:

1. An inventory file, updated daily, that is employed to determine product availability during daily operations.
2. A sales commission file, used to keep track of each salesperson's commissions. The file is updated at the time of sale from a point-of-sale data-entry terminal.
3. Goodrich Corporation stockholder file, updated weekly; employed for computing dividend checks, quarterly reports, and proxy requests.
4. A payroll file, used weekly to process payroll checks and used quarterly to aid in the processing of tax reports.
5. A customer account file at a major city bank, updated daily based on customer withdrawals and deposits, used monthly to generate monthly statements on each customer account.

9-4 The Elkin Corporation of Atlanta, Georgia, is a progressive and fast-growing company. The company's executive board consists of five members: the president, the vice-president of marketing, the vice-president of manufacturing, the vice-president of finance, and the vice-president of computing/information systems.

The marketing department is organized into nine territories and twenty-five sales offices. The vice-president of marketing wants the monthly reports to reflect those items for which the department is responsible and can control. The marketing department also wants information that identifies the most profitable products; this information is used to establish a discount policy that will enable the company to meet competition effectively. Monthly reports showing performance by territory and sales office would also be useful.

The vice-president of finance has recommended that the accounting system be revised so that reports would be prepared on a contribution margin basis. Furthermore, only those cost items that are controlled by the respective departments would appear on their reports. The monthly report for the manufacturing department would compare actual production costs with a budget containing the standard costs for the actual volume of production. The marketing department would be provided with the standard variable manufacturing cost for each product, so that it could calculate the variable contribution margin of each product. The monthly reports to the marketing department would reflect the variable contribution approach; the reports would present the net contribution to the department calculated by deducting standard variable manufacturing costs and marketing expenses (both variable and fixed) from sales.

A portion of Elkin's chart of accounts follows: Account Number and Description: 1000 for Sales, 1500 for Cost of sales, 2000 for Manufacturing expenses, 3000 for Engineering expenses, 4000 for Marketing expenses, and 5000 for Administrative expenses.

The company wants to retain the basic structure of the chart of accounts to minimize the number of changes in the system. However, the numbering system will have to be expanded in order to provide the additional information that is desired.

REQUIRED: Develop and explain a coding structure that will satisfy the needs of the marketing department management. Add any additional accounts that are needed to the chart of accounts. Be sure to provide some flexibility. Illustrate the new coding structure. (Adapted from the CMA examination.)

9-5 Ollie Mace has recently been appointed controller of a family-owned manufacturing enterprise. The firm, S. Dilley & Co., was founded by Mr. Dilley about twenty years ago, is 78 percent owned by Mr. Dilley, and has served the major automotive companies as a parts supplier. The firm's major operating divisions are heat treating, extruding, small-parts stamping, and specialized machining. Sales last year from the several divisions ranged from

$150,000 to over $3 million. The divisions are physically and managerially independent except for Mr. Dilley's constant surveillance. The accounting system for each division has evolved according to the division's own needs and according to the abilities of individual accountants or bookkeepers. Mr. Mace is the first controller in the firm's history to have responsibility for overall financial management. Mr. Dilley expects to retire within six years and has hired Mr. Mace to improve the firm's financial system.

Mr. Mace soon decides that he will need to design a new financial reporting system that will:

1. Give managers uniform, timely, and accurate reports on business activity. Monthly divisional reports should be uniform and available by the tenth of the following month. Companywide financial reports should also be prepared by the tenth.

2. Provide a basis for measuring return on investment by division. Divisional reports should show assets assigned to each division and revenue and expense measurement in each division.

3. Generate budget data for planning and decision-making purposes. The accounting system should provide for the preparation of budgets that recognize managerial responsibility, controllability of costs, and major product groups.

4. Allow for a uniform basis of evaluating performance and quick access to underlying data. Cost center variances should be measured and reported for operating and nonoperating units, including headquarters. Also, questions about levels of specific cost factors or product costs should be answerable quickly.

According to Mr. Mace, a new chart of accounts is essential to getting started on other critical financial problems. The present account codes used by divisions are not standard.

Mr. Mace sees a need to divide asset accounts into six major categories (i.e., current assets, plant and equipment, etc.). Within each of these categories, he sees a need for no more than ten control accounts. Based on his observations to date, one hundred subsidiary accounts are more than adequate for each control account.

No division now has more than five major product groups. The maximum number of cost centers Mr. Mace foresees within any product group is six, including operating and nonoperating groups. He views general divisional costs as a nonrevenue-producing group. Altogether, Mr. Mace estimates that about forty-four natural expense accounts plus about twelve specific accounts would be adequate.

Mr. Mace is planning to implement the new chart of accounts in an environment that at present includes manual records systems and one division that is using an EDP system. He expects that in the near future most accounting and reporting for all units will be automated. Therefore the chart of accounts should facilitate the processing of transactions manually or by machine. Efforts should be made, he believes, to restrict the length of the code for economy in processing and convenience in use.

REQUIRED:

1. Design a chart-of-accounts coding system that will meet Mr. Mace's requirements. Your answer should begin with a layout of the coding system. You should explain the coding method you have chosen and the reason for the size of your code elements. Explain your code as it would apply to asset and expense accounts.

2. Use your chart-of-accounts coding system to illustrate the code needed for the following data:

    a. In the small-parts stamping division, $100 was spent by foreman Bill Shaw in the polishing department of the Door Level Group on cleaning supplies. Code the expense item using the code you just developed.

    b. A new motorized sweeper has been purchased for the maintenance department of the extruding division, for $3,450. Code this asset item using the code you developed.
    (Adapted from the CMA examination.)

9-6 Main Construction Supply uses an index file structure to maintain its inventory records like that shown in Figure 9-5. The respective field (type and size) for PNUMBER, PNAME, SIZE, COST, PRICE QONHAND, QON-ORDER, VENDOR are: Character (4), Character

(10), Character (10), Numeric (6 with 2 decimals), Numeric (6 with 2 decimals), Numeric (5), Numeric (5), Character (20).

REQUIRED:

1. Using a microcomputer database package that has an index feature, set up the basic file in Figure 9-5.

2. Using the index feature of the database program, prepare a listing by PNAME and VENDOR.

3. Using a procedure to select a particular vendor, print out those products purchased from Maxwell Supply.

10

DATABASE ACCOUNTING INFORMATION SYSTEMS

INTRODUCTION

In the last chapter, single file management accounting information systems were presented. The structure of these files and method of access were tied directly to the informational requirements of a particular accounting application or set of applications. In this chapter we introduce database systems which can handle multiple files and support numerous applications without the degree of dependency present in file-oriented systems. In many accounting systems, transactions often require access to data in several files and result in posting several files. Moreover, management accounting reports often need to integrate data from several files to provide management with the information they need for decision making. As a result, there is a significant need for a system which can integrate multiple files. Database systems enable a firm to accomplish this data integration more easily than traditional file-oriented systems and are thus the cornerstone of many newer accounting information systems.

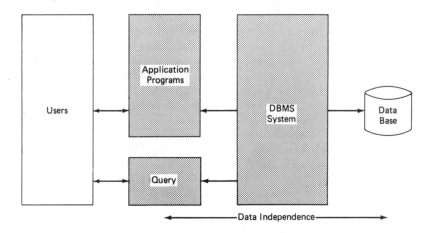

FIGURE 10-1   Database management system.

DATABASE PROCESSING

Database processing[1] or, more specifically, database management systems (DBMS) have emerged as the means to overcome some of the inherent limitations in the traditional single-file-oriented data processing. A *database management system* is a set of software programs that serve as an interface between application programs and an integrated database, which may either be a set of coordinated and interlinked physical files or a set of data tables which are related through a series of relationships. A database is not merely an accumulation of separate files as is the case with single file systems. The data may be stored as tables of data items or as collections of data items, analogous to the master files in single-file-oriented systems, linked with various pointers and chaining schemes similar to those used in linked lists. These structures help minimize redundancy and support unanticipated retrieval of related information. The logical organization of the data will be a function of the types of structure used by the database management system. Figure 10-1 illustrates a database management system.

In comparing Figure 10-1 with Figure 9-1, two changes are apparent. First, the individual data items or master files have been integrated into a database. (Note that we did not label the data as Accounts Receivable Data File, Accounts Payable Data File, and Payroll Data File, but instead we simply used the term *database.*) Second, a database management system module has been inserted between the data and the application programs. The accounts receivable, accounts payable, and payroll application programs still perform their original functions, but the database management system is called upon to retrieve the data from the database. The data used by these programs have been processed and stored by the database management system prior to being retrieved for use by the respec-

---

[1] See Date, C. J., *An Introduction to Database Systems,* 1990, Reading, Mass.: Addison-Wesley, for a complete introduction to database systems.

tive programs; therefore all the data are integrated and compatible. If a report were desired that called for a combination of, and/or integration of, accounts receivable and accounts payable data to help plan cash flows, this could be generated in most cases without changing the database. It would simply require the writing of an application program to access the database via the database management system. (We will see shortly that many database management systems provide a query language or a report generator whereby it is possible to generate "special reports" on line without writing a special application program. Moreover, many database management systems have a programmable command language which may be used by managers, accountants and other users to write their own programs because the people who use the information in decision-making actually write their own programs. This is called end-user programming.)

COMPONENTS OF DATABASE PROCESSING

The database environment involves four components: (1) the user (which includes application programmers, actual application programs, and end users); (2) the database administrator; (3) the database, and (4) the database management system. These are shown in Figure 10-2.

The user is involved with the development of application programs, defines the contents of the database (by specifying the needs of his or her programs), interacts with the database as an end user, defines relationships between data items, and by working with the database administrator brings about modifications to the database.

The database administrator is the custodian of the database. He or she is responsible for controlling the use of the database, its security, and maintenance of its integrity.

The database management system (DBMS) is a set of software programs that interacts with the database (i.e., manipulates data) in accordance with user commands. It is used to reference, add, delete, and/or modify data items for an application. The database is simply a collection of all the data necessary to support user needs, organized so as to minimize data redundancy, make the most efficient use of storage devices and space, and provide easy retrieval. Figure 10-2 illustrates the interrelationships of these components. To better understand the database processing environment, we will examine each component in detail.

Users

The term *user* generally refers to traditional users, such as departmental managers, accounting personnel, and other individuals outside the information system area who use application programs to interact with the database. Application programmers are also considered users. In addition, due to recent developments in database systems, particularly microcomputer software, traditional users have become their own application programmers; these users are called *end users.*

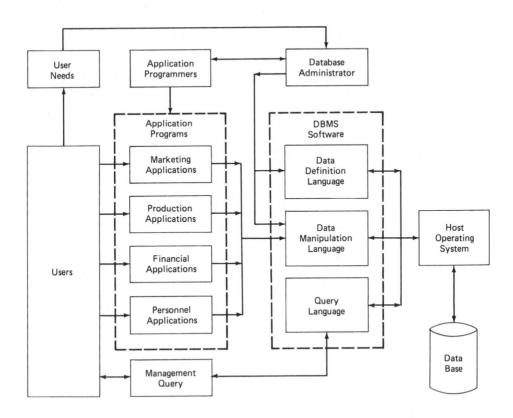

FIGURE 10-2   DBMS components and interaction.

Users have four means by which they can interact with the database management system: (1) directly, by using English-like commands known as a query language or by menus which respond to user requests; (2) by communicating with an application program, which in turn interacts with the database management system; (3) by using a report generator; or (4) by writing their own applications or requests as an end user. Much of this is feasible due to the availability of high-level languages supported by DBMS software. The query language is generally used for one-time or ad hoc applications where the particular use does not justify a written program. One benefit of the query language is that it makes the database accessible for end users who have limited or no background in computer programming. In the past, the majority of users have interfaced with the database through application programs rather than through the query mode. However, with the current trend in microcomputers, decision support systems, and terminal technology, this is changing fast; more and more use will be made of the query language and of end-user software which enables users to write their own applications.

Database Administrator

The database administrator is, as we have noted, the custodian of the database and controls the overall logical and physical structure of the database. Being custodian of the data does not mean that he or she is the owner. The data contained in the database are neither owned nor used by the database administrator. Actually the data is not even owned by department or individual, because it is common to all in the organization. Individuals and departments control access and use of specific data, however. The database administrator will know, for example, that the payroll portion of the database contains a payroll record that contains salary data, but he or she will not know the value recorded in the data item if the access to that value is restricted. Unless the person who controls access to that data has so specified, the database administrator cannot read the values of a given data item. But if the data item must be expanded in order to hold a larger value (for example, if the salary data item needed to be expanded from five digits to seven digits), only the database administrator has the responsibility and authority for making the change.

The database administrator is responsible for the overall configuration of the database structure. He or she, therefore, encourages standardization of data items and specifies the data structures and layouts that are best for the data users as a group. If an individual user wishes to create a new type of record, change an existing record by including new data items, or expand the size of a data item, the database administrator must be requested to make the change. The database administrator evaluates all requests and modifies the data structure only when it is best for the organization as a whole. An application programmer or any other user working on an individual application is not permitted to change the overall data structure even if an individual application program can benefit; the database administrator must take an organizational point of view. A key function of a database administrator is the settling of differences between groups or individuals who have requested the data to be defined, represented, and/or stored differently. A problem that often arises is whether data should be shared between departments who have previously not shared. Also, the converting of a database from an existing file-oriented system often causes problems because the process necessitates the restructuring of files and the rewriting of many programs. Department managers often argue vehemently about these changes for they are reluctant to release control of departmental data and have difficulty understanding why changes are required. For example, an old sales order file management system and an old inventory management system may have been controlled by the sales and purchasing departments respectively. Each had its own unique and different definition of a product and neither is willing to add or maintain move and now consistent detail for the benefit of the other. In addition to resolving conflicts over data control and demonstrating the need for certain changes or certain forms of data structure, the database administrator provides a number of basic services. He or she plans the file-addressing schemes for the database, the logical structure, the physical data layout, security procedures, and a means for recovery after failures occur. He or she also selects and provides data management software that can aid end users in using the database and provides consulting services to end users and systems analysts who write applications programs. End users often need support in understanding what data can be made available and the procedures (query language) for accessing the data. Application programmers must be assisted with data definitions in order to understand the structure of the database.

For a large organization that requires a complex database, these responsibilities are not carried out by a single individual. It is unlikely that a single individual would have the technical expertise, the knowledge of the data, and the communication skills to handle all these tasks. However, if there is to be a total integrated system, then a centralized database is required and these functions must be provided. For a centralized integrated online processing systems, a database administrative *unit* made up of several individuals will be required. This would probably include an overall database administrator, a database design analyst, a data definition analyst, a data operations supervisor, and a security officer.

The Database

The third component of database processing is the database itself (refer to Figure 10-2). As we noted in comparing the structure of a file-oriented system with that of a database processing system, the database is not simply a collection of the files that exist in a file-oriented system. Rather, it is a collection of data items linked together to serve numerous applications in an optimal fashion. The data are stored so that they are independent of the application programs and users. Operating procedures are used to add new data and/or modify and retrieve existing data within the database.

To better understand the structure (often called the architecture) of a database, we need to examine some basic concepts. Briefly there are three levels or views of a database. There is the user's view, which is in terms of the application program, programming language, or query language. Then there is the conceptual or logical view or structure of the database which defines the way data are organized and accessed. This often called the data model. Finally, there is the physical view which is the actual storage of data. These three views are shown in Figure 10-3. In the following subsections we will explain the differences between these views and the *schema* and *subschema* used to show logical relationships between items of data. This will be followed by a section on database structure or data models.

LOGICAL DATA AND PHYSICAL DATA. The arrangement of data as viewed by the application program or user may differ significantly from how it is physically stored. An application programmer organizes his or her data to fit the needs of a specific program. Data in a database are organized to maximize storage efficiency, reduce data duplication, and provide ease of access. The two views may differ significantly. The data view that an application program employs is called a *logical structure,* usually called the structure or the data model. The data organization employed in storing data, regardless of whether it is in tape, disk, or some other medium, is called a *physical structure,* as shown in Figure 10-4. Stated another way, *logical* refers to the manner in which a user views data and *physical* refers to the manner in which the data are stored.

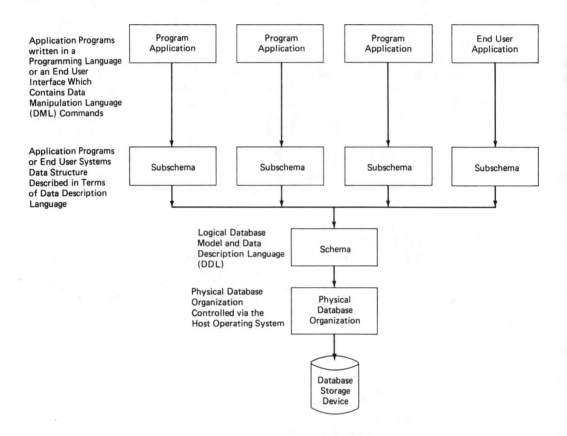

FIGURE 10-3   Relationship between applications subschema, schema, and the physical database.

As illustrated in Figure 10-4, an application program employs six records. The application program uses a logical order in which the records are structured and employed in the program. Physical data, on the other hand, are stored in the database (in this case a disk) in an order different from that viewed by the programmer and they may be intermixed with the physical data items used by other applications. To provide the logical (database) records, the physical records are organized via specified relations or linked together by a series of pointers. The relations are specified by the application or the user at the program level and the database software provides the method for forming the relationships among data items for the specific application. The linking mechanism (via pointers or relational algebra—discussed later) is also provided by database system software, and the programmer needs no knowledge of the linking mechanism in order to access data.

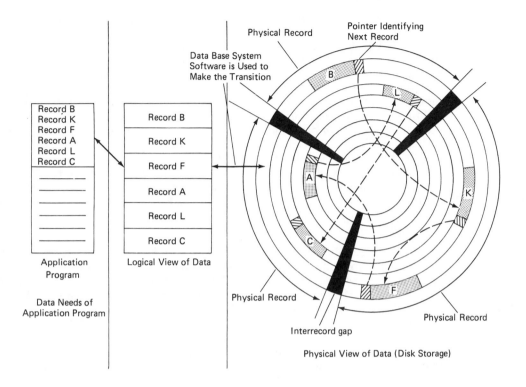

FIGURE 10-4   Logical vs. physical view of data.

Since different application programs will probably require different data, the database system software must be able to handle many requests. Also, since a user operating in a query mode may wish to access specific data items within physical database records, the software must have this level of capability.

SCHEMA AND SUBSCHEMAS.   To logically describe the data in the database requires a *schema* and *subschema*. A *schema* describes the logical view of the entire database. The schema is often expressed using descriptions of the data structure, data model, or a *data dictionary* (which lists all the data items in the database, their associated definitions, sources, and uses). These will be discussed later in this chapter. A *subschema* is that portion of the schema that is of interest to a particular user or application. In a sense, a schema is analogous to the map of a city, and the subschema is that portion of the map that includes a given individual's subdivision, a neighborhood, and/or area of interest. Figure 10-3 illustrates the relationship between schema and subschema (the diagram actually shows the relationship between data, physical database description, schema, and subschema, and application/user programs).

The concept of a schema and separate subschema allows the separation of the descriptions of the entire database from the descriptions of portions of the database employed by individual users. This is important for several reasons. First, since the database will probably contain data that are relevant to and shared by, multiple applications, subschema allow individual users to focus only on that portion of the database that is relevant to their program. This eases the writing, debugging, and maintaining of programs. Second, the employment of subschema automatically ensures a certain level of privacy and integrity of the database, since individual programs access that portion of the database identified by the subschema. Third, a certain degree of data independence is provided because changes may be made to the schema for the database and the database itself that will not affect programs that are linked to the data via subschema. Fourth, it allows a common language to be employed in defining the entire database while a variety of languages, based upon the desires or needs of the individual user, can be used to describe the subportion of the data needed by a given program.

Data Structure

As we noted earlier, sequential, indexed-sequential, direct-access random files are employed in traditional file-oriented systems. In addition to these file concepts, a variety of data structures (models) are employed in database processing. These include: (1) relational; (2) hierarchical or trees; and (3) networks. As a general framework for illustrating these structures we will consider the same sales and customer data for each data model.

The major difference between a relational database and all other databases is the extent to which data and links between data are essential.[2] Links are characterized by indexes and pointers. Essential means that a loss of an object (data or link) would result in the loss of data. For example, a record would be essential in any database if its loss would constitute the loss of data. Whereas in other databases the loss of a link between data items would result in the inability to access those data items; thus one would lose those data items. In a relational database the only essential object is the data itself. Linkages are derived as needs arise and are not essential. In a hierarchical and network structure, linkages are essential to the operation of the database. These linkages lead to the complexity of these other database structures and require additional operations to use the database.

HIERARCHY (TREE).   A tree is a hierarchical, logical data structure consisting of nodes connected by branches as shown in Figure 10-5. There is a *root* node, which is the record type, by which one initially accesses the hierarchy. In this example it is the customer record. Each descendent node has only one *parent* and all the parents are descendants of one root node. Descendant nodes are often referred to as *children*. A parent node may have an unlimited number of descendant nodes. These nodes refer to the type of record. Hierarchical structures are distinguishable from other structures in that every node with exception of the root node is dependent on its parent node. This means that one can only access data through parent (root) nodes. This structure resembles a tree as it is often called.

---

[2] See Date, C. J., *An Introduction to Database Systems*, Reading, Mass.: Addison-Wesley, 1990 for a complete discussion of relational and other databases.

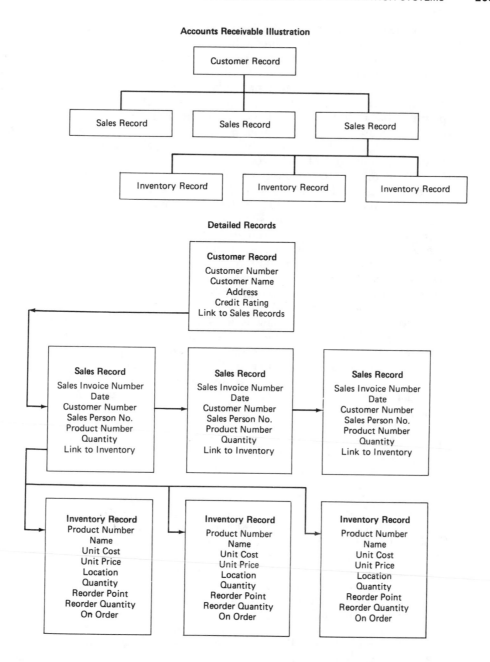

FIGURE 10-5   Hierarchical database structure.

Figure 10-5 illustrates the hierarchical structure. Consider the customer, sales invoice, and inventory hierarchy as shown in Figure 10-5. The customer record may include fields for a customer number, name, address, credit rating, as well as a pointer to a sales file via the customer number. This would indicate unpaid sales invoices for this particular customer with corresponding dates, product numbers, and quantities. In addition each sales record would have pointers that would lead to other sales records for the same customer. In turn, the sales records in this file contain pointers which reference the appropriate inventory records in the inventory file. This file contains all the inventory data including the unit price of each product.

To compile the accounts receivable information, this hierarchical (tree) structure and its references to more and more detailed information can be used effectively. Management could access information through this structure to create reports such as a monthly statement for merchandise purchased at a retail store. A manager could also assemble all the sales invoices for each customer in the customer file in order to compile a sales history report by customer, even through each customer has numerous purchases and the customer file and the sales invoice file reside in different segments of the database. The sales history subschema would manage the pointers which could be used to link the data to assemble this information. This hierarchical structure is fine provided the only need to use the inventory data is in conjunction with customer information. Management must have the appropriate customer number and invoice number to access the inventory information via this hierarchical path (schema). This path (linkage) is thus essential to that particular use of the database. The problem arises when you want to use the inventory information for other uses. For example, management may want to access the customers through the inventory parts numbers to list all customers who purchased a certain inventory item. To do this efficiently you need a different hierarchy. This can be done with several access paths. The problem is that a new hierarchy must be described for each application that requires a different access path. As a result, a much more complex structure such as a *network* may be needed.

NETWORKS. A network structure, like a hierarchical or tree structure, is composed of nodes and branches; but unlike a tree, a network can have multiple parents—that is, different types of parents or root nodes. The relationship from child to parent and from parent to child thus can be one-to-many in a network. Figure 10-6 illustrates a network structure. In this network, management can access the inventory record and determine which customers have purchased which parts in order to help the customer service department send out periodic maintenance information. Moreover, using this network of pointers, management can use inventory information for many uses without going through customer records, as would be the case using the tree network.

Many other forms of networks can be derived to meet management needs. One of the problems is that the complexity of the network can increase dramatically making it more and more difficult to maintain and operate. Networks, however, are widely used in business to organize data for a wide variety of managerial needs. One of the most popular network databases is IDMS from Cullinet Software. The important point here is that logical relationships can be repre-

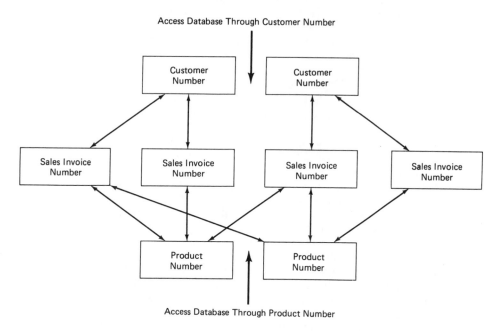

FIGURE 10-6   Network structure.

sented in the form of networks, regardless of the complexity involved. The problem is that each of these logical relationships (links) are essential for accessing data for a particular application. Thus, while the network reduces many of the problems of redundancy, independence, and flexibility it still falls short of the complete logical data independence provided by the relational structure where the links between data and applications are not essential. Not only are these links in hierarchical and network databases essential, they are explicitly predetermined. Thus, networks lack the flexibility needed in many organizations where accounting information requirements cannot be easily specified and incorporated into the database in advance.

RELATIONAL DATABASE.   The majority of new database systems are relational because they minimize the redundancy, data integration, dependence, and flexibility problems noted in Chapter 9. This is achieved by implicitly determining data relationships from data which are stored in logically independent flat files to meet information needs as they occur. This independence is manifested in the fact that in a relational database only data items are essential. In contrast to hierarchical and network structures, there are no essential linkages between data items. Thus a relational database is composed of relations which look like simple flat files or tables of attributes for data items. Each row (a record in a file-oriented application) is called a tuple; the columns are attributes (fields in a file-oriented application) with specified domains (data types and ranges). Each table looks like a flat file. Each has a primary key which represents a unique identifier. For example, in Figure 10-7 a sales invoice relation is composed of the sales invoice number, which represents a primary key used to access the data in the table, and a set of attributes about the sales invoice. In this example these attributes are: the date, customer number, product number, salesperson number, department number, and quantity sold.

This relationship represents the *logical view* of customer data not the physical view. There are no preconceived constructs such as lists, pointers, and other organization structures as there are in other database models. The user of the application is free to organize these tables using the database software. This software uses relational operations (algebra or calculus) to organize these tables to make the information useful to the user by presenting different views of the data tables or combinations of the data tables. These operations are called projection, join, and selection. Projection operations reduce the number of fields (columns or domains, as they are sometimes called) to those of interest to the user or needed by the report; thus reducing the data to those relevant fields. Join operations combine all the data from two or more relations by matching the primary keys of one relation with secondary keys of another relation. The result is the creation of one large combined relation containing all the data in each of the individual relations. The select operation then is used to identify those records (rows or tuples, as they are called) that satisfy the user or reports criteria. For example, using the data in Figure 10-7 a listing of Patrick, C.'s accounts receivable is prepared as shown in Figure 10-8. First only those columns that are relevant for the sales, customer, and stock relations are projected to form new projected tables in Figure 10-8a. Next the customer projected table is joined to the sales projected table via customer number to obtain the customer name for the sale. Next the stock projected table is joined to this combined table to add unit price information via stock numbers. These two joins together form the new relational table shown in Figure 10-8b. Finally the user is only interested in that information for Patrick, C.; therefore a select operation is used to select only those rows in the relation that meet this particular name criteria. The net result is the accounts receivable information shown in Figure 10-8c.

Relational databases follow certain data integrity rules which provide a more fundamental degree of data integrity than other structures and the traditional file-oriented systems. These rules include entity integrity and referential integrity. Entity integrity basically means that each row (record) in the relation is uniquely identified by a primary key. Referential integrity means that each reference from one relation to another must reference an actual primary key. The process of normalization[3] helps avoid violations of these rules. Without these rules accounting records such as a sale would not have a unique identification such as an invoice number and a customer record could reference a nonexistent invoice number.

Many relations can be developed from these basic tabular views of data. Application or end-user inquires are not restricted to any predetermined path through the data, such as a set of pointers which characterize the hierarchical, network, or file structures described in this text. As a result the relational data-

---

[3] See Date, C. J., op. cit., for a complete discussion of integrity rules and normalization.

Sales Relation

Sales Invoice No.	Date	Customer Number	Product Number	Salesperson Number	Department Number	Quantity
1101	4/16/91	9867	78	11	5	1
1102	4/16/91	3457	188	10	5	1
1103	4/16/91	7534	178	13	5	1
1104	4/16/91	7534	98	13	5	1
1105	4/16/91	3567	61	12	5	1
1106	4/16/91	2579	78	10	5	1
1107	4/16/91	5375	61	10	5	1
1108	4/16/91	5375	98	10	5	1
1109	4/16/91	2264	188	11	5	1
1110	4/16/91	4482	78	13	5	1

Customer Relation

Customer Number	Customer Name	Customer Address	Credit Rating
2264	Brown, B.	400 Toms Creek Rd., Blacksbury, Va.	A
2579	Myers, C.	150 Lee Street, Newton, Va.	A
3457	Smith, S.	100 Main Street, Pulasky, Va.	A
3567	Hyatt, A.	25 Ashlawn St., Blacksburg Va.	A
4482	Martin, C.	25 Laurel Ridge, Blacksburg, Va.	A
5375	Sims, A.	200 Radford Hwy. Christansburg, Va.	A
7534	Patrick, C.	501 North Street, Floyd, Va.	C
9867	Jones, R.	20 Mt. Vernon Way, Blacksburg, Va.	A

Stock Relation

Product Number	Product Name	Unit Cost	Unit Price	Location	Quantity	Reorder Point	Reorder Quantity
61	Garden Tractor-12 Hp	1250	1675	Warehouse	3	2	3
78	Lawn Tractor-10 Hp	950	1199	Store	5	4	10
98	Riding Mower-6 Hp	575	673	Store	10	6	15
178	Lawn Tractor-12 Hp	1000	1299	Warehouse	10	4	10
188	Garden Tractor-10 Hp	1150	1485	Store	3	2	8

Personnel Relation

Salesperson Number	SSN	Name	Address	Commission Rate
10	476-34-1704	Solberg, Hans	57 Lee St. Apt. 35, Blacksburg, Va.	10.00%
11	345-67-8764	Smith, Paula	45 S. Main, Blacksburg, Va.	10.00%
12	258-78-4720	Golf, Andy	34 Hill St., Radford, Va.	7.50%
13	458-42-4006	Kim, Ho	700 Radford Hwy. Christiansburg, Va.	7.50%

FIGURE 10-7   Sales order processing and inventory relations.

bases are more logically independent of applications than other structures. In summary the relational structure provides a conceptually simple view of the data, that is, a series of tables.

PROJECTIONS*

Sales Projection
(Cust. No., Prod. No. & Quantity)

Customer Number	Product Number	Quantity
9867	78	1
3457	188	1
7534	178	1
7534	98	1
3567	61	1
2579	78	1
5375	61	1
5375	98	1
2264	188	1
4482	78	1

Customer Projection
(Number and Name)

Customer Number	Customer Name
2264	Brown, B.
2579	Myers, C.
3457	Smith, S.
3567	Hyatt, A.
4482	Martin, C.
5375	Sims, A.
7534	Patrick, C.
9867	Jones, R.

Stock Projection
(Number & Price)

Product Number	Unit Price
61	1675
78	1199
98	673
178	1299
188	1485

*Projection operation separates out that information that is relevant to accounts receivable.
Only those columns that contain relevent information remain

(a)

JOIN OPERATIONS**

Join of Customer, Sales and Stock Projections

Customer Number	Customer Name	Product Number	Quantity	Unit Price
9867	Jones, R.	78	1	1199
3457	Smith, S.	188	1	1485
7534	Patrick, C.	178	1	1299
7534	Patrick, C.	98	1	673
3567	Hyatt, A.	61	1	1675
2579	Myers, C.	78	1	1199
5375	Sims, A.	61	1	1675
5375	Sims, A.	98	1	673
2264	Brown, B.	188	1	1485
4482	Martin, C.	78	1	1199

**Join operations combine the remaining information using customer number and product keys.

(b)

SELECT OPERATION***

Customer Number	Customer Name	Product Number	Quantity	Unit Price
7534	Patrick, C.	178	1	1299
7534	Patrick, C.	98	1	673

***Selection considers only those relevant rows.

(c)

FIGURE 10-8 Accounts receivable projection, join and select operations.

Database Management System (DBMS)

The fourth component of the database processing environment is the database management system (refer to Figure 10-2). A variety of database management systems exist; however, most systems have at least two common components: (1) a *data definition language* (DDL); and (2) a *data manipulation language* (DML). Some systems also contain an interactive inquiry facility, built around a *query* language. The query language employs a variety of commands for searching the database. These may use complex search strategies to satisfy the data needs of management. In this chapter we will focus most of our comments on the data definition and data manipulation languages and describe how these are employed in the database management system. We will also examine conceptually how the database system responds to a user data request.

Before we examine the DDL and DML, we need to examine briefly what is termed a *database manager* (DBM). A database manager is not the same as database administrator that we discussed earlier. The DBM is not a person; instead it is software. It is the part of the database management system that actually controls the database storage and access. The DBM communicates with the computer's operating system in carrying out data storage and retrieval functions. Other labels such as *data management routines* (DMR) and *data manager* (DM) are often used instead of *database manager* (DBM).

As illustrated in Figure 10-9, the database management system includes the database manager module which handles all queries, data definitions, and data manipulation. Since the DBM is the control mechanism for the database management system, communication must exist between the DBM and the operating system, between the DBM and the DDL and DML languages, and between the DBM and the telecommunications system which is used for queries. Each of these points of communication is depicted by a double arrow.

DATA DEFINITION LANGUAGE (DDL). The DDL is a key component in the link between the logical and the physical representation of data. As we noted in the previous section of the chapter, *logical* refers to the manner in which the user views data, and *physical* refers to the manner in which the data are stored. Users describe the logical structure of the data'ase with the DDL. Given the DDL, application programs are not constrained or locked into a particular physical representation of data as they are with a file-oriented system. The physical structure of the data can change, but the application logic can remain unchanged.

The DDL provides a number of specific functions in serving and in describing the structure of the database. First, it can define the characteristics of each record in the database, that is, the name and data type of each field. The DDL can also specify the way in which fields are grouped into records or relational tables and can identify primary and secondary keys. Fourth, it can describe the schema and subschema for the database. Finally, the DDL can specify limits and integrity features for the database. Thus the DDL, through inputs from the user, can indicate the fields or records that are limited in terms of activity and access and the type of restrictions (read or write only, or both read and write). It will generally require that each record (tuple as it is called in a relational system) have a primary key for maintenance of data integrity.

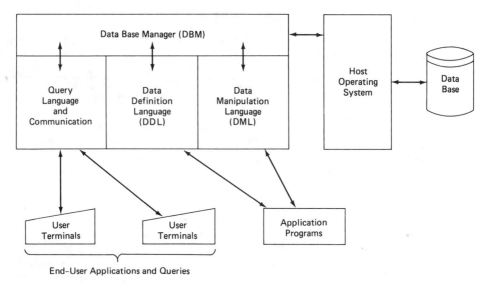

FIGURE 10-9 Database management system and its associated components.

Thus the primary functions of the DDL are as follows:

1. Define the characteristics of each field.
2. Specify the grouping of fields into records.
3. Identify the keys of the record.
4. Provide a means to specify the relationships among data tables or records.
5. Describe the schema and subschema.
6. Provide for data security.

To illustrate some of the functions of the DDL, we will assume that the database consists of three records: sales, customers, and parts inventory. To describe the database, we must first use the DDL to develop the schema. Figure 10-10 shows how the record layout might appear for parts inventory. Note that the DDL describes the name, type, width, and decimal characteristics of the inventory record. One item that is not defined in this example is the relationship between the two records. The DDL employs common labels to refer to the different fields of the record; thus, no tie is made to any physical structure or physical file. The records can reside in any order and on any type of storage device (disk, drums, data cell, etc.).

For every application program that accesses the database, a subschema must be structured. The subschema, as we noted earlier, is the descriptive layout of the relation, record, or records employed by the program. Figure 10-10 illus-

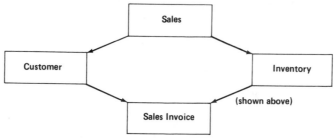

Data Definition Language DDL

Name	Part Number	Description	Quantity	Quantity On Order	Cost	Location
Data Type	Numeric	Character	Numeric	Numeric	Numeric	Character
Field Length decimals	10	25	5	5	7.2	10

SUBSCHEMA FOR SALES TRANSACTION
(Logical path showing the sequence of relational tables used to process transaction)

FIGURE 10-10 Data definition language and subschema illustration.

trated one possible subschema expressing a sales transaction for this database, using a relational structure. When the application program requests the data during execution, the database system will extract the values of the data items from the appropriate database tables or records and place them in the order noted by the subschema. Note that this particular example of a DDL is not structured around a particular database management system.

DATA MANIPULATION LANGUAGE (DML). The DML is used to describe the manner in which the database is processed; that is, it provides the techniques for processing the database, such as REPLACE, UPDATE, GROUP SELECT, READ, APPEND, COPY, FROM, USE, etc. To provide these capabilities, the DML employs a variety of manipulation verbs and associated operands for these verbs. Figure 10-11 shows some typical verbs and operands which are used by SQL database software. These are often called the commands. The structure of the operand associated with a particular verb depends upon the action taken by the verb (command). The SELECT verb requires a field such as sales person and criteria, for example.

By employing the manipulation verbs and the associated operands of the DML, a user is able to work with the database in logical or symbolic terms rather than physical terms. The DML also frees the user from making all the structural changes associated with a modification of the database. For example, when a record is added to a set, the database system will make all the necessary changes. The user simply issues the appropriate command.

```
SELECT SALES_PERSON, COUNT(NAME)
FROM SALES
GROUP BY SALES_PERSON
HAVING COUNT(NAME) >
  (SELECT COUNT(NAME)
  WHERE SALES_PERSON = 'JONES'
SALES_PERSON  COUNT(NAME)
============  ===========

MCPHERSON     35
DENT          50
WILLIAMS      75
```

This query using select, from, group, where, and count will select all sales persons who have sold more than Jones.

FIGURE 10-11 Data manipulation language SQL.

In summary, the DML is designed to do the following:

1. Provide data manipulation techniques such as joining, retrieving, replacing, selecting, sorting, and deleting.
2. Provide a means to work with the database in logical and symbolic terms rather than physical terms.
3. Allow the user to be independent of physical data structure and database structure maintenance.
4. Provide flexibility in the use of the DML with standard symbolic languages.

CONCEPTUAL VIEW. To better understand how the DDL and DML work in conjunction with the database management system, we will examine the steps required to read an accounts receivable record from the database. We will assume that a READ command (verb) has been employed by the user, along with the appropriate operand arguments. The numbers in bold indicate the order of the events in Figure 10-12. The sequence is follows:

1. The user program instructs the database management system to read a customer record. The program provides the record key (account number) and all associated data required for the application, such as name, address, and amount due.
2. The database management system examines the subschema associated with the accounts receivable application program and examines the records needed to respond to the user's request.
3. The database management system examines the schema to determine which records are needed.

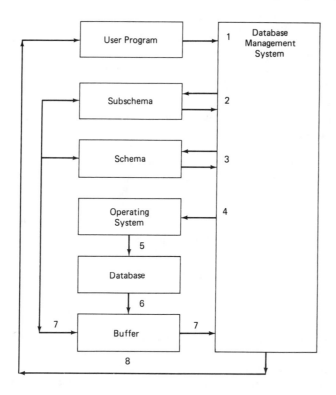

FIGURE 10-12   Conceptual view of an application program reading a record from a database.

4. The database management system passes control to the operating system after requesting the appropriate records.
5. The operating system interacts with the storage device on which the database resides and extracts the appropriate data.
6. The data are transferred from the database to the system buffer.
7. By comparing the subschema and the schema, the database management system extracts the data required by the accounts receivable program.
8. The data are then transferred to the application and displayed in the manner requested by the user.

DATA DICTIONARIES.   In our initial discussion of database processing, we did not identify a data dictionary as a processing component. This was not because of oversight; it was simply because all database systems do not employ data dictionaries.

A *data dictionary* is a software package used by some DBMS to assist in the construction and management of the database. It is a repository of data about data. A data dictionary could easily contain a catalog of the following data:

1. Data item (field)
2. Data classification and type
3. Subschema associated with each data item, such as the record name and application where it is used
4. Schema record associated with each data item, such as the record, file, or relational table that indicates the logical location of each item
5. Source of data (data input)

The data dictionary can be used by the database administrator, the systems staff, and the user (managers) and can be accessed by application packages. The data dictionary can help to ensure data definition consistency. It can help users determine what data are available for specific applications and the labels and types of data involved. It can show where data are used and where it originates. It can also guide a user in interrogation of the database.

OPERATION AND USE OF DATABASE PROCESSING

We have devoted a large portion of this chapter to examining the components that go together to make up a database processing system, but we have said very little about the use of such systems. In this section we will focus on some factors related to the operation and use of database systems. Specifically we will examine requirements for database use and discuss backup and recovery. Database security issues are discussed in the next chapter on control structure under the advanced computer control section.

Database Use

Earlier in the chapter we noted that users have four means by which they can interact with the database management system: (1) directly, by using a query language, (2) by communicating with an application program, which in turn interacts with the database management system; (3) by using a report generator; or (4) by writing their own applications or requests as an end user.

Using a database system, however, requires more than simply a language or a means of access. In actuality, five elements are involved in a user's interaction with a database systems.

The first is the *method of access.* This may be a query language; it may involve writing an application program using a host computer language such as COBOL, FORTRAN, or PASCAL. It may also involve the user writing a simple set of software commands or the user using report generating software to access data.

The second is the *mode of access or processing.* This refers to whether *batch* or *on-line* (interactive) processing is employed. Some individuals erroneously assume that database processing involves only on-line processing. Database processing, however, can be batch, on line, or a mixture of both.

The third element, the *nature of the request,* refers to whether the user's request is *fixed* or *dynamic.* In most systems a user is permitted to make certain specific fixed requests. However, many permit dynamic requests. An airlines ticketing agent making an inquiry to determine the availability of seats and a bank teller making an inquiry to determine the account balance of a customer are examples of users making fixed requests. An example of a dynamic request would be a marketing manager who is examining different combinations of sales data (by territory, by salesperson, by product type, by a ratio of product type to salesperson, etc.) in order to evaluate a market situation.

The *range of data that is referenced* refers to the extent to which the data base is employed. In some cases the user may need and have approval to access a large part or all of the database (schema). In other cases the user may need access to only a small portion of the database (subschema). If a user is given access to a portion (subschema) of the database needed by an application or query, only data in the defined area or areas can be referenced or modified. Security procedures, such as those reviewed in Chapter 11, are available to mask data in the database so that the users are restricted to defined subsets of data. For example, customer representatives could only view a small set of the customer database and they could only view certain items, such as the customer payment and charge history. They would have no access to other portions of the database or to confidential information on the customer income or personal data.

The last element employed in interacting with the database system is labeled the *access privileges*. This refers to whether the user inquiry involves actual access of data, changing data values, or modification of data structure (relationships) of the database. One marketing manager may only be able to access the database to retrieve data relating to sales by salesperson, sales by territory, or some other set of data. Another may be able to access and change commission rates. However, if the sales territories or the territory-to-salesperson relationships within the organization change, the structure of database would need to be changed to correspond to the organization. A marketing manager could, if given the proper security clearance, make data structure modifications. However, this responsibility is more appropriately that of the database administrator.

To illustrate how these five elements are employed by a database system user, consider the following. Assume that an individual calls an airline office to inquire about the availability of seats on a given flight. The caller talks with a reservations agent who has access to a database. The agent is the database system user; more specifically, the agent is a query language access/on line mode/fixed/subschema/data user. Under this arrangement the agent will use query language statements in an interactive on-line mode to access specific items of information. The database that the agent accesses may contain a vast amount of data relating to the operations as well as financial performance of the airline; however, the agent will only examine a subset of the database. The agent can only access and modify data in that subset. In terms of database use, it is expected that end-user applications will continue to grow very rapidly with the extensive use of microcomputers and networks which interface with minicomputers and mainframes. Newer database software is easy to use, and as a result of microcomputer access and the advent of relational databases, many users are able to write their own inquiries and applications. The net result is increasingly less reliance on the IS department for access to data and more widespread use of information heretofore inaccessible on a timely basis for decision making.

Backup and Recovery

One of the key elements of a successful database system is the backup and recovery procedure. Since databases are vulnerable, the lack of backup and recovery procedures can be catastrophic.

A number of problems that require backup and recovery can occur. First, it may be discovered that erroneous data exist in the database. This may be discovered in a database inquiry, in an output report, or simply in an edit check of the database. The origin of the data error is probably unknown; the data error is simply recognized. Second, a mistake in a program modification, an improper use of a program, or the simple inputting of data may result in the loading of erroneous data into the database. Third, an I/O parity error, a bad disk, a bad tape, as well as failures in hardware storage units, can result in lost data. In such cases the database is incorrect because parts or all of the data changes were not made. Finally, a power failure or machine malfunction can result in partial or complete loss of data. This is particularly true if the storage device on which the data are located "crashes."

Fortunately, procedures have been developed whereby recovery can be made from these types of problems. Two distinct and separate items are necessary for backup and recovery: (1) a backup database; and (2) a transaction log or a modification activity file. A backup database can be created by periodically dumping the database onto an alternative (backup) storage device. The frequency with which the dump is made depends upon how frequently changes are made to the database and the cost associated with the recovery process. The older the backup database, the greater the cost will be when recovery is required. Tests need to be run to be sure that the backup is valid.

After the valid backup database has been created, the second item that is used in a recovery process must be developed; this involves the creation of a transaction log or a database modification activity file. This log (activity file) is used to store information associated with database modifications. A transaction log is a simple recording of changes between periodic backups. A modification activity file on the other hand is more complex. When a change or a modification in the database occurs, data values (images) *before* and *after* the change are recorded in the activity file, along with the date, the time, the area of the database where the change was made (location), the software program employed in the change, and any other associated information. The more information collected and stored in the activity file, the easier the recovery process will be when restoration is needed. However, the more elaborate the activity file, the greater the operating cost. Larger files take more time to create and require more storage space. Recovery procedures, then, use the periodic backups and either a transaction log or modification activity file to reconstruct the database.

As is obvious from this very brief overview, backup and recovery are an important element in database processing. The methods discussed here are by no means the only procedures used in practice; however, they are used by a number of organizations. A great deal of research is currently being conducted to find more efficient, more reliable, and less expensive procedures.

ADVANTAGES	DISADVANTAGES
1. Reduction of Data Duplication	1. Complexity of Operating System
2. Data Integration	2. Increase in Expenses due to Complexity
3. Program and Data Independence	3. Complex Backup and Recovery
4. Reduced Cost of Program Development and Maintenance Due to Independence	4. Vulnerability Due to Data Concentration
5. Better Data Management	5. Difficult to Implement
6. More Rapid Retrieval of Information	
7. Increased Security Provisions	

FIGURE 10-13   Potential advantages and disadvantages of database systems.

SUMMARY OF ADVANTAGES AND DISADVANTAGES OF DATABASE PROCESSING

From the materials surveyed throughout this and the last chapter, the reader could either mistakenly conclude that database processing is a complex as well as an expensive process or conclude that it is the only rational choice for all data processing requirements. To avoid this misconception, we will highlight some of the advantages and disadvantages, shown on Figure 10-13, of employing a database management system. These are important, because, according to the contingency theory of accounting systems, the most appropriate system is a function of the nature of advantages and disadvantages like these.

Advantages

Reduction of data duplication. Duplicate data that traditionally exist in file processing systems can be reduced significantly by a database management system. Data need only be recorded once. This results in lower storage costs; but, more important, it provides a higher level of data consistency and integrity. If the same data item exists in two or more places, it is possible to change the data in one place but not the other. If this occurs, conflicting reports can result because one software program may access the updated data item while a second program accesses the incorrect data item. Database processing minimizes the possibility of this occurring.

Data integration. Since data is stored in only one place and not duplicated in multiple files, it is much easier to integrate accounting applications. The database management system can be used to efficiently access any data item regardless of the application or query. These applications, further, can be more easily integrated because they share a common data set. For example, the sales, accounts receivable, and inventory applications can be easily integrated to access common customer and stock data and to post sales transactions to the common data set. As a result the application and data are integrated rather than separate.

③ *Program/data independence.* Because the database management system interfaces between the database and the user, physical storage and logical storage structures are separated; therefore, software programs and data are more data independent. This is particularly true for relational database systems. Programs can be changed without changing data files, and data files can be changed without changing programs.

Because changes in the content of the database do not have an impact on the programs that access it, the overall system is more efficient. Updating and/or reorganizing the database requires only changes in the database management system; rewriting application programs is not required unless the logical structure is changed. Also, unlike a file-oriented system, a database can expand without having to be reorganized. For example, data fields can readily be added or deleted; the only change required is in the logical definition of the information in the database.

④ *Better data management.* When the data management responsibilities are centralized (not necessarily physically) data can be distributed, database processing can lead to better data management. It is more efficient and less expensive to have one department manage database activities than to have several staffs managing a portion of the data. The department can specify data standards and ensure that all data utilized in the database adhere to the standards. With a file-oriented system, several departments or areas might have to be contacted in developing a single application program, particularly if the program cuts across several organizational lines. With database processing, data requirements can be handled by contacting a single departmental unit.

From a managerial perspective, the integration of data in a common data base management system enables management to more easily access data from a number of divisions and functions to help managers make better decisions.

Disadvantages

① *Complexity.* Database processing is complex because of its very nature. Larger quantities of data, expressed in several different application formats, may require the access of data from numerous files or relational data tables. As a result, the database management system must be able to use complicated data structures and to process varied data requests. Thus sophisticated design and programming skills are required in developing a database management system. Likewise, because of the complexity of the overall process, application programs (with the exception of end-user applications) may take a lengthy period of time, and highly qualified programming personnel to develop.

② *Expense.* Due to their complexity database systems are expensive. The software cost of a mainframe system could be as much as $500,000. The software alone, however, is only part of the total expense. Since the database system will reside on disk, additional disk drives may be required. In some cases it may even be necessary to upgrade to a larger computer. Processing cost with a database management system will also probably be greater because more complex activities are involved. This is also the case for small companies that are switching from a manual file-oriented system to a computerized database system even though microcomputer software costs can start as low as $100.

Backup and recovery. Because several users may be operating with the database management system concurrently and because of the complexity in general of the entire system, backup and recovery can be a difficult process. Two general problems exist: (1) when a failure or an error occurs, the status of the database must be determined; and (2) assuming that the status of the database can be determined, the task is then to determine what should be done to rectify the error or errors in the data. Both problems can require considerable time and effort.

Vulnerability. Because the database management system is at the center of database processing, a malfunction in any component of the system can have an impact on the database as well as other users and may bring the entire system to a halt. And because several users may access the database concurrently, an error in one program can create problems in others. For example, if user A attempts to modify several records in the database but an error occurs in his or her application program, then invalid data may be placed in the database. If user B reads the records immediately after the modifications take place, then invalid data will be accessed by B. There are systems to prevent this but they are complex and costly.

Comparison of Advantages and Disadvantages

Figure 10-13 summarizes both the advantages and the disadvantages of database processing. If one is considering moving to a database system environment, these factors should be carefully examined and weighed.

SUMMARY

Database systems input, process, and access data in a way quite different than traditional single-file-oriented systems that were discussed in the last chapter. In general, a database management system is used to bridge the gap between the logic of an application and the actual storage of the data. This concept is called data independence. The components of a database system include the user, the database administrator, the database management system, and the database. The database management system consists of a database manager for controlling its operations, a data definition language to describe the data details and structure, a data manipulation language to use the database, and a query language to gain quick access to data. The more commonly used data structures included the hierarchy (tree), the network, and the relational data models, all of which provide a logical view of the data for effective use by management.

Database processing can reduce data redundancy, provide for the integration of data for many applications, provide more program/data independence, and provide better data management. However, there are some disadvantages to such a system, such as expense and complexity. Because backup and recovery and security are also major problems, we examined these in detail in this chapter and will consider them again in the next chapter on the control environment.

SELECTED REFERENCES

CHEN, PETER PIN-SHAN, "The Entity-Relationship Model—Toward a Unified View of Data," *ACM Transactions on Database Systems*, Vol. 1, No., 1 March 1976, pp 9–36.

CODASYL (Conference on Data Systems and Languages), "Data Base Task Group Report, 1971," New York: Association for Computing Machinery, April 1971.

DATE, C. J., *An Introduction to Database Systems*, 5th ed., Reading, Mass.: Addison-Wesley, 1990.

EVERST, G. C., and R. WEBER, "A Relational Approach to Accounting Models," *The Accounting Review*, April 1977, pp. 340–359.

FARIN, JEFF, and AMOR NAZARIO, "DBMS Basics," *Infosystems*, June 1986.

KROENKE, DAVID, *Database Processing*. Chicago: Science Research Associates, 1977.

MARTIN, JAMES, *Principles of Data Base Management*. Englewood Cliffs, N.J.: Prentice-Hall, 1976.

McCARTHY, W. E., "An Entity-Relationship View of Accounting Modeling," *The Accounting Review*, October 1979, pp. 667–686.

McCARTHY, W. E., "The REA Accounting Model: A Generalized Framework for Accounting Systems in a Shared Data Environment," *The Accounting Review*, July 1982, pp. 554–578.

NUSBAUM, EDWARD E., ANDREW D. BAILEY, JR., and ANDREW B. WHINSTON. "Data Base Management Accounting and Accountants," *Management Accounting*, 58 (May 1978), 35–38.

SMITH, JAMES F., and AMER MUFTI, "Using the Relational Data Base," *Management Accounting*, 1985.

WEBER, RON, "Data Models Research in Accounting: An Evaluation of Wholesale Distribution Software," *The Accounting Review*, July 1986, pp. 498–518.

REVIEW QUESTIONS

1. Differentiate between a file oriented approach and a database approach to data management.

2. Identify the major components of a database management system.

3. What are the responsibilities of a database administrator?

4. In what ways can a user interact with data in a database management system?

5. Differentiate between a logical view of data and the physical organization of data.

6. What is a schema and a subschema?

7. Describe the major characteristics of a hierarchical, network, and a relational database.

8. What characteristic makes the relational database the most flexible of the models (structures) presented in this chapter?

9. Describe the three major operations used to retrieve data from a relational database. Give an example of how they would work.

10. What are the functions of the data definition language (DDL)? Give an example.

11. What are the functions of the data manipulation language? Give an example.

12. Explain how the DDL and the DML work in

conjunction with the DBMS to execute a command such as READ.

13. What is the purpose of the data dictionary?

14. Explain how you would reconstruct a database after it was discovered that an error existed in the data.

15. What are the advantages and the disadvantages of database processing?

APPENDIX

REA ACCOUNTING MODEL

McCarthy[A1] proposed an extension to the entity-relationship (E-R) model called the REA model. REA represents economic *R*esources, economic *E*vents and economic *A*gents. This model takes the requirements analysis of what is needed in an economic entity, develops a logical view of the data base necessary to provide the information to users, organizes these views and data elements, constructs a data base from these elements, and uses this database for supporting transaction processing, reporting, and decision making needs of management.

The model consists of the following components as shown in Figure A-1 where the basic components in the general model are shown in parallel with examples of these components in a sales order entry system. Briefly these components are defined below.

Economic resources are objects which are scarce, have utility, and can be used by the enterprise. For example cash, inventory, and other assets except claims such as accounts receivable which will be discussed later.

Economic events are those activities that result in changes in economic resources from production, sale, use, and distribution. An example would be the sale of stock as shown in the illustration.

Stock Flows represent goods and services which flow throughout the system and thus represent relationships between the economic resources and events.

Duality is the relational concept that for each increase in the resource set of an enterprise there is a correspondingly decrease in the set of economic resources. In the example for the reduction in inventory there is a corresponding increase in cash as shown by the cash receipt and resulting payment. In other words the duality concept models debits and credits. In this simple model there are no accruals such as receivables or payables; these will be discussed later in this brief overview. The primary and the dual economic events are generally recorded as debits and credits in an accounting system.

Economic agents include persons or agencies who participate in economic events. In general they refer to those agents outside the organization. They have the power to use or dispose of economic resources, such as customers as illustrated in Figure A10-1.

[A1] See McCarthy, W. E., "An Entity-Relationship View of Accounting Models," *The Accounting Review*, October 1979, pp. 667–686, and McCarthy, W. E., "The REA Accounting Model: a Generalized Framework for Accounting Systems in a Shared Data Environment," *The Accounting Review*, July 1982, pp. 554–578 for a complete discussion of this model.

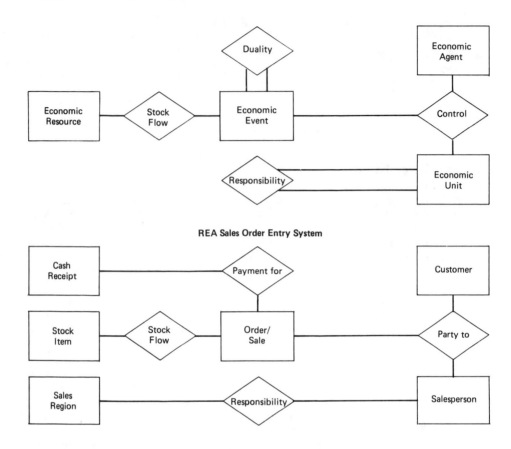

FIGURE A10-1   General REA accounting model.
Source: Weber, R., "Data Models Research in Accounting: An Evaluation of Wholesale Distribution Software", *The Accounting Review,* July 1986, pp. 498–518.

Economic units are those economic agents, such as salespersons, within the organization who participate in economic events.

Control is the association between an economic event (which describes the increase or decrease in an economic resource), the economic unit (inside party), and the economic agent (outside party). The accounting system illustrated may record this type of activity by simply recording the sale along with the salesperson's identity and the customer's identity.

Responsibility relationships indicate a higher level of control such as a superior and subordinate relation as indicated in the example by the region and salesperson relation. This type of relationship may be achieved via a reporting mechanism.

Duality imbalances in amount and timing between outflow and inflow economic events such as the sale of stock and the payment for the stock represent accruals such as accounts receivable.

Using these relationships developed by McCarthy one can describe the transaction processing as well as the reporting aspects of an accounting system. The flows between economic events capture the essence of the transaction systems whereas the control and responsibility components capture the essence of managerial accounting control and responsibility systems. As a result this model can serve as a basis for developing a database.

CASES

10-1 Mariposa Products, a textile and apparel manufacturer, acquired its own computer in 1988. The first application to be developed and implemented was production and inventory control. Other applications that were added in succession were payroll, accounts receivable, and accounts payable.

The applications were not integrated due to the piecemeal manner in which they were developed and implemented. Nevertheless, the system proved satisfactory for several years. Generally, reports were prepared on time, and information was readily accessible.

Mariposa operates in a very competitive industry. A combination of increased operating costs and the competitive nature of the industry have had an adverse effect on profit margins and operating profits. Ed Wilde, Mariposa's president, suggested that some special analyses be prepared in an attempt to provide information that would help management improve operations. Unfortunately, some of the data were not consistent among the reports. In addition, the reports did not include data by product line or department. The problems were attributable to the fact that Mariposa's applications were developed piecemeal and, as a consequence, duplicate data that were not necessarily consistent existed on Mariposa's computer system.

Wilde was concerned that Mariposa's computer system was not able to generate the information his managers needed to make decisions. He called a meeting of his top management and certain data processing personnel to discuss potential solutions to Mariposa's problems. The outcome of the meeting was that a new information system that would integrate Mariposa's applications was needed.

Mariposa's controller suggested that the company consider a database system that all departments would use. As a first step, the controller proposed hiring a database administrator on a consulting basis to determine the feasibility of converting to a database system.

REQUIRED:

1. Identify the components that comprise a database system.

2. Discuss the advantages and disadvantages of a database system for Mariposa Products.

3. List the factors that Mariposa Products should consider before converting to a database system.

4. Describe the duties of a database administrator.
   (CMA Adapted with permission.)

10-2 Tillman's Textiles manufactures a line of quality children's wear. They exhibit their merchandise at all trade shows in New York, Chicago, Atlanta, Dallas, and San Francisco. They sell through major department stores and children's wear specialty stores. They have over four thousand customers throughout the nation. They currently use some antiquated batch processing equipment, and they are considering installing a new system to manage their customer base. They want it to interface with a new accounts receivable system which they will write specifically for their needs. They would like to be able to maintain data on each customer for selected product promotions, credit ratings, billing, and sales history information. Each transaction must be kept for an audit trail and for customer inquiry. Management would also like to be able to change their reports and data to keep up with changing information needs. Moreover, management would like to be able to access the data for managerial decision-making needs that are not supported by routine reports. The management of Tillman's Textile Company has engaged you to suggest a database management and replaced accounts receivable and billing system. You have concluded that they need a relational database system to be able to merge the customer data file and the accounts receivable file and have the degree of data independence required for flexibility in reporting and managerial inquiry.

REQUIRED: As part of your proposal you need to explain why a relational database system, which has programming language that can be used by managers, is needed for the management of Tillman's Textile.

10-3 Maxwells Lumber is a general all-purpose hardware and building supply store. Their main clients are local building contracts, although they do maintain a reasonably large retail clientele. They are located in an industrial park near most of the contractors' offices. They stock a wide variety of building materials. They have everything from the foundation material through light fixtures and major appliances. Many of the local builders do all their business at Maxwells on credit, so Maxwells maintains an extensive accounts receivable system. Since Maxwells has a liberal return policy, the accounts receivable system must maintain an open item system. Moreover, it must interface with a sales order and inventory system. Currently they use a manual system to process all these transactions. Lately this manual system has "bogged down" due to the volume of business, and Maxwells is considering automation.

1. As their accountant and given your experience in retail accounting systems, list the data elements you would maintain in a database which would be necessary to support sales, inventory, accounts receivable, and accounts payable systems.

2. Identify the likely source of each data element.

3. How could these data elements be structured into tables for a relational database?

10-4 Peterson Construction Company currently uses a job-cost system for tracking construction costs for each of their construction jobs. This consists of a set of records for each job and resembles a large job-cost sheet. They use this information to estimate the progress of each job for financial reporting purposes and for bank financing. They also have a payroll system which consists of a set of records on each employee. This file is used to process weekly and biweekly payroll. They have an accounts payable system for the purchase of building materials and for subcontract work. They must run their accounts payable and their payroll files on their microcomputer prior to running their job-cost system in order to obtain accurate charges for their labor, material, and subcontracting costs. This is done biweekly and at the end of the month.

They have several problems with this system. One, they need up-to-date job-costs information more frequently. Two, they would like to use the information in other ways, such as in estimation for new jobs. This requires the writing of special programs for analysis of the data. Three, the payroll and accounts payable files are not organized in a way which makes it easy to transfer the costs to the appropriate jobs.

Mr. Peterson has just returned from a homebuilders convention where he was exposed to some new database software which seemed to resolve some of the updating, programming, and flexibility problems he is having. The problem is that he was too confused by all the discussion of schema and operating systems to understand how it could help.

REQUIRED: As Mr. Peterson's accountant explain how such a database system could be used to help him. Explain the theoretical reasons why it would help. Explain the various components of a database management system and how they can help with his problem.

10-5 Inventory database case (requires knowledge of a database package for a microcomputer).

REQUIRED: Develop a database package that will have the following features:

1. Perform the following functions which are typical of inventory operations:

   a. Record shipment and sales transactions in a journal file.

   b. Record receipts of inventory items in a journal file.

   c. Update receipts of inventory items to the inventory master file.

   d. Update shipping (or sales) transactions to the inventory master.

   e. Produce a listing of the contents of the master file in inventory number order with item descriptions and quantities on hand.

2. Use the following files with the following field names, type, and data width:

10-6 Progress in the design and development of computer-based management information systems has been impressive in the past three decades. Traditionally, computer-based data

1. Inventory master (INVMSTR).

Field	Field Name	Type	Width	Decimal
1	CODE	Numeric	4	
2	QTY	Numeric	4	
3	REORDER_PT	Numeric	2	
4	ORDER_DATE	Date	8	
5	ORDER_Q	Numeric	3	
6	COST	Numeric	5	2
7	VENDOR	Numeric	4	

2. Sales (SALES).

Field	Field Name	Type	Width	Decimal
1	CODE	Numeric	4	
2	QTY	Numeric	5	
3	PRICE	Numeric	5	2
4	DATE	Date	8	

3. Receiving (RECVNG).

Field	Field Name	Type	Width	Decimal
1	CODE	Numeric	4	
2	QTY	Numeric	4	
3	PO_NO	Numeric	6	
4	DATE_REC	Date	8	

4. Code listing (CODELIST)

Field	Field Name	Type	Width	Decimal
1	CODE	Numeric	4	
2	DESCRIPT	Character	10	

Use the following index files:
1. SINDEX for SALES
2. MINDEX for INVMSTR
3. RINDEX for RECVNG
4. CODE for CODELIST

processing systems were arranged by departments and applications. Computers were applied to single, large-volume applications such as inventory control or customer billing. Other applications were added once the first applications were operating smoothly.

As more applications were added, problems in data management developed. Businesses looked for ways to integrate the data processing systems to make them more comprehensive and to have shorter response times. As a consequence, the database systems were developed.

REQUIRED:

1. Explain the basic differences between the traditional approach to data processing and the use of the database system in terms of

   a. File structure

   b. Processing of data

2. Many practitioners have asserted that security in a database system is of greater importance than in traditional systems. Explain the importance of back up and recovery plans.

3. Identify and discuss the favorable and unfavorable issues other than security that a company should consider before implementing a database system.
   (Adapted from the CMA examination.)

10-7 Howell and Mitchell, a large regional architecture and engineering firm with sales approaching fifty million a year, currently uses a file-oriented microcomputer system. At the present time it retains separate files (diskettes) for clients or customer receivables, supplier payables, inventory, job specification, job bids and costs payroll, and standard engineering design specifications. In other words, it currently uses an antiquated file oriented system. To support routine operational and managerial decision making, it needs the following information on a regular basis:

1. Cost data to determine the profit or loss and percent completion for all jobs

2. Cost data to prepare bids on new jobs

3. Job specifications for bidding, cost analysis, and on-the-job instructions

4. Payroll reports and cash disbursements by jobs and by employees

5. Inventory and purchase requests

6. Accounts receivable and collection information for each job and each client

7. Accounts payable analysis disbursements information

8. Cash flow analysis and forecasts

9. Financial statements

It has been very awkward and time consuming for the computer operators to handle the files manually for the preparation of each of these reports, even though there is a straightforward procedures manual and a set of application programs for each report.

The problem is compounded by the need for information on a random basis. The job supervisor or the engineer often has specific requests about the status of an item, cost to date of a project, or other query involving more than one file. For many of these requests, several files must be handled, a program must be written, and a procedural manual must be referenced. However, this is seldom the case and managers must assemble the data from separate reports manually to satisfy their needs. The problem has been further compounded during the annual audit when it was discovered that the payroll, the job bid, and the cost files did not reconcile.

Mr. Mitchell has attended a seminar at the national meeting of building contractors and has listened to a discussion about a DBMS for a microcomputer. He has asked you, as his accountant, to advise him on the pros and cons of a DBMS and to explain to him, in language he can understand, how such a system would eliminate the obvious data update problems, the excessive procedural efforts needed to prepare reports, and the need on the part of management to assemble data manually when requesting information involving more than one file.

REQUIRED:

1. Write a brief report to Mr. Mitchell to answer his questions

2. Also explain to Mr. Mitchell the need to upgrade the microhardware to accommodate the larger data set necessary to sup-

port a DBMS and the costs associated with this upgrading.

10-8 The Community Savings Bank is a large bank based in Sydney with branches scattered throughout Australia. The bank uses an on-line update system for its customer accounts system. The branches are connected via a telecommunications network to a centralized database in the head office. The bank uses a database management system to manage its data.

As a member of the external audit firm of the bank, you are reviewing the adequacy of backup and recovery procedures for the on-line real-time update system. During an interview with the database administrator, she explains to you that when a system crash occurs, the computer operators attempt to restart the system immediately because downtime is intolerable with the system. Since the database management system used by the bank establishes relationships between entities via pointers, you express your concern to her about the possibility of pointers in the database not having been updated (that is, an update is in progress when the crash occurs and the database is in an inconsistent state). The database administrator concedes this point. Nevertheless, she argues that it is a relatively minor problem. When the system is restarted, tellers are supposed to check whether the last transaction they submitted was posted. If it was not posted, they resubmit the transaction. An inquiry transaction will also identify inconsistent or corrupted pointers. If the database is in an inconsistent state, since it is unlikely that another transaction will occur for the customer's account during that day, backup and recovery are left until the night shift.

REQUIRED: Write a brief report for your manager commenting on the adequacy of backup and recovery procedures for the on-line system. Make any suggestions that you feel would improve the adequacy of backup and recovery procedures for the system.

10-9 The Thomas Company is a medium-sized manufacturer of high-pressure valves. All products are produced on a job-order basis and are sold on account to other companies which incorporate them into final products. Thomas has been using data processing systems for the past ten years and is generally innovative in terms of applying current computer technology. The company is currently considering the installation of a DBMS in the raw material, production, order shipping, and accounts receivable areas.

1. What factors should the company consider before opting for the DBMS approach?

2. Assuming that Thomas decides to install a DBMS, what files would you recommend? What would be the contents of these records within these files? Identify which related records would be associated and indicate how "pointers" could be used to link the data.

3. How would the DDL of the DBMS be used in setting up the system?

4. What reports would probably be required?

5. Would the DML portion of the DBMS be employed? Give an example.

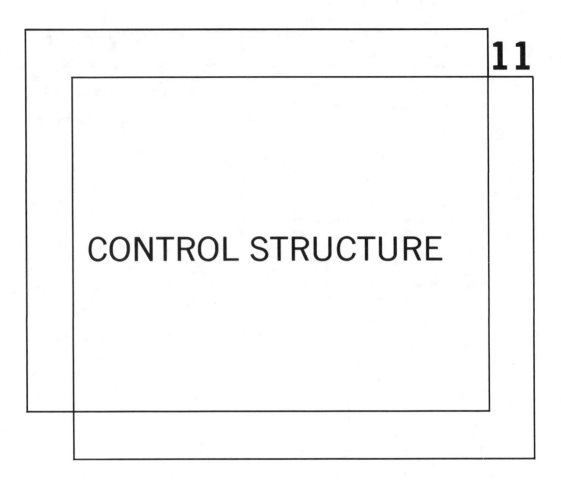

CONTROL STRUCTURE

INTERNAL CONTROL AND RISK

From a management perspective, risk is the potential for loss. It includes the potential exposure to loss and the probability associated with that potential. If an organization's controls are not adequate, the accounting information system is vulnerable to a number of potential problems that may result in a loss. The users of financial statements and the auditors who attest to the validity of financial statements are also at risk and subject to a potential loss. An effective and efficient control structure is necessary to minimize this risk.

Objective of Control Systems

The *Statement on Auditing Standards No. 1* gives the following definition of internal control:

> Internal control comprises the plan of organization and all of the co-ordinate methods and measures adopted within a business to safeguard its assets, check the accuracy and reliability of its accounting data, promote

operational efficiency, and encourage adherence to prescribed managerial policies.[1]

This definition recognizes the broad responsibility of public and private accountants for the organization's control structure. The design of the control structure is a function of many factors. These include the nature of the organization's objectives and environment, the size and structure of the organization, the extent and nature of computer processing, and the exposure of the organization to various risks. These risks vary for each organization and for each transaction, reporting requirement, and decision in the organization. In addition, the degree of exposure will be a function of the frequency of exposure, such as the number of on-line terminals; the vulnerability of the asset, such as cash; the size (value) of the asset; and the nature of the transaction or decision. These risks can result from fraud, security breach (unauthorized access), unintentional error, deliberate error, unintentional loss of assets such as data, an act of violence or a natural disaster. In sum, the nature of this exposure will differ for every organization and the exposure will impact the accounting information system in terms of its ability to comply with the transaction processing, reporting, and decision-making requirements of the organization. Moreover, what constitutes an excellent control structure for one organization may be weak for another.

Auditors are concerned about *audit risk* which is defined by the AICPA in the *Statement on Auditing Standards No. 47* [2] as the risk that an auditor may unknowingly fail to appropriately modify his or her opinion on financial statements that are materially misstated. The AICPA further suggests in SAS No. 47 that audit risk is composed of three components. These are inherent risk, control risk, and detection risk. These are described further in Chapter 20 on computer auditing. Briefly, inherent risk refers to the general business and economic environment and its impact on the exposure of various accounts and transactions to various risks resulting from the environmental conditions. Detection risk is the risk of not detecting an error during an audit and is discussed in Chapter 20. Control risk is defined by the AICPA as "the risk that misstatements that could occur in an account balance or class of transactions and that could be material, when aggregated with misstatements in other balances or classes, will not be prevented or detected and corrected on a timely basis by the entity's control structure."[3]

The assessment of control risk is straightforward in manual and traditional file-oriented systems and for the assessment of financial statements. At the other extreme in database environments this aggregation can take many forms based

---

[1] AICPA, *Codification of Auditing Standards and Procedures, Statement on Auditing Standards No. 1* (AU 320.08) New York: American Institute of Certified Public Accountants, Inc., copyright (1972), reprinted with permission.

[2] *Audit Risk and Materiality in Conducting an Audit, Statement on Auditing Standards No. 47,* (AU 312.03) Auditing Standards Board, American Institute of Certified Public Accountants, New York, N.Y., 1983.

[3] See SAS No. 47 (AU 312.20), *Consideration of the Internal Control in a Financial Statement Audit,* Statement on Auditing Standards (SAS) No. 55, Auditing Standards Board, American Institute of Certified Public Accountants, New York, N.Y., 1988. See also *The Auditor's Responsibility for Assessing Control Risk, Proposed Statement on Auditing Standards—Exposure Draft* (ARACR), Auditing Standards Board, AICPA, January 1987.

on user's information needs, as shown in Chapter 10. Thus, control risk is difficult to assess for decision-making needs in such an environment.

In complex information system (IS) environments, there is an increased potential for risk in many areas which are not as susceptible to risk in traditional manual accounting systems or in very simple computerized information systems which process information just like a manual system. These include the following:

1. User requirements may not be met by the information being generated by the accounting information system. This may result from a lack of understanding on the part of accountants and managers about technical aspects of computer systems and on the part of systems analysts about management and accounting problems.

2. In manual systems errors usually only happen once. In a computer system they can repeat themselves each time a transaction is processed with an erroneous program. Moreover, they can repeat themselves at a high speed.

3. Because of the integration of software, errors in one file can impact the integrity of other files that are linked to the erroneous file. A large portion of the database can be thus corrupted and reports based on the database may be in error.

4. Data are not readily observable. As a result errors such as those above can go undetected for a long time. They may have influenced numerous decisions, since the erroneous data formed the basis for the decisions.

5. Remote terminals, telecommunications, unprotected passwords, on-line terminals, critical files, end-user access to the database, and electronic data interchange all expose a computer system to numerous access risks. Those gaining unauthorized access can perpetrate fraud, use information to the detriment of the organization, use information for personal gain, and even disrupt the activities of the organization.

6. Procedural errors can result in lost data during file transfers and from using the wrong tape, disk, or file. Often this loss follows from incorrect labeling of files and disks. Data can easily become lost or compromised when it is communicated between units within the computer system or between different locations.

7. The concentration of data processing and of data also poses a significant risk. In a computerized accounting information system there is no segregation of duties in the traditional sense. Most of the transaction activities are under the control of the computer and as result new ways need to be devised to assign responsibilities to reduce risk. Also because the data is concentrated it is easy for perpetrators to locate data and to modify it if there are not sufficient controls. In fact, perpetrators can delete any trace of their unauthorized access by erasing the appropriate data. Moreover this concentration of data makes the system more vulnerable to catastrophic events such as fire. It is imperative that all accounting systems have backup procedures to guard against these risks.

8. Improper testing or modification procedures for programs can lead to considerable risks. Programs can process data incorrectly. Program changes in

one program may impact records in an unanticipated way. Appropriate controls may not have been included to guard against certain risks. Wrong assumptions may be used to generate reports and thus give users information that is different than that they think they are receiving.

9. Since their is often very little in the way of a document paper trail in a computerized accounting system, audit trails are more difficult to develop than they are in manual systems. Audit trails are needed not only for an audit but for normal business activity. Management must be able to trace transactions to deal with vendors and customers. Transaction listings (called logs) form the basis of these computer audit trails.

In general, the difficulty in controlling the system, due to its complexity, increases the risk to the organization, to users of financial statements and to the auditors. The system can fail in many ways and incorrectly process information without proper control. A good control structure is necessary to minimize this failure and its resulting risk to management, owners, and auditors.

CONTROL STRUCTURE

The control structure of an entity according to the AICPA[4]

consists of the policies and procedures established to provide reasonable assurance that its established objectives will be achieved. The control structure may include a wide variety of objectives and related policies and procedures, only some of which may be relevant to the examination of financial statements. Generally, the relevant policies and procedures are those that pertain to the entity's ability to record, process, summarize, and report financial data consistent with management's assertions embodied in the financial statements.

For the other transaction processing, reporting, and decision-making objectives of the accounting system, a much larger set of relevant policies and procedures will need to be present in the control structure. The entity's control structure, as stated by the AICPA,[5] consists of the control environment, the accounting system, and the control procedures, as shown in Figure 11-1.

In general, an accounting information system can be viewed as an integrated information network that provides information for transaction processing, reporting, and decision making. There will be critical junctures within this network where controls need to be established to provide an effective control structure. This structure will differ according to the nature of the organization and its information system requirements. In particular, it will be quite different for a manual system than for a computer system because the risks of exposure are different and arise from different kinds of activities, as indicated previously. Thus in a traditional manual transaction processing cycle, for example, the initial recording of the transaction, the transfer of an asset to another individual,

---

[4] ARACR and SAS No. 55, p. 4.
[5] ARACR and SAS No. 55, p. 5.

Control Structure Elements

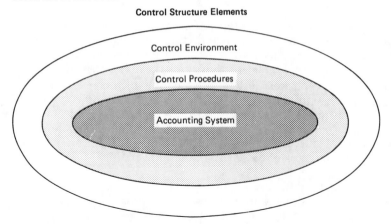

FIGURE 11-1   Control structure elements.

and the authorization for payment would be critical control points where some form of control should be established because these are the areas in the process where the system is exposed to errors and possible fraudulent activities. In summary, the recording, custody, and authorization should be separated in a manual system. On the other hand, in a computer system (1) many files are often impacted by one transaction; (2) files are readable only by machine; (3) information is generated automatically with little human intervention; (4) errors are not easily observable and can easily go undetected; (5) program changes can be erased without a trace; (6) audit trails are difficult to establish to trace transactions; and (7) control procedures are not always visible. In general, the computer is used to process the entire transaction, to make decisions authorizing the transfer of assets, and to review such transactions and decisions.

As a result, in a computer system the focus of control shifts from traditional custodial, authorization, and recording controls, consisting of a system of authorization, organizational independence, and close supervision, to the computer system. Figure 11-2 portrays the control structure for a computer system. It consists of (1) the control environment with its general controls shown across the top of the figure; (2) the accounting system and its elements shown by the rectangles; and (3) the control procedures represented by the circled areas and are within the system. These control points are for the design and operations of the computer in general, and for the input, processing, and output of each application. In addition, there are control procedures for the handling of the data used in the system and for each application. This structure and its control points shown by the circles are quite different than that used by a simple manual transaction processing system.

An integrated system of controls is essential to support the decision-making, transaction processing, and reporting requirements in an organization. Assume, for example, an integrated system consists of five controls of various types related to the environment, the accounting system, and specific procedures. Let each, for discussion purposes, have a 90 percent probability of catching a particular error or irregularity. This means that there is only one chance in ten that a particular error will escape detection and/or correction by the control. If all five

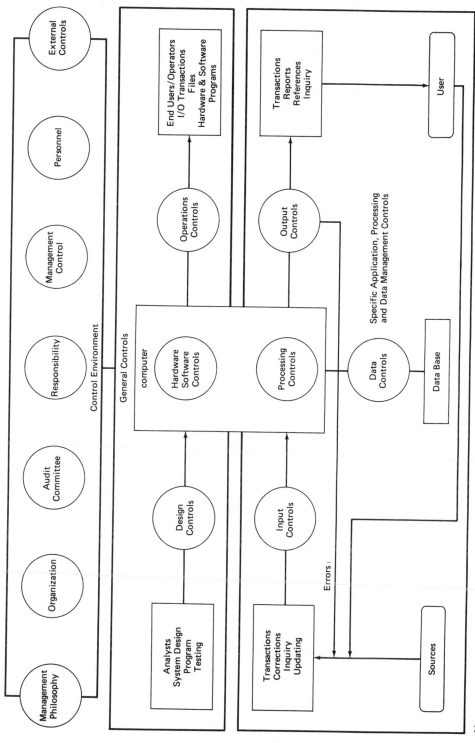

FIGURE 11-2 Control structure computer systems control points.

controls were independent, the result would be a $1/10 \times 1/10 \times 1/10 \times 1/10 \times 1/10$, or $1/100,000$, probability of having a particular error. If these are synergistic (each contributes to the other's effectiveness, i.e., they are not independent), the probability of incurring that particular error is even less. Moreover, controls may be effective for *detecting* errors, *correcting* errors, or *preventing* errors or irregularities. Preventive controls prevent errors, detection controls find them, and correction controls correct them. A network composed of these three types of controls will provide much better control than one using individual unrelated controls.

As an example consider an inventory system. A few of the components of this network may be described as follows:

1. The assignment of responsibility helps control investment through effective and efficient purchasing of new stock and compliance with management policies.
2. Just-in-time (JIT) models can help comply with managerial objectives of minimizing inventory investment.
3. A physical inventory can reconcile differences in records and stock to control errors and possible misallocation of inventory.
4. Communication controls help prevent errors in ordering new stock via an electronic data interchange network.
5. The Information Systems department can be organized so that operators do not have access or knowledge to alter computer programs that process inventory.
6. Personnel are qualified to operate the computer and qualified to use the reports generated from the system for good inventory management.
7. Input controls are present to edit data, to verify stock numbers, and to batch transactions to control for missing or erroneous input, as will be illustrated later.

These control features along with the others, should be integrated so that their total effect is synergistic. This means that all the controls together produce greater control than the sum of their individual contributions.

As another example consider only the input, editing, and screening control procedures. These may be characterized like the system in Figure 11-3. In this system, information is entered through remote terminals; it is then transmitted to the computer center where it is stored in buffer storage awaiting processing. As it leaves the storage area, the information is checked for access authorization, completeness, reasonableness, and accuracy. Any errors in input data are displayed and relayed to a correction process, which may entail feedback to the remote terminal for correction if necessary. The system has several control procedures for detecting several types of potential errors and for affecting their correction. The controls complement each other and work as an integrated system to detect and correct potential errors, such as unauthorized, incomplete, unreasonable, and inaccurate input data. For example, an unauthorized user may have a password but may not have all the information necessary to enter a complete transaction and, therefore, what is entered is unreasonable. A transposition error may seem complete, but the transaction may be unreasonable. More-

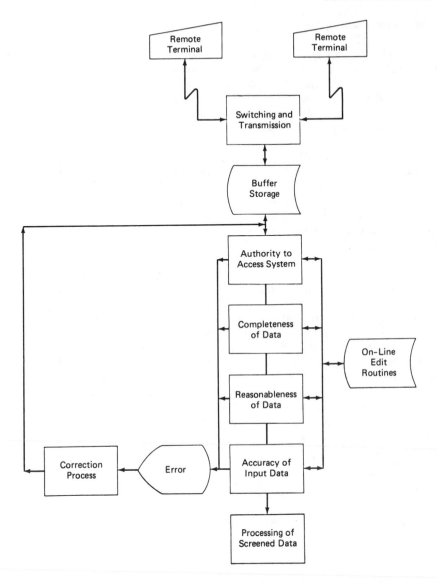

FIGURE 11-3 Control procedures for editing and screening of data entry.

over, these procedure controls just indicated are complemented by the accounting system and the control it affords in the control environment.

In summary, the control structure consists of the control environment, the accounting system, and the control procedures. An effective and efficient control structure will combine these components to achieve an effective and efficient synergistic network to minimize the risks associated with the organization's environment and type of business.

Control Environment

The control environment consists of the overall attitude, awareness, and actions of the board of directors, management, owners, and others concerning management philosophy and operating characteristics, organizational structure, role of audit committee, assignment of responsibility and authority to accomplish organizational objectives, management control procedures, personnel policies, and external or third party controls.[6]

MANAGEMENT PHILOSOPHY.   Management philosophy and operating style characteristics include management's attitudes and actions toward reporting and business risk, emphasis on budgets and other objectives, preference for organization structure (e.g., centralized or decentralized), and operating style such as a participatory or nonparticipatory. These characteristics have a significant impact on the exposure to various risks, on the nature of the accounting system, and on the control structure.

ORGANIZATION STRUCTURE.   The organization structure is a direct function of the organizational environment and the organization's business strategy for accomplishing its objectives, as discussed in Chapter 3. It provides the overall framework for planning, directing, and controlling the organization and it has a significant influence on the control environment. It specifies reporting, transaction processing, and decision-making relationships. These are couched in the assignment of responsibility and authority and supported by computer systems to provide information for these requirements.

AUDIT and STEERING COMMITTEES.   The *audit committee* of the board of directors oversees the accounting and reporting policies of the organization and they have a direct impact on the control structure. Auditors are required to report to the audit committee on the status of the control structure. Along these same lines, an information system *steering committee* (discussed in more detail in Chapter 12) is present in larger organizations to develop plans and determine policies for the entire information system for the organization.

RESPONSIBILITY AND AUTHORITY.   The assignment of responsibility and authority is important to the overall control structure and should include the consideration of the following:

1. Assignment of responsibility and delegation of authority to deal with organizational goals and objectives and operations.
2. Employee job descriptions delineating specific duties, reporting relationships, and constraints.
3. Policies regarding such matters as acceptable business practices, conflicts of interests, and codes of conduct.[7]

---

[6] This discussion of the various characteristics of the control environment is adapted from *The Auditor's Responsibility for Assessing Control Risk* (ARACR), and SAS No. 55, Ibid. with permission.

[7] ARACR and SAS No. 55, pp. 25–26.

MANAGEMENT CONTROL. Management control methods affect management's control over the authority delegated to others and its ability to supervise company activities effectively. These methods are important to the maintenance of the contractual (agreements) relationships necessary for control of organizations.[8] Effective management controls include:

1. Establishing planning, budgeting, and reporting systems that set forth management's plans and the results of actual performances.
2. Establishing methods that identify the status of actual performance and exceptions from planned performance, as well as communicating them to the appropriate levels of management.
3. Investigating variances and taking appropriate and timely corrective action.
4. Establishing and monitoring policies for developing and modifying accounting systems and control procedures, including the development, modification, and use of any related computer programs and data files.
5. Establishing an internal audit function with qualified personnel and with appropriate authority and reporting relationships.[9]

These management controls are essential for the transaction processing, reporting, and decision-making needs of management. Accountants and auditors need to be aware of them to ensure adherence to prescribed managerial policies. Many techniques are used to implement these controls and to monitor the activities of the various parties in the organization. In theory, owners (principals) must be able to monitor the performance and effort of employees (agents) to assess their compliance with managerial policies and objectives. This planning and monitoring process is a major component of the employment contract (agreement) and reward structure of the employee. These techniques can be characterized as feedback control systems and planning control systems.

The functional characteristics of a *feedback control system* are (1) an input/output process where input can be compared with output; (2) a standard by which the efficiency of this input conversion process can be measured; and (3) a measurement and reporting system, such as a standard cost system. This feedback is a key component of the monitoring process and the management accounting system of an organization.

The accountant or system analyst must make several decisions regarding feedback control systems used to monitor performance. What level of aggregation or detail should exist for each level in its organization? What constitutes a significant variance? What role should internal auditing play in the feedback control system? How accurate should the information system be? What is the value of the information? What does the system cost? These issues were discussed in detail in Chapters 3 and 4.

The *planning control system* is sometimes regarded as the primary control system for management. Management controls the firm's operations by way of a system of programs, plans, budgets, and agreements with members of the organization regarding adherence to these plans and budgets. These programs,

---

[8] This refers to contractual relationships which comprise an organization structure when it is viewed from a principal (owner) and agent (employee) perspective.
[9] ARACR and SAS No. 55, p. 26.

plans, and budgets are used to coordinate the firm's activities so that there is a cohesive effort to achieve its objectives. Techniques used in planning control systems include sales budgets, cash flow forecasts, inventory control models, research and development programs, promotion plans, production schedules, corporate planning models, and various mathematical and statistical planning models.

Establishing and monitoring policies for developing and modifying accounting systems and control procedures is important for an effective control structure. These include analysis and design, modification, and use of any related computer programs and data files. The objective of each analysis and design phase, as outlined in Chapter 2 and described in detail in Chapters 12 and 13, must be satisfied. Above all, the management information and accounting system must satisfy the needs of management in terms of helping management ensure that employees and units of the organization comply with managerial policies. The structured analysis presented in this text will ensure management participation, careful consideration of alternatives, inclusion of key decision variables, inclusion of the necessary internal controls, careful testing, coordinated conversion, and effective review of the system.

Specific control procedures that will promote effective and efficient analysis and design procedures include the following:

1. The procedures for system design, including the acquisition of software packages, should require active participation by user representatives and as appropriate the accounting department and internal auditors.
2. Each system should have written specifications which are reviewed and approved by an appropriate level of management and applicable user departments. These specifications serve as a standard for compliance reviews by management and auditors and should be kept up to date.
3. System testing should be a joint effort of users and information systems personnel and should include both the manual and computerized phases of the system. Users should make sure that all the specifications are met and that the interfaces between manual and computer systems operate smoothly.
4. Final approval should be obtained prior to placing the new system into operation.
5. All master file and transaction file conversions should be controlled to prevent unauthorized changes and to provide accurate and complete results. This will help prevent errors, which frequently occur at the time of conversion from an old procedure to a new procedure.
6. After a new system has been placed in operation, all program changes should be approved before implementation to determine whether they have been authorized, tested, and documented. There should be a formal system for requesting, authorizing, approving, testing, implementing, and reconciling changes. Management can run both the old and the new systems in parallel using actual data and test data to make sure the new system is working properly and that all differences between old and new results can be explained.

7. Management should require various levels of documentation and establish formal procedures to define the system at appropriate levels of detail.[10]

Controls such as these help ensure that the system design, development, and implementation process is executed as planned.

PERSONNEL MANAGEMENT.   A strong system of internal control depends on the employment of competent personnel who have the integrity and competence required to perform their given assignments. Misunderstanding, judgment mistakes, and carelessness on the part of incompetent employees can result in errors. Moreover, collusion can circumvent almost any control procedure. Sound personnel management methods are required to assure that personnel are assigned to roles in the organization that are commensurate with their ability. If this is not done, motivational problems can arise. Sound management policies here include those related to employment, training, evaluating, promoting, compensating, and supporting employees with the necessary resources to accomplish their assignments.

EXTERNAL CONTROLS.   Finally there are *external controls* imposed by outside or third parties on the operations and reporting policies of the entity. They arise from legislative bodies, regulatory agencies, financial institutions, and professional organizations. The reporting requirements of hospitals for Medicare and Medicaid are good examples of the reports and cost structure required by a hospital.

The factors comprising the control environment will differ markedly from one organization to another in terms of their importance to the overall control structure of the organization. A large publicly held manufacturing company will have a different environment than a small entrepreneurial enterprise, for example. In this chapter, control systems for larger organizations with large computer systems will be emphasized. The special characteristics of small entrepreneurial enterprises and their control environment, accounting systems, and control procedures will be emphasized in Chapter 19.

Accounting System

From the perspective of management, an effective accounting information system will be designed to support the transaction processing, reporting, and decision-making requirements of the organization's management system. The characteristics of the accounting system will be thus influenced extensively by the nature of the business, the organization's objectives, its size and complexity, its organizational structure and management style, its use of computers, and its need to comply with regulatory agencies.

From an auditing and financial reporting perspective, according to the AICPA, it includes appropriate methods and records that will

---

[10] With permission from the AICPA Computer Services Executives Committee, AICPA, *Auditor's Study and Evaluation of Internal Control in EDP Systems* (ASEIC), copyright (1977), pp. 31–36. Many of the controls outlined in this chapter follow those presented in this audit and accounting guide with the permission of the AICPA.

1. Identify and record all valid transactions.
2. Describe on a timely basis the type of transaction in sufficient detail to permit proper classification of the transaction for financial reporting.
3. Measure the value of the transaction in a manner that permits recording its monetary value in the financial statements.
4. Determine the time period in which the transaction occurred to permit recording of the transaction in the proper period.
5. Present properly the transaction and related disclosures in the financial statements.[11]

In general, measures should be implemented to give reasonable assurance that transactions have been recorded properly. Examples of general measures include (1) cash registers and other effective data gathering devices for accurate transaction recording; (2) well-designed forms and menus to ensure completeness of input data; (3) prenumbered forms and transactions to give reasonable assurance that all transactions have been accounted for; (4) a review of transactions by another individual or the editing of transactions by the computer prior to actual processing; (5) control totals; and (6) completeness checks. This is just a sampling of input controls. There are many other possible input controls for computer systems which will be noted later in this chapter.

Finally, the very presence of a well-designed accounting system and the coordination of all of its elements enhances the control structure in a major way. It establishes policies and procedures for the processing of transactions, inquiries, and reports. This means that every transaction, inquiry, or report will be processed in the same way each time, thus establishing very effective control over these activities. This is especially important in small businesses where manual systems tend to be sloppy. The presence of a well-designed microcomputer accounting system using good commercial software will bring order to the processing and reporting activities of the small business. Thus the accounting system can contribute significantly to the overall control structure of the organization.

Control Procedures

These are the policies and procedures applied by management to provide reasonable assurance that its objectives will be achieved and that the information that they obtain on the accomplishment of these objectives is reasonably accurate. In addition, effective procedures are necessary to ensure reasonable compliance with the agreements (contracts) between management (principals or owners) and employees (agents). Some of these control procedures apply to the accounting system in general and others apply to specific applications or combinations of applications. These control prodedures were previously classified as general and application controls.[12]

---

[11] ARACR and SAS No. 55, p.6.

[12] These controls were originally described in the *Statement on Auditing Standards No. 3* as *general controls* and *application controls* (AU 321.07-321.08), which is no longer in the code. Currently this distinction is defined in SAS No. 48, paragraph 34, footnote 3 (AU 1030.34, footnote 6); and in SAS No. 48, paragraph 58 (AU 1030.58) General Controls consist of:

    a. The plan of organization and operation of EDP activity

Generally *control procedures* may be categorized as procedures pertaining to:

1. Proper authorization of transactions and activities such as general or specific approval of transactions and approval for the reentry of transactions rejected by the computer.
2. Adequate segregation of duties, such as separating the responsibilities for custody of assets from the responsibility for the related record-keeping, and the separating computer programming from computer operations.
3. Adequate documents and records, such as prenumbered documents.
4. Adequate safeguards over access to and use of assets and records, such as secured facilities.
5. Independent checks on performance, such as clerical checks, reconciliations, computer-programmed edit controls, management review of reports that summarize the detail of account balances, such as an aged trial balance of accounts receivable, and user review of computer-generated reports.[13]

For example, detailed asset records, which include records for plant, equipment, inventory, and receivables, should be compared periodically with the actual assets. Moreover, these detailed records (subsidiary ledgers as they are often called) should reconcile to the general ledger control total. Someone other than the individuals who have asset custody and record-keeping responsibility should perform this function and reconcile any differences that are found.

In general, four different groups of employees within the organization share the responsibility for adequate control procedures.

1. User and data origination functions (groups) must maintain sufficient control procedures to satisfy themselves that they can rely on the quality of data input and the usefulness of the information produced.
2. System designers should ensure that the network of implemented control procedures is both effective and economical. Furthermore, they should prepare and update procedural manuals for training and consistent application of control procedures.
3. The Information Systems control group is accountable for all the data. They should schedule and log the flow of data and information in the computer operations. They must also secure authorization for input and ensure the reconciliation of any problems occurring during input, processing, and output. In a database system this function will probably be augmented by a

---

b. The procedures for documenting, reviewing, testing, and approving new systems or programs and changes in existing systems or programs

c. Controls built into the equipment by the manufacturer (commonly referred to as "hardware controls") and controls in the operating system

d. Controls over access to equipment and data files

e. Other data and procedural controls affecting overall EDP operations.

Application controls consisted of those controls applicable to specific applications.

[13] ASACR.

database administrator. In decentralized operations users are generally responsible for this function.

4. Computer operations personnel must comply with the set of instructions set forth in run manuals and other procedural directives.

As in the case of the accounting system used for the organization, the control procedures will differ substantially for each organization depending on its environment, organizational structure, size, and other factors that lead to the design of an accounting system which meets its needs. The structured design process is described in the next two chapters.

An understanding of the control structure of the entity is essential for the auditor to plan the audit engagement and in assessing the adequacy of the entity's internal control at various stages in the audit process. The importance of this to the audit process is described in Chapter 20. Moreover, this understanding is important to management and to internal auditors as they continually monitor the quality and the adequacy of the information they receive from the accounting information system they use for transaction processing, reporting, and decision making.

INFORMATION SYSTEMS (IS)—ORGANIZATION AND OPERATION. A well-planned and properly functioning IS organizaton is critical to good internal control. Several general organizational controls should be present in a system. The focus of the control in a system shifts from a system of authorizations and segregation of duties involving custody, recording, and authorization transactions to the computer system itself. Segregation of functions between the IS department and the system user is very important.

Specifically, the major functions within the IS department should be segregated as described in Chapter 3. These functions are (1) operations; (2) systems analysis and design; (3) control, and (4) librarian. A typical organization chart for small IS organizations is shown in Figure 11-4. The responsibility for systems analysis and design includes the development and maintenance of program logic, program coding, file record layout, program testing, operating instructions, and error and correction routines. To prevent unauthorized changes, systems and programming personnel must be separate from operations personnel because the former are aware of application program parameters and controls. The library function has custody of the data, files, and records. Two types of controls are generally part of this function. First, access to files and software is restricted to authorized users at scheduled times. Second, the use of records is monitored and backup files are provided. The control group has the responsibility for controlling the flow and balancing the transactions processed by the computer center. Part of this responsibility often includes the systematic disposition of errors. Moreover, provisions for general authorization over the execution of transactions will prevent the IS department from initiating and authorizing transactions, having custody over non-IS assets, having authority for master file changes, and establishing controls. Finally, in a database management system, another function of database administration is frequently added to oversee the database activities.

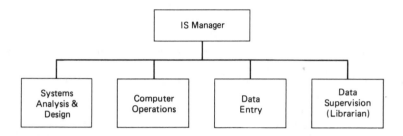

FIGURE 11-4   Structure of a small Information System (IS) Organization.

GENERAL HARDWARE AND SOFTWARE CONTROLS.   Control procedures for the hardware and operating system are usually provided by the vendor and are for the most part quite reliable. According to the AICPA:

> The control features inherent in the computer hardware, operating system, and other supporting software should be utilized to the maximum possible extent to provide control over operations and to detect and report hardware malfunctions. Furthermore: System software should be subjected to the same control procedures as those applied in installation of and changes to application programs.[14]

A formal control system for application software during system analysis and design should exist for system software.

GENERAL ACCESS CONTROL PROCEDURES.   To safeguard the system, the records maintained on the system, and the communications within the system network, it is important that access control procedures be used. Access controls should help prevent accidental errors, unauthorized use of program or a data file, improper use of a system's resources such as computer time and storage space, and unauthorized breach of communication within the system. Access controls can be characterized as follows:

1. Access to program documentation should be limited to those persons who require it in the performance of their duties.
2. Access to computer hardware should be limited to authorized individuals.
3. Access to data and programs should be limited to those individuals authorized to process or maintain particular systems.[15]

Access control procedures can be accomplished in part by physical security of the hardware, software, and data, and by good organization, specifically the use of a librarian. In addition, a system of passwords can be used effectively, even for small microcomputer systems to control access to program data and other sensitive information. A further discussion of access controls, such as passwords and problems unique to on-line, distributed, integrated and database sys-

---

[14] ASEIC.
[15] ASEIC.

tems, is included later in a section on advanced accounting and information systems.

DATA CONTROL PROCEDURES. Data control procedures involve accounting for all transactions. The reconciliation function is a key part of this control. The AICPA suggests that a control function should be responsible for receiving all data to be processed, for ensuring that all data are recorded, for following up on errors detected during processing to see that they are corrected and resubmitted by the proper party, and for verifying the proper distribution of output.[16] Other key data controls involve the use of batch totals which are detailed in another section and the use of backup procedures. These help ensure the integrity of the data files or the database. Most backup procedures are founded on the idea that several generations of master copies of files or databases (using a dump) and records of transactions between these copies are kept. If this is done one can reconstruct a file or even a database by using the most recent master copy and the transactions from the last copy. This is often called the grandfather, father, son (referring to three generations) back up procedure.

INPUT CONTROL PROCEDURES. More accurate data input can be ensured through input control procedures. According to the AICPA's *Statement on Auditing Standards No. 3:*

> Input controls are designed to provide reasonable assurance that data received for processing by EDP have been properly authorized, converted into machine sensible form and identified, and that data (including data transmitted over communication lines) have not been lost, suppressed, duplicated, or otherwise improperly changed. Input controls include controls that relate to rejection, correction, and resubmission of data that were initially correct.[17]

Basically, there are four types of input transactions: (1) updating and transaction entry; (2) file and database maintainance; (3) inquiry; and (4) error correction. In addition, there are many input methods. The accountant or systems designer must select the appropriate mode of input for each of the types of transactions based on the organization's processing needs, the control features, and the attributes associated with each input method. Figure 11-5 summarizes these attributes and, as can be seen, some of the attributes can effectively be used to enhance the validity and accuracy of data input.

More accurate data input can be ensured by the following: *Data entry controls* such as *standardized forms* designed for ease of data entry and, if possible, machine readability; *tutorial* (question and answer) *on-line input* capability; *sequencing* of input keys; *key verification;* precoded *turnaround documents* where only limited information is entered; and the generation of *machine-readable output at the point of the transaction.*

---

[16]ACEIC.

[17] AICPA, *The Effects of EDP on the Auditor's Study and Evaluation of Internal Control, Statement of Auditing Standards No. 3,* New York: American Institute of Certified Pubic Accountants, Inc., copyright (1972), reprinted with permission. See also SAS No. 48 for a general discussion.

DATA-ENTRY METHOD ／ INTERNAL CONTROL ATTRIBUTES	KEY TO TAPE (MAGNETIC)	KEY TO DISK	TURNAROUND DOCUMENT	MAGNETIC INK (MICR)	OPTICAL (OCR)	INTELLIGENT TERMINALS	POINT-OF-SALE (POS)	MICRO COMPUTER
Simple and flexible	+	+	+	−	−		−	+
Reduced human intervention				+	+	+	+	+
Cost	−	−		−	−	−	−	−
Ease of handling data								
Visibility of data				+	+			
Speed				+	+		+	+
Susceptible to damage								
Buffering	+	+		+	+	+	+	+
Validation editing and verification	+	+		+	+	+	+	+
Reliability				+	+	+	+	+
Machine readable	+	+		+	+	+	+	+
Reduced preparation errors			+	+	+	+	+	+
Display						+		+
Data captured at source						+	+	+

FIGURE 11-5 Major internal control advantages(+) and disadvantages (−) of data input devices.
Source: Adapted from Ron Weber, *EDP Auditing: Conceptual Framework and Practice*, New York: McGraw-Hill 1982, pp. 209–224. Reprinted with permission.

Validation of input data is also necessary for accurate transaction input. *Field checks* are designed to assess the validity of the field. Examples would consist of (1) a *master file reference* to ensure that an account number matches one on the master file; (2) a *check digit* (a mathematical combination of the other digits) to give reasonable assurance that transcription and transposition errors were not made; (3) a *completeness* test to ensure that all data in the field are present; (4) a *limit* test, which only allows transactions within specified bounds to be processed—for example, on a typical production day a maximum one thousand units could be processed; and (5) an *alphanumeric* check to ensure that data are either alphabetic or numeric, or both.

Record checks are designed to ensure that the *logical relationships* among fields are valid. Examples would consist of (1) a *completeness check* to ensure that all input fields were completed—for example, in a material requisition, the part number, job to which the cost should be allocated, number of items, and department should all be completed; (2) a *reasonableness* check to ensure that the interrelationships among the input data are reasonable—for example, each product order should consist of one engine, one handle, and four wheels; (3) a *sign test*— for example, debit or credit, to ensure that the sign is consistent with the nature of the transaction, such as a journal entry; and (4) a *sequence check* to ensure that all fields are properly sequenced for subsequent processing.

TRANSACTION NO.	ACCOUNT NO.	JOURNAL ENTRY	DR.	CR.
1	100	Cash	$1000	
	200	Fixed assets		$1000
2	100	Cash	2000	
	150	Accounts receivable		2000
3	150	Accounts receivable	2500	
	500	Sales		2500
3	1200		$5500	$5500
Transaction	Hash total		Dollar Amount	

FIGURE 11-6   Batch total illustration.

of the transaction, such as a journal entry; and (4) a *sequence check* to ensure that all fields are properly sequenced for subsequent processing.

Batch checks are used to establish controls over batches to further assist in controlling accuracy and completeness of fields and records as well as ensuring that all records are input into the processing cycle. *Control totals* such as *dollar amount, number of transactions,* and account number *hash* totals can be used to ensure that all the dollars were entered, all transactions were entered correctly, and account numbers were entered correctly. A *hash total* is a nonsense total of account numbers or other numbers to ensure that all numbers were correctly entered. Examples of these were given in Figure 11-6. The computer or mechanical input device should be programmed to ensure that batch totals agree with those calculated by the individual prior to entry of the data into the system for processing. For large volumes of information, tolerance limits for some discrepancies should be considered to expedite data processing, provided that errors can be cleared up at a later stage of processing, or the subset of data that is in error can be recycled. Other batch checks would entail provision for batch descriptions such as batch number, date, type of transaction, and origin.

File checks are useful for making sure the correct files are processed. Internal and external *file labels* and generation numbers can be used to ensure that the correct file or database is being updated. Another useful control to ensure that the correct file is processed is called an *anticipation control.* The computer is programmed to expect certain transactions and files to be accessed, such as a time card input for each employee and the payroll program run at a certain time during the week. Exceptions to the expectations will be investigated.

Finally other input controls include a *transaction log* to establish an audit trail. An *acknowledgement of receipt* is given to trace movement of data between one processing step and another, or between departments. And, correction and resubmission of all errors detected should be reviewed and controlled.

Error logs are generated by the computer and include complete details such as time, date, and type of error. Corrections are also logged. The computer can be used to keep track of both errors and subsequent corrections. This is not sufficient for a database environment as will be discussed later in the chapter.

Input Control Procedure Example.   Consider the input of credit card information to the accounts receivable master file of a large retail oil company (see Figure 11-7). Many of the controls we have just reviewed are present in this system. The input system is designed around a two-batch system. A batch total is prepared for each retail outlet each day. The batches are then mailed to the credit-card processing center where they are collected for processing. All charge slips are optically scanned and batch totals are keyed into the disk. An edit run is prepared where the computer prepares an independent batch total for each outlet and flags unreadable charge slips and all exceptions to batch totals are displayed for recalculation and correction. Errors may result from erroneous batch totals forwarded to the home office by a particular location or from a charge slip that is misread or lost. Each batch must ultimately balance. Corrections are made and keyed into the disk for another edit run. Once a batch is balanced it is transferred to the edited transactions file for an update of the accounts receivable master file.

Using this procedure, input is edited, completely accounted for, and corrected. Optical scanning equipment is programmed to reject any data that are not complete or are difficult to read. Moreover, such equipment reduces human errors. The result is a high level of assurance, although not absolute assurance, that input will be accurate.

PROCESSING CONTROL PROCEDURES.   Processing control procedures should provide reasonable assurance that processing is performed in compliance with management's specifications. There are basically five types of processing controls. These are transaction flow and validation, processing and logic, file and database, software, and hardware controls.

Transaction flow and validation control procedures include the *field, record, batch,* and *file* controls discussed earlier. Note, however, that they are useful throughout the entire information processing cycle including input, processing, and output. In addition, *transaction logs* must be generated for backup and recovery as well as the construction of an audit trail for management decision-making and auditing requirements. Moreover, an *error identification, reporting and correction procedure* must be present to account for all transactions, isolate errors, and reconcile differences as transactions are being processed.

Processing and logic controls primarily include the assurance that the system complied with the objectives set forth in the *structured analysis and design phases* summarized in Chapter 2 and detailed in Chapters 12 and 13. In other words, the system has been well designed and tested thoroughly. The testing cannot be overemphasized because a well-run accounting system, as noted earlier, is essential to the control structure. *Programming controls* should be present, such as: *sequence checks,* to match master and transaction files; *end-of-file* procedures to ensure that entire files are processed; *processing sequences,* such as changing master files prior to updating; and *run-to-run* totals to ensure that each program pro-

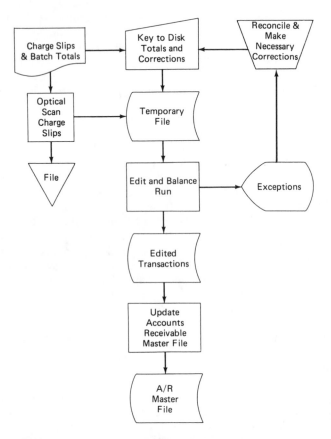

FIGURE 11-7 Credit card data input example.

cessed all the data at each stage in the processing cycle. Testing compliance with *logical relationships and limits* such as those noted earlier should be present. Often a *redundancy check* is useful here to *compare* details with control totals. *Concurrency controls,* such as *preempting,* for database systems must be present to prevent a deadlock when several users attempt to use the same set of data, interfere with each other or lockup.

File and *database controls* ensure that the correct files are processed and that files and databases are protected from compromise. Files have both *external* and *internal* (header and trailer) *labels* for file identification. For example, a program cannot be run if the label on the tape or disk does not agree with the program. Each file will have *file totals* to ensure that all records have been accounted for. A record of use will be maintained for each file. Other file and database controls are generally provided through the system hardware and software and access controls noted earlier in this chapter. Finally, *file and database maintenance procedures* will be established for changes to records.

The most important *processing software control* is the assurance that transactions and information for reporting and decision-making needs are processed in accordance with management's objectives. This assurance is only provided by following a well-planned system for *software development* and *implementation*, such as the one outlined in Chapter 2 and discussed in Chapters 12 and 13. Other software controls restrict *access* to the operating and database system and provide for *backup, recovery*, and *restart*. These are discussed elsewhere in this chapter. Finally, a useful control for detecting a compromise in software or the operating or database system is the *code comparison*. Programs can be periodically compared with a backup copy for differences, run against a test database and compared with previously generated reports, and reviewed for size changes to detect any evidence of a software change.

In addition to these processing controls, each manufacturer of hardware will provide for *overflow* and *read and write checks* to ensure that data are not lost and that input and output are accurate and free of transcription errors. *Dual read and write heads, echo checks, parity checks*, and *equipment checks* are also useful for this purpose.

OUTPUT CONTROL PROCEDURES.   Output control procedures are designed to assure the accuracy of the output such as the report, data update, or inquiry and to assure that only authorized personnel receive the results of the output.

First, output should be *reconciled* with input and processing control totals to help ensure that all transactions have been accounted for and processed in compliance with managerial objectives. Often this reconciliation will involve *procedures for error correction.* At the very least, exception information will be an integral part of the balancing process. Second, output should be scanned and tested to ensure that it has been properly processed. This can be done on a test basis. The extent of this testing will be a function of input and processing controls. Finally, output should be distributed only to authorized users. This latter objective is not difficult to achieve in an on-line system if there are appropriate access controls and the output is displayed on the terminal. It is difficult to detect in a processing system where reports are generated. In this latter case, controls must be maintained over (1) storage of output media such as payroll checks; (2) the report-generating program; (3) the report-printing program; (4) the actual printing operation; (5) the output distribution of multiple copies; (6) the review for errors; and (7) the storage and retention of output.[18]

PROCEDURAL AND DOCUMENTATION CONTROLS.   Documentation controls include the maintenance of up-to-date source documents, journals, ledgers, reports, chart of accounts, audit trails, procedures, database controls (which document the data structure), and job responsibilities. These may be in machine readable form. Procedure controls are characterized by written manuals that provide a step-by-step set of procedures to be followed by computer operators and accounting clerks for the smooth flow of information and the implementation of appropriate control features. These help to ensure compliance with control and policy directives of management.

The control and librarian functions shown in Figure 11-4 and described earlier are essential to ensuring compliance with prescribed procedures. In data-

---

[18] For more details, see Ron Weber, *EDP Auditing: Conceptual Foundations and Practice*, 2nd. ed. (New York: McGraw-Hill, 1988).

base systems the database administrator also plays an important role in procedural control. All processing activities should be scheduled. This schedule is used to route the flow of information and to authorize the use of data files and software packages.

PHYSICAL SECURITY. In addition to these reconciliation, balancing, and review procedures, physical security is important. Specifically, a system of physical control must provide for the following:

1. Prevention measures for physical access (discussed earlier), and malfunctions arising from fire, water, electrical problems, and climate control.
2. Protection to minimize the loss when a problem occurs. This is generally accomplished by maintaining duplicates of transaction files, databases, and programs off the premises and keeping them physically secured.
3. A plan of recovery to reconstruct the data or to use alternative facilities; this plan should be tested.
4. Insurance.

In database management systems, backup and recovery may be quite complex. These were outlined in Chapter 10.

CONTROL PROCEDURES FOR ADVANCED EDP SYSTEMS

In advanced computer systems, particularly those with remote terminals and communication networks and those that use a database management system, the risk to management, investors, and auditors is increased. This is due to the following significant developments:

1. The proliferation of remote terminals that gives employees easy access to corporate computer systems throughout the organization.
2. The concentration of information in an integrated database.
3. The increasing sophistication of employees' computing skills.
4. Off-site access via communications networks.

In summary, the risks associated with unauthorized access have been rapidly increasing due to the move toward distributed processing, more widespread knowledge about computer systems, and the presence of terminals that are a telephone call away.

Several penetration techniques can be used to secure access and enter unauthorized transactions. These are listed in Figure 11-8. Access to terminals is seldom tightly controlled, and the communication network may be entered when outsiders tap transmission lines. Cases have been recorded in which data have been manipulated and merchandise has been fraudulently sent to dummy warehouses. In general, a review of the largest computer frauds indicates that the most important area for improvement is the tightening of access controls to prevent manipulation of transactions. Unauthorized access was found to be the

PENETRATION TECHNIQUE	EXPLANATION
Browsing	Searching through residue such as magnetic tapes and wastebaskets for passwords and other sensitive information to gain access to the system.
Masquerading	Impersonating a legitimate user of the system to influence transaction processing, reporting, or decision-making activities.
Piggybacking	Modifying an intercepted communication by tapping communication lines.
Between Lines Entry	Addition of an unauthorized transaction by tapping lines between gaps in transactions as they are communicated.
Spoofing	Fooling the user into thinking he or she is interacting with the operating system. This compromises the system's security procedures.

FIGURE 11-8 Operating and communication system integrity penetration techniques.
Source: Adapted from R. Weber, *EDP Auditing: Conceptual Foundations and Practice,* New York: McGraw-Hill, 1982, p. 318. Reprinted with permission.

most frequent method of perpetrating fraud.[19]

On-Line Input Control Procedures (Passwords)

The following procedures can be used to reduce the risks associated with unauthorized use and modification of computer programs and information:

1. Restrict access of individuals to certain terminals, for certain types of transaction with specific portions of the data set or files.
2. Require passwords which indicate user access privileges.
3. Prevent confidential data from being displayed on unauthorized terminals.
4. Maintain security over passwords, such as frequent changing, combinations of passwords, responsibility assignment for passwords and changing procedures, terminal display protection via blackout and nondisplay on output, and encryption of data during transmission.
5. Enforce physical security of terminals.
6. Log terminal activity automatically.

A system of *passwords* for authorized users and restriction of access to certain types of data, such as payroll records from specific terminals, can be effective in an advanced on-line database environment. For an on-line system, a variety of passwords can be used; a single password can be used on the entire database, file passwords can be used on individual files, record passwords can be associated with each record, or passwords can be placed on specific fields within

---

[19] See Brandt Allen, "The Biggest Computer Fraud and Lessons for CPA's," *Journal of Accounting,* May 1977, pp. 52–62.

DATA FILE NAME / DATA BASE ACTIVITY	ACCOUNTS RECEIVABLE	PAYROLL	INVENTORY	BACK ORDER
Read	YES	YES	NO	NO
Delete	NO	YES	YES	YES
Modify	YES	NO	YES	YES

FIGURE 11-9   Password matrix for user KRD007.

records. In addition, the passwords can be set so that only read-access, write-access, or both read and write operations are possible.

Several modes of operation can be used in the password environment. First a *password matrix* can identify user activities (read, delete, and modify) and the areas of the database to which a user has access. Figure 11-9 illustrates a password matrix for the user with password KRD007. In this example the user can perform only certain functions on certain files or subschema; he or she can read the accounts receivable and payroll files but cannot read the inventory and back-order files, and so forth.

In addition to a password matrix, *passwords by content* or *passwords by combination* can be used. Passwords by content restrict access to certain values of data within a given field. For example, a teller at a bank may be given access to all customer savings accounts that are less than $2,500; accounts greater than this amount are referred to a vice-president. Passwords by combination give a user access to combinations of fields of data. For example, an individual involved with a payroll system might have access to employee name-address data, employee rate-per-hour data, and employee total monthly pay data, on an item-by-item basis but not simultaneously. Developing and maintaining a password by content or password by combination is very expensive; therefore, other forms of security are generally adopted before this form of data protection. A password, however, can be penetrated by experienced computer personnel because passwords are often found in wastebaskets and codes can be broken. Other methods such as badges, cards, dialogue, voice prints, and signatures of authorization of access to files can be used to overcome this problem. These may be compromised also, for example, by the loss of a card. To make penetration more difficult, the use of minicomputers as gatekeepers for the main CPU and data records has been suggested. However, a very experienced system programmer who has designed the system or a similar system, or who has knowledge of a particular vendor control procedure, will be able to circumvent any network of access controls. A *call-back* control procedure is where the receiving unit calls the sender back to make sure the source of the message is an authorized one.

The following control procedures can also be used to ensure complete and accurate data entry:

1. Use of control totals for future reconciliation by a person other than the one entering the data. These totals can be recorded for each terminal and programs can be written to tie them to daily activity in particular files or accounts. In other words all the debits to a particular account can be compared with the control totals for that account added over all the terminals for the day. This can be done by the computer.

2. Maintenance of a transaction log for all online processing. This can be tied to the control totals to catch any irregularities.

Audit trails are difficult to maintain in the on-line IS environment. The following procedures can help to establish effective audit trails:

1. Transaction codes which identify user, terminal, type of transaction, and sequential numbering of transactions within each classification such as purchase orders.

2. Confirmation feedback to the terminal operator for review prior to final data entry.

3. Periodic review by management or internal audit personnel of transactions and control totals.

4. Use of statistical sampling to monitor on-line transactions for input errors and to trace the transaction for processing irregularities using associated codes just noted.

5. Use of transaction logs which identify transactions. As in the case of database backup systems, these logs may be a listing of transactions or they may involve before and after imaging of the database.

6. Automatic notification of beginning and ending of transaction information.

Restarting an on-line system after a failure is a problem in complex on-line systems and good procedures need to be in effect so that operators can restart systems easily. These are discussed in the previous chapter.

Distributed Processing and Communication Procedures

With wide dispersion of the computing facilities and the access to databases from a large number of terminals, the risk is great for an unauthorized transaction or an error which may be fraudulent or impair the integrity of the database. Moreover there is increased risk of the data being compromised or read by an unauthorized user. Transactions must be authorized, complete, accurate, and secure. Procedures such as password matrices which specify access and activity, good local controls over access, and periodic reconciliation of local and centralized files and programs are essential for good control. Moreover, *concurrency control* procedures must be present to control the simultaneous usage of the same records, files, and data elements in a database. If concurrency controls are not present, a salesperson in Pennsylvania may try to access an inventory record at the same time as a salesperson in Ohio. Both may sell the entire stock of 100 items thinking that 100 items were actually available. The system would then either lock up if negative numbers are not permitted or try to ship 100 items to each of the two customers. Concurrency control procedures such as a priority system must be present to prevent the system from such a lock up and to ensure the integrity of the data.

Data coding, or *data encryption* as it is often called, can be effective in reducing the risk of possible access by means such as those noted in Figure 11-8. It involves the storing and/or transmitting of data in a coded format. Coding is relatively simple to incorporate into database processing and is effective against tapping and against accessing data directly from the database. However, the coding scheme itself must be protected if security is to be upheld. The primary disadvantages of data coding are that it requires additional CPU time. It is not effective against access made via a database management or operating system because the coding processes can be performed by software within the operating or database system.

Integrated Systems

Integrated systems such as the microcomputer integrated accounting software discussed in the appendix of Chapter 19 present another type of risk. No longer will an erroneous entry impact one file. It may compromise several files, data items, or the database and impact the validity of a multitude of reports which depend on the integrity of the data. Moreover, other files and data items may be updated based on this erreoneous entry. To do this, the accurate transfer of data within the database from one file to another is necessary. This requires an effective audit trail which tracks data as it moves from one file to another file, as it affects other data items, or as it moves one system to another system. For example, a sales order entry will affect inventory and receivable data. Moreover, procedures such as periodic reconciliation must exist to ensure that common data elements in different files are the same. As in the case for distributive systems, procedures must be used to make sure that other users are aware of changes in files and the database.

Database Control Procedures

All of the general controls just discussed, especially access and communications controls, are useful in maintaining database integrity and security.

If the data in a database are not coded or password protected, illegal access can easily result. Sometimes, the database system will be protected, when the data in the database are not. In these cases an offender can circumvent the database system protection by writing software programs to access the database files directly. To accomplish this requires knowledge of the structure of the data files. If a teleprocessing mode of operation is used to transfer data from the database to the user, then illegal access of data is possible by intercepting the transmissions between the authorized user and the computer. This risk must be controlled via the communication controls noted earlier.

If the offender is unable to obtain data directly from the database or by intercepting transmission in the teleprocessing operation, he or she might revert to modifying the database system software. If that portion of the system software that provides security protection can be changed, access to the data is possible.

As a result, it is important that several controls be present to ensure that the database management system operates effectively. These are part of that system and include the following:

1. Definition of each user's subschema, which limits that user's ability to enquire, add, modify, or delete data. The DBMS should check each transaction for these limits and check each user's password.

2. A utility program to check for the coherence of the internal pointers and report on broken links which describe links and relations.

3. DBMS control procedures to check every deletion to ensure that no dependent items will become inaccessible. These control procedures should follow from database integrity rules and adherence to normal forms in the design of a database. Normal forms and integrity rules are discussed in Chapter 10.

4. Lock-out procedures to provide automatic prevention of a computer lockup by DBMS of concurrent updating, which may occur when two users attempt to use the same item simultaneously.

5. Maintenance of transaction and recovery file logs that are separate from the database. The transaction log can be used effectively to audit access to the database. The log contains information such as the time, date, name of the user, type of inquiry or access mode, data accessed, location of data within the database, and name of the specific software programs used to access the data. At least two security procedures can be employed with a transaction log. First, the log can be reviewed at random time intervals, and any suspicious accesses or access to high-priority data areas could be investigated. Second, the database can be dumped at two separate and specific points in time and the log entries collected between the dumps. Using the first dump and the transaction log entries, a recreated database image is generated. If the recreation database image does not correspond with the second dump of the database, unauthorized modification may have occurred.

6. Periodic scans of the database contents carried out by a program which accumulates individual records, from agreement to control records, and copies of programs. Edit checks are very useful in accomplishing this task. They are performed to make copies and listings of files, data sets, and software to control for changes by using some form of comparison between the actual and the copy.

7. The presence of an effective database administrative function such as that discussed in Chapter 10. This function or person should be separate from the operational control of day-to-day operations, implementation and execution of control procedures, execution of restart and recovery procedures, design and coding of application programs, implementation of database definitions, systems analysis and programming, and user department management. The individual or function should be responsible for the design of the database schema (including data content, data structure, data storage and access methods), development and implementation of DBMS pro-

cedures, design and maintenance of the data dictionary, and the specification of control procedures.

8. Documented record of database structure and a data dictionary which describes each element, source, application programs associated with each element, interrelationships with other elements and records, edit and validation checks, and user authorization.

9. Backup and recovery controls, which are discussed in Chapter 10.[20]

Audit trails in a database system present a special problem. In a file-oriented system, corrections to an erroneous transaction can simply be made by a reversing entry; the resulting reports which are designed around the file structure were not affected. An audit trail thus simply listed all the good, the bad, and the correcting transactions. In a database environment, however, many users use the data elements for a wide variety of applications. It is often not enough to enter an adjusting entry and hope that the user application nets the incorrect with the adjusting entry or ignores both the original and reversing entry and only considers the new corrected entry. Often the application cannot distinguish what is good and what is not in terms of data elements. Thus, the original entry must be fixed so that only good data elements exist. This requires that the original entry be corrected and a record of this correction be made in an audit trail.

Regardless of whether passwords, data coding, transaction logs, edit checks, and/or backup and recovery are used, no database is completely secure. Also, it is desirable to modify the security procedures periodically, particularly if the database contains highly sensitive data.

Spreadsheet Controls

As in any system it is important that the system be designed well even though it is often a user-designed system. The risk with spreadsheets is that formulas, ranges, variables, tables, and so on may be misspecified. Moreover, when modifications are made many problems often occur related to ranges, formulas, variables, and functions because of poor documentation. Several suggestions are made for effective analysis, design, and implementation of spreadsheets at the end of Chapter 13. Foremost among these, is the need to fully test any spreadsheet to be sure it performs the calculations in the manner desired. It is also helpful to lock all the parts of a spreadsheet except input variables, to have a built in set of instructions, and to use macros so that clerical personnel who use it cannot modify the model without authorization.

Specifically, controls for spreadsheets may include:

1. Uniform procedures for the development and use throughout the organization.

2. A usage log should be maintained. It should include a record of any network or mainframe access or data interchange.

3. Passwords or personal identification may be used to restrict access to spreadsheets.

---

[20] Adapted with permission from *Evaluation and Testing of EDP Controls*, Price Waterhouse Audit Guidance Series, New York, NY.

4. Access may be controlled by locking up the spreadsheet program or restricting the portion of the disk that contains the spreadsheet.

5. A secure backup of the spreadsheet may be used to retain a good copy.

6. Users must be trained to use the spreadsheet software and applications.

7. The spreadsheet needs to contain a number of checks to be sure that it is properly performing the calculations.

8. Any changes must be authorized and tested.

9. The logic and proper use should be well documented if multiple users are anticipated.

10. Macros and provisions for restricting access to all but certain cells into which data can be entered, are important in multiuser environments.

Local Area Network Controls

The environment for a local area network is more complex than that for a stand-alone microcomputer system. In many ways it is like a distributed network where applications, data, and processing resources are shared. This requires the careful control of access to data and applications. Controls such as passwords and encryption of data are often necessary. Communication controls (protocols and address schemes) which manage the transmission of messages are also required so that messages do not collide. They get to the correct destination and the sender receives confirmation that the message was received intact. Also many networks use multiuser accounting and database packages, and as with any multiuser system, the software needs file locking and updating priority rules to manage concurrent update and use.

A LAN environment like most microcomputer environments usually suffers from the following: a small staff for effective segregation of duties, lack of good physical security to control access, ease of changing data, on-line access, limited documentation, poor audit trails, and very portable data which can easily be copied to diskettes. As is the case with most smaller systems, close supervision of activities and the assumption of key activities by management can reduce some of the risk due to the small size. Moreover, diskettes can be locked up and in some cases PCs without disk drives may be used to control access to data.

SUMMARY

In summary, an organization control structure is comprised of three major components. The first is the control environment which sets the stage with general controls and management policies. The second is the accounting system which, if well designated and tested, processes transactions and provides information in a consistent and reliable manner so users can place a considerable amount of faith in the information derived from the system. Finally, control procedures are used to reduce the risk of problems occurring in the accounting system, unauthorized access, data integrity, and fraudulent activities.

The control structure is an integral part of systems design, implementation, and operation and it is a function of the business environment. The design and implementation of controls requires active participation of the controller and the auditor. The absence of critical controls has left many organizations open to fraudulent activities. A system that provides unreliable data is also of little use in assisting management in making decisions that are in harmony with the enterprise's objectives.

Finally a system of controls should be devised so that any exposure to loss or fraud can be minimized by having a series of controls that may prevent, detect, and even correct any problem that can lead to a loss.

SELECTED REFERENCES

ALEXANDER, TOM, "Waiting for the Great Computer Rip-Off," *Fortune,* July 1978, pp. 143–52.

ALLEN, BRANDT, "The Biggest Computer Fraud: Lessons for CPAs," *Journal of Accountancy,* May 1977, pp. 52–62.

AMERICAN INSTITUTE OF CERTIFIED PUBLIC ACCOUNTANTS, *Audit Risk and Materiality in Conducting an Audit, Statement on Auditing Standards No. 47,* New York, N.Y., Auditing Standards Board, AICPA, 1983.

———, *Effects of Computer Processing on the Examination of Financial Statements, Statement on Auditing Standards No. 48,* New York, N.Y., Auditing Standards Board, AICPA, 1984.

———, *Consideration of the Internal Control in a Financial Statement Audit,* New York, N.Y., Statement on Auditing Standards (SAS) No. 55, AICPA, 1988.

———, *Report on the Special Advisory Committee on Internal Control,* New York: AICPA, Inc., 1978.

———, *Reporting on Internal Control, Statement on Auditing Standards No. 30,* New York: AICPA, Inc., 1980.

———, *The Auditor's Responsibility for Assessing Control Risk, Proposed Statement on Auditing Standards—Exposure Draft,* New York, N.Y., Auditing Standards Board, AICPA, January 1987.

———, *The Communication of Control Structure-Related Matters, Proposed Statement on Auditing Standards—Discussion Draft,* New York, N.Y., Auditing Standards Board, AICPA, December 1986.

———, AUDITING STANDARDS EXECUTIVE COMMITTEE, *Codification of Auditing Standards and Procedures,* Statement on Auditing Standards No. 1, New York: AICPA, Inc., 1972.

———, COMPUTER SERVICES EXECUTIVE COMMITTEE, *The Auditor's Study and Evaluation of Internal Control in EDP Systems,* New York: AICPA, Inc., 1977.

ARTHUR YOUNG AND COMPANY, *Foreign Corrupt Practices Act of 1977: Toward Compliance with the Accounting Provisions* (1978).

COMMITTEE OF SPONSORING ORGANIZATIONS OF THE TREADWAY COMMISSION (COSO), *Internal Control Integrated Framework, Exposure Act,* COSO, 1991.

CUSHING, BARRY E. "A Mathematical Approach to the Analysis and Design of Internal Control Systems," *The Accounting Review,* January 1974, pp. 24–41.

DAVIS, GORDON B., and RON WEBER. "The Impact of Advanced Computer Systems on Controls and Audit Procedures: A Theory and an Empirical Test," *Auditing: A Journal of Practice & Theory,* Spring 1986, pp 35–49.

GROLLMAN, WILLIAM K., and ROBERT W. COLLY, "Internal Control for Small Business," *Journal of Accountancy,* December 1978, pp. 64–67.

KNECHEL, ROBERT W. "A Stochastic Model of Error Generation in Accounting Systems," *Accounting and Business Research,* Summer 1985, pp. 211–222.

LEITCH, ROBERT A., GADIS J. DILLON, and SUE H. MCKINLEY, "Internal Control Weakness in Small Businesses," *Journal of Accountancy*, December 1981, pp. 97–101.

PORTER, W. THOMAS, and WILLIAM E. PERRY, *EDP Controls and Auditing*, 5th ed. Boston, Mass: Kent Publishing Company, 1987

SECURITIES EXCHANGE COMMISSION, *Foreign Corrupt Practices Act*, Washington: Securities Exchange Commission, 1977.

WEBER, RON, *EDP Auditing: Conceptual Foundations and Practice*, 2nd ed. New York: McGraw-Hill, 1988.

REVIEW QUESTIONS

1. What is the difference between the *control environment,* the *accounting system,* and a *control procedure?*

2. What is the impact of an assessment of risk on a control system?

3. Why is the accounting system important to internal control?

4. What are the key control points in an information system?

5. Explain why it is important to consider the system of controls and not just individual controls.

6. From an internal control perspective, why is it important that an information system be well designed and implemented?

7. Describe a set of input controls for an information system.

8. When converting a manual system to a batch processing system, is it good practice to maintain the same control procedures? Why or why not?

9. Explain how the information requirements of management are important to internal control.

10. Explain why there is a shift of internal control from a system of separation of duties and authorizations to the information system.

11. What are the components of the control environment?

12. How should an IS department be organized to promote good internal control?

13. Define the various components of audit risk.

14. Why are program change approvals necessary?

15. How can access to records be restricted?

16. Why are passwords necessary? Can they be compromised? How?

17. What is the major general control weakness leading to fraud?

18. What basic control procedures are useful in ensuring that all documents have been processed correctly?

19. What physical security steps must be taken with regard to critical files?

20. For what is the data control group responsible?

21. Name several input controls and describe how they can be used together to promote more effective control.

22. Why must there be a set of procedures for correction of exceptions?

23. What controls are necessary to ensure the integrity of a database?

24. What are some of the advantages of using a CRT that displays a form to be completed and upon completion exhibits summary information on inputs, compared with keying from handwritten source documents?

25. What controls can be used to protect against unauthorized access to data transmission?

26. Why is the organization of a control system given emphasis in the definition of internal control?

27. What control or controls would you recommend in a computer system to prevent the following situations from occurring?

    a. A computer programmer entered the computer room one night, selected a payroll tape, altered the payroll program, wrote a check for himself, restored the program to its original form to erase the evidence, and left.

b. The computer programmer left for another job, and no one in the firm could modify his program when management requested a modification.

c. An authorized change to a program was implemented for accounts payable. Upon the next run, checks of the wrong amount were sent to incorrect vendors.

d. A computer operator was selling the mailing lists of a large regional department store.

e. A systems programmer working for a large software vendor tied into an on-line inventory system via a remote terminal, cracked the password code, and generated the appropriate documents to cause the company to ship millions of dollars of merchandise to a warehouse he rented.

f. In an on-line accounts receivable database system, account representatives experienced deadlocks when trying to review multiple data sets at the same time that others were trying to access the same data.

g. In an inventory system, items were reordered automatically, on occasion, after they had been received. A study of the problem revealed that these particular

items were always on the exception list generated from the inventory update run.

h. The wrong size of materials often showed up at a work center in the production line. After a schedule was concluded, part numbers were keyed into the system for distribution to work centers.

i. When some invoices were missing, the accounts payable department passed the blame to the mail room.

j. One month, the wrong payroll tape was used to issue checks, resulting in underpayments to current employees and payments to terminated employees.

k. Once a critical receivable tape was used to copy an accounts payable transaction file.

l. Transmitted data always balanced when they left the district terminals, yet were sometimes out of balance when they were reviewed periodically at the home office.

28. What is different in a spreadsheet control environment from an environment that uses a commercial program or staff-designed information system? What special precautions (controls) are necessary in this environment?

29. What controls are necessary in a LAN? What risks (potential problems) are they designed to prevent, detect, or correct?

CASES

11-1 Consider the following independent situations:

1. A financial planner embezzled $1 million over six years. The embezzler, who was supposed to use a computer for financial modeling, changed accounts receivable and payable records which would go undetected to perpetrate the fraud.

2. Two engineers accidentally used a password one character different than theirs. It belonged to the president of the time-sharing firm and allowed access to privileged time-sharing customer and accounting data. Thus it allowed the engineers to use computer resources without being charged and to obtain customer

information and proprietary program listings.

3. Several county department of social service employees used terminated state welfare numbers, changing names and addresses, to issue checks to themselves.

4. A tape librarian, disgruntled because of being fired, replaced all of the magnetic tapes in the vault with new, blank tapes during the 30-day notice period.

REQUIRED: In each of the situations described, indicate the specific control techniques that could have prevented or detected the situation. (CIA adapted)

11-2 A bank provides services such as money transfers, letters of credit, and foreign exchange for its customers who maintain minimum balances in demand deposit accounts (DDA). Earnings on DDA balances compensate the bank for the services and contribute to income. The amount of income earned by DDA balances, however, is a function of variable interest rates. These are beyond the bank's control, and the bank cannot continually change minimum balance requirements as interest rates fluctuate.

The bank uses a spreadsheet model on a microcomputer to help it plan changes in minimum balances. The spreadsheet model projects operating results for different minimum balances. As interest rates fall, larger balances are required to produce the same income. The costs of the services include fixed costs and variable costs which are linear functions of volume.

REQUIRED: Identify preventive, detective, and corrective controls for this application and the exposures controlled by each. Present your response in three segments, one segment for each control type. Identify the control in the left column and the exposure in the right column, as shown.
(CIA adapted)

	CONTROL	EXPOSURE
Preventive:		
Detective:		
Corrective:		

11-3 Good Lumber Company is a large regional dealer of building materials that requires an elaborate system of internal controls. The flowchart of the purchasing activities is presented in Figure C11-1.

The activities in the Purchasing Department start with the receipt of an approved copy of the purchase requisition (PR) from the Budget Department. After reviewing the purchase requisition, a prenumbered purchase order (PO) is issued in multiple copies. Two copies are sent to the vendor, one retained in the Purchasing Department, and the remainder distributed to other departments of Good Lumber. The second copy of the purchase order is to be returned by the vendor to confirm the receipt of the order; this copy is filed according to PO number in the PO file.

A receiving report (RR) is completed in the Receiving Department when shipments of materials arrive from vendors. A copy of the receiving report is sent to the Purchasing Department and attached to the purchase order and purchase requisition in the vendor's file.

The Accounts Payable Department normally receives two copies of a vendor's invoice. These two copies, with various documents related to the order, are forwarded to the Purchasing Department for review. Purchasing will either institute authorization procedures for the payment of the invoice or recommend exception procedures.

REQUIRED:

1. A primary purpose for preparing a flowchart is to identify system control procedure. Explain what a control procedure is.

2. Control procedures are not specifically identified in the flowchart presented for the Purchasing Department of Good Lumber Company. Review the flowchart and identify where control procedures exist. For each control procedure:

   a. Identify where the control procedure exists in the flowchart. Use the reference number that appears to the left of each symbol.

   b. Describe the nature of the control procedure required for each control point.

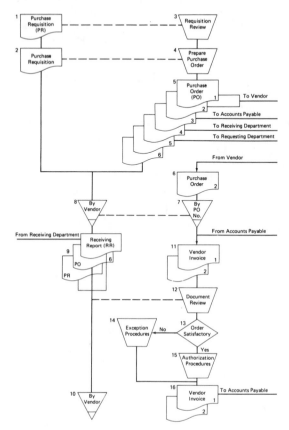

FIGURE C11-1
Purchasing department–
Good Lumber Company.

c. Explain the purpose of, or justification in terms of risk reduction for, each control procedure.

Use the following format in preparing your answer:

Reference Number	Control Procedure	Purpose or Justification

(CMA adapted with permission.)

11-4 Simmons Corporation is a multilocation retailing concern with stores and warehouses throughout the United States. The company is designing a new integrated computer-based information system. In conjunction with the design of the new system, the company's man-

agement is reviewing the IS security to determine what new control features should be incorporated. Two areas of specific concern are (1) the confidentiality of company and customer records; and (2) the safekeeping of computer equipment, files, and IS facilities.

The new information system will process all company records, which include sales, purchase, financial, budget, customer, creditor, and personnel information. The stores and warehouses will be linked to the main computer at corporate headquarters by a system of remote terminals. This will permit data to be communicated directly to corporate headquarters or to any other location from each location through the terminal network.

At the present time, certain reports have restricted distribution because not all levels of management need to receive them or because they contain confidential information. The introduction of remote terminals in the new system may provide access to this restricted data by unauthorized personnel. Simmons's top management is concerned that confidential information may become accessible and may be used improperly.

The company also is concerned about potential physical threats to the system, such as sabotage, fire damage, water damage, power failure, or magnetic radiation. Should any of these events occur in the present system and cause a computer shutdown, adequate backup records are available so that the company could reconstruct necessary information at a reasonable cost on a timely basis. With the new system, however, a computer shutdown would severely limit company activities until the system could become operational again.

REQUIRED:

1. Identify and briefly explain the problems Simmons Corporation could experience with respect to the confidentiality of information and records in the new system.
2. Recommend measures Simmons Corporation could incorporate into the new system which would ensure the confidentiality of information and records in the new system.
3. What safeguards can Simmons Corporation develop to provide physical security for its (1) computer equipment; (2) files; and (3) EDP facilities?

Adapted from the CMA examination.

11-5 Imtex Corporation is a multinational company with approximately 100 subsidiaries and divisions, referred to as reporting units. Each reporting unit operates autonomously and maintains its own accounting information system. Each month, the reporting units prepare the basic financial statements and other key financial data on prescribed forms. These statements and related data are either mailed or telexed to corporate headquarters in New York City for entry into the corporate database. Top and middle management at corporate head-

quarters use the database to plan and direct corporate operations and objectives.

Under the current system, the statements and data are to be received at corporate headquarters by the twelfth working day following the end of the month. The reports are logged, batched, and taken to the Data Processing Department for coding and entry into the database. Approximately 15 percent of the reporting units are delinquent in submitting their data, and three to four days are required to receive all of the data. After the data are loaded into the system, data vertification programs are run to check footings, cross-statement consistency, and dollar range limits. Any errors in the data are traced and corrected, and reporting units are notified of all errors by form letters.

Imtex Corporation has decided to upgrade its computer communication network. The new system would allow data to be received on a more timely basis at corporate headquarters and provide numerous benefits to each of the reporting units.

The Systems Department at corporate headquarters is responsible for the overall design and implementation of the new system. The Systems Department will install microcomputer terminals at all reporting units. These terminals will provide two-way computer communications, and also serve as stand-alone work stations for spreadsheets and other applications software. As part of the initial use of the system, the data collection for the corporate database would be performed with these microcomputers.

The financial data currently mailed or telexed would be entered via microcomputer terminals. The required forms would initially be transmitted (downloaded) from the headquarters computer to the microcomputer of each report unit and stored permanently on disk. Data would be entered on the forms appearing on the reporting unit's microcomputer terminal and stored under a separate file for transmission after the data are checked.

The data edit program would also be downloaded to the reporting units so the data could be verified at the unit location. All corrections would be made before the data are transmitted to headquarters. The data would be stored on disk in proper format to maintain a unit file. Data would either be transmitted to corporate headquarters immediately or retrieved by computer at corporate headquarters as needed. Therefore, data arriving at corporate headquarters would be free from errors and ready to be used in reports.

Charlotte Edwards, Imtex's controller, is very pleased with the prospects of the new system. She believes data will be received from the reporting units two to three days faster, and that the accuracy of the data will be much improved. However, Edwards is concerned about data security and integrity during the transmission of data between the reporting units and corporate headquarters. She has scheduled a meeting with key personnel from the Systems Department to discuss these concerns.

RISK AND PROBLEM IDENTIFICATION

(CMA adapted.)

11-6 It is estimated that several hundred million dollars are lost annually through computer crime. The first conviction of a computer "hacker" under the Computer Fraud and Abuse Act of 1986 occurred in 1988. There have been other cases of computer break-ins reported in the news, as well as stories of viruses spreading throughout vital networks. While these cases make the headlines, most experts maintain that the number of computer crimes publicly revealed represent only the tip of the iceberg. Companies have been victims of crimes but have not acknowledged them in order to avoid adverse publicity and not advertise their vulnerability.

Although the threat to security is seen as external, through outside penetration, the more dangerous threats are of internal origin.

REQUIRED: Imtex could experience data security and integrity problems when transmitting data between the reporting units and corporate headquarters.

1. Identify and explain the data security and integrity risks and problems that could occur.

2. For each problem identified, identify and explain a control procedure that could be employed to minimize or eliminate the problem.

Use the following format to present your response:

CONTROL PROCEDURE AND EXPLANATION

Management must recognize these problems and commit to the development and enforcement of security programs to deal with the many types of fraud that computer systems are susceptible to on a daily basis. The primary types of computer systems fraud include (1) input manipulation, (2) program alteration, (3) file alteration, (4) data theft, (5) sabotage, and (6) theft of computer time.

REQUIRED: For the six types of fraud identified above, explain how each may be committed. Also, identify a different method of protection for each type of fraud, describing how the protection method operates. The same protection method should *not* be used for more than one type of fraud, i.e., six different methods must be identified and described.

Use the following format:
(CMA adapted)

TYPE OF FRAUD	EXPLANATION	IDENTIFICATION AND DESCRIPTION OF PROTECTION METHODS
1.		
2.		
3.		
4.		
5.		
6.		

11-7 George Beemster, CPA, is examining the financial statements of the Louisville Sales Corporation, which recently installed an electronic computer. The following comments have been extracted from Mr. Beemster's notes on computer operations and the processing and control of shipping notices and customers' invoices:

—To minimize inconvenience, Louisville converted without change its existing data processing system, which used tabulating equipment. The computer company supervised the conversion and has provided training to all computer department employees (except key operators) in systems design, operations, and programming.

—Each computer run is assigned to a specific employee, who is responsible for making program changes, running the program, and answering questions. This procedure has the advantage of eliminating the need for records of computer operations because each employee is responsible for his or her own computer runs.

—At least one computer department employee remains in the computer room during office hours, and only computer department employees have keys to the computer room.

—System documentation consists of those materials furnished by the computer company—a set of record formats and program listings. These and the disk and tape library are kept in a corner of the computer department.

—The company considered the desirability of programmed controls but decided to retain the manual controls from its existing system.

—Company products are shipped directly from public warehouses, which forward shipping notices to general accounting. There, a billing clerk enters the price of the item and accounts for the numerical sequence of shipping notices from each warehouse. The billing clerk also prepares daily adding machine tapes ("control tapes") of the units shipped and the unit process.

—Shipping notices and control tapes are forwarded to the computer department for data entry and processing. Extensions are made on the computer. Output consists of invoices (in six copies) and a daily sales register. The daily sales register shows the aggregate totals of units shipped and unit prices, which the computer operator compares with the control tapes.

—All copies of the invoices are returned to the billing clerk. The clerk mails three copies to the customer, forwards one copy to the warehouse, maintains one copy in the numerical file, and retains one copy in an open invoice file that serves as a detailed account receivable record.

REQUIRED: Describe weaknesses in internal control structure over information and data flows and the procedures for processing shipping notices and customer invoices, and recommend improvements in control and processing procedures. Organize your answer sheets as follows:

WEAKNESSES	RECOMMENDED IMPROVEMENT

(AICPA adapted.)

11-8 VBR Company has recently installed a new computer system that has on-line capability. Terminals are used for data entry and inquiry. A new cash receipts and accounts receivable file maintenance system has been designed and implemented for use with this new equipment. All programs have been written and tested, and the new system is being run in parallel with the old system. After two weeks of parallel operation, no differences have been observed between the two systems other than keypunch errors on the old systems.

Al Brand, the data processing manager, is enthusiastic about the new equipment and system. He reveals that the system was designed, coded, compiled, debugged, and tested by programmers using an on-line CRT terminal installed specifically for around-the-clock use by the programming staff. He claims that this access to the computer saved one-third in programming elapsed time. All files, including accounts receivable, are on line at all times as the firm moves toward a full database mode. All programs, new and old, are available at all times for scheduled operating use or for program maintenance. Program documentation and actual tests confirm that data-entry editing procedures in the new system include all conventional data error and validity checking procedures appropriate to the system.

Inquiries have confirmed that the new system conforms precisely to the flowcharts, a portion of which is shown in Figure C11-2. A turnaround copy of the invoice is used as a remittance advice (R/A) by 99 percent of the customers; if the R/A is missing, the cashier applies the payment to a selected invoice. Sales terms are net sixty days, but payment patterns are sporadic. Statements are not mailed to customers. Late payments are commonplace and are not vigorously pursued. VBR does not have a bad debt problem because bad debt losses average only 0.5 percent of sales.

Before authorizing the termination of the old system, Carol Darden, the controller, has requested a review of the internal control procedures that have been designed for the new system. Security against unauthorized access and fraudulent actions, assurance of the integrity of the files, and protection of the firm's assets should be provided by the internal controls.

REQUIRED: Based upon the description of VBR Company's new system and the flowchart that has been presented:

1. Describe the control structure defects that exist in the system.
2. Suggest how each defect you identified could be corrected.

(Adapted from the CMA examination.)

11-9 The Department of Taxation of one state is developing a new computer system for processing state income tax returns of individuals and corporations. The new system features direct data input and inquiry capabilities. Identification of taxpayers is provided by using the Social Security number for individuals and federal identification number for corporations. The new system should be fully implemented in time for the next tax season.

The new system will serve three primary purposes:

1. Data will be input into the system directly from tax returns through microcomputers located at the central headquarters of the Department of Taxation. Mathematical accuracy will be checked at the time of entry by the microcomputer software.

2. The returns will be processed using the main computer facilities at central headquarters. The processing includes

   a. Auditing the reasonableness of deductions, tax due, and so forth, through the use of edit routines; these routines also include a comparison of the current year's data with the prior years' data.

   b. Identifying the returns that should be considered for audit by revenue agents of the department.

   c. Issuing refund checks to taxpayers.

3. Inquiry service will be provided taxpayers upon request through the assistance of tax department personnel at five regional offices. A total of fifty microcomputers will be placed at the regional offices for inquiry, data entry, and editing. A taxpayer will be allowed to determine the status of his or her return or get information from the last three years' returns by calling or visiting one of the department's regional offices.

The state commissioner of taxation is concerned about data security during input and processing over and above protection against natural hazards such as fire and floods. This includes protection against the loss or damage of data during data input or processing or the improper input or processing of data. In addition, the tax commissioner and the state attorney general have discussed the general problem of data confidentiality that may arise from the nature and operation of the new system. Both individuals want to have all potential problems identified before the system is fully developed and implemented so that the proper control procedures can be incorporated into the new system.

REQUIRED:

1. Describe the potential confidentiality

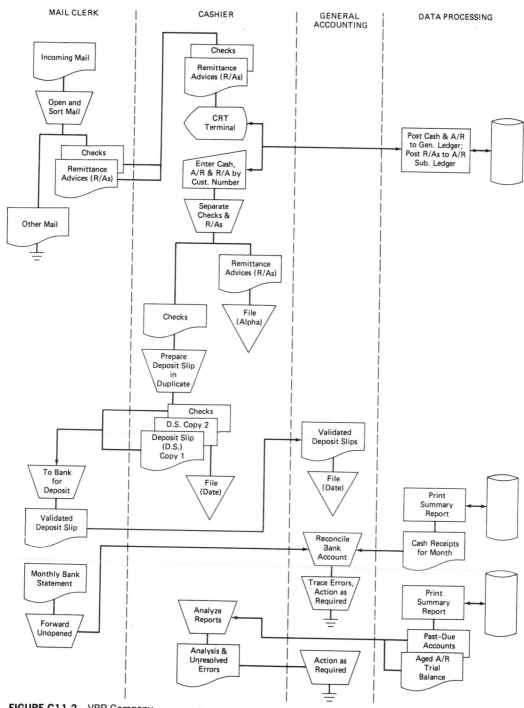

FIGURE C11-2   VBR Company.

problems their associated risks that could arise in each of the following three areas of processing. Recommend the corrective action or actions to solve the problem.

a. Data input

b. Processing of returns

c. Data inquiry

2. The State Tax Commission wants to incorporate control procedures to provide data security against the loss, damage, or improper input or use of data during data input and processing. Identify the potential risks and problems (outside of such natural hazards as fire and floods) for which the Department of Taxation should develop controls, and recommend the possible control procedures for each problem identified.

(Adapted from the CMA examination.)

11-10 The National Commercial Bank has fifteen branches, and maintains a mainframe computer system at its corporate headquarters. National has recently undergone an examination by the state banking examiners, and the examiners have some concerns about National's computer operations.

During the last few years, each branch has purchased an ample number of microcomputers in order to communicate with the mainframe in the emulation mode. The branch also uses these microcomputers to download information from the mainframe and, in the local mode, manipulate customer data to make banking decisions at the branch level. Each microcomputer is initially supplied with a word processing application package to formulate correspondence to the customers, a spreadsheet package to perform credit and financial loan analyses beyond the basic credit analysis package on the mainframe, and a database management package to formulate customer market and sensitivity information. National's centralized Data Processing Department is only responsible for mainframe operations; microcomputer security is the responsibility of each branch.

Because the bank examiners believe National is at risk, they have advised National to review the recommendations suggested in a letter issued by regulatory agencies in 1988. This informative letter emphasizes the risks as-

sociated with end-user operations and encourages banking management to establish sound control policies. More specifically, microcomputer end-user operations have outpaced the implementation of adequate controls and have taken processing control out of the centralized environment, introducing vulnerability in new areas of the bank.

The letter also emphasizes that the responsibility for corporate policies identifying management control practices for all areas of information processing activities resides with the Board of Directors. The existence, adequacy, and compliance with these policies and practices will be part of the regular banking examiners' review. The three required control groups for adequate information system security as they relate to National are

a. processing controls.

b. physical and environmental controls.

c. spreadsheet program-development controls.

REQUIRED: For each of the three control groups listed,

1. Identify three types of controls for microcomputer end-user operations where National Commercial Bank might be at risk, and

2. Recommend a specific control procedure that National Commercial Bank should implement for each type of control you identified in Requirement 1. Use the following format for your answer.

CONTROL TYPES	RECOMMENDED PROCEDURES
a. Processing controls	

(CMA adapted)

11-11 Jem Clothes Inc. is a 25 store chain, concentrated in the northeast, that sells ready-to-wear clothes for young men and women. Each store has a full-time manager and an assistant manager, both of whom are paid on a salary basis. The cashiers and sales personnel are typically young people working part time, who are paid an hourly wage plus a commission based on sales volume. The flow chart in Figure C11-3 depicts the flow of a sales transac-

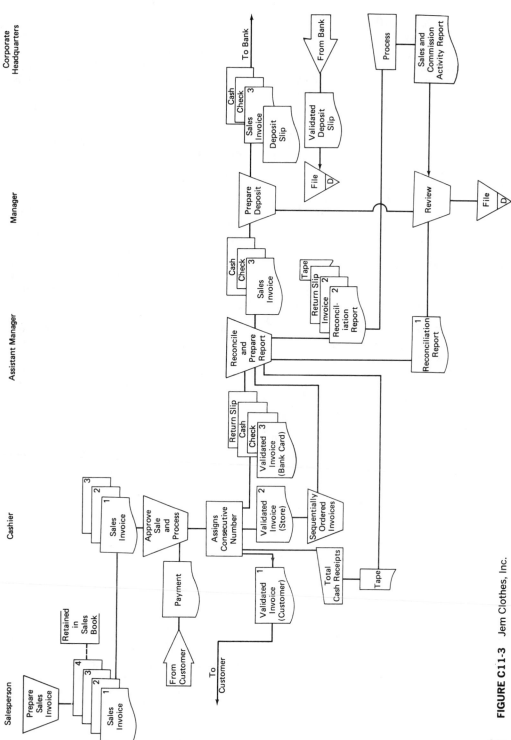

FIGURE C11-3 Jem Clothes, Inc.

329

tion through the organization of a typical store. The company uses unsophisticated cash registers with four-part sales invoices to record each transaction. These sales invoices are used regardless of the payment type (cash, check, or bank card).

On the sales floor, the salesperson manually records his/her employee number and the transaction (clothes class, description, quantity, and unit price), totals the sales invoice, calculates the discount when appropriate, calculates the sales tax, and prepares the grand total. The salesperson then gives the sales invoice to the cashier, retaining one copy in the sales book.

The cashier reviews the invoice and inputs the sale. The cash register mechanically validates the invoice by automatically assigning a consecutive number to the transaction. The cashier is also responsible for getting credit approval on charge sales and approving sales paid by customer check. The cashier gives one copy of the invoice to the customer, retains the second copy as a store copy, and retains the third copy for bank card deposit if needed. Returns are handled in exactly the reverse manner with the cashier issuing a return slip when necessary.

At the end of each day, the cashier sequentially orders the sales invoices and gets cash register totals for cash, bank card, and check sales, and cash and bank card returns. These totals are reconciled by the assistant manager to the cash register tapes, the total of the consecutively numbered sales invoices, and the return slips. The assistant manager prepares a daily Reconciliation Report for the store manager's review.

Cash sales, check sales, and bank card sales are reviewed by the manager who then prepares the daily bank deposit (bank card sales invoices are included in the deposit). The manager makes the deposit at the bank and files the validated deposit slip.

The cash register tapes, sales invoices, and return slips are then forwarded daily to the central Data Processing Department at corporate headquarters for processing. The Data Processing Department returns a weekly Sales and Commission Activity Report to the manager for review.

REQUIRED: Each store in the Jem Clothes chain follows this sales and cash receipts system for control of sales transactions.

1. Identify six strengths in the Jem Clothes system for controlling sales transactions.

2. For each strength identified, explain what problem(s) Jem Cloths has avoided by incorporating the strength in the system for controlling sales transactions.

Use the following format in preparing your answer. (CMA adapted)

1. <u>STRENGTH</u>   2. <u>PROBLEM(S) AVOIDED</u>

11-12 O'Brien Corporation is a medium-sized, privately owned industrial instrument manufacturer supplying precision equipment manufacturers in the Midwest. The corporation is ten years old and operates a centralized accounting and information system. The administrative offices are located in a downtown building while the production, shipping, and receiving departments are housed in a renovated warehouse a few blocks away. The shipping and receiving areas share one end of the warehouse.

O'Brien Corporation has grown rapidly. Sales have increased by 25 percent each year for the last three years, and the company is now shipping approximately $80,000 of its products each week. James Fox, O'Brien's controller, purchased and installed a computer last year to process the payroll and inventory. Fox plans to fully integrate the accounting information system within the next five years.

The Marketing Department consists of four salespersons. Upon obtaining an order, usually over the telephone, a salesperson manually prepares a prenumbered, two-part sales order. One copy of the order is filed by date and the second copy is sent to the Shipping Department. All sales are on credit, f.o.b. destination. Because of the recent increase in sales, the four salespersons have not had time to check credit histories. As a result, 15 percent of credit sales are either late collections or uncollectible.

The Shipping Department receives the sales orders and packages the goods from the warehouse, noting any items that are out of stock. The terminal in the Shipping Department is used to update the perpetual inventory records of each item as it is removed from the shelf. The packages are placed near the loading dock door in alphabetical order by customer name. The sales order is signed by a shipping clerk, indicating that the order is filled and ready to send. The sales order is forwarded to the Billing Department where a two-part sales invoice is prepared. The sales invoice is only prepared upon receipt of the sales order from the Shipping Department so that the customer is billed just for the items that were sent, not for back orders. Billing sends the customer's copy of the invoice back to Shipping. The customer's copy of the invoice serves as a billing copy, and the shipping clerk inserts it into a special envelope on the package in order to save postage. The carrier of the customer's choice is then contracted to pick up the goods, In the past, goods were shipped within two working days of the receipt of the customer's order; however, shipping dates now average six working days after receipt of the order. One reason is that there are two new shipping clerks who are still undergoing training. Because the two shipping clerks have fallen behind, the two clerks in the Receiving Department, who are experienced, have been assisting the shipping clerks.

The Receiving Department is located adjacent to the shipping dock, and merchandise is received daily by many different carriers. The clerks share the computer terminal with the Shipping Department. The date, vendor, and number of items received are entered upon receipt in order to keep the perpetual inventory records current.

Hard copy of the changes in inventory (additions and shipments) is printed once a month. The receiving supervisor makes sure the additions are reasonable and forwards the printout to the shipping supervisor who is responsible for checking the reasonableness of the deductions from inventory (shipments). The inventory printout is stored in the Shipping Department by date. A complete inventory list is only printed once a year when the physical inventory is taken.

Figure C11-4 presents the document flows employed by O'Brien Corporation.

REQUIRED: O'Brien Corporation's marketing, shipping, billing, and receiving information system has some weaknesses. For each weakness in the system:

1. Identify each weakness and describe the potential risk(s), problem(s) caused by each weakness.

2. Recommend control procedures or changes in the accounting system to correct each weakness.

Use the following format in preparing your answer:

WEAKNESSES AND POTENTIAL RISK(S) AND PROBLEM(S)	RECOMMENDATION(S) TO CORRECT WEAKNESSES

(CMA adapted)

11-13 Aidbart Company has recently installed a new on-line, database computer system. CRT units are located thoughout the company with at least one CRT unit located in each department. Jane Lanta, vice-president of finance, has overall responsibility for the company's management information system, but she relies heavily on Ivan West, director of MIS, for technical assistance and direction.

Lanta was one of the primary supporters of the new system because she knew it would provide labor savings. However, she is concerned about security of the new system. Lanta was walking through the Purchasing Department recently when she observed an Aidbart buyer using a CRT unit to inquire about the current price for a specific part used by Aidbart. The new system enabled the buyer to have the data regarding the part brought up on the screen as well as each Aidpart product that used the part and the total manufacturing cost of the products using the part. The buyer told Lanta that, in addition to inquiring about the part, he could also change the cost of parts.

Lanta scheduled a meeting with West to review her concerns regarding the new system. Lanta stated, "Ivan, I am concerned about the type and amount of data that can be accessed through the CRTs. How can we protect ourselves against unauthorized access to data in our computer file? Also, what happens if we have a natural disaster such as a fire, a passive threat such as a power outage, or some active threat resulting in malicious damage—could we continue to operate? We need to show management that we are on top of these things. Would you please outline the procedures we now have, or need to have, to protect ourselves."

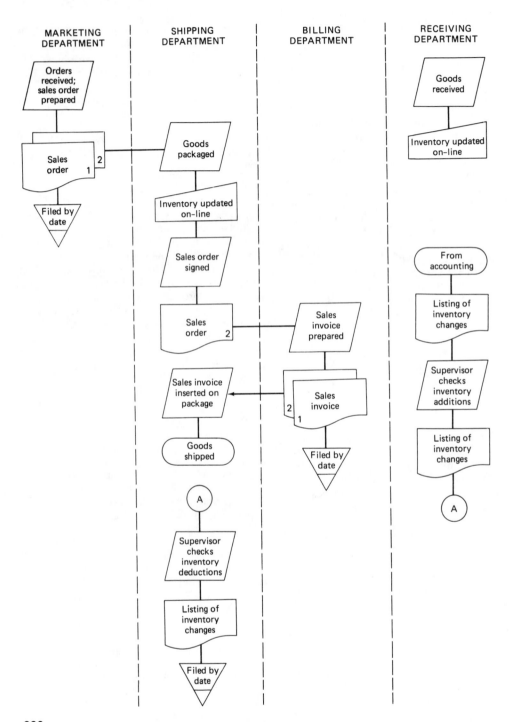

MARKETING DEPARTMENT

Orders received; sales order prepared

Sales order 1 2

Filed by date

SHIPPING DEPARTMENT

Goods packaged

Inventory updated on-line

Sales order signed

Sales order 2

Sales invoice inserted on package

Goods shipped

A

Supervisor checks inventory deductions

Listing of inventory changes

Filed by date

BILLING DEPARTMENT

Sales invoice prepared

Sales invoice 2 1

Filed by date

RECEIVING DEPARTMENT

Goods received

Inventory updated on-line

From accounting

Listing of inventory changes

Supervisor checks inventory additions

Listing of inventory changes

A

FIGURE C11-4 O'Brien Corporation.

West responded by saying, "Jane, there are areas of vulnerability in the design and implementation of any IS system. Some of these are more prevalent in on-line systems such as ours—especially with respect to privacy, integrity, and confidentiality of data. The four major points of vulnerability with which we should be concerned are the hardware, the software, the people, and the network."

REQUIRED:

For each of the four major points of vulnerability identified by Ivan West,

    a. Give one potential threat to the system, and

    b. Identify action to be taken to protect the system from the threat.

(CMA adapted with permission.)

11-14 Lexsteel Corporation is a leading manufacturer of steel furniture. While the company has manufacturing plants and distribution facilities throughout the United States, the purchasing, accounting, and treasury functions are centralized at corporate headquarters.

While discussing the management letter with the external auditors, Ray Landsdown, controller of Lexsteel, became aware of potential problems with the accounts payable system. The auditors had to perform additional audit procedures in order to attest to the validity of accounts payable and cutoff procedures. The auditors have recommended that a detailed systems study be made of the current procedures. Such a study would not only assess the exposure of the company to potential embezzlement and fraud, but would also identify ways to improve management controls.

Landsdown has assigned the study task to Dolores Smith, a relatively new accountant in the department. Because Smith could not find adequate documentation of the accounts payable procedures, she interviewed those employees involved and constructed a flowchart of the current system. This flowchart and descriptions of the current procedures are presented in Figure C11-5.

Computer Resources Available. The host computer mainframe is located at corporate headquarters with interactive, remote job entry terminals at each branch location. In general, data entry occurs at the source and is transmitted to an integrated database maintained on the host computer. Data transmission is made between the branch offices and the host computer over leased telephone lines. The software allows flexibility for managing user access and ending data input.

Procedures for Purchasing Raw Materials. Production orders and appropriate bills of material are generated by the host computer at corporate headquarters. Based on these bills of material, purchase orders for raw materials are generated by the centralized purchasing function and mailed directly to the vendors. Each purchase order instructs the vendor to ship the materials directly to the appropriate manufacturing plant. The manufacturing plants, assuming that the necessary purchase orders have been issued, proceed with the production orders received from corporate headquarters.

When goods are received, the manufacturing plant examines and verifies the count to the packing slip and transmits the receiving data to accounts payable at corporate headquarters. In the event that raw material deliveries fall behind production, each branch manager is given the authority to order materials and issue emergency purchase orders directly to the vendors. Data about the emergency orders and verification of materials receipt are transmitted via computer to accounts payable at corporate headquarters. Since the company employs a computerized perpetual inventory system, physical counts of raw materials are deemed not to be cost effective and are not performed.

Accounts Payable Procedures. Vendor invoices are mailed directly to corporate headquarters and entered by accounts payable personnel when received; this often occurs before the receiving data are transmitted from the branch offices. The final day of the invoice term for payment is entered as the payment due date. This due date must often be calculated by the data entry person using information listed on the invoice.

Once a week, invoices due the following week are printed in chronological entry order on a payment listing, and the corresponding

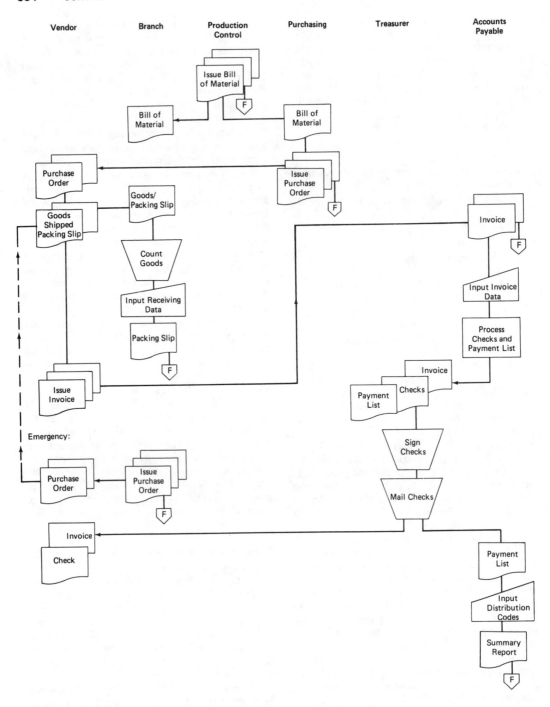

FIGURE C11-5   Lexsteel Corporation.

checks are drawn. The checks and the payment listing are sent to the treasurer's office for signature and mailing to the payee. The check number is printed by the computer and displayed on the check and the payment listing, and is validated as the checks are signed. After the checks are mailed, the payment listing is returned to accounts payable for filing. When there is insufficient cash to pay all the invoices, certain checks and the payment listing are retained by the treasurer until all checks can be paid. When the remaining checks are mailed, the listing is then returned to accounts payable. Often, weekly check mailings include a few checks from the previous week, but rarely are there more than two weekly listings involved.

When accounts payable receives the payment listing back from the treasurer's office, the expenses are distributed, coded, and posted to the appropriate plant/cost center accounts. Weekly summary performance reports are processed by accounts payable for each cost center and branch location reflecting all data entry to that point.

REQUIRED:

1. Identify and discuss three areas where Lexsteel Corporation may be exposed to fraud or embezzlement due to weaknesses in the procedures described, and recommend improvements to correct these weaknesses.

2. Describe three areas where management information could be distorted due to weaknesses in the procedures described, and recommend improvements to correct these weaknesses.

3. Identify three strengths in the procedures described and explain why they are strengths.

(CMA adapted)

11-15 The customer billing and collection functions of the Robinson Company, a small paint manufacturer, are attended to by a receptionist, an accounts receivable clerk, a general ledger clerk, and a cashier who also serves as a secretary. The company's paint products are sold to wholesalers and retail stores.

The following list describes *all* the procedures performed by the Robinson Company's employees pertaining to the customer billings and collections:

1. The mail is opened by the receptionist, who gives the customers' purchase orders to the accounts receivable clerk. Fifteen to twenty orders are received each day. Under instructions to expedite the shipment of orders, the accounts receivable clerk immediately prepares a five-copy sales invoice form which is distributed as follows:

   a. Copy 1 is the customer billing copy and is held by the accounts receivable clerk until notice of shipment is received.

   b. Copy 2 is the accounts receivable department copy and is held for ultimate posting of the accounts receivable records.

   c. Copies 3 and 4 are sent to the shipping department.

   d. Copy 5 is sent to the storeroom as authority for release of the goods to the shipping department.

2. After the paint ordered has been moved from the storeroom to the shipping department, the shipping department prepares the bills of lading and labels the cartons. Sales invoice copy 4 is sent to the storeroom as authority for release of the goods to the shipping department.
   Sales invoice copy 4 is inserted into a carton as a packing slip. After the trucker has picked up the shipment, the customer's copy of the bill of lading and copy 3, on which are noted any undershipments, are returned to the accounts receivable clerk. The trucker retains a copy of the bill of lading. The company does not "back-order" in the event of undershipments; customers are expected to reorder the merchandise. The Robinson Company's copy of the bill of lading is filed by the shipping department.

3. When copy 3 and the customer's copy of the bill of lading are received by the accounts receivable clerk, copies 1 and 2 are completed by numbering them and inserting quantities shipped, unit prices, extensions, discounts, and totals. The accounts receivable clerk then mails copy

2 and the copy of the bill of lading to the customer. Copies 2 and 3 are stapled together.

4. The individual accounts receivable ledger cards are posted by the accounts receivable clerk by a bookkeeping machine procedure whereby the sales register is prepared as a carbon copy of the postings. Postings are made from copy 2 which is then filed, along with staple-attached copy 3, in numerical order. Once a month, the general ledger clerk summarizes the sales register for posting to the general ledger.

5. Since the Robinson Company is short of cash, the deposit of receipts is also expedited. The receptionist turns over all mail receipts and related correspondence to the accounts receivable clerk, who examines the checks and determines that the accompanying vouchers or correspondence contains enough detail to permit posting of the accounts. The accounts receivable clerk then endorses the checks and gives them to the cashier, who prepares the daily deposit. No currency is received in the mail and no paint is sold over the counter at the factory.

6. The accounts receivable clerk uses the vouchers or correspondence that accompanied the checks to post the accounts receivable ledger cards. The bookkeeping machine prepares a cash receipts register as a carbon copy of the postings. Once a month, the general ledger clerk summarizes the cash receipts registers for posting to the general ledger accounts. The accounts receivable clerk also corresponds with customers about unauthorized deductions for discounts, freight or advertising allowances, returns, and so forth, and prepares the appropriate credit memos. Disputed items of large amount are turned over to the sales manager for settlement. Each month the accounts receivable clerk prepares a trial balance of the open accounts receivable and compares the resultant total with the general ledger control account for accounts receivable.

REQUIRED:

1. Flowchart the customer billing and collection system for Robinson Company. Use a document systems flowchart.

2. Discuss the control structure weaknesses in the procedures related to customer billings and remittances and the accounting for these transactions. In your discussion, in addition to identifying the weaknesses, explain what could happen (ie., the potential risks) as a result of each weakness.

(AICPA adapted.)

11-16   The accounting system and internal control procedures relating to purchases of materials by the Branden Company, a medium-sized concern manufacturing special machinery to order, have been described by your junior accountant in the following terms:

After approval by manufacturing department supervisors, material purchase requisitions are forwarded to the purchasing department supervisor, who distributes such requisitions to purchasing department employees. The purchasing employees prepare prenumbered purchase orders in triplicate, account for all numbers, and send the original purchase order to the vendor. One copy of the purchase order is sent to the receiving department where it is used as a receiving report. The other copy is filed in the purchasing department.

When the materials are received, they are moved directly to the storeroom and issued to the supervisors on informal requests. The receiving department sends a receiving report (with its copy of the purchase order attached) to the purchasing department and sends copies of the receiving report to the storeroom and to the accounting department.

Vendors' invoices for material purchases, received in duplicate in the mail room, are sent to the purchasing department and directed to the employee who placed the related order. The employee then compares the invoice with the copy of the purchase order on file in the purchasing department for price and terms and compares the invoice quantity with the quantity received as reported by the shipping and receiving department on its copy of the purchase order. The purchasing department employee also checks discounts, footings, and extensions and then initials the invoice to indicate approval for payment. The invoice is then sent to the voucher section of the accounting department, where it is coded for account distribution, assigned a voucher number, entered in the voucher register, and filed according to payment due date.

On payment dates, prenumbered checks are requisitioned by the voucher section from the cashier and prepared except for signature. After the checks have been prepared they are returned to the cashier, who puts them through a check-signing machine, accounts for the sequence of numbers, and passes them to the cash disbursements bookkeeper for entry in the cash disbursement book. The cash disbursements bookkeeper then returns the checks to the voucher section, which then notes payment dates in the voucher register, places the checks in envelopes, and sends them to the mail room. The vouchers are then filed in numerical sequence. At the end of each month one of the voucher clerks prepares an adding machine tape of unpaid items in the voucher register and compares the total thereof with the general ledger balance and investigates any difference disclosed by such comparison.

REQUIRED: Discuss the control weaknesses, if any, in Branden's purchasing and subsequent procedures and suggest supplementary or revised procedures for remedying each weakness with regard to

1. Requisition of materials
2. Receipt and storage of materials
3. Functions of the purchasing department
4. Functions of the accounting department

(AICPA adapted.)

11-17 In connection with an examination of the financial statements of the Olympia Manufacturing Company, a CPA is reviewing the accounting system for accumulating direct-labor hours. The CPA learns that all production is by job order and that all employees are paid hourly wages, with time-and-one-half for overtime hours.

Olympia's direct-labor-hour input process for payroll and job-cost determination is summarized in the flowchart shown in Figure C11-6.

Steps A and C are performed in timekeeping, step B in the factory operating departments, step D in payroll audit and control, step E in data preparation (keypunch), and step F in computer operations.

REQUIRED: For each input process step (A through E):

1. List the possible errors or discrepancies that may occur and which may result in increased risk to Olympia Manufacturing Co.
2. Cite the corresponding control procedure that should be in effect for each error or discrepancy.

Note: Your discussion of Olympia's procedures should be limited to the input process or direct-labor hours, as shown in steps A through F in the flowchart. Do not discuss personnel procedures for hiring, promotion, termination, and pay rate authorization. In step F, do not discuss equipment, computer program, and general computer operational controls.

Organize your answer for each input-processing step as follows:

STEP	POSSIBLE ERRORS DISCREPANCIES	CONTROL PROCEDURES

(AICPA adapted)

11-18 The Y Company, a client of your firm, has come to you with the following problem. It has three clerical employees who must perform the following functions:

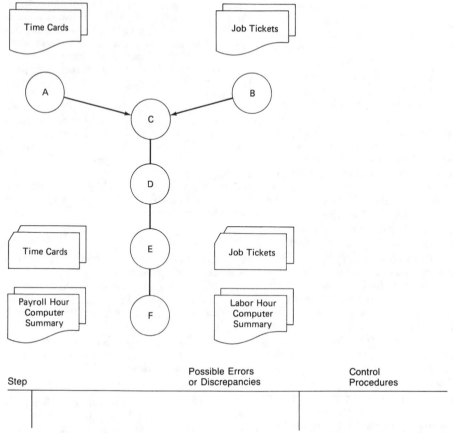

Step	Possible Errors or Discrepancies	Control Procedures

FIGURE C11-6 Olympia Manufacturing.
Source: AICPA adapted.

1. Maintain general ledger
2. Maintain accounts payable ledger
3. Maintain accounts receivable ledger
4. Prepare checks for signature
5. Maintain disbursements journal
6. Issue credits on returns and allowances
7. Reconcile the bank account
8. Handle and deposit cash receipts

Assuming that there is no problem as to the ability of any of the employees, the company requests that you assign these functions to the three employees in such a manner as to achieve the highest degree of internal control. It may be assumed that these employees will perform no other accounting functions than the ones listed and that any accounting functions not listed will be performed by persons other than these three employees.

REQUIRED: State how you would distribute the eight functions among the three employees. Assume that, with the exception of the nominal jobs of the bank reconciliation and the issuance of credits on returns and allowances, all functions require an equal amount of time. (AICPA adapted.)

11-19 Design and development progress in computer-based management information systems has been impressive in the past two decades. Traditionally, computer-based data processing systems were arranged by departments and applications. Computers were applied to single, large-volume applications such as inventory control or customer billing. Large files were built for each application.

As more applications were added, problems on data management developed. Many files contained redundant data. Businesses looked for ways to integrate the data processing systems to support management needs for decision making and on-line inquiry. As a consequence, the database system composed of the database itself, the database management systems, and the individual application programs were developed. Moreover, distributed processing and local area network systems have been developed where managers can interact with their own database or the corporate database via communication lines or network software.

REQUIRED:

1. Identify special control features a company should consider incorporating into its database system.

2. Identify special control features a company should consider to prevent access to its telecommunications and network data transmissions.

(Adapted from the CMA examination.)

11-20 Oxford Pharmaceutical Company has the following accounting system for billing and recording accounts receivable:

1. An incoming customer's purchase order is received in sales by a clerk who prepares a prenumbered company sales order form in which is inserted the pertinent information, such as the customer's name and address, customer's account number, and quantity and items ordered. After the sales order form has been prepared, the customer's purchase order is stapled to it.

2. The sales order form is then passed to the credit department for credit approval. Rough approximation of the billing values of the orders are made in the credit department for those accounts on which credit limitations are imposed. After investigation, credit approval is noted on the form.

3. Next the sales order form is passed to the billing department where a clerk keys in the order on a microcomputer system. The computer cross-multiplies the number of items and the unit price, and it then adds this automatically extended amount for each line to obtain the total amount of the order. The unit prices for the items are stored in the computer on a diskette and do not need to be keyed in unless they change. Sales order information is stored on a temporary transaction file. All information is posted to sales, accounts receivable, and inventory files during a daily computer run, and transaction lists are provided for the sales department.

The computer program automatically accumulates daily batch totals of customer account numbers and invoice amounts. After the sales orders have been processed by the computer, they are placed in files and held for about two years. The following copies of an invoice are printed on prenumbered forms during the daily billing run:

a. Customer's copy which is sent to billing

b. Shipping department copy, which serves as a shipping order

4. The bills of lading are generated by another computer run are then sent to the shipping department. After the order has been shipped, a copy of the bill of lading is returned to the billing department. The shipping department copy of the invoice is filed in the shipping department along with the bill of lading.

5. In the billing department a copy of the bill of lading is attached to the customer's copy of the invoice and both are mailed to the customer.

6. The microcomputer system uses this sales input for preparing and updating the sales journal, subsidiary accounts receivable ledger, and perpetual inventory records. Invoice information may be referenced by management at any time from the microcomputer system using the invoice number.

REQUIRED:

1. Flowchart the billing system as a means of understanding the system.

2. List the areas where Oxford Pharmaceutical Company is exposed to significant risk.

3. Itemize the control weaknesses in this system and the procedures that should have been used to reduce the risk associated with these weakness.

4. Describe an on-line system that would eliminate most of the "paperwork" using a systems flowchart.

5. List the internal control procedures that should be present over this revised on-line sales and billing system

(AICPA adapted.)

11-21 Until recently, Consolidated Electricity Company employed a batch processing system for recording the receipt of customer payments. See Case 8-10 in Chapter 8, and the accompanying figure for details of the procedures involved in the batch processing system.

REQUIRED:

1. Using the symbols provided in Chapter 8, prepare a systems flowchart of Consolidated Electricity Company's new on-line cash receipt processing system.

2. Have the new cash receipt accounting procedures as designed and implemented by Consolidated Electricity Company created any internal and systems control problems for the company? Explain your answer.

(Adapted from the CMA examination.)

11-22 Southern Insurers has a customer base of several thousand. They manage the insurance for a variety of clients and write policies of several companies. They have been using antiquated dumb terminals to enter transaction data. These transactions consist of new policies, modifications to existing policies, claims, payments, and inquiries about rates and status of policies and claims. They are considering the use of a local area network for their customer representatives. They feel it is essential that representatives have their own data on their set of clients, that they have access to company-wide information to answer questions and that they have smart terminals that can edit transaction information. Moreover Southern Insurers feels that security is important given the sensitivity of the data and the transaction amounts. They have many questions regarding the pros and cons of the various ways that they can configure their system of terminals of PCs in their offices.

REQUIRED:

1. Describe the data preparation and access controls you would recommend if they adopt a LAN.

2. Describe the communication controls you would use for the transmission of information on policies to the various insurance companies.

3. Can they link two Lans? What would they use if they consist of the same type of PCs and what would they use to link the

LAN to the mainframe with a different operating system protocol?

11-23 (Risk and information Systems) Sure Track Tire has operated a dozen tire outlets in the Chicago area for twenty years. They sell a variety of tires at discount prices. They have been considering changing from a manual accounting system where each retail location does its own accounting to a countywide EDP network.

Each outlet currently sends profit and loss statements as well as sales and inventory statistics once a month to the company office located at the main midtown location. The new system that they are considering would have a common relational database located at the company office and each store would have a microcomputer and a modem to process transactions as they occur during the course of business. The company and retail outlet managers would be able to access information anytime for reports such as sales and inventory and decision-making needs.

REQUIRED: List the potential risks and suggest at least one control procedure which would help reduce the potential risk to the integrity of the company's database.

RISK	CONTROL PROCEDURE

11-24 The flowchart in Figure C11-7 depicts the activities relating to the shipping, billing, and collecting processes used by Smallco Lumber, Inc.

REQUIRED: Identify weaknesses in the system of internal accounting control relating to the activities of

1. Warehouse clerk
2. Bookkeeper #1
3. Bookkeeper #2
4. Collection clerk

(AICPA adapted)

11-25 The following multiple-choice questions have been adapted from questions on CMA exams. Select the best answer.

1. The data control group of Burch Company has determined upon investigation that a large portion of the errors in processing payroll result from incorrectly recorded employee numbers. What method of control should Burch Co. install to reduce the chance of error?

   a. Sequence check
   b. Reasonableness test
   c. Check digit verification
   d. File protection ring
   e. Batch total

2. The management of Kusbar Co. has reason to suspect that someone is tampering with pay rates by entering changes through the company's remote terminals located in the factory. The method Kusbar Co. should implement to protect the system from these unauthorized alterations to the system's files is

   a. Batch totals
   b. Checkpoint recovery
   c. Passwords
   d. Record counts
   e. Parity checks

3. A source document with an invalid number of hours worked for one week, i.e., 93 hours instead of 39, would be best detected by

   a. Data-entry controls
   b. A limit test in an edit run

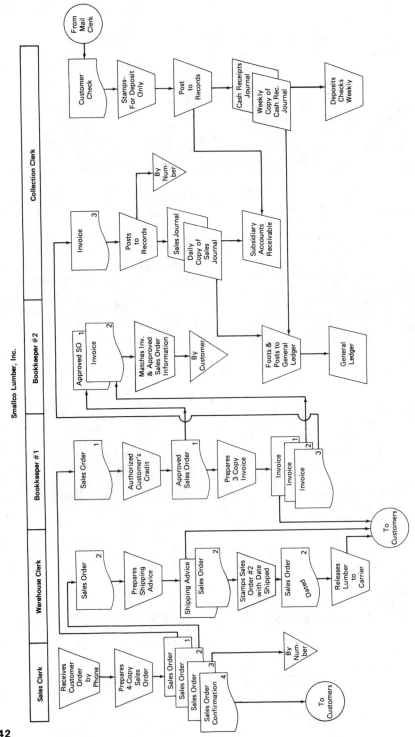

FIGURE C11-7 Smallco Lumber, Inc.

342

c. Hash total of hours worked

d. Record count total

e. Key verifying control

4. A transaction involving a charge to a non-existent customer account was entered into an accounts receivable and billing system that was batch processed. This error should be detected by the computer system and appear in

a. The sort run error printout

b. The edit run error printout

c. The customer statements printout

d. The master file update run error printout

e. Some error printout other than those mentioned above

5. A company's computer facilities and computer room conceivably could be destroyed completely by fire. The most appropriate action a company could take in an attempt to prepare for and protect itself from such a disaster as this would be

a. To have backup computer facilities at the same site.

b. To have off-site backup computer facilities

c. To have a reconstruction and recovery plan which outlines the procedures for reconstruction of files and use of alternate facilities

d. To have a contractual agreement with the manufacturer or another company to use its facilities

e. To have the grandfather-father-son concept implemented for all files stored on magnetic tapes

6. Transactions which were erroneous and had been previously rejected by the computer system apparently were not being reentered and reprocessed once they had

been corrected. This erroneous condition is best controlled by

a. Comparing a record count of transactions input into the system

b. A comparison of the batch controls totals

c. Scanning the error control log

d. Scanning the console log

e. Desk checking

7. An operator inadvertently has mounted the wrong master tape file. Which one of the following controls is most likely to detect such an error?

a. Password control procedures

b. Header label control procedures

c. Library control procedures

d. Trailer label control procedures

e. Control procedures of the input/output control group

8. In an on-line system which of the following would be most likely to be used as a backup for an application's master file maintained on magnetic disk?

a. At specified periods the disk files would be dumped to (copied on) magnetic tape along with the period's transactions

b. A duplicate disk file would be maintained and all activity would be copied on magnetic tape continuously

c. The grandfather-father-son technique would be employed to retain disk files

d. All source douments for transactions would be retained

e. The disk files would be copies to magnetic tape continuously

9. Jonkers, Inc., a large retail chain, is installing a computerized accounts receivable system employing a batch mode of

processing with sequential files. The program which will process receipts on account should include an input edit routine to assure

a. Proper sequencing of data

.b. Header and trailer label accuracy

c. The amount received is recorded correctly

d. The existence of control totals

e. Proper operator intervention

10. The internal auditors of the Zebra Company have expressed concern that the new computerized purchase order system does not permit them to trace through the system from the source document to the final report. The item about which the auditors have expressed concern is the nonexistence of

a. Test data
b. Operations manuals
c. System flowcharts
d. Internal file labels
e. Audit trails

12

STRUCTURED SYSTEMS ANALYSIS AND DESIGN CONCEPTS: ANALYSIS AND DEFINITION OF THE SYSTEM

INTRODUCTION

As a resource, accounting information should be used effectively to help management achieve the firm's objectives. This can be accomplished by designing an effective and efficient information system that supports the management decision-making, reporting, and transaction processing systems of the organization. Design of an information system, however, is not a simple task. Management should have a master plan for the system. It is necessary to recognize that a well-designed information system requires careful planning, organizing, staffing, coordinating, directing, and controlling of all the elements that will be integrated to form the system. These elements include personnel, hardware, software, and procedures.

The analysis and design of an information system involves much more than the physical aspects of design. It involves careful and logical consideration of accounting information system needs and the components of the system outlined earlier. The most widely applied design approach used in today's complex information system environment is the *structured approach to systems analysis and de-*

sign.[1] This process of analysis and design involves the seven phases outlined in Figure 12-1, and described briefly in Chapter 2. These phases are traditionally divided into two segments: (1) *structured systems definition and analysis* where management must define the problem and what must be done to resolve it; and (2) *structured system design and implementation* where management must decide how to solve the problem and implement the solution.

The American Institute of Certified Public Accountants, in its *Guidelines for Development and Implementation of Computer-Based Application Systems,*[2] differs slightly from the phases outlined in Figure 12-1 and includes two phases in systems analysis and definition. They are (1) the requirements definition and alternative approaches phases—which are equivalent to the first three phases in Figure 12-1; and (2) the general systems design phase—which is equivalent to the same phase in Figure 12-1. The overall sequence is the same as in the structured approach.

Systems analysis, design, and implementation is the process of actually creating the new system or modifying the existing system. Often this whole process is called systems development. In each case, design and implementation builds on careful systems analysis and definition. Systems design and implementation should not be confused with the collective use of the term *systems design.* Many authors use the term *systems design* to refer to both *analysis* and *design* of an information system. These are the two distinct segments of the overall development process. The first describes logically *what* must be done to solve the problem; and the second describes *how* to accomplish the mission and to implement the solution. In this chapter the procedures and steps for systems definition and analysis will be developed. In the next chapter, the actual design and implementation procedures will be developed.

Alternatives to the traditional structured approach are also used and they are discussed in the next chapter. These include the use of database and spreadsheet software by end users, and prototype and computer aided systems engineering CASE by systems development personnel. Briefly, a prototype approach is an iterative approach where the bare basics (skeleton) of the system is implemented very quickly and modified (added to) as management further defines their needs as they use the system. This modified system is then further modified after some more use. This iterative process is continued until management is satisfied. CASE stands for computer-aided systems engineering. It is a computer-aided process used to automate systems development. Each of these is founded on the basic theory of the structured approach. They simply expedite or automate the analysis and design process. End user, development is valuable

[1] George R. Marshall, *Systems Analysis and Design: Alternative Structured Approaches* (Englewood Cliffs, N.J.: Prentice Hall, 1986); Edward Yourdon, and Larry L. Constantine, *Structured Design* (Englewood Cliffs, N.J.: Prentice Hall, 1979), and William S. Davis, *Systems Analysis and Design: A Structured Approach* (Reading, Mass: Addison-Wesley Publishing Co., 1983.)

[2] AICPA, *Guidelines for Development and Implementation of Computer-Based Application Systems,* Management Advisory Services Guideline Service No. 4 (New York: American Institute of Certified Public Accountants, copyright 1976). The structured framework used in this chapter parallels and is adapted with permission from AICPA, *Guidelines for Development and Implementation of Computer-Based Application Systems.* Phase I, II, and IX are discussed in this chapter. Phases III through VIII of the AICPA framework are discussed in the next chapter. The discussion is supplemented extensively with permission from Charles L. Biggs, Evan G. Birks, and William Atkins, *Managing the System Development Process* (Englewood Cliffs, N.J.: Touche Ross & Co., and Prentice Hall, 1980).

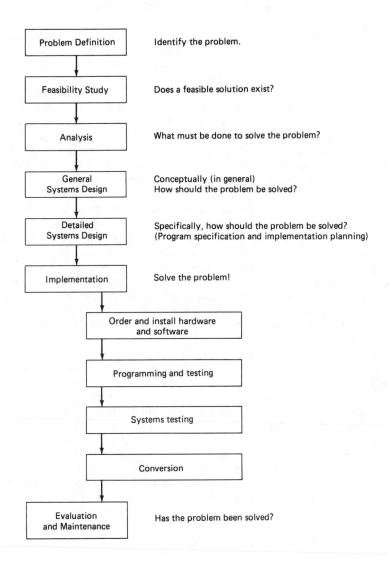

FIGURE 12-1   Structured systems analysis and design.

in situations which are simple enough for end users to do their own analysis and design. Prototyping is useful where the development must be very rapid, yet need not be as well designed, to meet management's information needs.

GENERAL APPROACHES TO SYSTEMS ANALYSIS AND DESIGN

There are several general approaches to systems analysis and design. This is true regardless of whether the accounting system is a manual, a personal computer, or a sophisticated on-line database system. Moreover, this is true whether a system currently exists or it is a completely new system.

The need for systems analysis has been widely accepted as an integral part of systems development. However, there is continuing debate regarding the approach or procedures with which the activities of systems definition and analysis are conducted. Some authors limit definition and analysis to the existing system; we take a broader perspective and apply the concepts of analysis to proposed new systems as well. This means that the analyst can and perhaps should view systems analysis from a fresh perspective, without being tied to past transaction processing, reporting, and decision-making procedures.

Due to natural growth patterns in business, many information systems have evolved over time as described in Chapter 7. Computers were programmed to support various transaction processing operations; many of these operations were in accounting because of the formal structure of the accounting process. As businesses grew, complex data processing equipment became less expensive, management became more familiar with computer operations, and data files formerly used only to support transaction processing operations were put into a common database for management use. Management began to use the information that was generated by transaction processing and stored in the computer for decision making.

Following this development, simple decision models that used database information were added to the system. Operational activities such as sales, inventory, and purchasing were integrated so that a single transaction, such as a sales order, would update inventory files and accounts receivable records and possibly initiate a purchase order via a programmed decision model. Operational control was thus achieved by many firms as their respective systems evolved from a data bank system to a predictive and decision-making system.

More complex models, such as those that integrated marketing, planning, and production scheduling, were added to these operational activities. This enabled management to plan production schedules based on incoming orders and sales projections, thereby enhancing management's control of the business. Finally, attempts were made to use the transaction processing system and the data and reports generated from it to support long-range planning and strategic policy formulation activities. System analysis and design procedures followed this evolutionary process.

The philosophy of this *evolutionary data analysis* [3] approach is most appealing. A system is built upon what is currently in use in the way of transaction processing procedures, decision models, and data files. The literature is replete with discussions that support this approach, which is often called a *bottom-up* or a *data analysis* approach. A summary statement would read as follows. Before designing a new system or adding to an old system, the analyst must understand the cur-

---

[3] See Gordon B. Davis, *Management Information Systems: Conceptual Foundations, Structure, and Development* (New York: McGraw-Hill, 1974) for a more complete description of the evolutionary process.

rent system. Therefore, the analyst proceeds to study documents, reports, data files, information flows, and organization charts in order to understand and build upon the current system.

This approach may be defined by beginning with transaction and reporting data and summing these activities upward through the organization. This approach also suggests that the analysis and definition procedures start with the analysis of the existing decision-making, reporting, and transaction processing system.

Another general approach is where information needs associated with the various levels of decision making become the starting point in defining a new or modified system. This is often called the *top-down* or *decision analysis* approach. Using this decision analysis philosophy, the accountant or systems designer does not start with the existing system and its related data and information flows. He or she begins with an analysis of the decisions needed to control the various activities of the organization and their related reporting and transaction requirements. In other words, the analyst starts with a more global definition of what must be done to satisfy management's information needs rather than simply revising the current system to somehow satisfy these requirements. The existing system then becomes only *one* piece of evidence regarding information requirements.

STRUCTURED APPROACH TO SYSTEMS ANALYSIS AND DESIGN

There must be a coordinated master plan for the accounting information system in the organization. Neither of the approaches to system analysis and definition just discussed will suffice. An integrated plan that includes the best of both is needed. Management cannot start from scratch for every modification of the system as suggested by decision analysis. The piece-by-piece evolutionary process, which is used in data analysis to continually add to the current system, is dangerous. In the latter case, several key factors are overlooked. More than likely irrelevant data had been collected, processed, and reported. Previously used data will become useless as business changes. Provisions to add new and relevant data will be founded on current practice rather than on future managerial needs for decision making. Moreover, technology will quickly outdate past transaction processing and reporting modes, data collection methods, communication procedures, and storage media. For example, consider the advent of microcomputers and its impact on small businesses. Given the restrictions on manual systems, they are not very good models for new microcomputer-based accounting systems.

The problem associated with the evolutionary data analysis approach has been expressed as follows:

> The corporate MIS did not deliver the full promise of management support. Instead, MIS printed seemingly endless stacks of reports that managers were supposed to use in decision making. Overwhelmed by data not

directly usable by them, managers lost interest and MIS became synonymous with EDP.[4]

And:

Most MIS designers "determine" what information is needed by asking managers what information they would like to have. This is based on the assumption that managers know what information they need and want. For a manager to know what information he needs he must be aware of each type of decision he should make and he must have an adequate model of each. These conditions are seldom satisfied. Most managers have some conception of at least some of the types of decisions they must make. Their conceptions, however, are likely to be deficient in a very critical way, a way that follows from an important principle of scientific economy: the less we understand a phenomenon, the more variables we require to explain it. Hence, the manager who does not understand the phenomenon he controls plays it "safe" and, with respect to information, wants "everything." The MIS designer, who has even less understanding of the relevant phenomenon than the manager, tries to provide even more than everything. He thereby increases what is already an overload of irrelevant information....

The moral is simple: one cannot specify what information is required for decision making until an explanatory model of the decision process and the system involved has been constructed and tested. Information systems are subsystems of control systems. They cannot be designed adequately without taking control into account.[5]

We propose a structured approach to systems analysis and design to resolve these dilemmas.

The key elements of this procedure are:

1. The philosophy that a firm's information system should be founded on decision-making, reporting, and transaction processing needs and to some extent on the strategic use of accounting information.

2. A feedback system that signals the need for an operational review and evaluation, leading to possible modification or complete redesign of the system.

3. The framework that begins with logical analysis of *what* must be done and then concludes with design and implementation of a system.

4. Decision-making, reporting, and transaction processing needs as the basic justification for every element of the system that the system be cost beneficial.

---

[4] G. R. Wagner, "The Future of Corporate Planning and Modeling Software Systems" (unpublished paper presented at the Corporate Planning Model Conference at Duke University, Dallas: Execucom, June 1981.

[5] Russell L. Ackoff, "Management Misinformation Systems," *Management Science*, 14, No. 4 (December 1967), B147–56.

A master framework is needed to enable a firm to react to changes in the business environment, and to meet the ever increasing needs of management for transaction processing, operational, managerial, and strategic decision making.

The objective is to have a functioning information system that is both effective and efficient. An *effective system* is one that (1) provides management with necessary information for planning and control; (2) stores sufficient historical information for future decision and reporting needs; and (3) processes transactions necessary for ongoing business operations. An *efficient system* is one that uses all the system's elements and the most up-to-date technology to accomplish these tasks in the most economical and expedient manner.

The basic precept of the structured approach to systems analysis is that an information system should provide management with relevant information for all decision-making needs. These may be internal for management needs or external for agencies such as the Securities and Exchange Commission, Interstate Commerce Commission, Internal Revenue Service, and Public Service Commission, and for other stakeholders, such as investors and creditors. Combined internal and external information is needed for intercompany transactions. The use of electronic data interchange (EDI) to accomplish this later objective is becoming much more common. This is a lofty goal which requires careful planning and analysis.

Ackoff[6] suggests that this goal can be accomplished using the following procedure:

1. Analysis of the Decision Systems—"Each (or at least each important) type of managerial decision required by the organization under study should be identified and the relationships between them should be determined and flow charted."

2. Analysis of Information Requirements—"Decisions for which models can or cannot be constructed to support the decisions, need to be analyzed and the type of system [as detailed in Chapter 4] with its related requirements needs to be determined."

3. Aggregation of Decisions—"Decisions with the same or largely overlapping informational requirements should be grouped together as a single manager's task. This will reduce the information a manager requires to do his or her job and is likely to increase his or her understanding of it."

4. Design of Information Processing—"Now the procedure for collecting, storing, retrieving and treating information can be designed."

5. Design of the Control System—". . . it is necessary to identify the ways in which it [systems] may be deficient, to design procedures for detecting its deficiencies, and for correcting the system so as to remove or reduce them."

The focus of the structured analysis and design philosophy must therefore be on the decision-making, reporting, and transaction processing networks of the firm. Special emphasis must be given to those decisions that are critical to

---

[6] Ibid.

the firm's success. Eventually all system expenditures will be justified by management's decision-making, reporting, and transaction processing needs.

The cost/benefit element of our approach to systems analysis and design is perhaps the most important aspect of the structured approach. Every expenditure should result in some identifiable benefit to the organization. All programs and activities, including information processing, should be coordinated by a steering committee or top management to achieve the organization's goals. As we have already emphasized, this will not happen by chance; an integrated master plan is needed, and it is the role of the steering committee or top management to oversee this plan.

The structured approach presented in this and in the next chapter will integrate both of the general approaches. It starts with the definition of the problem. It is then followed by a logical analysis of what must be done to solve the problem. The problem definition and the subsequent analysis may begin with an analysis of decisions or it may begin with an analysis of existing systems which are not meeting the requirements of management. Only after a logical analysis can the designer of an accounting information system begin to determine how to design a system. And only after it is designed can it be successfully implemented.

Not following this structured sequence which starts with the logical thought process and concludes in the physical design and implementation would be like a contractor building a structure without considering its use, without developing plans and without using blueprints to build it. The result would be a structure poorly built and not designed to meet the requirements of the users. It is essential that the analysis and design procedure be well organized and follow a structured approach, whether it be for a building, a bridge, or for an accounting information system. If it does not, all kinds of problems can result. In practice, many accounting systems have failed because their designers failed to follow such a structured approach or one of the alternative procedures outlined in the next chapter, which are designed to expedite some of the structured approach's steps.

Steering Committee and Project Teams

There must be a master plan for any systems definition and analysis. To develop a master plan, management must participate in, understand, and render full support to the structured approach. Strong consideration must be given to the factors that affect the social environment of the organization in the physical design and implementation of information systems. Organizational, behavioral, and decision-making concepts are extremely important. For this reason, the accountant or systems analyst should not attempt to change or modify the management system and supporting information system without the active participation of management. Chapter 3 emphasized the need for this cooperation. Typically, consideration of the organizational behavior and decision-making concepts is done by a top-level *steering committee* which guides the planning, development, and implementation of systems. Members of this committee should include top management and other managers with relevant experience, as outlined in Chapter 3. Moreover, the members must have (1) knowledge of strategic, managerial, and operational plans to assess a project's compliance with these plans; (2) objectivity in assessing corporate priorities; and (3) considerable experience.[7]

Perhaps the best way to alleviate many of the problems cited in Chapter 3, and to satisfy many of the decision-making requirements cited in Chapter 4, is to involve all the key personnel who will be affected by the system. This *project team* will consist of a key representative of top management (for support and direction), the managers who will eventually use the information to make decisions and issue reports, the controller, the manager of information systems, technical advisers (operations research, IS, training, and accountants, for example), and, if feasible, the firm's independent auditors. As a matter of practice, these individuals may send their representatives to routine meetings, but they must themselves be involved in all key decisions if the systems development and implementation process is to be successful. In larger organizations these teams will probably report to the steering committee.

In summary, all parties who are involved in the decision-making and reporting process supported by the system must participate in its analysis, design, and implementation phases. Moreover, all phases must have top management support. A steering committee and the project team must lay a foundation for the systems analysis and design phases.

Systems Boundaries

Before one can even start with the structured analysis and design of a system, the *boundaries* of the system of subsystem under review must be defined. The boundaries of the firm's accounting information system, the management (decision-making) system, and the environment must be specified. The boundaries between the environment and the accounting information and decision systems were discussed in Chapter 2 and 4; we will focus on boundaries between accounting information systems in this chapter.

Since the object of systems design should be to structure a well-planned and coordinated system, attention must be given to the procedures for *factoring* the firm's system into manageable modules or subsystems. If each subsystem, its associated boundaries, and the resulting interfaces are not identified and clearly defined, coordination of the resulting subsystems will be difficult. Figure 12-2, for example, shows that sales will interface with all other subsystems of the firm. As can be seen in the figure, the number of interfaces increases geometrically with the number of subsystems. Design problems can quickly become unmanageable.

The tightly linked system shown at the top of Figure 12-2 is said to be tightly *coupled*. It requires precise coordination for all factors or components to operate efficiently. The system can be simplified, however, by *clustering* the marketing subsystems and the production subsystems, as illustrated at the bottom of Figure 12-2. Close coordination can be maintained within each cluster, but not between a subsystem of one cluster and that of another cluster. There will be *one* interface between clusters. Clustering, therefore, results in *decoupling*. Sales, for example, will no longer be tightly coordinated with inventory; sales will be loosely coordinated with production activities via the marketing-production cluster interface.

---

[7] Biggs, Birks, and Atkins, *Managing the Systems Development Process*, p. 51.

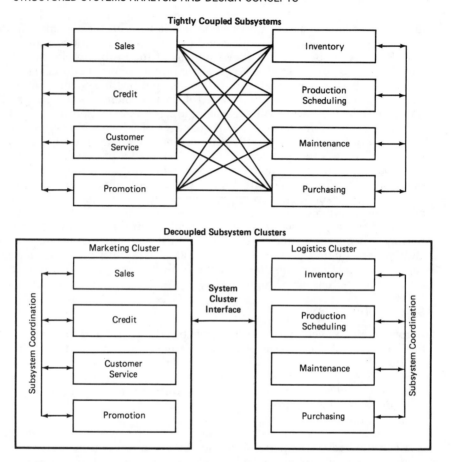

FIGURE 12-2 Tightly coupled subsystems and decoupled subsystem clusters.

In the process of logically defining a system, and in the general design phase, the cost of tight coordination should be compared with the cost of the resources necessary to decouple subsystems as alternatives are considered. This comparison should be made before selecting the final design framework for the proposed system. The cost comparison must, however, also consider the cost of communication hardware and software. The firm's accounting system can be used as the focal point for each cluster interface. Therefore, either the planning and budgeting system or the transaction processing system, with its various reports and files, can serve as a reasonable structure upon which to build an interface between organizational units. Profitability and responsibility accounting systems with their accompanying data organization structures also can serve as a basis for clustering various functions within the organization.

In summary, the system will need to be factored into subsystems so that the scope of the analysis and design process will be manageable. Each subsystem must be clearly defined. The systems analysis and design activities must further

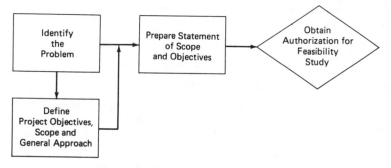

FIGURE 12-3   Problem definition.

describe the boundaries as well as the specification of requirements, decoupling resources, and interfaces with all subsystems.

Problem Definition

The first phase in structured analysis and design is the recognition and subsequent definition of the problem. It is essential that management monitor its accounting information system to determine changing requirements and the need for new information or modifications in existing information. In other words the problem, in many cases an opportunity, must be identified as shown in Figure 12-3.

Once a problem is identified it must be brought to the attention of management, or if the organization is large enough, the steering committee. This is done, as shown in Figure 12-3, by the initiating agent (users, managers, IS personnel or the steering committee itself). The person or group needs to then define the project's objective, scope, and general approach as shown in Figure 12-4. For example, a manufacturer of patio furniture (called Patio Furniture) has been experiencing excessive inventory buildups between departments. They manufacture their own line as well as house brands for large department stores. The production superintendent prepares a statement of scope and objectives for the organization's information systems committee. A projects' scope is defined as those subsystems in an organization affected by the project and its expected cost. This committee consists of the IS manager, who is an assistant controller; the controller; the marketing manager; and the manufacturing vice-president. The statement looks like the one in Figure 12-4. The project is titled Work in Process Inventory. The general problem which needs resolving is excess in-process inventory. The objectives are to reduce costs, eliminate clutter, and conserve space by reducing inventory levels. The superintendent estimates that cutting back on inventory would save the organization in excess of $90,000 over three years. She has read that good material requirement planning systems are available for personal computers and thinks that such a system may do the job effectively. She is willing to spend at least $7,000 to investigate the feasibility of such a system. She believes that the initial scope of the project should be limited to those that affect work in process inventory. This investigation could be accomplished in a month by a project team consisting of an analyst, an accountant,

---

STATEMENT OF SCOPE AND OBJECTIVES: March 21, 1990

The Project:	Work in Process Inventory
The Problem:	Excessive Inventory between Departments
Project Objectives:	Reduce Inventory Levels to a Minimum.
Project Scope:	The cost should not exceed the cost of the capital tied up in inventory over a 3-year period; this is $90,000. It should be linked to those systems that affect work in process inventory.
Preliminary Ideas:	Microcomputer Material Requirements Planning System
Feasibility Study:	One-month feasibility study using a project team consisting of a systems analyst, a staff accountant, and an industrial engineer will cost $7,000.

FIGURE 12-4   Objective, scope, and general approach to the problem.

and an industrial engineer. This report is than analyzed in light of the overall objectives of the organization with respect to its information system.

Feasibility Study

Given the initial description of the scope and nature of the problem, management or the steering committee acting on the behalf of management will authorize a feasibility study like the one illustrated in Figure 12-5. This may be done by a small project team, systems analyst, or a member of the controller's staff, depending on the organization. In this illustration it would be the project team. The feasibility study is a brief overview of the entire analysis and design process. Management simply wants to know if there is a feasible solution to the problem and that it is likely to be cost beneficial.

Assuming management adopts the structured analysis approach, the project team, analyst, or accountant must acquire a complete understanding of not only the firm's objectives, policies, and resources but also the nature of the business in which the firm is operating. This is most important if the feasibility study is being conducted by a consulting firm or a CPA firm. Environmental questions such as the following should be examined to assess the critical decisions, reports, and transaction flows:

1. What are the organization's structural, behavioral, and decision-making characteristics?
2. What are the firm's objectives?
3. Who are the customers and how can they be characterized demographically?
4. What are the products and how are they distributed with regard to sales and types of customers?

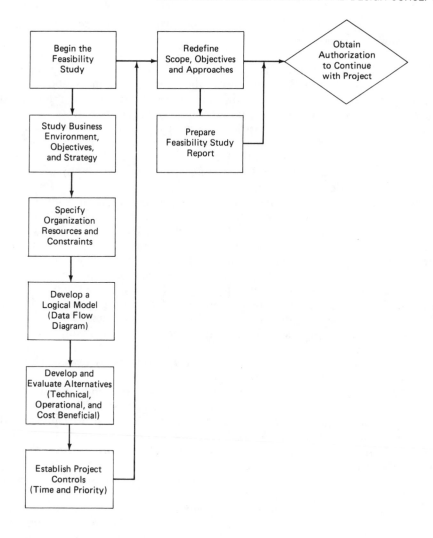

FIGURE 12-5   Feasibility study.

5. What are the firm's market characteristics, such as competition and price elasticity?

6. What is the demand forecast?

7. What are the firm's resources, such as capital, goods, personnel, customer goodwill, research capabilities, reputation, and financial management?

8. How are these resources being used and allocated?

9. What are management's policies?

10. What is the firm's interface with government and regulatory agencies?

11. What factors are critical to success, given the nature of the firm and the business environment?

From this analysis, the organizational and resource constraints can be specified. In the example for Patio Furniture, the project team must understand the manufacturing and marketing organization and how they interface during order processing. They must know the nature of the market and the product. They must know what is important to the success of the business, e.g., quality, customer service or product line breadth. Moreover, an understanding of organizational policies and resources is critical.

Next the team working on the feasibility study must study the nature of the problem in more depth. They must understand what must be done, for example, to cut work in process inventory. To gain this understanding they must do some fact finding to follow up on the expressed need for modification or revision of the system. Interviews must be conducted with top and middle managers who initiated the request and who will be affected by any change. The fact-finding interviews should clarify the problems, the information needs, the organizational units affected, the current procedures used to provide the information, and the relationship between the proposed project and the long-range goals of the organization. Often at this stage it is useful to study the existing system to determine what is currently done to deal with the information problems. This may or may not involve flowcharting the existing system as described in Chapter 8.

Next they must develop a high-level logical model of the system to describe what must be accomplished by the new or revised system. Such a model helps determine the major user requirements.

Data flow diagrams like those outlined in Chapter 8 and illustrated in Figure 12-6 are typically used for this high-level logical model. This model should indicate output objectives, input sources, all transaction processing and decision-making activities and data needed to support these activities. This model will enable management and the project team, analyst, or controller to better discuss the problem with management and refine the possible solutions to the problem. It should be augmented by consideration of organizational, environmental, and technological implications.

Consider again Patio Furniture's production schedule decision, which involves the in-process inventory problem noted earlier. The project team decided to enlarge the scope of the problem because it was determined that the inventory problem was most likely related to production scheduling. The team concluded that Patio Furniture produced products to order as well as for forecasted demand because of the seasonal nature of the product and the need to smooth production effort throughout the year.

Customer and economic information comprised much of their data source. From the economic information they prepared a sales forecast (see Figure 12-6). As customer orders came in, they processed orders by first checking finished goods stock. If the goods were in stock, they established a shipping date. Based on jobs in process, material inventory, assembly specifications, finished goods, shipping information such as required delivery dates, and the overall sales forecast, optimal production runs and schedules are prepared. From this decision and its output information, shipping dates are designated, production depart-

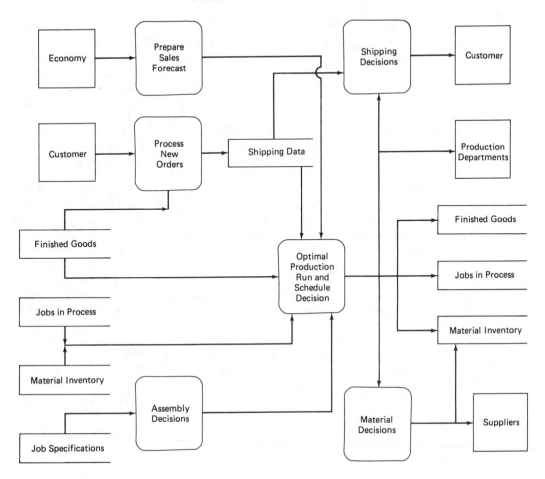

FIGURE 12-6 Data flow diagram production schedule.

ments are issued scheduling assignments, and material requisitions are prepared for needed material not in stock. Moreover, finished goods, jobs-in-process, and material inventory information is updated to reflect projected changes in stock levels for the next production run and order processing decision.

This logical model does not specify any method of processing, data storage mode, decision-making frequency, or reporting frequency. Nor does it specify any equipment requirements. It only describes *what* must be done in terms of the information.

From this logical model, alternative proposals can be developed to solve the problem. These proposals are tentative and are used to determine if there is a feasible solution to the problem before a full-scale analysis and design process is initiated. These proposals must be technically feasible in terms of hardware, software and personnel. They must be operationally feasible in terms of the organization's other activities and behavioral constraints. They must also be economically feasible in terms of a rough cost-benefit analysis. For example, given the scope of the job, it is economically infeasible for Patio Furniture to consider a large mainframe computer for its material requirements planning system.

Also before any study commences, project controls—such as projected times, project task analysis, personnel assignment and workload analysis, and project status reports—must also be formalized to help manage the system development project. These plans will be useful for checking compliance with design schedules, assessing staff requirements, and determining project check points, which evolve as development progresses.

Finally after this study the scope, objectives, and the various approaches to the project are revised in light of the new information obtained during the feasibility study. In the case of Patio Furniture the scope has been enlarged to include the entire scheduling system and not just the work in-process inventory problem. The estimated total savings is now in the neighborhood of $200,000 and not $90,000. Top management generally through the steering committee, must be informed of these changes to the scope, objectives, benefits, and general nature and cost of the project. Particular attention must be given to the boundaries of the system and the interfaces with other systems. Deadlines and priorities should be detailed with respect to completion of various phases of the project. Techniques such as PERT may be useful for scheduling. PERT is described in this context in the appendix of Chapter 13. Moreover, the project's objectives need to be reconciled with the long-range objectives of the organization. Often the steering committee must help with the reconciliation.

Concluding this set of steps, a feasibility study report is prepared by the project team, analyst, or consultant. Authorization to continue the project is then obtained based on this report.

Analysis

Management must next determine *what* must be done to solve the problem through a detailed analysis of the situation, such as that shown in Figure 12-7. This stage of the decision analysis approach requires an analysis of the management decision-making activities, the transaction processing requirements, and the reporting requirements of the firm as suggested by Ackoff earlier in the chapter. This analysis requires the organization of a project team and the commitment of resources by management to perform the necessary analysis of the problem. To accomplish this, decision-making processes or activities must be identified, information requirements for the process must be specified, and the characteristics of each type of information must be spelled out. A study of the existing system may aid in a general understanding of what decisions must be made, the transactions involved, and the reports that must be generated. Inputs such as documents, records, files, and data, as well as characteristics such as volume, media, origin, and location of this input, should be identified.

In general, the following analysis must be made:

1. Major decision-making process and activities

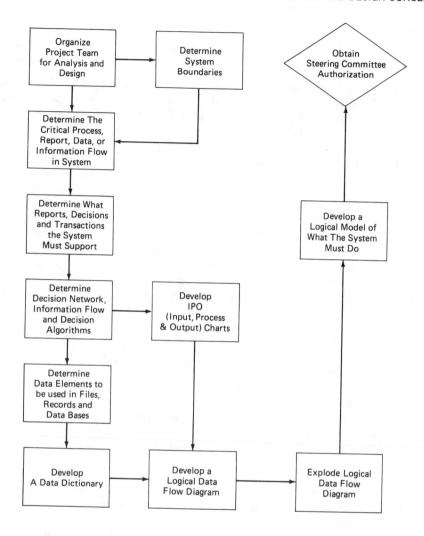

FIGURE 12-7   Analysis.

2. Information requirements for these decisions
3. Information generated by decisions
4. Other reporting requirements
5. Transaction records necessary to support both information and reporting requirements
6. Sensitivity analysis of information requirements
7. Aggregation requirements
8. Timing requirements

9. Economic analysis
10. Model specifications
11. Data source specifications

From an analysis of these requirements, a logical model of what the new or revised system must do is developed for use in the subsequent design stages. The system boundaries may be redefined in light of the feasibility study as illustrated earlier. The critical (most important to the success of the organization) processes, reports, data, and information flows are determined. The other reports, decisions, and transactions the system must support are likewise determined. These may be beyond the boundaries of the system being designed. A logical information flow, from sources, through various decision-making, reporting, and transaction processing steps, to destinations, must be determined. This is done by using techniques such as high-level data flow diagrams to describe this flow, such as that illustrated in Figure 12-6 in the initial feasibility study.

Often it is helpful to analyze each processing activity using an input-processing-output (IPO) chart to describe what is done at each processing node in the decision-making, reporting, and transaction processing network. From this, data elements can be determined and organized into files, records, and databases depending on their characteristics as described in the chapter on databases. Often the data are described using a data dictionary, which is simply a description of the various characteristics of the data, where the data elements come from, and where they are used. Much of this is generally captured in a data flow diagram to describe to management what the system must do, and it is used as the basis for design. Often each process in the data flow diagram is exploded (described in more detail) for the system designers to develop controls, refine data requirements, and possibly write programs for the various processes.

This analysis usually includes a minimum set of objectives for the proposed or modified system to provide a base for the design. All alternative designs, whether developed in the organization by writing programs or purchased from various vendors, must meet these minimum requirements.

For a better understanding of these activities, consider again the production scheduling network in the data flow diagram in Figure 12-6. The key decision is the preparation of the production schedule. This is what must be done by the system. The sales forecast for routine production of stock products, the processing of customers orders and the assembly sequence provides the basis for production decisions, shipping decisions, and the material ordering decisions. In general, the sources of information for this processing network consists of customer orders, economic information for forecasting customer demand, the specifications related to each job or product manufactured, and the status of the various inventories. Output generally consists of a report to the production department on what to produce and when, orders for raw material to be sent to suppliers, shipping information to customers, and an update of the various inventory status records. All this comprises the overall decision network and the information flows within the network. It should be noted that the information output from one process is often the input to the next decision, report, or transaction.

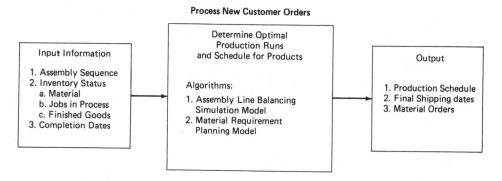

FIGURE 12-8   Input-process-output (IPO) chart.

In Figure 12-8 an IPO (input-processing-output) chart is illustrated for the key decision. It describes the algorithms used by management for decision making and the necessary input for these algorithms. It also describes the output from the algorithms. These charts are useful in describing the nature, frequency, and volumes of information which must flow through the system and be stored in the database.

Sensitivity analysis is often useful to analyze these flows and their frequency. One decision may be very insensitive to daily fluctuations, such as the sales forecast which is used to produce finished goods which are in general demand. Thus the volume and frequency of information here will be low. On the other hand, the scheduling decision must be made daily based on new orders, stock levels, material availability, shipping requirements, assembly sequences, and current work in process inventory. All this information should be incorporated into the IPO chart and its related data dictionary.

Figure 12-9 illustrates an example of a data dictionary, which describes the characteristics of the data stored in the materials inventory database. As can be seen in Figure 12-9, the data structure, which is a key component of a data dictionary, includes the part number, name, the number of units on hand, the number on order, and the lead time for shipping. Moreover, there is an indication of the part number's relation to sales, to products using a specification file and to vendors using a vendor file. These relations are typical in a database in a material requirement planning system. Note that each item listed in the structure is followed by a field size and data type code. These illustrations are typical of microcomputer software and the methods used to describe data about data, i.e., a data dictionary.

Flow charts, called hierarchy charts of the decision network, are helpful in assessing what must be done and how to arrange program modules and their interfaces. An example is shown in Figure 12-10. For example, the overall schedule is a function of the sales forecast, new orders, and the assembly decision. This schedule then impacts shipping decisions and material requisition decisions as shown. All of this comprises the overall production scheduling process.

NAME	PART NUMBER (10 N)	NAME (25 C)	UNITS ON HANDS (5 N)	QUANTITY ON ORDER (5 N)	COST (7.2 N)	LEAD TIME (5 N)
SOURCE	Inventory	Inventory	Sales & Receiving	Calculated	Vendor	Historical Vendor Information
USE	Sales Product Specification (Manufacturing) Vendor Selection (Purchasing)	Sales Product Specification (Manufacturing) Vendor Selection (Purchasing)	Sales Product Specification (Manufacturing) Vendor Selection (Purchasing)	Product Specification (Manufacturing) Vendor Selection (Purchasing)	Product Specification (Manufacturing) Vendor Selection (Purchasing)	Product Specification (Manufacturing) Vendor Selection (Purchasing)

FIGURE 12-9 Data dictionary.

In addition, matrices which show all the input down the left-hand column and output across the top, with an X where each input is used in an output, are frequently used to describe the flow of information between various sources and destinations. These may be useful for summarizing the detail presented in the IPO charts and the data dictionary. They are quite useful in the design phases which follow because the project team can get a good overview of the data required by the system.

Systems Evaluation and Operational Review

Even though this chapter is primarily concerned wtih the problem definition and analysis phases, the entire feedback evaluation structure is presented here. Various phases in the analysis and design process can be periodically audited or continually monitored by management, the controller's department, the IS organization, or the steering committee. This monitoring and audit process is often referred to as an operational review.[8] An operational review includes an assessment of performance and an identification of opportunities for improvement.

A regular schedule is suggested for such a review, but the need will clearly be a function of organizational circumstances. Certain situations will dictate examination of isolated check points in the systems analysis and design life cycle. Check points are those critical objectives which must be satisfied to go on to the next phase such as operational feasibility. The following are examples of situations noted by the AICPA:

1. Excessive costs of IS services
2. A major shift in corporate strategy or organization

---

[8] See American Institute of Certified Public Accountants, a Management Advisory Services Special Report, *Operational Review of the Electronic Data Processing Function* (New York: copyright 1978 AICPA), for a complete discussion.

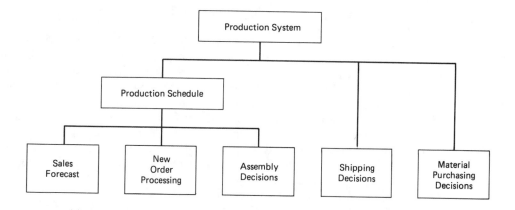

FIGURE 12-10 Production system hierarchy chart.

3. A major hardware or software upgrade or acquisition proposal
4. An inability to attract and retain competent IS executives
5. A new IS executive's need for an intensive assessment
6. An inordinate amount of personnel turnover within the IS department
7. A proposal to consolidate or distribute IS resources
8. Major systems that appear unresponsive to needs or are difficult to enhance or maintain
9. An excessive or increasing number of user complaints[9]

In other words, when a system ceases to be effective and efficient, an operational review is in order. The objective of the review is to determine which objectives are no longer being met. This is tantamount to a definition of a problem which can be further defined in phase 1. The scope of the review may involve the whole spectrum of controls noted in Chapter 11; a major systems operations including input, processing, storage and output activities; IS operations including hardware and software; or systems development policies. At the other extreme, the scope may be limited to a small subset of any of these activities. Thus an operational review may lead to either a modification or a complete revision of the system.

A feedback loop linked to the structured approach in Figure 12-1 will help in the review process. Management need only examine the criteria used in each step to develop the system to find those aspects of the system that do not comply with the effectiveness and efficiency guidelines. For example, does the old system still provide management with needed information. In other cases the impetus for the change may come from a manager of a user department. Such a letter should contain (1) a definition of the problem; (2) the objectives of the modification; (3) the expected economic and operational, managerial, and stra-

---

[9] Ibid.

tegic decision-making benefits; and (4) the subset of the organization that will be affected by the proposed change.

Sometimes only minor modification will be required to comply with the objectives of the system and the structured approach can be shortened considerably. As an illustration of this situation, many organizations require that requests from management for system changes be initially routed to the systems department to determine if the proposed modification can be achieved by a simple enhancement such as an additional terminal for the existing system.[10] In other situations the entire system will have to be redesigned and the complete structured approach will need to be used. Even though the structured approach is often shortened because of the nature of the modification, the concept of the structured approach remains intact because the overall framework for the system and most of the objectives are not changed by the modification.

For example, if the production decision network no longer satisfies specific management needs, a minor modification, such as a report design simplification and addition of a tape drive, may satisfy the need for more understandable reports and increased model specification storage requirements. In this case the basic set of decisions, logic, and information network remain effective and efficient. On the other hand, if the firm acquires a new product line that requires continual rescheduling of production to serve customers in the new market, it is likely that most of the objective criteria will not be satisfied because the old system is no longer effective. Under these conditions the firm must redesign the entire system using the structured approach. To add to the old system would probably result in an ineffective and inefficient system because the nature of the business has undergone a substantial change. A new system scheduling algorithm may be much more complex and may even provide "what if" feedback for sales personnel so that customers can be informed of the status of orders. The new system may be interactive rather than batch, and the level of support the information system gives the management system (decision maker) may change from data and prediction-inference to a decision-support system as discussed in Chapter 4.

SUMMARY

In order to analyze and design an effective and efficient accounting information system, it is imperative that a structured approach be followed. The definition and analysis phases must precede the design and implementation phases outlined in the next chapter. The problem must be defined. The economic, technical, and operational feasibility must be assessed. What must be done to solve the problem must be determined through a careful systems analysis.

All this must be done before the project team can decide how to design and implement the new or revised system. In addition the entire process must fit the overall master information system plan for the organization.

---

[10] Biggs, Birks, and Atkins, *Managing the Systems Development Process.*

APPENDIX

SHARED DATA ENVIRONMENT—ANALYSIS AND DESIGN

In a database environment where many applications share a common database, the analysis becomes more basic and entails the data and the database management system for the entire organization.[11] These systems must be designed around what data are required for many current as well as future applications. Thus the project team or the steering committee must carefully analyze the data requirements of the entire operation which will ultimately use the database. A centralized data dictionary is needed. Careful attention must be given to data *objects* such as equipment, inventory, and cash; *events* such as sale, purchase and cash receipt; *agents* such as employee, customer, and owner; and the potential *relationships* of these entities. A database must be conceived which will enable managers to establish relationships between events and their impact on objects and agents. An example would be the sale of merchandise. This event involves relationships between inventory, cash or accounts receivable, the customer, and the owner. Entity-relationship diagrams, such as those in the appendix to Chapter 10, can be drawn. These can be used to analyze what must be done by the accounting system to satisfy management's transaction processing, reporting, and decision-making needs. These then can be used to construct a common database which may be used by many. It may be flexible enough to enable end users to analyze their own needs and write their own programs to access the database using the database reporting and file manipulation software.

As a result end users such as managers, engineers, and accountants can analyze and design much of their own software to satisfy their needs. The structured approach is and should still be followed, however. The nature of the shared database and its related software for end-user usage is still determined using the structured approach and the users who use it should still assess their requirements before designing (writing) their reports or software to access the information on the database.

SELECTED REFERENCES

ACKOFF, RUSSELL L., "Management Misinformation Systems," *Management Science*, 14, no. 4 (December 1967), B147–56.

AMERICAN INSTITUTE OF CERTIFIED PUBLIC ACCOUNTANTS, *Guidelines for Development and Implementation of Computer-Based Application Systems*, Management Advisory Services Guideline Series Number 4. New York: AICPA, 1976.

———, *Operational Review of the Electronic Data Processing Function*, Management Advisory Services Special Report. New York: AICPA, 1978.

---

[11] See William E. McCarthy, "An Entity-Relationship View of Accounting Models," *The Accounting Review*, October 1979, pp. 667–86; and William E. McCarthy, "The REA Accounting Model: A Generalized Framework for Accounting Systems in a Shared Data Environment," *The Accounting Review*, July 1982, pp. 554–78.

BIGGS, CHARLES L., EVAN G. BIRKS, and WILLIAM ATKINS, *Managing the Systems Development Process.* Englewood Cliffs, N.J.: Prentice Hall, 1980.

BORTHICK, A. FAYE, and JAMES H. SCHEINER, "Selection of Small Business Computer Systems: Structuring a Multi-Criteria Approach," *The Journal of Information Systems*, 3, no. 1 (Fall 1988).

BROWN, ROBERT M., and BERNADETTE RUF, "Applying Software Design Principles to Accounting Software: A Direct Approach," *The Journal of Information Systems*, 4, no. 1 (Fall 1989).

DAVIS, WILLIAM S., *Systems Analysis and Design: a Structured Approach:* Addison-Wesley, Reading, Mass.: 1983.

GREER, WILLIS R., and HOWARD ROCKNESS, "Management Decision Support Systems for a Medical Group Practice," *The Journal of Information Systems*, 1, no. 2 (Spring 1987).

GROSSMAN, THEODORE, and SHAILENDRA PALVIA, "The Design and Implementation of a Multidimensional Retail Merchandising Information System," *The Journal of Information Systems*, 3, no. 1 (Fall 1988).

KING, WILLIAM R., and DAVID I. CLELAND. "The Design of Management Information Systems: An Information Analysis Approach," *Management Science*, 22 (November 1975), 286–97.

MCCARTHY, WILLIAM E. "Accounting Information Systems: Research Directions and Perspective," *The Journal of Information Systems*, 2, no. 1 (Fall 1987).

———"An Entity-Relationship View of Accounting Models," *The Accounting Review*, October 1979, pp. 667–86.

———"The REA Accounting Model: A Generalized Framework for Accounting Systems in a Shared Data Environment," *The Accounting Review*, July 1982, pp. 554–78.

MARSHALL, GEORGE R., *Systems Analysis and Design: Alternative Structured Approaches*, Englewood Cliffs, N.J.: Prentice Hall, 1986.

MERCURIO, V. J., B. F. MEYERS, A. M. NISBET, and G. RADIN, "AD/Cycle Strategy and Architecture," *IBM Systems Journal*, 29, no. 2 (1990), pp. 120–88.

ROCKART, JOHN F., "Chief Executives Define Their Own Data Needs," *Harvard Business Review*, March–April 1979, pp. 81–93.

SENA, JAMES A., and LAWRENCE M. SMITH, "Designing and Implementing an Integrated Job Cost Accounting System," *The Journal of Information Systems*, 1, no. 1 (Fall 1986).

WAGNER, G. R., "The Future of Corporate Planning and Modeling Software Systems." Paper presented at the Conference on Corporate Planning Models at Duke University, June 1981.

WHITTEN, JEFFREY L., LONNIE D. BENTLEY, and VICTOR M. BARLOW, *Systems Analysis and Design Methods*, 2nd ed. Homewood, Ill: Richard D. Irwin, 1989.

WILKINSON, JOSEPH W., "Specifying Management's Information Needs," *Cost and Management*, 48 (September–October 1974), 7–13.

WONG-ON-WING, BERNARD, "User Involvement in Systems Development: An Attributional Approach," *The Journal of Information Systems*, 2, no. 2 (Spring 1988).

YOURDON, EDWARD, and CONSTANTINE, LARRY L. *Structured Design*, Englewood Cliffs, N.J.: Prentice Hall, 1979.

REVIEW QUESTIONS

1. List the structured analysis and design phases and indicate which are considered part of analysis and which are considered part of design and implementation. Indicate what must be done for each phase and indicate how it can be done and ultimately implemented?

2. What problems can arise from an inap-

propriate use of the evolutionary approach to systems analysis and design?

3. Define an effective and an efficient information system.

4. What is the most important aspect of every phase of the structured approach?

5. What is the steering committee and what members of the management team typically make up a steering committee?

6. What is the project team and who typically participates on a project team?

7. What does a tightly coupled system require and how can clustering alleviate problems encountered by tightly coupled systems?

8. What is a feasibility study and what three types of feasibility are important in consideration of potential feasible alternative solutions to the problem?

9. Why are data flow diagrams used in the feasibility study to define major user requirements?

10. Briefly note the major tasks in the analysis phase of a structured analysis and design approach to systems development.

11. What flow chart or diagram technique is more appropriate to use in the analysis

phase and why? What is an IPO chart and how can it be used in this phase?

12. List several situations which may prompt management to review their accounting information system.

13. What costs are associated with integrated systems that are tightly coupled? How can these costs be reduced?

14. What is the basic philosophy behind the structured approach to analysis and design?

15. How can a firm's controller monitor a system to ensure compliance with the firm's decision needs and economic objectives?

16. Give several examples of environmental considerations for systems definition and further analysis. Why is each important in the context of a management (decision) system supported by an information system?

17. What pitfall is involved in starting the definition of a system with an analysis of the current system?

18. Are there other system development procedures? How do they differ and how are they the same as the structured approach?

CASES

12-1 Parker Drugs has engaged your firm in an analysis and design project involving the processing of prescription drugs in the pharmacy. In the analysis phase, you determine the following from a review of the old system and your discussions with management.

1. Parker Drugs maintains a drug inventory file, a patient record and receivable file, and a purchase order file. They all comply with state regulations.

2. Upon receipt of a prescription from a customer, the pharmacist must first determine, from inventory records, that the drug is in stock. If it is out of stock, the pharmacist orders a new supply from the pharmaceutical company. Further, if it is out of stock the pharmacist checks an alternate drug listing. If there is an alterna-

tive, it is used; if not, the customer is advised to consult their doctor.

3. If it is in stock or there is a suitable alternative, the pharmacist then checks the patient's records for drug incompatibility. If it is incompatible, the customer is advised to consult their doctor.

4. If it is compatible, the patient's records are updated, the prescription is filled using the data in the drug inventory file, the drugs are dispensed to the customer, and inventory records are updated to reflect the appropriate reduction in stock.

5. When drugs are received from a supplier such as one of the pharmaceutical companies, they are verified by checking them against the shipping lists and purchase

orders. Then they are added to stock and inventory is updated.

6. When a customer purchases on credit, it is entered when the details of the purchase are entered in the patient records. When payments are received, they are also entered into the patient records.

REQUIRED: Prepare a data flow diagram as part of your analysis of Parker Drugs pharmacy operations.

12-2 Visual Image Corporation of Monterey, California, manufactures and sells projection equipment, scanners and plotters for the microcomputer industry. Their equipment is compatible with most of the major microcomputers on the market today. Most sales are made through regional offices located in Atlanta, Boston, Philadelphia, St. Louis, Dallas, Denver, and San Francisco. Some sales are made directly to large microcomputer chains and large corporate customers.

All manufacturing is done in a single plant near Monterey. The plant is highly automated. There are several departments through which products pass. Many of the electronic components are purchased from outside vendors; these are costly and every effort is made to keep these inventories low yet sufficient so as not to halt production. The plant also has several support departments. They are engineering, maintenance, quality control, scheduling, and cost accounting. Research and development, which is also located at the plant site, assists with many technical problems.

As a result of these needs and the exponential growth of the microcomputer industry, Visual Image purchased an advanced computer system in 1984 and installed it in early 1985. This new machine was to handle all the processing for the plant as well as for all the regional sales offices. Management felt that such centralization would enhance the coordination efforts of marketing, production, and research. Prior to this time the regional sales managers, plant manager, and the manager of R&D had considerable authority to run their own operations and prepare their own plans. These plans followed the general guidelines from top management. A new MIS manager was charged with the responsibility of implementing this

new computer. He had complete authority, moreover, to purchase the software necessary to support all the sales, production, and research functions of the organization.

During the implementation of the new system in 1985, the analysts who worked for the MIS manager reviewed all the functions and redesigned the entire information system for Visual Image. The planning and control system was centralized. The scheduling was keyed to regional sales' decisions to reduce finished goods inventory. An on-line inquiry system was installed so that regional sales representatives could see exactly what was about to be shipped or, for larger customers, where their particular order happened to be in the manufacturing process. All plant employees now key into CRTs, located on the plant floor, their detailed activities. Material and parts were scheduled tightly so that excess stock is not sitting around. An automatic purchase order system was installed to order quantities of parts when they got too low and when they were needed for future production runs.

The president of Visual Image Corporation is very pleased with the new system. He stated that the new system should solve all their problems and make their company the most cost efficient producer in the market.

A recent conversation between Bob Johns, the sales manager in San Francisco, and Howard Black, the plant manager, went like this:

Johns: You never produce enough plotters. Our orders are uneven and the forecasts generated by the new system never seem to even come close to the demand fluctuation we have for the product. Our market is quite competitive and customers are much more sensitive to product features and availability than they are to marginal cost differences. A $100 difference in a $2,700 color plotter just doesn't matter as much as its features and availability.

Black: Yes, I know the new system doesn't allow for much slack. We have the same problem. The supply of microchips and other electronic components is so sporadic that we often have to deviate from the schedule to keep employees working when parts don't arrive as expected.

Johns: I understand, but you don't even produce enough of the scanners. I know the parts for those are plentiful. You know, I liked the old system better where we had some authority to make our own decisions and coordinate our own efforts.

Black: I agree; sometimes I feel like a droid obeying the master computer. I've been thinking about quitting and working for Color Plotters, Inc., where they let their plant manager really manage their facilities and they don't worry so much about spending a few dollars extra on their high-tech products.

REQUIRED: Explain what went wrong with their new system which sounds so good and why the new system has not solved all the problems as the president seems to think. In your explanation consider both analysis and behavioral issues. Could these problems have been foreseen during a feasibility study?

12-3 Bio Tech Industries uses a large database system. The software has been developed to generate statistics on a wide variety of company activities for management to use in decision making. These statistics include inventory status, customer order status, pricing and product specification information, competitor prices and product specifications, economic forecasts, financial statements, manufacturing specifications, sales statistics, cost statistics for each department, and research and development expenditures.

Management has been comfortable with this information system for some time now. However, the bio tech field has become much more competitive in the last year and management must now concentrate on the profitability of current products and the probable success of new products under development. They don't seem to be able to sort through the mound of statistics to determine this information.

REQUIRED:

1. Does the old system meet the information needs of management? As part of a feasibility study can you, as their accountant, suggest some improvement in the type of decision support system they use to help them meet these new competitive challenges?

2. Suppose the systems you suggest in the feasibility study require a reorganization

from a centralized functional organization form to a division structure in order to respond better to the market. What impact can organizational and behavioral problems have on a systems feasibility?

3. In describing a new system to management prior to the actual design, would you use a system flowchart or a data flow diagram? Why?

12-4 Nashville Recording Company operates a mail-order division. Nashville purchases country music tapes and CDs in volume. The savings are passed on to its country music club members. Club members are solicited via direct mail, newspapers, selected publications, and radio and television advertising. New members are offered six tapes or CDs for five dollars, providing they purchase at least six tapes or CDs during a two-year period. After that they are given a bonus selection on the purchase of four recordings at the regular club price. On occasion, special discounts are offered to club members on slow-moving recordings.

Each month a club member is sent a card stating the monthly selection along with alternative selections. The member indicates on the card whether the regular selection, an alternative, or no selection is desired that month. Upon receipt of this card, Nashville Recording then sends the appropriate selection. No tape or CD is sent unless a card is received; a positive response is required from the customer. The customer may return the recording if it has not been opened.

Your firm has been engaged to design a computerized billing and inventory system.

REQUIRED:

1. What key managerial or operating decisions will influence the success of the firm?

2. How can a computerized billing and inventory system support these decisions?

3. Identify the master data files required to support these decisions.

4. Identify the sources from which these files can be compiled.

5. Prepare a data flow diagram of what must be done in the billing and inventory system.

12-5 Greenway Manufacturing experiences a very seasonal demand for the products in its lawn mower division. Most mowers are purchased in the early spring. Greenway's plant is highly automated, and a large portion of its manufacturing costs are fixed. The labor required is skilled, and training workers is expensive. The current practice in the industry is to sell to distributors, who then either sell or consign merchandise to retail hardware or discount stores. Due to the bulky nature of the product, warehouse costs at either Greenway or its distributors are high.

REQUIRED: You have been engaged to develop a production-scheduling algorithm for Greenway Manufacturing. As part of this assignment, you must specify the interface between production and marketing. What issues are involved?

12-6 Consider again the Wright Manufacturing Company (Case 4-3). From a structured analysis and design perspective, what steps were missing in the initial analysis and subsequent modifications which may have led to the general demise of the system? Would an operational review have helped? How?
(Adapted from the CMA examination.)

12-7 Custom Frames is a small framing shop in State College, Pa. They offer a variety of services to the public including custom matting and framing and the facilities for customers to build their own frames to save on labor. Custom Frames is owned by two individuals who have extensive decorating experience to help customers select the appropriate mats and frames. In addition, they employ eight part-time students during busy times in the evening and on weekends. The majority of their business is cash, although they extend credit to local business customers.

Their inventory currently runs around 300 items. The inventory consists of raw materials used to construct frames, including mats, framing material, and glass. They also carry a line of inexpensive ready-made frames. Construction materials such as glue and nails are expensed as they are purchased. They have found inventory difficult to control because scrap from large mats becomes the raw material

for smaller mats and scrap from framing material is also put to good use in smaller frames. Their other accounting activities are typical of those of most small business.

As an initial step in the analysis, a staff person from your firm prepared the data flow diagram (See Figure C12-1) of their current system in order to gain a perspective on what was done in the way of accounting activities. All accounting records were kept by a local CPA because the owners did not know any accounting. Each time a sale was initiated, the stock was checked for the appropriate raw material. When a particular item became low or when large mats became scarce, the item was added to an order. These accumulated material needs were then sent periodically to the supplier. Orders and sales information were sent to a local CPA for accounting. In addition, receiving information on purchases and payroll information were sent to the CPA for updating Custom Frames' records and issuing checks to employees and suppliers, as shown in the data flow diagram.

The owners of Custom Frames would like to automate their financial operations and stop relying on their CPA to prepare periodic financial statements. They need to know, for example, what is in inventory and what is on order so they don't run out of inventory and can serve customers better. They also have a problem with the placement of duplicate orders because of their lack of records. Prior to each order they actually take a physical count of inventory. They would like to eliminate the cost of the bookkeeping, yet have a system that is so user friendly that they still would have time to serve customer needs. The CPA service is costing them $300 per month. They feel that a new system would be beneficial if it could be purchased and installed for less than $12,000. In their opinion, previously lost sales would make up the difference between the cost savings from eliminating of the CPA write-up service and the cost limit of $12,000 since they would be better able to serve customers. The new system, in their opinion, should handle on-line inventory, accounts receivable, sales order entry and point of sale invoicing, payroll, and accounts payable.

REQUIRED: Prepare a revised statement of scope and objectives for Custom Frames.

Sales Order Entry, Purchasing and Inventory

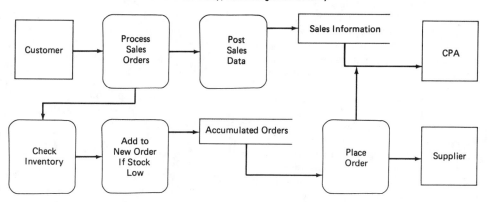

Inventory, Payroll and Cash Disbursements

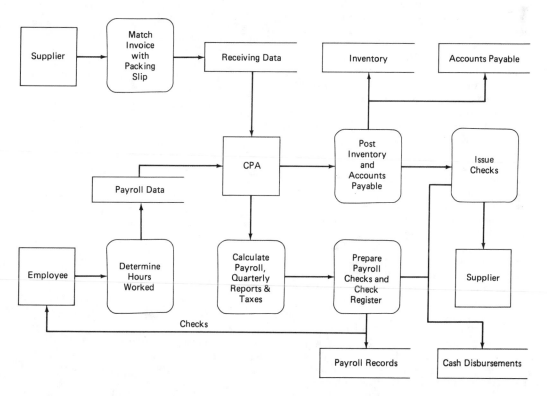

FIGURE C12-1   Custom Frames current system data flow diagram.

12-8   Audio Visual Corporation of Wooster, MA, manufactures and sells visual display equipment. Most sales are made through seven geographical sales offices located in Los Angeles, Seattle, Minneapolis, Cleveland, Dallas, Boston, and Atlanta. Each sales office has a warehouse located nearby to carry an inventory of new equipment and replacement parts. The remaining sales are made through manufacturers' representatives.

Audio Visual's manufacturing operations are conducted in a single plant, which is highly departmentalized. In addition to the assembly department, there are several departments responsible for various components used in the visual display equipment. The plant also has maintenance, engineering, scheduling, and cost accounting departments.

Early in 1989, management decided that its management information system (MIS) needed upgrading. As a result, the company ordered an advanced computer in 1989, and it was installed in July 1990. The main processing equipment is still located at corporate headquarters, and each of the seven sales offices is connected with the main processing unit by remote terminals.

The integration of the new computer into the Audio Visual information system was carried out by the MIS staff. The MIS manager and the four systems analysts who had the major responsibility for the integration were hired by the company in the spring of 1990. The department's other employees—programmers, machine operators, and keypunch operators—have been with the company for several years.

During its early years, Audio Visual had a centralized decision-making organization. Top management formulated all plans and directed all operations. As the company expanded, some of the decision making was decentralized, although the information processing was still highly centralized. Departments had to coordinate their plans with the corporate office, but they had more freedom in developing their sales programs. However, as the company expanded, information problems developed. As a consequence, the MIS department was given the responsibility for improving the company's information processing system when the new equipment was installed.

The MIS analysts reviewed the information system in existence prior to the acquisition of the new computer and identified weaknesses. To overcome the weaknesses, they redesigned old applications and designed new applications. During the eighteen months since the acquisition of the new equipment, the following applications have been redesigned or developed and are now operational: payroll, production scheduling, financial statement preparation, customer billing, raw material usage in production, and finished goods inventory by warehouse. The operating departments of Audio Visual that were affected by the systems changes were rarely consulted or contacted until the system was operational and the new reports had been distributed to the operating departments.

The president of Audio Visual is very pleased with the work of the MIS department. During a recent conversation with an individual who was interested in Audio Visual's new system, the president stated: "The MIS people are doing a good job and I have full confidence in their work. We paid a lot of money for the new equipment and the MIS people certainly cost enough, but the combination of the new equipment and new MIS staff should solve all of our problems."

Recently two additional conversations regarding the computer and information system have taken place. One was between Jerry Adams, plant manager, and Bill Taylor, the MIS manager; the other was between Adams and Terry Williams, the new personnel manager.

TAYLOR–ADAMS CONVERSATION

Adams: Bill, you're trying to run my plant for me. I'm supposed to be the manager, yet you keep interfering. I wish you would mind your own business.

Taylor: You've got a job to do, but so does my department. As we analyzed the information needed for production scheduling and by top management, we saw where improvements could be made in the work flow. Now that the system is operational, you can't reroute work and change procedures because that would destroy the value of the information we're processing. And while I'm on that subject, it's getting to the point where we can't trust the information we're getting from production. The mark-sense cards we receive from production contain a lot of errors.

Adams: I'm responsible for the efficient operation of production. Quite frankly, I think I'm the best judge of production efficiency. The system you installed has reduced my work force and increased the workload of the remaining employees, but I don't see that this has improved anything. In fact, it might explain the high error rate in the cards.

Taylor: This new computer costs a lot of money and I'm trying to be sure that the company gets its money's worth.

Adams–Williams Conversation

Adams: My best production assistant, the one I'm grooming to be a supervisor when the next opening occurs, came to me today and said he was thinking of quitting. When I asked him why, he said he didn't enjoy the work anymore. He's not the only one who is unhappy. The supervisors and department heads no longer have a voice in establishing production schedules. This new computer system has taken away the contribution we used to make to the company planning and direction. We seem to be going way back to the days when top management made all the decisions. I have more production problems now than I used to. I think it boils down to a lack of interest on the part of my management team. I know the problem is within my area, but I think you might be able to help me.

Williams: I have no recommendations for you now but I've had similar complaints from purchasing and shipping. I think we should get your concerns on the agenda for our next plant management meeting.

Required:

1. Apparently the development of and transition to the new computer-based system has created problems among the personnel of Audio Visual Corporation. Identify and briefly discuss the apparent causes of these problems.

2. How could the company have avoided the problems? What steps should be taken to avoid such problems in the future? (Adapted from the CMA examinations.)

12-9 Marine Products, a manufacturer of supplies for the Gulf fishing industry, has a large manufacturing plant near New Orleans and sales offices in many of the port cities along the Gulf of Mexico. The production vice-president, on the advice of top management, plans production runs for a wide variety of fishing gear and other marine supplies. The marketing vice-president conducts all the promotion, distribution, and sales activities. The marketing manager prepares a sales forecast by product line and presents it to top management. Management then adds its input and informs the production vice-president on production requirements. This is done once a year at budget time and has apparently worked well for several years.

As their auditor, however, you have noticed a large increase in inventory and an increase in stockouts. You are aware of an increase in competition from overseas suppliers and of the many improvements in technology in the fishing industry.

They have asked your firm to render some assistance with their inventory problems. Specifically they think that a new computer with on-line access to inventory records will help keep costs down. Marketing personnel will know what is available and thus be able to push items which are overstocked and know when items are in short supply.

Required:

1. What is the problem?

2. How would you proceed to analyze their needs after the problem is specified?

12-10 Channel 7 in Center City, an affiliate of a national television network, broadcasts both local and national shows. The primary source of Channel 7's revenue is spot advertising, and the station's inventory consists of ten-, twenty-, and thirty-second advertising time slots. Management has two primary objectives: to maximize profits and to provide a service to the community.

It is the practice of the industry to place different values on different time slots. A thirty-second commercial, for example, will cost less at 2:00 A.M. than during prime time. Shows with higher ratings command a higher price for their associated commercial time slots than do less popular programs. Moreover, it is the practice of the industry to have a priority system for guaranteeing time slots. A higher price is paid for a ten-second guaranteed slot during the 6:00 P.M. news than for a ten-second slot at the same time that is not guaranteed and may be bumped by another commercial. A commercial may be bumped for another that costs more or by a public service announcement. Because of the diversity in changes in time slots, the station salespeople are constantly trying to obtain the greatest amount of revenue for the array of time slots available.

Currently the station does all the scheduling of commercials and public service announcements by hand using a large PC spreadsheet that eventually becomes a report for the FCC. Records of each time slot's usage must be filed with the FCC, and each customer must have a record of his or her actual commercial time and cost.

Channel 7 must cut off sales one week prior to broadcast time in order to prepare the programming constraints, such as the same time each night for some spots and sufficient time duration between conflicting spots. Due to this time delay, sales that could increase the

station's profits are lost. Moreover, prior to the cutoff, salespeople are often not aware of available time.

REQUIRED: You have been engaged in a problem definition and feasibility study phase of systems analysis to assess the problem Channel 7 is having and to prepare a feasibility study.

1. Prepare a statement of scope and objectives.

2. As part of the feasibility study, describe the general reporting requirements, major decision-making activities, information processing modes, and general hardware and software requirements that may be necessary. Do not do a detailed analysis and system design, a data flow diagram is optional at this stage.

12-11 Citizens' Gas Company, a small gas distribution company, provides natural gas service to approximately 200,000 customers. The customer base is divided into three revenue classes. Data by customer class are as follows:

CLASS	CUSTOMERS	SALES IN CUBIC FEET	REVENUE
Residential	160,000	180 billion	$160 million
Commercial	38,000	15	25
Industrial	2,000	50	65
	200,000	145 billion	$250 million

Residential customer gas usage is primarily for residence heating purposes and consequently is highly correlated to the weather—i.e., temperature. Commercial and industrial customers, on the other hand, may or may not use gas for heating purposes, and consumption is not necessarily correlated to the weather.

The largest twenty-five industrial customers of the 200,000 total account for $30 million of the industrial revenues. Each of these twenty-five customers uses gas for both heating and industrial purposes and has a consumption pattern that is governed almost entirely by

business factors.

The company obtains its gas supply from ten major pipeline companies. The pipeline companies provide gas in amounts specified in contracts that extend over periods ranging from five to fifteen years. For some contracts the supply is in equal monthly increments, while for others the supply varies in accordance with the heating season. Supply above the contract amounts is not available, and some contracts contain take-or-pay clauses—the company must pay for the volumes specified in the contract, whether or not it can take the gas.

To assist in matching customer demand with supply, the company maintains a gas storage field. Gas can be pumped into the storage field when supply exceeds customer demand, and gas can also be obtained when demand exceeds supply. There are no restrictions on the use of the gas storage field except that the field must be filled to capacity at the beginning of each gas year (September 1). Consequently, whenever the contractual supply of gas for the remainder of the gas year is less than that required to satisfy projected demand and replenish the storage field, the company must curtail service to the industrial customers (except for quantities that are used for heating). The curtailments must be carefully controlled so that an oversupply does not occur at year-end. Similarly, care must be taken to ensure that curtailments are adequate during the year to protect against the need to curtail commercial or residential customers in order to replenish the storage field at year-end.

In recent years the company's planning efforts have not provided a firm basis for the establishment of long-term contracts. The current year has been no different. Planning efforts have not been adequate to control the supply during the current gas year. Customer demand has been projected only as a function of the total number of customers. Commercial and industrial customers' demand for gas has been curtailed excessively. This has resulted in lost sales and has caused an excess of supply at the end of the gas year.

In an attempt to correct these problems, the president of Citizens' Gas has hired a new director of corporate planning and has instructed the director to develop a logical concept and several design alternatives for a system that can be used to analyze the supply and demand of natural gas. The system should provide a monthly gas plan for each of the next five years, with particular emphasis on the first year. The plan should provide a set of reports that will assist in the decision-making process and contain all necessary supporting schedules. The system must provide for the use of actual data during the course of the first year to project demand for the rest of the year and the year in total. The president has indicated to the director that he will base his decisions on the effect on operating income of alternative plans.

REQUIRED:

1. What planning reports should be generated by the system and what level of inquiry capability should be present to support decision requirements?

2. Identify the major data items that should be incorporated into Citizens' Gas Company's new system to provide adequate planning capability.

3. In general, what hardware configurations and processing modes do you as director expect to utilize?
(Adapted from the CMA examination.)

12-12 Interstate Transfer is a regional moving and storage firm located in the Midwest. It has been growing at a rapid rate over the past several years and has been having increasing difficulty scheduling its trucks. Customers have had to wait several days for delivery of their furniture, and trucks have frequently been operating with partial loads. A management consultant was hired by the firm to help resolve this scheduling problem. The consultant decided that the firm could schedule its operations much more effectively by using a linear-programming algorithm. To support this model, Interstate would need to lease a small computer. To further justify the computer cost, the firm would automate its current billing, payroll, and payables systems. Using this computerized accounting system, management could make better decisions because information would be readily available.

REQUIRED: Comment on the appropriateness of the system analysis approach used here.

12-13 For several years, Brown's Department Store has been using magnetic tape to store its accounts receivable records. The credit department has been complaining about the increase in bad debts over the past year. The company has one location, and its computer is on the premises. You have been called upon to help Brown's Department Store with its problem.

REQUIRED: Prepare a statement of scope and objectives.

12-14 Business organizations are required to

modify or replace a portion or all of their financial information system in order to keep pace with their growth and to take advantage of improved information technology. The process involved in modifying or replacing an information system, especially if computer equipment is utilized, requires a substantial commitment of time and resources. When an organization undertakes a change in its information system, a series of steps or phases is taken. The following steps or phases are commonly included in a systems study:

1. Survey of the existing system
2. Analysis of information collected in the survey and development of recommendations for corrective action
3. Design of a new or modified system
4. Equipment study and acquisition
5. Implementation of a new or modified system

These steps or phases tend to overlap rather than be separate and distinct. In addition, the effort required in each step or phase varies from one systems change to another depending upon such factors as the extent of the changes or the need for different equipment.

REQUIRED:

1. Explain what problems may exist by starting with an analysis of the existing system. What step would you replace it with and why? When would you suggest starting with the existing system?

2. Identify and explain the general activities and techniques that are commonly used during the systems analysis phase of systems development.

3. The system analysis phase of a financial information system study is often carried out by a project team composed of a systems analyst, a management accountant, and other persons in the company who would be knowledgeable and helpful in the systems study. What would be the role of the management accountant in these phases of a financial information systems study?

(Adapted form the CMA examination.)

12-15 Refer back to Case 11-7, George Beemster, CPA. In your opinion, did the Louisville Sales Corporation use an evolutionary data analysis or a decision analysis approach in designing its system? What problems resulted and what effectiveness and efficiency opportunities were overlooked by Louisville Sales Corporation?

13

STRUCTURED SYSTEMS ANALYSIS AND DESIGN CONCEPTS: DESIGN AND IMPLEMENTATION

OBJECTIVE OF SYSTEMS DESIGN AND IMPLEMENTATION

The overall objective of the design and implementation of accounting information systems is the ultimate satisfaction of decision, transaction, and reporting needs of management. This objective must dominate all the work and the discussion by the accountants and systems analysts as they interact with management to improve the information system. Accomplishment of this objective requires careful planning, organizing, staffing, coordinating, directing, and controlling of all the elements that will be integrated into the information system, which in turn will support the management system of the organization.

In Chapter 12 we focused on the problem definition and analysis phases of this process, which is reviewed again in Figure 13-1. These steps must be followed to accomplish the overall design and implementation objective. The objective of the first three phases discussed in Chapter 12 was to define the problem or opportunity, assess the feasibility of solving the problem or responding to an opportunity, and analyze what must be done to either solve the problem or to respond to an opportunity.

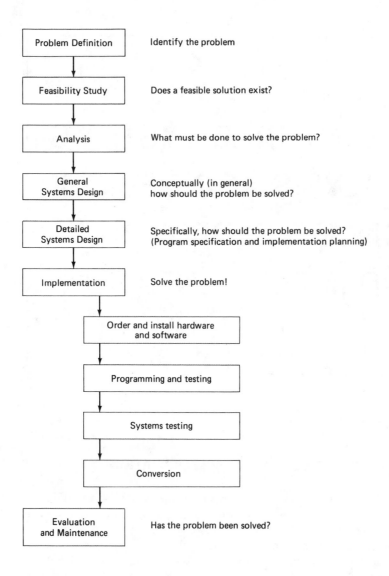

FIGURE 13-1 Structured systems analysis and design.

In this chapter we will review a strategy for change. Then we will review the key aspects of the actual physical design and implementation phases of the structured design shown in Figure 13-1. These phases describe *how* the problem is to be solved and the actual implementation of the new system that was designed to accomplish the objectives set forth in the first three phases. This review will carefully consider *economic, behavioral,* and *technical constraints,* which were also discussed in earlier chapters of this text. For example, the actual detailed design of the system may require a slightly different configuration of hardware for economic and technological reasons than originally thought during the feasibility study. Moreover, certain behavioral problems may lead to a slightly different organization of the data structure than previously conceptualized in the feasibility study and in the analysis process. Alternative analysis and design procedures will also be presented at the end of this chapter. In general, these enable users and systems analysts to expedite the structured approach when necessary.

From the auditor's perspective, it is important that these sequential phases be followed. In Chapter 11 we pointed out that one of the most important facets of good internal control is the set of procedures used to develop and implement the accounting and, in a larger sense, the information system of the organization. If these procedures are followed, there is a greater likelihood that a sound accounting and an effective control system will follow.

STRATEGY FOR CHANGE

Strong consideration must be given to the factors that affect the social environment of the organization in the physical design and implementation of information systems. Organizational, behavioral, and decision-making concepts are extremely important. For this reason, the accountant or systems analyst should not attempt to change or modify the management system and supporting information system without the active participation of management through project teams and the steering committee. Furthermore, it is much easier to change segments of the system successively rather than the entire system, although this approach does have its drawbacks, as will be noted later.

Modular Concept

System boundaries were reviewed in Chapter 12. We noted that it is often infeasible to modify or change an entire system at one time. Management should change only a subset of the system at one time. In this way the project is made more manageable. Clear objectives can be set, and design and implementation can proceed in an orderly fashion under the direction of the project team and steering committee.

There is a cost associated with this procedure, however, and it should be recognized. Any time a subset of the entire system is considered, the interface with other systems and the slack resources that will probably be required to accommodate this interface must be considered, if the modules are loosely coupled. Moreover, if the modules modified are too small, management will probably get the impression that the system will be in a continuous state of change. This will lead to overall disenchantment with the accounting system. As a matter of practice, it is necessary in an organization of any size to use the modular approach, but there are financial, organizational, and behavioral limits to its application.

Planning Change

In the structured approach there are many planning steps involved in the analysis, design, and implementation phases. The number of steps emphasizes the careful planning required in analysis, design, and implementation. Network analysis such as the *Program Evaluation Review Technique* (PERT) is most useful in this overall planning process. This procedure will be reviewed in the appendix to this chapter after all the necessary activity, planning, and decision steps have been explained.

STRUCTURED DESIGN[1]

General (Conceptual) Systems Design

Given authorization by management to continue the analysis and design, the general (conceptual) design phase can begin. After a thorough analysis of decision requirements and corresponding reporting and transaction processing needs, several alternative designs should be identified. These describe, in general, *how* the problem can be solved or how one can take advantage of an opportunity. This must be a very creative process. Many ideas should be pursued. At the end of this phase, one of the alternative designs should be selected and recommended to management. The general systems design follows the steps outlined in Figure 13-2.

Based on the analysis of the information requirements, the project team needs to develop a general plan to implement the logical design developed in the previous phase. It has been determined what has to be done and it is time now to develop alternative systems for accomplishing the task.

Organizational constraints related to decision making, subsystem coordination, and interfaces with other systems must be considered prior to alternative development. Behavioral constraints related to the implementation of change, decision-making activity, and the organization structure, such as those outlined in Chapter 3, must also be considered.

Hardware and software configurations, and operational proceedings must also be given careful thought. For example, what hardware is available, what are the characteristics of available software, what is practical with respect to new programs, and what is practical with respect to the current or future operation of the information system.

DEVELOP SEVERAL ALTERNATIVES. Several alternative conceptual designs should be developed. The systems requirements, such as those illustrated in the production scheduling example, should be spelled out in more detail. Particular attention should be given to *how* the organization can input, store, process, com-

---

[1] For a comprehensive discussion of systems design. See AICPA, *Guidelines for Development and Implementation of Computer-Based Application Systems,* Management Advisory Services Guidelines Series Number 4 (New York: American Institute of Certified Public Accountants, 1976); Davis, William S., *Systems Analysis and Design: A Structured Approach* (Reading Mass.: Addison-Wesley, 1983); Chris Gane and Trish Sarson, *Structured Systems Analysis: Tools and Techniques* (New York: Improved System Technologies, 1979); and Charles L. Biggs, Evan G. Birks, and William Atkins, *Managing the Systems Development Process* (Englewood Cliffs, N.J.: Touche Ross & Co. and Prentice Hall, 1980).

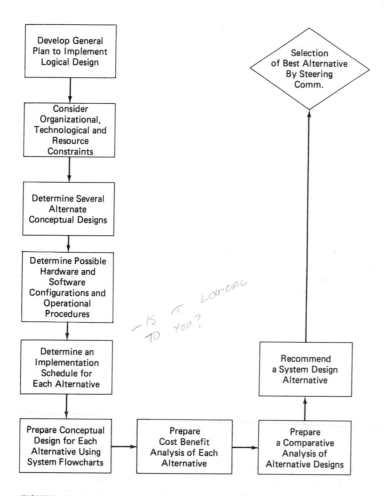

FIGURE 13-2   General (conceptual) systems design.

municate with, and operate the system. At this stage the project team should begin to concentrate on the physical aspects of the system.

Technical support for each alternative should be specified. For larger, more complex systems, this will involve specifications for data management such as structures and updating requirements. The mode of processing proposed will also lead to hardware and software requirements. Finally, for some systems such as the distributed processing systems, communication requirements will need to be specified in greater detail. For some systems, an alternative may be the purchase of an existing commercially available application package. Any such package must at least meet the minimum objectives of the system in order to be considered. Attention should also be directed to internal control features of the proposed alternatives.

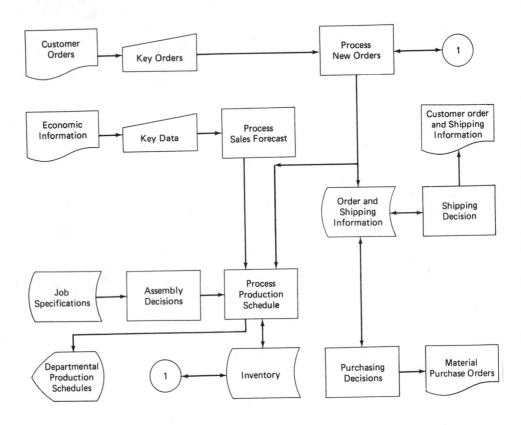

FIGURE 13-3 Production schedule: system flowchart.

Moreover, resources, specifications, and schedules for conversion, implementation, operation, and maintenance should be estimated for each alternative. It may be that one alternative can be operational in one month using commercially available software for production scheduling, for example; whereas one that meets the information requirements better must be programmed and will take six months to implement. These differences could be very important in selecting the best alternative.

Next, general system flowcharts of each alternative should be prepared to communicate the various aspects of each alternative to management or to the steering committee for final approval. An example of such a flowchart for one alternative for the production scheduling example is shown in Figure 13-3. This alternative uses: a random access database for job specification, inventory, and order information; on-line input for order processing and economic information; video display output on the shop floor production schedules; and printed reports and purchase orders for customers and suppliers respectively.

ANALYSIS OF ALTERNATIVES. Next the costs, benefits, and limitations of each alternative should be explored. Estimates of tangible and intangible costs

Development Costs	$40,000
Annual Cost Savings	
Inventory Reduction	$40,000
Clerical Savings	$15,000
Benefits	
Increased Sales Contribution Margin	$30,000
Less Annual Cost Increases	$10,000
Net Annual Benefits and Costs	$20,000

Net Present Value Analysis	Interest	10%	
YEAR	NET ANNUAL BENEFIT	PRESENT VALUE	CUMULATIVE
1	$20,000	$18,182	$18,182
2	$20,000	$16,529	$34,711
3	$20,000	$15,026	$49,737
5	$20,000	$12,418	$62,155
Less Development Costs			$40,000
Net Present Value			$22,155

FIGURE 13-4 Cost benefit analysis for production scheduling example.

and benefits should be made. These should include current as well as future estimates. Figure 13-4 illustrates this for the production scheduling example presented here.

Given this analysis of each conceptual design, a comparative analysis is prepared for each general design. An example is one illustrated in Figure 13-5. Based on this comparative analysis and a careful assessment of the organizations' environmental, organizational, and behavioral factors, a final recommendation should be prepared and presented to management or the steering committee for approval. This report is the culmination of the creative effort of the project team, analyst, or accountant and great care should be taken presenting its recommendations. The project team should refrain from giving the steering committee (management) only one alternative. While a clear and unambiguous recommendation is necessary, it is also important to ensure that all major alternatives are presented fairly in a way that permits easy comparison.

The actual detailed physical design (detailed systems design, implementation, programming and testing, and conversion) follow management's approval and confirmation of the alternative recommended by the project team.

Detailed Systems Design and Vendor Selection

In this phase of structure systems analysis and design, the project team, systems analyst, controller, or accounting firm doing the actual design work must state *specifically how* the problem should be solved or how the organization can take advantage of an opportunity.

CRITERIA	SYSTEM		
	A	B	C
MRP Scheduling Procedure			
Optimization	Yes	Yes	No
Simulation	Yes	No	No
On-Line	Yes	Yes	No
Batch	Yes	Yes	Yes
Inventory System			
On-Line	Yes	Yes	No
Number of Items	100,000	50,000	20,000
MRP	Yes	Yes	Yes
Optimized	Yes	No	No
JIT Capability	Yes	Yes	No
Standard Costs	Yes	Yes	Yes
Actual Costs	Yes	Yes	Yes
Multiple vendors	Yes	Yes	Yes
Forecasting			
On-Line Access to Cost Data	Yes	Yes	No
Economic Data Analysis	Yes	Yes	No
Market Analysis	Yes	Yes	No
Customer Order System			
On-Line	Yes	Yes	No
Automatic Schedule Update	Yes	No	No
Purchasing			
Automatic	Yes	Yes	Yes
JIT	Yes	Yes	No
Shipping			
Automatic	Yes	Yes	Yes
Optimized	Yes	No	No
Assembly			
Cost Optimization	Yes	No	No
Production Smoothing	Yes	No	No
Development Costs	$80,000	$40,000	$20,000
Annual Cost Savings			
Inventory Reduction	$60,000	$40,000	$10,000
Clerical Savings	$25,000	$15,000	$ 5,000
Benefits			
Increased Contribution	$60,000	$30,000	$10,000
Less Annual Cost Increases	$25,000	$10,000	$ 5,000
Net Present Value	$28,772	$22,115	($ 4,461)

FIGURE 13-5 Comparative analysis.

The detailed steps of this phase using the structured approach are outlined in Figure 13-6. According to the AICPA guidelines,[2] which parallel the steps recommended in the structured approach to analysis and design, the principal objectives of this phase are to (1) design a network of information flows and decision-making activities, specify the interfaces with other systems, and begin the specific selection of software and hardware; (2) establish the specifications for files, processing, and control; and (3) plan the programming, conversion, and training.

First, a plan and schedule for design and implementation must be prepared. This plan is based on the recommended conceptual design developed in the general design phase and the documented requirements associated with the chosen design. Next, this plan, along with all its prescribed conventions, standards, and restrictions, should be communicated in writing to all personnel involved in the project. Progress reports should also be sent to all company personnel who will be affected to keep them informed. This action will ease some of the anxiety associated with change.

DETERMINE SYSTEM SPECIFICATIONS. User decision-making models, reporting, and transaction processing requirements must be defined more precisely than they were in the general (conceptual) design phase. There must be a thorough definition of each decision model, report, and transaction to be processed to ensure that alternative technical approaches can be evaluated on how effectively and efficiently they meet these requirements. Outputs to be generated by the system must be described in terms of their purpose, frequency, and distribution using IPO charts and possibly input and output matrices. Data elements required must be defined in a data dictionary by a systemwide identification, format, source, content, and edit criteria.[3] Inputs required must be described using IPO charts and a data dictionary as follows:

1. Source, including form name and responsibility for completing the form.
2. Data elements included.
3. Method of data collection [e.g., remote terminals, Optical Character Recognition (OCR), etc.].
4. Manual processing, including editing procedures and distribution.
5. Control required, both manual and automated.[4]

Behavioral consideration should be given to the user's interface with the system input and output. Furthermore, the preliminary organization of required data elements into logical records should be established. Finally, volumes of transactions now and in the future should be estimated. For example, in the Patio Furniture illustration, a study of the work flow may indicate that daily revisions are necessary to optimize the production runs. These, for example, may be necessary because of short lead times in orders and material inventory systems.

---

[2] AICPA Guidelines for Development and Implementation of Computer-Based Applications Systems opt. cite.

[3] Biggs, Birks, and Atkins, *Managing the Systems Development Process.* pp. 94-95.

[4] Ibid.

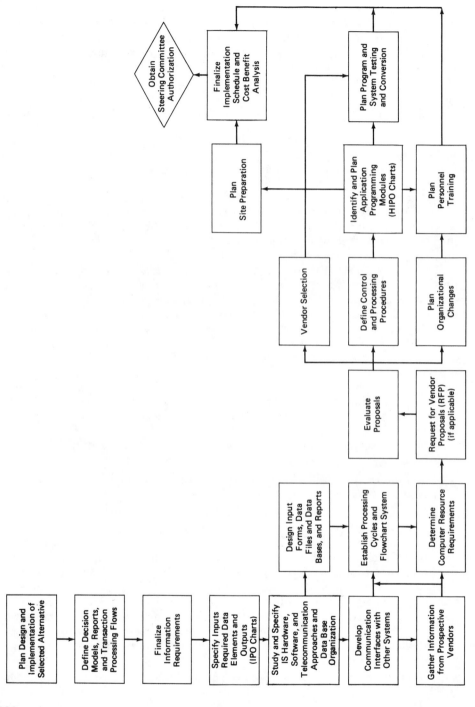

FIGURE 13-6 Detailed systems design.

After the accounting information system requirements have been fixed, the project team, analyst, or accountant should study various software approaches, with supporting hardware, and specify the needs of the system with respect to the hardware, software, telecommunication, and database organization. Various communication networks, file and database structures, and types of operating and database systems that meet the general requirements previously specified should be considered. Special attention should be paid to the features of these which are outlined in earlier chapters of this text.

Input forms, data files or database structures, and reports must be designed for the accounting information system. Often it is useful to assemble a database on an on-line operating system to verify operating assumptions prior to any applications programming.[5] Reports and other output media are designed along with distribution specifications. Input methods and procedures may furthermore be designed in detail given the preliminary specifications of hardware and software that have been developed thus far.

While input and output formats, decision models, and data files or data structures are being designed, the hardware, software, and communications equipment as well as systems interfaces need to be specified. For example, in the production scheduling illustration, the sales order and accounts receivable processing interfaces should be specified.

At this juncture, information from prospective vendors may be sought. Consideration should be given to commercially available application software that may meet the requirements of the recommended conceptual decision-making, reporting, and transaction processing systems. The objective is to obtain a description of commercial software that may meet the requirements of the system.

Systems flowcharts must then be revised to indicate the flow of transactions and information through the transaction processing and decision-making network of the organization. At this point, organizations can describe in detail all the specifications for hardware and software, and the system and its various interfaces with management and other systems.

Using the information on one prospective system and a set of systems flowcharts, processing cycles can be established in terms of frequency, time, data, and reports. From this detail, estimates can be made for the computer, software, and telecommunication resources that will be required for the system. Advice from prospective vendors may be helpful here for many firms that do not have a great deal of technical expertise.

REQUESTS FOR PROPOSALS (RFP). After this is done, the computer resources can be estimated so that requests can be made for vendor proposals, if applicable. These are often called RFPs (request for proposals). There are a wide variety of vendors and procedures for vendor selection. In this structured design sequence, it is assumed that the client or organization has sufficient expertise to propose a specific hardware/software configuration to several vendors and to request bids from these vendors. Moreover, it is assumed that the vendor will be selling, renting, or leasing the hardware and software to the organization.

---

[5] Ibid., p. 146.

Depending on the organization's information systems expertise, there are many other alternatives to this scenario.

In the computer industry, there are many types of vendors. An impression of vendors and their products and services should have been obtained as the organization or the outside analysts studied and estimated hardware, software, and communication requirements. There are *large computer* manufacturers that manufacture, sell, rent, and lease CPUs and a wide variety of peripheral equipment. For smaller clients and companies and for distributed processing systems, there are many (including some of the large computer manufacturers) *mini* and *micro computer* manufacturers and distributors as well as *supply* vendors. Finally, there are *software vendors* for database, operating systems, and application systems. Many have products designed for specific business markets and specific hardware manufacturers. For example, in the production scheduling example for Patio Furniture, there are many software vendors which specialize in MRP (material requirement planning) systems designed to do the type of tasks suggested in the data flow diagram. Much of this hardware, peripheral equipment, and software can even be made available to a firm through *leasing companies, service bureaus,* and *time-sharing* arrangements. Finally, to help a client or company with all of the phases of systems development and implementation or just a few steps, such as equipment selection, there are many systems *consulting firms.* These include all the large CPA firms.

There are several ways in which vendors can be approached. These approaches may take place at different points in the system development and implementation network. First, as is suggested here, a client or organization should approach vendors with *specific configuration proposals* that will satisfy the company's systems design. Configuration and financial arrangement bids should be sought for specific requirements for input, output, storage, interface, processing cycles, volume of processing, input and output activity, controls, communications, conversion, training, testing, and backup systems.

Another alternative, which might give vendors more creative latitude in using their hardware and software expertise, would be to translate the company's requirements into *performance objectives* and obtain configuration proposals on this basis. This may be done earlier in the design stage, after the finalization of the systems requirements shown in Figure 13-6. These performance objectives should be accompanied by all the data flow diagrams and the other analysis detail to aid the vendor in proposing a solution to the problem.

A company with little in-house expertise and without access to the expertise of an accountant or other consultant may choose to work closely with *one vendor* from the outset of the general design process. Finally a company may elect not to purchase their software because no package meets their needs. They may decide to write it themselves or have some one else develop it for them. The advantage of using commercial software though, is the fact that there is a large client base and it is usually well tested.

EVALUATE VENDOR PROPOSALS.   Next, all the vendors' proposals which meet the specified systems requirements directly or proposals that set forth reasonable alternative configurations and software packages should be evaluated. Second, all key aspects of a vendor's hardware and software should be evaluated. Evaluation criteria can include such items as (1) price; (2) lease or rent payments; (3) maintenance contracts; (4) storage capacity in each storage device; (5) access speed for each storage device; (6) processing speed; (7) speed of input and output devices—CRT, printer, card reader, etc.; (8) number of input and output terminals that can be supported; (9) hardware controls; (10) backup systems; (11) compatibility with other manufacturers in terms of hardware and software programs; (12) software support; (13) vendor support; (14) modularity to enable additional components and peripheral support to be added; (15) reliability statistics on downtime; (16) implementation support; (17) testing and conversion support; (18) initial and continued training; (19) documentation flowcharts and operation manuals; and (20) reputation of the vendor.

It may be useful to lay out a table, such as the one shown in Figure 13-7, for vendor comparisons. Evaluation should be based on an array of variables, with key variables being given more weight. As indicated in Figure 13-7, which represents three microcomputer configurations, the task of vendor selection is not easy because there are so many intangible factors. At this point in the detailed systems design stage, these resource requirement estimates must be carefully reviewed by the project team, the steering committee (management), the systems analyst, and the accounting personnel. They need to be sure that the computer, software, and storage and telecommunication resources exist and that they are economical, serviceable, effective, and easy to use given the availability of personnel. In other words, strict attention must be given to the technological and behavioral constraints mentioned in the earlier chapters on behavior, computer equipment, and databases.

VENDOR SELECTION.   Final vendor selection should follow these steps if possible. If feasible, the *equipment should be tested prior* to final vendor selection. Two basic procedures are used. Typical *benchmark* problems and sets of transactions can be run on the configuration suggested by the vendor to test input/output devices, controls, software, operating systems, database systems, and utility packages for the handling of transaction volume and anticipated problems. This testing can usually be done at the vendor's location and is excellent for evaluating batch processing systems. As an alternative, models may be used to evaluate storage, access, and processing structures. Based on these models, *simulation* may be used to predict response time, transaction processing time, and turnaround time for an on-line system. Following this evaluation and testing of hardware, software, and other critical characteristics of vendors' systems, the best vendor is selected, after receiving management's approval.

Once a vendor has been selected, a mode of financing must be selected. Consideration must be given to the following variables: ability to change equipment, expected value of the equipment at the end of the time period, risk of obsolescence, life of hardware and software relative to the company's needs, availability of lease and rental contracts, clauses, cancelability, maintenance provided, and, finally, cost. A capital budgeting approach using present value to assess cash flows for hardware, software, maintenance, installation, training, conversion, implementation, programming, testing, personnel, and the overall development and implementation process, is useful here.

CRITERIA	VENDOR		
	A	B	C
1. Price	$4,000	$3,000	$2,000
2. Lease payments	$1,000/yr.	$750/yr.	$500/yr.
3. Maintenance	$100/mo.	$150/mo.	$50/mo.
4. Storage	2M	1M	512K
5. Access	Same	Same	Same
6. Processing speed	N/A	N/A	N/A
7. Hard Disk	80 M	40 M	20 M
8. Network	30	12	None
9. Hardware controls	Excellent	Good	Good
10. Backup system	Not local	Local	Not local
11. Compatibility	Yes	No	Yes
12. Software support	Good	Good	Poor
13. Vendor support	Excellent	Excellent	Good
14. Modularity	Yes	No	Yes
15. Reliability	Excellent	Excellent	Excellent
16. Implementation	Fair	Good	Fair
17. Testing and conversion	Fair	Good	Fair
18. Training	Excellent	Good	Little
19. Documentation	Poor	Poor	Poor
20. Reputation	Nationally known	Nationally known	Good locally

FIGURE 13-7 Vendor selection criteria.

Generally speaking, purchase arrangements are superior if equipment will be kept for several years and there is an upgrade path. Cancelable leases offer more flexibility and often have purchase clauses at the end of the lease period; but cash outflows may be higher here than with a purchase. A company may also opt for the most flexible of all arrangements which is renting the equipment from month to month. Renting will result in the highest cash outflow. Another alternative is to rent, lease, and purchase various components based on their expected life and flexibility attributes.

With the essence of the system designed and considerable thought given to the nature of the hardware, site planning or preparation may be necessary at this time, especially if more space, different air conditioning, fire protection, or special security is required.

DEFINE CONTROL AND PROCESSING PROCEDURES.   Next, control and processing procedures can be designed in accordance with the basic principles and concepts. General control procedures need to be developed for users so that they can effectively use the new system. Input and output controls such as batching, verification, correction, resubmission, and balancing must be specified for users. Procedures for maintenance of database and data file integrity, including backup procedures, must be developed. Procedures must be designed to process transactions in accordance with the desires of management and generally accepted accounting principles. Finally, access controls such as passwords and physical access to terminals must be developed.

Concurrently, the project team should prepare for any organizational changes. It is important that the project team quickly and accurately communicate the nature of these changes, along with the compelling reasons for the changes, to personnel. In Chapter 3 we noted that these systems changes can often alter the social structure of the organization and cause a great deal of frustration and anxiety. Therefore consideration must be given to the behavioral constraints and principles.

PROGRAM SPECIFICATIONS.   Next, program requirements for each application module should be specified and plans should be made to schedule all programming tasks for each module needed in the system. Hierarchical input processing and output charts (HIPO charts) are useful in organizing the programming tasks. They are a natural extension of the IPO, charts which describe the processing steps, data flow diagrams, system flowcharts, and hierarchy charts which describe the overall processing steps. They illustrate all the processing tasks and the hierarchy of each of these tasks. Programmers can use this hierarchy to develop program modules which will fit together into an effective overall program. An example of a hierarchy chart was shown in the last chapter for production scheduling tasks for patio furniture. These program specifications must include the (1) purpose; (2) logic; (3) coding specifications; (4) testing specifications; and (5) criteria and conversion specifications. Specification must be done in terms of the logic, input, output, files, decision tables, formulas, and algorithms.

Concurrently, plans should be made for training. Personnel requirements, location, duties, and topics to be covered must be communicated. (Training procedures will be discussed later.)

PLAN CONVERSION AND IMPLEMENTATION.   Following the planning of application programming modules and concurrent with personnel planning, the project team, accountant, or systems designer should then plan systems conversion and backup systems. The precise details of the conversion plan and schedule must be specified. PERT may be used extensively here. The backup plan must detail recovery and alternative processing plans for the proposed system.

The last step in the detailed design phase is the preparation of an updated conversion and implementation budget, along with a cost-benefit revision for the system. The system must ultimately be justified on a cost-benefit basis. As illustrated in Chapter 4, all benefits must be considered in light of the potential value of the information obtained from the accounting system. The value of the system to the firm includes impact on both the reporting and information needs and the management decisions. The benefits to be derived must be compared with the estimated cost of the system. If the cost exceeds the expected benefits, then a revision in the detailed systems design is necessary before the design and implementation phases of the system can continue. In other words, in terms of the economic constraint, the benefits (value) of the information derived from the system must exceed the cost. The plans, design, and cost-benefit budget analysis set forth in this detailed systems design must then be approved by management.

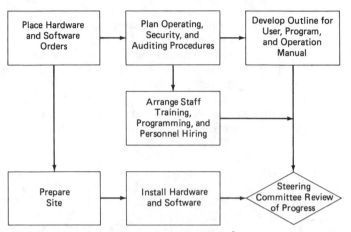

FIGURE 13-8   Implementation-planning and hardware and software ordered and installed.

Implementation

PLANNING AND HARDWARE AND SOFTWARE INSTALLATION.   Following the approval of management or the steering committee, implementation of the accounting information system should commence. After financial arrangements have been made, hardware, software, communication equipment, and forms should be ordered, as shown in Figure 13-8. Operating, security, and auditing procedures should be planned. Arrangements should be made with the vendor and within the organization for staff training and programming. A training schedule should be finalized so that all personnel, not only programmers, will be familiar with objectives, software, standards, documentation, procedures, data organization, and testing and conversion requirements. At this time an outline should be given to the vendor spelling out any requirements the company has regarding a user's manual and other documentation. If new staff are required, new personnel should be selected. Great care should be taken to obtain well-qualified personnel.

Finally the site should be prepared while all these activities are progressing. When this is accomplished, the hardware and software should be installed. Hardware should then be tested to ensure that all maintenance, operating, utility, and other routines provided by the vendor are functioning as specified. Again the steering committee and management should review the implementation progress of the new or revised accounting information system.

PROGRAMMING AND TESTING.   After all programs and data files have been specified and hardware and vendor software have been installed, programs must be coded and program and string tested, as shown in Figure 13-9. This phase requires active participation on the part of the ultimate decision makers and auditors to ensure that the results conform to the requirements of the information system and that adequate controls are present in the process.

First, programming logic must be completed and documented with descriptions and program flowcharts. These should be keyed to systems flow-

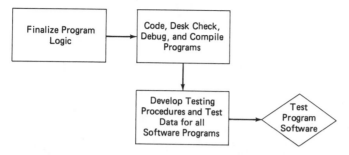

FIGURE 13-9 Implementation: programming and testing.

charts, IPO charts and hierarchical charts developed earlier using the structured approach to design. Modules must be assigned to programmers. It may be most effective to program and test the higher level, more frequently used application modules first. Programs must then be coded, checked for logic, and compiled.

Using the structured approach, programmers should verify that actual programming complies with the objectives of each module and that the modules are compatible with other modules, database or files, and procedures. Concurrent with this test, procedures must be derived to ensure that each program functions as specified by itself as well as in conjunction with other programs and files with which it interfaces. There are several types of test procedures which may be used by systems analysts. These include the following:

1. Desk check: review of program logic
2. Debugging: use of vendor hardware and software to check program logic as programs are being compiled and run on test data
3. Random transactions and inquiries: processing a sample of transactions and inquiries to make sure the program logic is functioning
4. Actual data: processing live groups of data to make sure all data are being processed as planned
5. Controlled test data: testing of all possible permutations of transactions and inquiries that are good and bad to test actual processing and control procedures

Moreover, each *program,* as well as combinations (*strings*) of programs and data files that are tightly coupled or integrated, must be tested using these procedures. Various combinations of these tests are generally performed. It should be remembered that no amount of testing will guarantee the complete elimination of errors. Extensive testing only detects those errors represented by test transactions.

If test data are required, they must be developed. As will be explained, especially in Chapter 20, test data can be a set of random transactions, an actual group of transactions, or a set of controlled fictitious good and bad transactions.

Given the programs, procedures, and test data, the programs and strings can now be thoroughly tested. As we noted in Chapter 11 on internal control,

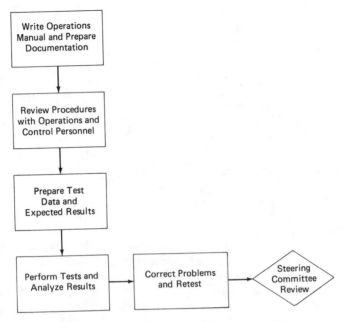

FIGURE 13-10 Implementation: system testing.

this testing is an important aspect of the overall system of controls. These test results are an important part of the system's documentation.

SYSTEMS TESTING. Finally, all programs and strings of programs and data files must be tested together as an entire system to ensure compliance with management's expectations and control procedures, as shown in Figure 13-10. Emphasis here is on the interface between strings of programs, the operating system, database systems, internal controls, and the various other systems of the organization.

The operations manual and documentation must be written. It must be reviewed with computer operators and control personnel to be sure that utility program support, operating rules, restart procedures, processing options, and systems controls are clear. Procedures and assignment of responsibility for obtaining data must be prepared. Test data representing a full range of valid and invalid operational possibilities must be prepared with the full cooperation of users, auditors, and management. Test data may come from master and transaction files. Great care must be used in controlling the integrity of these files in the data collection and testing process. The limits of the system must be determined here. These include: (1) the capacity, such as throughput, turnaround, and access time; (2) the entire system's ability to handle the typical volume of transactions; and (3) its ability to restart and recover when it does crash. In the Patio Furniture example, the system must be able to (1) handle rush orders, material shortages, and production breakdowns; (2) save sufficient information to restart the system; and (3) flag erroneous input to the system.

After all procedures are working well, the data are available, and the programs have been tested, the systems test is performed. The results are thoroughly reviewed by decision makers, systems personnel, accountants, and outside auditors to be sure everything is functioning in accordance with definition and design specifications. All problems are reconciled, and corrections to programs and procedures are made. The system is retested as often as necessary, for it must satisfy the requirements of management for effectiveness and efficiency and maintain data integrity through good controls. Following this test, the results must be reviewed by management or their representatives on the steering committee.

CONVERSION AND FINAL TESTING. This is the transition stage between the old way and the new way accounting information is provided to management for decision-making, transaction processing, and reporting requirements. The principal objectives of this phase are as follows:

1. Complete systems documentation and training manuals
2. Convert and verify files and data in the database
3. Perform final testing
4. Complete user training
5. Start operating the system
6. Obtain user acceptance and approval.

First, the conversion plan must be completed, as shown in Figure 13-11. Objectives must be communicated and responsibilities assigned. Timetables for file and program conversion must be prepared. Error and reconciliation procedures must be detailed. Moreover, specific rules for maintenance of old and new file and program integrity must be set forth.

The actual conversion approach may vary depending on the situation. A *direct approach* to stopping the old system and implementing the new system may be applicable when the differences between the old and new information system are so great that any comparison would be meaningless.

Most often, however, a *parallel conversion* is used where both old and new systems are operated simultaneously, results are compared and reconciled, and the new system is corrected for differences if necessary. This parallel operation may be run on old or current inquiries and transactions. This procedure is costly, but it offers considerable protection for the company and its records.

Another approach is to use a branch or small subset of the organization in which to implement the new system as a *pilot* system. Using this method, all risk is localized and problems can be corrected in the pilot situation prior to organizationwide implementation.

Finally, *phase-in conversion* can be used where small subsystems are implemented one at a time. This method has the major disadvantage of dealing with too many subsystem interfaces and the perpetual lack of a complete system. The job may never be finished, and a piecemeal system is likely to result.

After the conversion plan has been completed, procedures for the creation of new files must be determined and prescribed. Regardless of the approach

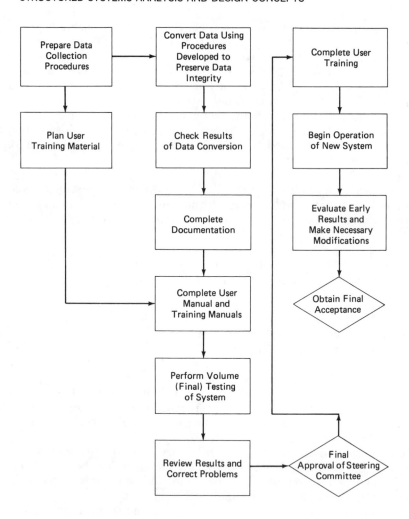

FIGURE 13-11 Implementation: conversion and volume (final) testing.

used, careful attention must be given to data files. They must be free of problems prior to conversion. The integrity of all the old files must be preserved while new ones are being created. After the procedures have been outlined for data conversion, the file conversion programs are run and the results are thoroughly checked.

At this time, computer operation documentation must be completed with specific instructions for operating the system. Database and file requirements, hardware and software constraints, restart procedures, paper requirements, file labeling, and retention requirements must be detailed.

User training procedures and schedules should also be completed. Personnel to be trained should also be chosen by this time. This training can be accomplished in many ways, as will be noted later. A major part of training will involve complete familiarization with the user's manual. The user's manual should be completed at this stage in systems development.

A final (sometimes called a *volume*) test is performed, applying one or more of the approaches noted earlier, to test the system in a live environment using all the converted files. All deficiencies are reconciled and corrected at this point. Often a parallel test is used to accomplish this final test. This is where the old and the new systems are operated in parallel for several accounting cycles and differences are reconciled. The test stage may run for several months before the new information system is finally approved and implemented. All problems must be resolved and the system must function in accordance with the design specification.

User training should be completed. This training may take the form of group seminars, individual study of procedure manuals, individual tutorials for more complex and complicated procedures (such as using the CRT for the first time), games or simulation for problem-solving routines, and on-the-job training. An example of on-the-job training would be the use of the video display in each department for scheduling; employees must know how to use it effectively. It is important that this training continue throughout the use of the system.

Next, the operations of the new information system should be started and the use of the old system should cease according to schedule. The early results should be evaluated with users who no longer rely on the old system. Any adjustments to fine-tune the system should be made at this point. After these minor modifications, the system should be turned over to the users and written acceptance obtained in the cases where the work was performed by third parties such as CPA or consulting firms. As time passes, the system should go through a postimplementation evaluation (often called an operational review), as described in Chapter 12.

ALTERNATE SYSTEMS ANALYSIS AND DESIGN

Prototyping

With the high-level design and programming tools available to systems designers and programmers today, the very basic elements of an accounting system can be designed, developed, and implemented prior to a complete analysis of the problem and preparation of a complete set of design specifications. The basic elements are the very fundamental transactions, records, files, and reports. For example, the basic elements of a sales transaction will only debit sales, credit finished goods for the amount of the sale, and report the total sales for the day. These basic elements can then be used and changed to meet more of the information requirements of management, such as salesperson information, customer information, quantities, and item descriptions. Each of these can in turn be used for payroll, accounts receivable, and inventory systems which may be added later. After these are added to the prototype, it can be used again, then modified some more to create more comprehensive sales, payroll, accounts receivable, and inventory systems, for example. In general, management starts with the minimum essential elements of the new system and adds to them or changes them in an iterative fashion until they obtain the system they want. This approach is particularly effective when management cannot define their needs and must get some system running as soon as possible. Changes can be made gradually and the system can evolve into a complete system as management's needs come into focus through the use of the prototype. This is quite different from defining the systems requirements at the outset of the formal structured analysis and design process.

This approach is particularly useful in decision support systems. For example, consider a database system designed using microcomputer database software. Management decides that its aging report should contain the following information: name of customer, address, invoice numbers, date, due date, amount, and a distribution of amounts by past due categories. They decide at a later date that they would like the terms and the salespersons' codes added; all they do is adjust the report format using the software procedures to include these items of information and retest the system.

At each step in the prototype design, the system still must be tested, data are sometimes converted, and results are evaluated as in the use of the structured approach. The basic difference is that all the information requirements are not known at the beginning of the development of the system as they are in the traditional structured approach. The overall result of using this approach is that some semblance of the system becomes operational at a much earlier stage because the analysis phase is shortened and the initial prototype is generally much simpler than the final system. Prototyping does create some problems from an internal control perspective. First, the final product will not be as well thought out and designed as one using a formal structural approach. Second, the system is in a continual state of change during the iterations. Finally, testing and conversion procedures must be replicated frequently; in practice this may not be the case.

End-User Development

In the shared database environment noted in Chapter 10, end users such as managers, engineers or accountants can easily write their own application systems. They can do this by using the database software or a spreadsheet package. The process of using database software to accomplish this is described in more detail in Chapter 10. For example, a marketing manager can simply design a report format that shows the sales, by territory, of each product line and plots the sales trend by product line for the last twelve months. This is feasible because these database management systems have independent data; that is, data are not dependent on the application. The data, for example, may be founded on entities which are called data objects (inventory and equipment and other physical assets); agents (employees, owners, and customers); and events such as sales and purchases. The end user then models the relationships between and among these entities using application software, a report generator, or a query language that generally accompanies the database. Many software packages are available now for microcomputers as well as mainframes that enable the manager to accomplish this task easily.

The end user using these software development systems and the shared database can, in many cases, develop much of his or her own software using the relationships that are allowable by the database structure. As pointed out in Chapter 10, some structures are more flexible than others; in particular the relational structure is the most flexible for end users to work with. Such a design procedure must still be structured, however. Otherwise the system will not meet user needs in a reliable manner. An analysis is necessary to determine what information is required. Design and implementation steps are necessary to develop the reports and the data analysis necessary to generate the information for these reports or inquiries. The same steps are present; only the way the steps are performed differ in end-user development because end users do much of the design work themselves.

CASE

In today's changing environment, informational needs are rapidly changing and systems development personnel and users must have the capability to develop new systems and to modify systems very quickly. Database software and end-user software provide this capability, in part, for simpler applications which can access data via query languages, construct simple reports via report generators, analyze data via user friendly database software, and analyze information via spreadsheets. But these are, for the most part, ad hoc remedies for simpler informational requirements. There is a need for systems development personnel to shorten the development life cycle for larger systems. To resolve this problem, several vendors have developed Computer Aided Systems Engineering (CASE) packages.

CASE systems automate the analysis and design process so that new systems can be more rapidly developed. Using CASE, a systems designer can analyze the information needs of management by displaying sample output, determining the processing and decision-making steps or algorithms needed to provide this output, determining the necessary data to support these processing steps, and developing the file structure or database needed to supply the necessary data. In many cases this can all be done graphically using CASE software which displays data flow diagrams, systems flowcharts, IPO charts, input data, and output. Using a concept of reverse engineering, these CASE systems can start with the needed informational output and sketch an entire system that will produce the needed output. In fact, several alternatives can be generated either in final form or in a prototype form and when one is selected the software can be used to write the accounting software programs that will be needed to operate and to control the system.

All this can be done in a computerized environment, thereby greatly reducing development time. These time reductions result from (1) significant reduction in lengthy feasibility studies because several potential systems can be explored for their feasibility using the software; (2) inferring from management's reaction to several alternative means for solving their informational or decision-making problems, their information requirements; and (3) automatic development of structured programs and data requirements from the alternative designs selected by management. In addition, via the discipline inherent in CASE, accounting software can be easily modified because it was developed using computerized tools and because the programs will be highly structured. Because of this, CASE is often used in developing prototype systems for further modification as management more finely determines their needs. Some think that along with CD–ROMs used to store data, fourth-generation query languages making data easier to access, and relational databases making data more accessible for a variety of uses, CASE technology will have a major impact on information systems in the near future because it has the potential significantly reducing the development life cycle.

Spreadsheet Analysis and Design

One of the most common software development packages used by accountants is the spreadsheet. A spreadsheet is an array of cells which are logically related via a series of formulas which are developed using the software. It may be used for analysis of financial information in decision support mode, a file management system that serves as a repository of data, and a completely automatic accounting system complete with menus and macros so that clerical personnel can operate the system to post transactions and to generate financial statements and managerial reports. End users can design these decision support and accounting and file management systems themselves.

Unfortunately, this ease of development can lead to many problems if appropriate design procedures are not followed. Mistakes in logic, incorrect cell references in formulas, incorrect ranges, confused range names, incorrect formats, misuse of built-in functions, accidental overwriting of formulas, reference to the wrong data set, incorrect references in macros, and many other logical and programming mistakes can lead to numerous errors in the results. Moreover, lack of documentation can lead to many of these problems as users attempt to modify an existing spreadsheet. Some of the major characteristics of spreadsheet analysis and design and their implications are:

1. Users tend to be noninformation systems specialists and do not realize the problems associated with informal approaches to software development.
2. Users hurry the development and don't take the time to document what they are doing.
3. Spreadsheets are easy to modify and therefore they are often modified with very little thought to the consequences of the modification and to adequate testing and approval of modifications.
4. Due to the personal nature of the development, very little consideration is given to the possibility of others using the software. Thus, they fail to see the need for any formal or uniform approach to development.

Just as in the case with those larger information systems designed by systems professionals, spreadsheet systems can benefit from a structured approach to analysis and design. Such a structured approach for spreadsheets must follow the basic structured approach, yet be modified to the unique objectives of spreadsheets and the need to quickly generate useful software, else the benefits

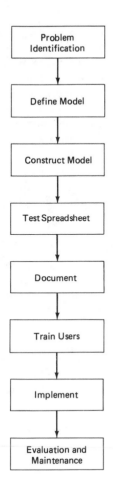

FIGURE 13-12 The spreadsheet development life cycle.

of end-user design will disappear. A set of suggested steps which parallel those in Figure 13-1 would be as follows and are diagramed in Figure 13-12:

1. Problem identification. The problem must be identified as in any systems analysis, for the solution to meet the needs of management.

2. Definition of model and decision variables. Since spreadsheets are primarily models that are used by management. These models, with their required input and variables comprise the information needs of the system and, as in any analysis phase, these must be identified. Sometimes the menus and macros which constitute the operational process used to manipulate the data, run the analysis, and generate the required output must also be identified.

3. Construct the model. This is analogous to the design and programming steps in traditional analysis and design. It involves the actual construction

of the spreadsheet and the necessary menus and macros needed to operate it. This, like the structured programs, needs some structure. It is suggested that there be (1) an identification section with names, users, revision dates, and file names; (2) a section for macros and menus; (3) a description of the model and its logic; (4) identification of model parameters, assumptions, and input variables; and (5) the spreadsheet itself with its formulas, input, decision, parameter, and output arrays or matrices. In summary, it is much easier to use, modify, and audit a spreadsheet if one can easily follow its logic.

4. Testing. As with any system, it should be tested by checking each calculation independently. Test using extreme and bogus data to see if the system will fail under stress and flag bogus transactions or data. There should also be an audit trail where one can follow a transaction or a calculation to trace its logic.

5. Documentation and operating instructions. Text should be included to explain its operating procedures, formulas, macros, various assumptions, models logic, and the various input and output information. As in all documentation, operators should only have access to operating instructions.

6. User Training, if needed.

7. Installation and use.

If these steps[6] are followed to the extent they are applicable, many of the problems noted earlier will be avoided and users will have developed systems that will serve their needs and be more robust over time as they are used and modified.

SUMMARY

In order to analyze and design an effective and efficient accounting information system, it is imperative that a structured approach be followed. The design and implementation phases must follow the definition and analysis phases outlined in Chapter 12. The problem definition, feasibility study, and the analysis phases describe in logical terms what must be done and assess the feasibility of proceeding with the project. In the design phases, the project team first decides how to solve the problem in general. Then, in the detailed design stage, they decide specifically how to solve the problem. Then they implement their new system by converting and testing it to see if it complies with the standards set by management. Finally, they operate and maintain it. In addition to the structural approach, prototyping, end-user, and CASE alternatives were presented. These can be used effectively to expedite the structural approach to analysis and design.

---

[6] See Boaz Ronen, Michael A. Palley, and Henry C. Lucas, Jr., "Spreadsheet Analysis and Design," *Communications of the ACM*, 32, no. 1 (January 1989), 86, 88 for a complete discussion of spreadsheet analysis and design.

APPENDIX

SCHEDULING THE ANALYSIS, DEFINITION, DESIGN, AND IMPLEMENTATION OF INFORMATION SYSTEMS—PERT

The definition, analysis, design, and implementation process outlined in Chapter 12 and in this chapter considers a series of activities and decision nodes. The various figures in Chapters 12 and 13 outlined the general sequence of these activities and decisions. More than once, planning activities were noted where the next sequence of activities and plans were to be scheduled.

A useful technique for scheduling activities in complex programs is PERT (Program Evaluation Review Technique). PERT is especially useful where there is a large network of tasks, such as the structured approach outlined in this text. This network has many such nodes and activities, and each activity unit precedes or follows other activities. A node begins and completes each activity, such as programming.

As an example in Table A13-1, letters designate activities; and numbered nodes denote the beginning and ending of activities. For each activity to commence, another activity or set of activities must be completed. This is denoted in the preceding activity column. For example, to begin activity *O* (writing of programs), *N*, *I*, and *F* must be complete. Note also that estimated times are shown in Figure A13-1.

As these activities are being completed, comparisons can be made between planned times and actual times. Moreover, these times and their network can be used to compute the critical path (as shown in Figure A13-1.) The *critical path* is

FIGURE A13-1   PERT diagram.

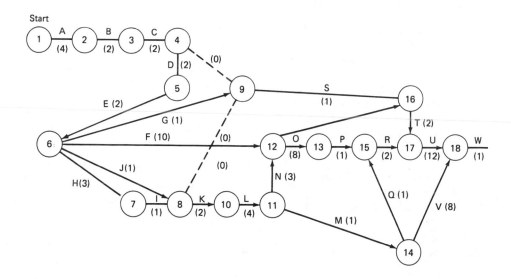

the path through the network with the least estimated time for completion. Any delay along this path will delay implementation of the entire system. In this example, the critical path is *A B C D E H I L N O P R U W*, which takes a total of 48 weeks to complete. Any activity not on this path has some slack time. For example, item *F* has a three-week slack time, for the longest time along the critical path from node 6 to node 12 is twelve weeks and activity *F* is ten weeks. Management could start *F* two weeks late and still not delay the entire project. If, however, *F* is started three weeks late, then it becomes part of a new critical path.

Using this scheduling procedure, the accountant, systems designer, and managers involved in the systems development project can track the progress of the development and implementation steps. They can pay particular attention to the activities on the critical path and be more flexible with those items where slack is present. In summary, PERT has proved useful for the design and development of large complex information systems.

Table A13-1 Activities and their Expected Time of Completion.

DESCRIPTION	ACTIVITY	TIME (IN WEEKS)	PRECEDING ACTIVITY
Design the decision model	A	4	General design
Design the input and report forms	B	2	A
Design the file	C	2	B
Develop the interface	D	2	C
Establish control procedures	E	2	D
Prepare the site	F	10	E
Plan conversion and backup	G	1	E
Plan training	H	3	E
Plan programming	I	1	J
Identify program module and flow	J	1	E
Prepare specifications and budget	K	2	E,G,H,I,J
Select vendor	L	4	K
Outline user, operation, and program manuals	M	1	L
Prepare detailed program specifications	N	3	L
Write programs	O	8	N,I,F
Test programs	P	1	O
Review operations manual documentation	Q	1	M
Test the systems	R	2	P,Q
Collect data for conversion	S	1	C,Q
Convert data files	T	2	S
Conversion volume test (parallel runs)	U	12	R,T
Complete user training	V	8	J,M
Implement system	W	1	V,U

SELECTED REFERENCES

AMERICAN INSTITUTE OF CERTIFIED PUBLIC ACCOUNTANTS, *Guidelines for Development and Implementation of Computer-Based Application Systems.*, Management Advisory Services Guidelines Series Number 4. New York: AICPA, 1976.

BIGGS, CHARLES L., EVAN G. BIRKS, and WILLIAM ATKINS, *Managing the Systems Development Process.* Englewood Cliffs, N.J.: Prentice Hall, 1980.

BORTHICK, A. FAYE, and JAMES H. SCHEINER, "Selection of Small Business Computer Systems, Structuring a Multi-Criteria Approach," *The Journal of Information Systems,* 3, no. 1 (Fall 1988).

BROWN, ROBERT M., and BERNADETTE RUF, "Applying Software Design Principles to Accounting Software: A Direct Approach," *The Journal of Information Systems,* 4, no. 1 (Fall 1989).

DAVIS, WILLIAM S., *Systems Analysis and Design: A Structured Approach.* Reading, Mass.: Addison-Wesley, 1983.

GREEN, GARY I., and EARL A. WILCOX, "Find the Right Software through Specifications," *Management Accounting,* January 1981, pp. 43–49.

GREER, WILLIS R., and HOWARD ROCKNESS, "Management Decision Support Systems for a Medical Group Practice," *The Journal of Information Systems,* 1, no. 2 (Spring 1987).

GROSSMAN, THEODORE, and SHAILENDRA PALVIA, "The Design and Implementation of a Multidimensional Retail Merchandising Information System," *The Journal of Information Systems,* 3, no. 1 (Fall 1988).

McCARTHY, WILLIAM E., "Accounting Information Systems: Research Directions and Perspective," *The Journal of Information Systems,* 2. no. 1, (Fall 1987).

———, An Entity-Relationship View of Accounting Models, *The Accounting Review,* October 1979, pp. 667–86.

———, The REA Accounting Model: A Generalized Framework for Accounting systems in a Shared Data Environment, *The Accounting Review,* July 1982, pp. 554–78.

MARSHALL, GEORGE R., *Systems Analysis and Design: Alternative Structured Approaches.* Englewood Cliffs, N.J.: Prentice Hall, 1986.

MERCURIO, V. J., B. F. MEYERS, A. M. NISBET, and G. RADIN, "AD/Cycle Strategy and Architecture," *IBM Systems Journal,* 29, no. 2 (1990), 170–88.

NANMANN, J. D., and A. M. JENKINS, "Prototyping the New Paradigm for Systems Development," *MIS Quarterly,* September 1982, pp. 29–44.

RONEN, BOAZ, MICHAEL A. PALLEY, and HENRY C. LUCAS, JR., "Spreadsheet Analysis and Design," *Communications of the ACM,* 32, no. 1 (January 1989), pp. 84–93.

SENA, JAMES A., and LAWRENCE M. SMITH, "Designing and Implementing an Integrated Job-Cost Accounting System," *The Journal of Information Systems,* 1, no. 1 (Fall 1986).

WONG-ON-WING, BERNARD, "User Involvement in Systems Development: An Attributional Approach," *The Journal of Information Systems,* 2, no. 2 (Spring 1988).

REVIEW QUESTIONS

1. What constraints should be considered in the final detailed design of an accounting information system?

2. What is the major difference between the analysis phase and design phase?

3. Why is the modular concept necessary?

4. At what point in the systems design phase must the decision models be fully specified and why?

5. At what point in the systems design phase must the data files be specified and why?

6. Why are systems flowcharts used in the systems design phase?

7. When are detailed accounting and administrative controls considered in the design process? Why?

8. Discuss the variety of vendor options available to the potential IS user.

9. When would you use benchmark problems in vendor selection?

10. Discuss the purpose of each test procedure.

11. What is meant by systems testing?

12. What are the advantages and disadvantages of the various conversion procedures? What is a volume test?

13. What is meant by prototyping?

14. What is the difference between structured analysis and design and end-user development?

15. What tool is there for planning and scheduling design and implementation procedures and how does it work?

16. What are the major tasks in the general design stage and what is their general sequence?

17. How can IPO charts and data dictionaries assist in describing the flow of information to be used in design?

18. What is the general sequence of activities in the detailed design phase?

19. List the tasks in each of the major implementation phases.

20. How can CASE be used to expedite the development process?

CASES

13-1   Manchester Supplies of Phoenix, Arizona, a supplier of data processing supplies to large companies and institutions, uses a batch processing purchasing and accounts payable system. They have generally been pleased with it to date. However, the present system has evolved through practice. They have just added equipment as needed. No formal design has ever been done. Consequently, the system is inadequate for the current volume of activity and management's decisions, and it needs to be redesigned.

The following is a description of the *present* system. Whenever the quantity of an item is low, the computer program prepares a purchase order in duplicate. The purchase order and accounts payable file is updated. The original is sent to the supplier; the copy is retained in the purchasing department filed in numerical order. When the shipment arrives, the inventory supervisor sees that each item received is checked off on the packing slip that accompanies the shipment. The packing slip is then forwarded to the accounts payable department where the information on it is keyed into the purchase order and accounts payable file. When the invoice arrives, it is likewise keyed into the purchase order and accounts payable file. The packing slip information is then compared with the invoice and the purchase order information by the computer. After any differences between the packing slip and the invoice are reconciled by the accounts payable department, the computer is given the "green light" to print a check.

REQUIRED: As part of your systems design, of an on-line purchase order and accounts payable system prepare.

1. A systems flowchart of the old system

2. An IPO chart of (1) the inventory reorder process; and (2) purchase order, packing slip, and invoice comparison processes in the following form:

Module _____
Called or Invoked by   Calls or Invokes
_____   _____

Inputs   Outputs
_____   _____

_____   _____

_____   _____

Process

13.2 Cosmic Signal, an electronics firm in Atlanta, specializes in the production and service of communication satellites and their related broadcasting equipment. Their growth has been rapid and they believe they have the need for an advanced decision support system in order to compete in the future. As their accounting firm, you have been asked to assist in this process. It has proceeded smoothly through the feasibility study and the analysis. In the general design stage it was determined that a database system would be necessary. In terms of the detailed design you have identified the tasks that must be accomplished for completion of the project. (Table C13-1).

REQUIRED: Assuming that you could start at the first of the year, (the beginning of week 1), how long would it be before the system would be operational and what steps would be critical to meeting this target? Prepare a PERT diagram to illustrate your results, assuming, for simplicity, five-day work weeks and no

holidays for the period. If for some reason Cosmic Signal cannot begin to collect data for conversion until the end of week 32, will the implementation be delayed or not? If for some reason they cannot begin to test the computer programs because of the availability of computer personnel until the end of week 37, will that change the critical path and delay the final completion of the project?

13-3 Consider again the Custom Frames Company (Case 12-7). During the analysis of the Custom Frames situation, the staff of your firm has come up with the data flow diagram (Figure C13-1) of what must be done to operate their own accounting system. Furthermore, during the general design stage your firm found two viable alternatives. These are listed next.

1. An automated point-of-sale and inventory system for small retail establishments was the first alternative. It would update inventory automatically at the time of sale

Table C13-1 Cosmic Signal.

ACTIVITY	DESCRIPTION	TIME	PRECEDING
A	Decision requirements	4	General design
B	Reporting requirements	5	General design
C	Database design	6	A & B
D	Identify data flow	4	A & B
E	Control procedures	3	C & D
F	Program modules needed	2	E
G	Prepare hardware and software specifications	4	F
H	Plan conversion	1	G
I	Plan training	1	G
J	Plan programming specifications	4	G
K	Select vendor	1	G
L	Site preparation	4	G
M	Collect date for conversion	6	H
N	Write programs	10	J
O	Install equipment	3	K & L
P	Convert data	1	M
Q	Training	3	I & R
R	Prepare user, operations, and program manuals	4	N
S	Test programs	2	N & O
T	Complete documentation	2	R & U
U	Systems test	2	S
V	Parallel conversion	12	P, Q, & T

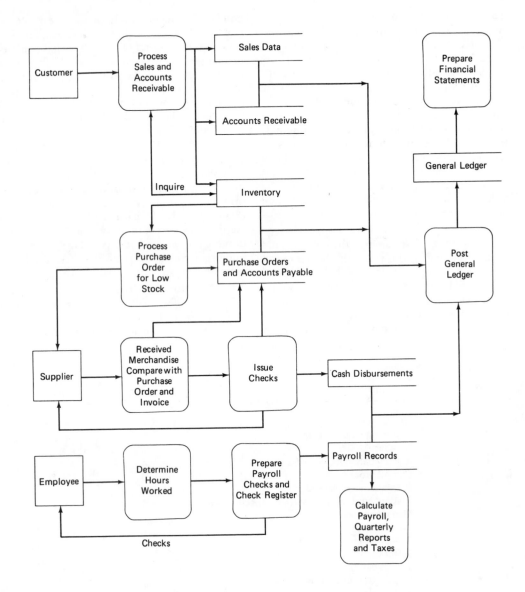

FIGURE C13-1 Custom Frames Company.

and give management on-line access to the quantity of merchandise on hand and automatically reorder material when necessary. It also permitted adjustments for scrap reentered into the inventory for smaller jobs. This system would not save any time or resources with respect to the other accounting and reporting activities provided by the CPA. For this system the software would cost $1,200 to purchase, test, and install. The hardware needed for it to operate would cost $5,000 for the microcomputer, printer, and disk drives. It would save $5,000 in terms of previously lost sales and salespersons' time that was spent in the past contending with the antiquated ordering ASN sales system. The savings with respect to the CPA bookkeeping and write-up service would be minimal.

2. An integrated alternative system would do the same basic procedures as the first, but it would also save all the outside bookkeeping and write-up costs now incurred. Moreover, it would enable Custom Frames to automate the entire accounting and inventory systems using an on-line integrated accounting system with a common integrated database for all applications. It would cost more to purchase, test, and install the software, however. The total software cost would be $3,000 and the hardware cost would be $1,500 more than it would be for alternative 1. The savings with respect to inventory and salespersons would remain the same as in alternative 1.

REQUIRED:

1. Prepare a system flowchart for alternative 2: the computerized on-line accounting system for Custom Frames.

2. Assume that the feasibility study actually costs $750; the analysis of the problem costs $500; the design is expected to cost $1,000; and the expected implementation (exclusive of the software testing and installation) cost will run $500 for both systems. Also assume annual supplies maintenance and utilities will run approximately $1,000 for both alternatives. What is the net present value, assuming a 10 percent cost of capital and a 5-year time horizon for both alternatives? Based on this analysis, which alternative would you select for detailed analysis and why?

13-4 (Cost-Benefit Analysis of Alternatives) Lancaster Building Supplies is located in eastern Pennsylvania. They operate five retail outlets and one large warehouse in suburban Philadelphia. The corporate office is at the warehouse. Most of their customers are other retail building supply and hardware stores. They carry a large inventory, and it's their pol-

icy to deliver anything that is in short supply within 24 hours. Thus their customers can minimize their inventory. Their profit margins have been shrinking over the past several years, however, because the premium they once charged for their service has virtually vanished due to some new competition. Currently they use an old batch processing computer system. Inventory and accounts receivable records are kept on magnetic tape and information is key punched as transactions are processed. This takes a considerable amount of time and effort and they are always behind in paperwork.

Once a week management gets the following:

1. A stock status report for making sales, purchasing, and promotional decisions

2. An accounts payable report for making decisions on which suppliers to pay

3. An accounts receivable report for credit and collection decisions

4. A payroll register for 25 home-office and warehouse, and 50 retail outlet employees

Monthly, they get the following:

1. An updated general ledger

2. Summary reports for each of the weekly reports

3. An aging schedule

4. A payroll register for 25 monthly employees

The current system processes the following daily transactions:

1. Sales orders

2. Accounts receivable and inventory updates for sales

3. Invoices for sales

4. Purchase orders

5. Receiving reports

6. Hours worked by hourly employees

7. Stock receipts and distributions

Except for payroll, all retail store activity is handled locally. After an analysis of the system, you have proposed three different microcomputer systems to help them manage their inventory, receivables, payables, payroll, and general ledger.

The first alternative you prepare is a simple inventory system using a small microcomputer. The configuration is shown in Table C13.2:

Table C13-2 Simple Inventory System.

DESCRIPTION OF EQUIPMENT	NUMBER	UNIT PRICE
Small Micro with Hard Drive	1	$2,600
Color Graphics Card	1	200
Memory Card	1	650
Monitor	1	200
Laser Printer	1	1,550
SOFTWARE		
DOS	1	50
Inventory System	1	100
Database Package	1	600
Spreadsheet	1	300
Installation and Data Conversion		750

You estimate that this will save $1,500 the first year and $2,000 per year for the next four years by enabling them to have on-line access to inventory records at the warehouse to make more up-to-date data purchasing decisions and thus reduce carrying costs. They would continue to operate the rest of their system using their current batch processing system.

As a second alternative you recommend that they purchase the following configuration which will support a comprehensive accounting system including a budget system (Table C13-3).

You estimate that this will save $5,000 the first year; $7,500 the second year; and $10,000 in the next three years because all systems will be on PC's and management will be better able to take appropriate measures to manage accounts receivable, payable, and to tie their overall operations to a budget system. You also recommend a more comprehensive inventory system using a 100 MB hard disk connected to a PC. In other words, they will be better able to adjust their plans and adhere to them as they conduct their daily business affairs. Again, except for payroll, all retail outlet accounting will be done locally.

Table C13-3 Comprehensive Accounting System.

DESCRIPTION OF EQUIPMENT	NUMBER	UNIT PRICE
Small Micro with Hard Drive	4	$2,600
Small Micro/Small Hard Drive	1	1,200
Color Graphics Card	5	200
Memory Card	5	650
Monitor	5	200
Large Hard Disk (100MB)	1	2,000
Dot Matrix Printer	5	400
Switch for Laser and Dot Matrix	1	150
Laser Printer	1	1,550
SOFTWARE		
DOS	5	50
Nonintegrated Accounting Software	1	500
Database Package	5	600
Spreadsheet Package	5	300
Installation and Data Conversion		1,500

As a last alternative you recommend a network system with appropriate hardware so that you can install an integrated accounting package and so that all five retail outlets will be part of the system. Currently the retail outlets have their own system. This system will support color graphics for promotional efforts, a comprehensive inventory system for the warehouse as well as each store, and an integrated multiuser accounting software package. The configuration is shown in Table C13-4.

You estimate that this will save $15,000 the first year; $25,000 the second; $25,000 the third; $30,000 the fourth; and $25,000 the fifth year.

This system will enable management to control their entire operation and have on-line access to all relevant information.

REQUIRED: Prepare a cost-benefit analysis for Lancaster using the present value of these alternatives. Assume that the cost of capital for Lancaster is 10 percent.

13-5 Mickie Louderman is the new assistant controller of Pickens Publishers, a growing company with sales of $35 million. She was for-

Table C13-4 Network Accounting System.

DESCRIPTION OF EQUIPMENT	NUMBER	UNIT PRICE
Large Microcomputer with Hard Drive	1	$3,200
Small Micro with Small Hard Drive	9	1,200
Color Graphics Card	10	200
Memory Card	9	650
Monitor	10	200
Hard Disk (200 MB)	1	5,500
Network Cards	5	600
Laser Printer	2	1,550
Color Printer	1	1,000
Modem	6	400
Dot Matrix Printer	5	200

SOFTWARE		
DOS	10	50
PC Network Software	1	350
Integrated Multiuser Accounting Software	1	2,750
Database Package	10	600
Comprehensive Spreadsheet	10	600
Installation and Data Conversion		5,000

merly the controller of a smaller company in a similar industry where she was in charge of accounting and data processing, and had considerable influence over the entire computer center operation. Prior to Louderman's arrival at Pickens, the company revamped its entire computer operations center, placing increased emphasis on decentralized data access, microcomputers with mainframe access, and online systems.

The controller of Pickens, John Richards, has been with the company for 28 years and is near retirement. He has given Louderman managerial authority over both the implementation of the new system and the integration of the company's accounting-related functions. Her promotion to controller will be dependent on the success of the new accounting information system (AIS).

Louderman began to develop the new system at Pickens by using the same design characteristics and reporting formats that she had developed at her former company. She sent details of the new accounting information system to the departments that interfaced with accounting, including inventory control, purchasing, personnel, production control, and marketing. If they did not respond with suggestions by a prescribed date, she would continue the development process. Louderman and Richards determined a new schedule for many of the reports, changing the frequency from weekly to monthly. After a meeting with the director of computer operations, she selected a programmer to help her with the details of the new reporting formats.

Most of the control features of the old system were maintained to decrease the initial installation time, while a few new ones were added for unusual situations; however, the procedures for maintaining the controls were substantially changed. Louderman appointed herself the decisive authority for all control changes and program testing that related to the AIS, including screening the control features that related to batch totals for payroll, inventory control, accounts receivable, cash deposits, and accounts payable.

As each module was completed by the programmer, Louderman told the department to implement the change immediately, in order to incorporate immediate labor savings. There were incomplete instructions accompanying these changes, and specific implementation responsibility was not assigned to departmental personnel. Louderman believes that each operations person should "learn as they go," reporting errors as they occur.

Accounts payable and inventory control were the initial areas of the AIS to be implemented; several problems arose in both of these areas. Louderman was disturbed that the semi-monthly runs of payroll, which were weekly under the old system, had abundant errors and, consequently, required numerous manual paychecks. Frequently, the control totals of a payroll run would take hours to reconcile with the computer printout. To expedite matters, Louderman authorized the payroll clerk to prepare journal entries for payroll processing.

The new inventory control system failed to improve the carrying stock level of many items, causing several critical raw material stockouts that resulted in expensive rush orders. The primary control procedure under the new system was the availability of ordering and usage information to both inventory control personnel and purchasing personnel by direct access terminals so that both departments could issue purchase orders on a timely basis. The inventory levels were updated daily, so the previously weekly report was discontinued by Louderman.

Because of these problems, system documentation is behind schedule and proper backup procedures have not been implemented in many areas. Louderman has requested budget approval to hire two systems analysts, an accountant, and an administrative assistant to help her implement the new system. Richards is disturbed by her request since her predecessor had only one part-time employee as his assistant.

REQUIRED:

1. List the major steps Mickie Louderman should have taken during the analysis, design, and implementation of the accounting information system to ensure that end-user needs were satisfied.

2. Identify and describe three areas were Mickie Louderman has violated the basic principles of internal control during the implementation of the new accounting information system.

3. By referring to Mickie Louderman's approach to implementing the new accounting information system,

   a. identify and describe the weaknesses.

   b. make recommendations that would help Louderman improve the situation and continue with the development of the remaining areas of the accounting information system at Pickens Publishers. (CMA adapted)

13-6 Refer back to Nashville Recording in Case 12-4 and the solution to parts 1 through 5 which describe what has to be accomplished to support their decision-making, transaction, and reporting needs.

REQUIRED:

1. Prepare a systems flowchart for an alternative billing and inventory system.

2. Briefly identify the hardware configuration you envision to be necessary to support that alternative system.

13-7 (Requires knowledge of PERT in Appendix) Smith and Smith, CPAs, have been asked to help May's Industries investigate the possibility of computerizing their inventory system. They conclude that the tasks shown in Table C13-5 need to be performed to fully implement the system.

REQUIRED: How long will it take and what tasks are critical to completing the engagement on time? Prepare a PERT diagram as part of your solution.

13-8 Blackstone General Contractors has the following information needs:

1. Information that will allow a competitive bid to be submitted for a construction job

2. Internal accumulation and control of costs related to a specific job

3. Planning and budgeting information for scheduling jobs and resource allocation

The initial information requirement in the estimation process is a knowledge of the construction jobs that are "up for bid." This knowledge is gathered primarily from trade journals and weekly listings of new construction jobs in the metropolitan area. These provide a brief description of the job. Specialized blueprints for the job must then be obtained from the architect (or owner) for a specified charge. Next the actual bid is prepared by an estimator. The estimator will consider the amount of materials needed, the amount of labor needed, the bids received from the various subcontractors, and an appropriate allowance for overhead and profit. An important factor to be considered is the price of materials. Supplies used in the building industry are sometimes subject to violent fluctuation on a daily basis. For this reason, the estimator will not compute the material costs until moments before the bid is telephoned in. The most recent prices available are used for the bid. If the bid is accepted, the estimator will immediately place an order with suppliers for the amount of materials needed. This establishes the price for the materials at the price quoted in the bid.

Table C13-5   May's Industries (Smith & Smith CPA's).

ACTIVITY CODE	DESCRIPTION OF ACTIVITY	DAYS
A	Start	0
B	Plan, design, and program modules	30
C	Prepare site	30
D	Hardware selection	40
E	Write programs	40
F	Personnel selection	20
G	Program testing	15
H	Equipment installation	20
I	Documentation and user manual	20
J	Training	20
K	System testing	10
L	File conversion	20
M	Parallel operation	60
N	Stop	0

Cost information in the construction industry is of primary importance for three types of users. Estimators need relevant information on past costs of completed contracts in order to make estimates for bidding on future contracts. Managers use cost information in order to monitor the progress of the contract by comparing estimated cost figures with actual cost figures. Cost figures are also important in preparing income tax returns.

If the analysis of costs is to be useful, it is important to know how costs are allocated to each job. Direct costs are a function of subcontractors' costs, direct labor, direct materials, and equipment charges. Subcontractors' costs are allocated on the basis of the contract price and are readily verified. Direct labor is a function of time spent on a job by the contractor's employees and the rate of pay. This information is assembled on timecards that show (1) how long the employee worked; (2) which job was worked on; and (3) the rate of pay. Direct materials are purchased for a specific job following the estimator's analysis. Materials are charged to the job for which they were purchased. Equipment charges are divided into three categories: durable and standard equipment, special equipment, and perishable equipment. Durable and standard equipment charges for trucks, cranes, and bulldozers are made for each job on the basis of the fair amount of rent that would be paid to an outside equipment rental concern less any profit that would be incurred. Special equipment is equipment that can be used only on a particular project. This equipment would be rented and the rental payments would be charged to the job for which it was used less any residual value remaining after the job has been completed.

Indirect costs are charged on the basis of a fixed overhead rate. Costs of the estimating department are recorded on the basis of time spent on a successful bid. Costs of unsuccessful bids are considered general administrative expenses and are charged out using the fixed overhead rate.

The division of costs by elements is important as a guide in future construction of the same nature. Also, if analyzed on a fairly current basis, these unit costs can indicate whether the contract is running in excess of the estimate. It is important that a periodical accumulation of actual costs on each project be submitted by the accounting department. These reports should be analyzed by cost classifications on each job and compared with the total bid estimate using the same classifications.

REQUIRED: As part of the design team of a CPA firm, you have been assigned to recommend some alternative systems to meet Blackstone's information requirements.

1. What data elements would you suggest Blackstone keep on current jobs and past jobs to enhance the future estimation process and other cost accounting needs?

2. Would you recommend a relational database system over a simple file system and why?

3. What would be the pros and cons of using commercially available software?

4. How would you use a data dictionary and IPO charts to help you in the detailed design process?

5. How would IPO charts enhance any programming effort which may follow as part of implementation?

6. (Optional) Explain how a microcomputer database package could be used in accumulating costs for each job and, using this information, for estimating costs for new jobs.

13-9 Easy Way Builders, a regional building and supply retailer with outlets in several southeastern states, recently decided to install small microcomputers at each location and to tie these via modems to the home office. Sales data are transmitted once each day to the home office for the day's activities after closing. The home offices computer system accumulated local sales statistics and kept a perpetual inventory of building supplies better than the old manual system previously used by each location. With this new system, billing was handled out of the home office instead of from each location. This relieved each manager of a large volume of paper work.

Initially, considerable cost savings were realized. Lower stock levels were achieved with the new perpetual inventory system and better sales forecasting was achieved due to the availability of companywide sales data. Problems developed, however. Easy Way started to lose its market share. Managers complained that many of their larger customers (builders) had a difficult time in communicating and resolving problems related to their monthly statements. Moreover, these builders detested paper work and preferred to resolve problems and misunderstandings on a face-to-face basis. Generally these problems arose because the supplies ordered were excessive or the wrong items were delivered. Returns and exchanges were common.

REQUIRED:

1. Itemize any failures that may have occurred in the initial phases of problem definition through the analysis in the systems development. Indicate what should have been done to prevent these possible failures.

2. Do the same thing for the design and implementation phases of systems development.

3. Indicate how a distributed processing computer system may resolve some of these problems.

4. What can the organization do now about the mess they are in?

13-10 Whitson Company has just ordered a new computer for its financial information system. The present computer is fully utilized and no longer adequate for all of the financial applications Whitson would like to implement. The present financial system applications must all be modified before they can be run on the new computer. Additionally, new applications which Whitson would like to have developed and implemented have been identified and ranked according to priority.

Sally Rose, Manager of data processing, is responsible for implementing the new computer system. Rose listed the specific activities which had to be completed and determined the estimated time to complete each activity. In addition, she prepared a network diagram to aid in the coordination of the activities. The activity list (Table C13-6) follows and the network diagram is shown in Figure C13-2.

REQUIRED:

1. Determine the number of weeks which will be required to implement fully Whitson Company's financial information sys-

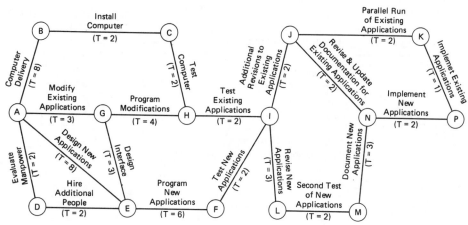

T = Expected time in weeks to complete activity

FIGURE C13-2   Whitson Company network diagram.

tem (i.e., both existing and new applications) on its new computer. Identify the activities which are critical to completing the project.

2. The term *slack time* is often used in conjunction with network analysis.

   a. Explain what is meant by slack time.

   b. Identify an activity which has slack time and indicate the amount of slack time available for that activity.

3. Whitson Company's top management would like to reduce the time necessary to begin operation of the entire system.

   a. Which activities should Sally Rose attempt to reduce in order to implement the system sooner? Explain your answer.

   b. Discuss how Sally Rose might proceed to reduce the time of these activities.

4. The general accounting manager would like the existing financial information system applications to be modified and operational in 22 weeks. Determine the number of weeks which will be required to modify the existing financial informa-

tion system applications and make them operational. (CMA adapted)

13-11   After deciding that its decision-making, transaction processing, and reporting needs required a new microprocessing system, Platte River Contractors purchased a system well suited to its needs, from a leading supplier of such systems for Platte River's type and size of business. All programs and their combinations were well tested by the software supplier. Given their lack of expertise, Platte River's managers decided to select a proven vendor for general contractors of their size.

Given their confidence in the system and its ease of operation, they terminated their bookkeeper. The receptionist was given the user's manual and told to enter the information on the CRT during her free time, which averaged six to seven hours per day. Moreover, the day the system arrived, Platte River's management personnel ceased operations of the old manual payroll, accounts receivable (contracts), purchasing and inventory, equipment scheduling, and asset systems. They immediately started using the new system.

Table 13-6 Whitson Company

ACTIVITY	DESCRIPTION ACTIVITY	EXPECTED TIME REQUIRED TO COMPLETE (IN WEEKS)
AB	Wait for delivery of computer from manufacturer	8
BC	Install computer	2
CH	General test of computer	2
AD	Complete an evaluation of manpower requirements	2
DE	Hire additional programmers and operators	2
AG	Design modifications to existing applications	3
GH	Program modifications to existing applications	4
HI	Test applications on new computer	2
IJ	Revise existing applications as needed	2
JN	Revise and update documentation for existing applications as modified	2
JK	Run existing applications in parallel on new and old computers	2
KP	Implement existing applications as modified on the new computer	1
AE	Design new applications	8
GE	Design interface between existing and new applications	3
EF	Program new applications	6
FI	Test new applications on new computer	2
IL	Revise new applications as needed	3
LM	Conduct second test of new applications on new computer	2
MN	Prepare documentation for the new applications	3
NP	Implement new applications on the new computer	2

Within a month, the company's auditors (one of the "big six") were called in to send out confirmations to its suppliers to clean up an awful mess. Platte River had completely lost track of its accounts payable records and was in the embarrassing position of having to ask each of its suppliers for the information.

REQUIRED: What went wrong? What should the company have done to prevent this problem?

13-12 Soft and Tender Footware, a manufacturer of bedroom slippers for ladies, recently fired its controller and EDP manager, who had been with the company for several years. To take his place, it sent one of its operations managers to school to learn all about the minicomputer hardware it was using. The company justifiably felt that, aside from the transaction processing and report generation of the minicomputer and supporting software, most of which has been programmed by the former controller, all accounting needs could be handled by several bookkeepers and the advice of a local CPA.

Subsequent to this, the CPA began to ask various questions about some of the output from the system, and the new Information System (IS) manager could not answer these questions. In fact, every time the IS manager needed to find out how a program worked or how it interfaced with other programs, he had to request a code listing and proceed from there. On each of these listings, he found a considerable amount of what he termed "excess baggage," or programming steps without apparent use. Upon hearing all of this, the president of the company was furious and threatened to "chuck" the accounting information system, hire several bookkeepers, and return to an old manual system where the mode of transaction processing was clear-cut and easy to see.

REQUIRED: What action on the part of the former controller would have prevented this problem? Why? Other than scrapping the accounting information system, what should management first do to get its system in order?

13-13 (Requires knowledge of Appendix) Ross and Montgomery, CPAs, are advising one of their clients about the acquisition of a new data processing system. To assist in scheduling the major tasks involved in design and development, they are using PERT. Their estimation of

their client's major activities and the weeks required to accomplish these activities is shown in Figure C13-3.

REQUIRED: What is the earliest date for the completion of system implementation? Where is the slack in the system? What assumptions did you make in your analysis?

13-14 Financial Alternatives Washington Farm Supply, a farm supply distributor for the upper Midwest, has decided to acquire a microcomputer, printer storage devices and software to process its accounting transactions, post the general ledger; and to prepare stock status reports, accounts receivable, and purchase activity reports on a daily basis for management's decisions needs. It can rent or purchase or lease the equipment and software. The following information is given on the four available alternatives:

1. Rent for $4,000 per year.
2. Lease for $2,000 per year for three years with an option to purchase at the end of three years for $4,000. Maintenance contract costs $1,500 per year for the life of the lease, and $1,000 per year when the purchase option is exercised at the end of three years. Assume cash flow at end of the year.
3. The same as alternative 2, with the option to purchase at the end of three years for $4,000 is not exercised.
4. Purchase for $8,000, with a maintenance contract costing $1,200 per year. The cost of capital is 10 percent. Other costs will be the same.

REQUIRED: What is the most desirable contract if Washington intends to keep the hardware and software from one to eight years and the exact number of years is unknown at the present time? Due to rapid technology changes, salvage value will be negligible.

13-15 (Analysis and Design Problems) Quasar Air, a freight company, guaranteed overnight delivery of all packages in the continental United States. It would pick up and deliver door-to-door in select U.S. cities, place packages on the plane, fly the planes to an old air

ACTIVITY		TIME (IN WEEKS)
A	Select vendor	2
B	Prepare site	7
C	Define system requirements	4
D	Determine specifications for system	3
E	Analyze decision and transaction processing network	6
F	Determine general approach to data processing	5
G	Write programs	5
H	Install hardware	2
I	Purchase hardware and software	1
J	Test (programs and systems)	6
K	Design database	3
L	Parallel conversion	8
M	Switch from old to new system	1
N	Train employees	4

FIGURE C13-3 Estimated times for each design and implementation activity.

force base south of St. Louis, sort all packages, fly to select destinations, and deliver packages the next morning at these various cities.

The company started out with a few major cities and eventually gained an excellent reputation. Its stock joined the list of other glamour companies on Wall Street. It easily raised more equity and expanded rapidly. Soon its scheduling and delivery routing problem became a nightmare. It began to have some trouble and frequently fell short of its goal of 100 percent overnight delivery because of scheduling and delivery problems.

Management was beginning to consider deleting some routes in order to assign more aircraft to high-volume traffic areas. The problem here was that the company controller could not determine the contribution to profit (if any) each route made because the cost system was so full of allocation assumptions and other dependent cost relationships.

Management had heard of some new operations research procedures that could resolve the company's traffic routing problems and had read about some new cost-allocation schemes that could help it get a better handle on contribution to actual profit of the various routes. Management decided to engage the services of Operations Research Systems. Operations Re-

search Systems' managers recommended a software package they had used before, called Traffic Scheduler–III, and a flexible standard cost system that they had sold to a wide variety of clients.

Mr. Blake, president of Quasar Air, decided that these two systems would meet the company's needs, so he purchased the systems and instructed Mr. Simmons, his controller who was responsible for all data processing, to install the systems and begin using them. This was done as soon as each had been compiled and run on Quasar's computer system. The programs worked well.

The conversion step was skipped because the programs ran so smoothly, and they were immediately implemented. Disaster struck next.

1. The schedule was fairly good from a distribution perspective under normal circumstances, but resulted in costly mistakes such as routing one plane for St. Louis to Miami to San Francisco to Toronto and back.

2. The schedule could not handle adverse weather conditions, which frequently socked in upper Midwest airports.

3. The schedule algorithm broke down when no solution was feasible and the "best" alternative was needed because it

was a linear programming optimization model. This occurred when more than one plane was in maintenance and a peak traffic load occurred.

4. The cost system did not interface with the scheduling algorithm to cost various routes over a range of potential routing patterns. The cost system did not interface with the general ledger system. Input actually had to be keyed into the general ledger package from reports generated by the cost system. The maintenance system did not interface with the scheduling algorithm, and there was no way to determine an optimal maintenance program for the fleet.

5. The amount of time needed to input delivery location data into the delivery algorithm on busy days took three hours at some locations and it was 9:00 A.M. before the trucks could leave to deliver the packages, resulting in many late deliveries.

The president, given these and many more problems, fired Mr. Simmons for failing to implement the new systems properly.

REQUIRED:

1. List any weaknesses in systems development implementation and state what should have been done to correct the weaknesses. Use the following format:

WEAKNESS	WHAT SHOULD HAVE BEEN DONE

2. As Quasar's accountant, where do you suggest it begin to clean up this mess? Outline your suggestions step by step and briefly explain the reason for each step.

13-16 The Reed Company of Winnipeg, Manitoba, has yearly sales close to $40 million. All of its business activities are conducted from one location. Currently, office workers manually perform all operations in accounts payable, accounts receivable, general ledger, and invoicing. The amount of work that the office staff performs is increasing each year and the staff, which now numbers 15 people, is finding it difficult to keep up with the excess workload. Reporting deadlines are often missed. Additional clerical help is not the solution and the manager recognizes that automation of the firm's procedures is essential.

In the existing system, orders are received through the mail. Clerks pull customers' records to check for poor credit risks and delinquent accounts. These are then referred to the manager.

Each customer record is updated manually and an entry is made in the sales summary. An invoice and bill of lading are made up and the latter is sent to the warehouse for assembly of the order. The products are picked from the inventory, and product cards are changed to reflect the change in inventory. If a product is not in stock, the office is notified and the invoice is adjusted. The return of a copy of the bill of lading to the office to advise that the order has been filled serves as authorization for sending the invoice to the customer.

At present, there are 6,000 customers for whom records are kept (200 characters of data per customer) and 500 products for which product ledger cards are kept (100 characters of data per product).

The design objectives are that the proposed system must be able to handle the existing order-entry and invoicing applications as well as improved inventory control function. It would also be desirable if some other basic functions could be handled. Moreover, the system must be designed to operate without a team of expensive IS personnel. No in-house programming or operation talent is available and training such a staff is not planned.

After a study of the system requirements and the potential benefits, two alternative system designs are proposed. One approach is to use a simple minicomputer file-oriented system that handles the several applications. The applications will be handled sequentially in a batch mode, and no internal processing interfaces are needed between applications. Although several terminals will be used, it is not a multiuser system because there is no concurrent sharing of data or applications software. All essential functions can be handled, although some cannot be handled as completely as desired. The back-order and future-order functions, for example, cannot be satisfactorily handled automatically, and so they will be maintained manually. Commissions and accounts payable will not be handled initially. Also, there is no possibility of handling the sales analysis requirements of the company.

In this first alternative, 10 megabyte removable floppy disks are used as the storage medium. There is a record for each customer and for each product. Batch processing is performed on one application at a time. When the accounts receivable or invoicing program is loaded into the computer, only that application can be run. The input is menu driven. Transaction output is printed as transactions are processed, for an effective audit trail. The supplier provides the basic business software with the minicomputer and charges $3 per instruction when deviations from the standard program are required. It appears that approximately 2,500 instructions will need to be modified in these programs to accommodate the special reporting requirements of the Reed Company. The hardware configuration—consisting of three microcomputer terminals, a small minicomputer and software, and a laser printer—has a purchase price of $32,000. On a five-year purchase plan the monthly payments are $800. Monthly maintenance is $100. Installation can be accomplished in three months. The supplier will supply four additional weeks of programmer training for the user, at any time the user desires. This system requires 100 square feet of space.

The other proposed system uses a relatively sophisticated on-line random access relational database minicomputer system with a data stored on a large hard disk. This system is a multiuser integrated system; more than one application can be run at one time and several users can share data and applications. This system is also menu driven. When an order arrives, the operator enters the customer's identification. The software will validate this identification, check the customer's credit, and then notify the input clerk whether to proceed with the first product ordered or to take the order to the manager to be handled manually. Assuming that the customer has a good credit rating, the operator will then enter the product number and the quantity desired, wait for the program to check if enough inventory is available to fill the order, and then enter the next product ordered. This procedure is repeated until the entire order is entered. The input clerk is notified if special action is required (such as excluding an item from the order because of insufficient inventory). Items which must be reordered are printed daily. Invoicing for all deliverable items is performed automatically as is the preparation of shipping documents. The preceding procedures initiate other functions which interface with the system.

The proposed on-line interactive database minicomputer system includes the processor, three microcomputer terminals, a laser printer, and a large disk drive. This hardware costs $56,000, or $1,400 per month on a five-year monthly installment plan. Maintenance is $250 per month. Application software will have to be developed in its entirety to make the integrated approach work. This cost is estimated to be $70,000, despite the use of much of the manufacturer's software. It is estimated that the installation time for such a system would be nine months. Also, this minicomputer would require 200 square feet of space.

The manufacturer of the small file-oriented minicomputer provides, at a $750 charge, the means to convert Reed's customer and product files to disks. With respect to the on-line interactive minicomputer system, the software developed for processing the sales data can also be used to convert the data to disk storage. (However, the data in the present files will still need to be keyed into the computer system via the microcomputer terminals.)

Current space costs are $2 per square foot per month. Keying and verifying rates are $7 per hour at a rated speed of 10,000 keystrokes per hour.

REQUIRED: Which alternative system should the manager choose? Justify your answer in quantitative and qualitative terms. Use a three-year horizon. SMAC adapted.

13-17 Pickering Nursery has retained you to design an accounts receivable and billing system. They are a major supplier of nursery products to builders in the Charlotte, NC, area. They maintain a retail location, but it's strictly cash and carry and credit card business. Their major problem is with business accounts receivable. They currently use an old MAX-10 microcomputer for their inventory system and would like their accounts receivable system to be compatible. They have a 10 megabyte disk on the MAX-10, and it is taxed to the limit to handle the inventory system. You have determined that the solution to their problem is feasible given their initial limit of $5,000 for the installation of such a system. You have also analyzed their system and have determined that they need the following data to service their customer base:

Customer number	5 bytes
Customer name	25 bytes
Customer address	32 bytes
Phone number	10 bytes
For each transaction	
Order (invoice) number	5 bytes
Date	6 bytes
Amount of purchase	8 bytes
For each product	
quantity	5 bytes
description	10 bytes
price	6 bytes
Current balance	8 bytes
Previous balance	8 bytes
Customer payment history (12 months)	
Date	6 bytes
Amount	8 bytes
Credit limit	8 bytes
Service charges	6 bytes

You estimate that they have approximately 500 potential credit customers and that sufficient storage should be allocated for 25 transactions per customer and 10 products per order. The system should be user friendly because Mr. Pickering is still a novice at using the PC. Customer query is a must for granting credit. The system should be able to accumulate totals for analysis of sales and automatically print monthly statements. Backup is essential to maintain data integrity. A customer list is needed for promotion efforts and an aging schedule is needed for collections. The system should be designed so that accounts receivable and inventory are integrated, i.e., one transaction input will update both systems.

You will be expected to design, start up, and install the entire system. You must test it and you must make sure it has adequate internal controls.

REQUIRED:

1. Given the hardware and software specifications prepare a RFP.

2. Suggest a set of control procedures for insuring data integrity and reliability of operations.

13-18 The St. Anne Hospital of Ottawa, Ontario, has decided to develop and implement a computer-based information system as soon as it is feasible. St. Anne's controller has identified the following activities, with their expected durations and interdependencies, that would be involved in the undertaking (Figure C13-4).

REQUIRED:

1. Prepare a network diagram and specify the activities on the critical path.

2. What is the minimum number of days required to design and implement this system? *Hint:* Refer to the appendix on PERT.
(SMAC adapted.)

13-19 As a CPA advising a client in the design and development of a new system, how would you explain to the client the need to follow the structured phases in systems analysis and design suggested in this chapter? Keep in mind that the client is not impressed with academic reasons for all this effort and wants to know why he just can't go and lease an accounting system like his friend at the Rotary Club. Also, keep in mind that you will need to justify your billing time.

13-20 Metro Ad Agency performs market analysis and develops promotion and marketing strategies for several hundred clients in the Dallas–Ft. Worth area of Texas. They have been using a mainframe system for designing various market and promotion models with good success for several years. These models incorporate fiscal accounting information, inventory and sales statistics, market data, and economic information. Metro has been satisfied with this procedure. Recently, however, one of their competitors has started using microcom-

ACTIVITY CODE	DESCRIPTION OF ACTIVITY	EXPECTED ACTIVITY DURATION (DAYS)	CODES OF PREDECESSOR ACTIVITIES*
A	Prepare system requirements	10	
B	Plan design phase	3	A
C	Design system	20	B,F
D	Verify feasibility	2	C
E	Organize project	5	A
F	Establish plans and controls	3	E
G	Prepare design specifications	2	C
H	Prepare audit and control specifications	4	G
I	Prepare job descriptions for new employees	3	H
J	Prepare training guides	3	I
K	Prepare logic diagrams and programs	20	D
L	Prepare test data	4	K
M	Perform program testing and debugging	5	L
N	Select and order system resources	20	D
O	Install computer system	12	N
P	Perform system testing and debugging	5	M,O
Q	Prepare program documentation	5	M,O
R	Prepare system documentation	3	J,Q
S	Plan for system support	2	R
T	Perform final checkout and cutover	3	Q

* Activities that must be completed *prior* to starting the listed activity.

FIGURE C13-4   St. Anne's hospital.

puters to comply with changing the client market. So Metro replaced each mainframe terminal with a microcomputer to keep up with competition.

REQUIRED: They have been using the structured approach to systems development and using the DIS department to do the analysis, design, and programming. This has been too slow to respond to changes in their clients' markets. Suggest a different analysis and design procedure.

13-21 Tulsa Underwriters has a customer base of several thousand. They manage the in-

surance for a wide variety of clients and write policies for many companies. They have been using antiquated terminals to enter transaction data. These transactions consist of new policies, modifications to existing policies, claims, payments, and inquiries about rates and status of policies and claims. They are considering either the use of multiuser software with a small mainframe and "smart" terminals system or a local area network of microcomputers for their customer representatives. They feel it is essential that each representative be able to access their own data on their set of clients, that they have access to companywide information to answer questions, and that they have either smart terminals or microcomputers that can edit transaction information. Moreover, they feel that security is important given the sensitivity of the data and the transaction amounts. They have many questions regarding the pros and cons of the various ways that they can configure their system of terminals or PCs in their offices.

REQUIRED:

1. As their accountant, describe for them the differences between local area networks and multiuser systems.

2. Describe the analysis and design steps they would use to make a decision between these alternatives.

3. Describe the data preparation and access controls you would recommend if they adopt a multiuser system with smart terminals.

4. How would these controls differ for a LAN? Can they link LANs?

5. Describe the communication controls you would use for the transmission of information on policies to the various insurance companies.

14

PRODUCTION AND INVENTORY SYSTEMS

OBJECTIVE

Over the last several years there has been an increased awareness of the vital role production and inventory logistics systems play in the successful operations of an organization. It is imperative that products and services be produced efficiently, delivered on time, in sufficient quantity, with high quality, and with minimum waste. Many companies have failed to do this and have fallen by the wayside to global and local competition. Six major trends[1] have had a significant impact on the production and inventory systems of an organization. These are: increased quality, reduced inventory, flexible manufacturing flow, automation, product line organization, and effective use of information. In general, it is no longer enough to simply produce goods for inventory and charge the marketing department with the responsibility of selling the product or service. These products need to be well designed so that they meet consumer needs and so that they can be manufactured efficiently.

---

[1] Robert A. Howell, and Stephen R. Soucy, "Major Trends for Management Accounting," *Management Accounting*, July 1987, pp. 21–27.

In this chapter, traditional production and inventory accounting systems will be presented because many systems still use traditional planning, cost and inventory control procedures. Accountants and auditors need to fully understand these traditional systems and their informational needs. More contemporary systems will also be presented. These may lead to a more competitive position in the market. Accountants must also understand the informational needs of these more contemporary production and inventory systems. Therefore, we review the basic decision and transaction characteristics of both the traditional and more contemporary systems used in the process of converting resources into goods and services. These involve: production, planning and scheduling, engineering and product design, maintenance, quality control, purchasing, and inventory systems. Microcomputer, batch, and on-line systems are illustrated.

Traditional Production and Inventory Systems

The objective of a traditional production and inventory logistics information system is to support the decision-making, transaction processing, and reporting requirements of production, inventory, and quality control. These requirements are a function of the management's strategy and objectives. In a traditional production system, management needs inventory to absorb fluctuations in the supply of raw material and subassemblies and to meet the demand for finished goods. Economical production runs and production line balancing need inventory in a traditional logistics system to support long-run efficient operation. Marketing management needs inventory to smooth fluctuations in its traditional distribution system and in sales demand in order to better serve customers. Inventory has also been useful in more traditional systems in decoupling parts of an organization such as marketing and production. It serves as a buffer between those areas that would be too costly and impractical to tightly couple or coordinate.

In developing an inventory system, the level of service provided as well as the cost of that service is very important. The cost of service can increase astronomically; therefore, the traditional inventory accounting information (control) system must be designed to enhance management's control over inventory levels and costs. Traditional inventory control systems vary in complexity from those using simple status reports, reorder points, and economic lot sizes to those using mathematical and statistical models. Regardless of the inventory control system's complexity, it must be designed to provide information to support the various activity levels within each function (primarily the logistics and marketing functions in this illustration), and it must link all the elements of the system in the most efficient way.

The basic objective of a traditional production control system is to support efficient production operations through the efficient use of company resources such as plant and equipment, financial, raw material, labor, and supporting overhead. Such a system must support planning and controlling activities. To accomplish this objective, management needs accurate, timely, and relevant information including production orders, the demand for products, product and quality specifications, manufacturing sequence specifications, labor efficiency data, and resource availability information.

The basic objective of a traditional purchasing accounting information (control) system is to ensure that production and inventory systems have sufficient raw material, supplies, equipment, and inventory to operate effectively and efficiently.

Planning objectives are generally executed using budget or responsibility accounting systems, scheduling procedures, or mathematical models such as those reviewed in Chapter 17. Cost control objectives are traditionally achieved through a system of overhead budgets and through the use of standard costs and the subsequent variance feedback information. Quality control objectives are accomplished using a series of inspection points throughout the plant.

Contemporary Production and Inventory Systems

In contrast, contemporary production and inventory systems seek to tightly coordinate and to integrate the objectives just discussed. This includes the use of just-in-time (JIT) systems, material requirement planning systems (MRP), flexible manufacturing systems (FMS) or computer-aided design and computer-aided manufacturing (CAD/CAM) production management systems. All of these attempt to closely link the logistics objectives, through carefully integrated production planning, engineering, and control. Accounting information (control) systems are a key element of the information needed to coordinate (link) these logistics activities.

For example, in contemporary (just-in-time) logistics systems the objective is to reduce all non-value-added activities to zero (this includes inventory). Thus, inventory is minimized, setup time is minimized, transit time is minimized, and defective products or unsatisfactory service is minimized. The overall objective is to deliver a quality product or service to the customer or client on time and in sufficient quantity with minimum effort. Often the inventory system consists of the bare minimum such as a simple count of inventory, because there isn't much to account for. Production is typically scheduled to eliminate waste in setup time and in work-in-process inventory. Purchasing is often prearranged with a fewer number of vendors so that parts arrive only as needed and material inventory is greatly reduced. Often, no formal purchase order system such as those outlined in other chapters in this text is required because the organization has signed an agreement (contract) ahead of time to provide a certain amount of material or components just as they are needed.

The objective in planning is to integrate the various production and inventory systems with marketing and to reduce the planning time horizon, to reduce forecast errors which traditionally required inventory to act as a buffer between production and marketing. This reduction is accomplished via setup time reduction, attention to quality to reduce waste, and flexible manufacturing systems to quickly adjust to demand changes. Also computer-aided design and manufacturing have enabled firms to more quickly adjust to market changes.

Plant capacity	Customer characteristics	Quality expectations
Competitive environment	Distribution system	Product design
Resource availability	Labor requirements	Manufacturing process
Financial capability	Technology level	JIT philosophy
Product life cycle	Uniqueness of product	Prices
Product options	Economy	Computer system
Obsolescence	Government regulation	Customer service
Product mix	Government influence	Supply of components
Styles and colors	Seasonality	Quality of labor
Inventory policy	Ownership	Maintenance

FIGURE 14-1   Common environmental characteristics.

DECISION AND TRANSACTION PROCESSING CHARACTERISTICS

Basic Environmental Considerations

We cannot easily specify a general accounting system for production and inventory management because each firm operates in a unique and often vastly different environment. Thus, as we noted in earlier chapters, environmental characteristics play a major role in information system development and implementation. An accountant, therefore, must understand the decision-making, reporting, and transaction processing environment of the business so he or she can design a system that is contingent upon these key factors. Figure 14-1 outlines some common characteristics that have a bearing on traditional and contemporary logistics management systems. For example, an accountant who is advising a utility organization must be cognizant of such key environmental characteristics as governmental regulations, public rate-making activities, the assets involved and the effect of technology on these assets, classes of customers, electrical distributive systems and backup capabilities, supplies of fuel, and capital requirements for future expansion. The information system must be designed to satisfy decision-making, processing, and reporting needs in this context. Therefore, studies of the economic and decision-making environment must precede an analysis of decision-making and transaction processing networks.

In traditional batch processing manufacturing and inventory systems, the environment may be such that scheduling and ordering decisions are made weekly. In these cases, daily economic activities have little effect on management decisions. Changes in plans are very infrequent. Weekly stock reports on material, work in process, and finished goods suffice for most decision-making requirements. Prices and costs are relatively stable and can be published once a week for marketing decisions. A batch processing or manual system that generates reports following traditional lines of authority and responsibility will be likely to satisfy management's information needs.

In a highly competitive contemporary logistics environment, however, prices, costs, product mix, and demand fluctuate daily. Profitability and forecasting decisions are more difficult to make. Most likely this type of environment will require a more contemporary logistics system such as just-in-time (JIT), manufacturing resource planning or material requirement planning (MRP), or flexible manufacturing systems (FMS), which may be linked together into some form of computer integrated manufacturing (CIM). A system is required that can constantly monitor the environment and alert managers to changing economic events in order to allow timely scheduling decisions. This type of environment will often require that a manager take an integrated view of manufacturing that crosses traditional management functions. This means that management must integrate all functions from product development through the actual delivery of the product or service. To support these coordinated activities, an information system must be able to support a product or matrix organization structure. The system may require on-line data processing capability. In some situations, such as MRP, complex database management systems such as outlined in Chapter 10 may be required.

Traditionally, production operations may follow a set sequence of steps where work is done to the product as it moves down an assembly line, or as it moves from workstation to workstation in batches (jobs) in a job shop model. Often at the end of each production run in the process system or at the end of each job (batch), significant setup times are required because of the specialized nature of the production (workstation) equipment. In more contemporary systems, flexible manufacturing systems (FMS) may be used along with computer-aided manufacturing (CAM) to control the flow of work on the factory floor.

WORLD CLASS PRODUCTION SYSTEMS AND COST DRIVERS.   In order to be more competitive in world markets, production, and in a broader sense logistics systems, have had to shift their emphasis from traditional planning of production runs based on forecasted demand, the stockpiling of inventory for distribution, and using standard cost systems for controlling material, labor, and overhead costs. In such systems, very little consideration was given to the cost of inventory, related obsolescence, and markdowns. The total cost of low quality and related repairs, customer ill will, warranties, inspection, rework costs and production downtime, setups, lost sales, lost market share, decreased manufacturing flexibility, reduced throughput, and incentive schemes are much more important. In a traditional manufacturing environment these costs were masked by excessive inventory at every stage in the process.

To be competitive, renewed emphasis had to be made to cut out all non-value-added costs. These include among other items: inventory costs, inspection costs, rework costs, and setup time costs. In general, a much larger set of cost drivers must be considered in planning and controlling the logistics aspects of an organization. These are the real determinants (called cost drivers) of product costs in competitive global markets. These include:

1. Process time used to add value or to work on the product.
2. Inspection and time needed to insure the material and product is up to standard.
3. Reworking time needed to restore product to acceptable standards.
4. Move time needed to transport components and product from the beginning to the end of the manufacturing and distribution cycle.
5. Queuing time needed for the product to wait for the next step in process-

ing or in distribution. This is a component in material, work in process and finished goods inventory.

6. Storage time of materials, components, in process products and finished goods which are stockpiled for the next stage in the logistics cycle. This is another component of inventory.
7. Variety of products and related components.
8. Schedule changes.
9. Changes in product or options resulting in set-up times.
10. Lead times and their related uncertainty for components and finished products.
11. Customer satisfaction.
12. Maintenance and machine down time.[2]

Of these, only the processing and move time can add value to the product; move time can sometimes add location value. These should be as efficient as possible. The other cost drivers just suggested need to be minimized for a company to be as efficient as possible. It should be noted that many of these are related to quality and time. Figure 14-2 compares traditional cost accounting information with the new information requirements of an organization desiring to monitor and control the variety of cost drivers indicated above. As can be seen from this figure, the management of time is becoming very important in the logistics function of an organization.

The implications for an accounting information system are that the system must begin to measure these additional cost drivers, or surrogates for them, in order to provide management with relevant information to control the physical

FIGURE 14-2   Examples of information requirements for traditional vs. contemporary logistics systems.

TRADITIONAL	CONTEMPORARY JIT, MRP, AND FMS
Inventory levels	Schedule attainment
Actual costs by work center:	Conversion costs by product
Material	Cost of quality
Labor	Level of customer service
Overhead idle time	On-time delivery of product
Rework and scrap	Part lead times
Standard costs	Set-time reduction
Work center variances for:	Number of customer complaints
Material	Group performance evaluation
Labor	Competitors' costs
Overhead	Product cycle time
Purchase price variances	Transition time to respond to
Machine utilization	changing customer demand
Inventory turnover	Time for inspection and movement
Individual performance evaluation	Number of changes in schedule

[2] Robert D. McIlhattan, "The JIT Philosophy, "*Management Accounting,* September, 1987, pp. 20–26.

(logistical) activities of the organization. Control of these is necessary for the organization to compete effectively.

DECISION NETWORK.   The objective of a logistics and production information system is to provide management with the information necessary to make operational, planning, and strategic decisions, report the results of operations to third parties, and to process transactions. These transactions undergird the information system because summaries of transaction data are often used to make decisions. However, such information is often irrelevant for decision making or is in a form not useful for levels of management other than the operations level. The accountant and the system analyst must therefore design the system around the decision and reporting network and not around the flow of transactions, although transaction information is necessary to value inventory in traditional systems and to track the flow of products in more contemporary systems.

As outlined in earlier chapters, the economic, business, and information environment must also be reviewed in designing the system. The business strategy and organization within which the system must function is a key facet of this environment. A traditional organization chart is illustrated in Figure 14-3. The production vice-president is responsible for providing corporate headquarters with information for strategic planning. The vice-president also needs information for managerial decisions and for working with the marketing and finance organizational units. Each plant manager and each staff manager is responsible for supplying the production vice-president with sufficient information for these decision-making and reporting requirements. Department supervisors and various department heads in turn supply information to the plant managers.

Depending on the firm and its economic environment, the department heads in traditional settings may be responsible for such activities as purchasing, production, maintenance, inventory control, engineering, cost accounting, personnel, and scheduling. The department heads need information for operational decisions, and they must also supply information to the plant manager for decisions and reporting needs. The logistics information system must therefore satisfy the information requirements of all levels within the organization.

In more contemporary settings, each product or type of service will have a product manager whose sole responsibility will include all logistical operations and in many cases all marketing and financial functions as well. In some cases, minifactories will exist within a total factory where all operations pertaining to one product will be grouped to reduce move time. This is in contrast to more traditional settings where processes are grouped by the type of process. In general, the plant will be organized around product flows.

Logistics Subsystems

There can be many logistics subsystems depending on the organization and business strategy these typically include: engineering and product design, production operations, quality control, purchasing, maintenance, personnel inventory control. Purchasing is discussed in the next chapter in the expenditures cycle and personnel is discussed in the chapter on financial accounting information systems. Each has a characteristic set of information sources, data

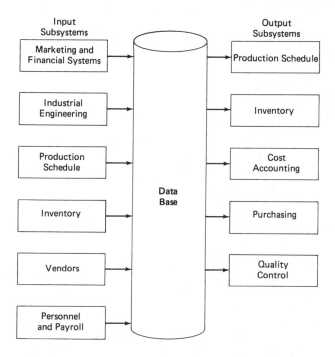

FIGURE 14-3   Production and inventory logistics organization.

files, decisions, and information requirements. Figure 14-4 outlines many of these sources and their destinations. Traditionally these are all separate functions; but in many more contemporary environments they are integrated. A discussion of integrated systems such as those used in computer integrated manufacturing (CIM) will follow.

Production Operations

Production operation involves both planning and actual manufacturing. The objective of a traditional production operation is to schedule production operations and to efficiently produce products. Given a set of constraints on equipment, personnel, supplies, and financial resources, management must meet sales and distribution system stock demands. Management can use a variety of methods to accomplish this objective. Many of these are very traditional; others use sophisticated computer software to schedule production. They can vary from a review of inventory status reports to sophisticated mathematical models which use simulation and linear programming. This is followed by several scheduling models. These include material requirement planning (MRP), just-in-time (JIT) Kanban and math programming. Computer-aided design (CAD) and computer-aided manufacturing (CAM), can be used to design products to expedite these and to plan and control all of these operations.

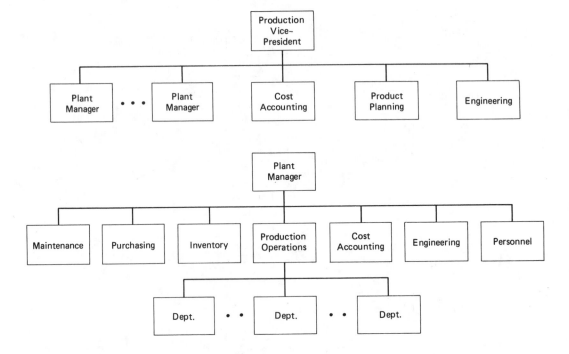

FIGURE 14-4 Production management systems.

Flexible Manufacturing Systems (FMS)

FMS attempts to reduce setup times to the absolute minimum so that the same machinery can be used for a variety of products with very little lost time. This is in contrast to traditional manufacturing systems where jobs move down an assembly line through a series of workstations which do a particular task. In many situations the machines used in an FMS system are automatic and can easily be switched from one product or from one operation to another; but not always. Often just changes in scheduling will remove or at least lessen the impact of bottlenecks. Then a few procedural changes aimed at the remaining bottlenecks may increase throughput, reduce work in process inventory, and increase flexibility in the manufacturing process. Priorities and careful scheduling are important in implementing such a system.

A list of benefits which accrue to FMS systems include:

1. Ability to produce a wide range of products.
2. Ability to respond quickly to customer demands and product changes.
3. Ease of adding new products and changes in volume of existing products.
4. Reduced labor as computerized material handling systems and machines, such as numerical control machines and robots, are used to replace human operators.

5. Improved quality as machine certainty replaces human uncertainty in quality.

6. Less set up time due to scheduling, product design set up operations located at the loading and unloading stations and not at the machine work stations, and flexibility of the machines.

7. Increased machine use due to machine scheduling, no set up time at machines, efficient movement of products from one work center to another.

8. Lower work in process inventory due to computer scheduling of manufacturing operations, less set up time, and more efficient material handling.

9. Less space due to reduced inventory and the use of fewer, more flexible machines.

10. Reduced direct labor costs.

11. More effective response to machine down time due to the flexibility of machines to pick up the operations of the equipment under repair.

12. Better information on production, systems utilization, tooling, and maintenance, for example.[3]

Additional information is required to effectively operate an FMS system. This system must be able to schedule, control, and monitor many machines and FMS workcenters as illustrated in Figure 14-5.

Planning and Scheduling

The actual manufacturing process must be carefully planned and scheduled.[4] Traditionally, this is accomplished using sales order and inventory reports, but in today's competitive environment a computer is frequently used in this planning and scheduling process. Material requirement planning (MRP) or just-in-time (JIT) systems are widely used to accomplish this. MRP is a traditional push type of system which develops production plans based on sales forecasts and stock levels, whereas JIT is a pull type of system in which each step, in the flow, requests the components or material from the previous step when it is ready to use it (work on it or sell it). The latter, theoretically, will reduce inventory to zero.

MATERIALS REQUIREMENTS PLANNING (MRP).   A MRP system can be used to track the progress of a production (work) order and to make sure needed material and components arrive at each workstation in sufficient time to smooth production. A smooth production system maximizes efficiency by minimizing down time and stockouts.

MRP systems can take uneven demand, determine a production schedule and order the necessary material to smooth and maximize the efficiency of the production line. To do this requires a bill of materials for each product. The linkage between the bill of materials and production requirements is called ex-

---

[3] Robert E. Bennett, and James A. Hendricks, "Automated Equipment," *Management Accounting*, July 1987, pp. 39–46.

[4] See Sumer C. Aggarwal, "MRP, JIT, OPT, FMS? Making Sense of Production Operations Systems," *Harvard Business Review*, September-October, 1985, for a complete discussion of these procedures.

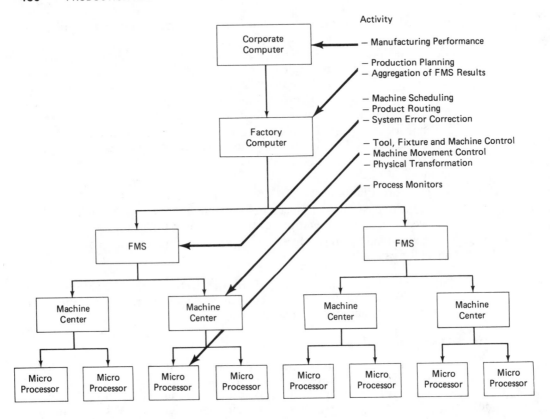

FIGURE 14-5 Information flows for flexible manufacturing system.
Source: Dilts, D. M. and G. W. Russell, "Accounting for the Factory of the Future", *Management Accounting*, April, 1985, p. 3.

ploding the bill of materials. This simply means that one looks at the detailed material requirements of a product. This is the basis for determining what materials or components are needed and where they are needed at each stage in production. The MRP system also requires inventory and finished goods status information, including open purchase orders; that is, materials on order and when they are expected to arrive.

A MRP system produces to meet a master production schedule based on sales order or a forecast and inventory. This way inventory shortages, production bottlenecks, and potential down time are spotted in advance. To minimize these problems material can be expedited and completion dates can be adjusted accordingly. The system is good for companies with mass production assembly lines. It will help control inventories, improve labor efficiency, and help schedule the production process. Information requirements are elaborate, extensive, and complex. These requirements include job order and routing sheets. MRP systems automated these.

From:	Part Number:	Kanban Number: 5
Housing	34500	
Assembly	Name:	Type:
	30cc Engine	Gas 2 Cycle Engine
To:	Quantity:	Location:	Workstation:
Inspection	50	Aisle A6	Electrical Assembly

FIGURE 14-6 Kanban control card ticket.

JUST-IN-TIME (JIT) AND KANBAN.   In contrast, just in time (JIT) is based on demand to pull the product through the system. JIT/Kanban systems are an attempt to reduce inventories, reduce setup times, reduce overall costs, and increases the velocity of product flow through the production process. The Kanban move ticket replaces the job orders and routing sheets of more traditional systems. It emphasizes small lot sizes. The system requires short lead times, which translate into small inventories at every stage. Because a chain of move tickets connects all stages from suppliers to retailers, companies never need additional paperwork for planning and control. It requires far less information than MRP. Figure 14-6 illustrates such a ticket. A typical Kanban system using such tickets is illustrated in Figure 14-7.

In the Kanban system, customer orders are keyed into the computer as they arrive and approved suppliers are immediately informed that certain components (parts or material) are needed. Arrangements are made with the supplier to furnish the components just-in-time (JIT) for production so that stores inventory is virtually eliminated. The supplier immediately ships the necessary components along with a bill of lading. No formal purchase order is necessary in this system. Parts arrive on a predetermined schedule (say, one day). At that time a Kanban card describing the part to be manufactured, its production sequence, its required components, and its delivery schedule, is then sent to the first processing step in time to meet its scheduled delivery date.

As the component in the last step is completed, the card is sent to be keyed into the system to indicate compliance with the schedule and to generate an invoice. Upon its completion, the computer then requests the component from process 2 along with the necessary parts to complete process 3. In turn, as component leaves process 2 a request is made for the next component from process 1. In this way products are pulled through the system and components and the necessary parts arrive just-in-time (JIT) for production. This procedure greatly reduces in process inventory. Along the way, if a component fails to meet inspection standards the whole process is stopped to fix the problem. In this way no wasted effort is put forth to produce more defective units in subsequent processing steps.

The scheduling and the tracking of the movement of products is accomplished by using the feedback system shown in Figure 14-7. It should be noted that no job-cost sheet follows the product because all the labor and overhead are applied for the *entire* process (instead of each workstation) to the product. This is in contrast to traditional systems which apply these conversion costs via over-

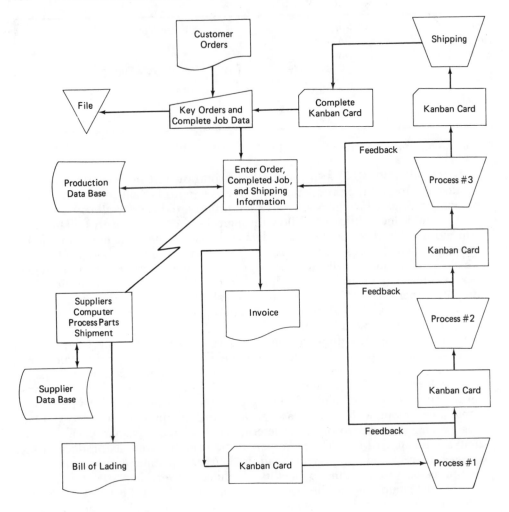

FIGURE 14-7 JIT/Kanban system.

head rates for each processing step. Kanban cards are simply used to describe the product, its production sequence, and its components.

In summary, the system simply counts the products as they are completed and describes the work to be done at each processing step. It is a much simpler system than a traditional job-cost system with a job-cost sheet which is used to tally all the costs at each workstation (process).

MATH PROGRAMMING SCHEDULING ALGORITHM. Mathematical scheduling algorithms may be used in any of these scheduling systems. To demonstrate the concepts of a *mathematical decision model* applied to production, consider the following problem. Assume that a production process exists in which three separate and distinct products can be produced. The only limited resource is labor; 400 labor hours are available. From prior experience it is known that product 1 requires eight hours of labor per unit of product output, product 2 requires four hours per unit of output, and product 3 requires two hours per unit of output. Product 1 contributes \$12 per unit to profits, product 2 contributes \$10 per unit, and product 3 contributes \$8 per unit. Based upon these data, we might conclude that as many units as possible of product 1 should be produced because this product contributes the most per unit to profit. Upon examining the labor requirements, however, we can see that product 1 has the highest per-unit labor requirement.

A decision model approach to the problem would be to express the problem as a linear programming model and solve via the SIMPLEX method. Expressed mathematically, the problem is:

$$\text{Maximize } z = 12x_1 + 10x_2 + 8x_3$$

$$\text{Subject to: } 8x_1 + 4x_2 + 2x_3 \leq 400$$

where

x_1 = number of units of product 1 to produce

x_2 = number of units of product 2 to produce

x_3 = number of units of product 3 to produce

z = total profits resulting from the production of x_1, x_2, and x_3

The optimal solution to the problem, resulting from employing the SIMPLEX algorithm, is $x_1 = 0$, $x_2 = 0$, $x_3 = 200$ units; and $z = \$1600$.

Engineering and Product Design

Production operations may have an engineering support subsystem. The objective of an engineering and product design system is to: provide product specifications, develop effective production sequences, prepare bills of material, specify quality controls, determine subassembly requirements, specify a scheduling algorithm, and design efficiency into the product. Information from this support system is often key input information for operations decisions. In more contemporary systems, a CAD/CAM design and control system may be an integral part of the logistics system, as shown in Figure 14-8.

A list of benefits which often accrue to an organization which uses CAD/CAM include the following:

1. Improved design and product drawings.
2. Early discovery and reduction of errors.
3. Integration of design and analysis activities.

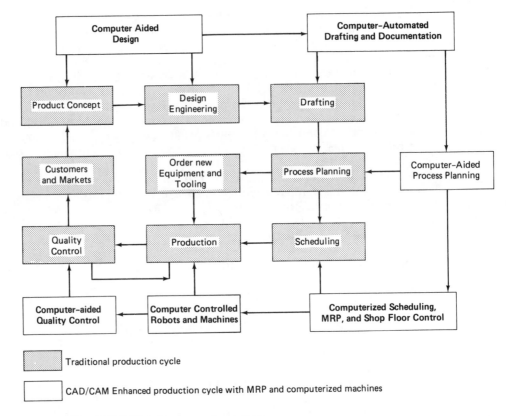

FIGURE 14-8 CAM/CAD design and control system.
Source: Groover, Mikell P. and Emory W. Zimmers, Jr. *CAD/CAM Computer-Aided Design and Manufacturing*, ©
1984. Adapted by permission of Prentice Hall, Englewood Cliffs, New Jersey.

4. Increased design productivity and shorter lead times.
5. Reduced training time.
6. Reduced numerical control machine programming costs via program libraries.
7. Better control of machine tool and fixture design for manufacturing.
8. Improved quality control.
9. More efficient material handling.
10. Shorter manufacturing lead times.
11. Reduced set up times.
12. Reduced costs and more competitive products.[5]

The net result can be an increase in productivity, efficiency, and effectiveness through faster throughput, increased quality and reduced defects, reduced inventories, improved scheduling of parts and product distribution.

---

[5] Bennett, "Automated Equipment," pp. 39–46.

COMPUTER AIDED DESIGN (CAD).   Computer-aided design uses computers in the developing, analyzing, and modifying of a product design including the actual drafting and documentation. This can be seen in Figure 14-8 which shows the enhancements needed to convert the traditional production cycle into a CAD/CAM system. At the very beginning, the computer is used to build production efficiency, which is important to JIT and FMS systems, into the design of the product. This can be used to simplify the products, to reduce the number of components, and reduce setup times. This can be accomplished by considering the characteristics of the product as well as the characteristics of the manufacturing process in the design process. Moreover the design process is automated so that modifications are simple and can still consider the constraints just noted.

COMPUTER-AIDED MANUFACTURING (CAM).   Computer-aided manufacturing uses the computer to plan, implement, and control production operations using the resources available to the organization. CAM may use one of the planning and scheduling procedures such as MRP. Combining CAD with CAM can result in maximum use of the computer and its ability to analyze information and in some cases seek the best design or production schedule to improve the efficiency and the effectiveness of the manufacturing process. The whole manufacturing process is computerized via a scheduling scheme to monitor via feedback information systems from the manufacturing and distribution process. These feedback systems can monitor inventory levels, product flow, quality and can catch bottlenecks and problems and provide information so that the CAM system can adjust the production and distribution plans accordingly.

Maintenance

The objective of the *maintenance system* is to keep the logistics system operating. The effectiveness of the production system is very much a function of maintenance. Decisions concerning the timing and amount of maintenance to be performed must be made periodically as well as when breakdowns occur. As before, an information system must be designed and implemented to support the decision-making network of the maintenance system. Preventive and routine maintenance is often planned; but, an information system must clearly monitor the logistics (operations) process so that management can react when problems occur. Production and performance records can be used as early warning signals of potential problems and be used to schedule preventative maintenance.

Quality Control

The objective of the quality control system is to (1) ensure that material and components which enter the production process meet the quality standards of the organization; (2) make sure that the components as they go from one workstation to another meet the standards of the organization; and (3) finally make sure that finished products meet the quality standards of the organization prior to shipment (or delivery of the service if the organization provides a service). These objectives are generally carried out in a traditional system using a series of inspection points at the beginning, throughout the process, and at the end of the production cycle to test and inspect the product. Defective units are then returned for rework, scrapped, or sometimes sold as seconds. In traditional systems, the cost of quality control is relatively easy to assess but it may be incomplete. As will be discussed later, in more contemporary systems the cost of quality is much more complex because it is much more extensive and gathering quality information extends well beyond the bounds of the production facility.

Purchasing

The objective of a purchasing system is to ensure that production operations either have available or can readily obtain the necessary raw material components, supplies, and equipment. The purchasing department is charged with selecting the order quantities, vendors, prices, and mode of shipment.

Decision models used in purchasing can range from the visual scanning of production schedules, parts requisitions, stock status reports, and the stock itself, to complex mathematical and statistical models for reorder quantity, to automated MRP and JIT systems. When mathematical models are used, purchase orders are usually generated automatically once inventory reaches a certain reorder point. Inventory records, vendor price, product availability, delivery schedules, history, economic forecasts, and cash forecasts are some of the prime sources of the information needed as input for these decision models. In JIT systems an organization's computer may simply send an electronic request to the vendor.

An example of an inventory purchase order and vendor record is shown in Figure 14-9. Generally the record is identified by part number, but it may be sorted by vendor name or number for accounts payable information. Some of the more contemporary systems actually eliminate the need for a formal purchase order. Approved vendors are on line to the production system and under a predetermined agreement with the organization, the vendor simply ships the required amount of parts or material. No formal purchase order is necessary. Even a small microcomputer system, for example, has available the following random access data and reports to facilitate the purchasing manager's decision process:

1. Inventory listing: item code, description, number in stock, number ordered, number sold and number returned, purchase price, unit list price, total purchase price, unit profit, total profit, and percent profit.
2. Vendor listing: name, address, prices, discount and terms, history of transactions (number ordered, back orders, number returned, lead time, quality).
3. Inventory on order list; item code, description, vendor, date ordered, lead time, when overdue, number ordered, unit price, total price, overdue items, and days late.
4. Inventory value: item code, description, number in stock, unit cost, total cost, unit list price, total list price, gross profit, percent gross profit, and vendor breakdown.
5. Accounts payable aging report.
6. Inventory and vendor agreements for JIT supply.

With this information, purchasing should be able to make more intelligent decisions with regard to what, from whom, and when to order. In many traditional systems, transaction records and simple economic order quantity (EOQ) models can also be used to supply much of this information. In more sophisticated systems, which will be noted next, much of this will be prearranged and happen automatically and inventory will arrive just-in-time to replenish raw material stock level, for example. A manual illustration of basic purchasing procedures is presented in the appendix.

Inventory

The traditional objective of the inventory management subsystem has been to ensure that an adequate stock of raw material, parts, subassemblies, and buffer stock exists to support production operations adequately and to make finished goods available at convenient locations in the company's distribution system. This objective has been constrained by the investment in inventory and other carrying costs. Traditionally, a balance has been achieved between these costs and the cost of production interruptions, lost sales, and late deliveries. Traditionally, decision models, were directly or indirectly based on the traditional ABC system which in inventory items are classified as an ABC system: A (high cost $\times$ high volume = high total cost); B (high cost $\times$ low volume or low cost $\times$ high volume = medium total cost); and C (low cost $\times$ low volume = low total cost). The level of sophistication of the inventory system is a function of the amount of inventory in each of these classifications as well as the size of the firm's inventory. For a large firm, all inventory may be in class A. For a very small firm, most of the inventory may be in class C where inventory control systems may be relatively simple. In the typical firm, all three types of inventory will be present. Mathematical and statistical models can be used to control those items with a high total cost, such as engines and transmissions in a firm that manufactures garden tractors. Casual inspection or periodic ordering based on the department supervisor's requisitions, can be used for small cost items such as hand tools. Complex systems can only be justified where they can economically help management control costs and provide service. A wide variety of inventory models based on production line balancing, economic order quantity, and simulation techniques have been used in more complex situations.

Traditionally, determining the quantity of inventory that should be ordered is part of the decision process. Management needs to know when to order or when to produce. Reorder points need to be set so that when stock reaches a certain level, a new production run is scheduled or purchase orders are initiated. This decision is a function of demand, seasonal fluctuations, suppliers' lead time, and desired safety stock levels. However, since some of these factors are often uncertain, sophisticated models based on statistical decision theory are often used to determine reorder points.

In addition to using decision models, management can often use status reports similar to those outlined in the purchasing discussion. These reports are based on the types of records outlined earlier in Figure 14-9. They are often the only reports that small firms use in decision making. In those firms, the data sources for decisions are day-to-day transaction and production records. Other

INVENTORY STOCK, PURCHASE
ORDER, AND VENDOR RECORD

Part Description
    Part Number—key field
      for identification
    Part Name and Description
    Price
    Cost
    Location
Order Information
    Vendor Name and Number
    Lead Time
    Order Frequency
    Order Quantity
    Reorder Point
    Safety Stock
    Forecast
    Purchase Price
    Maximum Discount Allowed

Current Activity
    Quantity on Hand
    Quantity on Order
    Purchase Order Numbers
    Dates
    Vendors
    Receiving Report Number
    Number Received
    Dates Received
Historical Detail
    Quantity Purchased
      in last 12 Months
    Purchase Order Numbers
    Quantity per Order
    Vendor Delivery Information
    Number Received
    Profit per Item

FINISHED GOODS INVENTORY
RECORD

Production Order (Job)—Key
Production Number
Cost
    Material
    Labor
    Overhead Applied

Price
Location
Quantity Completed
Requirements
Shipment Date
Production Quantity

FIGURE 14-9 Inventory, purchase order, and vendor record and finished goods inventory record.

information can be calculated and extracted from basic source documents such as receiving reports and purchase orders. However, it should be clear that these sources do not always provide enough information for sophisticated models, which often require marketing information.

In more contemporary systems, such as those which will be discussed next, inventory records are minimized. In many cases, this is because there isn't much inventory to account for and as a result simpler systems are desirable from a cost and benefit perspective.

Information Systems

In addition to the production, quality control, purchasing, and inventory subsystems, a logistics management system requires supporting information subsystems. These may be engineering, cost accounting, maintenance and personnel as shown. The decision network and set of cost accounting transaction requirements in a particular production allocation subsystem must be supported by the information system. Several records are often necessary to support this information subsystem. Generally, in traditional systems, production records such as the production order record, production information record, production schedule, and performance record are often required in addition to other records from the inventory subsystem. Remember that even though all the records here are set up for traditional file storage, each element of each record could be assigned a location in a database system and accessed randomly. This organization logic was described in Chapter 10.

Day-to-day transactions provide the source of much of the information required for production operation decisions. However, daily transactions are not sufficient for more complex systems. Planning information in the form of standard cost data, work sequences, production requirements, expected selling prices, and standard times and standard material requirements is required to support logistical decisions. Moreover, it may be necessary to draw from other functions in order to generate a database that can support the logistical decisions of many companies. For example, a production order (number, quantity, and completion dates) may be generated by the marketing function.

Cost Accounting System

Cost accounting systems, which compare planned operations with actual results by using a set of standards and resulting variances for a variety of cost drivers such as those noted earlier, provide a key role in supporting logistical operations. The objective of a cost accounting support system is twofold. First, it is an effective control device because it provides standards with which logistics personnel can control various cost drivers. Second, through a comparison of standards and logistics data, problem areas can be detected. With this information, management can take corrective action. For example, excessive labor variances may signal the need for increased maintenance for a particular type of machine in the manufacturing process. In another example, excessive delivery times for finished products may signal a scheduling problem. The cost system can also be used in the traditional sense to value inventory and determine the cost of goods sold. Multiple uses of cost systems can be more easily implemented by using a relational database, as discussed in the database chapter.

Transaction Processing Networks

A logistical transaction processing network is necessary (1) to support the decision-making requirements of a logistical system; (2) to supply key data elements for many of the records and reports noted in this chapter; and (3) to provide information necessary for financial reporting and managerial evaluations of the whole logistical process. In general for traditional job-cost systems, all costs, direct (or standard) and applied, are accumulated by job-on-job cost sheets (or an equivalent computer record) like the one illustrated in Figure 14-10. This is also the work-in-process inventory record. In a standard cost system, actual and standard usage and the associated costs are accumulated by department or job for variance analysis. At the very least, a traditional logistics information system must contain the necessary features to record the flow of costs through a job-cost system, maintain the inventory records, and generate reports for inventory

JOB COST SHEET							

Production Order No. _____ Page _____
Product _____
Date Started _____
Date Completed _____
Routing Departments _____

Department _____

Material			Labor			Overhead	
Date	Ref.	Amount	Date	Ref.	Amount	Date	Amount

Department _____

Material			Labor			Overhead	
Date	Ref.	Amount	Date	Ref.	Amount	Date	Amount

FIGURE 14-10   Job-cost sheet.

valuation and cost control. Thus the information set shown in Figure 14-9 is basic to any production inventory system if management is to properly record the transactions that relate to the flow of costs through a job-cost system. Accounting for a process cost system will be similar to accounting for a job cost system. More contemporary systems attempt to minimize the amount of data recorded because excessive data does not add value to the product. Theoretically, work in process will be minimized and job cost sheets which represent WIP detail are not nearly as important as other time-based indicators.

Information Retrieval Considerations

Information retrieval needs will be a function of the type of logistic management activity. Strategic, managerial, and operational and transaction processing activities have a major impact on these needs in terms of frequency of use, level of aggregation, scope, and accuracy of information. In many situations, periodic status reports can be used to meet these decision-making, reporting, and transaction processing needs. In other situations, managers will need on-line, up-to-date information on inventory and production status in order to react to environmental changes. In some situations, this quick response may be required at all three managerial activity levels.

TRADITIONAL JOB-COST SYSTEM: MICROCOMPUTER ILLUSTRATION

Typical job-cost systems[8] for a microcomputer have the following features:

1. New or in-process jobs can be easily entered and edited.
2. Labor, material, subcontract costs and other cost types can be entered and tracked by management.
3. Budgets for all costs are available for control purposes and actual costs can be compared to the budgets.
4. Complete estimates may be entered for any phase of the job.
5. Detailed on-line inquiry is provided.
6. Complete job information is saved for job extensions, customer inquiry, or for cost estimation purposes.
7. Reports such as job status, job performance, job profitability, and cost analysis can be printed.
8. An interface is provided with other software such as accounts receivable, accounts payable, general ledger, payroll, inventory, invoicing, and purchasing.
9. An interface is provided so that data can be used in a word processor.

Most of the microcomputer job-cost packages are menu driven and display useful managerial and reporting information, such as that shown in Figure 14-11a, where there are several different options. The core of the system is shown in Figure 14-11b where job information and cost data are shown. Transactions are generally entered using a menu (such as that shown in Figure 14-11c), then edited and listed. An interface is provided with the billing system to invoice customers or clients for work or services performed. Management is often provided with the ability to view the activities related to a particular job and status of that job in a format such as that shown in Figure 14-11d, and reports such as the job status report (Figure 14-12) can be printed at any time. Regardless of what system is used the job cost sheet (a manual version is shown in Figure 14-10) is at the core of all traditional job-cost systems. All charges to jobs are recorded on the job cost sheet (or the equivalent record in the computer) as the job passes from one workstation or department to another.

---

[8] For more details of the system from which this illustration was drawn see *RealWorld Software*, RealWorld Corporation, Concord NH, 1988.

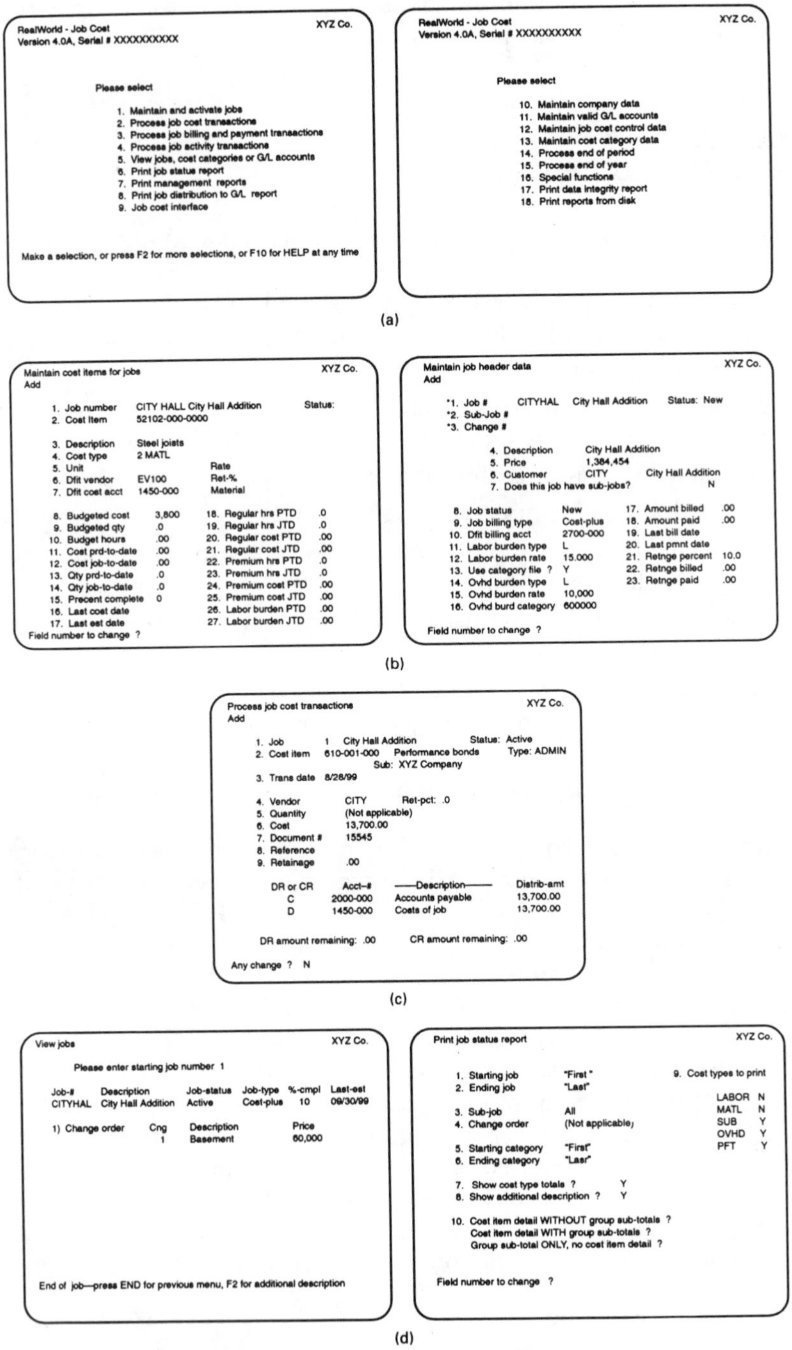

(a)

(b)

(c)

(d)

FIGURE 14-11 Menus for a microcomputer job-cost system.
Source: RealWorld Corporation. Reprinted with permission.

JOB STATUS REPORT

Cost-item	Description Type / Unit	Budgeted Outstd-PO	Actual costs Job-to-dat / Prd-to-dat	Total	Estimates Pct compl	Cost to-compl	Tot-cost	Over/(under) Pct	Cost
Job: CITYHAL	City Hall addition	Cost-plus	Customer: CITY	City of St. Louis			Active		
6108-000-000	Performance bonds ADMN	13,563	13,700 / 13,700	13,700	100		13,700	1	137
6502-000-000	Insurance MATL	2,000	2,000 / 2,000	2,000	100		2,000		
6608-000-000	City building permits ADMN	1,100	1,100 / 1,100	1,100	100		1,100		
10501-000-000	Supervision LABOR	19,200	600 / 600	600	3	16,800	17,400	(9)	(1,800)
14112-000-000	Concrete testing – matl MATL	330			0	330	330		
14122-000-000	Soil testing MATL	150			100			(100)	(150)
15122-000-000	Temporary electricity MATL	1,200	200 / 200	200	17	1,000	1,200		
15132-000-000	Temporary toilet MATL	800	800 / 800	800	100		800		
15142-000-000	Temporary phone MATL	350	100 / 100	100	29	250	350		

FIGURE 14-12 Job status report.

Source: Reprinted with permission from RealWorld Corporation, 1988.

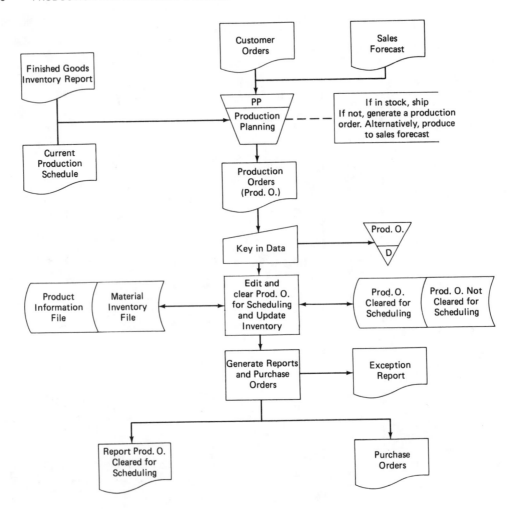

FIGURE 14-13 Production planning.

TRADITIONAL BATCH PROCESSING ILLUSTRATION

The flow of transactions, information, and internal control considerations, and the records used to support operational and managerial control activities in a typical batch processing system, are illustrated in this section. A production scheduling system is flowcharted in Figure 14-13. Weekly production scheduling runs are assumed.

First, the production planning department prepares production orders based on finished goods stock status, customer orders, sales forecasts, and the current production schedule. These orders are batched, and keyed into a disk file of pending orders. After a comparison with the production information specification file and the material inventory records, these new production orders are analyzed, along with those previously submitted but not yet scheduled, to determine whether to schedule them. There may be a delay in the scheduling of production orders (Prod. O. not cleared for schedule) because all the material is not on hand. If this is the case, purchase orders are generated for the purchasing department for those items not already on order. Some production orders are not scheduled because they have longer lead times and can wait until the next scheduling run. This analysis and comparison results in updated (1) materials inventory records; (2) files of production orders cleared for scheduling; and (3) files of production orders not cleared for scheduling. Reports are also prepared on orders cleared for scheduling and on processing exceptions arising from reconciliation of batch totals, missing input, or product information. In essence, the computer run verifies that all the needed information and materials are available prior to scheduling production and that only those requiring production before the next run are scheduled. The production order run results in production to be scheduled the following week.

The production schedule is run daily. Input includes work tickets that detail the preceding day's progress, the current production schedule, and all production orders cleared but not yet scheduled that detail product specifications.

Machine-readable work tickets serve as turnaround documents for collecting production data. Work tickets are accumulated each day from the shop and batched. The production data is then read optically. From each daily updating run, the following information is generated for shop supervisors and production management:

1. New work tickets for each production department. These will be used as turnaround documents for the next day's production.
2. A daily production schedule for each department, explaining what, when, and how much to produce.
3. An updated master production schedule.
4. Reports listing the production orders scheduled and those pending scheduling for production management.
5. A record of daily input on a backup disk to serve as an audit trail.
6. Exceptions between the current schedule, work tickets, and production orders. These are reviewed and corrected, if necessary, by management, and reentered during the next production run.
7. Material requisitions to be forwarded to the warehouse so that only those parts and materials necessary for each day's activities are issued from stores to the production departments. This scheduling process is illustrated in Figure 14-14.

After the work tickets have been used in the daily production run, they are processed, along with employee timecards and material requisition cards (which are also scanned optically) in a production control run shown in Figure 14-15 on page 453. The output of this processing procedure is a daily performed record which is stored on the disk. A hard copy input is filed for backup security measures and for audit purposes. Given this performance record and the current

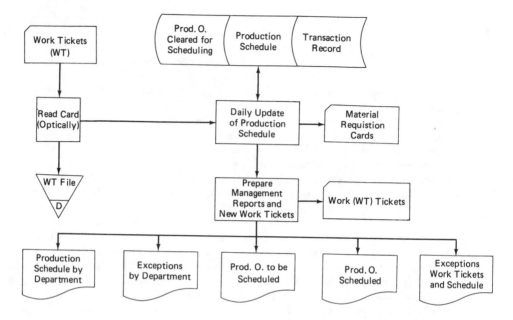

FIGURE 14-14   Production scheduling.

(not the updated) production schedule which details what should have been done, a daily control run is made for operational and management control activities.

In addition to a performance record (transaction file) and an exception listing, the following information is generated:

1. Completed production orders, which are sent to finished goods inventory.
2. Material usage reports for each department, manager, production order, or product.
3. Labor usage reports for each department, manager, production order, or product.
4. Reconciliation and resulting exceptions between the current schedule, the materials requisitioned, and employee time cards. The reconciliation and exceptions are produced by department and by product. Also, a reconciliation of the number and batch totals of work tickets, material requisitions, and timecards and the issuance of a report for correction and follow-up action.

By careful management planning at the outset of the process, and by employing a production schedule and turnaround documents, effective control of operational activities can be exercised. Feedback control is obtained through the various exception reports and comparisons. From a data processing perspective, effective control is achieved through a system of record retention, transaction records, key verification, comparison of data and batch totals, and turnaround documents such as requisitions and work tickets.

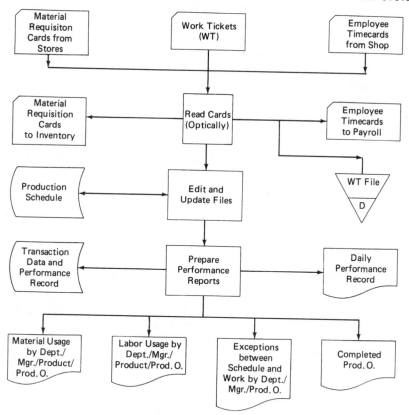

FIGURE 14-15   Production control.

DATABASE EXTENSION

The production scheduling problem can be reconsidered from the standpoint of an on-line real-time system database extension. A real-time system is under the control of the computer. Suppose the business environment has changed so that more and more production orders need to be expedited, customer sales representatives are increasingly calling to check on the status of production orders, and the business environment has become such that the plant needs to clear production orders for scheduling as soon as possible, not weekly as is the current practice. It has become apparent to management that more rapid response, more sophisticated algorithms, and instantaneous feedback are required for planning and dealing with customers.

A real-time database system that will satisfy the information requirements of the management system could consist of a set of on-line programs that will edit input, generate transaction records, periodically dump the database for control and security, clear orders for production when all materials are on hand, generate daily production schedules with the appropriate work tickets and material requisitions, update the status of materials and parts as supplies are received, and answer inquiries as they are received from management personnel. Such a set of programs would interface with a database (not a set of files) consisting of data elements that comprise the files noted earlier for the production schedule, materials inventory, product information, production orders, and finished goods inventory.

This system would have the necessary operations (joins, selections, and projections) or linkages (pointers) among the data elements to generate reports and other output needed by management. It would permit on-line input of customer orders, sales forecast changes, materials receipt, production plans, and expediting decisions. Moreover, due to its flexibility it would permit management to inquire into the status of materials, production orders, product specifications, finished goods, and the current data for scheduled production of a product. As in the batch system, work tickets and material requisitions could be generated as turnaround documents for the control of material flow in the plant. Terminals could be provided with menu input to accomplish the same input control. As before, any number of reports could be generated on a routine basis, such as the exception listings and the production schedules shown in the batch illustration.

In addition to faster input and inquiry capability, another advantage of the real-time system is that changes to the schedule can be made daily rather than weekly. Moreover, management can use the system in a simulation mode in order to experiment with different schedules, product configurations, manufacturing procedures, and size of production runs. Many "what if" questions can be asked.

As with the batch system, a daily control run is feasible. The difference is that unsorted input is used in conjunction with the random access database to store data elements which can be used in a wide variety of ways. These include routine reports like those discussed in the batch system, as well as on-line inquiries such as those related to differences between plans or standards and actual departmental output. Computer integrated manufacturing (CIM) can be used in conjunction with CAM, JIT, or MRP systems can be used to provide instantaneous feedback and control of the production operations.

RISK AND INTERNAL CONTROL

The potential risks associated with the logistics system which includes production and inventory are as follows:

1. Production of unauthorized products which may result in the waste of scarce personnel, capital and financial resources, dissatisfied customers, unwanted markdowns, and excessive inventory.
2. Incorrect cost allocation to goods and services produced resulting in potential errors in profitability analysis, performance analysis, and pricing of the goods and services.
3. Incorrect inventory status information resulting in downtime when mate-

rial was believed to be on hand, and excessive stock when it was believed to be in short supply.

4. Poor quality control resulting in excessive waste and rework costs or returns for services which were not performed up to standards, resulting in dissatisfied customers and excessive returns, and resulting in excessive downtime to fix problems.
5. Production for unauthorized customers resulting in fraud.
6. Inventory shrinkage and obsolescence resulting in lost sales, possible fraud, and waste.

These and other exposures to risk need to be considered carefully and an internal control system must be designed to control these risks and to provide management with sufficient information so that they can control the logistics operation so that risks due to mismanagement and possible fraud can be minimized.

SUMMARY

In this chapter we have highlighted the framework involved in designing and developing a logistics system. This framework integrates all the subfunctions, levels of management activity, and data processing elements associated with the logistics function of a firm. Contemporary logistics systems attempt to integrate the production, engineering, and information component of the system. A batch and a real-time database production scheduling system, as well as a contemporary JIT/Kanban system, were described in detail in order to illustrate the integration of the different dimensions of a logistics system. Finally, because this area is undergoing some significant changes in procedures, key differences between traditional and contemporary logistics systems were emphasized.

APPENDIX

A MANUAL PURCHASING, RECEIVING, AND INVENTORY SYSTEM

To illustrate the flow of transactions, the records generated from this flow, internal control considerations, and the information used to make operational decisions, a *manual* purchasing, receiving, and inventory system is described in this section. The system flowchart is shown in Figures A14-1 and A14-2.

The manager reviews the sales forecast and the stock records that contain information similar to, but not as extensive as, that illustrated in Figure 14-9 on page 444. Here it is assumed that the records consist of the following:

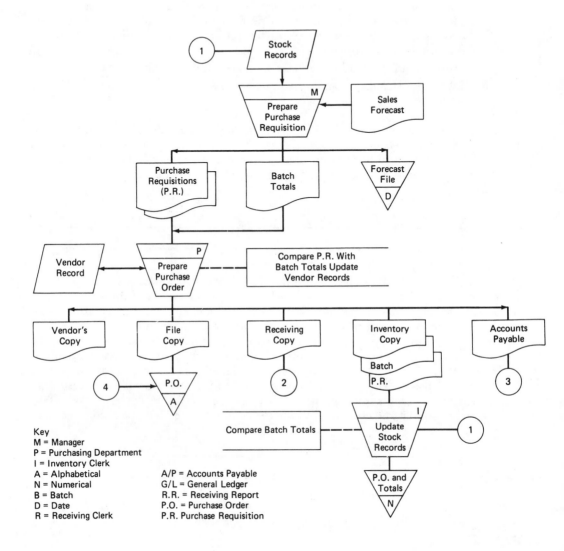

FIGURE A14-1   Manual purchasing, receiving, and inventory system.

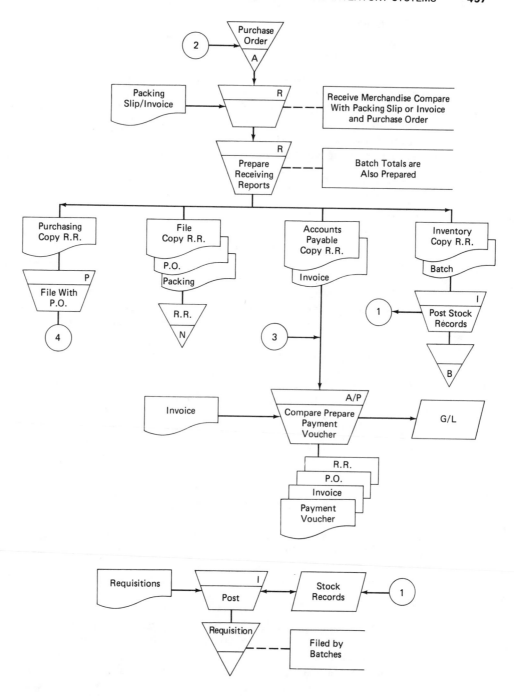

FIGURE A14-2 Manual purchasing, receiving, and inventory system, (continued).

1. Stock number
2. Name
3. Number on hand
4. Number on order

From this information, the manager manually prepares prenumbered purchase requisitions. These are batched by the manager, and control totals are run on the dollar amount and number of requisitions. From the purchase requisitions, the purchasing department then prepares five copies of prenumbered purchase orders, using separate vendor records consisting of the following:

1. Vendor number
2. Vendor name
3. Types of materials supplied
4. List of most recent prices
5. Number on order from each vendor
6. Possibly some note pertaining to delivery time and financial terms

The purchasing department compares the total number and dollar amounts of the purchase orders with the batch totals forwarded from the manager. The purchasing department updates these vendor records to reflect the new purchase orders.

The five purchase order copies are distributed as follows: (1) a vendor copy is sent to the vendor; (2) a file copy is filed alphabetically; (3) a copy is sent to the receiving department where it is filed alphabetically pending receipt of merchandise; (4) a copy is sent to the inventory clerk along with the batch totals and purchase requisitions to update stock records; and (5) a copy is sent to the accounts payable department pending receipt of an invoice from the vendor. The inventory clerk updates the stock records to reflect items on order, reconciles the changes with the batch totals, and files the purchase order and requisitions numerically.

Upon receipt of the merchandise, a receiving clerk compares the packing slip or invoice that accompanies the shipment with the purchase order on file, which is in alphabetical vendor order. Four copies of the prenumbered receiving report are prepared. One copy goes to purchasing for an alphabetical purchase order file by vendor. A file copy is kept in receiving and is filed numerically with the related purchase orders and packing slips. A third copy is forwarded, along with the invoice (if it accompanies the shipment), to the accounts payable department. The last copy, along with batch totals, is sent to the inventory manager for posting stock records and reconciliation of totals.

In the accounts payable department, a comparison is made between purchase orders, invoices, and receiving reports. Payment vouchers are prepared upon receipt of invoices which are supported by the purchase order and receiving report. Provisions can be made here for partial shipments and payments if necessary. The payment voucher, invoice, purchase order, and receiving report are all forwarded to the manager or owner for payment. The general ledger accounts are posted to reflect payment at this point in time. Numerical control is maintained on the payment vouchers. These last three payment steps are not shown in Figure A14-2.

In addition to updating inventory records for purchase orders and merchandise receipts, the inventory department also receives requisitions, which are used to update stock records when items are issued. These are batched for stock record control and filed by batches.

SELECTED REFERENCES

AGGARWAL, SUMER C., "MRP, JIT, OPT, FMS? Making Sense of Production Operations Systems," *Harvard Business Review*, September–October 1985, pp. 8–16.

BENNETT, ROBERT E., and JAMES A. HENDRICKS, "Automated Equipment," *Management Accounting*, July 1987, pp. 39–46.

BIGGS, JOSEPH, and ELLEN J. LONG, "Gaining the Competitive Edge with MRP/MRP II," *Management Accounting*, May 1988, pp. 27–32.

BOEING CO. and HEWLETT-PACKARD, "A Production Management System at Boeing," *Management Accounting*, April 1979, pp. 33–35.

BRIMSON, JAMES A., "How Advanced Manufacturing Technologies Are Reshaping Cost Management," *Management Accounting*, March 1986, pp. 25–29.

CAPETTINI, ROBERT, and DONALD K. CLANCY, eds., *Cost Accounting, Robotics and the New Manufacturing Environment*, American Accounting Association, 1987.

CARBONE, FRANK J., "Automated Job Costing Helps Mulack Steel Stay Competitive," *Management Accounting*, June 1980, pp. 29–31.

CHALOS, PETER, and ALLAN H. BADER, "High Tech Production: Impact of Cost Reporting Systems," *Journal of Accountancy*, March 1986, pp. 106–12.

COOPER, ROBIN, and ROBERT S. KAPLIN, "How Cost Accounting Distorts Product Costs," *Management Accounting*, April 1988, pp. 20–27.

DILTS, DAVID M., and GRANT W. RUSSELL, "Accounting for the Factory of the Future," *Management Accounting*, April 1985, pp. 34–40.

DOLL, WILLIAM J., and VONDEREUKE, MARK A., "Forging a Partnership to Achieve Competitive Advantage: The CIM Challenge," *MIS Quarterly*, II, no. 2 (June 1987); 210.

FOSTER, GEORGE, and CHARLES T. HORNGREN, "JIT Cost Accounting and Cost Management Issues," *Management Accounting*, June 1987. pp. 19–25.

GODFREY, JAMES T., and WILLIAM R. PASEWARK, "Controlling Quality Costs," *Management Accounting*, March 1988, pp. 48–51.

GROVER, M. P., and E. W. ZIMMERS, JR., *CAD/CAM Computer Aided Design and Manufacturing*. Englewood Cliffs, N.J.: Prentice Hall, 1984.

HOWELL, ROBERT A., and STEPHEN R. SOUCY, "Major Trends for Management Accounting," *Management Accounting*, July 1987, pp. 21–27.

KAPLAN, ROBERT, "Yesterday's Accounting Undermines Production," *Harvard Business Review*, July–August 1984, pp. 95–101.

MCILHATTAN, ROBERT D., "The JIT Philosophy," *Management Accounting*, September 1987, pp. 20–26.

NEWMAN, BRUCE R., and PAULINE R. JAOUEN, "Kanban, Zips and Cost Accounting: A Case Study," *Journal of Accountancy*, August 1986, pp. 132–39.

RealWorld Software, Concord, N.H.: RealWorld Corporation, 1988.

SENA, JAMES, A., and LAWRENCE M. SMITH, "Designing and Implementing an Integrated Job Cost Accounting System," *The Journal of Information Systems*, 1, no. 1 (Fall 1986), 102–12.

REVIEW QUESTIONS

1. What are the objectives of the various production and inventory subsystems?

2. What are the differences between traditional production systems and contemporary JIT systems?

3. Briefly describe the types of information that would be needed for an on-line traditional job-cost system and a JIT system?

4. Why is it important to consider the decision-making activities of the various levels of management in the design of inventory databases?

5. Outline the basic flow of transactions in a Kanban system.

6. Discuss the role of the job cost sheet in an traditional EDP batch processing system.

7. Briefly describe a MRP, JIT, FMS, and a CAD/CAM system.

8. What has been the impact on the inventory system of the new contemporary manufacturing systems?

9. How can linear programming models be used in production scheduling and planning?

10. Why would a database system be an improvement over a traditional file-oriented system for a computerized job cost shop that uses an FMS or any of the other newer systems to manage and control their manufacturing operations?

CASES

14-1 Valpaige Company of Omaha is an industrial machinery and equipment manufacturer with several production departments. The company employs automated and heavy equipment in its production departments. Consequently, Valpaige has a large repair and maintenance (R&M) department for servicing this equipment.

The operating efficiency of the R&M department has deteriorated over the past two years. Further, repair and maintenance costs seem to be climbing more rapidly than other department costs. The assistant controller has reviewed the operations of the R&M department and has concluded that the administrative procedures used since the early days of the department are outmoded due in part to the growth of the company. The two major causes for the deterioration, in the opinion of the assistant controller, are an antiquated scheduling system for repair and maintenance work, and the actual cost system to distribute the R&M department's costs to the production departments. The actual costs of the R&M department are allocated monthly to the production departments on the basis of the number of service calls made during each month.

The assistant controller has proposed that a formal work order system be implemented for the R&M department. The production departments would submit a service request to the R&M department for the repairs and/or maintenance to be completed, including a suggested time for having the work done. The supervisor of the R&M department would prepare a cost estimate on the service request for the work required (labor and materials) and indicate a suggested time for completing the work on the service request. The R&M supervisor would return the request to the production department which initiated the request. Once the production department okays the work by returning a copy of the service request, the R&M supervisor would prepare a repair and maintenance work order and schedule the job. This work order provides the repair worker with the details of the work to be done and is used to record maintenance hours worked and the materials and suppliers used.

Producing departments would be charged for actual labor hours worked at a predetermined standard rate for the type of work required. The parts and suppliers used would be charged to the production departments at cost.

The assistant controller believes that only two documents would be required in this new system—a repair maintenance service request initiated by the production departments and the repair maintenance work order initiated by the R&M department.

REQUIRED:

1. For the repair and maintenance work order document:

   a. Identify the data items which would be important to the repair and maintenance department and the production departments which should be incorporated into the work order.

   b. Indicate how many copies of the work order would be required and explain how each copy would be distributed.

2. Prepare a document flowchart to show how the repair and maintenance service request and the repair and maintenance work order should be coordinated and used among the departments of Valpaige Co. to request and complete the repair and maintenance work, to provide the basis for charging the production departments for the cost of the completed work, and to evaluate the performance of the repair and maintenance department. Provide explanations to the flowchart as appropriate. (CMA adapted)

14-2 Jefferson General Contractors has the following information needs: (1) information that will allow a competitive bid to be submitted for a construction job; (2) internal accumulation and control of costs related to a specific job; and (3) planning and budgeting information for scheduling job and resource allocation.

The initial information requirement in the estimation process is a knowledge of the construction jobs that are "up for bid." This knowledge is gathered primarily from trade journals and weekly listings of new construction jobs in the metropolitan area. These provide a brief description of the job. Specialized blueprints for the job must then be obtained from the architect (or owner) for a specific charge. Next the actual bid is prepared by an estimator. The estimator will consider the amount of materials needed, the amount of labor needed, the bids received from the various subcontractors,

and an appropriate allowance for overhead and profit. An important factor to be considered is the price of materials: Supplies used in the building industry are sometimes subject to violent fluctuation on a daily basis. For this reason, the estimator will not compute the material costs until moments before the bid is telephoned in. The most recent prices available are used for the bid. If the bid is accepted, the estimator will immediately place an order with suppliers for the amount of materials needed. This establishes the price for the materials at the price quoted in the bid.

Cost information in the construction industry is of primary importance for three types of users. Estimators need relevant information on past costs of completed contracts in order to make estimates for bidding on future contracts. Managers use cost information in order to monitor the progress of the contract by comparing estimated cost figures with actual cost figures. Cost figures are also important in preparing income tax returns.

If the analysis of costs is to be useful, it is important to know how they are allocated to each job. Direct costs are a function of subcontractors' costs, direct labor, direct materials, and equipment charges. Subcontractors' costs are allocated on the basis of the contract price and are readily verified. Direct labor is a function of time spent on a job by the contractor's employees and the rate of pay. This information is assembled on timecards that show (1) how long the employee worked; (2) which job was worked on; and (3) the rate of pay. Direct materials are purchased for a specific job following the estimator's analysis. Materials are charged to the job for which they were purchased. Equipment charges are divided into three categories: durable and standard equipment, special equipment, and perishable equipment. Durable and standard equipment charges for trucks, cranes, and bulldozers are made for each job on the basis of the fair amount of rent that would be paid to an outside equipment rental concern less any profit that would be incurred. Special equipment is equipment that can be used only on a particular project. This equipment would be rented and the rental payments would be charged to the job for which it was used less any residual value remaining after the job has been completed.

Indirect costs are charged on the basis of a fixed overhead rate. Costs of the estimating department are recorded on the basis of time spent on a successful bid. Costs of unsuccessful bids are considered general administrative expense and are charged out using the fixed overhead rate.

The division of costs by elements is important to a guide in future construction of the same nature. Also, if analyzed on a fairly current basis, these unit costs can indicate whether the contract is running in excess of the estimate. It is important that a periodical accumulation of actual costs on each project be submitted by the accounting department. These reports should be analyzed by cost classifications on each job and compared with the total bid estimate using the same classifications.

REQUIRED: As part of the design team of a CPA firm you have been assigned to recommend some alternative system to meet Jefferson's information requirements.

1. What data elements would you suggest Jefferson keep on current jobs and past jobs to enhance the future estimation process and other cost accounting needs?

2. Would you recommend a relational database system over a simple file system and why? Why, from the perspective of the advantages of using a database system in general, and from the perspective of using an implicit approach rather than an implicit approach to database management?

3. How would you use a data dictionary and IPO charts to help you in the design process?

4. How would IPO charts enhance any programming effort which may follow as part of implementation?

5. Explain how a relational database could be used in accumulating costs for each job and, using this information, for estimating costs for new jobs.

14-3 Direct Drive Electronics, a major producer of hard disks, has been using a traditional cost accounting system for several years. They use purchase orders to order inventory when stock gets below a certain level. The reorder level is based on an EOQ model. Vendors are selected from a vendor file. Lead times and costs vary considerably resulting in great uncertainty and large inventories of components.

The production process consists of three basic steps each with its own work center. A job cost sheet accompanies each batch or job throughout the process. All overhead is applied using a plantwide rate which is determined using the budgeted overhead and the expected level of direct labor hours for the year.

Actual direct labor is recorded by employees at each work center on the job cost sheets and a labor usage report. Setup time and idle time is also recorded on a labor usage report for each work center. The labor usage report is submitted to the controller at the end of each shift. Currently a considerable amount of idle time is present in the system because of a bottleneck in the process at work station number two. The result is a build up of work in process inventory. Finally an inspection takes place at the end of the process and defective units are returned to the appropriate workstation for rework.

The controller analyzes all the material components and labor used and the overhead applied and computes variances for each work station.

Direct Drive Electronics is considering implementing a JIT production and purchasing system. They plan to automate work station number two which will reduce the total amount of labor in the process to less than 10 percent of the total manufacturing cost. Moreover, they plan to incorporate some design changes to eliminate setup times between products. Also instead of producing for inventory to be sold, they will attempt to produce to actual orders as they are received. They expect this to greatly reduce finished goods inventory. Finally they plan to increase quality by inspecting components at the supplier's facility to reduce their rework efforts.

REQUIRED:

1. Flowchart the traditional job-cost system being used.

2. Suggest, via a systems flowchart, a new accounting information system which will provide management with information which is key to the control of a just-in-

time system. Make every effort to minimize the paper work in this proposal because paper work adds no value to the product.

14-4 In the manual illustration in the appendix, assume that the volume of paper work was becoming so large that more information, such as lead time and reorder points, was required to make purchasing decisions. Flowchart and describe appropriate internal control procedures for a batch processing procedure to replace the manual system illustrated. Use disks to store data.

14-5 Beccan Company, a discount tire dealer, operates twenty-five retail stores in the metropolitan area. Beccan sells both private brand and name brand tires. The company operates a centralized purchasing and warehousing facility and employs a perpetual inventory system. All purchases of tires and related supplies are placed through the company's central purchasing department to take advantage of quantity discounts. The tires and supplies are received at the central warehouse and distributed to the retail stores as needed. The perpetual inventory system at the central facility maintains current inventory records, designated reorder points, optimum order quantities, and continuous stocktakings for each type of tire and size and for other related supplies.

Beccan uses the following documents in its inventory control system:

Retail Stores Requisition. This document is submitted by the retail stores to the central warehouse whenever tires or supplies are needed at the stores. The shipping clerks in the warehouse department fill the orders from inventory and have them delivered to the stores.

Purchase Requisition. The inventory control clerk in the inventory control department prepares this document when the quantity on hand for an item falls below the designated reorder point. The document is forwarded to the purchasing department.

Purchase Order. The purchasing department prepares this document when items need to be ordered. The docu-

ment is submitted to an authorized vendor.

Receiving Report. The warehouse department prepares this document when ordered items are received from vendors. The receiving clerk completes the document by indicating the vendor's name, the date the shipment is received, and the quantity of each item received.

Invoice. An invoice is received from vendors specifying the amounts owed by Beccan.

The following departments are involved in Beccan's inventory control system:

Inventory Control Department. This department is responsible for the maintenance of all perpetual inventory records for all items carried in inventory. This includes current quantity on hand, reorder point, optimum order quantity, and quantity on order for each item carried.

Warehouse Department. This department maintains the physical inventory of all items carried in inventory. All orders from vendors are received (receiving clerk) and all distributions to retail stores are filled (shipping clerks) in this department.

Purchasing Department. This department places all orders for items needed by the company.

Accounts Payable Department. This department maintains all open accounts with vendors and other creditors. All payments are processed here.

REQUIRED:

1. Prepare a document flowchart to show how these documents should be coordinated and used among the departments at the central facility of Beccan Company to provide adequate internal control over the receipt, issuance, replenishment, and payment of tires and supplies. You can assume that the documents have a sufficient number of copies to ensure that the perpetual inventory system has the necessary basic internal controls.

2. (Optional) Using a system flowchart and

the information just given, describe the flow of information as it now exists and describe the flow of information that would be involved if you were designing a new system that made use of random access microcomputer software for inventory.

(Adapted from the CMA examination.)

14-6 You have been engaged by the management of Alden, Inc., to review its internal control over the purchase, receipt, storage, and issue of raw materials. You have prepared the following list, which describes Alden's procedures:

Raw materials, which consist mainly of high-cost electronic components, are kept in a locked storeroom. Storeroom personnel include a supervisor and four clerks. All are well trained, competent, and adequately bonded. Raw materials are removed from the storeroom only upon written or oral authorization of one of the production supervisors.

There are no perpetual inventory records; hence the storeroom clerks do not keep records of goods received or issued. To compensate for the lack of perpetual records, a physical inventory count is taken monthly by the storeroom clerks, who are well supervised. Appropriate procedures are followed in making the inventory count.

After the physical count, the storeroom supervisor matches quantities counted against a predetermined reorder level. If the count for a given part is below the reorder level, the supervisor enters the part number on a materials-requisition list and sends this list to the accounts payable clerk. The accounts payable clerk prepares a purchase order for a predetermined reorder quantity for each part and mails the purchase order to the vendor from whom the part was last purchased.

When ordered materials arrive at Alden, they are received by the storeroom clerks. The clerks count the merchandise and compare the counts with the shipper's bill of lading. All vendors' bills of lading are initialed, dated, and filed in the storeroom to serve as receiving reports.

REQUIRED: Describe the weaknesses in internal control and recommended improvements of Alden's procedures for the purchase, receipt, storage, and issue of raw materials. Organize your answer sheet as follows:

WEAKNESSES	RECOMMENDED IMPROVEMENTS

14-7 Anthony, CPA, prepared the flowchart shown in Chapter 8, Figure 8-10, which portrays the raw materials purchasing function of one of Anthony's clients, a medium-sized manufacturing company. The flowchart shows the preparation of initial documents through the vouching of invoices for payment in accounts payable. The flowchart was a portion of the work performed on the audit engagement to evaluate internal control.

REQUIRED: Identify and explain the systems and control weaknesses evident from the flowchart. Include those resulting from activities performed or not performed. All documents are prenumbered.

(AICPA adapted.)

14-8 Wekender Corporation owns and operates fifteen large departmentalized retail hardware stores in major metropolitan areas of the southwestern United States. The stores carry a wide variety of merchandise, but the major thrust is toward the weekend "do-it-yourselfer." The company's business has almost doubled since 1980.

Each retail store acquires its merchandise from the company's centrally located warehouse. Consequently, the warehouse must maintain an up-to-date and well-stocked inventory ready to meet the demands of the individual stores.

Wekender Corporation wishes to maintain its competitive position with similar type stores of other companies in its marketing area. Therefore, Wekender must improve its purchasing and inventory procedures. The company's stores must have the proper goods to meet customer demand, and the warehouse, in turn, must have the goods available. The number of company stores, the number of inventory items carried, the volume of business—all are providing pressures to change from basically manual data processing routines to mechanized data processing procedures. Recently the company has been investigating two different approaches to mechanization. The first is batch processing and the second is on-line processing. No decision has been reached on the approach to be followed.

Top management has determined that the following items should have high priority in the new system procedures:

1. Rapid ordering to replenish warehouse inventory stocks with as little delay as possible

2. Quick filling and shipping of merchandise to the stores (this involves determining whether sufficient stock exists)

3. Some indication of inventory activity

4. Perpetual records in order to quickly determine inventory level by item number

A description of the current warehousing and purchasing procedures is given next:

Warehouse Procedures. The stock is stored in bins and is located by an inventory number. The numbers are generally listed sequentially on the bins to facilitate locating items for shipment; frequently this system is not followed and, as a result, some items are difficult to locate.

Whenever a retail store needs merchandise, a three-part merchandise request form is completed—one copy is kept by the store and two copies are mailed to the warehouse the next day. If the merchandise requested is on hand, the goods are delivered to the store accompanied by the third copy of the request. The second copy is filed at the warehouse.

If the quantity of goods on hand is not sufficient to fill the order, the warehouse sends the quantity available and notes the quantity shipped by the warehouse. At the end of each day all the memos are sent to the purchasing department.

When the ordered goods are received, they are checked at the receiving area, and a receiving report is prepared. One copy of the receiving report is retained at the receiving area, one is forwarded to the accounts payable department, and one is filed at the warehouse with the purchase memorandum.

Purchasing Department Procedures. When the purchase memorandum are received from the warehouse, purchase orders are prepared. Vendor catalogs are used to select the best source for the requested goods, and the purchase order is prepared and mailed. Copies of the orders are sent to the accounts payable department and the receiving area; one copy is retained in the purchasing department.

When the receiving report arrives in the purchasing department, it is compared with the purchase order on file. The receiving report is also checked with the invoice before forwarding the invoice to the accounts payable department for payment.

The purchasing department strives periodically to evaluate the vendors for financial soundness, reliability, and trade relationships. However, because of the tremendous volume of requests received from the warehouse, this activity currently does not have a high priority.

Each week a report of the open purchase orders is prepared to determine if any action should be taken on overdue deliveries. This report is prepared manually from scanning the field of outstanding purchase orders.

REQUIRED:

1. Wekender Corporation is considering two possible automated data processing systems: batch processing system or on-line computer system.

   a. Which of these systems would best meet the needs of Wekender Corporation? Explain your answer. Flowchart your suggested system.

   b. Briefly describe the basic equipment configuration that Wekender would need for the system recommended in Question a.

2. Regardless of the type of system selected by the Wekender Corporation, data files will have to be established.

   a. Identify the data files that would be necessary.

   b. Briefly indicate the type of data that would be contained in each file.

3. (Optional; refer to Chapter 10) Assume

Wekender acquires a database management system. How would you organize (structure) and access the files to generate a set of reports and support management inquiries you expect Wekender to need and make?

(Adapted from the CMA examination.)

14-9 Peabock Company, a wholesaler of soft-goods, has an inventory composed of approximately 3,500 different items. The company employs a computerized batch processing system to maintain its perpetual inventory records. The system is run each weekend so that the inventory reports will be available on Monday morning for management use. The system has been functioning satisfactorily for the past fifteen months and has provided the company with accurate records and timely reports.

The preparation of purchase orders has been automatic as a part of the inventory system to ensure that the company will maintain enough inventory to meet customer demand. When an item of inventory falls below a predetermined level, a written record is made of the inventory item. This is used in conjunction with the vendor file to prepare the purchase orders.

Exception reports are prepared during the update of the inventory and the preparation of the purchase orders. These reports identify any errors or exceptions identified during the processing. In addition, the system provides for management approval of all purchase orders exceeding a specified amount. Any exceptions of items requiring management approval are handled by supplemental runs on Monday morning and are combined with the weekend results. A system flowchart of Peabock Company's inventory and purchase order procedure is shown in Figure C14-1.

REQUIRED: The illustrated system flowchart of Peabock Company's inventory and purchase order system was prepared before the system was fully operational. Several steps important to the successful operations of the system were inadvertently omitted. Indicate in narrative terms where the omissions have occurred. The flowchart does not need to be redrawn.

(Adapted from the CMA examination.)

14-10 Wooster Company is a beauty and barber supplies and equipment distributorship servicing a five-state area. Management has generally been pleased with the company's overall operations to date. However, the present purchasing system has evolved through practice rather than having been formally designed. Consequently it is inadequate and needs to be redesigned.

The present purchasing system can be described as follows. Whenever the quantity of an item is low, the inventory supervisor phones the purchasing department and gives the item description and quantity to be ordered. A purchase order is prepared in duplicate in the purchasing department. The original is sent to the vendor, and the copy is retained in the purchasing department and filed in numerical order. When the shipment arrives, the inventory supervisor sees that each item received is checked off on the packing slip that accompanies the shipment. The packing slip is then forwarded to the accounts payable department. When the invoice arrives, the packing slip is compared with the invoice in the accounts payable department. Once any differences between the packing slip and the invoice have been reconciled, a check is drawn for the appropriate amount and is mailed to the vendor with a copy of the invoice. The packing slip is attached to the invoice and is filed alphabetically in the paid invoice file.

REQUIRED: Wooster Company intends to redesign its purchasing system from the point in time when an item needs to be ordered until payment is made. The system should be designed to ensure that all the proper controls are incorporated into the system.

1. Identify the internally and externally generated documents that would be required to satisfy the minimum requirements of a traditional system and indicate the number of copies of each document that would be needed.

2. Explain how all of these documents should interrelate and flow among Wooster's various departments, including the final destination or file of each copy.

Adapted from the CMA examination.

14-11 Specialty Steel Corporation is a small

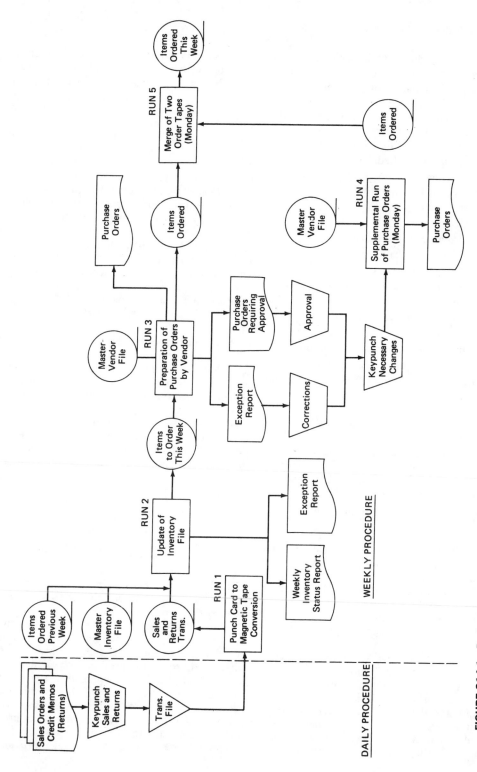

FIGURE C14-1 Peabock Company's inventory and purchase order procedure.

467

rolling mill in Sandusky, Ohio, which produces special steel alloy slabs, and plates. It is considering the implementation of a computer-based information system to support its logistics management system from order entry through the shipping of customer orders.

The objectives of the system are to:

1. Generate work schedules
2. Track work through production, inspection, and shipping facilities
3. Have on-line
   a. Order entry
   b. Order status monitoring
   c. Production planning
   d. Shipment planning
   e. Monitoring of finished goods inventory
4. Achieve processing improvements by
   a. Reducing waste
   b. Increasing equipment utilization
   c. Reducing labor requirements
5. Optimize slab-making throughputs while meeting specifications as closely as possible
6. Minimize the slabs not meeting specifications
7. Monitor customer orders, control processing, ensure correct routing, minimize delivery times, and provide for status inquiry in the heavy plate facility
8. Use the computer to plan weekly and daily schedules

REQUIRED: Discuss in general the data base requirements for transaction, operational, and managerial control of Speciality Steel's logistics function. Refer to Chapter 10 for details of database design to support your general discussion. Prepare a systems flowchart of the online function in objectives 3a and 3b.

14-12 Lawn Care Lawn Mower Company has a policy of using its distribution system to stock finished goods inventory. The company effectively accomplishes this objective by offering discounts and delayed invoice payments from its distributors to smooth its production over slack sales months. In the lawn mower industry, seasonality is a big problem. As a result, Lawn Care has very little space for finished goods inventory in its plant. The industry in recent years has suffered from large fluctuations in material prices, which are putting pressure on management to speculate in material purchases. To compound the logistics planning problems, sales often follow the pattern of housing starts. Competition is in terms of price, service, and quality. Thus Lawn Care must carefully plan and schedule its logistics operations. It must be able to act fast in response to changing supply and demand problems while producing for a season six months in the future at minimum cost.

Lawn Care manufactures three basic products: walk-behind lawn mowers, riding lawn mowers, rototillers. Each machine is produced in three sizes for a total of nine basic products. Various options are added to these basic products, and many parts are common among the products.

Production orders are received from distributors and approved by management as follows. Each week the production and sales management personnel review the production schedule for the next year. They prepare a list of changes and new production orders at this time. They also review the raw material status report weekly and override the automatic reorder system with an authorization to purchase so that the company can take advantage of lower costs or anticipated cost increases. The changes, new production orders, and purchase authorizations are keyed into the next daily production scheduling run.

Lawn Care uses a small mainframe with several disk drives for its programs and records. It uses a mathematical optimization model to maximize throughput in the proper mix of products while minimizing in-house inventory of raw material and finished goods, and delivery time to the distributors.

The daily production run accesses an operations specification list for each product and an open production order file, which indicates when each production order is to be scheduled for the next year. The mathematical algorithm then generates two copies of the production orders for the day, for the department supervisor and management. At the same time, production schedules for the day's activities are generated for each department and the plant.

Also, an update of the yearly production schedule is prepared for management. At the same time, operation cards are punched to be distributed to the factory departments. Material requisition cards are sent to the warehouse for the distribution of the raw materials to each department for that day's production. After the materials have been sent to the departments, these requisition cards are returned to data processing with a signature of compliance. The operation cards are marked as to indicate what actually occurred in terms of number of units produced, time consumed, and materials used in each department. They are returned each day to IS to be read into the computer.

Along with these three outputs of the daily scheduling run, an assembly order is generated for each mower to be assembled. This is used to ensure that the mower (tiller) is assembled to specifications. The assembly order is attached to each mower through the assembly process. When the mower is finished, the assembly order is removed and sent to IS.

REQUIRED:

1. Itemize the operational, managerial, and strategic control decision activities required for the operation of the firm.
2. Prepare a systems flowchart for all operations discussed.
3. Discuss several control policies and procedures that should be incorporated.

14-13 ABS Wholesalers distributes food products. The firm uses a perpetual inventory system with automated reorder points. Sales orders are received from salespeople and are approved for credit and stock availability. A stock status inquiry system is used for this purpose. On-line terminals interface with a random access inventory status file. Sales personnel also call the warehouse to write up a purchase order on an item they believe to be in short supply.

Sales orders are keyed into the terminal and processed. At this time, stock status data are updated. A shipping card, an invoice, and a packing slip are generated and used by warehouse personnel to process the order. Upon completion of the order, the shipping card is signed and returned to data processing for stock status update. The packing slip and invoice are sent to the customer with the merchandise.

Purchase orders are generated as necessary each time a stock status update run is made. Due to the size of the operation, stock status runs are made each hour.

REQUIRED:

1. Prepare a systems flowchart of the operations described.
2. Describe several control policies and procedures that should be incorporated into this computerized system.
3. Describe the stock status inventory record.

14-14 Consider again Jefferson General Contractor's Case 14-2:

REQUIRED:

1. From the information in 14-2, indicate what records may be useful in the estimation and bidding process.
2. Flowchart this process for Jefferson General Contractors.
3. Indicate the internal controls necessary in the manual computation of the above bid and estimation information to ensure a reasonable degree of accuracy.
4. Describe in general how a microcomputer using on-line programs can be used in this business environment to enhance management's decision making.

14-15 A description of Boeing Company's Commercial Electronic Manufacturing Division's Production Management System (PMS) follows.

Keeping track of every assembly being manufactured, not to mention every hex nut and cap screw going into it, can be an overwhelming task in a manufacturing plant. Even with huge computers such detailed information is difficult to keep current. Yet one plant in the Boeing Company's Commercial Electronic Manufacturing Division tracks not only every assembly but where every part is located, what has been purchased and received for it, for whom it is being built, what inspections have been performed on it, how many more parts can be built out of current inventory, and each payroll hour chargeable to any part or assembly constructed.

What It Needed. In establishing the PMS, Boeing management determined that it had to have an on-line system that could keep track of inventory and work-in-process while updating bills of materials, performing material requirements planning (MRP), and handling several accounting functions, including payroll accounting by job and contract from each work area.

The guidelines under which the PMS was written demanded that the system:

1. Justify its cost through measurable production cost reductions,

2. Prevent—or at least accurately predict—late end-item deliveries,

3. Function on-line, so as to respond to critical manufacturing needs, as well as routine production, and spot shop-flow bottlenecks early in either operation,

4. Respond to inquiries for any level of a bill of materials—whether full assembly, subassembly or part—as end-items in themselves, in order to fill order requirements,

5. Require minimum training for use by noncomputer people, including such things as providing displayed lists of options and resisting failure under operator error, and

6. Provide complete front-end error checking to preserve database integrity.

According to Ralph Baldwin, Automated Data Systems Manager for Electronics Manufacturing, "the criteria used for selection included processing speed, size of on-line storage, and operating system characteristics, with particular emphasis on after-sales support. They researched small computers thoroughly before deciding which computer to use. The operating system selected provided greater flexibility to do what they had in mind that any other looked at. And the database selected could be interrogated in almost any fashion to supply the answers people who use the system needed. Most of the users don't know anything about a computer, but they had to get data quickly in a form they could use."

What It Got. The Boeing department selected a computer system which is common in manufacturing settings. The computer system includes three large disc drives, two tape drives to record data for the company's mainframe accounting and payroll functions, a machine readable interface with Boeing's central procurement facility, and a printer. A total of 29 terminals are connected with the computer.

The new system included a multiprogramming executive operating system and an on-line text editor as well as other common utilities. These features provided the power Boeing needed to develop the system.

The database management system permits on-line access to the database in almost any fashion to dig out information for nonroutine as well as regular reports without having to redesign the application program. With the magnetic disk drives, the system provides virtual memory so that large programs can be executed without overrunning the main memory.

80% Use by Production. To ensure that the needs of those who generate the data are met (production people account for 80% of the data demands made on the system), production personnel at every level were consulted during the system's development. From their input, flowcharts showing every step in manufacturing were developed. These formed the basics of program development and highlighted internal control needs. The system was fully developed before it was put on-line to encourage user confidence in the program's capabilities from the outset.

To protect each portion of the database against unintentional or unauthorized entry, PMS includes password protection for user groups. The bill of materials, for instance, cannot be modified by quality control people, nor the inventory altered by production control employees.

PMS addresses most of the manufacturing aspects of the CEMD's inventory, bills of materials, master schedules, planning and ordering of parts, monitoring open job orders, recording and accumulating shop labor charges, measuring job standards performance, and monitoring shipping requirements and dates.

The material requirements planning module considers all on-hand inventories and open orders and plans additional orders so that both "make" and "buy" parts will be available at the proper time. Records of lead times are constantly updated by the module. Planning for any assembly follows a complicated path in which the computer spots any difficulty that might result in a late order shipment.

An accounting interface subsystem of PMS updates Boeing's larger financial accounting system. Data processed by the subsystem accumulate from other modules which monitor work flow on the factory floor. Daily, the accounting subsystem transmits actual labor hours to the payroll system, transmits data on material dollar transfers resulting from the transfer of purchased parts, and notifies the financial department of transactions concerning assemblies.

In addition to handling payroll accounting for employees on the floor, the system supplies daily reports to cost center foremen. These reports tell the foreman which jobs are in the shop and what priorities they have, what jobs will flow into the stop in the next five days along with their priorities, and what the performance has been on jobs just completed by the shop. All rework time and assemblies scrapped are logged and reported to foreman weekly to assist them in evaluating their own performance.

REQUIRED:

1. From the description just given, comment point by point on how the new system satisfies its stated requirements.

2. What internal control features were built into the system?

3. What report generation features are present in the system? Why are these features important for management decision making?

4. What is the interface with Boeing's accounting and payroll functions?

5. Given the system development phases outlined in Chapters 10 and 11, briefly discuss this system's compliance with those phases.[9]

---

[9] This case is based on and quoted from Boeing Company and Hewlett-Packard, "A Production Management System at Boeing," *Management Accounting*, April 1979, pp. 33-35. Reprinted with permission.

15

MARKETING SYSTEMS AND THE REVENUE CYCLE

OBJECTIVE

The overall objective of the marketing and revenue system is to generate sales and collect revenue from customers. To do this, a marketing and revenue system must support the decision-making, reporting, and transaction processing requirements of marketing and sales management. This includes the processing of sales orders and the management of accounts receivable for the organization. These requirements are a function of the management objectives, the organization's strategy for achieving these objectives, and the organizational structure designed to implement this strategy. The major objective of the marketing management system is to develop, promote, distribute, sell, and service the products of the organization. This must be done to return a profit that is sufficient to justify the organization's investment in the product. In addition to selling the product, the revenue cycle is not complete until cash is collected.

To accomplish this objective, marketing management needs to make effective marketing decisions in a dynamic environment that is often characterized by intense competition and technological change. These decisions span product planning and development, advertising and promotion, sales and distribution

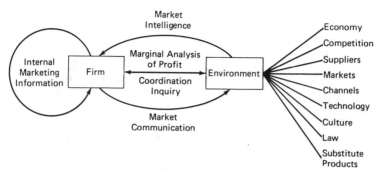

FIGURE 15-1 Marketing information flows.

including customer credit, and market research, and customer service functions. It also includes all levels of managerial activities. These decisions must often be made on the basis of market research, accounting information, and a wide variety of externally generated information. In addition, to accomplish this objective an effective and efficient sales order, accounts receivable, and cash receipts system must be in place. The transaction part of the system is generally called the revenue cycle. The objective of this chapter is to review accounting information systems used to support these decision making, reporting, and transaction processing needs.

DECISION AND TRANSACTION PROCESSING CHARACTERISTICS

Environmental Considerations and Information Flow

Over the past several years, management has become increasingly aware that (1) the success of an organization is largely a function of marketing success; and (2) marketing success requires management to focus more on customer needs and market demands than on manufacturing efficiency. In summary, those firms who serve the customers the best will be the most successful. The major implication of this development for accounting information systems is in the increase in the flow of information to and from the marketplace. In other words, intensive interaction with the environment is critical to the accomplishment of the objectives of marketing and sales management. This interaction is illustrated in Figure 15-1, in which three general flows of environmental and transactional information are indicated.

First, there is a continual monitoring of the environment through a marketing intelligence system. The system must gather information on trends that may have an impact on sales, competition, pricing, promotion activities, suppliers' activities, market trends, distribution problems, new developments stemming from technology changes with respect to markets and products, changes in cultural values and norms, legal requirements, and potential substitute products.

In addition to obtaining intelligence from the environment, the organization must be able to interact with the environment to perform marginal analysis on products and coordinate the activities of the organization. Negotiation of contracts for delivery, price, and quality specifications requires sales personnel to be able to coordinate their activities with production and inventory management in terms of inventory, production schedules, and cost data in order to determine the feasibility of the terms of the sale and the potential profitability of the contract. This coordination may require changes in production and shipment schedules. An assessment of the costs associated with such a change, for example, should consider a marginal analysis of the contract. For some organizations, this type of marginal analysis and production and marketing coordination may be so intense that on-line systems and mathematical models may be required. For other organizations, current cost data coupled with an occasional phone call to the production manager to review an upcoming production schedule may suffice. More and more organizations are using electronic data interchange (EDI) to coordinate these activities as described in Chapter 18.

Finally, marketing management and sales management must be able to make inquiries with respect to the availability of inventory and the status of sales or production orders, to be able to service customers. Customers need to know when they can expect delivery and the status of their orders that are being manufactured. These inquiries again require coordination of marketing and logistical systems.

In addition to these intelligence and inquiry flows, marketing management requires an internal accounting information system for the revenue cycle that is effective and efficient. This system must process sales, post receivables, generate invoices or monthly statements, and account for cash receipts, at a minimum. The data gathered in this system are very important in supporting management decision-making, reporting, and transaction processing activities. In general, the overall objective of a marketing and sales order processing information system is to provide marketing management with the information necessary to make operational, planning, and strategic decisions and to report the results of the operations to third parties.

In addition to the information flows from the environment and internal information flows used to satisfy decision-making needs, an organization must also consider its requirements for communication to the environment, as shown in Figure 15-1. Some of this communication is in the form of reports to third parties (including financial statements), reports to consumer agencies on product characteristics, and reports to various trade associations. Other information may be required to communicate to the organization's customers and the general public the merits of the firm's products and services through promotion and advertising. The information system must be capable of generating data to support all these information flows to the environment.

Market Decision Support Systems

Marketing management must carry out strategic, managerial, and operational planning in this dynamic and ever-changing environment. To do this marketing management uses a marketing decision support system with features like the planning model shown in Figure 15-2. Based on the inflow of information from the environment as customer needs, product characteristics, service, competitor

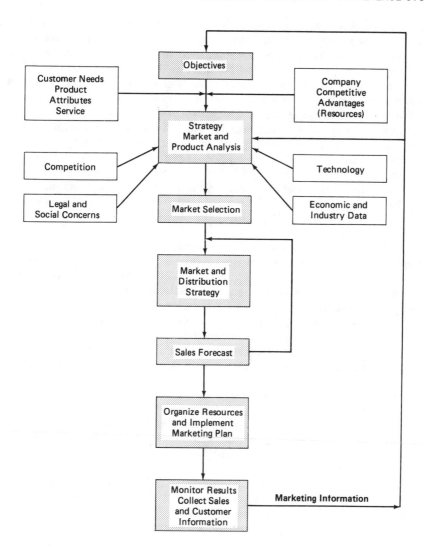

FIGURE 15-2 Marketing planning models.

actions, technological change, economic data, and specific industry information, and an analysis of the organization's capital, technological, human, and other resources, management must develop a strategy to implement its objectives. This market strategy generally specifies what products to introduce, develop, manufacture, purchase, promote, and service; and what markets to serve. This strategy also outlines general policies for sales, pricing, inventory, distribution channels, promotion, and customer service. For each product and market, management decisions must be made to determine what specific product marketing and distribution strategies are necessary to implement the organization's strategic plan. From this a sales forecast is developed which may result in a revision of the strategy, as shown by the feedback loop in Figure 15-2. This planning process requires access to much of the data used to set corporate strategy and access to operational data developed from an analysis of transactions. After this plan is developed, management must then organize its resources, such as the sales force, into an operational plan to implement its product strategy.

Finally, transaction systems, which process sales and accounts receivable transactions, and credit systems, which establish credit for customers, are used to monitor marketing operations. The accounting system used to process this information must be designed to support the strategic, managerial, and operational decisions shown in Figure 15-2. Sufficient data must be obtained at the point of sale, upon credit application, and upon the exercise of credit over time to support many of these decisions. (The major transaction processes that support the majority of marketing information systems are examined in the latter part of this chapter.)

Marketing functions can generally be classified as sales (including pricing, product mix, and distribution functions); product development; promotion and advertising; customer service; and market research. Within each of these functions, and for marketing management as a whole, information like that described in the previous section is required for operational, managerial, and strategic decision-making activities. Moreover, the accounting transaction processing and cost analysis subsystems must be designed to compile a transaction history, accounts receivable, credit, and cost analysis database to support the marketing information system and to monitor its progress shown in Figure 15-2. These transaction data can be obtained from credit data (generally part of the treasurer's function); the inventory subsystem; sales order transaction processing; and accounts receivable records and billing activities. We noted in an earlier chapter that the source of information for managerial and strategic decisions increasingly tends to be environmental and to follow from market research and intelligence. Operational decisions tend to rely more on the analysis of internal transaction sources.

The nature of the business, its objectives and business strategy will dictate the type of marketing decision support system (MDSS) and the nature of the information flows just outlined. The nature of the business will in turn be a function of the organization's products and markets, the nature of the competitive environment, the size of the organization, the resources available from subsystems, and finally, the management's expertise in the use of the information. These environmental characteristics are summarized in Figure 15-3. In general, however, the marketing (MDSS) system requires intensive *monitoring* of the environment, complex *retrieval systems*, and a vast database consisting not only of transaction accounting data, but market data as well to support intensive *inquiry* and *coordination* activities.

Marketing Decision Support System Illustration

U.S. Electronics uses a wide range of decision support systems for marketing management. They range all the way from simple database systems based on transaction processing data to sophisticated interactive decision models. They

Organization structure	Credit and collection practice
Volume and frequency of information flows	Advertising media
Competitive environment	Inventory policy
Resource availability	Distribution system
Financial capability	Technology level of product
Product attributes	Service requirements
Product life cycle	Mathematical and statistical expertise
Product seasonality	Pricing policies
Substitute products	Logistical support
Product line and variety	Cultural norms
Obsolescence and uniqueness	Legal requirements
Styles and colors	Economic conditions
Customer characteristics	Government influence and regulation
Promotion activity	

FIGURE 15-3   Environmental characteristics.

include the statistical analysis of data and "what if" planning models which can explore various strategic scenarios. The type of model and database used to support the model depends upon the nature of each division's business environment, objectives, and business strategy.

For example: (1) For the mature consumer products market, transaction data is stored in a database for analysis, budgeting and forecasting. Market segment and competitive information is also stored to enable U.S. Electronics to react effectively in today's dynamic, competitive, and technological consumer products market. (2) In some of the service divisions an on-line database is used to track customers, activity, and prospects. (3) In international divisions, sales data are used to analyze markets by region, product, and market segment. (4) Industrial sales data is used to track and forecast potential business. This data is augmented by sales representatives. It is used by marketing management to support their efforts and decision making. Industrial sales are also supported by order-entry and inventory systems for pricing and preparation of bids. (5) Several divisions are supported by a system designed to service customers with component parts. (6) An electronic data interchange (EDI) system is used to take customer product specifications, produce a bill of material and information for a bid, initiate raw material orders, and tie this information into computer-aided manufacturing as described in the previous chapter. (7) Interactive econometric forecasting, with on-line sales analysis, market research data for analysis, and alternative scenario models for distribution analysis is used by several consumer divisions. (8) The power generation division uses a model and database to assess generation capacity and to forecast energy needs bases on the present capacity, population trends, energy consumption, and GNP for various countries. (9) An industrial markets model exists for product managers to forecast future industrial market trends. (10) Finally the corporation uses product-pricing models based on product information and market characteristics. All of these systems enable U.S. Electronics to compete effectively in numerous market segments. Moreover, they enable U.S. Electronics to use information as a potent competition force.

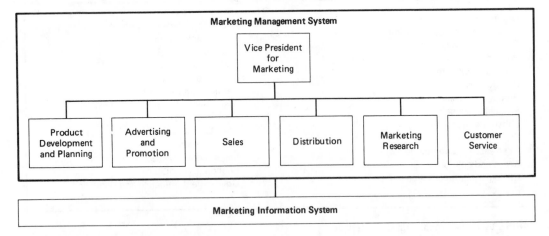

FIGURE 15-4 Marketing organization subsystems and supporting information systems.

These models depend on a well-designed database founded on the transactions generated in the organization via point-of-sales order-entry systems and inventory systems like those discussed in the previous chapter, as well as a wealth of economic and market information which must be collected and analyzed outside the normal sales transaction process.

Marketing Organization

Marketing management must organize its activities in an effective way to accomplish the objectives of the firm, as discussed in Chapter 3. In a functional organization such as the one illustrated in Figure 15-4, the vice-president is primarily responsible for the strategic planning activities and, in smaller organizations, the managerial planning, coordinating, and control of marketing activities. These activities must interface with logistical and financial activities and are often critical to the firm's overall success. Moreover, as shown in Figure 15-5, they contribute to the database upon which marketing decisions are made, reports are generated, and transactions are processed.

Each of the managers of the functional areas of product development and planning, advertising and promotion, sales, market research, and customer service is responsible for providing sufficient information, via the information system and its database, for decision making, reporting, and transaction processing. In turn, each of the managers of a functional subsystem or area will have an organization that will be responsible for providing sufficient information to him or her for managerial and operational decision-making activities.

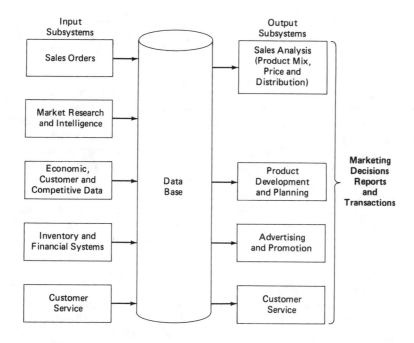

FIGURE 15-5   Sales, marketing, and customer service system.

Marketing Subsystems

SALES.   The objective of the sales manager is to coordinate the sales effort so that the long-run profitability of the company is maximized. Decisions must be made and implemented by the sales management system to ensure adequate stock, effective distribution channels and dealer location, effective motivation of sales personnel, promotion of more profitable products or product lines, profitable pricing of products, appropriate product mix, and good customer relations. These managerial decisions all require careful planning given the strategic objectives of the firm, its marketing plan, and its supporting sales forecast. Each decision of sales management must consider new products and product development, advertising and promotion activities, market research information, and customer service. Moreover, these decisions often require intensive interaction with the marketplace and coordination with logistical operations of inventory and production. Mathematical models such as those used to optimize distribution channels and set prices based on economic and competitive position may be used to assist with these decisions. In other cases, interactive decision support systems may be used to determine price, distribution channels, and product mix. Whether such decision aids are used or not, these decisions must be made by management. These decisions are often based on a set of internal reports.

One of the most useful of these reports is the *stock status report,* which indicates the number of items in stock, the price, and the cost (fixed and variable) if possible. This report is very useful for marginal analysis of the profitability of sales.

A *sales analysis report,* such as the one shown in Figure 15-6, is also quite useful because it details unit and dollar sales for the current period and the year to date, by location (department, store, or territory,) and by salesperson. Budgeted sales and last year's sales are often noted for comparisons. Other analyses, such as sales by product, are also feasible given the basic transaction data gathered at the point of sale. This sales analysis information may be merged with cost accounting and inventory records to prepare profitability analysis reports by location, salesperson, product, or any other category of interest as long as the raw data are collected.

As we can see, much of the information on these management reports is generated by the sales order, inventory, distribution, and accounts receivable transaction processing system. This information is invaluable for decision making.

DISTRIBUTION.   The distribution and transportation of an organization's products to the customer is clearly tied to sales. It is often the responsibility of the sales manager. The objective of the distribution system is the effective delivery of products to the customers. This may entail the shipment of sales orders or the stocking of warehouses or, in many cases, retail stores with adequate merchandise to satisfy customers demand. This objective must consider inventory levels and transportation costs and balance these with customer service objectives.

PRODUCT DEVELOPMENT AND PLANNING.   The product development and planning manager must provide marketing management with packaging, promotion, pricing, and style recommendations throughout the product's life cycle. This life cycle includes the test marketing of new products, the introduction of new products, the maintenance of each product, and finally, the phasing out of products or the substitution of alternative products. Often the product life cycle dominates marketing management's decisions. If it does, a project organization may be preferable to a functional organization.

Decisions that support these product recommendations may be based on marketing models. As in sales management, however, a series of inventory, sales, and profitability analysis reports often provide basic input into these decisions. Marginal analysis of sales revenue and costs is often quite useful in assessing the potential contribution of a product to the overall profitability of the organization. Environmental information is also critical to these decisions. Information on changing styles, customer demand, competitor actions, and new products, is very useful in assessing the strengths and weaknesses of an organization's products and in recommending various courses of action to marketing management.

Class Sku/Sty	Desc Cl Sz S	Current				Month-to-Date						Year-to-Date					
		Net Units	Net Sales	%Sls /Tot	%Ret /Sls	Net Units	Net Sales	%Sls Tot	%Ret Sls	%Diff Unit	Ty/Ly Dollar	Net Units	Net Sales	%Sls /Tot	%Ret /Sls	%Diff Unit	Ty/Ly Dollar
1643	Merchandise A	2	42	3.7	.3	6	125	3.6	.9	-5.1	-6.0	80	1080	5.1	1.0	.7	.6
1645	Merchandise B	2	15	1.3	.0	2	15	.4	.0	-2.5	-3.0	16	118	.6	.0	-2.9	-4.7
1759	Merchandise C	6	123	10.9	3.5	14	282	8.0	2.7	6.9	8.0	111	2313	10.9	2.5	1.5	2.3
1761	Merchandise D	11	78	6.9	.0	32	224	6.4	.0	1.2	2.0	220	1540	7.3	.0	6.8	5.3
1773	Merchandise E	17	181	16.1	1.2	96	1031	29.3	1.6	4.7	5.2	598	6362	30.0	1.7	5.8	6.4
1775	Merchandise F	12	96	8.5	.0	45	360	10.2	.0	1.4	1.0	333	2664	12.5	.0	3.0	2.1
1784	Merchandise G	10	90	24.1	.0	27	243	16.4	.0			123	1107	15.4	.0		
916120	BL/34/2	4	48	12.9	.0	23	276	18.6	.0			213	2556	35.7	.0		
916126	A B C Co.	2	20	5.4	.0	14	140	9.5	.0			124	1240	17.3	.0		
916127	X Y Z Co.	1	5	1.3	.0	2	46	3.1	.0			5	114	1.6	.0		
916128	Promotion	14	210	56.3	.9	41	615	41.5	.8			92	1380	19.3	.6		
916129	Bad Goods	0	0	.0	.0	3	161	10.9	.0			15	762	10.6	.0		
Class 1784 TOT		31	373	33.2	.9	110	1481	42.1	.8	3.7	4.0	572	7159	33.7	.6	4.8	5.0
Dept. 12 TOT		81	1123	25.7	.8	305	3518	19.4	.9	2.7	3.6	1930	21236	26.0TR.29.9		2.8	2.4
x				x				x						x			
x				x				x						x			
x				x				x						x			
Div. 5 TOT		693	4365	28.3	1.2	2596	18095	53.1	1.4	4.8	5.1	12491	81745	33.1	1.0	1.8	2.3
x				x				x						x			
x				x				x						x			
x				x				x						x			
Store 1 TOT		1289	15430	100	.8	3806	34102	100	1.0	2.6	3.5	23461	246698	100	1.0	2.9	3.1

FIGURE 15-6   Sales analysis report.

Source: NCR—*Retail Management Information System*, Dayton: NCR Corporation. Reprinted with permission.

Therefore, the database needed here includes not only internal information gathered at the point of sale and through the cost accounting system, but also considerable external information, which is needed by product planning and development managers. Market research can be quite instrumental in satisfying this need.

ADVERTISING AND PROMOTION.   The objective of the advertising and promotion manager is to plan, coordinate, execute, and evaluate advertising and promotion policy. Given a limited budget, advertising and promotion management must allocate resources in the most effective manner through a variety of media to products and locations (territories, regions, stores, etc.) to accomplish the overall sales objectives of marketing management. These decisions require careful planning and coordination of sales and product development. They are generally a function of a market's response to the various media, exposure to those media over time, and the product and market strategy of the organization.

Mathematical models have been used effectively for a number of years in helping advertising and promotional management to select the best type of media and exposure for various products. A subsequent evaluation of the impact of these efforts is necessary to refine these models for future use. The *sales analysis report* shown in Figure 15-6 can be used effectively in this evaluation process. It is essential that key sales statistics be collected at the point of sale or during the sales transaction process if advertising and promotion management is to make intelligent decisions on allocating the advertising and promotion budget. To further assist advertising and promotion management, the array of sales statistics on salespeople; locations (department, store, territory, etc.); products; styles; sizes; and so forth, should be in a database as shown in Figure 15-5. This is necessary so that planned and actual promotional efforts can be matched with their respective target populations to facilitate future decision making and the evaluation of past decisions.

As with product planning, promotional decisions require a considerable amount of external information, such as that noted earlier, which is often gathered by market research. The database as shown in Figure 15-5 therefore, not only must contain information about customers, competition, and the economic and legal environment, but also must be organized in such a way that it can facilitate information retrieval. Users may request information either in report form or via random inquiry.

MARKETING RESEARCH.   The objective of marketing research is to investigate problems confronting the other managers in the marketing organization. These problems may involve sales, product development, advertising and promotion, customer service, or general marketing management needs.

To satisfy these decision-making and reporting requirements, the market research department must, either periodically or upon demand for specifically commissioned assignments, gather information by a general scanning of the environment and by retrieval from the firm's database. This information must then be processed. This may entail evaluation of the various signals received and an abstraction of the relevant signals from a large set of data. This set of currently or potentially relevant data must be planned, indexed (coded), and logically organized. This organization is necessary for retention and retrieval purposes for responses to inquiries, solutions to problems, analysis of information, and generation of periodic reports to be disseminated to the appropriate decision makers or users.

The decision maker can use the information provided by marketing research in a number of ways, which generally parallel those used by the types of information systems outlined in Chapter 4. The information may be of value in its own right for decision making. It may be analyzed using statistical, economic, or psychometric models. It may be used in conjunction with models to enable marketing management to pursue "what if" questions. It may be used in corporate planning models such as those outlined in Chapter 17. Market research management will probably utilize all the mathematical and statistical techniques it can to provide the best possible information to the other areas of marketing management.

The database used by market research will include sales, inventory, and accounts receivable statistics which are generated from transaction data of the kind described later in this chapter. It will, moreover, require the set of external data noted earlier as shown in Figure 15-5 which is gathered via a continual monitoring of the environment through a marketing intelligence system. In fact, the management of this intelligence system may very well be the responsibility of marketing research.

CUSTOMER SERVICE. The goal of customer service is to serve the customer in such a way that he or she will be satisfied with the product. To do this, the objective of customer service management is to provide customers with technical assistance and product maintenance. Decisions must be made pertaining to the maintenance organization, training of service personnel, capabilities of equipment, and location of facilities to serve customers and assist in the dissemination of technical information to these customers. These management decisions must be congruent with the marketing management strategy regarding customer satisfaction and service.

Again, the basic sales, inventory, and accounts receivable transaction information is useful for customer service management. In addition, information on sales returns, customer complaints, and frequency and cause of repair by location, salesperson, and product is useful for making decisions and evaluating customer service policies. Most of these reports can be generated periodically. An on-line system may be needed for parts inventory and maintenance activities.

Finally, much of the information generated for decision making, reporting, and transaction processing may be used to add value to the product or service itself. For example, a system which tracks the availability of products in the distribution channel can be used to specify exact delivery times, thereby reducing customers' material inventory because their stock levels can be reduced given the increased certainty of delivery.

Transaction Processing Revenue Cycle

All marketing information systems are supported by a revenue cycle that includes the processing of sales transactions and the subsequent collection of receivables. This sales and collection cycle represents the prime source of internally generated data for the decision-making and reporting needs of marketing management.

These major subsystems generally provide this basic transaction information. They serve as prime inputs into the database or files utilized by product development, promotion, sales, market research, and customer service. These subsystems are the *sales order processing and accounts receivable and invoicing system;* and the *credit authorization and management system.*

At the point of sale, a considerable amount of information must often be gathered in addition to the dollar amount of the transaction. Due to the tremendous volume of this information, special data-entry point-of-sale systems that can capture large volumes of data economically and effectively have been developed in certain situations. These are a subset of the sales order processing system. Typical data-entry POS systems are illustrated first. Then a relatively complete sales order, accounts receivable, and cash receipts system is used to illustrate the key components of a typical sales order-entry system. A microcomputer example is used to highlight a portion of this illustration. Not all systems contain all the features illustrated and some contain many more.

DATA INPUT AND POINT-OF-SALE SYSTEMS.   Data entry can be very costly when either the amount of sales analysis detail to be collected for each transaction or the volume of these transactions is large. This is particularly true of many retail firms and food chains. There are numerous small transactions. For each transaction, data must be collected to be subsequently used to prepare sales analysis and inventory reports and to support random inquiry by marketing personnel. As we noted earlier, these reports and the need for such inquiry are essential for many marketing decisions.

The basic steps to data entry:

1. Record data at source
2. Input data into system
3. Edit, verify, validate, and correct data
4. Log transaction
5. Store data for future use

A simple sales order (in small systems this may be the invoice) that must subsequently be keyed into the system and processed only satisfies step one. During the past decade, however, equipment and procedures have been developed that can automate almost all of these steps in a cost-effective way. Sophisticated cash registers, intelligent terminals, or microcomputers can generate machine-readable output such as tape or disks for use in computer processing. Moreover, these cash registers, intelligent terminals, or microcomputers can be wired directly to a microcomputer or minicomputer in the store using a network like those described in earlier chapters. Hand-held optical scanning wands and holographic optical equipment have been developed to read codes directly from the merchandise or tags. Universal Product Codes have been developed and printed on the merchandise by the manufacturer for many items typically sold through supermarkets. Product codes, coupled with salesperson and location codes, enable a small microcomputer located in the store to perform all five data-entry steps as well as the local generation of sales and inventory reports.

The general differences between POS systems for supermarkets or discount department stores and traditional retail stores follow from the business environment for which they were designed.[1] The major impetus for supermarket POS systems was checkout productivity; whereas in retailing, inventory and other managerial support systems dominated the need for detailed sales and customer information. In a supermarket, Universal Product Codes and descriptions are used and are maintained on a random access file where they are matched with prices, which may vary from store to store and from day to day. The Universal Product Code is read by a holographic scanner built into the checkout counter. Prices need only be posted on shelves and not on the merchandise. Price and descriptive information is displayed and printed for customer use. The checkout clerk basically stays in one place and checks out large volumes of merchandise.

This is in contrast to a traditional retail department store where the salesclerk spends a considerable amount of time assisting customers. When a sale is consummated, a multitude of options such as sales discounts, charge, COD, layaway, and partial payments are available. Moreover, salesclerks are often temporary personnel who need assistance in processing transactions. Ticket marking or coding merchandise descriptions and possibly prices on sales tickets is a major task for retail stores compared with supermarkets and discount department stores that use a Universal Product Code. As a result of these characteristics, POS systems for retail stores tend to be intelligent terminals that "walk" salesclerks through a transaction by requesting a predetermined sequence of data input activities. The terminal or electronic cash register may use prompts to assist sales personnel in data input. They, however, may also have optical wands or magnetic character reading equipment designed to read the merchandise and price codes on the sales tickets.

A typical intelligent terminal or microcomputer with POS software uses a transaction sequence control and guides the cashier or operator through the steps of the transaction by using a sequence of messages. It is generally programmable by the user for many retail point-of-sale applications and includes features[2] such as:

1. Customized keyboard arrangement
2. Transaction sequence control and prompter display
3. Keylock mechanisms for use and programming control
4. Programming flexibility
5. Change computation

---

[1] This discussion is based on P.V. McEnroe, H.T. Huth, E.A. Moore, and W.W. Morris III, "Overview of the Supermarket and the Retail Store System," *IBM Systems Journal,* 15 no. 1 (1975), 3–15.

[2] NCR, *NCR 2151 Retail Terminal System* (Dayton: NCR Corporation).

6. High amount limit lockout
7. Layaway features
8. Merchandise tag reading
9. Check digit verification
10. Buffered keyboard
11. Programmable printing and format control
12. Document validation, sales check insertion, deposit payment, fee payment features
13. Tax calculation
14. Itemization and multiple price extension features
15. Deposit calculation
16. Automatic check endorsement
17. Automatic department sales person identification entry
18. Credit lookup and authorization display

Several equipment configurations may be used with these intelligent terminals or microcomputers and supermarket checkout scanners and registers. The terminals may be connected to a central computing facility for the organization, especially for credit authorizations, or via a network to a microcomputer in the particular location. They may also stand alone and generate machine-readable output for further batch processing at another location or in the store at a later point in time. In all of these configurations, each terminal must be able to stand alone or have sufficient backup. The backup computer may in some cases be at another location. This is necessary so that transactions can continue to be processed when a malfunction occurs in the system to which the POS terminal is networked.

SALES ORDER PROCESSING.   During the processing of the sales transaction, a large volume of data can be captured by using a sales order. In smaller systems such as the microcomputer software referenced here, the sales order and sales invoices may be the same document. Sales order processing systems can be manual, batch, or random access depending on the nature of the business, the strategy of the organization, and the structure of the organization. To illustrate the basic concept of a sales order processing and accounts receivable system, a typical system will be illustrated.[3] The cash receipts segment which completes the revenue cycle will follow later in the chapter with reference to the type of features provided by some microcomputer software. The system flowchart for a typical sales order entry system is shown in Figure 15-7. It contains features typical of small microcomputer systems as well as those found in larger systems. Both the more comprehensive and microcomputer illustrations are fairly complex system and require random access for reporting and transaction processing needs. The microcomputer illustrations are for National Athletic Distributors, a wholesale distributor of sporting goods. The microcomputer module with sev-

---

[3] The microcomputer system and its illustrations for National Athletic Distributors are adapted with permission from Peachtree Software Inc.'s INSIGHT Accounts Receivable System.

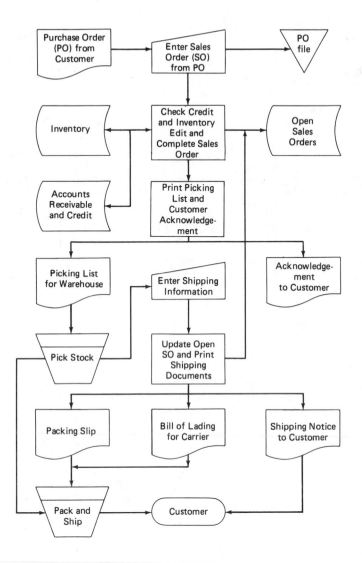

FIGURE 15-7 Typical sales order-entry system.

eral other modules ties directly into a general ledger module to complete an integrated accounting system.

First an organization receives a purchase order from a customer. Then a sales order is prepared and the accounts receivable database can be referenced in an interactive mode by the sales clerk to assess the credit standing of the customer. As shown in Figure 15-8, the credit limit, aging information, and previous sales history are available in the customer information file. All this information helps management determine the credit applicability of the customer. In this example, Feron's Racket and Tennis Shop seems to be a good customer

Customer Information Card									
Account	FERATE	Balance		24,486.00	Credit Limit		30,000.00	Open Item	X
Bill To:		Date Opened		06/15/86	Ship to:			Add New Address	
Name	**Feron's Racket and Tennis Shop**				Name				
Address	105 Newbury St. 14th floor				Address				
City	Boston				City				
State	MA	Zip Code	02120		State			Zip Code	
Telephone	617/392-3020	Ext	10		Discount Level	3		Statement Cycle	30
Attention	Mr. Edward Feron				Terms	30		Finance Charge Type	1
Territory	NE	Sales Rep	CEB	Division 1	Exempt #	45945-293		Tax Jurisdiction	

The following information can be modified only by 'Change History'.					
Balance Due	Current	31-60 days	61-90 days	Over 90 days	High Credit
24,486.00	15,756.50	8,729.50			43,898.25

	Sales	Cost	Profit		Last Payment	Last Invoice
MTD	15,756.50	8,897.25	6,859.25	Date	12/05/86	12/28/86
YTD	155,090.89	86,468.95	68,621.94	Amount	5,217.75	7,424.50
Last Year				Average Payment Days	48	

FIGURE 15-8 Customer information card.

Source: INSIGHT A/R System, Peachtree Software, Inc., 1988. Reprinted with permission

with a reasonably good credit record. However, in other cases, large 90-day balances and long periods since the last payment may cause National to cancel the sale. In addition to checking the credit, National has the ability to reference inventory data to check on product availability, price, discounts, and costs. Product information can be accessed by item name, as shown in the window on the screen in Figure 15-9. In more extensive systems, a separate file is kept on open sales orders. The order remains there until it is completely shipped and invoiced. Also in more extensive systems, the customer is notified by an order *acknowledgement* and a picking list is sent to the warehouse. A *picking list* will contain product data such as number, name, and number of units ordered by location (bin number) for efficient picking. In a more extensive system, once the shipment is picked the actual products to be shipped are keyed into the system and a packing slip and, a bill of lading are generated.

For small systems, such as the microcomputer system illustrated here, the *packing slip* is sometimes a copy of the sales order or sales invoices with the number shipped entered. It is enclosed with the shipment. The *bill of lading,* common in larger systems and shown in Figure 15-7, is intended for the common carrier. It tells the carrier the goods are legally on board, the freight has been paid or billed, the persons (company) authorized to receive shipment, and the destination of the shipment.

After the goods are shipped, the billing department is notified of the shipment. Sometimes this is done electronically. Also, in larger systems, the open sales order file is updated to reflect the shipment. Often a *shipping notice* is prepared, as shown in Figure 15-10. In some systems, this may be a copy of the bill of lading or even a copy of the sales order which indicates what has been shipped.

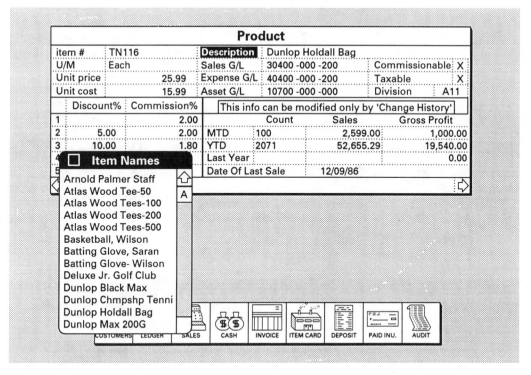

FIGURE 15-9 Product information card.
Source: INSIGHT A/R System, Peachtree Software, Inc., 1988. Reprinted with permission

Once this is received, the sales invoice can be completed. Sometimes the sales order itself can be completed and used as an invoice. It is the key document in the entire revenue cycle and contains the description of what was sold and the amount due. National can process the sales invoice on the microcomputer screen, as shown in Figure 15-10. In this process, invoice numbers are generated automatically for control and reference. Moreover, as is typical of microcomputer order-entry systems, customer information, terms and discount level, sales representative, territory, product description, and price extensions can be referenced directly from the accounts receivable and product data which may appear as separate windows on the screen. All the clerk needs to do is enter the customer account number (such as OTMNSH on Figure 15-10) or search a customer directory to enter it and then enter the product quantities and account numbers. The clerk may also search the directory to obtain the account number which in turn will be entered automatically. All extensions are made automatically and once the invoice is completed, it can be printed and be mailed or shipped with the product to the customer. The customer directory is simply a customer names file, like the product (item) names file shown in Figure 15-11. The invoice also includes pertinent information about the company, such as name, address, and telephone number.

Also after the goods are shipped the inventory is reduced to reflect the amount of goods shipped.

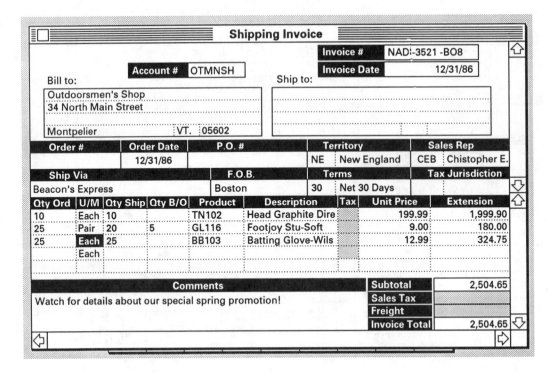

FIGURE 15-10   Shipping invoice.
Source: INSIGHT A/R System, Peachtree Software, Inc., 1988. Reprinted with permission

After the invoice has been prepared, the sales are posted to update the accounts receivable database. As is typical of many systems, this may be done on an individual sale-by-sale basis, or the sales journal may be posted and at the end of the day, the entire sales journal can be posted to accounts receivable data. When this is done, transaction listing (audit trail) can be provided for control purposes. The accounts receivable data, credit history, and customer data will normally contain the kind of data shown in Figures 15-8 and 15-11, the customer ledger record.

In summary, the following sequence of activities is followed in the revenue cycle: (1) receive purchase order from customer; (2) enter sales order; (3) check credit; (4) check inventory; (5) complete and acknowledge sales order; (6) select (pick) stock; (7) pack; (8) ship; (9) notify billing of amount shipped; (10) invoice customers; (11) send monthly statements to customers; (12) receive remittances; and (13) make bank deposit. Many small systems use the sales order as an invoice and many do not have a formal picking, packing, and bill of lading system because these are not needed. Nevertheless, a customer should not be billed until goods are shipped, otherwise the firm runs the risk of billing a customer for goods not shipped.

In general, there are three basic types of accounts receivable systems. One is an *open item system* in which there is a complete accounting of customer activity

Customer Ledger Card

Account	OTMNSH	Outdoorsmen's Shop	Current	
---------	--------	--------------------	---------	
Attention	Mr. George Shaw	34 North Main Street	31 - 60	
Telephone	802/887-9230	Montpelier VT 05602	61 - 90	
Territory	NE Salesperson CEB Cycle 30 Terms 30 Days 59		Over 90	

Date	Div	Invoice/Check	Amount	Payment	Balance	Comment	Sro	?
10/18/86	1	NADI-1209-BOS	428.50		428.50		N.Y	
12/20/86	1	NADI-1219-BOS	5,244.00	Part Payment	3,224.00		N.Y	
12/31/86	1	NADI-3521-BOS	2,504.65		2,504.65		N.Y	
12/31/86	1	2392	Fully Applied	2,000.00	0.00		C/R	
12/31/86	1				0.00		S/J	
16,000		Credit Limit	8,157.15	2,000.00	6,157.15			

Paid Invoice Journal

Name		Check #	Chk-Date	Original Amount	Amt Applied	Balance	
Outdoorsmen;s Shop		2392	12/31/86	2,000.00	2,000.00	0.00	

Name	Div	Invoice	Inv-Date	Original Amount	Discount	Amount Applied
Feron's Racket and	1	NADI-1203-BOS	11/05/86	8,729.50		4,193.26
Outdoorsmen;s Shop	1	NADI-1219-BOS	12/20/86	5,224.00		2,000.00

FIGURE 15-11   Customer ledger card.
Source: INSIGHT A/R Peachtree Software, Inc., 1988. Reprinted with permission

for all unpaid or uncontested invoices such as the one illustrated here. Credits are made either to specific invoices or to the oldest invoice as cash is remitted. Simpler systems only retain detail for the current month's activity and bring forward only the balance and past-due charges from previous months' activity. This type of system is called a *balance forward system*. Other systems record only the balance. This type of *balance only system* is frequently used by small retail stores and is supported by copies of the original invoice.

Customer statements can be printed with the appropriate finance charges and many other reports can be prepared for marketing management from the accounts receivable and product data which is maintained in the system. These are typical of most comprehensive microcomputer packages and would be more elaborate for large systems. Larger, more comprehensive systems will also provide for a tear-off portion (sometimes it is a separate card) of the statement to be returned with the customer's remittance. This contains the customer ID, amount due, and place for the customer to indicate the amount remitted. This is called a *remittance advice*. In this example, aging, credit, sales history, commissions, customer list, and inventory reports can be easily generated by management whenever they are needed or on a periodic basis. A typical sales history report is shown in Figure 15-12. Moreover, like many systems this small micro system even makes it easy to communicate with customers by providing a procedure for producing mailing labels to send out promotional material, for exam-

Sales History Report
Order by Account #

National Athletic Distributors
12/31/86   9:02:28 AM

Page
All Division:

Account	Sales Rep	Territory	MTD/YTD Sales	MTD/YTD Cost	MTD/YTD Profit	Last Sale
ACSPGD CEB Action Sporting Goods		NE	33,777.35 221,773.34	10,264.50 100,253.34	23.512.85 121,526.00	7,302.20 12/19/86
ADSPGD ADD Adams Sporting Goods		CEN				
BESPCT CEB Beacon Sports Center		NE	8,306.00 149,105.66	4,490.75 89,931.95	3,815.25 59,173.71	5,307.00 12/22/86
BESPSH ADD Beacon Sports Shop		CEN				
BURSPO BCW Burlington Sports		MID	12,999.00 173,882.90	4,845.00 92,757.55	8,154.00 81,125.35	12,999.00 12/19/86
CAHISP KAM Castle Hill Sporting Goods		NO				
COSPCO DBF Cohasset Sports Company		NCE				
CTSPGD DCO City Sporting Goods		NEA	122,055.20	65,254.75	56,800.45	4,606.00 12/01/86
FERATE CEB Feron's Racket and Tennis Shop		NE	19,949.76 159,284.15	11,628.75 89,200.45	8,321.01 70,083.70	4,193.26 12/31/86
FLFOIN ADD Fleet foot Inc.		CEN				
HEWOSP CEB Herman's World of Sporting Goods		NE	8,246.50 236,421.75	4,044.00 125,696.50	4,202.50 110,725.25	8,246.50 12/09/86
HOCOSP ADD Holvack & Coughlin Sporting Goods		CEN				
JAFBRI BCW James F. Brine		MID	7,098.00 185,349.65	4,119.00 100,680.45	2,979.00 84,669.20	7,098.00 12/21/86
JOSPGD KAM John's Sporting Goods		NO				
NEBODI DCO Nevada Bob's Discount Golf		NEA	13,900.00 185,704.14	7,800.00 107,155.39	6,100.00 78,548.75	13,900.00 12/23/86
NOSHSP DBF North Shore Sports		NCE				
OTMNSH CEB Outdoorsmen's Shop		NE	8,209.70 131,018.70	4,022.35 68,084.20	4,187.35 62,934.50	2,504.65 12/31/86

FIGURE 15-12 Sales history report.
Source: INSIGHT A/R System, Peachtree Software, Inc., 1988. Reprinted with permission.

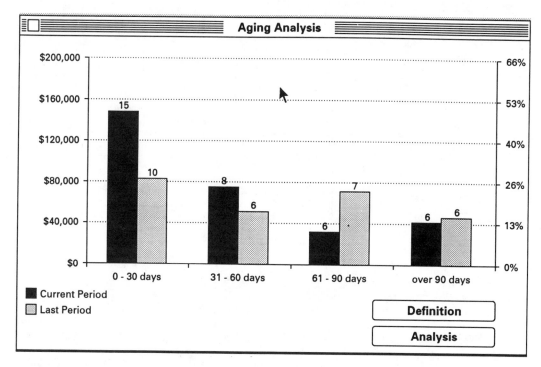

FIGURE 15-13   Aging analysis.
Source: INSIGHT A/R System, Peachtree Software, Inc., 1988. Reprinted with permission.

ple. Large systems have extensive database capability to help management to communicate with customers. As in any random access system such as this one, management can call up, assuming they have the appropriate password or clearance, any data item, record or file from the database and use the information for decision making. An example was given earlier with respect to inventory and credit checks.

· A helpful feature of this and other more advanced microcomputer accounting software is the ability to portray output in graphical form. Sales history, projections, and aging analyses are available here for management to assess trends and aid in the decision-making process. A comparative aging analysis is shown in Figure 15-13 as an example. It clearly shows management the that the aging situation in terms of the 60- to 90-day category is improved from the last period.

CASH RECEIPTS SYSTEM.   The revenue cycle is concluded with the receipt of payment for outstanding receivables, as shown in Figure 15-14. This system can apply the cash receipt to a single invoice or to an open balance. Checks are endorsed, and along with remittance advices (for more comprehensive systems), are posted to a cash receipts journal. Like sales they can be posted to the accounts receivable database as they occur or they can be accumulated in a journal and posted in batch at the end of the period. A period can be a day, week, or even a month. As in the posting of sales, an audit trail is often established using

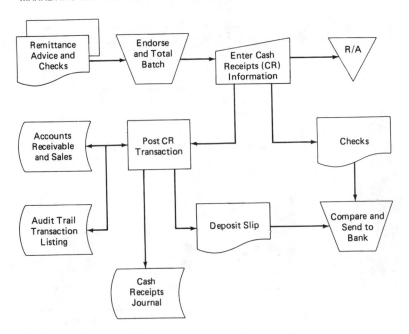

FIGURE 15-14 Accounts receivable system: cash receipts.

a transaction listing. Deposit slips are prepared, compared with check totals, and forwarded to the bank.

The microcomputer example, as can be seen from the examples of the sales order processing screens, makes good use of windows. This enables management to view or use several accounting subsystems and to reference several parts of the database at the same time. This feature is becoming more common in many advanced large-scale and micro systems. This greatly enhances the productivity of the user because all the related transactions in the sales order-entry system can be viewed at one time to deal with sales and customers in day-to-day activities in the business. The microcomputer illustration also permits the processing of back orders. In essence, these are unshipped sales orders which must be produced or ordered in order to complete a sales order.

Finally, inventory and general ledger files are updated when accounts receivable are updated, providing the other modules are tied into the integrated system. This is common in integrated accounting systems such as this one.

CREDIT AUTHORIZATION AND MANAGEMENT. Prior to the authorization of credit and the determination of the amount of credit, the firm's credit and collection department must review the credit history of old customers. This history is contained in the accounts receivable database and includes the basic elements previously illustrated. In larger systems there is much more information on collection patterns and sales history. For new customers, the application for credit must be reviewed and the credit-worthiness of the potential customer assessed. Mathematical models, such as multiple regression and discriminant analysis (a special case of multiple regression), are often used to forecast and classify a potential customer's credit risk. Multiple regression must be used because of the multiplicity of variables, most of which are gathered on the application and contribute to the overall credit rating of the potential customer. Examples of these variables are salary, age, education, marital status, outstanding debt, and other charge account numbers.

Credit management systems are important to retailers. The vast increase in the use of credit has expanded sales volumes throughout the country, but it has also led to increased collection problems, fraud, and bad debts. The retailer must therefore have a good system for scrutinizing credit purchases, such as that illustrated above in the POS and microcomputer example, so that these problems can be addressed. In general, this system must not interfere with customer service and must not cost more than the benefits derived from the system. There are many such on-line systems available today. A typical system:

1. Allows interaction between the sales personnel, credit, and customer data files.
2. Permits quick retrieval of customer records by the credit department.
3. Generates messages to sales personnel for credit authorization decisions. This relieves the sales personnel of this decision.
4. Protects the integrity and confidentiality of the data files via several levels of security and access codes.
5. Provides dynamic file updating to ensure that the credit authorization file is current via
   a. Data generated from an accounts receivable system
   b. On-line changes in customer records
   c. Point-of-sale transactions
6. Monitors check-cashing (credit card) activity via number of checks (transactions) and dollar amount[6]

Coordination of Subsystems and Supporting Systems

All of these decision-making and supporting transaction processing systems must be coordinated by marketing management to achieve the goals and policies set forth by the general management of the firm. To accomplish this, the management information system must be designed to communicate objectives and policies to and among the various marketing managers, such as those for the areas of responsibility illustrated in Figure 15-4. Generally, this is part of the budget process, and the controller plays a key role in this process. The coordination of the management subsystems can be further enhanced by using an integrated database (see Chapter 10) as illustrated in Figure 15-5. The result will be one common set of data from which each report is generated and to which inquiry is made. Finally, the centralization of the market intelligence activities under market research will aid in the coordination of these activities.

---

[6] Reprinted with permission, NCR, *Credit Management System* (Dayton: NCR Corporation). (emphasis added)

Interface with Production and Inventory Systems

An interface between the marketing and logistical systems is often necessary at all levels of management activity. Strategic planning must obviously consider marketing as well as production capabilities and constraints. Managerial activities must often span marketing and production, as well as financial, functions. This is the case when a manager is responsible for the coordination of all activities for one product, project, or location. Use of a product manager is common in many industries. If the organization is to function smoothly, the marketing and logistical activities must be coordinated to produce a product, meet sales forecasts or demands, and eventually ship to the customer. The budgeting process can be particularly effective in this type of situation.

A good example of the coordination necessary at the operational decision-making and transaction processing level is found in the typical on-line *order-entry system* just shown. Batch processing in a small manual system, illustrated in the appendix at the end of the chapter, likewise requires a significant amount of coordination.

Larger, more advanced systems like the one illustrated often employ direct data entry, random file access, and interactive processing for (1) order entry; (2) on-line inquiry and credit authorization; (3) on-line invoicing; (4) on-line inventory control; (5) shipment processing; (6) price changes and cost changes; (7) order statistics and inquiry; (8) customer payment entry; (9) posting stock orders; and (10) posting stock receipts. In addition to having inquiry capability, advanced systems can generate several reports. These may include sales order statistics, orders received, orders shipped, orders canceled, stock outs, credit limits exceeded, inventory stock status, buyer's reports, customer status and delivery, customer master list, accounts receivable, trial balance, aging report, and back order reports.

Marketing Systems' Inherent and Control Risks

A sales and marketing accounting information system is exposed to many risks which may cause the system to fail or to lose its data integrity. For example:

1. Sales may be made for inventory which is not in stock resulting in partial shipments, to the customer's surprise.
2. Credit may be granted to customers with poor credit ratings and result in excessive write-offs of receivables.
3. Shipping may be made too early or to late and violate the terms of the sale resulting in complete shipments or loss of customer good will.
4. Terms may be in error resulting in dissatisfied customers or loss of income.
5. Pricing and discount policies may be violated resulting in dissatisfied customers. Incorrect statement may result from these inaccuracies.
6. Returns may be mishandled resulting in incorrect granting of credit or incorrect inventory.

7. Write-offs of customer accounts may be in error resulting in the loss of income to the organization.
8. Sales analysis may be misleading resulting in poor management promotional, pricing, and other marketing decisions.
9. Inaccuracies in accounts receivable records can lead to inaccurate customer statements and misleading balances in the financial statements causing customer ill will and adjustments to receivable balances during the audit.

A control structure following the principles set forth in Chapter 11 needs to be designed to control for the risks like these which are common to many sales order, accounts receivable, and cash receipts systems.

SUMMARY

Marketing information systems must be carefully planned, designed, and implemented if they are to succeed in satisfying the varied decision-making and reporting needs of marketing management. To compound this problem, there is a further need for extensive coordination with other functions, a need for very intensive interactive inquiry, and a need to search the environment for relevant data that will be transformed into information useful for strategic, managerial, and operational decision making and reporting. As a result, marketing systems tend to require more complex hardware and software than many production and inventory systems in order to support the management system for which they are designed.

In summary, the sequence of steps and the associated forms (files) used in the revenue cycle is as follows:

1.	Receive customer purchase order	Customer's purchase order
2.	Enter sales orders	Sales order
3.	Check credit	A/R file
4.	Check inventory	Inventory file
5.	Acknowledgement	Acknowledgement
6.	Stock selection	Picking list
7.	Pack	Packing slip
8.	Ship	Bill of lading and Inventory file
9.	Notify billing of shipment	Shipping notices
10.	Prepare and send sales invoice	Invoice and A/R file
11.	Prepare monthly statement	Monthly statement
12.	Receive remittance	Check, remittance advice, A/R file
13.	Make deposit	Check, deposit slip, cash, receipt file

Manual System Illustration: Order Entry

To illustrate a manual system, a simple order-entry and invoicing system is shown in Figure A15-1. Assume that all sales are on account. An invoice is mailed once a month for the sales during the current month and for any past-due balance. All of these data are recorded on a card for each customer and filed alphabetically. After credit approval, one copy of the sales order is filed in a numerical file for future sales analysis and numerical control. A second copy is used by the accounting clerk to update the perpetual inventory records. This copy is then sent to shipping where the order is prepared. The second copy becomes the packing list for the shipment and is subsequently sent to the customer. The third copy is forwarded to accounting where the accounts receivable and general ledgers are posted. It is then temporarily filed alphabetically. At the end of the month, the third copy and the accounts receivable detail ledger are used to prepare two copies of the invoice (statement) which indicates current activity and any past-due amounts with appropriate interest. The third copy of the sales order and the second copy of the invoice are then filed alphabetically in a permanent file for reference. The original invoice is mailed to the customer.

Large manual systems follow the same sequence of steps outlined in the illustration in the text, except that all documents are filed manually and multiple copies are required for each user and the department originating the document. Each file is organized for numerical control or for easy reference by name, number, or date. Generally, all the documents are numbered for control and reference purposes.

Batch Processing Illustration: Order Entry, Accounts Receivable, and Sales Analysis

To illustrate batch processing concepts and issues in a marketing system, consider the simple order entry, accounts receivable, and sales analysis shown in Figure A15-2. This illustration uses cards and magnetic tapes which are rapidly being replaced by batch systems which use direct data entry into the computer via a menu driven screen and keyboard, and the storage of files on magnetic disk instead of magnetic tape. Cards and tape are simply used here to illustrate the batch processing concepts because the processing logic is easier to follow.

This type of system will be required when the volume of transactions involving sales, inventory, and accounts receivable exceeds that which can be processed manually. A batch processing system is also required when the volume of detail collected during the transaction process exceeds that which can be processed manually on an economical basis. A batch processing system is also necessary to support product, location, and salesperson analysis for marketing decisions, when the volume of detail required for those decisions exceeds that which can be processed manually on an economical basis.

In the system illustrated, approved sales orders are batched using dollar amount and transaction totals. They are sent to the data processing department for key punching onto cards and key verification. The original orders are filed by

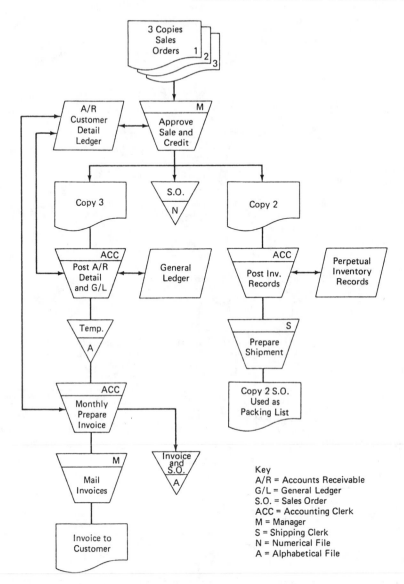

FIGURE A15-1 Manual order-entry and invoicing system.

sales order number for future reference and accountability. Each sales order contains the type of information shown in Figure 15-10. The sales order card deck is then sorted mechanically by customer number. These cards are processed to update both the current monthly sales tape and the accounts receivable master file. Cash sales (if any) are noted separately on the sales report and tape. In many other systems, this update of the accounts receivable records will

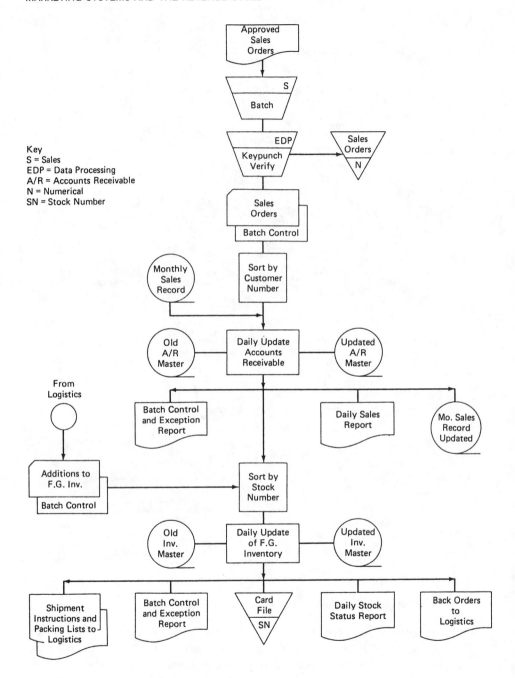

FIGURE A15-2 Batch processing daily sales order processing cycle.

include the update of a daily cash receipts file. For credit sales, accounts receivable records are posted. For all sales, the monthly sales record is updated for future analysis. Batch control totals and exceptions are reported to management for control and possible follow-up of errors. A daily sales report is generated for marketing management.

Sales order cards are then sorted by stock number along with batch control cards indicating additions to finished goods inventory from the logistical system. Once these cards have been sorted (finished goods additions are on tape in many batch processing systems), the old inventory master file is then updated to reflect additions to and reductions in inventory. As part of this update run, shipping instructions and packing lists are sent to the shipping department, batch control and exception reports are forwarded to management for review, cards are filed numerically by stock number for reference, daily stock status reports are given to marketing and production management for decision making and review, and a listing of back orders is forwarded to the production and sales departments.

In this illustration, billing is done once a month for all customers. In some firms, billing is done on a daily basis where statements are prepared for customers for certain billing cycles (segment of the accounts receivable master file) each day. The accounts receivable master file is run to prepare statements to be sent to customers. Aging reports of current and past-due accounts are also prepared for credit and sales management decision needs. For all runs, an exception and control report is given to management for review.

In addition to processing transactions and generating reports, this system is capable of taking the monthly sales record, which is updated daily, and sorting these data in a number of different ways to generate reports for management decision making. In this illustration, product, location, salesperson, and overall sales statistics are generated each month. These monthly sales statistics could be aggregated once a year and could be compared with monthly or yearly budget and historical data. This type of comparison is much more feasible and economical with a batch system than with a manual system. More details, a larger volume of data, and greater information needs are more easily handled because the data, in this case the monthly sales records, are easily sorted, aggregated, and compared because they are in machine-readable form. In this batch processing illustration, cards and magnetic tape were used as the storage media. The same systems could use magnetic disks to store the data in files and, except for sorting, still process all data the same way.

SELECTED REFERENCES

"Communication Firm Automates Accounts Receivable," *Computerworld*, May 14, 1984.

GULLO, KAREN, "AT&T Readies New Billing System," *Datamation*, December, 1987, pp. 24-25.

INSIGHT Accounts Receivable Package, Layered Inc., 1986, Division of Peachtree Software Atlanta, Ga.

Layered Inc., 1986, Division of Peachtree Software, Atlanta, GA.

McEnroe, P.V., H.T. Huth, E.A. Moore, and W. W. Morris, III, "Overview of the Supermarket System and the Retail Store System," *IBM Systems Journal*, 15, no. 1 (1975), 3–15.

Mitchell, William G., and Joseph W. Wilkinson, "POS Systems Revolutionize Retailing," *Journal of Systems Management*, 27 (April 1976), 34–41.

Montgomery, David B., and Glen L. Urban, "Marketing Decision—Information Systems: An Emerging View," *Journal of Marketing Research*, 7 (May 1970), 226–34.

NCR Credit Management System. Dayton: NCR Corporation

"Retail Terminals: a POS Survey,: *Datamation*, July 15, 1971, pp. 22-31.

Senn, James A., "Close to the Customer: IS Strategies for Marketing Success." *SIM Network* (May/June 1988): 2-5

REVIEW QUESTIONS

1. In terms of "success factors," what should be the focus of a marketing system? What are the implications of this for designers of accounting information systems?

2. What information flows are characteristic of a marketing information system? Contrast these with a logistical system.

3. What are the major features of a marketing decision support system? What are the information sources for this system?

4. Contrast the three types of accounts receivable systems.

5. Why are mathematical models useful in assessing a customer's credit risk?

6. For what decisions would sales analysis reports be useful?

7. List the objectives of the various functions, or subsystems, of marketing management.

8. What role does market research play in the company's information system and decision network?

9. Explain how customer information and product information can be effectively combined in processing a sales order (sales invoice).

10. Why is a highly automated point-of-sale system useful for retail stores and supermarket food chains? What internal control advantages does it have?

11. What can an intelligent terminal be programmed to do to assist a clerk who enters the sales data into the marketing information POS system?

12. How can the sales order processing system interface with the inventory system using microcomputer software?

13. How can a database be used effectively in a marketing system?

14. Illustrate how the concept of windows can be used by microcomputer software to aid in processing a sales order. Use the example in the text.

15. What are picking lists, packing slips, and bills of lading used for?

16. Indicate the correct sequence of the following sales order activities:

    a. Prepare sales invoices

    b. Prepare a packing slip

    c. Prepare a picking slip

    d. Prepare a sales order

    e. Check credit

    f. Check the availability of inventory

    g. Send shipping notices to billing

CASES

15-1 (POS System) Pinta Company is a regional discount chain in the Southeast selling general merchandise. The company is considering acquiring a point-of-sale (POS) system for use in its stores.

There are basically three types of firms

that currently use POS systems—large retailers, grocery stores, and fast food chains. Pinta would probably employ cash registers that use light pens to read the Universal Product Code (UPC) that is printed on packages.

Charles Brenski, President of Pinta, knows that the equipment is very expensive. He has asked his systems staff to prepare a report on POS systems including a survey as to what companies are employing POS systems and why they have adopted them.

REQUIRED:

1. Explain briefly how a POS system operates.

2. Identify the potential advantages and disadvantages of a POS system for a company's operations and record-keeping system.

3. Identify and explain the special control problems that POS system could present to Pinta Company's system personnel.

(CMA adapted with permission)

15-2 Value Clothing is a large distributor of all types of clothing acquired from buy-outs, overstocks, and factory seconds. All sales are on account with terms of net 30 days from date of monthly statement. The number of delinquent accounts and uncollectible accounts have increased significantly during the last twelve months. Management has determined that the information generated from the present accounts receivable system is inadequate and untimely. In addition, customers frequently complain of errors in their accounts.

The current accounts receivable system has not been changed since Value Clothing started its operations. A new computer was acquired eighteen months ago but no attempt has been made to revise the accounts receivable application because other applications were considered more important. The work schedule in the systems department has slackened slightly, enabling the staff to design a new accounts receivable system. Top management has requested that the new system satisfy the following objectives:

1. Produce current and timely reports regarding customers which would provide useful information to
   a. Aid in controlling bad debts.
   b. Notify the sales department of customer accounts which are delinquent (accounts which should lose charge privileges).
   c. Notify the sales department of customers whose accounts are considered uncollectible (accounts which should be closed and written off).

2. Produce timely notices to customers regarding
   a. Amounts owed to Value Clothing.
   b. A change of status of their accounts (loss of charge privileges, account closed).

3. Incorporate the necessary procedures and controls to minimize the chance for errors in customers' accounts.

Input data for the system would be taken from four source documents—credit applications, sales invoices, cash payment remittances, and credit memoranda. The accounts receivable master file will be maintained on a machine-readable master file by customer account number. The preliminary design of the new accounts receivable system has been completed by the systems department. A brief description of the proposed reports and other output generated by the system are detailed next.

1. Accounts Receivable Register—daily alphabetical listing of all customers' accounts which show a balance as of the last statement, activity since the last statement, and account balance.

2. Customer Statements—monthly statements for each customer showing activity since the last statement and account balance; the top portion of the statement is returned with the payment and serves as the cash payment remittance.

3. Aging Schedule, All Customers—a monthly schedule of all customers with outstanding balances displaying the total amount owed with the total classified into age groups 0–30 days, 30–60 days, 60–90 days, over 90 days; the schedule includes

totals and percentages for each age category.

4. Aging Schedule, Past-Due Customers—a schedule prepared monthly which includes only those customers whose accounts are past due (over 30 days outstanding), classified by age. The credit manager uses this schedule to decide which customers will receive delinquent notices, temporary suspension of charge privileges, or have their accounts closed.

5. Activity Reports—monthly reports which show

    a. Customers who have not purchased any merchandise for 90 days.

    b. Customers whose account balance exceeds their credit limit.

    c. Customers whose accounts are delinquent yet they have current sales on account.

6. Delinquency and Write-off Register—a monthly alphabetical listing of customers' accounts which are

    a. delinquent.

    b. closed.

    These listings show name, account number, and balance. Related notices are prepared and sent to these customers.

7. Summary Journal Entries—entries are prepared monthly to record write-offs to the accounts receivable file.

REQUIRED:

1. Identify the data which should be captured and stored in the computer-based file records for each customer.

2. Review the proposed reports to be generated by the new accounts receivable system.

    a. Discuss whether the proposed reports should be adequate to satisfy the objectives enumerated.

    b. Recommend changes, if any, which should be made in the proposed reporting structure generated by the new accounts receivable system.

    (CMA adapted)

15-3 High Top Chair Company manufactures a line of fine furniture for outlets across the country. They have been growing rapidly and their manual system for processing sales orders and managing accounts receivable has become overwhelmed with the volume of business. The result is that they are often behind in processing their invoices and in following up on their receivables. As their CPA, you prepared a systems flowchart to better understand their sales order processing system. This flowchart is shown in Figure C15-1. Five copies of sales invoices are prepared either from sales representatives, sales orders, or from customers who call in their order to a clerk. Two copies are sent to the shop to process the order. One copy is retained by the shop and the completed invoice is returned and matched by the shipping clerk with the other three copies to make sure everything is OK. Shipping information is added if necessary and labels are prepared for shipping. One copy, along with any sales order information, is sent to accounts receivable for posting: these are filed numerically. Two copies are mailed to the customer and one copy is sent to the shipping department for inclusion in the shipment.

REQUIRED: As High Top Chair's CPA, explain to management with a systems flowchart how they might use the microcomputer software presented in this chapter to resolve their problem. This explanation is to be part of a feasibility study and not the final design.

15-4 Feet of Champions is a chain of athletic footware and accessories located in prominent shopping malls throughout Florida. They are headquartered in Orlando, Florida. With the fitness craze their sales have been growing rapidly and they have expanded to ten stores. Each store has a microcomputer which can communicate with the home office via a modem and each cash register is an intelligent terminal connected to the microcomputer.

Feet of Champions' accounting system consists of the following transaction processing systems: sales, accounts receivable, inventory and purchasing, cash disbursements, and cash receipts.

A member of your audit staff has preceded you to the location of one of the stores and to the home office and has prepared the following written description of their transac-

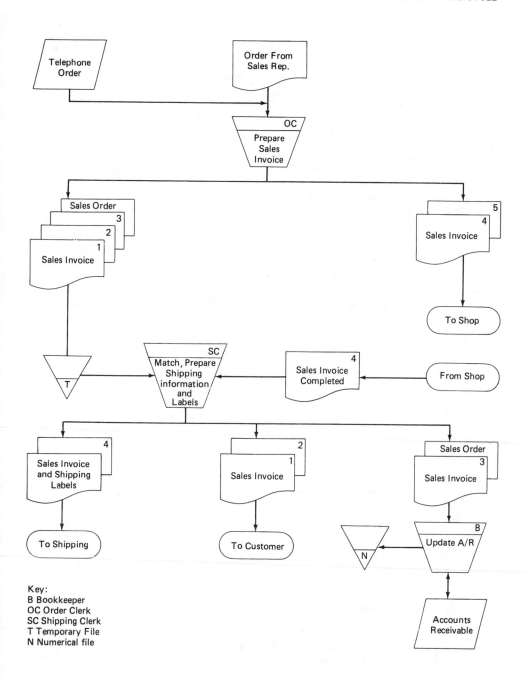

FIGURE C15-1   High Top Chair Company.

tion processing system.

Sales transactions are processed as follows. Sales are keyed into the cash register by the salespersons and the computer processes the sale and updates a transaction file which is stored on a hard disk. This transaction file will store the necessary information to update inventory, sales, and accounts receivable for credit sales. This includes who made the sale. The salesperson then completes the sales transaction by giving the customer a receipt and the appropriate amount of change if it is a cash sale. At the end of the day, the manager clears the register, counts the money, and keys in the totals to the computer which reconciles the count to its records. Each employee has his or her own cash drawer and only that drawer operates when they key in their employee ID number. The computer then generates a daily sales and commission report along with any exception by a salesperson. The sales report is filed by date and the exception report is filed alphabetically by name. In addition, a deposit slip is prepared daily in duplicate by the manager. One is filed and the other is taken to the bank for night deposit with the cash.

Management has the ability to access the transaction data for inquiry purposes to clarify sales transaction details and cash receipts.

Sales transaction information is communicated to the home office once a day. The store and home office computer exchange data via a modem. The home office computer accumulates all this transaction data and then updates the master database. In the sales transaction this will effect sales data, inventory data, and accounts receivable data.

Sales, inventory, and budget information is analyzed daily and then the results are communicated to the stores' microcomputer which generates the following reports: sales budget, inventory status, and accounts receivable.

All accounts receivable are handled at the home office. Monthly customer statements are prepared from the database, which contains receivable information on all credit customers. All statements contain a remittance advice to be returned with the customer payment. An aging report is also prepared for the use of management. When payments are received they are compared to the remittance, keyed into the computer, and the accounts receivable data is updated. Payments are applied against specific credit sales or, if they are not specified, the payment is applied against the oldest sales on the statement. In addition, a cash receipts journal is posted and at the end of the day a deposit slip is prepared. The duplicate information is retained in the cash receipt journal. Bank deposits are then made daily.

Purchase requisitions are originated at the local store. The manager reviews the inventory status report along with the sales budget or plan and makes ordering decisions. These are then transmitted to the home office. At the home office, purchasing management reviews the purchase requisition requests on line. If they are approved, a purchase order is prepared, inventory is updated with the purchase information, a vendor is selected, and accounts payable is updated by the computer. Two copies of the purchase order are prepared. One is sent to the vendor and the other is sent to the store for receiving information. A listing is also prepared of outstanding purchase orders for the purchasing department.

Inventory is received at each store where it is counted, compared with packing slips, and compared with the store's copy of the purchase order. A receiving report is then prepared indicating what was received and comparison information. This is keyed into the computer at the store by the manager, transmitted to the home office, and used to update the database information on inventory, accounts payable, and vendor. The packing slips, purchase orders, and receiving reports are filed by date for future reference.

When vendor invoices arrive by mail they are keyed into the system by a clerk in accounts payable. This information is then entered into the database. In this process original invoices are filed alphabetically for future reference.

When invoices are due based on the terms, a comparison is made of purchase order information, receiving information, and invoice information by the computer. Management then reviews this in an on-line mode and approves the preparation of cash disbursements. In most cases this is automatic, but on occasion a payment is withheld when a dispute arises with a vendor. The cash disbursement journal is then posted, a listing of the journal postings is printed out for management, and upon review of the listing the treasurer signs the disbursement checks which were printed out by the computer at the time of the posting.

Once a month the general ledger is posted with these transactions.

REQUIRED:

1. As part of the audit prepare a systems flowchart of: (1) the sales transaction processing system including the communication to the home office and the reports provided by the home office; (2) the home office accounts receivable and cash receipts system; (3) the inventory and purchase order system; and (4) the inventory, receiving, and cash disbursement system. The last two comprise an inventory and accounts payable system.

2. What internal controls would you look for to protect the integrity of the database? Consider transaction processing, communication from remote computers, and on-line management inquiry.

15-5 A partially completed document flowchart is shown in Figure C15-2. The flowchart depicts the charge sales activities of the Bottom Manufacturing Corporation. A customer's purchase order is received and a six-part sales order is then prepared. The six copies are initially distributed as follows:

Copy 1—Billing copy: to billing department

Copy 2—Shipping copy: to shipping department

Copy 3—Credit copy: to credit department

Copy 4—Stock request copy: to credit department

Copy 5—Customer copy: to customer

Copy 6—Sales order copy: file in sales order department

When each copy of the sales order reaches the applicable department or destination, it calls for specific internal control procedures and related documents. Some of the procedures and related documents are indicated on the flowchart. Others are labeled with letters *a* to *r*.

REQUIRED: List the procedures or the internal documents that are labeled letters with

a to *r* in the flowchart of Bottom Manufacturing Corporation's charge sales system. (AICPA adapted.)

15-6 Huron Company manufactures and sells eight major product lines with fifteen to twenty-five items in each product line. All sales are on credit, and orders are received by mail or telephone. Huron has a computer-based system that employs disk as a file medium.

All sales orders received during regular working hours are typed on Huron's own sales order form immediately. This typed form is the source document for the keying of a shipment or back-order information to a disk. This data are processed at night after-hours to complete all necessary record keeping for the current day and to facilitate the shipment of goods the following day. In summary, an order received one day is to be processed that day and night and shipped the next day.

The daily processing that has to be accomplished at night includes the following activities:

1. Preparing the invoice to be sent to the customer at the time of shipment
2. Updating the accounts receivable file
3. Updating the finished goods inventory
4. Listing of all items back ordered and short.

Each month the sales department would like to have a sales summary and analysis. At the end of each month, the monthly statements should be prepared and mailed to customers. Management also wants an aging of accounts receivable each month.

REQUIRED:

1. Identify the master files that Huron Company should maintain in this system to provide for the daily processing. Indicate the data content that should be included in each file and the order in which each file should be maintained.

2. Employing the symbols shown in the chapter on systems flowcharts, prepare a systems flowchart of the daily processing required to update the finished goods inventory records and to produce the necessary inventory reports. Use the annotation symbol to describe or explain

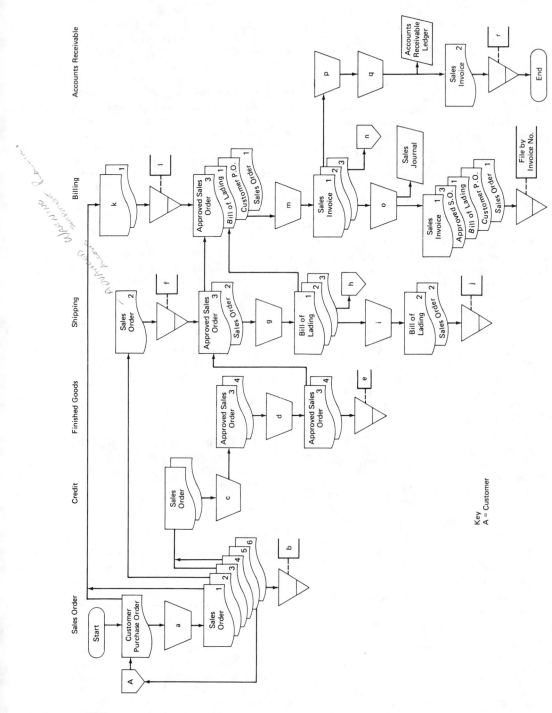

FIGURE C15-2 Bottom Manufacturing Corporation: flowchart of credit sales activities.

Key
A = Customer

508

any facts that cannot be detailed in the individual symbols.

3. Describe (1) the items that should appear in the monthly sales analysis report or reports that the sales department should have; and (2) the input data and master files that would have to be maintained to prepare these reports.

(Adapted from the CMA examination.)

15-7 Delmo, Inc., a wholesale distributor of automotive parts, serves customers in the states east of the Mississippi River. During the past twenty-five years the company has grown from a small regional distributorship in Michigan to its present size. It is still located in East Lansing, Michigan, where it was founded.

To service Delmo customers adequately, the states are divided into eight separate territories. Delmo salespersons regularly call upon current and prospective customers in each of the territories. Delmo customers are of four general types:

1. Automotive parts stores

2. Hardware stores with an automotive parts section

3. Independent garage owners

4. Buying groups for garages and filling stations

Because Delmo must stock such a large variety and quantity of automotive parts to accommodate its customers, the company acquired its own computer system very early. It implemented an inventory control system first. Other applications such as cash receipts and disbursements, sales analysis, accounts receivable, payroll, and accounts payable have since been added.

Delmo's inventory control system is comprised of an integrated purchase-order and perpetual inventory system. Each item of inventory is identified by an inventory code number; the code number identifies both the product line and the item itself. When the quantity-on-hand for an item falls below the specified stock level, a purchase order is automatically generated by the computer. The purchase order is sent to the vendor after approval by the purchasing manager. All receipts, issues, and returns are entered into the computer daily. A printout of all inventory items within product lines show-

ing receipts, issues, and current balance is prepared weekly. However, current status for a particular item carried in the inventory can be obtained daily if necessary.

Sales orders are filled within forty-eight hours of receipt. Sales invoices are prepared by the computer the same day that the merchandise is shipped. At the end of each month, several reports that summarize the monthly sales are produced. The current month's and year-to-date sales by product line, territory, and customer class are compared with the same figures from the previous year. In addition, reports showing only the monthly figures for product line within territory and customer class within territory are prepared. In all cases the reports provide summarized data—i.e., detailed data such as sales by individual customers or product are not listed. Terms of 2/10, net 30 are standard for all of Delmo's customers.

Customers' accounts receivable are updated daily for sales, sales returns and allowances, and payments on account. Monthly statements are computer prepared and mailed following completion of entries for the last day of the month. Each Friday, a schedule is prepared showing the total amount of accounts receivable outstanding by age—current accounts (0–30 days), slightly past-due accounts (31–90 days), and long overdue accounts (over 90 days).

Delmo, Inc., recently acquired Wenrock Company, a wholesale distributor of tools and light equipment. In addition to servicing the same type of customers as Delmo, Wenrock sells to equipment rental shops. Wenrock's sales region is not as extensive as Delmo's, but the Delmo management has encouraged Wenrock to expand the distribution of its products to all of Delmo's sales territories.

Wenrock Company uses a computer service bureau to aid in its accounting functions. For example, certain inventory activities are recorded by the service bureau. Each item carried by Wenrock is assigned a product code number that identifies the product and the product line. Data regarding shipments received from manufacturers, shipments to customers (sales), and any other physical inventory changes are delivered to the service bureau daily, and the service bureau updates Wenrock's inventory records. A weekly inventory listing showing the beginning balance, receipts, issues, and ending balance for each item in the inventory is provided to Wenrock on Monday morning.

Wenrock furnishes the service bureau with information about each sale of merchandise to a customer. The service bureau prepares a five-part invoice and records the sales. This processing is done at night, and all copies of each invoice are delivered to Wenrock the next morning. At the end of the month the service bureau provides Wenrock with a sales report classified by product line showing the sales in units and dollars for each item sold. Wenrock's sales terms are 2/10, net 30.

The accounts receivable function is still being handled by Wenrock's bookkeeper. Two copies of the invoice are mailed to the customer. Two of the remaining copies are filed—one numerically and the other alphabetically by customer. The alphabetic file represents the accounts receivable file. When a customer's payment is received, the invoice is marked "paid" and placed in a paid invoice file in alphabetical order. The bookkeeper mails monthly statements according to the following schedule:

10th of the month	A–G
20th of the month	H–O
30th of the month	P–Z

The final copy of the invoice is included with the merchandise when it is shipped.

Wenrock has continued to use its present accounting system, and it supplies Delmo management with monthly financial information developed from this system. However, Delmo management is anxious to have Wenrock use its computer and its information system because this will reduce accounting and computer costs, make Wenrock's financial reports more useful to Delmo management, and provide Wenrock personnel with better information to manage the company.

At the time that Delmo acquired Wenrock, it also hired a new marketing manager with experience in both product areas. The new manager wants Wenrock to organize its sales force using the same territorial distribution as Delmo to facilitate the managing of the two sales forces.

The new manager also believes that more useful sales information should be provided to individual salespersons and to the department. Although the monthly sales reports currently prepared provide adequate summary data, the manager thinks that additional details would aid the sales personnel.

The acquisition of Wenrock Company and the expansion of its sales to a larger geographic area have created a cash strain on Delmo, Inc., particularly in the short run. Consequently, cash management has become much more important than in prior years. A weekly report that presents a reliable estimate of daily cash receipts is needed. The treasurer heard that a local company had improved its cash forecasting system by studying the timing of customers' payments on account to see if a discernible payment pattern existed. The payment pattern became the model that was applied to outstanding invoices to estimate the daily cash receipts for the next week. The treasurer thinks that this is a good approach and wonders if it can be done at Delmo.

REQUIRED:

1. Identify and briefly describe the additional data Wenrock Company must collect and furnish in order to use the Delmo data processing system. Also identify the data, if any, currently accumulated by Wenrock which will no longer be needed due to the conversion to the Delmo system.

2. Using only the data currently available from the Delmo system, what additional reports could be prepared that would be useful to the marketing manager and the individual salespersons? Briefly explain how each report would be useful to the sales personnel.

3. If Delmo, Inc., were to use a cash forecasting system similar to the one suggested by the treasurer, describe:

   a. The data currently available in the system that would be used in preparing such a forecast

   b. The additional data that must be generated

   c. The modifications, if any, that would

be required in the Delmo data processing system.

4. (Optional) Develop codes for identifying inventory items and customers.

5. (Optional) What advantages would there be to Delmo-Wenrock to replacing the current system with a database management system? Describe the content of the database, the basic organization schema, the internal controls necessary for such a system, and flowchart the system. Assume Delmo, Inc., plans to implement a cash forecasting system similar to the one described.

(Adapted from the CMA examination.)

15-8 Forward Corporation is a progressive and fast-growing company. The company's executive committee consists of the president and the four vice-presidents who report to the president—marketing, manufacturing, finance, and systems. The company has ordered a new computer for use in processing its financial information. Because the computer acquisition required a substantial investment, the president wants to make certain that the computer is employed effectively.

The new computer will enable Forward to revise its financial information system so that the several departments will get more useful information. This should be especially helpful in marketing because its personnel are distributed widely throughout the country.

The marketing department is organized into nine territories and twenty-five sales offices. The vice-president of marketing wants the monthly reports to reflect those items for which the department is responsible and which it can control. The marketing department also wants information that identifies the most profitable products; this information is used to establish a discount policy that will enable the company to meet competition effectively. Monthly reports showing performance by territory and sales office would also be useful.

The vice-president of finance has recommended that the accounting system be revised so that reports would be prepared on a contribution margin basis. Furthermore, only those cost items that are controlled by the respective departments would appear on their reports. The monthly report for the manufacturing department would compare actual production costs with a budget containing the standard costs for the actual volume of production. The marketing department would be provided with the standard variable manufacturing cost for each product so that it could calculate the variable contribution margin of each product. The monthly reports to the marketing department would reflect the variable contribution approach; the reports would present the net contribution of the department calculated by deducting standard variable manufacturing costs and marketing expenses (both variable and fixed) from sales.

REQUIRED:

1. Given that Forward Corporation's system is file oriented, describe the contents of the sales and finished goods inventory files which are necessary to prepare the marginal analysis desired by management.

2. Describe the processing steps necessary to merge these files to produce the marketing reports.

3. Would Forward Corporation have been better off purchasing an on-line random access computer system to meet the requirements of management above? Would an increased awareness of the potential of on-line random access hardware and software alter the information requirements above? How and why?

4. Is there some potential for the use of a distributed system in this case? Why?

5. How could a database management system contribute to the ability of the marketing vice-president to manage the marketing function for Forward Corporation? (Adapted from CMA examination.)

15-9 Nelson's Pharmacy is a sole proprietorship owned by a practicing pharmacist. Nelson's offers a small lunch counter, an extensive line of cosmetics, and a wide range of sundry items in addition to its prescription service. Nelson's employs three pharmacists and six full-time sales clerks.

Mr. Nelson's wife and his son, Gordon, work in the business also. Mrs. Nelson posts accounts receivable and handles all billing.

Gordon Nelson opens all mail, deposits the daily cash receipts, and reconciles the monthly bank statements. A local CPA firm does write-up work for Nelson's at year end and handles all tax matters. Gordon sometimes prepares monthly financial statements. The accounting system is manual and double entry. A chart of accounts is used.

Short-term budgeting is used on an information basis. Weekly cash flow projections are made and compared with actual results. Monthly estimates of sales, stock levels, markups, and expenses are made by Mr. Nelson working with the personnel employed in the various departments of the business. These figures are compared with actual results and with industry averages.

The pharmacy has four cash registers: a register near the front door and one each in the lunch counter, cosmetic, and prescription departments. A base amount of cash is kept in each drawer to use in making change. All registers except the one near the door are closed out one hour before the business shuts down for the evening. The final register is closed out after business hours. Deposits are made each morning, and receipts are kept in a safe in the back of the store overnight. The base amount of money for change always stays in the drawer and never exceeds $30 per register.

When the cash registers are closed out for the day, all sales totals are broken down into cosmetics, food, sundry, prescriptions, and nonprescription drugs on a summary tape. The total amount of sales tax collected is also shown. If the contents of the register approximately equal the amount of cash sales rung up, the employee in the department in question places the cash and register tape in a bank bag and gives the bag to Mr. Nelson, who places it in the safe. Bank credit-card sales are also totaled, and the charge slips are placed in the safe. Credit-card sales are rung ug using a special key on the cash registers, and therefore they are included in the sales totals recorded on the cash register tape.

The next morning, Gordon Nelson removes all bank bags from the safe. He counts the money for deposit and sees that the total approximately agrees with the cash register tapes. He then enters cash, bank card and charge sales totals into a sales journal, fills out a deposit slip, and makes the deposit. Bank charge-card slips are accumulated for a week and then mailed to the appropriate banks.

Mr. Nelson feels that a definite problem exists with customers' checks being returned from the bank for lack of funds. He has established a lenient check-cashing policy and is reluctant to change this policy because he wants to maintain a good relationship with the local residents. At the present time two-party checks, payroll checks, and checks for more than the amount of purchase are accepted. Identification is required.

Mr. Nelson is also very lenient regarding the extension of credit to local customers. No credit check is performed. Uncollectible accounts are usually 1 percent of total sales. When a customer makes a credit purchase, a prenumbered credit invoice is signed. There are two copies of this invoice, both of which are filed alphabetically. The sale is keyed into the cash register using a special key. All credit sales are posted the next day to the sales journal and accounts receivable ledger card by Mrs. Nelson. Once a month, customers are sent statements and the original credit invoice is enclosed. Payment is received by mail or in person and is posted to the customer's account by Mrs. Nelson. The second copy of the credit invoice is permanently filed alphabetically by customer.

In all departments, vendors come to the store periodically and take a physical inventory of the supply of their products on hand. They then suggest purchases to the employees on duty. The vendor prepares the order using his or her own order form and it is approved by the employee on duty. For prescription drugs, Mr. Nelson assists in the inventory and the drugs are purchased through wholesalers. Narcotic drugs are purchased and inventoried, as required by law. No shopping around is done to get better prices on purchases. The employees analyze the profitability of their lines to see if maximum profit is being obtained for the shelf space used. Markdowns are used for promotions and to move slow items. No list is kept of goods marked down.

Order forms are filed by vendor. When goods are received, a clerk will count them and give the order form to Mrs. Nelson in most cases. Some items are paid for by cash directly from the cash register using the appropriate key. Checks are prepared for other vendors twice a month by one of the clerks. Either Mr.

Nelson or Mrs. Nelson must sign all checks. The Nelsons trust their employees and feel that this procedure is adequate. Order forms are thrown out after the check has been prepared. Suppliers' statements are discarded when received because all payments are made from order forms after the goods have been received.

REQUIRED: From the limited notes given, flowchart the system and describe the internal control weaknesses. Suggest how you might make use of intelligent terminals to help control sales, cash receipts, and inventory.

15-10 Knowledge of product line profitability and contribution margin concepts are needed to answer this question. Bundt Foods Company produces and sells many products in each of its thirty-five different product lines. From time to time a product or an entire product line is dropped because it has ceased to be profitable. The company does not have a formalized program for reviewing its products on a regular basis to identify those products that should be eliminated.

At a recent meeting of Bundt Foods Company's top management, one person stated that there probably were several products or possibly a product line that was unprofitable or producing an unsatisfactory return on investment. After considerable discussion, management decided that Bundt Foods should establish a formalized product discontinuance program. The purpose of the program would be to review the company's individual products and product lines on a regular and ongoing basis to identify problem areas.

The vice-president of finance has proposed that a person be assigned to the program on a full-time basis. This person would work closely with the marketing and accounting departments in determining (1) the factors that indicate when a product's importance is declining; and (2) the underlying data that would be required in evaluating whether a product or product line should be discontinued.

REQUIRED:

1. Identify and explain briefly the benefits, other than the identification of unprofitable products or product lines, that Bundt Foods Company can derive from a formalized product discontinuance program.

2. In developing Bundt Foods Company's product discontinuance program:
   a. Identify the factors that would indicate that a product's or product line's importance is diminishing.
   b. Identify the data that the accounting department would be able to provide for the purpose of evaluating a product or product line.

(Adapted from the CMA examination.)

15-11 Smith & Smith, a national mail-order house, is designing a new warehouse facility in Texas to serve the Southwest. Customer orders come in from retail outlets throughout the geographical territory and from customers via mail. The retail outlets each have a microprocessor that transmits these orders directly to the warehouse facility. Orders that come in through the mail are keyed onto a disk file, edited, and verified for current stock numbers.

Both sources of orders are then compared with an on-line inventory file to ensure that the item, style, and quantity are in stock. If the item is out of stock, an out-of-stock memo is generated, a copy of which is mailed to a mail-order customer or transmitted electronically to the retail outlet's microprocessor for subsequent memo generation for a customer at a retail outlet. Out-of-stock reports are generated concurrently with both sets of memos.

Those orders that can be filled are cleared. Reports are generated by the computer for each department indicating the sequence of order filling and the time at which each order is to be filled. A route slip is also printed to accompany each item of an order as it is pulled from stock. The route slips serve as a packing list and follow pulled items through the actual shipment to the store or individual. Clerks pull items to fill each of these orders and place the items on long conveyors that converge in a packing area. The orders are sequenced and timed so that all the items ordered by a store or by an individual arrive at the packing area at the same time. Items pulled for shipment are compared with the customer or store order to make sure that all goods "cleared" are included in the order. A listing of the order number and detail (items ordered, customer name, customer number, and store name and number, if applicable) was sent to each packing station at the beginning of each shift for this comparison. If the items and the order do not reconcile, the order is set aside and a call is made to the stock area from which the items should have been sent. If the error occurred there, the needed item is immediately sent to packing. If the error is in the order itself, an exception is noted on the order listing and these listings are returned to EDP where they are keyed into an error file. From these data an exception memo is transmitted to either the retail store or the mail-order customer, the packing manager, the warehouse stock manager, the EDP manager, and general management. A report that summarizes the substance of these exception memos is also prepared for management.

It is the objective of the distribution center to process these orders as effectively and efficiently as possible. The center's management strives for a 1 percent or less exception ratio.

REQUIRED:

1. Flowchart the system using a document flowchart to show the movement of documents as well as processing steps.
2. Describe the internal control procedures that should be used throughout the order processing cycle.
3. Describe the organization and content of a database (1) needed to operate the transaction processing system described; and (2) needed to support sales, promotion, and customer service management decisions.

15-12 Henderson, Inc., a distributor of institutional food to hospitals, schools, and restaurants in the metropolitan area, distributes an entire line of products including meat, fruit, fresh vegetables, canned goods, dairy products, and frozen food. Some of these items must be handled with special care; they are frozen and perishable, and special equipment is required to distribute and store these items. Henderson is particularly known for its large variety of fresh vegetables, and many customers buy from Henderson for this reason.

All of Henderson's sales are negotiated by ten salespeople, who use daily stock status reports to see what is on hand at the beginning of the day. Negotiated sales contracts (invoices) are based on monthly price and cost statistics for each food item stocked.

Fair Value Foods, a small, aggressive distributor, has been rapidly gaining in market share in the metropolitan area. Its gains have hurt several of Henderson's competitors and are beginning to attract some of Henderson's best customers. From inquiries, Henderson's sales personnel have received the following comments:

1. "Fair Value can give us a better price."
2. "Their meat, fruits, vegetables, and dairy products are fresher."
3. "Their variety is not as large, but it meets 95 percent of my needs."
4. "They never need to substitute a product [a common practice in this business] because they always know exactly what is on hand. All they do is call the office to find out the current stock status."
5. "Their service is as good as yours."

To compound this competitive problem, Henderson has been experiencing slow inventory turnover in the past several years, resulting in more spoilage. This spoilage has caused some pressure to negotiate higher prices. Currently Henderson uses a small batch processing system with input/output media consisting of cards and tapes to control inventory and generate reports.

REQUIRED: From a technological and reporting perspective, what would you, their CPA, suggest that Henderson consider in order to become competitive again? Why?

15-13 A credit authorization system is used by a large regional department store. Credit applications are submitted to the credit office, and responses to the questions listed below are weighted. Weights are determined by using discriminant analysis. Discriminant analysis assigns weights to factors, such as those in the following table, so that good and bad credit risks can be assessed with a high degree of statistical significance. The higher the score, the better the credit risk.

Factor	Weight
1. Age over twenty five	7
2. Own home	20

3. Own automobile 3
4. Employed with present company over three years 25
5. Has bank reference—account number 8
6. Lived at present address over two years 6
7. Married 5
8. Fewer than four children 5
9. Income over $20,000 15
10. Income over $10,000 6

a. Will these weights be appropriate a year from now? If not, what data must be maintained in the firm's database to reassess the credit granting model?

b. How can the data be obtained to update these weights for processing applications next year?

c. What subset of input data for a and b can be collected via transaction processing and what subset must be obtained from other sources?

15-14 Knowledge of sales forecasting models is necessary to answer this question. Daizy Shoes, a merchandiser of stylish and casual ladies' shoes, must order several lines of shoes from at least two dozen domestic and foreign manufacturers and ensure distribution to several hundred retail shoe stores located in shopping centers throughout the United States. Due to long lead times and the great risk of high-style items not selling, Daizy requires all its sales personnel to keep accurate records of sales at each retail outlet and report this to the home office in Sunnyville, Florida. Using these sales statistics, Daizy uses an exponential smoothing forecasting model which quickly adapts to changing trends and seasonal changes in sales data to give sales management guidance in reordering more of certain styles. This model was provided by the company's accounting firm and works extremely well. Daizy's management employees, most of whom have recent MBA degrees from well-known universities, have a great deal of faith in this forecasting technique.

Management, however, is still unhappy with the number of styles that must be marked down at the end of each season. Management has asked you, as the accountant who provided

the model it uses, what other information it needs to improve its forecasting and inventory control.

REQUIRED: Outline the information requirements, sources of the data procedures for obtaining the data, and methods of data storage for rapid retrieval of information for management decisions. Pay specific attention to the point-of-sale transaction date in your assessment of the problem.

15-15 West Montana Wire, Inc., (WMW) is a manufacturer of electrical wire and cable. Copper and aluminum are the two primary raw materials used in the production process and account for about 50 percent of the total cost of the finished goods. Because of the importance of these raw materials, a separate department has been set up to manage the contracts. To further control the cost of its copper input, WMW vertically integrated by constructing a copper refinery in Butte. The refinery smelts and refines copper scrap and virgin ore into pure copper, or copper cathode. In the remainder of the production process, the copper cathode is melted down, cast into continuous copper rod, drawn into wire, and finally stranded into cable or building wire. Some of the wire is then insulated.

The copper management department of West Montana Wire is responsible for the procurement of copper, inventory, and contracts until the copper is cast or reaches the drawing machines. Organizationally, copper management is directed by a corporate vice-president. The department seems very small to be under the control of a high ranking official, but its importance stems from the fact that it oversees nearly half of West Montana Wire's total annual expenditures of $400 million. The organization chart is shown in Figure C15-3. No formal job descriptions exist for the specific positions. All four managers and the two assistant managers can write sales orders, approve contracts, and approve release documents for shipment of copper from the refinery.

Copper is traded internationally as a commodity and as such experiences dramatic fluctuations in market price. Copper management uses several types of contracts to stabilize this price fluctuation. The manner in which a

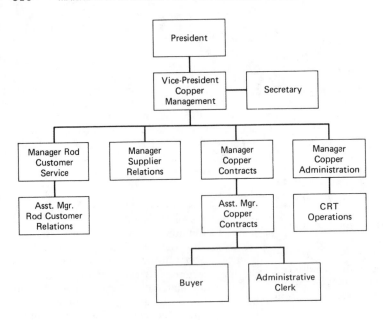

FIGURE C15-3 Organization chart for copper management.

transaction is processed through West Montana Wire's information system depends on the type of contract. The most common type of contract is a simple purchase contract, usually for thirty-day delivery. Conversion contracts, on the other hand, involve changing the form of copper owned by another party, and charging a fee for this service without ever taking title to the copper. Purchased conversion contracts are the opposite of conversion contracts. To alleviate a capacity shortage, WMW sends its metal to another smelter to be converted but retains title to it. Exchange contracts are used to trade one type of metal for another to save freight charges or correct a temporary inventory imbalance. Sales contracts are infrequently used; they involve the disposition of surplus raw materials when a favorable price can be obtained.

Copper management uses an on-line computer system for almost all of its information requirements. The information system is very specialized and was developed at West Montana Wire specifically for the copper management department.

The copper management information system operates as follows. Copper management personnel negotiate contracts with suppli-

ers. The pertinent contract information, including the type of contract, is given a unique contract number. The CRT operator then keys this information into the system. Purchase, conversion, purchase conversion, exchange, and sales contracts carry prefixes of P, C, O, E, and S, respectively. Each contract is numbered sequentially by type, using a five-digit code. An additional two digits are also added to indicate multiple batches for a contract. Eight additional spaces in the code allow for a contract data and batch receipt data, if applicable. Other pertinent information is also coded for reporting purposes. The type of contract code indicates the types of transactions which can validly be posted to that contract. The order-entry system is on-line and automatically updates the copper management information system for new contracts. All input data are edited and totals are logged in, as will be described later.

Upon receipt of copper ore or scrap, a transaction is required to update the quantity of metal received. A metals receipt document is created daily for receipt of each load of copper. These transactions, called assay transactions, specify the composition and tonnage of each batch of metal received. Each assay transaction must use the appropriate contract and batch code. If a purchase contract is involved, a payment authorization will be automatically generated. These authorizations are numbered sequentially. For other types of contracts, the perpetual inventory balance of metal due to or from the other party is updated.

Once a contract is received and a batch of metal has been assayed and a batch number is assigned and after a review of the various status reports (described later), smelting operations are scheduled by the refining department. Any member of copper management can determine at any time, through inquiry to its database, the status of any contract or batch or any transaction related to a contract. Examples of information which can be accessed through inquiry of the contract master file include information on all open contracts and batches along with all pertinent information on a specific contract and batch, shipping dates, inventory levels by location, and information on a specific receipt of inventory.

Several hard-copy reports are output from the copper management information system. The vendor listing provides trend analysis and demographic information about suppliers. The standard pricing report projects the expected costs for the next month. This information is used for determining the material costs in setting prices for finished goods. The metals position report compares the aggregate demand and supply expected for a particular type of copper input material. The active contract and batch report indicate the status of each contract in the refinery. An analysis of copper purchases report determines whether weekly procurement targets are being met. The conversion position report indicates the status of each conversion contract, including the balance due to or from a customer when the metal is due, and the particular form in which it is due.

The copper management system database includes the following random access files: contract master file, vendor master file, daily summary file, daily control totals file, inventory master file, and file of standard costs.

The system controls used include checks for valid codes, characters, field size and sign, transactions, and field combinations. Transactions are also checked for missing data fields. Limit checks, check digits, and passwords are used.

Totals (dollars, tons, and number transactions) are prepared by CRT operators to ensure the ultimate posting of transactions to reports and entering of all transactions, i.e., the system will not accept out-of-balance input where details do not match control tables. The control totals are kept in the temporary daily totals file. These totals are compared to a log book kept by the CRT operator at the end of the day, when the CRT operator enters number of transaction by type of contract, assay documents, and release documents. Dollar and tonnage totals are also entered for reconciliation at the end of the day. Errors are corrected before the nightly update of interfacing files. An audit tape is produced by the CPU for all transactions.

The copper management system interfaces with accounts payable and a separate batch system at the copper refinery, which maintains a perpetual refinery inventory of contract batches and their progress through the refinery. The accounts payable system is run once a day, in a batch processing mode, and the accounts payable vendor file is updated from the copper management information system daily transaction file.

REQUIRED:

1. Flowchart the system.
2. Describe the internal control strengths.
3. Describe the internal control weaknesses.
4. Describe the data content of each file necessary to generate the reports generated by the system.
5. How do these reports support operational, managerial, and strategic decision-making needs?
6. Should West Montana Wire consider a database management system? What would be the advantages of such a system to West Montana Wire?

15-16 While auditing Top Manufacturing Corporation the auditor prepared a flowchart (Figure C15-4) of credit sales activities. In this flowchart, Code Letter "A" represents CUSTOMER.

REQUIRED: Indicate what each of the code letters "B" through "P" represents. Do not discuss adequacies or inadequacies in the system of internal control.
(AICPA adapted.)

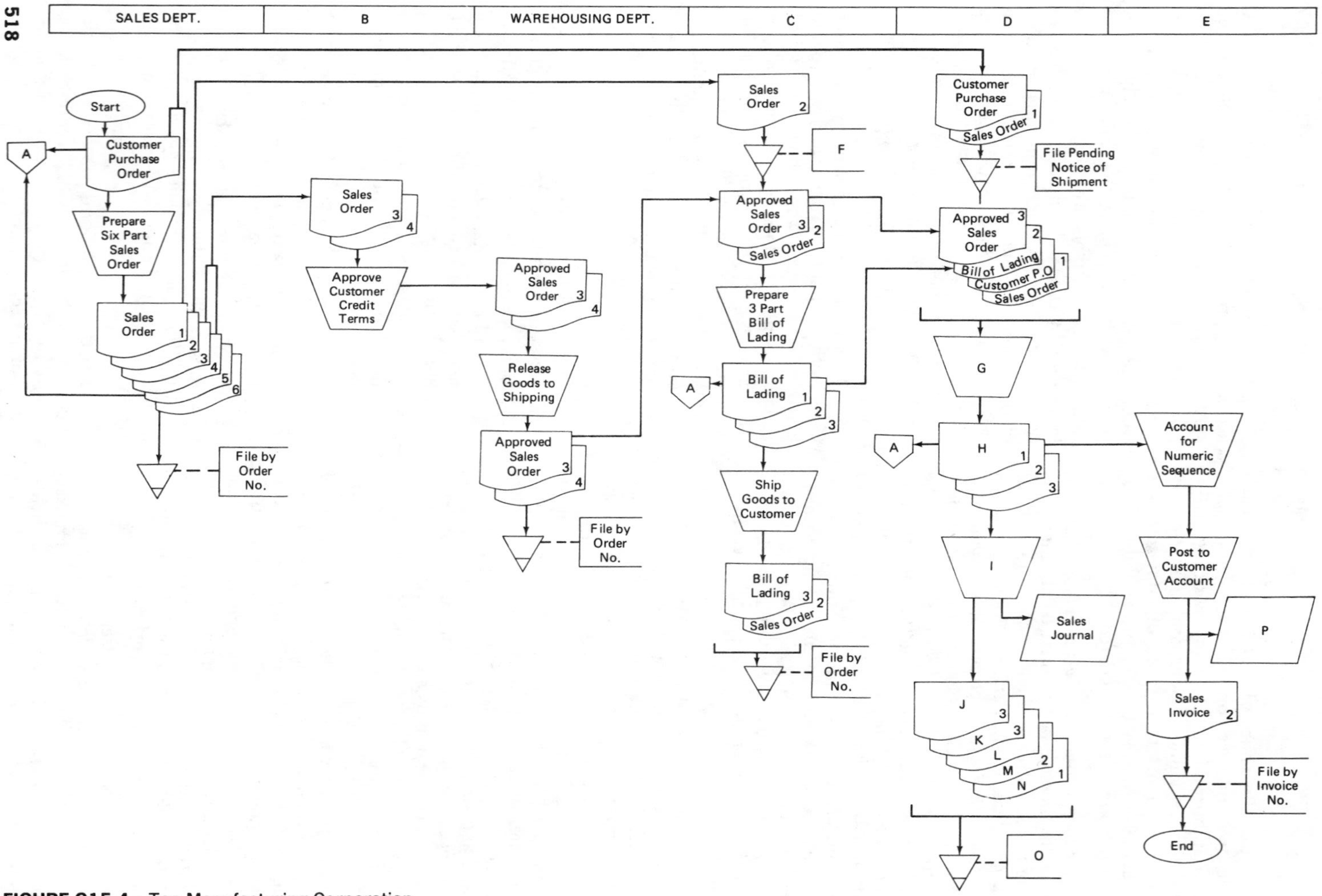

FIGURE C15-4 Top Manufacturing Corporation.

16

FINANCIAL INFORMATION SYSTEMS

OBJECTIVE

The objective of a financial information system is to support the decision-making, transaction processing, and reporting activities of the organization. The financial activities include financial planning and budgeting, cash management, capital acquisition, capital budgeting, and auditing. Information is needed to develop financial plans in conjunction with those plans that were formulated in the marketing and production sector of the organization. These plans usually take the form of budgets that are used as a basis for decision making. Information is also needed to manage cash to support these plans. Information is needed to acquire additional capital resources to implement marketing and production plans. In summary, all of these activities require extensive financial information. Finally, the financial affairs of the organization usually require an audit. In this chapter we review the informational needs of these different financial management activities. Auditing is discussed in Chapter 20.

In addition, the financial accounting information system provides information for these activities as well as those noted in the previous chapters. In particular the general ledger system is at the heart of any financial accounting system,

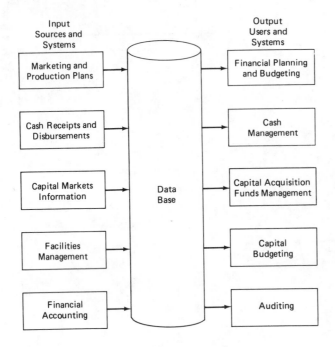

FIGURE 16-1 Financial management systems.

so particular emphasis is given to the general ledger system and those key systems that interface with it in this chapter. These related systems include: accounts receivable (detailed in the last chapter), inventory (detailed in an earlier chapter), purchasing, accounts payable, payroll, and facilities management. Particular emphasis is given to large comprehensive financial accounting systems in this chapter. A very small system for a microcomputer is outlined in Chapter 19 on small entrepreneurial systems.

FINANCIAL DECISION-MAKING ACTIVITIES

In general, the financial information system of the organization is needed to support financial management activities. These include planning and budgeting, cash management, capital acquisition, capital budgeting, and auditing. Figure 16-1 illustrates the sources and the uses of financial information. The individuals responsible for the financial management activities of the organization are the controller and the treasurer. Briefly, as noted in the organization chapter, the controller is responsible for the record keeping and financial planning activities, such as budgeting and transaction processing, and the treasurer is responsible for custodial activities, such as cash and funds management.

Financial Planning and Budgeting

Financial management's major activities involve planning and budgeting. Marketing and production plans are merged with each other and a financial management plan is developed from these management requirements. All of the firm's resources and constraints need to be considered in this planning process. These resources include: facilities, manpower, raw material, and finances. Market constraints such as competitor's actions, pricing, and consumer demand as well as production and distribution constraints must also be considered in this planning process. Information is needed on the marketing and production plans as well as on the resources available to the organization and it's market and operating constraints. Because financial planning models and decision-support systems play such a major role in supporting this process, the budgeting process is illustrated in the next chapter.

Cash Management and Funds Acquisition

A financial management plan must help management effectively manage cash, marketable securities, and other investments. On the other side of the balance sheet, it is equally important that it help managers to control corporate equity and debt. Budgeted activities and incoming resources need to be carefully analyzed. Resources need to be attained to support the ongoing activities and future capital improvements of the organization. Often this requires the securing of additional equity or debt. Information needs to be available on these plans, on their cash consequences, and on the equity and debt markets to achieve this objective.

Effective management (control) of a firm's cash resources is needed to achieve the financial support the rest of the organization's needs to carry out their activities. Cash receipts and disbursements need to be carefully monitored to see that they comply with planned expectations. Since the cash receipts and disbursements system interface with all other accounting and information systems, information needs to be received in a timely manner from sales, collections, purchasing, payroll, and all the other systems that receive cash and disburse cash. A comprehensive cash receipts system is outlined in Chapter 15 and a cash disbursement system will be illustrated later in this chapter. Also a cash disbursement system for a small microcomputer is illustrated in the appendix of Chapter 19. Financial management must also be aware of increasing needs in working capital and the need to acquire new facilities and equipment in order to plan cash needs adequately.

In summary, the financial manager of the organization must maintain and control the cash balances and the cash flow in the organization. He or she must be able to forecast future cash requirements and to make appropriate arrangements with lending institutions to ensure an adequate balance to maintain business activities.

Capital Budgeting

Management also needs information from production and marketing in order to make capital budgeting decisions. These decisions usually require cash flow forecasts from marketing based on the demand as well as cost forecasts from production regarding the new venture. In addition, information on the cost of equipment, interest rates, useful life, operating and maintenance costs, and savings to be generated by the new equipment are often important in a capital budgeting decision. Moreover, if the project is to be considered along with other investment options, information on the interaction between this project and current activities as well as on other future ventures may be important. In other words, information on the total investment portfolio may be important to the capital budgeting decision.

Environmental Considerations

It is difficult to specify a general financial information system and its financial accounting subsystem for all organizations because each serves management's needs in its own unique environment. This diversity has challenged software houses as they have attempted to develop and market software for financial management. As a result, many focus on vertical markets for various fields and professions such as medicine, construction, real estate, retail, and education in an effort to achieve some commonality. For example, the widely used financial accounting system for small businesses illustrated in the appendix to Chapter 19 would not meet the needs of management in many situations. Moreover, the large financial accounting system discussed in this chapter will not meet the needs of many organizations. First of all, it probably is too big and complex for many organizations.

Thus, environmental factors should be considered in the design of the financial information system. For example, one firm may have many credit customers with whom a high degree of interaction is necessary. Such a firm may need an on-line accounts receivable system to manage cash and credit such as that illustrated in Chapter 15. Another firm may have one primary customer, such as the U.S. Air Force, and thousands of employees working on various large complex jobs. In this latter case, the accounts receivable system will be very different and a complex job-order cost accounting system will be very important.

This diversity of needs is found even in small businesses. The financial accounting needs of a building contractor with many employees, many vendors, and a considerable capital investment are vastly different from those of a retail shoe store with one vendor, two employees, and cash or credit card customers. The accountant must be able to advise or assist management in a wide variety of situations with the selection of financial information systems that meet information processing requirements.

FINANCIAL ACCOUNTING INFORMATION SYSTEMS

Financial Accounting Transaction Processing Network

The typical financial accounting transaction processing network is composed of all the financial transactions of the organization. This system is at the heart of the financial information system of most organizations. It interacts with other aspects of the financial information system as well as the marketing and production information systems. The centerpiece of this network is the general ledger system. The general ledger accounts are control accounts and are supported by detailed subsidiary ledgers, which are necessary for management's use in dealing with vendors and customers. They are needed to make day-to-day operating decisions such as the granting of credit, payment of invoices, and ordering of inventory. In general, the general ledger and the journal entries (transactions) from which it is created are the very heart of the information system of the organization.

Reporting Needs and General Ledger

Most organizations require financial statements. The balance sheet and income statement are useful for many internal business decision-making needs. Often these are required on a monthly basis, by division, for management decisions. These two statements, along with the statement of cash flows, are required by stockholders, creditors, the Internal Revenue Service, the Securities and Exchange Commission, and many other third parties, depending on the nature of the business. Moreover, many derivatives of these statements, such as the 10-K and quarterly reports, are often required. These statements, along with many other reports that are useful for decision making and third-party reporting, all come from a general ledger system.

A typical general ledger system will interface with all the other financial accounting systems and management information systems, as illustrated in Figure 16-2. General ledger and financial systems can be completely integrated using a large complex database, or they can be modular so that they may be adapted to many types of business conditions and information requirements. All the data posted to the various accounts during the processing of sales and cash receipts; inventory, purchasing, and cash disbursements; conversion of material, labor, and overhead into products and revenues; payroll and fixed assets are posted to the general ledger account as shown in Figure 16-2.

Sometimes this posting is done concurrent with the transaction and sometimes it is done from periodic summaries of transactions. It depends on the system used. From this posting a journal entry file (listing) is posted. At the end of the month (accounting period), a trial balance is prepared for the accounting department. Then as shown in Figure 16-3, standard adjusting entries are posted from a file and adjusting journal entries are prepared and posted to the general ledger. From this, an adjusted trial balance is prepared with a listing of adjusting journal entries. From this adjusted trial balance, financial statements are prepared. In a typical large integrated applications package[1] for larger organizations, data are entered, maintained, and accessed in an on-line mode so information is always current. Such a large system may have the following features:

1. It would provide common reports such as: general ledger activity, a trial

---

[1] See Management Science America (MSA), *Cooperative Excellence in Application Software: MSA and NCR*, Atlanta, 1985 for a comprehensive discussion of features found in large main frame systems. The discussion here is in part based on this system. MSA is one of the largest business software houses in the world.

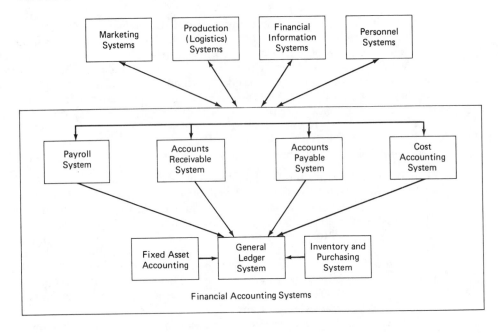

FIGURE 16-2   General ledger interface with other accounting and information systems.

balance, exception reports, posting journals, reconciliation reports, expense reports, account analysis, and cash flow reports.

2. It would provide comprehensive financial and managerial accounting functions including cost accounting functions.

3. It would provide financial analysis capabilities. This would include ratio and trend analysis. Managers would be able to analyze financial and nonfinancial information to evaluate performance based on the planned and actual results for a given period. It would support managerial needs at all levels in the organization.

4. In addition to routine reports, managers would be able to access information in an on-line mode and to generate their own reports as they need the information. These inquiry and report-writing features would enable the user to access the database any way he or she desires. The user would have a great deal of flexibility in formatting these reports. For example, comparisons, ratios, graphics, mathematical calculations, and ranges would be feasible in general ledger systems with good report generation features.

5. It would provide planning and budgeting capability to help managers plan for the future. It would support various levels of budgeting and support, financial and managerial decision support models such as those outlined in the next chapter. For example, it would support on-line spreadsheet analysis so that managers could ask "what if ?" questions concerning various options.

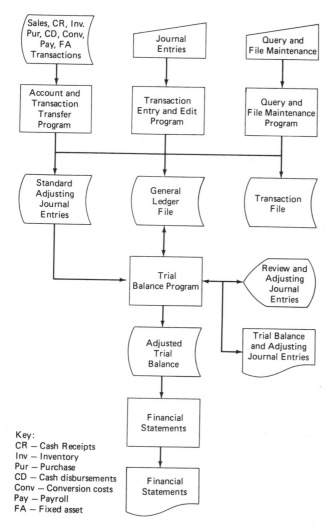

FIGURE 16-3   General ledger system.

6. It would provide cost allocation procedures necessary to allocate various costs to products.

7. It would help control the accounting process by maintaining transaction logs (lists or records) for a complete audit trail. Journal entries could be entered, edited, validated, and stored in an on-line mode. Batch controls would also be automatically compared to transaction totals and exception reports would be generated automatically for management review.

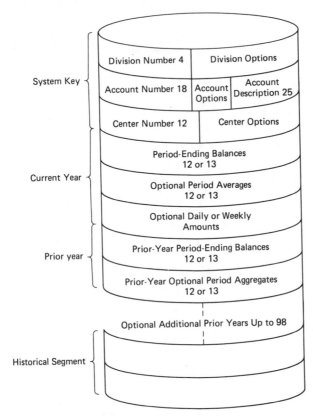

FIGURE 16-4 A segmented database.

Source: General Ledger Data Base, MSA, *General Ledger Accounting System.* Copyright 1981, Management Science America, Inc. Reprinted by permission.

Most contemporary general ledger systems share a database with the other components of the financial information as well as the management information system. This database may be organized in many different ways. A segmented database[2] with a separate file for each financial accounting component may be organized for a large divisional organization, as shown in Figure 16-4. A division may be any entity requiring a balanced set of books. It may be a legal entity, a division, a fund, a subsidiary, or an individual plant. It is identified by a code. A chart of accounts is defined for each division. A center, on the other hand, is the lowest level of detail for which detailed accounts are accumulated. It may be a cost center, a department, a shift, or even a person. All data in this example are stored at this lowest level of detail in the database for ease and flexibility of reporting.

In addition some of the more common options available in a general ledger system include the following:

---

[2] MSA, *General Ledger Accounting System,* copyright 1981, Management Science America, Inc. (Atlanta: Management Science America, Inc., 1981), p. 6.

1. Multiple years of history to be retained for each division.
2. Update procedure. This may be random or sequential depending on the needs of each division. This may differ for each division in the organization.
3. Edit controls.
4. Average balances and end-of-period balances.
5. Different fiscal calendars for different divisions.
6. Daily or weekly reporting.
7. Provision for maintaining nonfinancial information.
8. Exception or alert criteria along with the automatic processing or exception reports.
9. User-defined exception criteria.
10. Prior-year balances for either twelve- or thirteen-period ending balances.
11. Multiple organizational entities using the same database and automatic consolidation capabilities including standard elimination and adjusting entries.

Many such general ledger systems accommodate a wide variety of data entry including tape, key-to-tape, disk, key-to-disk, on-line, EDI, or an interface with a microcomputer network. Transactions generated by other components of the accounting system can generally be entered automatically either in an on-line mode or periodically without manual intervention.

Finally, in most cases sophisticated systems such as this edit and validate data prior to updating the database. Errors and out-of-balance conditions are reported and exceptions are determined. Distributions are often predefined and translation provisions are often present to translate one account number to another account number when necessary. This overview of a general ledger system demonstrates that the general ledger is the heart of the financial accounting system, the general accounting system, and the entire information system of the firm. (A microcomputer version of a general ledger system is illustrated in the appendix of Chapter 19.)

Accounts Receivable

Accounts receivable systems were discussed in Chapter 15. To obtain a complete picture of the financial accounting system, we review some of the key features of such a system here. For example, an accounts receivable system for larger organizations provides information management needs to manage receivables and help speed up the collection process. This includes instant on-line access to current customer balance, credit ratings, and comprehensive historical data. This allows management to make effective credit and collection decisions which in turn helps reduce bad debts and improve profitability.

Large accounts receivable systems have a provision for flagging problem accounts based on their particular credit policies. Management can then monitor these accounts. Credit and collection personnel can likewise follow these problem accounts, enter confidential data, and analyze payment history statistics. In larger systems an organization can spot changes in customer payment habits automatically and instantly to help avoid potential losses. In more comprehensive systems, management can easily tailor all correspondence to meet special requirements. For example, user-defined dunning letters, special billing cycles, and customized customer statements are usually feasible.

Larger more comprehensive systems have on-line cash collection capability to reduce the clerical effort required to process customer payments. These systems automatically calculate and process customer discounts, credits, and service charges. Moreover, to further simplify cash collection, large systems can automatically reconcile payments and credit the appropriate accounts, and particular invoices if necessary. Often large systems provide for split-payments and automated lockbox processing. In addition, these systems can produce cash receipt forecasts that give treasury personnel an accurate picture of short-term cash receipts.

Finally, on-line inquiry facilities give management instant access to open and paid items. These larger systems offer complete payment reconciliation information in order to eliminate the time-consuming research of manual files. This permits prompt responses to customer problems.

Inventory and Purchasing

An effective inventory and purchasing system is very important to the successful achievement of the objectives of many organizations. This was especially true as pointed out in the chapter on production and inventory systems. In fact, many new approaches such as JIT and MRP systems have been developed to manage this activity. These lead to the automatic generation of purchase orders or the notification via direct communication (sometimes from one computer to another computer) to the supplier of the need for parts or components.

Effective inventory and purchasing systems are just as important to merchandising firms. They need sufficient stock to display their merchandise and service customer demand. On the other hand, just as in a manufacturing organization, they need to control their investment in inventory due to its cost, potential obsolescence, and the space it requires.

A typical inventory and purchasing system for either a manufacturing or merchandising firm may be represented by the system flowchart depicted in Figure 16-5. First, a purchase requisition is initiated by the using department. It identifies the goods to be purchased, the quantity and the date needed. Once signed by the using department manager and sent to the purchasing department, it authorizes the purchasing department to place an order with the vendor (supplier). Sometimes it may suggest a potential vendor. Sometimes this request must also be approved by the purchasing department to be sure it falls within the using department's limits of authorization or budget.

Second, this approved request is keyed into the system to generate a prenumbered purchase order. Sometimes the generation of a purchase order (PO) is generated from a model, such as those described in Chapter 14, which automatically places an order when stock falls below a reorder point. Sometimes it is requested by a computerized MRP or JIT system. In most cases a purchase order is signed and forwarded to a supplier. In some new systems it is communi-

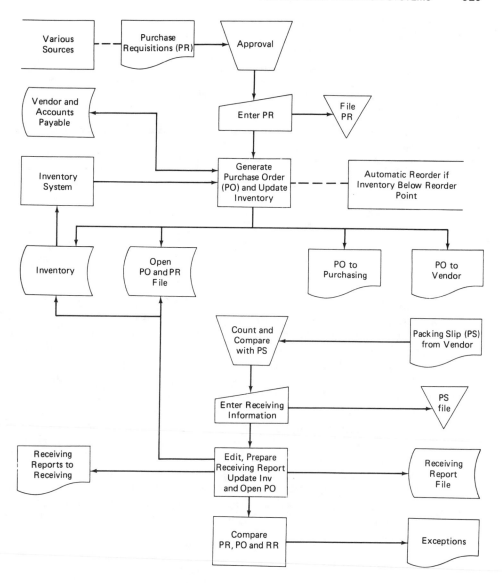

FIGURE 16-5   Purchasing, receiving, and inventory system.

cated to the vendor via electronic data interchange (EDI). It states the description, amount, and terms of the order and constitutes a legal commitment to pay for the goods or services once they are delivered. An example is shown in Figure 16-6. Sometimes multiple copies are used to inform the requesting department of the order, to keep a file copy in purchasing, and to inform receiving of a pending shipment (the receiving copy will have the quantity blacked out so as

Southwest Air Freight
400 S. Main, Alberque, NM
(800) 364–9004

Number: 3008
Date: 5/7/92

Requesting Department	Requisition Number	Account Number	Method of Shipment	Delivery Date
Maintenance	3800	400	UPS	5/21/92

Quantity	Part Number	Description	Unit Price	Total
10	XD700	Pistons	$135.00	$1,350.00
20	V2000	Valves	$125.00	$1,250.00

Total $2,600.00

Joe Davidson
Approved

FIGURE 16-6 Purchase order.

not to influence the receiving count). Also, in some systems an actual paper copy may not even exist because the supplier is notified via EDI. The inventory file is updated to reflect items on order and an open purchase order file is posted to indicate the presence of a PO and an accompanying purchase requisition.

Next, goods are received from the vendor. Normally the goods are accompanied by a packing slip. They must be counted, compared with the packing slip, if it exists, and entered into the receiving system. The receiving system generates a prenumbered receiving report in some cases, as illustrated, and stores the receiving data in a computer file. Receiving data will include the description of what is received, the date, and the quantity based on actual physical count. The receiving system then edits the input; updates the inventory and open purchase orders; compares the purchase requisition (PR), the purchase order (PO), and the receiving report (RR); and notes any exceptions, such as back orders. Management can follow up on exceptions such as shortages or wrong goods sent by the supplier. This information is stored pending the receipt of vendor's invoices or statement.

Accounts Payable

This system is important to the effective management of cash flow and to the timely processing of an organization's trade obligations. It interfaces directly with the logistics and purchases system noted earlier in Chapter 14 and in this chapter. Payment to vendors generally requires some form of authorization and supporting evidence that the material has been received or that the service has been performed in a satisfactory manner. The typical supporting documents consist of vendor invoices, matching prearranged agreements like those used in JIT systems or purchase orders, and receiving reports. All of these stem from the inventory and purchasing system outlined earlier.

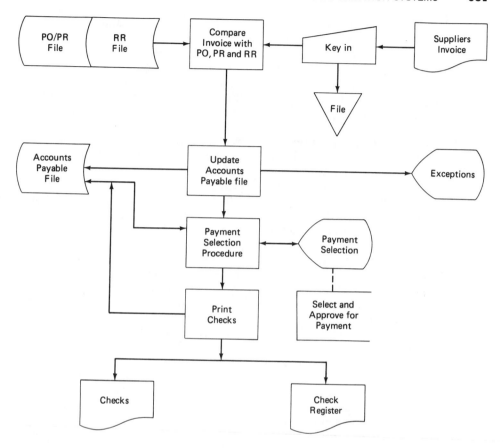

FIGURE 16-7   Accounts payable system.

An illustration of the typical functions found in an accounts payable system is presented in Figure 16-7. First an invoice is received from the vendor. It is keyed into the system and compared with the purchase requisition, purchase order, and receiving report data stored on the computer files. Exceptions are displayed for management to follow up on. If the invoice is correct, the accounts payable vendor records are updated.

Periodically, in many cases daily, those payables which are due or which should be paid to take advantage of various terms are displayed or posted and reviewed by management. Management selects (confirms the selection) those which should be paid. In many systems this may be done automatically.

Next, checks are printed along with a check register for those paid, and the accounts payable file is updated to reflect the amount and invoices paid. These checks are often signed by the computer if all the information and supporting documents match and management has approved the selection of invoices to be paid.

Sometimes a voucher system is used where a disbursement voucher for each invoice is prepared and approved prior to the issuance of a check. These checks are then signed by the appropriate management personnel upon receiving the supporting documents (sometimes including a disbursement voucher).

The distribution of charges to the appropriate accounts is an essential part of the accounts payable transaction processing system of any organization. For computerized systems such as the one illustrated at the end of Chapter 19 on small entrepreneurial systems, this process is essentially the same as a voucher system. Summary payable information is processed through that microcomputer system for overall control of expenditures and the accompanying distribution of charges to various departments in an organization. In many computerized systems a vendor file also includes open purchase orders and payables to control open liabilities, purchase or contractual commitments, and vendor history. This information helps the purchasing department deal with vendors and to make intelligent purchasing decisions. For example, the history of shipments from a vendor will enable the purchasing department to determine the timeliness and completeness of future shipments. These systems may seem simple but they must be able to effectively deal with many problems due to the nature of the business environment. For example, discrepancies may occur due to vendor price changes, overshipments and undershipments of merchandise, damaged or lost material, substitutions, incorrect routing and related problems in freight charges, and modifications in terms. Management needs information to deal with these common problems.

The data generated by this system are used in many reports. The essential operational reports include those which reflect: open liabilities with vendors and other contractors for goods and services, unfilled purchase orders or commitments, and account distribution of actual payments. In addition, good systems, as noted in the example, will flag invoices which are due in order to take advantage of the terms offered by various vendors. Most systems provide management with daily listings of payments, check registers, an aging report for unpaid invoices or accrued liabilities, and projected cash requirements given the nature of the unpaid liabilities.

In summary, where many vendors supply an organization with goods or services, a formalized accounts payable system will often be useful in decision making and transaction processing. Some of the more common operational and managerial decisions that may be supported by the accounts payable system are cash planning, bank relations, expense allocation or distribution, invoice payment selection, and purchasing. Some of the typical reports generated by these systems to assist in the decisions are: vendor lists which include pricing information and status data, transaction lists (logs), open purchase order reports, cash requirement reports, aged payables reports, check registers, payment selection lists, and summarized general ledger posting entries. Automatic transaction-by-transaction posting of payments (vouchers) and all their corresponding charges, and the printing of checks for invoices selected for payment, are essential for many firms with a large number of vendors. All of files generated by the inventory purchasing and accounts payable transactions are useful for queries by management on purchase order and vendor status. Some larger systems even have provisions like numerical control over cash disbursements to guard against invalid vendors, duplicate invoices, and invalid expense distribution. Many automatically calculate taxes, discounts, and freight amounts for invoice processing. Many larger systems generate appropriate journal entries for cash, expense, liability, tax, freight, discount, variance, intercompany, and project accounts. Many even distribute expenses over multiple accounting periods and automatically perform invoice reversals and payment cancellations. In general, a well designed accounts payable system enables management to manage its purchases, payables, and it's cash disbursements.

Payroll and Personnel

The payroll and personnel system is very important to many organizations. In those that are labor intensive, it may be the most important transaction processing system in the organization. Whether the organization is a labor intensive manufacturing company or a government agency, the system must be accurate and process payroll and disbursement information in a timely manner. The system, moreover, must produce a variety of reports, many of which are required by governmental and regulatory agencies. Moreover, as shown in Figure 16-2, the payroll system will interact in some way with most of the other systems in an organization.

Where an organization has many employees, such as a labor-intensive manufacturing company, or where the mode of payment or the reporting requirements are complex, a computerized payroll system will prove useful for personnel management and daily transaction processing. Information from such a system will be useful for strategic and managerial activities such as personnel planning, performance and employement policies, safety standards, and collective bargaining. Due to these demands, very stringent requirements are placed on a typical payroll department for confidentiality of information and for a wide variety of management information. First the department must have the necessary controls to protect the integrity of the information stored in the payroll database. General examples of these controls are discussed in Chapter 10. Commonly required transaction processing and management information requirements include the processing of payroll checks, check and payroll registers, payroll deductions, periodic reports on payroll and deductions, and labor distribution reports. Generally, the payroll system will interface with the other financial information systems, as illustrated in Figure 16-2.

For example, consider a typical payroll and labor distribution system for production operations. This system is shown in Figure 16-8. The employee master file is updated and remains current through on-line entry of personnel and payroll changes from these departments. This master file is used along with the production schedule, generated from systems such as those illustrated in Chapter 14, to prepare prepunched timecards and daily production schedules for employees and departments, respectively. The timecards are sent to timekeeping, and each employee punches in upon arrival at work and punches out upon termination of work for that day. The department foreman uses the production schedule to assign jobs to employees. Upon completion of each job, the employee keys in a set of information to a disk file. This information includes his or her employee number, department, job-order number, number of units that he

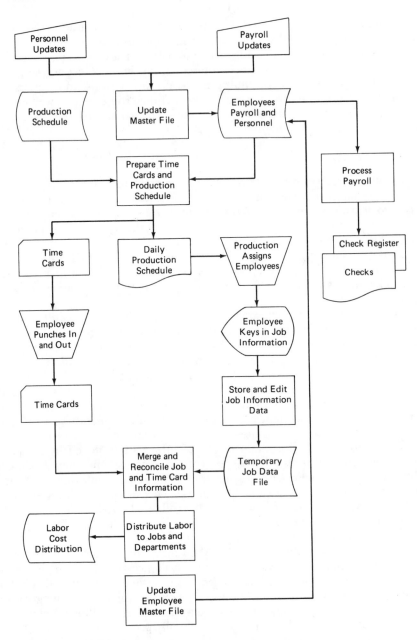

FIGURE 16-8 Payroll system.

or she completed, and time in hours spent on each job. Idle time and setup time are also reported, to account for all the time an employee spends in the plant. These data are edited and verified to ensure that all numbers are valid, logical (the employee is assigned to that department and the job is scheduled for that department), and reasonable. These data are stored on a temporary disk file, and at the end of the shift they are merged with completed timecards to reconcile employee time—that is, the hours must match for each employee, and the job assignments must match with the labor distribution data reported by the employee. Exceptions are reported and followed up by plant auditors and management. Major exceptions are corrected at this time before any further processing. Once the input data have been reconciled, job cost distributions are made and the employee master file is updated. Moreover, labor distribution along with other reports is issued to production supervisory personnel. Periodically the payroll is processed and checks are prepared. This may be weekly, biweekly, or monthly depending on the nature of the business and the employee classification. Checks and a check register are prepared at that time. Both the job cost data and the payroll are subsequently used to update the general ledger.

For many organizations, numerous reports are needed to help management control personnel activities and labor costs. At the operational level, the data collected can often be transformed into useful information for such management and accounting needs as career development, training, job scheduling, performance evaluation, medical and safety records, turnover problems, job costs, employee benefit programs, profit sharing, group insurance, ERISA compliance, employee selection, and affirmative action.

Large integrated payroll systems generally provide consistent and accurate data for all these human resource functions. These larger systems automatically update corresponding payroll information based on changes in personnel data. These systems automatically handle deductions and earnings calculations, and benefit deductions such as IRAs, 401(k)s, and "perks." In addition, these systems provide employees with complete and accurate earnings statements. These systems also provide an automatic earnings history for each employee.

These systems automatically allocate (distribute) labor costs down to project or work-order levels. They also provide payroll cost analyses and benefit planning reports, for use in manpower planning.

Moreover most large systems,[3] even some smaller systems, provide the following reports:

1. A Transaction Validation Report which provides a detailed analysis of all items processed and an explanation of any rejected items.
2. An Input Balancing Proof List Report which provides a permanent audit trail of current pay action transactions with system-produced totals and may be used by the Payroll Department to balance totals.
3. A W-2 Audit Report which provides a printout of W-2 data by employee, enabling management to audit tax records prior to printing W-2s on the specified form.
4. An Employee Master Profile Report which provides computer printouts of

---

[3] MSA, *Payroll Accounting System*, copyright 1981, Management Science America, Inc., Atlanta, Ga. Reprinted by permission.

employee information that includes administrative data and the frequency of specific deductions and/or other earnings.

5. A File Maintenance Report which furnishes an audit trail of all subsidiary and employee master file changes, including those generated by the system.

6. A Reversal Update Report which provides detailed and summary information on transactions entered to reverse specific checks and deposit records.

7. A Worker's Compensation Report which provides compensation information that makes compliance with state reporting requirements easier.

8. A Tax Distribution Summary Report which furnishes accrued federal, state, county, city, and provincial (Canadian) tax figures, which facilitates the necessary function of filing required tax reports to taxing authorities.

9. A W-2 Report which provides a wage and tax statement that complies with federal requirements.

10. A Form 1099 which reports compensation that is not required on either the W-2 or the W-2P Report to employees.

11. A Payroll Register which provides a recap of payment transactions for each employee and serves as an important part of the system audit trail.

12. A Check/Deposit Notification which provides an employee with check and deposit notification records when all or a portion of net pay is deposited to one or more banks or bank services.

13. An Hours Register which furnishes a listing of various hours categories, as well as available vacation and sick leave, by employee.

14. A Deductions/Earnings List which details individual employee deductions and other earnings in a user-defined format.

15. A Deductions/Other Earnings Register which details employee deductions and other earnings, providing a permanent employee record and supporting the totals provided on the Payroll Register.

16. A Labor Distribution Report which provides meaningful cost/labor distribution information for management and Accounting Department use.

17. An Earnings History Report which provides a listing of an employee's history of payment of earned wages. The detail of this report is an essential component of an employee's permanent records.

It is essential that the employee file or database be comprehensive and flexible so that these decision-making and reporting requirements can be satisfied. This file can include such items as: pay rates; tax information; benefit data; and as much history, skill, and performance data as management deems necessary. In addition, it is essential that current, monthly, and year-to-year pay records be complete and interface, if necessary, with the sales and manufacturing systems to efficiently capture commission, pay rates, overtime, and cost distribution information.

Facilities Management

For many firms, a formalized system for fixed asset accounting is necessary for property control, financial accounting, journal entries, tax accounting, and reporting to third parties and regulatory agencies. Facilities management systems must enable management to make replacement decisions, forecast future expenditures, plan maintenance operations, and purchase new assets. Moreover, the system should be detailed enough to help management decide on the various modes of asset financing and their impact on cash flow and on the financial statements of the business. At a minimum, the following information must be incorporated into the system: (1) location and descriptive information for property control; (2) depreciation information for multiple sets of books (tax and financial reporting); (3) lease accounting; (4) constant-dollar accounting information; and (5) tax information for various governmental and regulatory agencies. All information should be complete, timely, accurate, and flexible. A typical facilities management system would include those features found in Figure 16-9. First the amount, description, location, and other pertinent data would be keyed or transferred directly into the system from the accounts payable system. Also, disposal information and change (such as location change) are keyed into the facilities management system. The data is edited and posted to the fixed asset database and the general ledger system. From this, as shown in Figure 16-10 various reports such as depreciation schedules are prepared.

In addition to the features just noted, many fixed asset systems for large organizations provide the following:

1. Provisions for insurance revaluation based on historical cost, net book value, current replacement costs, and current insurable value.
2. Maintenance and repair cost statistics (including service contract information) for each asset.
3. Construction-in-progress reporting.
4. Reports on such data items as quantity, status, condition, serial number, vendor or manufacturer name, model name, and purchasing authority.
5. Transfers of location.
6. Journal entries for depreciation expense, additions, transfers, adjustments, and retirements.
7. Multiple depreciation methods and the necessary calculations so that the company can comply with various FASB pronouncements.
8. Incorporation of the most recent depreciation tax laws, calculation of investment tax credit and recapture information for management's needs, and calculation of gains and losses on the disposition of property.
9. Accounting for inflation via current value, replacement cost, or price-level adjustments as required.
10. Simple input, maintenance, and updating with complete audit trails.
11. A report generator for custom reporting to satisfy management's needs for decision making, reporting, and transaction processing.[4]

---

[4] MSA, *Fixed Asset Accounting System*, copyright 1981, Management Science America, Inc., Atlanta, Ga. Reprinted with permission.

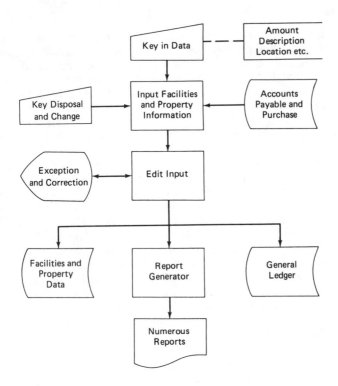

FIGURE 16-9 Facilities and property management systems.

ASSET CONTROL NUMBER	LOCATION	DESCRIPTION	DATE ACQUIRED	COST	DEPRECIATION METHOD	EXPECTED LIFE	CURRENT YEAR DEPRECIATION	ACCUMULATED DEPRECIATION
101	Casper	1988 Olds	1988	$14,000	SL	5 Years	2800	$11,200
208	Jackson Hole	1991 Ford	1991	$21,000	DDB	5 Years	5040	$13,440

FIGURE 16-10 Depreciation schedule.

In summary, contemporary facilities management systems help managers to control and to account for their investment in fixed assets.

SUMMARY

In this chapter we reviewed the various financial management systems in an organization and the information it takes to support them. Particular attention was given to the basic financial accounting system. This system is based on the general ledger system which is the foundation upon which an organization's financial statements are founded. The sales, accounts receivable, and cash receipts systems; the production, cost accounting, and inventory management systems; and the purchasing, accounts payable, and expenditures systems presented in this and earlier chapters tie directly into the general ledger systems. In addition, many firms have a personnel and payroll as well as a facilities management systems which may also be linked to the general ledger system. These transaction processing systems in turn provide the basis for marketing management, production and inventory management, and financial management of an organization.

SELECTED REFERENCES

"HRMS Meet Personnel Data Needs," Computerworld, May 13, 1985, pp. 1,23.

JURIS, ROBBIN, "Managing Human Resources On-line," *Computer Decisions,* January 14, 1986, pp. 44-52, 85.

"Management Science America", *Accounting Series 40,* Apple II Ed. Atlanta, Ga.: MSA, 1980.

————*Cooperative Excellence in Application Software: MSA and NCR.* Atlanta, Ga.: MSA, 1985.

————*Fixed Assets Accounting.* Atlanta, Ga.: MSA, 1981.

————*General Ledger Accounting System,* Atlanta, Ga.: MSA, 1981.

————*NCR Interactive Financial Management System.* Dayton, Ohio: NCR Corporation, 1979.

————*Payroll Accounting System.* Atlanta, Ga.: MSA, 1981.

————*Personnel Management and Reporting Systems.* Atlanta, Ga.: MSA, 1981.

SNYDERS, JAN. "A Company's Human Resource," *Infosystems,* March 1988, pp. 54-56.

REVIEW QUESTIONS

1. What are the advantages of an integrated financial accounting information system which is tied in an on-line mode to the general ledger versus a modular accounting system which links separate applications such as accounts receivable and payroll to the general ledger via monthly posting procedures? What are the disadvantages of such an integrated system?

2. What is the role of financial management in many organizations? Why are financial plans developed after tentative plans are available from marketing and production?

3. What information is needed to develop a capital budgeting proposal?

4. What information is typically needed to prepare a cash budget?

5. List the features found in a typical general ledger system for a large organization.

6. What characteristics should an on-line credit management and accounts receivable system have to help management manage its receivables?

7. What key comparison is usually required in accounts payable systems to ensure that invoices are correct prior to payment?

8. What key comparison is needed to be sure what was received is what was requested by a department?

9. What key reconciliation is necessary to be sure all hours are applied to some job or to some other activity in a manufacturing setting?

10. How can employees indicate when they begin and end a particular job so that the correct amount of labor is applied to that job?

11. What features are common in most computerized payroll systems?

12. What features are common in most computerized accounts payable systems?

13. What features are common in many fixed asset accounting information systems?

CASES

16-1 ConSport Corporation is a regional wholesaler of sporting goods. The systems flowchart in Figure C16-1 and the following description present ConSport's cash distribution system.

1. The accounts payable department approves for payment all Invoices (I) for the purchase of inventory. Invoices are matched with the purchase requisitions (PR), purchase orders (PO), and receiving reports (RR). The accounts payable clerks focus on vendor name and skim the documents when they are combined.

2. When all the documents for an invoice are assembled, a two-copy disbursement voucher (DV) is prepared and the transaction is recorded in the voucher register (VR). The disbursement voucher and supporting documents are then filed alphabetically by vendor.

3. A two-copy journal voucher (JV) that summarizes each day's entries in the voucher register is prepared daily. The first copy is sent to the general ledger department, and the second copy is filed in the accounts payable department by date.

4. The vendor file is searched daily for the disbursement vouchers of invoices that are due to be paid. Both copies of disbursement vouchers that are due to be paid are sent to the treasury department along with the supporting documents. The cashier prepares a check for each vendor, signs the check, and records it in the check register (CR). Copy 1 of the disbursement voucher is attached to the check copy and filed in check number order in the treasury department. Copy 2 and the supporting documents are returned to the accounts payable department and filed alphabetically by vendor.

5. A two-copy journal voucher that summarizes each day's checks is prepared. Copy 1 is sent to the general ledger department and Copy 2 is filed in the treasury department by date.

6. The cashier receives the monthly bank statement with cancelled checks and prepares the bank reconciliation (BR). If an adjustment is required as a consequence of the bank reconciliation, a two-copy journal voucher is prepared. Copy 1 is sent to the general ledger department. Copy 2 is attached to copy 1 of the bank reconciliation and filed by month in the treasury department. Copy 2 of the bank reconciliation is sent to the internal audit department.

REQUIRED: ConSport Corporation's cash disbursement system has some weaknesses. Review the *cash disbursement* system and for each weakness in the system:

1. Identify where the weakness exists by using the reference number that appears to the left of each symbol.

2. Describe the nature of the weakness.

3. Make a recommendation on how to correct the weakness.

Use the following format in preparing your answer:

REFERENCE NUMBER	NATURE OF WEAKNESS	RECOMMENDATION TO CORRECT WEAKNESS

(CMA adapted)

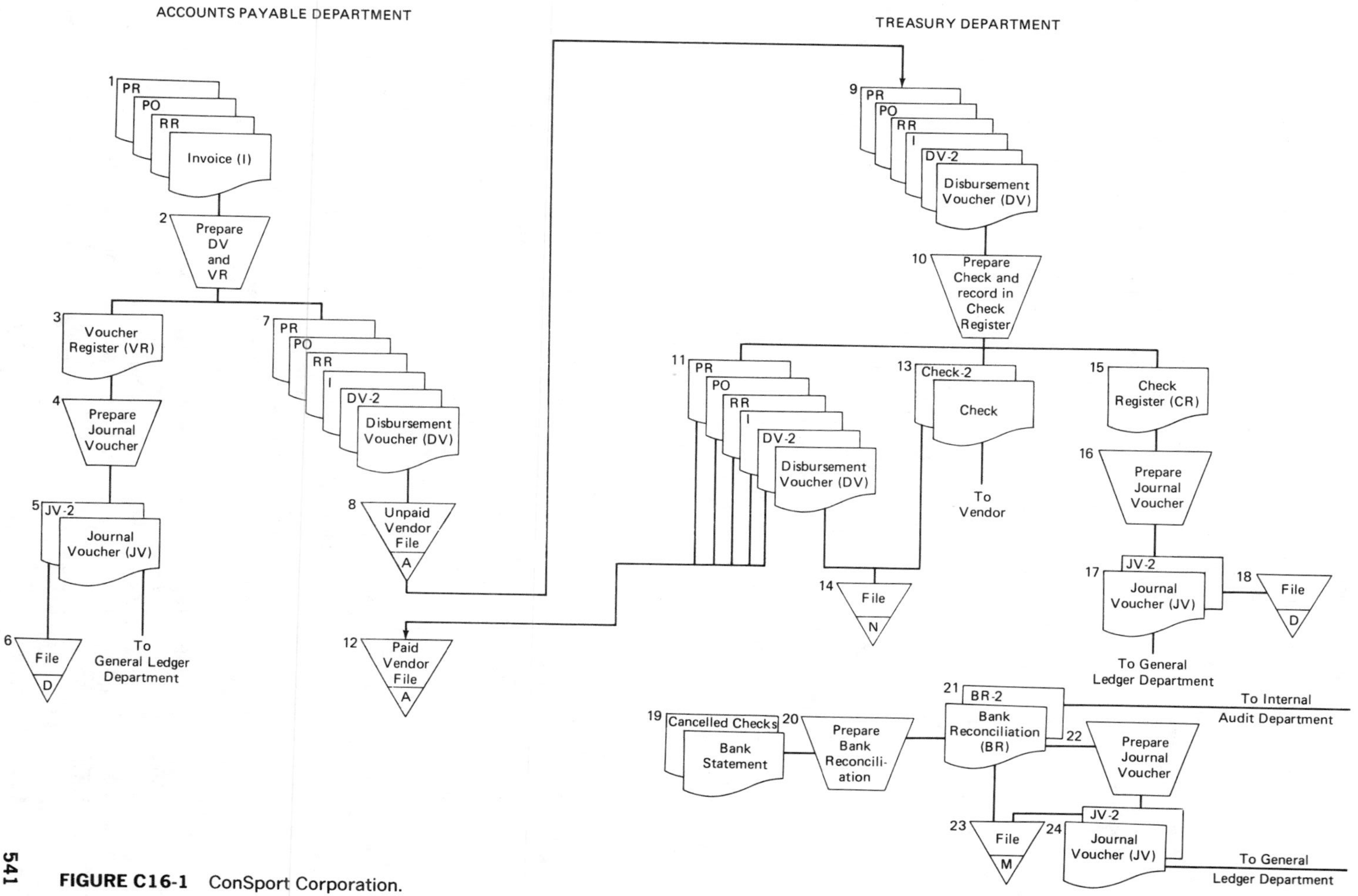

FIGURE C16-1 ConSport Corporation.

16-2 Rose Publishing Company devotes the bulk of its work to the development of high school and college texts. The printing division has several production departments and employs 400 persons, of which 95 percent are hourly rated production workers. Production workers may work on several projects in one day. They are paid weekly based on total hours worked.

A manual timecard system is used to collect data on time worked. Each employee punches in and out when entering or leaving the plant. The timekeeping department audits the timecards daily and prepares input sheets for the computerized functions of the payroll system.

Currently, a daily report of the previous day's clockcard information by department is sent to each departmental supervisor in the printing division for verification and approval. Any changes are made directly on the report, signed by the supervisor, and returned to the timekeeping department. The altered report serves as the input authorization for changes to the system. Because of the volume and frequently of reports, this report changing procedure is the most expensive process in the system.

Timekeeping submits the corrected hourly data to general accounting and cost accounting for further processing. General accounting maintains the payroll system that determines weekly payroll, prepares weekly checks, summarizes data for monthly, quarterly, and annual reports, and generates W-2 forms. A weekly and monthly payroll distribution report is prepared by the cost accounting department that shows the labor costs by department.

Competition in college textbook publishing has increased steadily in the last three years. While Rose has maintained its sales volume, profits have declined. Direct labor cost is believed to be the basic cause of this decline in profits, but insufficient detail on labor utilization is available to pinpoint the suspected inefficiencies. Chuck Hutchins, a systems consultant, was engaged to analyze the current system and to make recommendations for improving data collection and processing procedures. Excerpts from the report that Hutchins prepared are reproduced in Figure C16-2.

. . . An integrated Time and Attendance Labor Cost (TALC) system should be developed. Features of this system would include direct data entry; labor cost distribution by project as well as department; on-line access to time and attendance data for verification, correction, and update; and creation and maintenance of individual employee work history files for long-term analysis.

. . . The TALC system should incorporate uniquely encoded employee badges that would be used to electronically record entry to and exit from the plant directly into the data system.

. . . Labor cost records should be maintained at the employee level, showing the time worked in the department by project. Thus, labor costs can be fully analyzed. Responsibility for correct and timely entry must reside with the departmental supervisors and must be verified by project managers on a daily basis because projects involve several departments.

. . . On-line terminals should be available in each department for direct data entry. Access to the system will be limited to authorized users through a coded entry (password) system. Departmental supervisors will be allowed to inspect, correct, verify, and update only time and attendance information for employees in their respective departments. Project managers may access information recorded for their projects only and exceptions to such data must be certified outside the system and entered by the affected supervisor.

. . . Appropriate data should be maintained at the employee level to allow verification of employee personnel files and individual work-history by department and project. Access to employee master file data should be limited to the Personnel Department. Work-history data will be made available for analysis only at the project or departmental level, and only to departmental supervisors and project managers for whom an employee works.

FIGURE C16-2   TALC system.

REQUIRED:

1. Compared with traditional clockcard system, what are the advantages and disadvantages of the recommended system of electronically recording the entry to and exit from the plant?

2. Identify the items to be included in the individual employee's master file.

3. The TALC system allows the employee's departmental supervisor and the personnel department to examine the data contained in an individual employee's master file.

   a. Discuss the extent of the information each should be allowed to examine.

   b. Describe the safeguards that may be installed to prevent unauthorized access to the data.

(CMA adapted)

16-3 A CPA's audit working papers contain a narrative description of a segment of the Croyden, Inc., factory payroll system and an accompanying flowchart as follows. The internal control system with respect to the personnel department is functioning well and is *not* included in the accompanying flowchart (see Figure C16-3).

At the beginning of each workweek, payroll clerk no. 1 reviews the payroll department files to determine the employment status of factory employees and then prepares timecards and distributes them as each individual arrives at work. This payroll clerk, who is also responsible for custody of the signature stamp machine, verifies the identity of each payee before delivering signed checks to the foreman.

At the end of each workweek, the foreman distributes payroll checks for the preceding workweek. Concurrent with this activity, the foreman reviews the current week's employee timecards, notes the regular and overtime hours worked on a summary form, and initials the aforementioned timecard. The foreman then delivers all timecards and unclaimed payroll checks to payroll clerk no. 2.

REQUIRED:

1. Based upon the narrative and the flowchart in Figure C16-3, what are the weaknesses in Croyden's system of internal control?

2. Based upon the narrative and the flowchart, what inquiries should be made with respect to clarifying the existence of *possible additional* weaknesses in Croyden's system of internal control? (*Note:* Do not discuss the internal control system of the personnel department.)

(AICPA adapted.)

16-4 Deake Corporation in Eugene, Oregon, is a medium-sized, diversified manufacturing company. Fred Richards has recently been promoted to manager of the Property Accounting Section. Richards has had difficulty in responding to certain requests from individuals in some of Deake's other departments for information about the company's fixed assets. Some of the requests and problems Richards has had to cope with are as follows:

1. The controller has requested schedules of individual fixed assets to support the balances in the general ledger. Richards has furnished the necessary information, but he has always been late. The manner in which the records are organized makes it difficult to obtain information easily.

2. The maintenance manager wants to verify the existence of a punch press which he thinks was repaired twice. He has asked Richards to confirm the asset number and location of the press.

3. The insurance department wants data on the cost and book values of assets to include in its review of current insurance coverage.

4. The tax department wants data that can be used to determine when Deake should switch depreciation methods for tax purposes.

5. The company's internal auditors have spent a significant amount of time in the Property Accounting Section recently, attemping to confirm the annual depreciation expense.

The property account records that are at Richards's disposal consist of a set of manual books. These records show the date the asset was acquired, the account number to which the asset applies, the dollar amount capitalized, and the estimated useful life of the asset for depreciation purposes.

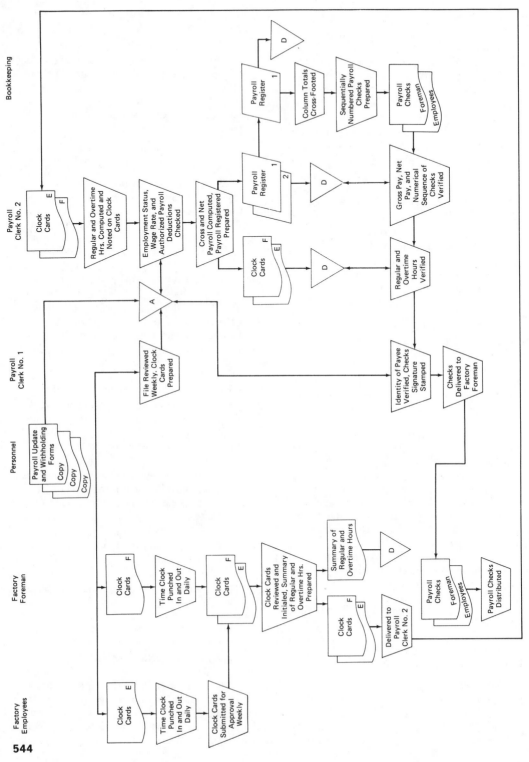

FIGURE C16-3   Croyden, Inc.

544

After many frustrations, Richards has realized that his records are inadequate and that he cannot easily supply the data when they are requested. He has decided to discuss his problems with the controller, Jim Castle.

Richards: Jim, something has got to give. My people are working overtime and can't keep up. You worked in Property Accounting before you became controller. You know I can't tell the tax, insurance, and maintenance people everything they need to know from my records. Also, that internal auditing team is living in my area and that slows down the work pace. The requests of these people are reasonable, and we should be able to answer these questions and provide the needed data. I think we need an automated property accounting system. I would like to talk to the information systems people to see if they can help me.

Castle: Fred, I think you have a good idea, but be sure you are personally involved in the design of any system so that you get all the information you need.

Required:

1. Identify and justify four objectives that Deake Corporation's automated property accounting system should attain in order to provide the data necessary to respond to the company personnel's requests for information.

2. Identify the data that should be included in the computer record for each asset included in the property account.

3. From the brief discussion of the MSA Fixed Asset Accounting System in the chapter, would that system be an option for Deake Corporation given the problems noted above? Why?

(Adapted from the CMA Examination.)

16-5 The Vane Corporation, a manufacturing concern, has been in business for the past eighteen years. During this period the company has grown from a very small family-owned operation to a medium-sized organization with several departments. Despite this growth, many of the procedures that Vane uses have been in effect since the company was founded. Just recently Vane computerized its payroll function.

The payroll function operates in the following manner. Each worker picks up a weekly timecard on Monday morning and writes in his or her name and identification number. These blank cards are kept near the factory entrance. The workers write on the timecard the time of their daily arrival and departure. On the following Monday, the factory foremen collect the completed time cards for the previous week and send them to data processing.

In data processing the timecards are used to prepare the weekly time file. This file is processed with the master payroll file, which is maintained on magnetic tape according to worker identification number. The checks are written by the computer on the regular checking account and imprinted with the treasurer's signature. After the payroll file has been updated and the checks have been prepared, the checks are sent to the factory foremen, who distribute them to the workers or hold them for the workers to pick up later if they are absent.

The foremen notify data processing of new employees and terminations. Any changes in hourly pay rate or any other changes affecting payroll are usually communicated to data processing by the foremen.

The workers also complete a job time ticket for each individual job they work on each day. The job time tickets are collected daily and are sent to cost accounting where they are used to prepare a cost distribution analysis.

Further analysis of the payroll function reveals the following:

1. A worker's gross wages never exceed $300 per week.

2. Raises never exceed $0.55 per hour for the factory workers.

3. No more than twenty hours of overtime is allowed per week.

4. The factory employs 150 workers in ten departments.

The payroll function has not been operating smoothly for some time, but even more problems have surfaced since the payroll was computerized. The foremen have indicated that they would like a weekly report indicating worker tardiness, absenteeism, and idle time so that they can determine the amount of productive time lost and the reason for the lost time. The following errors and inconsistencies have been encountered during the past few pay periods:

1. A worker's paycheck was not processed properly because he had transposed two numbers in his identification number when he filled out his time card.

2. A worker was issued a check for $1,531.80 when it should have been $153.81.

3. One worker's paycheck was not written, and this error was not detected until the paychecks for that department had been distributed by the foreman.

4. Part of the master payroll file was destroyed when the tape reel was inadvertently mounted on the wrong tape drive and used as a scratch tape. Data processing attempted to reestablish the destroyed portion from original source documents and other records.

5. One worker received a paycheck for an amount considerably larger than he should have. Further investigation revealed that 84 had been punched instead of 48 for hours worked.

6. Several records on the master payroll file were skipped and were not included on the updated master payroll file. This was not detected for several pay periods.

7. In processing nonroutine changes, a computer operator included a pay rate increase for one of his friends in the factory. This was discovered by chance by another employee.

REQUIRED: Identify the control weaknesses in the payroll procedure and in the computer processing as they are now being conducted by the Vane Corporation. Recommend the changes necessary to correct the system. Arrange your answer in the following columnar format:

CONTROL WEAKNESSES	RECOMMENDATIONS

(Adapted from CMA Exam)

16-6 Alichem is a chemical producer that has been in business for three years. Ed Caz was hired as Controller two months ago. Recently, when copies of the completed purchase orders arrived in the Accounting Department, Caz learned that the Processing Department was replacing some large machines. Caz had not approved these purchase orders. By questioning Sharon Price, Director of Purchasing, he learned that the orders had not been forwarded to him for approval. He discovered that, while the Purchasing Department negotiates and orders all direct materials and processing supplies, the procedure differs for the purchase of fixed assets. When fixed assets are to be acquired, the Purchasing Department issues and records a blank, prenumbered purchase order to the requesting user department. The user department handles its own purchasing arrangements. Through additional inquiries, Caz was able to identify the current procedures followed for fixed asset acquisition; these procedures are presented in the first column of Figure C16-4.

Caz believes that the acquisition procedure should be more efficiently distributed over the functions, thus providing the automatic implementation of new controls. Furthermore, he believes that a management group should review and approve requests for fixed assets before an order is placed.

In a manner similar to the description of the current procedures, Caz prepared the description of his proposed procedures presented in the second column of Figure C16-4.

REQUIRED:

1. Identify the strengths or improvements of Ed Caz's proposed procedures for fixed asset acquisition over the current procedures.

2. Identify and explain what further modifications, controls, or applications could be incorporated into the proposed procedures for fixed asset administration. (CMA adapted)

16-7 Rockmart Construction Company needs an accounts payable system that will let it manage its cash disbursements. It needs to know when to pay certain invoices to take advantage of discounts, and it needs a suspense system that will pay all invoices by their due date. It also needs to be able to make partial payments

Current Procedures

User Department

- Need determined, decision and approval to acquire made internally.
- Vendor bids requested and obtained for type and model of asset selected.
- Blank, prenumbered purchase order requested from Purchasing Department.

Purchasing Department

- Issue and log blank, prenumbered purchase order to user.

User Department

- Select best bid and place order.
- Prepare purchase order and distribute copies as follows:
  — Orginial and copy to vendor.
  — File copy for Receiving Department.
  — File copy for Accounting Department.
  — File copy retained for user department.

Receiving Department

- Asset arrives at Receiving Department's dock.
- Receiving notifies Accounting so that Accounting can verify that correct asset has been received and can issue brass tag number.
- Asset delivered to user department after verifications or returned to vendor if there is a problem.
- Send invoice to Accounting if packed with asset.

User Department

- User receives, installs, and tests the asset or receives notification of return.
- If asset malfunctions upon or shortly after installation, user deals with vendor and attempts to delay payment.

Accounting Department

- Verify asset, issue and record brass tag number.
- Receive and match invoice to purchase order copy.
- Forward invoice to Controller for approval.
- Payment approved by Controller.
- Check prepared and asset recorded unless user requests a delay of payment.
- Check mailed.
- Brass tagging of asset is verified.

Proposed Procedures

User Department

- Determine need.
- Obtain bids and select best vendor in consultation with Purchasing, as necessary.
- Prepare purchase request that includes type and model, bids, and justification.

Management Review

- Review justification.
- Assure that asset meets goals and objectives of the business and department.
- Verify that request is within existing guidelines.
- Approve or reject asset request.

Purchasing Department

- Receive approved requisition.
- Prepare prenumbered purchase order and place order with selected vendor.
- Negotiate financing with vendor, if necessary.
- Assume responsibility to follow up if delivery is delayed and distribute copies as follows.
  — Original and copy to vendor.
  — File copy for Receiving Department.
  — File copy for Accounting Department.
  — File copy for Purchasing Department.

Receiving Department

- Asset arrives.
- Prepare a receiving report including visible condition of asset upon receipt; copy sent to Accounting Department.
- Match original of receiving report with purchase order copy and file.
- Deliver assets to user.
- Deliver copy of receiving report and invoice, if received with asset, to Accounting.

User Department

- Receive, install, and test asset.
- Accept or reject asset.
- Prepare and send copy of acceptance report to Accounting and Purchasing indicating acceptance or rejection.
- Asset returned to vendor if rejected.

Purchasing Department

- Receive acceptance report from user department.
- Deal with vendor if asset rejected or fails shortly after installation.

Accounting Department

- Match accounting copies of purchase order, receiving report, acceptance report with invoice.
- If all reports are acceptable, prepare payment approval or else keep matched documents in open invoice file.
- Controller or delegate approves invoice for payment.
- Issue and mail check.
- Record asset.
- Issue brass tagging number and verify that asset is tagged.

FIGURE C16-4 Fixed asset acquisition procedures.

and select individual invoices to pay so that payments will not exceed available cash.

Considerable changes must be made to invoices because of the nature of the construction business. Rockmart needs to be able to implement these changes as they occur using an on-line system. Rockmart also needs to be able to document these changes so misunderstandings can be resolved by tracing transactions via the managerial audit trail.

REQUIRED:

1. What on-line information is required?

2. What reports will give management this accounts payable information? Is this information available given the system illustrated in the microcomputer system illustrated in the appendix of Chapter 19?

16-8 Arlington Industries manufactures and sells component engine parts for large industrial equipment. The company employs over 1,000 workers for three shifts, and most employees work overtime when necessary. Arlington has had major growth in its production and has purchased a mainframe computer to handle order processing, inventory management, production planning, distribution operations, and accounting applications. Michael Cromley, president of Arlington, suspects that there may be internal control weaknesses due to the quick implementation of the computer system. Cromley recently hired Kathleen Luddy as the internal control accountant.

Cromley asked Luddy to review the payroll processing system first. Luddy has reviewed the payroll process, interviewed the individuals involved, and compiled the flowchart displayed on the next page. Below is listed additional information concerning payroll processing.

- The Personnel Department determines the wage rate of all employees at Arlington. Personnel starts the process by sending an authorization form for adding an employee to the payroll to the payroll coordinator, Marjorie Adams. After Adams inputs this information into the system, the computer automatically determines the overtime and shift differential rates for the individual, updating the Payroll Master file.

- Arlington uses an external service to provide monthly payroll tax updates. The company receives a magnetic tape every month which the Data Processing Department installs to update the Payroll Master file for tax calculations.

- Employees at Arlington use a time clock to record the hours worked. Every Monday morning, Adams collects the previous week's time cards from the card bin, leaves the new week's time cards, and begins the computerized processing of payroll information in order to produce paychecks the following Friday. Adams reviews the time cards to ensure that the hours worked are correctly totaled; the system will determine whether overtime has been worked or a shift differential is required.

- All the other processes displayed on the flowchart are performed by Adams. The system automatically assigns a sequential number to each payroll check produced. The checks are stored in a box next to the computer printer to provide immediate access. After the checks are printed, Adams uses an automatic check-signing machine to sign the checks with an authorized signature plate that Adams keeps locked in a safe.

- After the check processing is completed, Adams distributes the checks to the employees, leaving the checks for the second-and third-shift employees with the appropriate shift supervisor. Adams then notifies the Data Processing Department that she is finished with her weekly processing, and they make a backup of the Payroll Master file to magnetic tape for storage on the tape shelves in the computer room.

REQUIRED: By referring to the information above and the flowchart in Figure C16-5 identify and describe:

1. Five different areas in Arlington Industries' payroll processing system where the system controls are inadequate.

2. Two different areas in Arlington Industries' payroll processing system where the system controls are satisfactory.
   (CMA adapted)

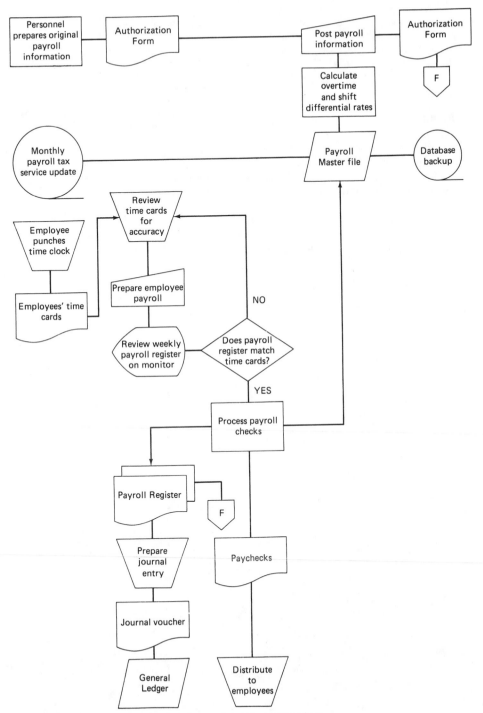

FIGURE C16-5   Arlington Industries' payroll processing flowchart.

16-9 A hotel chain in the upper Midwest continually needs to evaluate their investment decisions. They build and construct their own hotels. They are interested in a return on capital of more than 12 percent to keep their investors happy.

REQUIRED:

1. What data items (internal and external) would you consider to be important in forecasting their cash flows?
2. Would a planning model assist them in making these decisions? How?

16-10 Bob Peake Realtors buys and sells homes, rents property, and acts as an agent in the transfer of property. Their income is derived mainly from rental units, commissions for the sale of property, and from the sale of their own investments. Expenses include salaries, commissions, selling expenses, maintenance, interest, and capital outlays. They have a hard time managing cash flows since the sale of property is so seasonal and unpredictable. They have a microcomputer and know how to use one of the more popular comprehensive spreadsheet packages. They also have access to economic data via an industry service and can download that information via a modem and communication software.

REQUIRED: Suggest the characteristics needed in a cash flow forecasting system that they can be used to manage their financial affairs.

17

DECISION SUPPORT SYSTEMS

INTRODUCTION

The basic aspects of the decision-making process are outlined in Figure 17-1. First the problem is defined, relevant objects are observed and classified, measurements are taken of their activities and data are collected in a database or file so that the decision maker can understand the problem. From this data, functional relationships are developed from various patterns and predictions, or inferences are made. Criteria are selected for decision making and for enlisting various alternatives. From these criteria a decision model is used to select the best or the most satisfactory alternative or course of action. Management action is then taken. Finally, an accounting system is used to measure the outcome of the action and to feed the results back into the decision process for management to make the next decision. In some cases, many of these processing steps are automated. In other cases, they are done by the decision maker based on the information provided by the accounting information system and computer software used to assist management in the decision-making process. Throughout the decision-making process are communication channels through which information

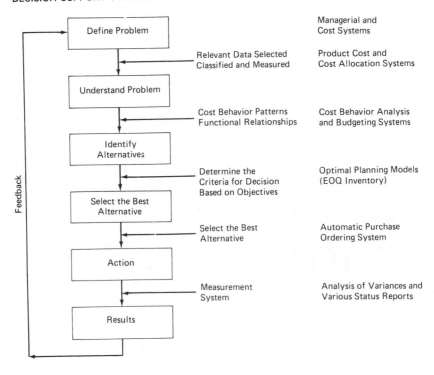

Define Problem	Managerial and Cost Systems
	Relevant Data Selected Classified and Measured — Product Cost and Cost Allocation Systems
Understand Problem	
	Cost Behavior Patterns Functional Relationships — Cost Behavior Analysis and Budgeting Systems
Identify Alternatives	
	Determine the Criteria for Decision Based on Objectives — Optimal Planning Models (EOQ Inventory)
Select the Best Alternative	
	Select the Best Alternative — Automatic Purchase Ordering System
Action	
	Measurement System — Analysis of Variances and Various Status Reports
Results	

FIGURE 17-1 Decision-making process: accounting information perspective.

flows, and there are numerous feedback loops for more information on the results of action and its bearing on future decisions.

In this chapter, we will examine several types of decision support systems (DSS). A decision support system is a system which aids management in some stage in the decision process in situations where some aspects of the process are not well structured or well defined. Decision support software can assist the decision maker in each of the steps in Figure 17-1. It can signal the need for a decision through an exception report. Software can be used to accumulate and organize the data so that management can better understand the nature of the problem. It can be used to model several alternative solutions using financial planning, mathematical models, statistical models, or simple spreadsheet. It can make comparisons between alternatives based on management's decision criteria. It can aid in selecting the best alternative and it can even implement the selected course of action. Finally, software can monitor and accumulate data on the outcome for future decision making.

In considering the level of support a decision support system can render in the decision-making process, we assume Simon's[1] principle of bounded rationality in decision making.

Decisions can be classified into the following classes:

---

[1] H. A. Simon, *The New Science of Management* (New York: Harper & Row, 1960).

1. *Structured* decisions where all the steps in the process are well structured.
2. *Semistructured* decisions where at least one of the steps, such as the criteria or the set of relevant data, is unstructured.
3. *Unstructured* where all the steps in the process are unstructured.

Managers make structured decisions using a well-defined set of data; with a well-defined process for analyzing the data; with a logical, often analytical, model; with well-defined selection criteria, such as optimizing the contribution to profit. Managers, on the other hand, make unstructured decisions based on heuristics which are founded on poorly organized and ill-defined data, which are often not quantifiable, and methods of analysis and alternative selection which are often based on heuristics founded upon judgment, experience, and intuition. Often, as explained in the appendix of Chapter 4 on decision theory, this is a sequential search for a satisfactory solution.

Structured decisions tend to be operational and based on factual internal information. Unstructured decisions are more likely to be related to managerial and strategic decisions which are dynamic and require a great deal of nonfinancial data which are laden with uncertainty and external data (variables). Thus, decision support systems must be designed to accommodate unstructured data related to various forecasts, exogenous information, such as economic indicators, and economic uncertainty. They must enable managers to act in a heuristic manner in a timely fashion on managerial and strategic issues. This requires a completely different system than that which provides managers with routine structured information for routine operational decision-making and reporting needs. This is not to say they are completely independent. Indeed, DSS rely heavily on the transaction processing and structured decision-making information base for much of its internal information, which complements the external information needed by management.

An effective DSS will provide management with a better understanding of the problem, the key variables associated with the issues, the alternative courses of action, and the impact on the organization and its vendors and customers. In general, it will not provide an answer, because it is designed to support decision-making and not to make decisions. It should be remembered that managers solve problems and make decisions.

The key components are described next.

1. The *user interface or dialogue subsystem* provides the user with flexible easy access to the DSS models and the database. Much of the power of a DSS is derived from the capabilities users have to interact with the decision support system. This interface includes input procedures (action language) which enable the user to interact with the system. Input procedures must present information in a form which is consistent with the user's background and experience. Often this is in the form of key input, a command language which is familiar to the user. An example will be given later in the discussion of planning and control systems and the Interactive Financial Planning System—IFPS. A set of menus that walk the user through a series of questions may also be used effectively. This interface also includes a

presentation language. Presentation can constitute printed output such as financial statements, graphical analysis, or simply output to the screen for immediate use in the decision process. It should present information in a form that is consistent with the user's experience and decision-making style. A complete discussion of this will be presented in the planning and control section of this chapter. The *user's knowledge base*, which is the user's experience in working with the set of problems and with the technology used in the DSS, is also an essential component of the user's interface. Advanced issues pertaining to this knowledge base are described in the expert systems section later in the chapter.

2. The *data subsystem (base)* comprises internal accounting and MIS data as well as external (exogenous) data relevant to the decision. The database must be based on the database concepts set forth in Chapter 10 in that it must be flexible and independent of applications and physical structures. It is usually much broader and includes nontransactional internal data such as production statistics, as well as external data such as economic indicators. This supporting database must be able to add and subtract data sources easily; it must be very flexible. It must be able to present logical data structures in ways users can understand, or be organized in a relational form so that relations can be easily constructed for a variety of uses. Figure 17-2a illustrates a DSS database. Database issues will likewise be discussed in the planning and control section.

3. The *model base* comprises a set of models which attempt to structure the relationships among the key variables to aid the decision maker in assessing the problem or various alternatives to the problem. The DSS must be flexible enough to create models using a modeling language such as IFPS, which will be reviewed later in this chapter. It should be able to integrate the models with the database and it should be able to assemble "model building blocks" into a system to support unstructured decisions. Often these building blocks include statistical analysis, what-if analysis, goal seeking models, deterministic and stochastic simulation models, and optimization models. Figure 17-2b illustrates the model base. A more complete discussion is presented in the planning and control section of this chapter.

Figure 17-3 presents a comparison of the characteristics of decision support systems (DDS) and more traditional structured decision systems (SDS). Both are components of MIS systems, and accounting information systems overlap both classifications.

In summary, decision support systems comprise a growing set of systems which are used to support management in its decision-making process. Decision support systems include financial planning models such as spreadsheets for microcomputers, and planning and control systems which we will review in the next section. Also included are expert systems based on artificial intelligence concepts which we will review later in this chapter.

The Data Subsystem

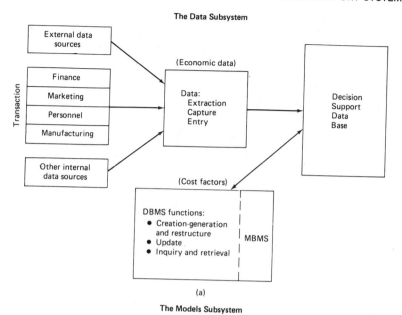

(a)

The Models Subsystem

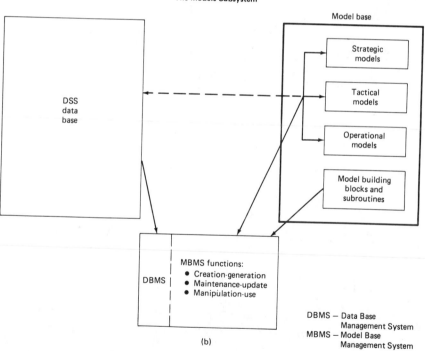

(b)

FIGURE 17-2   Decision data support system, database, and model base.
Source: R. Sprague and J. Carlson, *Building Effective Decision Support Systems,* © 1982, pp. 31-34. Reprinted by permission of Prentice Hall, Inc., Englewood Cliffs, N.J.

SUBJECT	SDS	DSS
I. The Final User/Decision Maker		
Decision-maker's environment (internal and external)	constant, simple	dynamic, complex
Decision-maker's level	operational control	strategic planning
System development initiative	to decision maker	from decision maker
Decision-maker's involvement in system development and use	passive	active
Decision-making style	predetermined	individual
II. The Decisions Supported by the System Structure	structured	unstructured
Time horizon	historical	future-oriented
Use	routine	ad hoc, unique
Decision-making process	defined, algorithmic, programmable	heuristic, iterative, exploratory, nonprogrammable
Importance to organization	local, operational	strategic, organizationwide
Decision phases supported	all phases	some phases
III. The Information System		
Data sources	largely internal	largely external
Design predetermination	structured	unstructured
Data base	well-defined, narrow, detailed	redundant, broad, integrated, aggregated
Model base	predetermined models, quantitative, universal O.R., explicit	tailor-made, qualitative model building blocks, heuristic, implicit
System design orientation	data orientation	decision oriented
Operating mode	batch	interactive
System success criteria	operational efficiency	flexibility
Frequency of use	predetermined	undefined frequency
IV. Information System Developers		
Organizational body	technicians, service unit	planners, staff unit
Involvement of developers in decision-making process	none	involved

FIGURE 17-3 Characteristics of SDS and DSS.

Source: S. Newman and M. Hadass. "DSS and Strategic Decision." Copyright 1980 by the Regents of the University of California. *California Management Review, Vol.* 22, No. 3, 77–84. Reprinted by permission of the Regents.

PLANNING AND CONTROL MODELS AND SYSTEMS

Corporate Planning and Control Systems

The planning and control process used by management to accomplish the objectives of the organization, as shown in Figure 17-4, consists of the planning; operation; and measurement, evaluation, and reporting system of the organization. *Planning* is the process of setting goals and objectives at the strategic level, making decisions on how to achieve these objectives, and the preparation of plans and budgets at the managerial level. *Operations* consists of the day-to-day process of implementing these plans through various decisions and actions. *Measurement* is the process of collecting information and assigning numerical values. These results are then reported back to management through performance reports and to external third parties through financial statements. These reports are then used in the *evaluation* process to adjust day-to-day operations through a *feedback* system, as shown in Figure 17-4, to help management implement the plans. This feedback information is also used to adjust objectives, decisions, and plans as technological and environmental changes occur.

Planning models help management in making decisions, in tracking the operations, and in measuring and evaluating the results of managerial actions. Full-blown corporate planning and control models and systems will probably encompass several subunits within the corporation. They are often an integrated model of the organization. To begin to understand how one goes about structuring or developing such models, we can break the problem into a number of manageable components or elements. For discussion purposes, we will subdivide the corporate planning and control modeling process and systems into four basic elements: (1) the planning system; (2) the information system; (3) the modeling system; and (4) the control system.[2] Each of these systems is made up of subcomponents or subelements. In the following sections we will examine these major systems and their associated components. Most of these components apply to DSS in general. An illustration of many of these components is presented in the discussion of IFPS which follows.

Expressed in a formal or "general model" framework, a *corporate model* can be defined as a set of relationships which represents the key activities in the organization. They relate input variables to output variables for each of these important activities, such as the input of labor, material, and overhead into the production (activity) of goods and services. Within this general model framework, the output variables are referred to as endogenous variables, and the input variables are classified as either exogenous or decision (policy) variables. During the modeling (evaluation) process, the values of the decisions and exogenous variables are known and are either held constant or are modeled via a stochastic process (using a probability distribution). The decision variables are chosen by the user to determine their influence on the output (endogenous) variables.

---

[2] T. H. Naylor, "Elements of a Planning and Modeling System," presents a detailed discussion of these basic principles, Corporate Economics Program, Duke University, North Carolina, June (1981) pp. 1017–26.

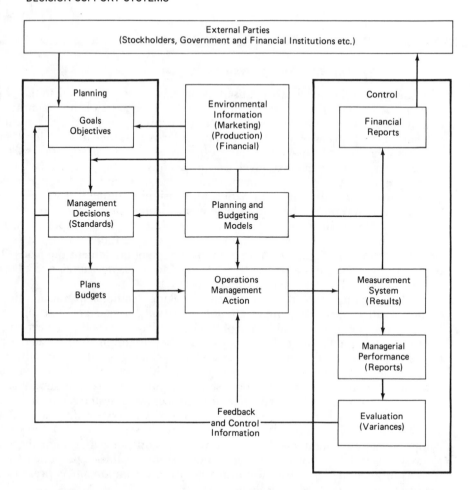

FIGURE 17-4 Planning and control process.

The values of the decision variables represent managerial or user decisions. Exogenous variables, on the other hand, are set by a firm's environment (which generally cannot be influenced by the decision maker). The values of the endogenous variables provide the answers to "what if" and other questions that can be addressed by the model.

Types of Analysis

The first type of investigation focuses on "what is" or "what has been" questions, such as the relationship between variables of the firm and macroeconomic variables like GNP or certain raw material prices. Generally, the goal in this type of analysis is to develop a data set and a set of relationships among the data elements.

The second type of investigation focuses on "what if" questions. This analysis often takes the following form: "What happens under a given set of assumptions if the decision variables are changed in a prescribed manner?" An analysis of this type is supposed to provide a quantitative answer to hypothetical entrepreneurial decisions.

Planning and control systems using this type of analysis can be deterministic or they can be stochastic. Deterministic systems use predetermined relationships between the various elements of the organization to construct a model of the organization's activities. For example, they would use a sales forecast to determine the production plan and then use the production plan to plan financing. All the sales, revenue, collection, cost, production specifications, and financial arrangements would be expressed as a set of equations. A deterministic set of output will be generated by this type of model. If any of the elements, such as variable costs or price, for example, are not known for certain, "what if" questions can be pursued by rerunning the model for the new set of circumstances to obtain revised output. If certain input information is not known for certain, the deterministic model can be run for a range of variables, say plus and minus 5 percent and 10 percent, for example, to test the model's output for the sensitivity of its input. Each deterministic output is compared with the original input to assess the sensitivity of input variables.

On the other hand, stochastic models treat any subset of the input data as random variables which may or may not follow a known statistical distribution, such as a normal distribution. Simulation is used to solve such models and output is in the form of a probability distribution, frequency tables, or percentiles based on the probability distribution.

The third type of investigation that can be addressed via modeling takes the following form: "What must be done in order to achieve an objective?" This is often called goal seeking. Today even some of the microcomputer spread sheets have this feature. Under this arrangement, the decision maker sets goals and uses the model to determine which decisions will achieve these goals. This type of analysis is more restrictive than the "what if" analysis because the range of values for the output or target values may be limited. If the model user chooses a goal that is outside the feasible range there will be no feasible way to achieve the objective. In the cases where feasible goals exist, the solutions to the input (decision variable) can be found by analysis or by experimentation (simulation). It should be recognized that with either solution process, the solution can be affected by the initial values of the exogenous input variables and the goals (target values of the endogenous output variables).

Planning System

The focal point of any corporate planning model is the planning system. Unless there is a formal planning system, there is probably little need to consider the modeling process. Obviously the planning system for any firm or corporation will be tailored to the particular needs of the organization. For illustrative purposes, however, we can assume that most firms will have financial, production, and marketing functions and that these must be linked somehow in the planning process. As a general example, we will assume that the company we will examine is a large decentralized firm with multiple divisions or strategic business units. Furthermore, we will assume that each division is autonomous and thus is responsible for its own marketing and production activities. The financial planning and cash management activities for the firm are handled at the corporate level, but each division is responsible for its own balance sheet and income statement.

At the beginning of the planning process, as shown in Figure 17-4, corporate goals and objectives are set by top management of the firm. These are conveyed to the divisional units by the corporate planning manager. The corporate goals may be specific target objectives for the company as a whole, which would require breaking them down to the division level, or they may be goals (target levels) for specific division. Typical goals could include return on investment (ROI), market share, sales growth, and cash flow. These targets might also include environmental, social, and political functions.

Regardless of whether there is a formal modeling process, the corporate planning department should design the final report formats to be employed by the business units in formulating their plans. Standardized reporting at the division level greatly facilitates the generation of a consolidated plan at the corporate level. Individual business units are allowed to make their own marketing, production, and other activity assumptions as long as these do not conflict with external assumptions about market activity or policies of the firm in general. Divisional financial plans must obviously follow from given assumptions about revenues and costs.

For our hypothetical example, we will assume that during the formal planning process, plans from the division are transmitted to the corporate planning department for consolidation, review, and evaluation. In the initial stages of the process, individual division plans will probably be returned to the respective unit for modification and/or reformulation. The iterative process will be replicated until all the division plans have been approved and consolidated into the corporate plan.

As we indicated earlier, the modeling process can only occur if a planning system exists; however, the modeling processes should coincide with the planning process. But it should not be concluded that the only time the modeling process is undertaken is during the formal planning process.

A group of divisional planning models (finance, marketing, and production) may exist for each division in an organization. These models can either be used on a stand-alone basis at the division level, or be used to generate information that can be consolidated and used at the corporate level. The objective of the separate divisional models is to generate alternative scenarios and plans based on various assumptions about divisional policies and the external environment of the corporation. Each of these follows the decision-making process outlined in Figure 17-1.

Examples of Planning Models

FINANCIAL MODELS.   Each division's financial model can be used to produce its own pro forma financial statements. The division financial models can be used to simulate the effects on net profits of alternative business strategies for the unit. The results generated by the divisional financial model, however, will be a function of the assumption relating to revenue and product cost projections, which are inputs to the model.

At the corporate level, the financial model can be used to generate consolidated pro forma financial statements. Some of the application programs employed at this level include (1) cash flow analysis; (2) profit planning; (3) budgeting; (4) investment analysis; and (5) merger-acquisition analysis.

MARKETING MODELS.   For most firms, revenue projections must be made during the formal planning process. The marketing model, which may include economic indicators, sales forecasts, and cash collections for each of the divisions, may be used to accomplish this task. Two alternative projection methods are available. These are forecasting models and econometric models.

Forecasting models are time-series techniques that attempt to forecast next-period sales in terms of prior sales. These forecasts are basically a function of past data. The output from these sales forecasts, however, will often require adjustments for changing economic conditions, promotional effort, or product mixes.

Econometric models can be used for "what if" analyses. Such models can be used to simulate the effect on sales volume or market share of alternative pricing and advertising strategies. In addition, such models can be used to link market forecasts to the national and regional economics. But the results from such models are no better than the accuracy of the policy assumptions and the assumptions about the firm's external environment. (Additional comments relating to forecasting and econometric models will be made in the section entitled "Modeling System.")

PRODUCTION MODELS.   An effective production model can provide management with the production cost associated with a given level of demand. Given a divisional forecast, the production model can generate the cost of goods sold associated with the forecast. An extended analysis, linked with this basic analysis, would even generate the minimum cost production plan associated with a set of demand levels that match all the products in the business unit. We will note in the "Modeling System" section later in the chapter that this latter alternative can be accomplished by mathematical optimization techniques (such as linear programming).

Information System

The information system is an integral part of corporate planning and modeling systems and decision support systems. The elements that make up the information system are (1) data and the associated database; (2) a database management system; (3) control structure; (4) a report generator; and (5) graphics.

DATABASE.   Before a corporate model can be developed and used effectively, the variables and the structure of the model must be specified. The numeric values for the input variables (exogenous and decision) of the model must be supplied, and the values of model parameters and the initial values or goals (target values of the endogenous variables) must be identified.

Numeric input data are obtained from a variety of sources including decisions of the model user. These include measurements of historical data or forecasts of future values of variables that are needed.

Statistical sampling is often used in collecting and generating data. For example, macroeconomic exogenous data or marketing data may be collected from government statistics or consumer panel data.

The amount of data required to support a corporate modeling system will depend on the variables involved and the type of model. A minimum of three or four years of historical financial data is often required. Even more data is generally required if the model is used to generate monthly or quarterly reports. Econometric marketing models should have twenty-five to thirty observations of historical data.

Although most firms have little difficulty in meeting the data requirements for financial modeling, data problems are often severe in the cases of marketing and/or production modeling. One means for circumventing this problem is to rely on external sources for data. A number of service bureaus provide national historical macroeconomic data and econometric forecasts to their clients. The major disadvantages of these services, however, are that they are quite expensive and they have not been consistently accurate. An inexpensive alternative is to subscribe to the historical database of the National Bureau of Economic Research (NBER). The cost associated with the NBER database is nominal, and the database includes over twenty-two hundred economic and time series values. It is available through most time-sharing bureaus and it can be installed on a user's own computer.

DATABASE MANAGEMENT SYSTEM.   Regardless of the source of the data for a planning and modeling system, users should be able to view the data as a database, which gives them maximum flexibility. Most commercially available software modeling languages feature a database management system that meets this objective. There are some differences in the internal data structure of the database systems in these modeling software packages. At least four different structures have emerged: (1) a matrix structure; (2) a row-column structure; (3) a record-file structure; and (4) a relational structure.

Many FORTRAN-based planning and modeling systems use matrices in reading data into the system. The database management and modeling functions are likewise carried out using matrix manipulations. This type of structure is familiar to a scientific programmer. However, for corporate planners, accountants, and financial analysts who are neither mathematicians nor scientific programmers, the martix structure of data handling and manipulation may be difficult to use.

A number of planning and modeling systems make use of row numbers and column letters in formulating models, creating and loading databases, and generating reports. The row-column structure is much easier to work with than the matrix arrangement, particularly for accountants who are accustomed to working with financial spreadsheets. Econometric and production data, however, do not necessarily lend themselves to this arrangement.

The third type of database management structure is a record-file arrangement. Under this structure, a record is the basic unit of data. This type of structure was discussed in depth in the chapter on data files. Time series data such as sales, costs, and profits are often stored in such a file. Under a record-file arrangement, each model may have one or more files. For example, for a given model, one file may contain actual historical data; another file, budgeted data; and a third file, simulated data. As stated in Chapters 9 and 10 this type of structure can result in lack of flexibility and data dependence.

The fourth type of structure is relational. It offers the most flexibility and is the most independent, as discussed in the database chapter.

CONTROL STRUCTURE.   A key element of the information system component of a planning and modeling system is the control system. Some means must exist for controlling access to files, records, models, and reports. Division managers should be able to access their own models and reports and should have access to or be able to view the files or data bases segments they need to use. They should be restricted from accessing other data they do not need to use. Control structures for databases were discussed in Chapter 10.

REPORT GENERATOR.   As is the case in database management systems, the report generator should be an integral part of any planning and control system. To be effective, the report generator should be flexible and easy to use and should not impose any restrictions on the type of report produced by the system. If the planning system is to be used effectively to support a wide variety of decisions such as those summarized earlier in this chapter, the generator should be able to produce any type of report format desired.

GRAPHICS.   The tabular form of presenting information, particularly financial information, is traditionally employed throughout industry. However, with recent developments in graphic technology it is now possible, and in many cases more cost effective, to employ full-color charts and graphs to present the data. Graphics can be particularly important in planning and modeling systems because results displayed from different types of analyses are easier to comprehend than actual numbers, particularly if rapid "what if" types of analyses are being conducted. Graphics software has become so important that a whole class of software has evolved called "presentation graphics."

Modeling Systems

Almost every corporate planning model consists in part of a set of simple equations that express the basic activities and relationships in the organization. These are often financial and accounting relationships. The solution to these equations is often the basis of the model. In general, however, the modeling system component of a corporate model involves much more than solving these equations. A number of features should be available to support the modeling effort. These include (1) sequential modeling capabilities; (2) ability to handle simultaneous equations; (3) logical models; (4) risk analysis; (5) optimization; (6) goal seeking; (7) forecasting; and (8) econometric modeling. We will discuss each of these briefly.

Many of the financial models that have been developed are sequential models. A *sequential (recursive) model* is one in which, by placing the equations of the model in the proper order, it is possible to solve each equation individually in a step-by-step fashion by substituting the solution values of previous equations into the equation being solved. The advantage of sequential models is that matrix inversion or some other simultaneous equation solution technique is not required in order to solve the model.

Ideally, every corporate model should have a sequential decision structure. Unfortunately, this is not always the case. For this reason a corporate modeling system should include the capabilities for handling the solution of *simultaneous equations*. To illustrate the need for a simultaneous equation solution technique, consider the following basic model:

EQUATION NO.	EQUATION
1	$PROFIT_t = REVENUE_t - COGS_t - INT_t - TAX_t$
2	$INT_t = 0.16 * DEBT_t$
3	$DEBT_t = DEBT_{t-1} + NDEBT_t$
4	$CASH_t = CASH_{t-1} + PROFIT_t + NDEBT_t$
5	$NDEBT_t = MBAL_t - CASH_t$

For this case, equation 1 defines profit during the current time period t ($PROFIT_t$) as revenue for the period ($REVENUE_t$) less cost of goods sold ($COGS_t$), interest (INT_t), and taxes (TAX_t) for the period. While cost of goods sold and taxes ($COGS_t$, TAX_t) could be inputs, interest for the time period (INT_1) depends on total indebtedness for the period ($DEBT_t$), as defined by equation 2. But indebtedness for the period ($DEBT_t$) is dependent upon indebtedness from the prior period ($DEBT_{t-1}$) plus new debt for the current period ($NDEBT_t$), as expressed in equation 3. New debt for the period ($NDEBT_t$) is defined in equation 5 as the firm's minimum required cash balance for the period ($MBAL_t$) less the cash balance for the period ($CASH_t$). ($NEDBT_t$) may be negotiated to reflect the payments of debt in equations 3, 4 and 5. In equation 4, cash balance for the period ($CASH_t$) is defined as the cash balance for the previous period ($CASH_{t-1}$) plus profits and new debt for the period ($PROFIT_t$, $NDEBT_t$).

It is impossible to solve the model sequentially by simply ordering the equations. To solve the model requires the use of a technique capable of solving simultaneous equations. Most of the more sophisticated planning and control modeling software packages have the capabilities for solving simultaneous systems of equations. Even some of the newer versions of the more comprehensive spreadsheet packages for microcomputers have this capability. Some can solve linear as well as nonlinear simultaneous equations.

In some modeling situations the user must sometimes be able to determine whether a variable has dropped below some predetermined minimum level or to select the maximum or minimum values. An example would be to determine whether a cash balance or an inventory level has dropped to a previously established critical level. *Logical* commands such as an IF, GOTO, MAX or MIN statements can be used to design logical expressions and submodels within the overall model.

Obviously some of the variables in the real world are probabilistic in nature and should be treated as such in the modeling process. *Risk analysis* is the formal process used in modeling to handle such situations. Risk analysis is also useful in testing the sensitivity of the model to random variations, developing confidence intervals, and testing hypotheses. Probabilistic models can be very useful in decision support systems in dealing with uncertainty.

In the Lin and Watkins[3] study of the use of mathematical models in the 1,000 largest firms, widespread use of *optimization (mathematical) models* was found. An optimization model is designed to find the best solution given some optimization criteria such as the maximization of contribution to profit. This is a major change from earlier studies which found limited use. A sample of those commonly employed throughout the organization are shown in Figure 17-5. As before, it is probably true that most of these were used in the divisional level due to the information demands and structure of the models. For example, virtually every major oil refinery in the world uses optimization techniques to schedule its operations. And, every major airline in the world uses optimization methods for route design and scheduling. All of these optimization models have the ability to consider marketing, production and financial constraints. This feature is one of the most valuable aspects of these models because most business activity is constrained in some way. Optimization models are, thus, widely used for small segments of the organization.

The disadvantage with using optimization techniques to develop optimal plans for a corporation as a whole is that the size of the problem can be enormous and the corporation as a whole may have multiple objectives (criteria). If a company is to be successful, it must deal with a whole host of objectives such as profits, return on investment, market share, sales growth, and cash flow, as well as all the line items of the income statement and balance sheet. To develop a model that incorporates all these and other objectives requires a lot of assumptions about conditions and interrelationships. Even if the model can be developed, the problem of multiple objectives must be addressed. Goal programming, utility theory, and multiobjective linear programming[4] are three optimization techniques that can be used to aid in examining multiple objectives. Most of these can only be used for smaller problems such as those noted in Figure 17-5.

The ability to generate short-term *forecasts* for variables that appear to have reasonably stable relationships with respect to time is useful in planning and modeling systems. Such techniques can be used for marketing planning models, financial forecasting, and determining trends in variable performance. A variety of forecasting methods exist, although all are not available in every software modeling package. The most basic forecasting models are simple linear, quadratic, exponential, or logarithmic trends. For the user who wishes to employ a weighted forecasting method, exponential smoothing is available. This method employs a set of weighting schemes that assign the greatest weight to the most recent historical observation. Adaptive forecasting models provide methods

---

[3] W. Thomas Lin and Paul R. Watkins, *The Use of Mathematical Models* (Montvale, N.J.: The National Association of Accountants, 1986).

[4] Corporate models may also contain non-linear equations or constraints. Typically nonlinear mathematical-programming techniques are required in solving these models. This material is beyond the scope of this chapter; only structural equations will be examined.

Revenue Forecasting
Regression analysis
Internally developed models
Quarterly forecasting
Financial statement projections
Microcomputer financial models
Simulation
Computer time-sharing models
Asset-liability software packages
Correlation
Probability theory
Time-series models
Computer-based financial planning models
Linear and goal programming
Leading indicator models
Vepco base revenue model
Virginia economic model
Vepco energy sales model
Econometric models
Discounted cash flow model
Manual projections
Heuristic interactive financial model
Engineering models
Mathematical extrapolation
Consensus analysis
Revenue deterministic models
Bottom-up forecasting model
Product mix models
Experience curve analysis
Integer programming
Breakeven analysis
PERT/CPM models
In-house custom models
Microcomputer spreadsheet analysis
Judgmental

Cost Estimation
Regression
PERT
Time series
Time and motion studies
In-house models
Simulation
Historical trend analysis
Indexing
Linear programming
Ratio analysis

Contract planning model
Breakeven analysis
Discounted cash flow
Product movement modeling
Correlation analysis
Engineered models
Life cycle costing model
Experience curves
Econometric modeling
Manual, judgmental models
Actuarial rate-making models
Probability theory
Microcomputer spreadsheet analysis
EOQ inventory models
Cost/price projection models
Integer programming
Goal programming
Production costing models

Production Planning and Product-Mix Decisions
Linear programming
MRP
Simulation
Economic lot scheduling
Correlation
Probabilistic modeling
EOQ modeling
Goal programming
Breakeven analysis
PERT/CPM
Forecasting algorithms
Judgmental
DCF
Box-Jenkins modeling
Business unit planning models
Integer programming
Deterministic what-if models
Product line planning model

Budgeting and Financial Planning
Regression analysis
Simulation
DCF
Linear programming
Goal programming
Integer programming
Time series
Financial planning models

Simulation
In-house modeling software
Manual procedures
Experience curve analysis
Econometric models
Breakeven models
Correlation analysis
Microcomputer spreadsheet analysis
Probability theory
Dynamic forecasting
Heuristic interactive financial
Asset-liability management models
Budget planning models
Corporate financial models
Business planning model
PERT
Judgmental

Evaluation of Policy Alternatives
Multiple criteria decision making
Breakeven analysis
DCF
Regression analysis
Correlation analysis
Time series
Simulation
Manual methods
Factor analysis
Multivariate scaling
Input- output analysis
Linear programming
Goal programming
Corporate financial models
In-house proprietary models
Financial planning model
Heuristic interactive financial modeling
Probability analysis
Capital planning model
Asset liability model
Profit planning model
Scenario analysis
Ratio analysis
Conjoint analysis
Judgmental models
Decision tree analysis

Merger and Acquisition
In-house proprietary
DCF

Simulation
Financial planning models
Probability theory
Business and capital evaluation models
Breakeven analysis
Regression and correlation
Deterministic financial models
Portfolio analysis
Judgmental
Operations network models
Actuarial valuation models
Microcomputer spreadsheet models
Goal programming
PERT
Financial forecasting models
Dilution analysis
Ratio analysis
ROI analysis
Merger and acquisition modeling
Sampling
Linear programming
Capital structure analysis

Inventory Planning and Control
ELQ
MRP
Simulation
EOQ
Linear programming
Integer programming
Goal programming
PERT/CPM models
In-house proprietary
Production information system
Queuing
Optimum cost models
Manual analysis
Probability theory
Qualitative forecasting methods
Time phase planning models
Economic lot scheduling
Microcomputer spreadsheet analysis
Time series
Financial planning models
Regression analysis
Heuristic interactive financial
Heuristic programming
Automated inventory control system
Input-output analysis
DCF
Breakeven analysis

FIGURE 17-5 Typical applications supported by mathematical and mathematical related models/procedures.
Source: W. Thomas Lin and Paul R. Watkins, *The Use of Mathematical Models* (Montvale, N.J.: The National Association of Accountants, 1986), pp. 33–37.

whereby the models themselves have the ability to "self-correct" if the forecast is not tracking the actual occurrences.

The majority of corporate modeling systems employ sequential models or require simultaneous equation solution techniques. In-depth modeling capabilities, however, are available only through *econometric modeling*. Pricing, advertising, and competitive strategies can be evaluated via such techniques; and a better understanding of the market behavior of specific products or groups of products can be obtained by employing such models.

Econometric modeling, however, is much more detailed, complex, and time consuming than most other modeling tools. The methodology for the process involves a four-step framework: (1) model specification; (2) parameter specification; (3) validation; and (4) simulation. Data for building such models are vast and are likely to be in the form of a market or economic database. Fortunately many of the existing corporate modeling software packages are flexible enough to support the steps necessary to link together the required databases. Thus it is possible for a user to move in a step-by-step fashion to design, test, and implement a model, all within the corporate modeling system. Some systems even contain commands that enable the user to save the structural specifications and parameter estimates of submodels. With this feature, it is much easier to integrate marketing, production, and financial submodels.

General models employing many of the features just discussed have been developed for widespread use. On the other hand, many organizations must develop their own specific models. In these later cases, the use of software with a modeling language is helpful in the development of these specialized applications. Such languages generally require interactive hardware and a database system with a good query language. Sometimes these are part of the modeling software.

Many general modeling software packages that support corporate planning and modeling systems are now available in the market. Because so many packages are available, one needs to be cautious in selecting software and make certain that the software will indeed support the modeling effort. Two key factors that should be considered in evaluating modeling software are whether it supports a modular design structure and whether it is adaptive. A corporate model is often likely to be a large model. To facilitate the control and debugging of such a model, a structured and modular program design is needed. The same is true of the modeling software. In addition, it is unlikely that a firm's internal structure and its external environment and market will remain fixed for very long. Thus a corporate model must be adaptive in the sense that it can track and represent such changes. This, together with the fact that a decentralized organization may want to build corporate models for different subunits, means that the modeling software package must be very flexible.

Adaptability and modularity are the key factors that should be considered in examining modeling support software; however, these are by no means the only factors. Other key factors that must be considered in the selection of a corporate model include: availability of macros, databases, ease of use, graphics capabilities, statistical subroutines, report generators, query capabilities, cost, and hardware requirements.

Equations

Regardless of the type of model developed, most will be made up of structural equations that represent various activities and relationships in an organization. We can classify the structural equations into the following four categories: (1) economic and behavior relationships; (2) identities or definitions; (3) technological and institutional relationships; and (4) equilibrium conditions and constraints.

Economic and behavior relations are used to express hypotheses about the economic behavior of the entity (firm) being modeled or its environment. Equations that contain decision variables or random variables can be classified as behavioral equations. An example of a behavioral equation is a demand function (equation). It expresses a relationship about the reaction of a market (demand) to a firm's price decisions.

Identities, or definitional equations are used to define a variable such as CASH. They are usually employed in the financial portions of a corporate model. For example, an identity would be used to equate total assets and total liabilities in a balance sheet. Following are two simple examples of identities:

$$\text{NET INCOME}_t = \text{SALES}_t - \text{COSTS}_t$$
and
$$\text{CASH}_t = \text{CASH}_{t-1} + \text{CASH INCREASE}_t - \text{CASH DECREASE}_t$$

Technological equations are used to describe various activities. Various production factors are combined in the production process to provide a given quantity of finished product or service. For example, it takes 3 direct labor hours and 4 pounds of material to manufacture a part. It is assumed that the combination is accomplished in such a way that some objective of either optimization or satisfaction is attained.

Institutional relations, like technological equations, relate internal (endogenous) and external (exogenous) variables of a model. They describe the relationships between model variables and a firm's environment. Expressions that describe taxes or insurance that a company must pay are institutional variables.

Equilibrium conditions relate endogenous variables at any point in time to other endogenous or exogenous variables. A typical short-term equilibrium condition would be the following:

$$I_t = \Sigma S_t / 12$$

where

I_t = inventory at time t

S_t = sales for month t

This equation states that at time t (yearly), the firm adjusts its inventory level I_t so that it is equal to average monthly sales (total sales divided by twelve—$\Sigma S_t/12$).

Constraints correspond to short- or medium-range equilibrium conditions. However, they differ from general equilibrium conditions in that they are expressed as inequalities. They restrict the values of the endogenous variables in a solution only when the strict equality in an inequality is approached. For example, sales of product X will be greater than 1,000 because there is a contract to sell at least 1000 X to the state. This is expressed as SALES $X_t \geq 1,000$. In summary, most planning and control, as well as many decision support systems, will include many of these equations.

Control Structure

The control structure is an integral part of the planning and control and it generally involves feedback on the results of the planning process. This feedback is an important part of the decision-making process and often entails financial information such as variances from plans and, at the operational level in the organization, variances from standards. The planning and control system must be designed to accommodate this feedback information. Much of this is related to cost accounting information and other performance indicators, as was indicated in Figure 17-4. The planning aspects, however, are considered to be an important component of control because they specify the direction of the organization and provide essential information for the coordination of subunits within the organization.

In summary, DSS models are used extensively in budgeting, cash flow analysis, investment decisions, merger and acquisition analysis, financial planning, tax planning, forecasting, and corporate planning. Auditing firms even use DSS extensively in analytical review and audit planning.

BUDGET PROCESS

The most widely used planning and control system is the budget process. Several illustrations are presented in sections which follow. The budget process is illustrated in Figure 17-6. Briefly, the budget is the overall plan expressed in financial terms. It is comprehensive and consists of many supporting schedules as will be outlined later in the example shown in the appendix and in the spreadsheet application which follows. Often there are supporting schedules for several operating units or divisions in the organization. The *profit plan* is that part of the master budget which details the operating plan and supporting schedules for generating revenue and expenses associated with this process. Often this plan is detailed by areas of responsibility such as divisions or products using responsibility accounting systems such as those described earlier in this text. The *cash budget* is that part of the master budget which details the cash receipts and disbursements pertaining to the overall plan and details of the financial requirements associated with the master budget. Finally the master budget includes *financial statement forecasts* for the organization.

In general the following steps, shown in Figure 17-6, are followed in the preparation of the master budget:

1. Forecast sales.
2. Develop a production plan and inventory plan to meet the sales forecast.
3. Develop a manufacturing plan for materials, labor, and factory overhead.

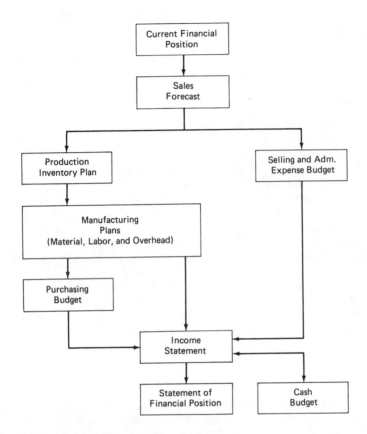

FIGURE 17-6 The budget process.

4. Develop a purchasing budget for components.
5. Develop a selling and administrative expense budget.
6. Develop an income statement.
7. Develop a cash flow budget for financing requirements.
8. Develop statement of financial position for the end of the period.

SPREADSHEETS

Spreadsheets can be used effectively for planning and control activities such as budgeting and analysis of feedback information. The illustration presented in the appendix shows a spreadsheet that uses a sales forecast based on regression analysis, develops a production plan from this forecast and product specifications and costs, generates a purchasing plan, estimates cash collections, and formulates a financial plan for the organization. Moreover, a set of forecasted financial statements are generated from the results.

As an illustration, a cash collection plan is prepared using the following set of assumptions:

1. A sales forecast is provided by the marketing department and is expressed in another part of the spreadsheet.
2. The historical cash collection pattern has been that 30% of current sales are collected during the current period, 50% of the current period's sales are collected in the next period, and 20% of the sales are collected after two periods. This means that:

$C_t = .2S_{t-2} + .5S_{t-1} + .3S_t$; where C and S are collections and sales respectively and t refers to the current month.

In the example shown in Figure 17-7a, March collections are:

.2 * \$12,000 + .5 * \$12,000 + .3 * \$6,000 = \$10,200; where \$12,000, \$12,000 and \$6,000 are sales forecasts for January, February, and March respectively.

This formula is couched in terms of the spreadsheet locations of the variables. For example, as can be seen from Figure 17-7b, which shows the spreadsheet equations, total collections for March are expressed as: @SUM(E318...E322) which means the summation of all the collections from past periods sales from line 318 through line 322 in column E of the spreadsheet. Some of the lines are zero, meaning that according to past patterns no collections were received from those periods. For March's collections, column E, the portion of sales collected from February sales is shown by the equation in cell 321 which is: +\$A\$328*\$B\$321 which means that the absolute value (denoted by the spreadsheet software with a \$ sign) in cell B321 is multiplied by the absolute value in cell A328; in other words February sales of \$12,000 are multiplied by .5 or 50% to obtain a value shown in Figure 17-7 of \$6,000.

Another example of the construction of a spreadsheet is shown in Figure 17-8a/b for inventory and production requirements. Here production:

$$P_t = (S_t + .5S_{t+1})\text{-}EI_{t-1}$$

which means that the organization has a production policy that production must equal sales for the period plus a target ending inventory for the period less beginning inventory. In terms of the model, ending inventory must be equal to 50% of next periods sales, hence ending inventory must equal $.5S_{t+1}$ and beginning inventory must equal ending inventory from the previous period or EI_{t-1}. In terms of the spreadsheet software, shown in Figure 17-8b, this is expressed in terms of the cells which contain the values above. Thus, production for February in cell:

MONTH	SALES	JANUARY	COLLECTIONS FEBRUARY	MARCH	A/R
Oct	$24,600				
Nov	23,400	$4,680	$0	$0	
Dec	16,200	8,100	3,240	0	$16,020
Jan	12,000	3,600	6,000	2,400	11,640
Feb	12,000	0	3,600	6,000	10,800
March	6,000	0	0	1,800	6,600
Total		$16,380	$12,840	$10,200	

Collection Pattern:
   30.0% in Month of Sale
   50.0% in Month after Sale
   20.0% Two Months after Sale

FIGURE 17-7a   Arctic Air Products cash collection budget first quarter 19X7 (000).

A	B	C	D	E	F
MONTH	SALES	JANUARY	COLLECTIONS FEBRUARY	MARCH	A/R
317 Oct	24600				
318 Nov	23400	+$A$329*$B318	0	0	
319 Dec	16200	+$A$328*$B319	+$A$329*$B319	0	+C318+C319+D319
320 Jan	+F105	+$A$327*$B320	+$A$328*$B320	+$A$329*$B320	+D319+D320+E320
321 Feb	+F106 -	0	+$A$327*$B321	+$A$328*$B321	+E320+B321−D321
322 Mar	+F107 -	0	0	+$A$327*$B322	+B322−E322+B321−D321 −E321
323					
324 Total		@SUM (C318..C322)	@SUM (D318..D322)	@SUM (E318..E322)	
325					

326 Collection Pattern:
327   0.3 in Month of Sale
328   0.5 in Month after Sale
329   0.2 Two Months after Sale

FIGURE 17-7b   Arctic Air Products cash collection budget first quarter 19X7 (000).

	DECEMBER	JANUARY	FEBRUARY	MARCH	APRIL	MAY
Sales in Thousands	27	20	20	10	16	24
Ending Inventory *	10	10	5	8	12	
Finished Goods Required	37	30	25	18	28	
Beginning Inventory	13	10	10	5	8	
Production Requirements	24	20	15	13	20	

*Policy: 50 Percent of Next Periods Sales

FIGURE 17-8a   Spreadsheet example for inventory and production for Arctic Air Products.

		D	E	F	G	H	I
		DECEMBER	JANUARY	FEBRUARY	MARCH	APRIL	MAY
134	Sales in Thousands	27	+D105	+D106	+D107	+D108	+D109
135	Ending Inventory *	10	0.5*F134	0.5*G134	0.5*H134	0.5*I134	
136	Finished Goods	37	@SUM(E134+E135)	@SUM(F134+F135)	@SUM(G134+G135)	@SUM(H134+H135)	
137	Beginning Inventory	13	+D135	+E135	+F135	+G135	
138	Production Requirements	24	+E136−E137	+F136−F137	+G136−G137	+H136−H137	

*Policy: 50 Percent of Next Periods Sales

FIGURE 17-8b Spreadsheet software for Arctic Air Products.

$F138 = F136\text{-}F137$ = finished goods required less beginning inventory where F137 is defined as E135 or ending inventory from January, and F136 is defined by the spreadsheet as @SUM(F134+F135) or sales + desired ending inventory. Moreover, F134 is defined as D106 which is sales in units from another part of the spreadsheet and F135 is defined as .5* G134 which is 50% of March's sales shown in cell G134.

These are two illustrations of how a spreadsheet is constructed from the known relationships in a financial planning model. In this fashion, an entire budget can be developed as illustrated in the appendix. These are only two schedules from that budget. Although the notation is tedious, the spreadsheet software makes it easy to express these relationships through simple pointing and clicking or movement of the cursor to the cells that belong in the equations. Moreover, once a relationship is established for one period, it can be copied with ease to other like periods. As a result, spreadsheets can easily be constructed for planning and control purposes.

Once constructed, spreadsheet models can be used for many planning and control activities. They can be used to create a financial plan as illustrated in the appendix. They can be used to ask "what if" questions about various management options. For example, an assessment of new collection policies can be explored by simply changing the collection pattern or the impact on the financial statements of different sales projections based on a different pricing policies. Moreover, sensitivity analysis can be performed on the different variables and most software will enable management to view the impact of variations in variables on key output values such as net income or cash flow. In addition, management can try out various policies and assess their impact on the bottom line. For example, what would be the impact of a level production plan? This would require redoing the logic of the production plan shown in Figure 17-8a and b. This is easy to do using the facilities available to users of spreadsheets.

Once spreadsheets are developed, they may be operated with macros. Macros define a series of input and operating steps so that users can use the spreadsheet easily. They enable the user to extract data for use from databases, run the spreadsheet, and print the results without ever knowing the details about how it works. In fact, the actual model (sets of relationships or equations) can be locked so that users cannot alter the relationships among the variables. The use of macros and the locking feature offers a good set of controls over spreadsheet use.

The previous example can be combined with a database that incorporates a variety of statistics on market conditions, customers and their preferences, products and their characteristics, costs and supplier information, as well as feedback information on past performances to provide a rich set of information upon which to plan. This can be done using an integrated software package which enables users to integrate database information with spreadsheet analysis or a financial planning model.

In addition, a variety of graphic output can be used with most integrated software to enable managers to better communicate their plans and the results of their actions for future planning cycles. Further, the results can even be integrated into reports which focus on the issues using tables (spreadsheets), graphs, and word processing software for effective presentation. Finally, some of the more sophisticated integrated software enables users to communicate results and download data over telephone lines and FAX modems.

In general, integrated software enables managers to effectively support a wide variety of planning and control needs.

SIMULATION

In many decision support and budgeting situations, simulation analysis can be used effectively. Simulation enables a manager to model a real-world system and change the model to represent different conditions. He or she can then gain some insight as to how the real-world system might behave under these conditions. This way a manager can try out different alternative strategies and assess their outcomes without actually implementing the alternative strategies. Many simulation models may use a "what if" approach such as that illustrated using a spreadsheet or they may use a probabilistic (Monte Carlo) approach. Using this probabilistic technique, a manager, can use estimates of the expected values and estimated variances of sales, prices, and various cost items to construct an expected plan. He or she can also obtain a probability distribution of profit or other output variables of interest to management. Input probability distributions can be easily determined by simply asking managers their expected sales and costs along with their assessment of the chances that these will exceed or be less than certain amounts. Today this assessment can often be generated using graphic input. Such an assessment can be used to construct a cumulative frequency distribution or to construct a probability distribution if the sales or costs, for example, behave like a normal distribution. Random observations can be drawn from these cumulative distributions which may or may not be normal distributions. These can, for example, be used to determine what profit would be for that random observation. Several hundred such random observations are calculated in this manner and the result will be a probability distribution of profit. Management can then assess the probability of achieving certain profit levels, such as the probability of breaking even. In a sense Monte Carlo simulation analysis is like asking "what if" for several hundred situations all drawn from an estimated probability distribution(s) of input variables such as sales and costs. This type of analysis can only be done effectively on the computer because of the number of situations considered.

As can be seen from Figure 17-5, simulation is used on a widespread basis in industry to assess a number of important decisions. Monte Carlo simulation analysis can be used with the interactive financial planning system (IFPS) described in the next section.

FINANCIAL PLANNING SYSTEM

Financial planning languages constitute a large and widely used class of decision support systems. They were developed in the 1970s to enable managers to interact with financial models and data which was stored in the computer. These are end-user systems in that the need for an intermediary is not required, although they are sometimes used.

There are several of these and IFPS (interactive financial planning system) discussed here[5] is one of the more popular. It has been ported over to microcomputers from the mainframe for which it was developed. IFPS is interactive. It is designed to support the construction of ad hoc planning and budgeting models. In a record and table line-oriented fashion, it is used primarily to support the formulation, evaluation, and solution of financial identities and statements.

It is written in English for ease of use by a variety of end users. It has the potential to do "what if" analysis. It can provide sensitivity analysis and even deal with uncertainties via deterministic analysis of the best and worst case scenarios. It can also simulate a business environment. Moreover, it has the capability to set forth courses of action to achieve specified goals.

It is a column-oriented language. Each column represents a time period and it is thus well suited for financial planning. The language is nonprocedural, which means the user need not pay careful attention to the sequence in which the program is written. The language is definitional and only requires that each variable be defined at some place in the program. This makes it easy to use for the novice end user.

IFPS incorporates five subsystems: (1) executive; (2) modeling language; (3) report generator; (4) data file; and (5) command file.

The executive subsystem is used to call the other subsystems by EXECUTIVE commands. It contains commands to specify data files, to list, delete, copy, and combine, as well as consolidate IFPS models and reports. The latter two commands are sufficiently flexible to allow decision tree calculations and hierarchical modeling.

The modeling language is used to create, edit, solve, and print the results from IFPS models. Models consist of definitional statements in the IFPS language. They are written, processed, and stored in a similar fashion.

[5] The source of much of this discussion is from Paul Gray, *Student Guide to IFPS* (New York: McGraw-Hill, 1983); See also, Paul Gray, "Using the Interactive Financial Planning System (IFPS) for Stochastic Simulation," *SIMULATION*, December 1984, pp 286–292; and EXECUCOM, "Interactive Financial Planning System User's Manual" (Austin, Tex., EXECUCOM Systems Corporation, 1976).

The language possesses a number of built-in functions and subroutines to perform frequently encountered modeling tasks. Examples are commands to perform totalling; built-in functions, financial calculations, and random number generators for risk analysis; and subroutines to calculate depreciation schedules. The analyst may call on user-written FORTRAN functions and subroutines from an IFPS program.

The language subsystem incorporates commands to experiment with a model. The modeling steps of equation specification and solution are separated. The latter can be implemented by a SOLVE command. IFPS incorporates algorithms to handle the sequencing of sequential equations, an iterative process to handle the solution of simultaneous linear equations, a simulation process, and a procedure to determine goal-oriented solutions. There are several built-in statistical (uniform, triangular, normal, and user-designed cumulative distributions) and financial functions which make it easy to use. Several "what if" investigations of a model can be formulated by using a specific "what if" command and statements of the language.

The IFPS report generator subsystem incorporates commands to specify, format, and print customized reports that cannot be written using statements of the modeling language subsystems.

The data file subsystem allows the creation, updating, deleting, and editing of permanent IFPS data files. The subsystem contains commands that permit the storage of alternative model solutions.

The command file subsystem operates with permanent files on which IFPS commands and directives can be stored. The execution of the stored commands can be initiated by other IFPS commands, thus reducing the effort needed to specify operations that use many commands.

In summary, IFPS is an easy to use nonprocedural modeling language. It has many features designed to support financial planning. These include the ability to write code in plain English; to solve equations; to handle uncertainty via high low (best and worst case) scenarios and via simulation analysis; to use subroutines written in other formats; to determine a course of action to achieve a goal; to generate a wide variety of reports including frequency distributions of simulated results; and to use a database. Moreover, any of the parameters can easily be changed to ask "what if" questions. IFPS is a very powerful decision support system. It can provide management with a potent planning and analysis tool that can be used very effectively to support managerial decisions.

ARTIFICIAL INTELLIGENCE AND EXPERT SYSTEMS

Artificial intelligence (AI) is the mimicking of intelligent human behavior by a computer. AI takes a knowledge base and acts on this base according to a set of heuristics (decision rules) which search for a satisfactory solution to a problem. The most common manifestation of AI in business is in the form of an *expert system* (ES). In an expert system the knowledge base is founded upon the knowledge of experts in the specific area (called a domain). In other words, they are designed for specific problems.

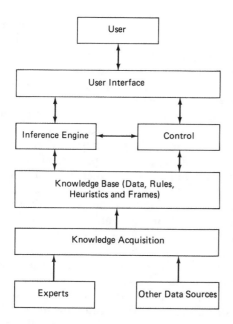

FIGURE 17-9 Components of an expert system.

The components of an expert system are shown in Figure 17-9. The knowledge base is at the heart of the system. It consists of facts about a specific decision environment such as accounting. Accounting principles, tax regulations, organization policies, production standards, and economic information are examples of the type of information one might find in the database supporting the knowledge base.

The other component of the knowledge base is the set of rules (heuristics) or frames used by experts to operate on this data. Heuristics are the set of search processes used by experts to search for a satisfactory solution in this particular problem environment. For example, the decision rules used by auditors to assess internal control reliability is based on sampling data and past experience with the client's system. Rules are structured in an "if . . . then . . ." format. For example, in the evaluation of internal control systems:

If:
Internal control software is sufficient, and
Compliance with internal control procedures is sufficient, and
Backup and recovery procedures are adequate, and
The audit trail is sufficient and
Then:
There is strong evidence that data loss controls are sufficient.

Frames are similar to a set of rules except they use a network structure to specify the relationships between and among the data elements or attributes of a specific problem—that is, they are more complex than simple "if . . . then . . ." relations.

In addition to these heuristics, mathematical and statistical functions are also used to express functional relationships such as accounting procedures or probability distributions used to express uncertainty.

The acquisition of a knowledge base is time consuming and difficult. A great deal of data can be obtained from the organization's own database. More facts and rules can be obtained from various written sources from the AICPA, SEC, FASB, and IRS, for example. Rules and frames can be inferred by observing the actions of experts and many of the rules can be based on optimization techniques and statistical procedures such as linear programming, matrix algebra, and regression analysis. To understand the cognitive process of how a decision maker thinks when searching for a solution to a problem or when diagnosing a situation, *protocol analysis* is often used. Experts describe their decision process as they make decisions; the verbalization of the process is recorded and coded into a decision rule such as an "if . . . then . . ." statement.

The next major component is the inference engine. This is part of the software and there are many such products on the market. The inference engine evaluates the heuristics and ties them together in a path that leads to a recommendation. In most cases this path can be traced so that the user can follow the logic of the inference engine. These inference procedures can be either forward-chaining, which is the appropriate strategy for poorly defined problems with no well-defined goal; or they can be backward-chaining for problems with well-defined goals.

Forward chaining is data driven. The facts and rules in the knowledge base are considered. These permit subgoals to be satisfied. Upon satisfaction of these an overall conclusion can be reached. For example, given a certain set of financial characteristics, a conclusion can be drawn about the viability of a new venture.

Backward chaining starts with the goal, such as a target sales volume, outlines subgoals needed to achieve this goal, and ultimately defines the actions and data values needed to achieve the ultimate objective.

Both processes are complex. As a result a development system called a shell is used to control the process of using the expert system from the user's perspective. This enables users to devote their time and effort to the acquisition of knowledge and the use of the expert system and not to its programming.

The use of expert systems has particular potential in a decision support framework where: (1) tasks can be decomposed into separate segments; (2) knowledge can be expressed in terms of rules and heuristics; and (3) expertise is scarce and expensive. Many management accounting situations and many auditing problems possess these characteristics. As a result there has been a considerable amount of interest in expert systems by the accounting profession. Computers cannot reason by analogy and are limited in the extent that they can detect complex patterns. Moreover, computers are limited in the extent they can learn. However, they can apply a set rules consistently and recognize simple relationships with great accuracy. As a result, expert systems have a valuable place in organizations in a diagnostic capacity, in training, in system evaluation, in planning and control activities, and in assisting in management decision making. Figures 17-10 and 17-11 illustrate some of the various prototype systems under development and in use in accounting. Many of these and similar systems will

SYSTEM NAME	FUNCTION	SUBJECT	LANGUAGE/SHELL	TYPE
AUDITOR— Dungan (1983)	Audit	Auditing allow- ance for bad debts	AL/X	ES
EDP AUDITOR— Hansen and Messier (1985a, 1985b)	EDP audit	Auditing advanced EDP systems	AL/X	ES
AGGREGATE— Munakata and O'Leary (1985)	Accounting information systems	System design of aggregated financial state- ments	Prolog	ES
ICE— Kelly (1984)	Audit	Audit planning process	INTERLISP	ES
TICOM— Bailey et al. (1985)	Audit	Internal control evaluation	PASCAL	AI*
TAXMAN— McCarty (1977)	Tax planning	Corporate reorganizations	MicroPLANNER /LISP	AI**
TAX ADVISOR— Michaelsen (1982a, 1982b)	Tax planning	Estate tax planning	EMYCIN	ES

*They suggest an interface with an ES.
**TAXMAN II is being developed (Miller 1984).

FIGURE 17-10 A summary of AI/ES prototype systems in accounting.
Source: Daniel E. O'Leary, "The Use of Artificial Intelligence in Accounting", *Expert Systems in Business,* Barry G. Silverman, ed., p. 89. Copyright © 1987, Addison Wesley: Reading, Mass., Reprinted with permission.

become operational in the near future.

There are many limitations to expert systems which have slowed their widespread use. These include:

1. Economic effort to build the system for a specific type of problem. This is compounded by the fact that accounting rules change so often it is difficult to keep the system current;

2. Large size of knowledge base;

3. User's and expert's use of natural languages and computer's use of programming languages this is compounded by the fact that the trace of the decision is often not a satisfactory explanation of the decision process;

4. Availability of experts to develop the knowledge base;

5. Lack of general knowledge to fall back on when specific knowledge is not sufficient; and

6. Ill-defined learning process.[6]

APPLICATION	DESCRIPTION
ANALYTIC REVIEW— Braun (1983)	A problem of concern to the external auditor/CPA. Emulates auditor decision used in determining the relative importance of analytic review information compared to other audit evidence.
PRICE ANALYSIS— Ramakrishna, et al. (1983) and Dillard, Ramakrishna, and Chandrasekaran (1983)	Primarily a concern of the internal auditor. The system would analyze prices for fairness and reasonableness. Developed for the U.S. government. A design only.
ACCOUNTANT'S OPINION FORMULATION— Dillard and Mutchler (1984)	A problem of concern to the external auditor/CPA. Reviews the question of how auditors form an opinion of the financial statements. Addresses the issue of going concern. A design only.
INTERNAL CONTROLS— Meservy (1984)	Designed to help auditors evaluate the quality of the internal control systems.
GOING CONCERN— Biggs (1985)	Addresses the issue of going concern judgment.
CAPITAL BUDGETING— Reitman (1985)	Designed for use by corporate management in the analysis of capital budgeting problems. Currently developing a prototype system in LISP.

FIGURE 17-11   A summary of reported AI/ES conceptual designs in accounting.
Source: Daniel E. O'Leary, "The Use of Artificial Intelligence in Accounting", *Expert System in Business,* Barry G. Silverman, ed., p. 90. Copyright © 1987, Addison Wesley: Reading, Mass. Reprinted with permission.

SUMMARY

In summary, decision support systems are designed to support management decision making when some part of the decision process is unstructured or the data may be uncertain. Many organizations have built DSS models of their organization to assist managers in making these decisions. A decision support system consists of a user interface that must be easy to use, a data base which usually includes external and forecast information, and a model base which contains the DSS model. Many corporate planning models including budget models are classified as DSS systems. These models may deal with a small portion of the business enterprise or they may include all the operations of the organization. They

[6] Daniel E. O'Leary, "The Use of Artificial Intelligence in Accounting" in, *Expert Systems in Business,* ed. Barry G. Silverman, (Reading, Mass.: Addison Wesley, 1987), pp. 93–94.

may be simple spreadsheets that will run on microcomputers or they may be very large complex mathematical programming models of the entire organization that need a large mainframe computer to run. Some may even enable managers to simulate various scenarios to evaluate their impact on their organization before they actually implement one of the courses of action. Some organizations have even begun to incorporate expert judgment into the modeling systems; these are called expert systems.

In general a great deal has been done to move information systems support to a higher level in the decision making process. In other words, systems can be devised to help management analyze complex interactions among marketing, production and financial variables; consider numerous constraints; and suggest courses of action based on some predetermined objective.

APPENDIX

MASTER BUDGET PREPARATION—ILLUSTRATION

To illustrate the preparation process for the master budget and its associated profit plan, consider Arctic Air Products (AAP). The budget is prepared using a popular spreadsheet program. All the schedules can be accessed via the main menu which is simply part of the spreadsheet.

This company assembles and sells air conditioning units to home building contractors. Its sales are seasonal and are very sensitive to financial and economic conditions such as interest rates. AAP does not manufacture any of its component parts. It purchases these components and assembles them into air conditioning units. AAP uses a standard cost system. For illustrative purposes we will assume that they manufacture only one product.

Current Financial Position

AAP's current financial position is presented in Schedule A-1. This statement describes the resources such as cash, receivables, inventory, and other assets available to AAP at the beginning of the period. It also details the financial obligations of the company as it begins a new year. Finished goods inventory and raw material inventory are shown at standard cost. Due to the nature of the assembly process, work in process inventory is insignificant.

Sales Forecast

The development of a sound sales forecast is the first step in the preparation of the master budget. This is a difficult task for AAP due to changing economic conditions. Sales are seasonal and the number of units sold can differ considerably with the strength of the housing market. For example, in 19X6 the economy was depressed and the overall market declined. Since most of the units are sold to contractors and published statistics are available for housing starts, it makes

Current Assets			
Cash		$ 5,000	
Accounts Receivable		16,020	
Inventory			
Raw Material (SCHEDULE A-6)	$ 525		
Finished Goods	3,100	3,625	$24,645
Fixed Assets			
Cost		10,000	
Acc Depreciation		(2,000)	8,000
Total Assets			32,645
Equities			
Accounts Payable (SCHEDULE A-6)			2,415
Taxes Payable			1,500
Loan Payable			8,000
Paid-in Capital in Excess of Par			10,000
Retained Earnings			10,730
Total Equities			$32,645

SCHEDULE A-1   Arctic Air Products statement of financial position December 31, 19X6 (000).

sense to explore the association between AAP's sales and this economic indicator. If housing starts are treated as a leading indicator with air conditioning sales lagging housing starts by three months, a strong linear relationship results. Thus, a simple regression analysis is used to determine the relationship between housing starts and units sold. The result is that the sales forecast for the month t was determined to be:

$$Y_t = a + b \times_{t-3} = .13 + .20 \times_{t-3}$$

or approximately 20 percent of the number of housing starts three months earlier (plus a small constant of .13). Using this set of equations and rounding to the nearest thousand, sales are forecast and shown in Schedule A-2 for the next year based on actual housing starts for the fourth quarter of 19X6 and the forecast of housing starts for 19X7.

Production Plan

AAP must next develop a production plan based on the sales forecast. This plan is based on the assumption that there must be enough finished goods in stock at the end of each month for 50 percent of the next month's sales. To determine the total requirements for the month, management must add the sales forecast to a desired ending finished goods inventory to calculate the total finished goods required for the period. From this, beginning inventory is subtracted to determine production requirements. The production plan is shown in Schedule A-3 (Figure 17-8a illustrated earlier in the chapter). It should be noted that the sales forecast for April is necessary for March's production plan.

Manufacturing Plan

Once AAP decides to manufacture the units noted in Schedule A-3, it must de-

	HOUSING STARTS FORECAST	UNITS	SALES* FORECAST DOLLARS
January	80	20	$ 12,000
February	120	20	12,000
March	200	10	6,000
April	250	16	9,600
May	275	24	14,400
June	325	40	24,000
July	275	50	30,000
August	225	55	33,000
September	175	65	39,000
October	150	55	33,000
November	125	45	27,000
December	100	35	21,000
Annual Sales Forecast		435	$261,000
Normal Month Activity		36	
* Selling Price = $600			

SCHEDULE A-2   Arctic Air Products sales forecast 19X7 (000).

termine the labor, material, and overhead costs for this plan. These costs are based on standard specifications and costs outlined in Schedule A-4. These total $120 for direct labor, $105 for direct material (components), and $25 for variable overhead. The variable standard cost applied totals $250. The number of units to be produced in each month is then multiplied by these variable standards, and the results are shown in Schedule A-5. For example, in February 15,000 units are to be produced; the total variable cost will be $250 * 15,000 = $3,750,000. This is added to fixed overhead of $2,175,000 to yield an expected manufacturing cost of $5,925,000 for the month. Notice that there will be a planned volume variance each month when the level of production differs from the normal activity level for the year, which is 435,000 units per 12 months or 36,250 units per month. This is $1,275,000 because only 15,000 units are manufactured instead of the average monthly number of 36,250 units and only $60 per unit manufactured are applied.

SCHEDULE A-3   Arctic Air Products production inventory plan 19X7 (000).

	DECEMBER	JANUARY	FEBRUARY	MARCH	APRIL	MAY
Sales in Thousands	27	20	20	10	16	24
Ending Inventory *	10	10	5	8	12	
Finished Goods Required	37	30	25	18	28	
Beginning Inventory	13	10	10	5	8	
Production Requirements	24	20	15	13	20	

*Policy: 50 Percent of Next Period's Sales

DIRECT LABOR	6.00 HR/UNIT	$20.00 PER HOUR		
Direct Material		BASE COST	INFLATION ADJUSTED	
Compressor		40	40	
Coil		20	20	
Electrical Equipment		25	25	
Housing		20	20	105
Variable Manufacturing Overhead				25
Total Variable Production Copsts				$250
Annual fixed Overhad		$26,100		
Fixed OH Application Rate		60		
Total Standard Costs Applied		$ 310		

SCHEDULE A-4   Arctic Air Products manufacturing specifications.

SCHEDULE A-5   Arctic Air Products manufacturing costs first quarter 19X7 (000).

		JANUARY	FEBRUARY	MARCH
Production Requirements		20	15	13
Variable Costs				
Direct Labor	$120	$2,400	$1,800	$1,560
Direct Material	105	2,100	1,575	1,365
Overhead	25	500	375	325
Total	$250	5,000	3,750	3,250
Fixed Overhead				
(Annual Fixed Overhead/12)		2,175	2,175	2,175
Total Manufacturing Costs		$7,175	$5,925	$5,425
Fixed Overhead Analysis				
Budgeted Amount		2,175	2,175	2,175
Application	$60 Per Unit	1,200	900	780
Planned Volume Variance		$975	$1,275	$1,395
Total Applied Costs (Variable Plus Fixed)		$6,200	$4,650	$4,030

Purchasing Budget

After determining the manufacturing requirements shown in Schedules A-3 and A-5, AAP must then prepare a purchasing budget. This is necessary to coordinate purchasing activity with production and sales to assure that sufficient units

	DECEMBER	JANUARY	FEBRUARY	MARCH	APRIL
	Components Needed for Manufacturing (000)				
All Components	24.00	20.00	15.00	13.00	20.00
Ending Inventory Requirements	5.00	3.75	3.25	5.00	
Total Inventory Required	29.00	23.75	18.25	18.00	
Beginning Inventory	6.00	5.00	3.75	3.25	
Purchase Requirements	23.00	18.75	14.50	14.75	
Components	Cost of Ending Inventory (000)				
Compressor	$200	$150	$130	$200	
Coil	100	75	65	100	
Electrical Equipment	125	94	81	125	
Housing	100	75	65	100	
Totals	$525	$394	$341	$525	
Components	Purchasing Costs (000)				
Compressor	$920	$750	$580	$590	
Coil	460	375	290	295	
Electrical Equipment	575	469	363	369	
Housing	460	375	290	295	
Total Purchasing Costs	$2,415	$1,969	$1,523	$1,549	
Cash Disbursements		$2,415	$1,969	$1,523	
Accounts Payable				$1,549	

Cash Disbursements Policy: 100 Percent in Month after Purchase
Inventory Policy (All Components):   25.0% of Next Period's Production

SCHEDULE A-6   Arctic Air Products analysis of material inventory and purchase requirements (000).

are manufactured to meet sales demand. This budget is shown in Schedule A-6. Based on a company policy of having an ending inventory equal to 25 percent of the next period's manufacturing requirements to act as a buffer for delivery uncertainties, AAP first determined the manufacturing requirements. Ending buffer inventory is then added to this for each component. This sum is the total which is needed to ensure smooth production. For example, 25 percent of March's requirement of 13,000 components is 3,250 components; this must be added to the 15,000 February components to obtain a total needed for February of 18,250. From this, beginning inventory is subtracted to obtain the purchase requirements. In February this is 3,750 components; thus the purchase requirements for February are $18,250 - 3,750 = 14,500$ components. Finally these requirements are converted to dollars for financial planning by extending the component purchase requirements by their respective standard costs from Schedules A-4 and A-5. For example, in February the purchase of 14,500 components will cost $105 * 14,500 = $1,523,000$.

	JANUARY	FEBRUARY	MARCH
Sales Forecast in Units	20	20	10
Sales Forecast in Dollars	$12,000	$12,000	$6,000
Selling and Administrative Exp.			
Variable*	$ 1,200	$ 1,200	$ 600
Fixed	2,000	2,000	2,000
Total	$ 3,200	$ 3,200	$2,600

*Sales Commission   10.0% Sales Dollars

SCHEDULE A-7   Arctic Air Products selling and administrative expenses (000).

Selling and Administrative Expense Budget

All nonmanufacturing expenses are treated as period costs. AAP pays a 10 percent commission to sales personnel, and all other selling and administrative expenses are assumed to be fixed committed or fixed discretionary costs including such items as rent, utilities, salaries, and depreciation. These costs are shown in Schedule A-7.

Income Statement

After revenue and expenses have been planned and forecast, the income statement forecast can be prepared. This forecast is shown in Schedule A-8 for the first quarter of 19X7. In February the total sales dollars are expected to be $600 per unit times 20,000 units or $12,000,000. From the schedule in Schedule A-7, $310 in standard costs are applied to each unit sold; this is expected to total $6,200,000 in February. Since all the fixed costs will not be applied an adjustment is necessary to reflect the total expected fixed costs for February of $2,175,000; this volume variance adjustment is $1,275,000 as shown in Schedule A-8. The cost of goods sold is thus expected to be $7,475,000 in February. From this, selling and administrative expenses along with interest expenses are subtracted. Interest expenses are a function of the amount of money which must be borrowed to finance operations and capital acquisitions. Interest is accrued based on the ending loan balance for that particular month. Thus the cash budget must be completed prior to the completion of this Income Statement Forecast. Taxes payable are accrued and assumed to be paid on the first day of the next quarter.

At this time management can view the results of the income statement forecast for the period and make changes to the production and marketing plans to adjust net income. For example, if net income is unsatisfactory, a different marketing plan may be developed such as lowering the price and selling more units. Using spreadsheet software makes the analysis of different plans an easy task.

Cash Budget

After the production plan is determined and purchase and other disbursements (including taxes) are planned, the cash budget can be determined. This is necessary for the management of cash flow and financial planning. It may be neces-

	JANUARY	FEBRUARY	MARCH	1ST QRT.
Unit Sales	20	20	10	50
Sales Dollars (SCHEDULE A-7)	$12,000	$12,000	$6,000	$30,000
Cost of Goods Sold				
Standard Applied Costs (SCHEDULE A-4)	$ 6,200	$ 6,200	$3,100	$15,500
Volume Variance Adjustment (SCHEDULE A-5)	975	1,275	1,395	3,645
Adjusted Cost of Goods Sold	$ 7,175	$ 7,475	$4,495	$19,145
Gross Margin	$ 4,825	$ 4,525	$1,505	$10,855
Selling and Administrative Expenses (SCHEDULE A-7)	3,200	3,200	2,600	9,000
Interest Expenses	80	41	41	162
Net Income before Taxes	$ 1,545	$ 1,284	($1,136)	$ 1,693
Income Tax (Rate = 40.0%)	618	514	(454)	677
Net Income after Tax	$ 927	$ 771	($ 682)	$ 1,016

SCHEDULE A-8   Arctic air products income statement first quarter 19X7 (000).

sary to obtain short-term financing or there may be sufficient cash resources to invest some of the cash. It may also be necessary to alter some of their earlier plans to adjust for cash-flow problems at this time. The cash budget can help management make these decisions. Again, the whole process can be automated so that management can even ask "what if" questions to determine the effect of policy changes on cash flows.

To plan cash flows AAP must first determine expected cash receipts. This can be done by analyzing historical collection patterns and applying these to sales. Schedule A-9 shows the cash collection forecast for the next quarter and the resulting accounts receivable balances at the end of each month. The collection patterns are simply applied to the sales forecast; for example, collections in January would be equal to .2 November sales +.5 December sales +.3 January sales for a total of $16,380,000, and the accounts receivable balance at the end of March consists of .7 March sales +.2 February sales. This equals $6,600,000.

Next the cash budget can be prepared as illustrated in Schedule A-10. Beginning cash is obtained from the balance sheet. Cash receipts are obtained from the schedule in Schedule A-9 and added to the beginning cash balance to obtain the cash available. The total cash disbursements are obtained from the various schedules for wages, purchases, overhead (an adjustment is made to back out depreciation), other planned cash outlays such as the purchase of equipment in February, and selling and administration expenses for the period. The total disbursements are then subtracted from the cash available to determine the need to borrow or the ability to repay financial obligations while maintaining a minimum cash balance of $3,000,000 for contingencies.

All borrowing and repayment is assumed to be done in increments of $1,000,000. For example, in January Arctic Air Products can repay $6,000,000 in

		COLLECTIONS			
MONTH	SALES	JANUARY	FEBRUARY	MARCH	A/R
Oct	$24,600				
Nov	23,400	$ 4,680	$ 0	$ 0	
Dec	16,200	8,100	3,240	0	$16,020
Jan	12,000	3,600	6,000	2,400	11,640
Feb	12,000	0	3,600	6,000	10,800
March	6,000	0	0	1,800	6,600
Total		$16,380	$12,840	$10,200	

Collection Pattern:
   30.0% in Month of Sale
   50.0% in Month after Sale
   20.0% Two Months after Sale

SCHEDULE A-9   Arctic Air Products cash collection budget first quarter 19X7 (000).

financial obligations; whereas in February they must borrow $2,000,000 in order to maintain a minimum cash reserve. For planning purposes, interest is accrued monthly on the loan balance at the end of the month. This is shown in the financial summary and for the month of January the accrued interest expense is $80,000.

The net income before taxes (Schedule A-8) and taxes payable are both functions of the interest expense just mentioned. As a result, net income cannot be determined until the cash budget is complete; using a computer spreadsheet program this is easy to accomplish. Moreover, a few iterations of the cash budget may be necessary to achieve management's objectives. This too is easy to accomplish using spreadsheet software. For planning purposes in this illustration it is assumed that fixed manufacturing overhead consists mainly of cash disbursements except for the depreciation.

Statement of Changes in Financial Position

Finally, after the financial decisions have been made and the income statement adjusted accordingly to reflect financial decisions, the statement of financial position forecast (Schedule A-11) can be prepared at the end of the quarter. Again, management may wish to review the financial position at the end of the period and make any necessary adjustments in policies or decisions which are reflected in various plans and schedules prepared prior to this.

Decision Making and Sensitivity Analysis

Upon the initial development of the master budget and its associated profit plan, cash budget, and financial statement forecast, management may want to use the financial framework provided by the budget model to help in further developing and ultimately finalizing its plans or to explore the consequences of alternative plans of action. These activities are important elements of the planning and con-

	JANUARY	FEBRUARY	MARCH
Beginning Cash Balance	$ 5,000	$ 3,290	$ 3,761
Cash Receipts	16,380	12,840	10,200
(SCHEDULE A-9)			
Total Cash Available	$21,380	$16,130	$13,961
Cash Disbursements			
Manufacturing Wages	$ 2,400	$ 1,800	$ 1,560
(SCHEDULE A-5)			
Material Purchases	2,415	1,969	1,523
(SCHEDULE A-6)			
Manufacturing Var. Oh.	500	375	325
Fixed Mfg. Oh.	2,175	2,175	2,175
(SCHEDULE A-5)			
(Less Noncash Depreciation)	(100)	(150)	(150)
Equipment Purchases	0	5,000	0
Selling and Adm. Expenses			
Variable (SCHEDULE A-7)	1,200	1,200	600
Fixed	2,000	2,000	2,000
Taxes Paid	1,500	0	0
Total Disbursements	$12,090	$14,369	$ 8,033
Cash Available-Disbursements	$ 9,290	$ 1,761	$ 5,929
Minimum Cash Balance	3,000	3,000	3,000
Financing Requirements			
Borrowing	0	2,000	0
Repayment	6,000	0	2,000
Total Financing	(6,000)	2,000	(2,000)
Cash Balance	$ 3,290	$ 3,761	$ 3,929

Plant and Equipment	DECEMBER	JANUARY	FEBRUARY	MARCH
	$10,000	$10,000	$15,000	$15,000
Acc. Depreciation	(2,000)	(2,100)	(2,250)	(2,400)

FINANCIAL SUMMARY			
Beginning Loan Payable	$8,000	$2,080	$4,121
Ending Loan Prior to any Repayment	8,000	4,080	4,121
Interest Expense*	80	41	41
Ending Loan after Repayment	2,000	4,080	2,121
Accrued Loan and Interest Payable	$2,080	$4,121	$2,162

Minimum Cash Balance Policy $3,000
*Interest Rate Monthly is   1.0% on Loan Balance Prior to Repayment
Assume Repayments are at the End of the Period and All Borrowing is at the Beginning of the Period for Planning.

SCHEDULE A-10   Arctic Air Products Cash Budget First Quarter 19X7 (000).

trol system as shown in Figure 17-4 and are especially easy to accommodate in today's technological environment. The budget officer or controller merely de-

Current Assets			
Cash (SCHEDULE A-10)		$3,929	
Accounts Receivable (SCHEDULE A-6)		6,600	
Inventory			
Raw Material (SCHEDULE A-7)	$525		
Finished Goods	2,480	3,005	$13,534
(Ending Balance * Standard Cost)			
Fixed Assets			
Cost		$15,000	
Acc. Depreciation		(2,400)	12,600
Total Assets			$26,134
Equities			
Accounts Payable			$1,549
Taxes Payable			677
Loan Payable			2,162
Paid-in Capital in Excess of Par			10,000
Retained Earnings			11,746
Total Equities			$26,134
Statement of Retained Earnings			
Beginning Retained Earnings			$10,730
Net Income after Tax			1,016
Ending Retained Earnings			$11,746

SCHEDULE A-11   Arctic Air Products proforma statement of financial position March 31, 19X7 (000).

velops the schedules presented thus far using any number of computer spreadsheet programs.

The budget presented here was developed using a spreadsheet and is made up of sets of relationships or equations which can easily be manipulated to express different conditions, policies, and economic factors. Through this manipulation process management can easily ask "what if" questions.

The planning and control system used by management, its associated master budget model, and its related accounting system must be justified on an economical basis. To make this assessment management must assess the accuracy—that is, the quality of the system required—for each assumption, constraint, variable, and parameter of the budget or, more specifically, the budget model. Sensitivity analysis can be used to assess the impact variances in each assumption, constant, variable, or parameter on the results such as the estimate of net income or cash flow. Those pieces of input data for which the results are more sensitive may require more precise systems for gathering or estimating the data. The cost of more accurate systems can then be compared with its impact on the decision. Some of the spreadsheets have features that facilitate sensitivity analysis and help management make such an assessment.

REFERENCES

BORTHICK, A. FAYE, "Artificial Intelligence in Auditing: Assumptions and Preliminary Development", *Advances in Accounting* (1987).

EDWARDS, ALEX, AND N. A. D. CONNELL, *Expert Systems in Accounting*, Englewood Cliffs, N.J.: Prentice Hall, 1989.

GRAY, PAUL, Using the Interactive Financial Planning System (IFPS) for Stochastic Simulation, *SIMULATION*, December 1984, pp. 286–292.

GREER, WILLIS R., AND HOWARD ROCKNESS, "Management Decision Support Systems for a Medical Group Practice," *Journal of Information Systems*, Spring 1987, pp. 65–79.

GROSSMAN, THEODORE, AND SHAILENDRA PALVIA, "The Design and Implementation of a Multidimensional Retail Merchandising Information System," *Journal of Information Systems*, Fall 1988, pp. 119–131.

IFPS *Cases and Models*, Austin, Tex.: Execucom Systems Corporation, 1981.

MOSER, JORGE G., "Integration of Artificial Intelligence and Simulation in a Comprehensive Decision-Support System," *Simulation*, 47, (December 1986), 223–229.

NAYLOR, T. H., AND M. H. MANN, "A Comparison of Eight Planning and Modeling Software Systems," Corporate Economics Program, Duke University, North Carolina, (June 1981).

O'LEARY, DANIEL E., "The Use of Artificial Intelligence in Accounting," in *Expert Systems in Business*, ed. Barry G. Silverman, Reading, Mass.: Addison-Wesley, 1987.

SILVERMAN, BARRY G., ed., *Expert Systems in Business*, Reading, Mass.: Addison-Wesley, 1987.

SIMON, H. A., *The New Science of Management*, New York: Harper & Row, 1960.

TAYLOR, JAROD, AND WILLIAM TAYLOR, "Searching for Solutions," *P.C. Magazine*, September 15, 1987.

REVIEW QUESTIONS

1. What are the major components of a decision support system? How can such a system contribute to each step in the decision-making process? Decision support systems are used extensively for planning and control systems (budgeting). In this regard, (referring back to chapter 3), how may they coupled with monitoring (feedback) information be used to assist principals and agents in planning and controlling the activities of an organization?

2. What are the major components of an expert system? What is the purpose of each?

3. What types of decision making activities are expert systems designed to assist?

4. What is the function of each of the components of a decision support system?

5. Suggest several ways a DSS can help in planning corporate strategy?

6. What types of analysis can be supported by DSS? Name the different types of models that can be used to support these types of analysis.

7. What is the basis of many of the corporate planning models?

8. How can the budget process be enhanced by using a DSS planning model?

9. What is the value of simulation in the planning process?

10. How can spreadsheets be used to support decision-making in an unstructured environment?

CASES

17-1 Bio Tech Industries uses a large database system. The software has been developed to generate statistics on a wide variety company activities for management to use in decision making. These statistics include inventory status, customer order status, pricing and product specification information, competitor prices and product specifications, economic forecasts, financial statements, manufacturing specifications, sales statistics, cost statistics for each department, and research and development expenditures.

Management has been comfortable with this information system for some time now. However, the bio tech field has become much more competitive in the last several years and management must now concentrate on the profitability of current products and the probable success of new products under development. They don't seem to be able to sort through the mound of statistics to determine this information.

REQUIRED:

1. Does the old system meet the information needs of management? Can you as their accountant suggest some improvement in the type of decision support they use to help them meet these new competitive challenges?

2. Suppose the system you suggest required a reorganization from a centralized functional organization to a division structure in order to respond better to the market. What behavioral problems will occur and why?

3. In describing a new system to management prior to the actual design, would you use a system flowchart or a data flow diagram? Why?

17-2 Hartwell Jewelers was established in 1980 when Keith Richmond purchased two small jewelry stores that were going out of business. Three additional stores have since been added to the chain. Richmond built Hartwell's reputation by offering fair prices for quality engagement and wedding rings, and these items currently comprise 60 percent of Hartwell's sales.

In 1985, Hartwell began offering discounts on wedding rings to purchasers of engagement rings in order to stimulate follow-up business. A couple that purchases one wedding ring within one year of the purchase of the engagement ring receives a 20 percent discount. For the purchase of two wedding rings, the couple receives a 30 percent discount. The discount program has been successful, and Hartwell's sales have increased steadily.

In order to offer the discounts and maintain Hartwell's profit of margin, Richmond must plan the purchase of engagement and wedding rings carefully. To take advantage of wholesale discounts, Richmond purchases, each January and July, all the engagement and wedding rings that Hartwell expects to sell in the coming six months. Richmond has decided to develop a model based on Hartwell's past sales experience to enable him to more accurately forecast the sales of engagement and wedding rings. He has gathered the following information from his analysis of historical data.

* Of the couples who purchase silver engagement rings at Hartwell, 35 percent return to purchase a single wedding ring, while 45 percent return for a pair of wedding rings.

* Purchasers of gold engagement rings return to buy a single wedding ring 45 percent of the time, and buy a pair of wedding rings 50 percent of the time.

* The average period between the sale of engagement rings and the follow-up sale of wedding rings is six months.

* Customers do not switch to a different type of ring once they have purchased an engagement ring—that is, a customer who purchases a gold engagement ring will only purchase gold wedding rings, if any, and not silver wedding rings.

* The demand for gold or silver rings is affected by the market price of gold at the time of the initial purchase of a ring. If the market price of gold rises above a certain level, customers are

Market Price of Gold per Ounce	X	Y
$305 and below	−880	+1,240
$305.01–315.00	−480	+750
$315.01–325.00	0	0
$325.01–335.00	600	−500
Above $335.00	1100	−1800

Table C17-1 Adjustment factors for the market price of gold.

more likely to buy silver rings than gold rings. If the market price of gold drops below a certain level, gold rings are more popular than silver rings.

* Additional wedding ring sales are derived from customers who did not purchase engagement rings at Hartwell. These sales equal 80 percent of the number of wedding rings sold by Hartwell as follow-up business in both the silver and gold categories.

* Total unit sales of engagement rings (gold and silver combined) have increased at a 5 percent growth for each six-month period since the discount plan was adopted.

Richmond's model is a function of engagement ring sales during each prior six-month period before he buys rings in January and July. Richmond has been able to quantify the impact of the market price of gold as an adjustment factor and incorporate this adjustment factor into the model. Richmond's model and the adjustment factors for the market price of gold are presented in Table C17-1.

$$W_s = 1.25 \sum_{n=1}^{6} S_n + .8[(1.25 \sum_{n=1}^{6} S_n) + X]$$

$$W_g = 1.45 \sum_{n=1}^{6} G_n + .8[(1.45 \sum_{n=1}^{6} G_n) + Y]$$

$$E_s = 1.05[(\sum_{n=7}^{12} S_n) + X]$$

$$E_g = 1.05[(\sum_{n=7}^{12} G_n) + Y]$$

where:

W_s = sales forecast for silver wedding rings for the next six months

E_s = sales forecast for silver engagement rings for the next six months

S_n = actual monthly sales for silver engagement rings

X = adjustment factor that quantifies the impact of the market price of gold on the demand for silver rings

W_g = sales forecast for gold wedding rings for the next six months

E_g sales forecast for gold engagement rings for the next six months

G_n = actual monthly sales for gold engagement rings

Y = adjustment factor that quantifies the impact of the market price of gold on the demand for gold rings.

Hartwell's actual sales of engagement and wedding rings for the past twelve months are presented in Table C17-2. The average price of gold for the first six months of 1991 was $340.00 per ounce. Richmond estimates that the average price of gold will drop to $330.00 per ounce during the last six months of 1991.

REQUIRED:

1. Keith Richmond plans to use his new model to estimate the number of rings Hartwell Jewelers should purchase in July 1991 for resale during the last six months of 1991. Using the model, or a spreadsheet version of the model, calculate the

	ENGAGEMENT RINGS		WEDDING RINGS	
	Silver	*Gold*	*Silver*	*Gold*
July 1990	400	350	820	790
August	450	400	900	790
September	350	350	700	810
October	350	350	590	750
November	300	350	620	770
December	450	500	880	1,120
January 1991	350	400	730	880
February	300	400	600	850
March	300	350	650	840
April	400	400	840	750
May	400	450	790	1,010
June	450	600	920	1,350

Table C17-2   Hartwell Jeweler's actual sales.

estimated purchases that would be made in July 1991 of:

  a. silver wedding rings

  b. gold engagement rings.

2. A colleague of Keith Richmond's has suggested that the gold price adjustment factor is too dependent on a single price prediction and should be replaced by a factor incorporating probabilities. For example, the model could consider predictions that are pessimistic, most likely, and optimistic. Discussed how this change could improve the accuracy of Richmond's model.

3. Describe how Keith Richmond could test the sensitivity of his new model.
   (CMA adapted)

17-3 Shotz Company of St. Louis, Missouri, is a major producer and distributor of a regional brand of beer. The beer is marketed in ten states in the Midwest and Great Plains. Recent decisions by some states to ban nonreturnable bottles and cans and the expectation that more states will do the same have led the Shotz management to reappraise the company's bottling function. Shotz has automatic bottling and canning facilities that can handle three sizes of nonreturnable bottles and two sizes of cans.

Demand for beer in cans and nonreturnable bottles will be reduced drastically in the next few years, because of the ban on nonreturnables. However, demand for beer in returnable bottles is expected to increase sufficiently to offset the reduced sales of beer in nonreturnables. The present canning equipment cannot be adapted for use in the returnable-container environment. The bottling equipment can be adapted for use in bottling returnable bottles. Therefore, the company will have to acquire more automated bottling equipment to replace the capacity lost from the discarded canning equipment. The new equipment should enable the company to have adequate capacity for the next five years. Should returnable cans be developed, the company would be prepared to invest in the necessary equipment five years from now.

The company's largest bottling plant, located in Jefferson City, produces approximately 75 percent of the firm's total output, split evenly between bottles and cans. The present canning equipment will be replaced by new automated bottling equipment. The new equipment is technologically superior to the present automated bottling equipment. The major decision plan management must now make is how large the Jefferson City plant's maintenance and repair staff should be to keep both the new and adapted automated equipment running efficiently.

The maintenance and repair staff is responsible both for the preventive maintenance conducted according to the planning schedule, and for the repairs arising from any breakdowns. There are comprehensive accounting records regarding the maintenance and repair function for the past five years of operations. Records on the number of breakdowns for each three-month quarter during the past five years are classified by kind, length of time, and type of product being processed (bottle or can identified by size). Total costs of the maintenance and repair department, consisting of labor, supplies, equipment, and an allocation of general factory overhead, have averaged $500,000 a year for the past five years.

Two separate ten-person maintenance and repair staffs have been used to service the bottling and canning operations for each of the two eight-hour shifts. The total staff has averaged forty persons for the past five years.

There no longer will be any need for two separate maintenance and repair staffs on each shift, because the canning equipment is to be replaced by new bottling equipment. Furthermore, the management believes that it may be able to reduce the size of the maintenance and repair staff on each shift to fewer than twenty persons. However, the staff will not be reduced unless operations can be maintained as efficiently as in the past. The plant will not be able to hire temporary service persons, because the servicing of the automatic bottling equipment requires a relatively high level of skill.

Since a great deal of uncertainty is associated with this decision, plant management has decided to use a computerized simulation

model in its analysis. Simulation models have been used by the company in the past to analyze other problems, and they have proven very useful.

REQUIRED:

1. Identify the different types of costs that should be included in the simulation model used to analyze the size of the maintenance and repair staff, and briefly justify their inclusion.

2. Indicate the source for each of the cost inputs identified.

3. Assuming the decision problem can be simulated adequately, explain the typical types of information generated by the simulation model that will assist the Jefferson City plant management in its decision regarding the appropriate size of the maintenance and repair staff.

4. Describe the design features of a decision support system that can aid Shotz in making decisions of a similar type in the future. (CMA adapted)

17-4 The Glenall Company is a maker of numerous small industrial items. In some cases the items are sold individually, but most are sold in combinations. The market for these products is extremely competitive. Recently, the company has been losing sales because of stock shortages. The product demand, production, and inventory history by month for the 1990-1991 fiscal year are reproduced in Table C17-3.

Table C17-3 Glenall Company

MONTH	SALES DEMAND	PRODUCTION	ENDING INVENTORY
July	9,400	10,000	5,600
August	10,200	10,000	5,400
September	10,200	10,000	5,200
October	15,300	12,000	1,900
November	15,600	12,000	0
December	15,800	16,000	200
January	18,300	16,000	0
February	19,300	18,500	0
March	19,600	19,500	0
April	15,900	19,500	3,600
May	16,200	16,000	3,400
June	17,200	16,000	2,200

All production schedules for each product are planned by an ad hoc committee composed of both production and sales personnel. On the fifth of every month, production is determined for the coming month. Demand is determined for the coming month. Demand is determined by actual sales and unfilled orders received since the fifth of the prior month. There are no back orders. Thus, sales that cannot be filled within 60 days of receipt are lost. Once production runs are determined, they cannot be easily changed without substantial setup, sequencing, and raw material carrying costs.

The production manager blames faulty demand forecasts for the current crisis, while the sales manager blames the production manager for not keeping enough safety stock on hand to satisfy customer demand. Company officials are not satisfied with the current forecasting method and have decided that a more sophisticated basis should be employed. Two models that have been proposed are a three-month moving average and a time series regression.

Amy Chew of Glenall's Planning Department was assigned to develop both models and was told that both models are to be based on historical data. She developed the moving average model to forecast demand for the coming month based upon the actual sales demand for the prior three months, as shown in the following equation:

$$D_t = \sum_{i=1}^{3} D_{t\text{-}i} / 3$$

where: D_t = forecasted sales demand for coming month

$D_{t\text{-}i}$ = actual sales demand for prior month i

The model based on the time series analysis was developed through the use of the least squares method. The demand was regressed on a trend with four seasonal components—that is, each quarter of the year was considered a seasonal component. The fourth quarter seasonal factor was actually incorporated into the intercept term. The resulting time series model is reproduced next:

$D_t = 11,000 + 488\, t + S_i$
D_t = forecasted sales demand for month t
t = the month in the time series (e.g. July 1990)
S_i = seasonal factor for quarter i
i = applicable quarter; i = 1, 2, 3, or 4
S_1 = seasonal factor for first quarter (July, August, September);
   value = $-2,110$
S_2 = seasonal factor for second quarter (October, November, December);
   value = $+2,060$
S_3 = seasonal factor for third quarter (January, February, March);
   value = $+4,100$
S_4 = 0 because it's built into the intercept
r^2 = .99
F-statistic = 467

The seasonal factor to be used in the model depends upon the month for which the sales demand is being forecasted—that is, the forecast for January means the third quarter seasonal factor would be applicable.

REQUIRED:

1. Forecast Glenall Company's sales demand for July 1991 using

   a. the moving average model.
   b. the model based on the time series analysis.

2. Compare and contrast, in general terms, the model based on the time series analysis with the moving average model with respect to

   a. complexity.
   b. applicability to Glenall Company.

3. If past sales trends continue for Glenall Company in the future, which of the two models will yield the more accurate forecast for future sales demand? Explain your answer. (CMA adapted)

17-5 Precision Tillers Inc. (PTI) is a small manufacturer of rototillers. PTI's business is very seasonal requiring careful attention to cash management. The controller of PTI begins the cash management task with an annual projection of unit sales. Production is scheduled for the month prior to sale. Materials must be ordered two months before they are scheduled for use, received a month after they are ordered, and paid for a month after receipt. Material costs averaged 30 percent of the product's selling price. Labor and the variable overhead requiring the expenditure of cash average 25 percent of sales. The amounts are paid for during the month of production. Fixed costs requiring the expenditure of cash total $3000 per month. This figure includes all fixed costs other than those specifically mentioned next. Half of PTI's sales are for cash, the other half are on account. Receivable collections normally occur as follows:

During month after sale	80%
Two months after sale	15%
Three months after sale	3%
Uncollectible	2%

PTI pays royalties to the designer of its rototiller. The royalty amounts to 2 percent of sales. The total royalty for each quarter is paid during the first month of the next quarter. PTI pays a regular cash dividend of $.25/share/quarter on each of its 100,000 outstanding shares. This dividend is paid during the first month of each quarter. Monthly depreciation charges amount to $1,500. Planned capital expenditures of $25,000 in June and $25,000 in August of the next year will not affect this amount. PTI must make a $60,000 payment to a bank to settle the balance due on a note payable in September. The controller is aware the PTI's investment tax credit carry-forwards will eliminate any tax obligations for the next year. To assist in the cash management task for next year, the controller wants to develop a model. The model should permit the controller to determine the cash inflows and outflows for each component and the net cash flow for each month. The model is to be stated in terms of sales using the following notation: S = sales for a month and t = time. For example, S_t would stand for sales during month t. If a cash flow in month t depended upon a sale made in the second prior month, the appropriate notation would be S_{t-2}.

REQUIRED:

1. For each of the items enumerated next, develop the appropriate notation for use in the controllers cash flow model. The notation should include an algebraic sign $(+, -)$ and be stated in terms of S and t where applicable. Indicate whether the item is used each month or is only used for specific months (i.e., if an item is used for all months, show $t = 1\text{-}12$; if an item is used for a specific month or months, e.g., June and July, show $t = 6,7$. Use the following format for presenting your answer:

ESTIMATED CASH FLOW ITEM	NOTATION	APPLICABLE MONTHS
1. Materials		
2. Labor and variable overhead		
3. Fixed costs		
4. Cash sales		
5. Collections of accounts receivable		
6. Royalties		
7. Regular dividend		
8. Capital expenditures		
9. Debt repayment		

2. How can PTI use simulation to test the model and in using the model to evaluate cash flows when sales are uncertain?

17-6 Fred Adamson manages a large door-to-door selling organization. The pattern of weekly sales is quite seasonal, but not highly predictable. The typical annual pattern is shown in Figure C17-1.

Adamson's most difficult problem is cash management. He often experiences either a cash shortage or has idle reserves. The cash outflows are not a problem because Adamson has a set payment schedule. The sales force is paid its 10 percent commission weekly and Adamson's suppliers are paid five weeks after the sale.

The problem arises from Adamson's inability to predict accurately the cash collections from sales. All sales are made on account, and the customers are asked to remit their payments by mail within four weeks. If Adamson fails to receive the payment within eight weeks, he sends customers personalized form letters threatening legal action. Six percent of the payments are never received, but legal action is not actually taken due to its high cost.

Adamson has maintained collection experience records which have allowed him to specify a frequency distribution for the collection lag. This frequency distribution is presented in the following schedule.

COLLECTION LAG (NUMBER OF WEEKS FROM SALE UNTIL ACTUAL COLLECTION)	PERCENTAGE OF ACCOUNTS
1	2%
2	4
3	8
4	16
5	18
6	12
7	8
8	6
9	4
10	8
11	6
12	2
Uncollectible	6
	100%

Adamson has discussed his cash management problem with a business acquaintance who is a consultant. The consultant has suggested that Adamson consider using simulation analysis.

REQUIRED:

1. Explain what is meant by simulation analysis and discuss why the computer is a

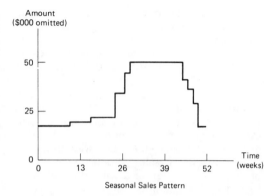

FIGURE C17-1 Typical annual pattern.

useful tool in performing a simulation.

2. Explain why computer simulation would be an appropriate analysis technique for Fred Adamson to use in an attempt to solve his cash management problem.

3. Explain the basic structure of a simulation model which would address Fred Adamson's cash management problem.

17-7 The planning process at the Best Company consists of a network of interrelated decisions that can be summarized in the form of budgets. These budgets are related to each other in a manner similar to that shown in Figure C17-2.

A synopsis of the budgeting process follows: Long-range sales forecasts and corporate policies are determined. Capital projects are then outlined in a capital planning budget; afterward a periodic sales budget is prepared. The sales budget is then used as a basis for determining inventory levels. Based on the inventory levels, the production requirements are established. From the production requirements, direct material requirements and purchases can be planned, labor needs can be determined, and overhead needs can be budgeted. Also, given the sales budget, cash receipts can be estimated. And given: the capital budget; the production budget for material, labor, and overhead; and planned selling and expenditures; cash disbursements can be estimated. From estimated receipts and disbursements, a cash budget can be prepared. The cash budget allows the organization to plan for effective use of cash resources and prepare ef-

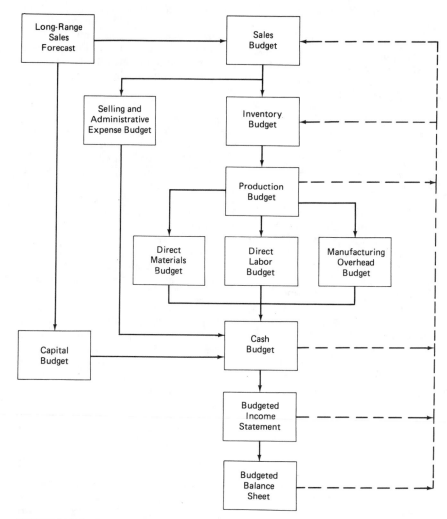

FIGURE C17-2   Budget flowchart.

fectively for the acquisition of additional cash resources as the need arises. Given the sales, inventory, production, selling, and administrative expense, along with capital and cash budgets, a pro forma income statement and balance sheet can be prepared.

Best's budget process for the first quarter of 19X4 is as follows: First a *sales forecast* is prepared from historical sales patterns and from an assessment of the economic and competitive outlook for Best's product. Best's sales were 30,000; 20,000; and 10,000 units in October,

November, and December 19X3, respectively. It has forecast that sales will be 20,000; 25,000; 30,000; 50,000; 50,000; and 40,000 for the next six months. Best anticipates no change in price over the next six months, which has been $4 per unit for the past six months. Furthermore, based on last year's experience, Best forecast that its collection pattern would be 60 percent in the month of the sale, 20 percent the following month, and the remaining 20 percent the month after that.

REQUIRED (either using a spreadsheet package or sets of equations):

1. From these data prepare a *Sales Budget* and *Cash Collection Budget* for the first quarter of 19X4. The accounts receivable from November and December 19X3 sales are shown in Table C17-4.

Table C17-4 Best Company's accounts receivable.

| | | 19X4 | |
FROM	12/31	JAN.	FEB.
Nov. sales	16,000	16,000	
Dec. sales	40,000	8,000	8,000

2. Following the preparation of the sales budget, the *Production Budget* can be prepared, but several decisions must be made prior to this. First, an inventory policy must be set, based on the degree of uncertainty in the sales forecast and production operations and on the need for a buffer stock of finished goods. Best has decided that to avoid lost sales and ensure adequate distribution to retail centers, the company should end each month with at least 50 percent of next month's sales inventory. From this information, December 31, 19X3 balance of 20,000 units and sales production requirements for the next three months can be planned. Develop the production requirements portion of the budget. Inv. Bal. 12/31/19X3 = 5,000 units.

3. Given (1) the production requirements; (2) an estimated need of two pounds of material (per unit) at $0.25 per pound; and (3) material is purchased as it is used, the monthly *acquisition of raw material* (expressed in terms of units) and *cash disbursements* for these purchases can be determined. Prepare this portion of the budget. Assume that all materials will be paid for in the month following the purchase.

4. Best uses an industrial engineering study and concludes that it will take one quarter of an hour of labor at $6.00 per hour, or $1.50 per unit, to manufacture its product. Given the number of units to be produced in the production requirements portion of the Production Budget, *labor costs* and *disbursements* can be completed, assuming that cash disbursements for labor are made for all practical purposes in the same month in which the labor cost is incurred. Compute this portion of the budget.

5. Best uses direct labor hours to allocate variable factory overhead at $1 per direct labor hour. Therefore, upon completion of the direct labor requirement (in part 4), *variable overhead* expenses can be determined. To these, fixed overhead expenses, or $2000, can be added. Assuming that overhead expenses are paid for in the month in which they are incurred (by subtracting depreciation from the budgeted overhead), cash disbursements for manufacturing overhead can be determined. Computer the manufacturing overhead portion of the Production Budget.

6. Given the sales patterns, the behavior of selling and administrative costs based on these patterns, and the planned discretionary expenses for promotion and other expenditures, the *selling and administrative expense budget* can be computed. Develop this budget by assuming that variable selling/administrative expenses are $0.25 per unit sold and all selling and administrative expenses are paid in the month in which they are incurred.

7. Prepare a cash budget for the Best Company. In January, February, and March 19X4, no capital additions are planned. Assume that Best has a policy of borrowing and repaying in $500 increments with a 12 percent annual interest rate. The interest paid monthly is on the maximum balance during the month, and all borrowing takes place at the beginning of the month and all repayments are made at the end of the month. A $5,000 minimum cash balance is required by Best as a contingency against uncertainties. The cash budget is prepared as follows: (1) expected cash receipts from the cash collection schedule (prepared in part 1 are added to the beginning balance to determine the total cash available; (2) all disbursements from the Production Budgets

and the Selling and Administrative Expense Budget are added to obtain total cash disbursements; (3) any excess or deficiency is adjusted by a minimum balance required to obtain a net excess of deficiency; (4) cash borrowing or repayment and interest expenditures are then planned to maintain a minimum cash balance. Cash balance 12/31 = $5,000.

8. Develop a set of recursive equations that can be used to generate each of the budgets developed in parts 1 through 7.*

17-8 (Knowledge of simple probility and decision trees is required) Brandon Appliance Corporation, a predominant producer of microwave ovens, is considering the introduction of a new product. The new product is a microwave oven that will defrost, cook, brown, and broil food as well as sense when the food is done.

Brandon must decide on a course of action for impelementing this new product line. An initial decision must be made whether or not to (1) market the product at all, (2) introduce the product in a marketing test, or (3) nationally distribute the product from the onset. If a marketing test is conducted, Brandon must then decide whether it wishes to abondon the product line or make it available for national distribution.

The finance department has provided some cost information and probability estimates relating to this decision. The preliminary costs for research and development have already been incurred and are considered irrelavant to the marketing decision. A success nationally will increase profits by $5,000,000, and a failure will reduce them by $1,000,000, while abandoning the product will not affect profits. The test market analysis will cost Brandon an additional $100,000.

If a market test is not performed, the probability of success in a national campaign is estimated to be 45 percent. If the market test is performed, the probability of a favorable test result is 60 percent. With favorable test results, the probability for national success is estimated to be 80 percent. However, if the test results are unfavorable, the national success probability is only 10 percent.

REQUIRED:
Determine the course of action Brandon Appliance Corporation should follow for the introduction of its new product line by first constructing a decision tree diagram that analyzes all the alternatives (paths) presented above.

Decision trees such as this are the backbone of most AI models. Using this tree perform backward induction to determine the optimal course of action using the net change in profits as the payoff. The objective is to maximize profits. (CMA Adapted)

17-9 Always Safe Inc. (ASI) manufacturers and sells alarm systems for home use. Purchasers of the alarm systems are connected to ASI's central alarm center on a subscription basis. When activated, ASI intercepts the alarm signal to determine whether the signal is valid or caused by an equipment malfunction before alerting the police.

Most of ASI's revenues are derived from the manufacture and sale of alarm systems, and ASI has developed guidelines for managing inventory and production levels. The controller has asked Jack Ray, a recently employed accountant with in-depth modeling experience, to develop a PC-based financial model to help plan and control operations.

The guidelines ASI developed for Jack Ray are as follows:

- Finished goods inventory at the end of a month should be equal to 30 percent of the next month's sales.

- Work-in-process inventory at the end of a month should be equal to 20 percent of the next month's expected sales. The work-in-process inventory should include 100 percent of direct materials and be 70 percent complete as to manufacturing effort.

- Direct materials inventory at the end of a month should equal the quantity needed to complete the coming month's expected sales plus the direct materials required to fulfill the finished goods inventory as of the end of the coming month.

- Production for the month should result

---

* The original case upon which this case is based is from Charles T. Horngren, *Accounting for Management Control*, 3rd Ed. (Englewood Cliffs, N.J.: Prentice Hall, 1974), p. 205.

in the quantity of units required to meet both the expected sales and inventory levels for the month.

- During the year, direct material purchases and production requirements for a month are adjusted for any differences between the expected and actual sales of the prior month.

Based on these guidelines, Jack Ray developed the following formulas for the financial planning model. Ray has not yet developed the formula for the equivalent production of non-material manufacturing costs (M_n) for the alarm systems. The explanation of the notations used follow the formulas.

FORMULAS

$$ES_n = \sum_{i=1}^{3} S_{ni} P_i$$

$$FG_n = .30ES_{n+1}$$

$$WIP_n = .20ES_{n+1}$$

$$DM_n = .50ES_{n+1} + .30ES_{n+2}$$

$$P_n = .70ES_{n+1} + .30ES_{n+2}$$

$$P'_n = .70ES_{n+1} + .30ES_{n+2}$$
$$+ (AS_{n-1} - ES_{n-1})$$

NOTATIONS

n	=	current month (e.g., 1 = January, 2 = February, etc.)
i	=	one of three probability levels (i.e., optimistic, average, pessimistic).
S_{ni}	=	one of three estimated sales volumes for a month.
P_1	=	one of three probability levels for estimated sales volume for a month.
ES_n	=	expected unit sales for a month.
FG_n	=	finished goods inventory in units at the end of a month.
WIP_n	=	work-in-process inventory in units at the end of a month.
DM_n	=	direct materials inventory in units at the end of a month.
P_n	=	units of direct material to purchase in a month (no adjustment factor included because prior month's actual sales are not known).
P'_n	=	units of direct material to purchase in a month when actual sales from a prior

month are known (adjustment factor included).

AS_n	=	actual unit sales for a month.
$(AS_{n-1}-ES_{n-1})$	=	adjustment factor for month n when actual sales differ from expected sales in month $n-1$.
M_n	=	equivalent unit production for non-material manufacturing costs during a month.

ASI's estimated unit sales for the first six months of 1991 and the standard cost for an alarm system are presented below.

ESTIMATED UNIT SALES VOLUME

	Optimistic (p = .2)	Average (p = .6)	Pessimistic (p = .2)
January	1,400	1,200	1,000
February	1,400	1,200	1,000
March	1,500	1,300	1,100
April	1,700	1,400	1,200
May	2,000	1,700	1,400
June	2,500	2,100	1,800

STANDARD COST PER UNIT

Direct material	
Electronics	$600.00
Alarm housing steel (1.2 lb. @ $5.50/lb.)	6.60
Direct labor (2.5 hr. @ $20.00/hr.)	50.00
Manufacturing overhead (2.5 hr. @ $2.80/hr.)	7.00₆.
Total standard cost per unit	**$663.60**

REQUIRED:

1. Using the formulas that Jay Ray has developed, calculate the following items for April 1991.

   a. The number of alarm systems that should be in the finished goods inventory at the end of April.

   b. The number of alarm systems that should be in the work-in-process inventory at the end of April.

   c. The pounds of steel that should be in the direct materials inventory at the end of April.

2. Prepare a spreadsheet from these formulas.

3. Assume that Always Safe Inc. (ASI) actually sold 1,300 systems in January, 1,400 in February, and 1,400 in March of 1991. Calculate the dollar value of electronics that ASI would need to purchase in April 1991 in this situation.

18

LARGE-SCALE SYSTEMS

INTRODUCTION

Large organizations can have operations scattered around the world. They can have several manufacturing sites that are vertically integrated where materials and components are obtained in one location, assembled in other locations, and finished in a third location. All of these locations may even be in different countries so that the organization can take advantage of the market imperfections between each country. Market imperfections often manifest themselves in the forms of different tax structures, resources, and wage rates. They may even serve several global markets and need to satisfy consumers in each of these markets. Managing such a far flung operation is very difficult. Management needs an information system to coordinate all these activities and meet the local needs in each location or country.

In addition to the vastness of the operations in many large organizations, these organizations process millions of transactions and transfer billions in funds during the course of a year. Thus they need systems that are sweeping in terms of geography that can handle millions of transactions. Again thousands of these transactions may need to be coordinated with other aspects of the organization. This will require large computer systems that are connected by telecommunication systems that can handle thousands of transactions between different divisions. Some of these divisions may be scattered around the world.

In earlier chapters we discussed the advantages and disadvantages as well as the evolution of centralized and distributed systems. In this chapter we will examine applications of some of these concepts to large integrated information systems. Sometimes large distributed systems are denoted as "wide area networks" because of the communication network needed to coordinate a global network of operations. In addition these large organizations are using electronic data interchange (EDI) because of the huge volume of transactions between different segments of the organization and between the organization, its customers and vendors. Although this concept was noted in earlier chapters it will be discussed in more depth in this chapter because it is vital to the efficient operation of large systems.

Five different examples are given in the chapter. Two examples are used to illustrate EDI, two illustrate integrated manufacturing, and another illustrates a worldwide distributed processing system. A paper manufacturer, test equipment, and computer manufacturer are illustrated in the cases. Each example provides a unique or different systems application. Electronic data interchange is discussed first because large organizations are becoming more and more dependent on this form of communication because of the volume of their transactions.

ELECTRONIC DATA INTERCHANGE

Electronic data interchange is the communication of transactions and information between two computers. It usually refers to the interchange of electronic documents such as purchase orders, shipping notices, invoices, and payments. With EDI, transmitted data replaces documents such as those illustrated in earlier chapters and EDI may be used between organizations or within the same organization. When EDI is used to effect a *payment* it must flow through the banking system. To use EDI, standard formats must be used, otherwise receiving divisions or organizations will not recognize or be able to translate incoming messages from other divisions or companies. The American National Standards Institute (ANSI), in recognition of this problem, has sanctioned a committee designated X12 to develop a framework of standards. Many benefits can accrue to an organization that uses electronic data interchange (EDI). A summary of these includes the following:

1. Improved seller's response time to orders
2. Reduced clerical expense by eliminating paper documents
3. Reduced copying errors due to data entry and copying
4. Savings in forms and mailings
5. Better implementation of just-in-time systems
6. Reduced inventory lead time
7. Reduced information float thus improving cash and inventory management
8. Reduced uncertainty in cash transfer time, i.e., check clearings
9. Reduced cycle time from receipt of order to cash receipt

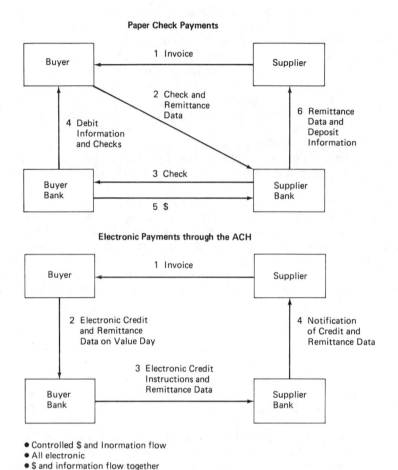

Paper Check Payments

Electronic Payments through the ACH

- Controlled $ and Inormation flow
- All electronic
- $ and information flow together

FIGURE 18-1   The automated clearing house can simplify corporate trade payments.
Source: The Globecon Group, Ltd., *Electronic Data Interchange and Corporate Trade Payments,* Financial Executives Research Foundation (FERF), Morristown, N.J., p. 16 and The First National Bank of Chicago, 1988.

The major benefits can be summed up in Figure 18-1 which compares the use of paper check payments with the use of electronic payment using the Automated Clearing House (ACH), which is the banking systems, EDI system designed to replace checks.

Figure 18-2 illustrates many of the potential uses of electronic data transfers of information in business. To appreciate the magnitude of the potential benefits that can be reaped from an EDI system, it is generally held that approximately 70 percent of all computer input is from other computers. Thus, the po-

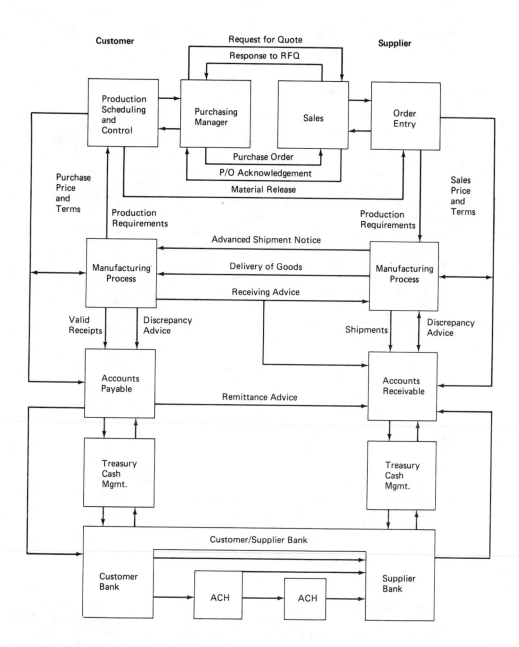

FIGURE 18-2 EDI business transaction information flow.
Source: The Globecon Globe, Ltd., *Electronic Data Interchange and Corporate Trade Payments*, Financial Executive Research Foundation (FERF), Morristown, N.J., 1988, p. 64 and Corporate Controller, Navistar International Corporation.

tential is enormous. The challenge will be to standardize these various flows so that transaction information can be transmitted without paper documents and the corresponding delay and clerical errors associated with paper documents can be reduced.

EDI Analysis and Design

Analysis, design, and implementation of EDI projects tend to follow the pilot approach. This is because formal feasible studies are difficult to do because the whole area of electronic data interchange is so new. There is very little evidence upon which to assess the feasibility of new projects in terms of economic, operational or technical feasibility. Indeed, one of the main reasons many companies have not started to use EDI is due to the lack of standardization, making system operation infeasible. On the other hand, some very large automotive and merchandise organizations have developed their own proprietary systems to implement EDI within their own organizations and with their suppliers. In the analysis and design of EDI systems, special emphasis needs to be given to the interface with those whom the organization will be communicating. In some cases if the organization is large enough they have mandated that suppliers use EDI. Contractual agreements such as those suggested in the logistics chapter may need to be designed to use EDI to implement a JIT inventory system as another example. Sometimes translation software may need to be written to translate data received from a customer so that an organization can comply with an electronic request on a timely basis. This is an example of the need to extend the bounds of analysis to include suppliers and customers in the design of an electronic data interchange system.

To resolve some of the data translation problems, especially for small vendors who must deal with several customers who may be using different formats, third party and value added networks have evolved. A value added network, such as those provided by some of the communication giants, provides a "mail box" where electronic documents can be stored for future access by the other party. This alleviates the need to maintain in constant communication with a vendor or suppliers' computer. These value added networks also provide a translation service that can deal with different message protocols and formats. These are especially valuable for JIT suppliers. A third party network functions as a communication service bureau. They not only provide the "mail box" features and the translation service, they also handle the entire communication process including all the communication links.

EDI Risk and Control

Corporations face the potential of great loss in terms of dollars that may be misdirected, of lost sales transactions, and of production disruptions due to lost material requisitions. In addition, they face losses due to fraudulent access to the communication network. To protect themselves from these and other losses due to miscommunication or fraudulent communication, several controls can be used to help reduce the risk. First, transactions must be authorized before they are entered. Second, identification measures need to be in place along with reliable communication channels to insure those messages received are valid and correct. Finally, unauthorized access to terminals or to transmission lines needs to be prevented. Numerous means are available to implement these controls. Passwords, data encryption, and echo checks are but a few of those mentioned in the internal control chapter that are useful in communication networks.

Electronic Data Interchange Applications

It is estimated that the auto industry wastes 2 billion dollars a year shuffling paper. Using EDI to eliminate much of this would save approximately $200 per car. All the big three automobile companies are actively working on various projects. Similar savings can accrue to firms in the grocery industry. We discuss these[1] in general terms here.

AUTOMOTIVE INDUSTRY.   The auto industry has basically mandated that all of its suppliers communicate electronically. The big three in the auto industry are currently using EDI for a range of transactions. This range includes[2]: material releases, shipment notices, purchase orders, supplier invoices, interdivision invoices, purchase requests, quotations and responses to quotes, electronic funds transfers, and evaluated receipt settlements. Standards have been developed for a number of these transactions. To aid in implementation of EDI and the ultimate standardization of EDI in the automotive industry they have formed an organization called AIAG (Automotive Industry Action Group).

Since all three automakers are basically mandating the use of EDI and electronic funds transfer industry wide, this will involve hundreds of thousands of monthly payments totaling billions of dollars. Several value added and third party vendors (often telecommunication giants and financial institutions) are setting up networks that can expedite the transfer of information and the translation of data into a common protocol and format.

As an example, one of the larger automotive corporations has developed an electronic payments system with a network of several banks. It will transmit all payments electronically. Different divisions may transmit to different banks in the network. Suppliers have been encouraged to receive payments through one of these banks. The banks have arranged to make payments through the EDI system and to send hard copy information in the mail to those that do not want to establish relationships with one of those banks. Many of the suppliers in the system will still receive payments from banks outside the network, because they are often reluctant to disturb relationships with banks that are extending credit to them. This software will have authentication and encryption facilities. The ultimate goal of this particular automaker is for EDI to eliminate 300,000 paper checks to over five thousand vendors.

As another example, automakers are trying to develop evaluated receipt settlements which eliminate all the paperwork in receiving invoices, reconciling accounts payables and receivables as well as executing payments. As a result a

---

[1] The source of many of the facts in this discussion of the auto and grocery industries was The Globecon Group, Ltd., *Electronic Data Interchange and Corporate Trade Payments*, Financial Executives Research Foundation (FERF), Morristown, N.J., 1988 and Willenz, Nicole V. "Electronic Data Interchange: A Quiet Revolution," *Price Waterhouse Review*, 1988, No. 3, pp. 33-45.

[2] These are discussed in Sadhwani, Arjan T. and M. H. Sarhan, "Electronic Systems Enhance JIT Operations," *Management Accounting*, 1987.

shipment may simply be inspected using a bar code to ensure that the shipment agrees with the electronic advanced shipment notice. This input will trigger all the necessary data interchange that previously involved purchase orders, receiving reports, invoices, and the reconciliation of these for the authorization of a cash disbursement. Even the check will be written automatically if everything agrees with the supplier agreements.

GROCERY INDUSTRY.   In 1978 the consulting firm of Arthur D. Little, Inc. was commissioned by the trade associations of the grocery industry to study the feasibility of using EDI. In the grocery industry:

1. A large number of manufacturers, distributors, brokers, and retailers interact with each other;
2. There is high volume of transactions;
3. Margins are thin making a small savings per transaction very important;
4. There is a need for an efficient distribution system that minimizes inventory.

As a result this industry is particularly well suited for EDI.

A 1980 feasibility study[3] focused on wholesale transactions between manufacturers and brokers or distributors. It estimated fifteen million orders with a value of $105 million flowed between 5,000 manufacturers and 2,400 distributors and 3,000 brokers. These orders generated ninety million orders, order adjustments, bills of lading, invoices, invoice adjustments, payments, price changes, and promotion announcements transactions.

The study found that even though significant progress had been made in using computers, routine business transactions such as purchase orders and invoices, were usually manually processed then mailed or telephoned before being keyed into the other company's computer. The study concluded that manufacturers, distributors, and brokers could save hundreds of millions per year if EDI was even partially implemented. The benefits would include the majority of those noted earlier.

The study concluded that implementing such a system in the grocery industry with its large number of participants would be difficult because some were already using proprietary systems and there were no common message formats or communication standards. To help resolve the standardization problem, the trade associations that commissioned the study formed the Uniform Communications Standards Committee (UCS) in 1980 to develop a common format for the entire grocery industry. The Committee developed and pilot tested a series of message formats. Over sixty manufacturing, broker, wholesale, and retail companies participated before pilot projects began. In early 1987, Arthur D. Little completed another study[4] on the application of EDI to direct store delivery.

---

[3] This study is discussed fully in The Globecon Group, Ltd., *Electronic Data Interchange and Corporate Trade Payments,* Financial Executives Research Foundation (FERF), Morristown, N.J., 1988. Only some of the key facts are noted here.

[4] This second study is discussed fully in The Globecon Group, Ltd., *Electronic Data Interchange and Corporate Trade Payments.* Financial Executives Research Foundation (FERF), Morristown, N.J., 1988. Only some of the key facts are noted here.

In direct store delivery, manufacturers ship directly to individual stores, bypassing brokers, distributors, and retail warehouses. There were 500 million direct shipments each year involving billions of line items. Direct store deliveries present major control problems because there are opportunities for theft and cheating. The study recommended a direct computer to computer interface or a direct interface using a smart card to record and control the transfer delivery data. A smart card has logic coded on a memory chip. The supplier codes the smart card with delivering data at the warehouse. The retailer, upon delivery, uses data from the smart card to record the delivery and acknowledge receipt. The study estimated that retailers and suppliers could save hundreds of millions per year with such a system.

Since these studies some of the larger grocery vendors have realized many of the benefits of EDI as outlined in these studies as well as some of the benefits listed earlier which normally accrue to those who use EDI systems. For example, one large chain saves $1.30 per purchase order and $10 per invoice, totaling $600,000 per year. Other industries such as the aircraft, retail merchandise, food, and railroad have also realized substantial savings from the use of EDI.

AN INTEGRATED MANUFACTURING COMPANY

In Chapters 14, 15, 16, and 17, accounting systems were considered for each functional area and for managerial decision making. In this section an example of an integrated manufacturing company is presented to illustrate how the majority of these activities flow together into a coordinated accounting and information system for operational control. This is followed by an example of a worldwide distributed network using telecommunication and electronic data interchange. Finally, a third example is provided to illustrate a distributed material requirement planning system which links sales, company forecasts, and factory flows in a distribution system.

General Products Corporation[5] specializes in the manufacture of products for the consumer market. The company's sales were $198 million per annum in 1986 and were projected to be about $220 million by 1991. Its product line consists of twelve products divided among three product groups. For large orders, products are shipped directly to the customer from the company's manufacturing plants. All other orders are shipped from the company's warehouses to retailers. Experience has shown that 20 percent of the company's dollar volume represents direct shipments from the plants and 80 percent represents shipments through the company's warehouses.

Corporate headquarters are located in Minneapolis; manufacturing plants are located in Birmingham, Philadelphia, and Portland. Wherever a manufacturing plant is located, a warehouse is attached. The present employment level for the entire firm is approximately three thousand employees.

The organization of General Products is such that the president (the chief executive officer) reports to the board of directors and is assisted by the corporate planning group. The executive vice-president, in turn, reports to the presi-

---

[5] This example is an updated example from Robert J. Thierant *Distributed Processing Systems* © 1978, pp. 136-152. Adapted by permission of Prentice-Hall, Inc., Englewood Cliffs, N.J.

dent. In a similar manner, nine vice-presidents (marketing, research and development/engineering, manufacturing, purchasing and inventory, physical distribution, accounting, finance, personnel, and management information system) report to the executive vice-president. Various corporate managers, plant managers, and warehouse managers report to the respective vice-presidents.

General has progressed through a series of data processing systems over the years. The company first used a batch processing management information system. They are converting to an interactive on-line processing system.

The main reasons for selecting an interactive distributed processing system are:

1. Better customer service and improved selling efficiency.
2. More timely and improved management information analysis and reporting at the plant and home office levels.
3. Improved coordination and control of the overall organization and its individual parts.
4. Better opportunity to match demand with production.
5. On-line information available from a distributed database for management analysis of the organization's operations and prospective operations.

The Distributed Processing Environment

To implement the distributed processing system the company selected a computer system that integrated satellite minicomputers at each of the three manufacturing plants, including the attached warehouses, with a centralized computer system. At each of the plants with attached warehouses, four terminals have been installed for use in sales order processing plus four for accounting. In a similar manner, fourteen have been installed for manufacturing and physical distribution. Within this hardware configuration, the organization was able to distribute its database and application programs to the appropriate remote locations. Figure 18-3 illustrates the hierarchical or tree network utilized by the corporation.

The operating system software for the host computer system controls, schedules, and monitors all activities and adjusts processing activity to changing demands. Processing modes include transaction processing, database inquiry, time sharing, interactive job entry and execution, and batch processing. These modes are available at the central site and remotely via the communication facilities, using the corporate database.

The particular distributed processing system software selected was designed for high-volume on-line transaction processing and efficient, interactive query and reporting. It uses a common language for defining, managing, and directing data and provides a standard user interface that is simple and logical. Additionally, it allows a common file description to govern the structure of all data. It gives organizational personnel timely access to vital information and provides data integrity protection, security, and automatic recovery and restart. A distributed communications network was selected to accommodate the heavy traffic in the distributed operating environment.

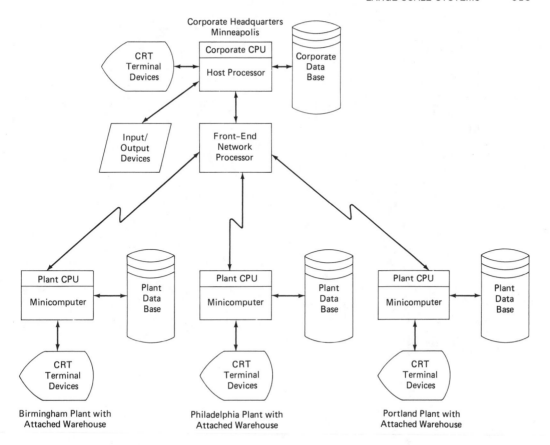

FIGURE 18-3   Overview of distributed processing system (General Products Corporation).

Overview of Major Subsystems

From an overview standpoint, General Products can be described as a *materials-flow company*. This concept is illustrated in Figure 18-4 as a double-line arrow on the outer rim of the flowchart. Purchased materials, and manufactured materials for stock flow into the various stages of the production process; here, the materials take on a variety of forms and shapes until they become finished goods. Next, the finished products flow through the distribution system, either directly via direct shipments or indirectly through company-owned warehouses, until they reach the customer. In this materials-flow concept, several of the corporation's subsystems are thus involved, namely, purchasing, inventory, manufacturing, and physical distribution.

Coupled with the materials flow in Figure 18-4 is a corresponding information flow. Materials-flow information is an important factor in coordinating the diversified activities of the three manufacturing plants and attached warehouses with corporate headquarters. The information must be comprehensive, thereby integrating decision making throughout the entire materials-flow process. With

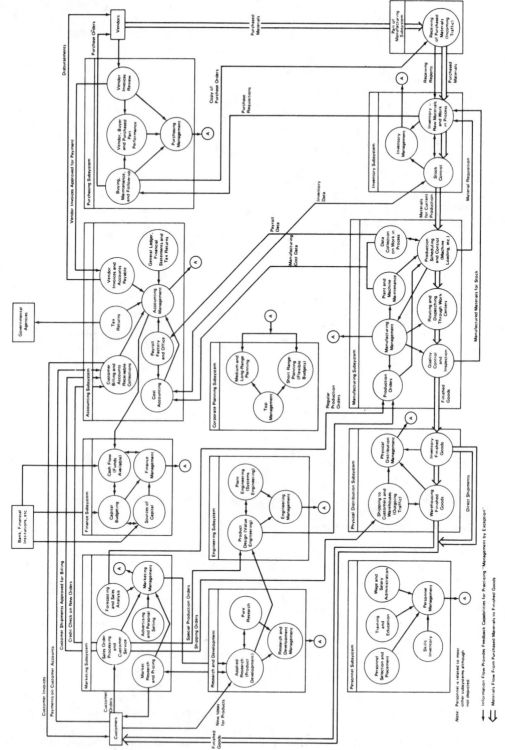

FIGURE 18-4 Flowchart depicting the major subsystems (General Products Corporation).

614

an integrated flow of essential information, management and operating personnel can make adjustments swiftly and effectively in response to the ever-changing business environment. The materials-flow approach is therefore an essential part of the distributed processing system.

From Figure 18-5 it can be seen that the quarterly sales forecast (marketing subsystem), based on external and internal factors, affects the quantity of finished goods to be produced (physical distribution subsystem). This, in turn, affects materials to be purchased from outside suppliers (purchasing subsystem) and to be manufactured within the company (manufacturing subsystem) by future planning periods. Goods purchased or manufactured are produced as needed using a material requirements (MRP) planning system, and are eventually handled by the inventory section (inventory subsystem). They are requisitioned to meet the manufacturing requirements in accordance with the schedule of master operations (manufacturing subsystem) and to meet future material needs. The operational or shop status of the final product, material, labor, and similar items is used for operations evaluation control at the manufacturing level. In some cases, operating information is significant enough for review by middle and top management. If this happens, feedback may make it necessary to review future plans (corporate planning subsystem). Also, it may be necessary to revise future sales forecasts. It is important to note that the manufacturing plan is a function of shipments as well as stock levels. Also materials and parts are a function of this plan as well as stock levels. Finally, finished goods are shipped directly to the customers or through plant-attached warehouses.

Due to space limitations, we will not explore all of the major subsystems for General Products. Rather, only the basic subsystems (namely, marketing, manufacturing, physical distribution, and accounting) are discussed. The analysis and design of these selected subsystems serve to highlight the distributed nature of interrelationships between local processing (plants with attached warehouses) and centralized processing (corporate headquarters).

MARKETING SUBSYSTEM. The firm's marketing subsystem consists of several modules:

1. Forecasting and sales analysis
2. Sales order processing and customer service
3. Advertising and personal selling
4. Market research and pricing

To illustrate how the subparts operate, let us consider sales order processing. The block diagram (an overview of information processing), Figure 18-6, indicates that orders are received and appropriate order forms are prepared and edited before the customer credit is checked. If the order is not accepted because of poor credit, it is returned to the customer and the reason is noted. Generally the order is approved for order entry whereby appropriate files (customer, pricing, and finished goods) are referenced for preparing shipping papers. Shipping papers are then forwarded to the appropriate warehouses for regular shipment or to a particular plant for direct shipment.

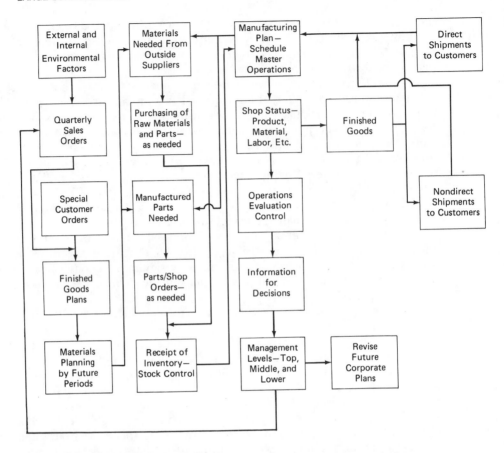

FIGURE 18-5 The integrated flow of information (General Products Corporation).

At this point, other major subsystems interact with sales order processing (marketing subsystem). Shipping documents provide the basis for preparing customer invoices that are eventually used for aging accounts receivable and processing checks received from customers (accounting subsystem). In addition, they are used for assembling goods at the warehouse and plant levels. If items are available for shipment as noted by the perpetual finished goods inventory records during the sales order processing phase, the file is changed from "finished goods on order" to "finished goods shipped" (physical distribution subsystem). Engineering also comes into contact with sales order processing through the receipt of special customer orders which require engineering work for their modification.

MANUFACTURING SUBSYSTEM. The next key subsystem for getting regular or special production orders produced is manufacturing. Its essential subparts are as follows:

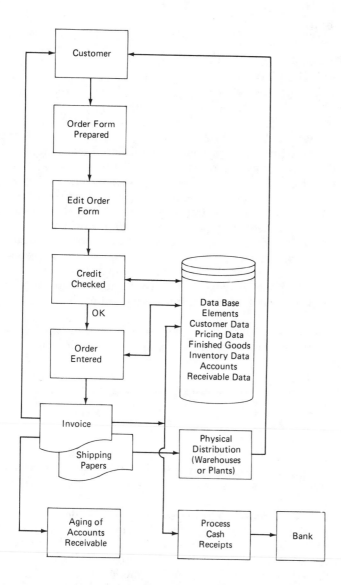

FIGURE 18-6   Sales order processing—a subelement of the marketing subsystem (General Products Corporation).

1.   Receiving
2.   Production scheduling and control
3.   Manufacturing operations:

    a. Machine shop

    b. Assembly—major and minor

    c. Plant and machine maintenance

4. Quality control and inspection

5. Data collection system

The manufacturing process is a continuation of the forecasted finished goods marketing subsystem. As illustrated in Figure 18-7, raw materials are ordered as needed using the purchasing system which is based on the manufacturing plan and the other flow indicators in the database. Upon receipt, the raw materials are placed under the supervision of stock control (inventory subsystem). Data on the flow of products is used to move material and work in process to the appropriate work center and to the distribution system as needed. This data also provides input for the manufacturing plan of the production scheduling and control section, whose job is to schedule, route, and dispatch orders through the various manufacturing work centers. The quality control section is responsible for making appropriate tests of manufactured and finished products before forwarding them to the warehouse or customer (physical distribution subsystem). As illustrated, feedback of critical information is used to adjust operations.

PHYSICAL DISTRIBUTION SUBSYSTEM. The handling of finished goods after manufacturing is the responsibility of the physical distribution subsystem. It includes:

1. Shipping to customers and warehouses (outgoing traffic)

2. Warehousing—finished goods

3. Inventory—finished goods

The manufacturing process culminates in having the finished goods transported from one of the three manufacturing plants to the customers directly (direct shipments) or to one or more of the plant-attached warehouses (nondirect shipments).

The shipment must be reflected in the company's data files. Likewise, certain data on routing finished goods are utilized in obtaining the lowest total shipping and storage costs. These files, as shown in Figure 18-8, are referenced when finished goods are shipped to customers via order processing (marketing subsystem). As indicated in Figure 18-6, shipping papers, initiated by the physical distribution subsystem, start the customer billing and collection process (accounting subsystem).

ACCOUNTING SUBSYSTEM. The sales and cost factors, generated by the previous subsystems, are accounted for and reported by the accounting subsystem. They provide the required inputs for the following accounting subparts:

1. Receivables and payables

2. Payroll

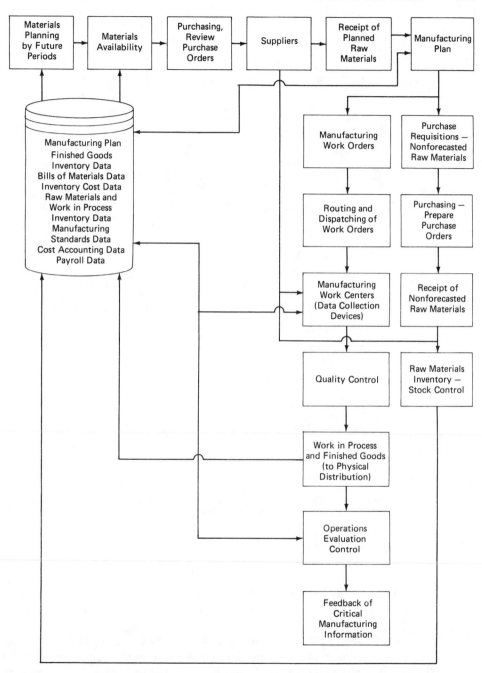

FIGURE 18-7 Work in process and finished goods—a subelement of manufacturing, inventory, and purchasing subsystems (General Products Corporation).

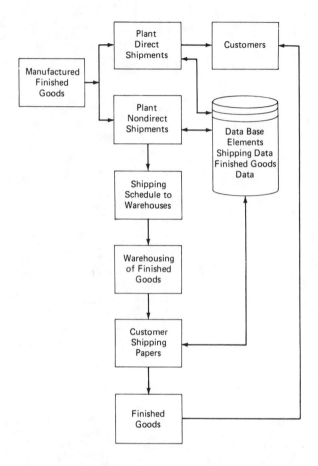

FIGURE 18-8   Distribution of finished goods from plants to warehouses and customers—the main subelement of the physical distribution subsystem (General Products Corporation).

3. Cost accounting
4. Financial statements and tax returns

The accounting subsystem, which involves keeping records, billing customers, arranging payments, and costing products, among others, is a myriad of details.

Generally, accounting activities, as set forth in Figure 18-9, center on those of recording and reporting sales and costs (expenses). Sales revenue and manufacturing cost data—raw materials, labor, and overhead—as well as marketing and general and administrative expenses provide the necessary inputs per the general ledger for producing periodic—overall and detailed—income statements. Cash, receivables, payables, and other accounts are recorded in the gen-

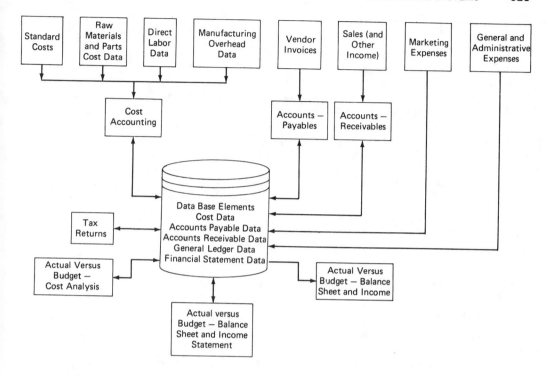

FIGURE 18-9 Sales and cost data—essential components of the accounting subsystem (General Products Corporation).

eral ledger for producing the balance sheet. These financial statements provide inputs for intermediate and long-range analysis (corporate planning subsystem). In a similar manner, detailed income and cost (expense) analyses are helpful in determining future cash flow and capital budgets (finance subsystem).

WORLDWIDE DISTRIBUTED PROCESSING

Florida Semiconductor (FS)[6] is a multinational electronics firm with fifty plants in twenty-five different countries. The systems problem associated with linking these diverse locations is a major task because the company is in a variety of product markets, including the consumer market, and is experiencing such a tremendous growth that it has projected a fivefold increase in net sales billed in the next decade. FS employs a large distributed processing network to link its plants and activities.

---

[6] This example is based on a Texas Instruments example from *Datamation* ® magazine © copyright by Technical Publishing Company, A Dunn & Bradstreet Company, (April, 1979), updated with permission.

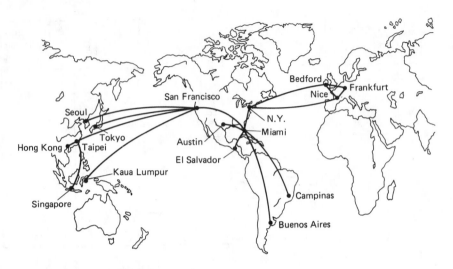

FIGURE 18-10   FS Communication Grid (FSCOG).

Overview

FS's distributed network currently links several small mainframes, minicomputers, approximately 20,000 PC terminals and 200 RJE (remote job entry) stations.

The Corporate Information Center (CIC) in Miami is host to the distributed network. It handles the corporate database and information common to many of the distributed systems. This host computer has several gigabytes of storage that handles thousands of jobs a day. Its capabilities include RJE batch processing, on-line inquiry, time sharing, communication with all the small mainframes, minicomputers and 20,000 microcomputer terminals. It also controls EDI connections with a whole host of suppliers and customers. FS calls each cluster of mainframes, minicomputers, and PC terminals a data exchange system (DXS). Figure 18-10 shows the land line and satellite communciation channels used by Europe, Asia, and Latin America for the communication network.

The functions of these computers and terminals include: concurrent batch, interactive communications, and transaction processing; local database capability local and remote data collection; interface to a host via EDI; multitasking; storing and running the application programs; and special inquiries.

A DXS can be configured with one or more CPUs. For example, one CPU can be designated to handle applications, one to handle PC terminal polling, and another to control host communications with divisions and external parties. The use of multiple CPUs increases throughout and creates communication redundancy in the system. If a local DXS processor goes down, the communication redundancy allows work to continue on another network's DXS or a mainframe host. Some DXSs can support up to thirty thousand transactions per day. On the average, the transaction level for DXS is approximately ten thousand per day; but with the large growth in distributed processing at FS, the number of transactions is increasing 20 percent to 100 percent per year.

The company uses distributed processing in a wide variety of applications, including automated design of printed circuit boards using interactive graphics. This graphics capability is also used to do design editing on integrated circuits. The database contains a standard parts library needed for this purpose. Another application is a work-in-progress schedule and control system used in production planning that generates statistical data for analysis. Mechanical controls for processing are also controlled by this front-end process system. The company also has an on-line system which shows job status, shop load analysis and permits on-line work sequencing.

Two of FS's more interesting applications are an on-line system for customer service management in the field and a factory distributed processing system.

The Field Information System (FIS)

Historically, a major problem for all customer service organizatons has been information on the status of customer problems. In batch systems, when a customer or management makes an inquiry into a problem's status, a major time lag exists between the inquiry, research of the status, and feedback. The resulting time lag causes management inefficiency and customer frustration.

Florida Semiconductors CARE system addresses this problem. CARE includes toll-free EDI centralized service dispatch, on-line status on each service request, service history on all equipment, inventory control of service parts and equipment, and preventive maintenance planning. Also, field engineers can change work-order scheduling to meet customer needs.

The Field Information System (FIS) is used to implement CARE. FIS is a distributed transaction processing EDI network that allows data collection, scheduling, and resource management of any particular service call in the United States. The need for each dispatcher and manager to know the location of each of his or her field engineers and the current status of all customer requests led to the development of CARE and FIS.

For ease of use, FS decided to design the system so that the customer with a problem could call or communicate with via EDI any dispatch center in the United States and receive a response to his or her needs. System response had to be quick to reduce both frustration and cost, since either a client or the customer engineer service were probably waiting on the phone. CARE and FIS also enables customer computers to talk to the FS computer via EDI to receive status information.

The Field Information System (FIS) was built around the Service Ticket (or the EDI equivalent) used to generate a customer request. When an equipment serial number is entered via service engineers or via EDI, all recent information on that piece of equipment becomes available. To ease the generation of this equipment database, much of the information is entered when a piece of equipment leaves the loading dock. The Factory Order Control System, which controls factory packaging and shipping, automatically enters equipment data into the FIS when equipment is shipped. This information contains factory ship dates, warranty dates, warranty status, contract status, coverage hours, and the like.

The dispatcher or the customer (via EDI) only needs to enter a service number. The FIS then assigns a ticket to the job request and computes the closest service office by using telephone prefixes laid over a geographic grid of the entire United States. This means that a customer can call any of the dispatch centers and the appropriate service office will receive the service request. After selection of the nearest service office, FIS transfers the service ticket, often via EDI, into the nearest office's work queue.

When the service engineer (SE) becomes available, he or she calls into the service office. There the work queue displayed on the CRT shows the work tickets in order of receipt, the equipment model number, the status of the work ticket, and the location of the equipment. From this information the dispatcher can decide which job to assign.

After responding to the request, the service engineer (SE) enters that information into a portable microcomputer and updates the data bank and work queue. The SE then receives his or her next assignment. During all of this, FIS has kept track of service inventories down to the service engineer level. Part of the inventory control system in FIS is an automatic reordering system. When an inventory falls below a predetermined level, it is automatically reordered, in a standard quantity, from the factory warehouse and shipped to the location where it is needed.

The system has also been storing all the transaction data for use in computing indices used to manage the service organization. The performance indices calculated by CARE include: the number of incident reports, tickets, trips, and calls; the number of calls requiring parts, the number of calls where parts are not available, and the number of parts rushed from each stocking location; the mean time to travel, repair, dispatch, diagnose, and complete; the mean miles traveled and the actual miles traveled; the percentage of recalls and the calls per day; the cost in dollars per hour and in dollars per call; and the number of tickets in each billing status. All of these are cost driven and are monitored closely by management.

The host DXS system contains a centralized database which is downloaded daily to the dispatch centers that use smaller DXSs. The localized databases and communication redundancy make a highly reliable combination. For example, the dispatch DXSs in use include two CPUs; one acts as the applicable processor and the other handles terminal polling and communication routing. Should malfunctions occur, this feature allows terminals to continue functioning by immediately rerouting communication around the malfunctioning CPU to another CPU in the network. Thus, even when a network node goes down, the system remains viable and functioning and terminals can still enter tickets and dispatch SEs. The local database means that each dispatch center can operate autonomously for extended periods even if it loses all communication with the host or other dispatch centers.

As each transaction takes place at the dispatch DXS, the transaction is spooled and transmitted to the host DXS in Miami via the EDI. The host in turn replies with any new information that will update the district database. All of this takes place in a few seconds so the DXSs are effectively communicating real time. This provides the advantage that customers can call any service center and find out the status of their request.

Microcomputer terminals, in conjunction with DXS, are also used to communicate with the Corporate Information Center's database. This means that the FIS network both collects field data and gives the field inquiry status to the corporate database. Information needed by corporate level managers is available on an on-line basis, whereas the access of corporate data is restricted to selected FIS terminals.

In-Factory Distributed Processing

Florida Semiconductor uses an in-factory application of distributed processing known as the Distributed Application Processing System (DAPS). DAPS is based on the belief that proper management of operation flow is the prime factor in minimizing material buildup in an area and smoothing the work load. To do this they use a just-in-time system such as that outlined in an earlier chapter, where a component is not started into production until it is needed by the next operation.

DAPS provides the capability of tracking a part number and quantity through a series of work stations relative to a designated cycle time. The system is linked to the Corporate Information Center. Input to the DAPS computer is through microcomputers located on the factory floor. By keeping careful control over the flow and by not starting component manufacturing until needed, work in process is minimized. Hard-copy scheduling, work status, and problem job reports can be delivered on a daily basis. The increased visibility and on-line mode allow flexible rescheduling and priority expediting if the need arises. Scheduling and managing are also easier because shop load versus shop capacity is now visible. Summary data in the form of schedules, starts, and completions are automatically sent to the Material Control System.

This system replaced an old manual logging of assemblies as they move through the manufacturing stations, and it eliminated the need for slow verbal and written communication to dispatchers. It also addresses such common production questions as: What is the latest schedule? Where is the part? What do I do next? What are the problems? What is hot? Can we meet the schedule workload?

In addition to on-line information available, customized data listings are distributed to support project and shop management. The Active Record Status report is printed every weekday evening and contains estimated times of arrival, commit dates, job statistics, and so forth. A Run History shows the history of work completion. A Shop Load report contains past and future projections of work hours for each work station.

DAPS is made up of distinct units. The largest unit, the shop, is a separate facility or easily identified subset of a fabrication facility or supply organization. A group of stations composes a shop. Stations perform a single operation or series of related operations inside one shop. The station's capacity is expressed in parts per day and hours per day. The specific sequence of stations that a category or family of parts must proceed through is called a *flow type*. The time necessary for completing a certain operation is called *cycle time*. The cycle time for a specific flow type is the sum of the station cycle times for that flow type. This cycle time includes wait, setup, run, and move times for each station.

The DAPS system is on-line on DXS; however, changes are only made to the Corporation Information Center's system when the Material Control System is updated nightly. The shipping and packaging system, FOCS (Factory Order and Control System), works in conjunction with DAPS. Together they link numerous computers and terminals located at several sites spread over several cities. Both DAPS and FOCS have access to host computers. The DAPS runs on DXS and keeps track of 25,000 to 30,000 lots distributed throughout the 660 stations within twenty-five shops. The DAPS and FOCS operate twenty-four hours a day, seven days a week with time off only for preventive maintenance and backup procedures.

CAROLINA WOOD PRODUCTS

Carolina Wood Products's production[7], inventory, and distribution systems used to run on a mountain of paper work. Errors were made and important business decisions were delayed while the necessary paper-based data made its way to Winston-Salem and waited for keypunch operators to enter it into the corporation's mainframe.

The objective of Carolina's new MRP system it developed a few years ago was to eliminate all of the paper trails, so that when a transaction occurs, it is recorded in the computer at that moment. But eliminating paper work wasn't the primary aim of the MRP system. Carolina Wood Products wanted to be more efficient at its business. Eventually, that means a distributed corporatewide system is needed, with some functions, such as master scheduling, running in Winston-Salem and other functions, such as inventory control, running at each factory. The idea was to locate each application where the user is located.

Although the system today remains a long way from the fully distributed MRP the company is shooting for, the changes in place are already generating major benefits. Inventory records are more accurate, customer service has improved, and divisions are more likely to meet standards. Almost immediately, the company improved its inventory control, as production became more closely aligned with sales through the distributed MRP system.

Large multisite manufacturers like Carolina Wood Products usually adopted a centralized first-generation MRP approach where a mainframe would run all of the MRP applications for an entire company. Carolina Wood did not do this. However, when manufacturing companies began moving business responsibility and control out to individual business units in the 1970s, second-generation MRP approaches were developed, where each plant would implement its own autonomous system.

These second-generation MRP systems did not turn out to be satisfactory solutions for many organizations because of system inconsistency between the plants. As a result there was no way of really communicating between various parts of the organization.

A distributed MRP system, which is what Carolina Wood is attempting, combines aspects of the first two generations; some aspects are used at the plant

---

[7] This example is founded upon Simla, Chris, "Georgia-Pacific's MRP II Test," Datamation, Nov. 15, 1989.

(decentralized) level and other aspects are centralized. The completed system should link sales and forecasting done at corporate headquarters to the factory floor, and then link data from production and distribution back to the corporate financial applications. The plan is to go through three phases one plant at a time. In phase one, some functions, particularly master scheduling, remain at corporate headquarters. The pieces needed to meet that schedule, like purchasing and distribution, run at the plants. Phase two will add shop floor control to increase automation at the plants and link more of the actual production to the MRP system. Phase three will be the fully implemented distributed MRP system linking the five company plants to Winston-Salem.

For a traditional information system (IS) shop, running a centralized system, the distribution of such major applications means major operational changes. And these changes faced a reluctant IS department. Some behavorial problems resulted from these changes. For example, data entry, plus access and control of the database, are moving out of IS control. This is an entirely new concept to a lot of MIS departments. In the good old days of centralization, managers used to go to MIS and say "please give me this report." Decentralized managers using distributed systems don't do that any more, so the MIS people feel somewhat threatened.

The initial distributed MRP system ran into some initial resistance in several departments. A bar-coding system now keeps track of inventory, eliminating a physical count that used to be performed by the plant's purchasing department. When purchasing personnel found that they were running low on an item, they bought more of it, but the decision as to how much to buy was based on past needs, not projected sales. Now, materials handlers keep track of inventory using laser scanners. Corporate headquarters has access to updated inventory every five minutes and planners in Winston-Salem decide purchasing needs based on that data and future sales. Such a detailed level of data allows planners to purchase inventory more often in smaller quantities to approach JIT objectives. But such an approach required the purchasing department to move away from its traditional batch-purchasing approach. As a result, the purchasing department's job changed so that they end up working more with the vendor to schedule material and lower inventory levels. It's a more efficient way of doing business, but it has created the need for some cultural adjustments within the purchasing department.

In summary, several phases have been fully implemented at a few plants. Managers really like the new system because substantial savings have occurred. The home office is still not a believer in the distributed MRP system, however.

SUMMARY

In summary large companies are often geographically disbursed, consist of many divisions, and process huge numbers of transactions. As a result their management needs large complex information systems to deal with widespread operations. These information systems are generally integrated so that the organization can coordinate its activities. These systems need complex communication structures for management and their computer systems to communicate. Often this involves distributed processing and distributed databases. In many cases this involves EDI systems to handle the volume of communication between the organization's own divisions and between the organization and its suppliers and customers. These communication and EDI systems have saved these large organizations hundreds of thousands of dollars through reduced paperwork and improved operations such as JIT inventory systems. As a result integrated wide area communication networks have become a new way of doing business for many large organizations.

SELECTED REFERENCES

THE GLOBECON GROUP, LTD., *Electronic Data Interchange and Corporate Trade Payments*, Financial Executives Research Foundation, Morristown, N.J., 1988.

HEIDKAMP, MARTHA M., "Reaping the Benefits of Financial EDI," *Management Accounting*, May 1991, pp. 39-43.

MAYER, JAMES A., "MIS at International Paper: An Integrated Teleprocessing Network," *Management Accounting*, April 1979.

PERSON, RON, "How TI Distributes Its Processing," *Datamation*, April 1979.

SADHWANI, ARJAN T. and M. H. SARHAN, "Electronic Systems Enhance JIT Operations," *Management Accounting*, 1987.

SIMLA, CHRIS, "Georgia-Pacific's MRP II Test," *Datamation*, November 15, 1989.

VANRENSSELAER, CURT, "Centralize? Decentralize? Distribute?" *Datamation*, April 1979.

WILLENZ, NICOLE V., "Electronic Data Interchange: A Quiet Revolution," *Price Waterhouse Review*, 1988, No. 3, pp. 33-45.

REVIEW QUESTIONS

1. What is electronic data interchange (EDI)? What benefits can an industry gain from adopting EDI?

2. What barriers stand in the way of companies adopting EDI? How can third party vendors of communication specialists aid in making EDI easier for small organizations to achieve who deal with many customers that are in a variety of industries?

3. How can large organizations deal with divisions scattered throughout the world? How can they save money by reducing their transaction costs when customers and vendors, as well as their own divisions with whom they buy and sell, are scattered throughout the world?

4. Name some examples where EDI has improved the processing of transactions in the automotive industry.

5. What characteristics of the grocery industry make it a very likely candidate to benefit from widespread use of EDI?

6. Why is it important to integrate the systems in the integrated manufacturing example? How can the system and the database be integrated and distributed at the same time? What would happen if they were not integrated?

7. What is the nature of the communication network in a worldwide distributed processing situation? How can the use of EDI and other telecommunication systems help companies spread over a wide area serve customers?

8. How can MRP help large organizations control their productive activities?

CASES

18-1 Garden State Chemicals produces many of the chemicals used in the manufacture of plastics. Several of its customers have started to use electronic data interchange and have adapted the CIDX standards for the chemical industry in 1984. They would receive orders, send invoices, and receive payments using this standard. Mr. Bailey, the chief accountant of Garden State, is reluctant to adopt EDI because of the risks and the lack of standardization.

REQUIRED: As Garden State's accountant, draft a memo regarding standardization, third party translation, and communication specialists and controls that can be used to lessen the risks to help Mr. Bailey better develop a position regarding EDI.

18-2 Big Bird Food's controller has studied the experiences of other similar grocers who have adopted EDI. Big Bird has approximately 5,000 purchase orders per week and processes 400 invoices per week which need to be reconciled in their accounts payable system.

REQUIRED: Based on the experience of others, how much could Big Bird expect to save using EDI (ignoring the cost of such a system) assuming a 52-week year?

18-3 World Wide Paper Company is a large multinational forest products corporation, with over $6.5 billion in sales in 1990.* The company is the largest North American producer of paperboard, paper, and pulp products but is also involved in health-care and wood products as well as exploration for oil, gas, and minerals.

In the early 1980s the company's information systems were essentially decentralized with little corporate reporting and control. The only companywide telecommunications facility was an antiquated network for administrative messages, order entry, and intracompany data flow. From an information systems standpoint, most operating unit locations were on their own; a total of twenty-three separate computer

centers and roughly twenty-six mainframes existed. In effect, the limitations in effective telecommunications prevented any real integration of computer functions.

This environment created problems in the flow of information. Systems at the division level met the requirements of local managements but had no built-in linkages to corporate level information systems. Passing information from the division level to business-unit and corporate management levels was complex, subject to errors and delay. As a result, planning and decision making were being inhibited unnecessarily.

In 1981, WWP's senior management directed the financial organization to set an overall direction for MIS activity—with consolidation of the twenty-three data centers and an integrated companywide information system in mind. To achieve these objectives, WWP needed to integrate existing systems or provide a new framework for information companywide. The result was an "Integrated Information Systems" (IIS) plan. In simple terms, IIS was a plan to feed operating and planning data up through the organization to provide business unit and corporate managers with the information they needed to do their jobs.

Obviously the goal was worthy and the task was complex. It meant not only defining information needs at all organization levels and designing application systems to support those needs, but establishing an appropriate technical environment to accommodate the data transfer needs of the corporation on a cost-effective basis. In 1986, WWP reorganized from a functional structure to one along lines-of-business units—again calling for a better means of distributing information throughout the company.

The first step was consolidation of twenty-three decentralized computer centers into four and, subsequently, three regional computer centers. In effect, the company consolidated the data into mainframes in Danville, Virginia, Stockton, California, and Mobile, Alabama. Corporate Management Information

---

* This case has been updated, adapted and reprinted, in part, by permission from, "MIS at International Paper: An Integrated Teleprocessing Network" by James A. Mayer appearing in the April 1979 issue of *Management Accounting*, published by Institute of Management Accountants (formerly The National Association of Accountants), Montvale, N.J., pp. 24-27.

Systems (CMIS) planned and coordinated the move at WWP headquarters in Manhattan, providing consolidated computing resources to the corporate staff and seventy-nine WWP facilities in the United States.

This, of course, did not solve all of WWP's problems. The company had centralized the data but did not have an effective way of moving these data between locations. More than seventeen software technicians were assigned pure maintenance and liaison with locations. Moreover, total voice and data communication costs had increased 122 percent. Data communications costs were also $4 million, rising much faster than overhead. In addition, the company was being pressured to add on-line order entry and other applications without disrupting existing operations. It was difficult to meet those demands and get information to existing locations at the same time.

The second step, therefore, was implementation of ITN (Integrated Teleprocessing Network), an under-one-roof approach to data communications. To understand ITN, one has to look at the telecommunications facilities WWP had at the time and the objectives of the proposed integrated network.

Historically, commercial teleprocessing environments reflected a lack of overall direction. Software was usually designed and developed for specific user applications without an overall structure in mind. WWP was no exception. Each major systems group developed its own application and teleprocessing support. A lot of software development depended strictly on personalities. Nobody really knew exactly what was "out there." To improve an application, or to interface it with similar work at another facility, required costly changes in application code, communication software, and terminal equipment. Any change in mill applications required a system that could communicate with older information systems. New applications like on-line order entry had to interface with a number of different manufacturing systems.

In effect, WWP was a company of single-application terminal types, with no common standardized teleprocessing software. The company actually had four different networks, each developed and maintained separately, each with its own software, lines, and terminals. The administrative message switch network, the only network serving intracompany communications, serviced low-speed terminals and high-speed computer mainframe links to the old regional mainframes. The data-entry network serviced forty-seven remote terminals, handling a light volume of data from many locations. Another network supported on-line transactions, mainly file updates. A fourth supported remote job entry for a total of twenty-eight sites.

If viewed separately, none of these networks was deficient; they accommodated the data transfer needs of the users for which they were designed. However, it took three different teleprocessing access methods, five separate teleprocessing control programs, and five data networks to get the job done. It also required some locations to have as many as four different terminals, one for each teleprocessing application. Network integration did not exist.

To solve these technical problems, WWP set the following objectives:

1. Single base telecommunications software to support company needs including diverse terminal types, microcomputer, and networking requirements.

2. Reliable transfer of data from any terminal to any other terminal or data stored in the computer.

3. Cost reduction and cost avoidance.

In September 1986, WWP set up a group to develop and implement an integrated teleprocessing network to meet these objectives. Two documents resulted. The first was functional specifications for ITN, submitted to five telecommunications vendors. The second evaluated vendor proposals and subsequently recommended the concept of IBM's SNA (System Network Architecture) as the direction for teleprocessing at WWP. The SNA approach is basically common teleprocessing software and simplification of all the technical considerations facing a data communications user. With this SNA concept, all data transfer concerns such as line protocol and access methods, and even the choice of the most economical transmission facilities, are "transparent" to the user. For WWP this meant that an IBM 3270 terminal or microcomputer—or almost any terminal for that matter—could be used to communicate with the company's regional mainframe computers. The application did not matter. A person could log onto a 3270 terminal for order entry, switch over to check stock availability, and wind up sending an administrative message—all in one session at one terminal.

In effect, SNA came closest to meeting the ITN objectives. It allowed the company to grow into an integrated network by keeping the application code considerably separate from teleprocessing support.

Corporate systems development manager Jerry Helems sums it up well: "What is key to me is that we can establish input criteria at any location without worrying about which network is involved. In the past we had separate networks for most of our teleprocessing applications. Applications people had to worry about everything from line protocol to access methods and data reliability—in effect all data transfer concerns are used. Now we provide the format specified to get into ITN and the destination of the data, whether a terminal or an application at one of the computers. In either situation, ITN delivers it. The information is received, it is sent, and everything in between is transparent."

Using SNA, WWP implemented ITN in two phases, and the network is now fully in place. Results range from outright savings in hardware and line costs to the reduced costs of application development. All levels at WWP have been affected. This includes applications development staff, computer center operations, end users, and general management. WWP is truly one company from a data communications standpoint.

A byproduct of ITN and SNA was a reversal of the trend toward centralization of data processing at WWP—through distributed processing. SNA makes this possible. The company has shifted some processing to remote sites. Thirty communications systems have been installed at the Container Division plant locations. Instead of processing all data at regional data centers, plants do remote editing for applications like roll stock inventories, general ledger, and accounts payable. The host computer in Danville provides major data on customers and items as well as network support.

ITN has also helped WWP remove most of the antiquated data input/output facilities. For locations without a terminal operating under SNA and suitable for administrative traffic, the company has installed keyboard printer terminals and similar devices. Some sixty terminals have been eliminated.

REQUIRED:

1. Prepare a system flowchart showing the initial information systems employed by WWP.

2. Prepare a system flowchart for the integrated teleprocessing network.

3. In the last section of the WWP overview the statement was made that ITN and SNA had led to a distributed processing arrangement. Explain this in light of the fact that in 1981 the company established an Integrated Information Systems (IIS) plan.

18-4 The Hewlett-Packard Company manufactures more than 4,000 products for wide-ranging markets that are primarily in manufacturing-related industries.[†] The company has thirty-eight manufacturing facilities and 172 sales and service offices around the world; together these employ about 45,000 people. The company has experienced a growth of about 20 percent per year, culminating in sales of $1.7 billion in 1978.

To support the business at that time, HP had some 11,400 computers. Of these 85 percent were used to support engineering and production applications, dedicated to specific tasks or arranged in networks. A number of them were also used in computer-aided design applications as front-end processors for large mainframes. The remaining 200 computers were used to support business applications. The largest was an Amdahl 470/V6 located in Palo Alto, California. There were nine medium-sized IBM systems in other large facilities. Seventy HP 3000s were used in HP's factories and larger sales offices, and 125 HP 1000s were scattered about for data entry, data retrieval, and data communications work.

Generally speaking, the HP computers were oriented toward on-line applications and the large mainframes toward batch processing (although three also supported on-line applications). In addition, HP used about 2,500 CRT terminals in business applications alone.

[†] Reprinted with permission of Datamation magazine, copyright by Technical Publishing Company, a Dunn & Bradstreet Company, (April 1979), all rights reserved.

The network tying all this together consisted of 110 data communications facilities located at sales and service offices, at manufacturing plants, and at corporate offices in northern California and Switzerland.

After careful analysis and study, management at HP concluded that systems should be centralized, decentralized, or distributed depending on management needs. The following four examples describe specific HP information systems or facilities and show how they matched the organization needs. The first deals with the communication system, which is the heart of a minicomputer network. The second and third examples are of two systems having distributed databases, one with central master files (at two locations) and the other with both central and dispersed masters. The final example deals with decentralized systems which interface some distributed systems.

110-Node Network

The communications system that supports HP's computing network employed minicomputers at 110 worldwide locations. These minis took care of a number of data communication functions. They handled data entry, formatted data for transmission, automatically detected and corrected errors, and adapted transmission protocols to meet the requirements of various countries. In addition, the minis supported on-line access to local databases.

The company began to build the network in the late 1960s to support a communications network with intelligent terminals. The network was successful right from the start. HP had continuously been adding to the locations served. In 1974 HP began to install display terminals on the network. Then distributed databases and an inquiry capability were added.

The average worldwide data volume for the network was about 140 million characters per day in the late 1970's. This translates into about 100,000 messages. Line cost ran under $50,000 per month, which was very economical compared with the communication costs of other companies at the time using on-line systems at similar data volumes.

The largest communication system applications were for marketing (60 percent of the traffic), accounting (15 percent), employee information (10 percent), and administrative messages (15 percent). About a million orders

per year were transmitted over the network and about three million invoices; almost 50 percent of which originated outside the United States. The network was also used extensively for file transmission.

The system has provided an excellent means for transmitting administrative messages (electronic mail) and has been particularly effective for overseas communication, where the telephone is costly and inconvenient because of time zone differences. Using the system, the cost of transmitting a letter-size message overseas is typically thirty cents. This low cost, coupled with the system's speed and convenience, has resulted in a large increase in day-to-day communication between people at the operations level in the company's U.S. and overseas offices.

Marketing Administration System

The second application system example is a distributed marketing administration system, which supports the sales and service organization. The primary objective of the marketing system was to provide accurate and consistent information to support customers on a worldwide basis. To do this required a centrally managed distributed system.

The system was such that centralized, decentralized, and distributed processing all went on simultaneously. Decentralized processing was used for production planning, product configuring, and shipment scheduling at the manufacturing sites, and for order entry and service scheduling at the sales and service offices. Centralized processing was used for such functions as financial and legal reporting and administration of the employee benefits program at corporate headquarters.

Some forms of distributed processing were employed for maintaining and accessing distributed databases. All the data for customer records originated at the sales offices, for example, and parts of the customer database were kept in each sales office, but a complete customer database was simultaneously maintained at corporate headquarters and parts of the database also existed at the manufacturing plants.

All the data for product records originated at the sales offices, for another example, and parts of the product database were kept at each plant, but complete product databases are simultaneously maintained at corporate headquarters and at each sales office.

Orders and changes were entered at the sales and service offices, transmitted to headquarters where they were entered on central files, and then sent on to the factories for acceptance and delivery acknowledgment. Company order, shipment, and backlog status was maintained centrally to provide information to top management. Delivery information was transmitted from the manufacturing divisions back to the sales offices where orders are acknowledged.

Invoices were centrally processed in Palo Alto and Geneva. The credit and collection functions were decentralized to the sales offices, which central reporting of receivables status to provide financial control.

Files of European open orders were maintained in both Geneva and Palo Alto. An order from a European sales office containing items to be supplied from a European factory and a U.S. factory was processed in Geneva. Complete detail pertaining to the U.S.-supplied items was transmitted to Palo Alto; however, only order statistics were sent to Palo Alto for the European-supplied items. Order status information was transmitted back and forth daily to keep the two files in sync, and a monthly audit procedure ensured that nothing has been overlooked in the daily updates.

Up-to-date order status change information was transmitted daily from the Palo Alto headquarters to the larger U.S. sales offices to provide on-line access for response to customer inquiries. The remote files were synchronized with the master files by computer control. That is, the update program requires each batch update to be performed in the right order. (The January 17 update could not be performed before the January 16 update.) Local files could be recreated from the central files should recovery be necessary.

Although data communication was handled in a batch mode, the system operated in the same manner as an on-line distributed system in which a significant portion of the data processing is done at more than one location. Data was batch communicated because this was the most economical method to employ with currently available communication facilities.

Personnel/Payroll System

To comply with local laws and customs, an independent personnel/payroll system was maintained by HP in each country in which it had operations. In the United States HP had a distributed system that payed about 25,000 employees. The pay information was entered on display terminals at about thirty remote locations, each with its own daily update disk file. The data were transmitted to Palo Alto monthly, where the payroll was processed. The paychecks were either transmitted back to the originating locations for printing or directly deposited in the employee's bank account.

The distributed database that supported the payroll/personnel system operated in a different mode from that which was used for the sales and service system. Each division was responsible for the accuracy of the data relating to its employees. The data were kept on local HP 3000 disk files updated daily. Changes made to these files were transmitted to Palo Alto several times a month, where they were used to update a central file prior to payroll processing.

The audit and control procedure that ensured that the central and remote files were synchronized worked in the following manner. After the central file had been updated, the modified records were transmitted back to the local entity for comparison. Any discrepancies were then reported.

Discrepancies could arise from two causes. First, somewhat more stringent edit routines could be applied centrally, so an unedited error was occasionally detected. Second, certain changes to employees' records could be made centrally and these were sometimes not recorded in the local files. A small, but significant number of errors were detected by this audit and control procedure.

The payroll/personnel system served a number of departments: finance, accounting, personnel, and tax. An advisory board consisting of members of each of those departments reviewed and approved changes to the system's programs, which number several hundred per year.

Eighty-five percent of HP's U.S. employees were paid by this system. The other 15 percent were located in manufacturing divisions that elected to run their payrolls locally. Personnel data for this 15 percent was still maintained in the central file to take care of the centrally administered benefit programs. Keeping these independently prepared data accurate and consistent with the data prepared centrally was a significant challenge. This experience dramatized the advantage of sharing common data used by different functions. The discipline of the payroll system proved to be invaluable in keeping central personnel records up to date and accurate.

The remote personnel files of both kinds permitted local entities to produce reports on their employees. In addition, they provided a timely interface to local systems such as cost accounting. The remotely used software was centrally supported, and changes were released periodically.

Factory Management System

The last application system to be described was the factory management system, which was implemented on HP 3000 hardware. This decentralized system supported the functions of order processing, materials management and purchasing, production planning, product assurance, service support, and accounting.

The factory management system consisted of a group of functional modules which accessed a central database that served as an information resource for the division. As mentioned earlier, most systems used by manufacturing divisions were decentralized and locally managed. Although each HP division had unique requirements that had to be satisfied by its local support systems, there was a remarkable similarity between the needs of the different divisions. Most HP divisions were oriented largely toward assembly operations, so manufacturing support systems were designed around a bill-of-materials processor. As a general rule, 80 percent of a division's needs could be satisfied with the basic system. HP developed the factory management system to multiply the return on development and support costs by sharing systems between these decentralized locations.

The factory management system was developed over a five-year period, one module at a time. (An example of a system module would be materials management, production planning, or cost accounting.) The development

was accomplished by development teams consisting of division personnel responsible for providing the specifications and ensuring that the system meets their functional needs, and of central data processing specialists who made sure that the modules operated efficiently and properly interfaced other system modules. On completion each module could be shared by other divisions on a voluntary basis.

HP did not attempt to solve all system problems in each module; instead it followed the 80–20 rule, taking care of major requirements that were common to a number of divisions. In fact, HP encouraged sharing divisions to add unique features required to meet their local needs. Quite often these unique features were of value to other divisions and later got incorporated into the "standard" modules.

This approach to shareable system design was very successful. The company found that the shared modules save up to 75 percent over the cost of local development and that they can be implemented in a fraction of the time. At that time, over half of HP's thirty-eight divisions elected to participate in this, and nearly all had plans eventually to use some parts of the system.

The factory management system had been especially useful to new divisions (which were being added at a rate of about three per year). It permitted managers in these divisions to have a high level of systems support capability early in their growth cycle. On the other hand, the system had been much less useful to older, established divisions with mature systems. These entities found it difficult to justify the cost of change (especially retraining people), even though on-line operation and other enhancements would have been desirable.

REQUIRED:

1. Compare the communication network of the World Wide Paper Company (Case 18-3) with that of the Hewlett-Packard Company. How do the communication needs of the two companies differ?

2. Describe some of the problems that might exist in the *marketing administration* system in regard to new applications and/or changes in the system. What types of problems probably existed because of the international scope of the systems

activities? What, if any, justifications exist for a more distributed system?

3. What would justify HP's decision to process all payrolls at Palo Alto rather than at remote locations?

4. What advantages are present in the factory management system because it used a common shareable system design?

19

SYSTEMS FOR SMALL ENTREPRENEURIAL ENTERPRISES

INTRODUCTION

Small entrepreneurial enterprises which effectively harness the capabilities of microcomputer systems to establish better links with customers, control costs, and in general make better management decisions have a distinct competitive advantage over rivals and larger organizations. This is true whether the organization produces goods or services.

Like large organizations, small entrepreneurial enterprises must follow the structured approach to system design in theory. Because of their size they probably will not formalize all the steps but their thought process must be consistent with good design theory. First, they must determine a business strategy. This should be founded upon critical success factors for their particular business environment, management style, and other competitive strengths. This business strategy should not be a copy of a large business or even a competitor, because their business environment and set of strengths and weaknesses will be quite different. Second, they need to understand their information needs for operating the business, processing transactions, reporting, and decisions making. Again, because of the special characteristics of small firms, these will most likely be different than for large organizations. Like large organizations they need to develop an information strategy to satisfy these requirements. This is followed by a system design which follows this strategy. Finally, they need to carefully implement their strategy and accounting information system. Thus, even though their competitive, organizational, and social environment will be quite different in many cases from their larger counterparts, small entrepreneurial enterprises still need to carefully plan and implement their accounting and information systems. If this is done, their information can be used as a competitive weapon to enhance their business.

In summary, a well-designed, effective accounting system is essential to the continued success of a small entrepreneurial organization. On the negative side, many small businesses fail because of the lack of an effective accounting system that provides management and owners with information for decision-making and reporting requirements. Even small businesses with an efficient, well-designed manual or computer system may fail because management does not know how to effectively use the information provided by the system.

CHARACTERISTICS OF THE SMALL ENTREPRENEURIAL BUSINESS ENVIRONMENT

A small entrepreneurial enterprise can best be described by characteristics[1] other than sales or assets in dollars, even though these figures are generally small in comparison with those in a large, more established business. Moreover, entrepreneurial businesses are not always new ventures; many older small businesses have these characteristics. These characteristics lead to specific design, implementation, and control problems not discussed in earlier chapters.

First, a small entrepreneurial manager or owner is likely to have a direct understanding of the market (customers, products, and prices) being served and may not need an expensive, highly structured system to provide much of this information.

Second, entrepreneurial enterprises are characterized by their ability to react quickly to market conditions with new products and services. Their systems need to provide this flexibility to take initiatives quickly and not hinder these initiatives with elaborate controls.

Third, a small business is generally a high-risk venture with little capital and a great deal of enthusiasm. Often the business is relatively new. Thus there often are not enough funds to support expensive systems and the personnel to run these systems. Many small businesses have only a part-time clerk rather than a controller to operate the entire accounting information system. However, the owners are often quite active in the affairs of the business and may not need a financial officer to analyze, interpret, and report information for decision making.

---

[1] Characteristics are based on Donald R. Smith, "Information Systems for the Entrepreneurial Enterprise," *Today's Executive* (Summer–Autumn 1986), Price Waterhouse, New York, NY, pp. 3–17; and William K. Grollman and Robert W. Colby, "Internal Control for Small Businesses," *The Journal of Accountancy.* Copyright © (1978) by the American Institute of Certified Public Accountants, Inc., December 1978, pp. 64–67.

Fourth, managers and owners of small businesses tend to be aggressive risk takers despite the fact that even minor reversals can be catastrophic. They operate much more on intuition rather than on the numbers for decision making, as is often the case for larger more established organizations. They will assimilate much of their day-to-day operating information through direct observation. This direct, hands-on style of management will have an impact on decision needs and the type of system desired to support these needs.

Fifth, the key personnel who run the business tend to have marketing, engineering, mechanical, and artistic talents, for example, rather than financial or accounting expertise. They exercise personal leadership in the areas that are critical to the success of the business. These key personnel often either are not interested in accounting and financial systems or, if they have these systems, do not know how to use them. They can, however, be greatly assisted if the accounting system provides information about the success factors critical to the organization's success.

Sixth, executives and managers, as well as their families, are likely to own most or a controlling part of the business. Because of family ownership, reports to the owners are often unnecessary because they are so actively involved in day-to-day operations.

Seventh, due to their talents and degree of ownership, these small-business executives or owners tend to dominate the affairs of the company. For example, if the owner is an engineer, the basic characteristic of the firm and all of the decisions will reflect the technical side of the business, not the marketing or financial aspects. This is the way it should be for this is likely to be the key to business success.

Eighth, generally the business is not very complicated. This means that the accounting system required and the reports generated by the system are not as complicated as those for large businesses. The owner or manager is likely to know key customers and vendors and not need such an extensive information system to track customer credit activities, for example.

Ninth, generally small businesses are informal in decision and reporting style, making it difficult to implement a complicated accounting system with a great deal of structure. Highly structured control systems would probably hinder the entrepreneurial spirit of the organization.

Tenth, as with large businesses, many reports still must be prepared for managers, creditors, owners, and governmental agencies. These reporting requirements have increased in complexity but not to the same extent as for large businesses. Typical reports are shown in Figure 19-1.

In summary, the major differences characterizing large businesses and small entrepreneurial enterprises result from the dominant influence of the owners and/or managers on the business environment and the need to support the information requirements related to these critical factors for success. In a large business, owners and managers are often dominated by the business and its environment. Moreover, in small businesses there is less of a need for a formal financial reporting system for the owners (principals) to monitor the activities of the managers (agents). This difference has major implications for accountants as they design and develop information systems for small entrepreneurial enterprises.

Sales Analysis (by location, merchandise, and salesperson)
Accounts Receivable (including aging and write-offs)
Accounts Payable
Inventory Status (perpetual inventory)
    Inventory on order
    Inventory on hand
    Reorders
Cash Receipts
Cash Disbursements
Cash Forecast and Budget
Asset and Depreciation Records
Budgets
    Sales—forecast
    Purchase or production
    Cash
Payroll Register
Financial Statements
Other Special Reports for the Type of Business
    Reports to third parties
        tax returns
        banking requirements
        government regulation

FIGURE 19-1 Typical reports for small businesses.

Entrepreneurial Strategy and Organization

A small entrepreneurial enterprise must determine its business strategy. As discussed in earlier chapters, this is similar to large organization's requirement, but the choice of strategy will be quite different because of the special characteristics just outlined. This strategy should be based on the special talents and abilities of the owners and key employees and their knowledge of the market, customers, product, and other firsthand information. These keys to success should dictate the business organization, decision-making requirements, and type of information to be provided by the organization's accounting information system to support the transaction processing, decision-making, and reporting needs of the enterprise.

A small entrepreneurial enterprise could be organized along functional lines, by projects, or by a matrix structure. In general, the organization should retain of organizational flexibility such as that provided by the matrix or project organization so that the enterprise can react quickly to new opportunities. In very small firms, the organization will probably be much less formal and will consist of a manager (often the owner) to whom all employees report. Slightly larger businesses may have a few functional, product, project, departmental, store, or regional managers. In all cases the organization will be small and often informal, rendering the traditional systems concepts of responsibility and segregation of duties ineffective. This is usually counteracted, in part, by the active participation of the manager and owner in most aspects of the business.

Entrepreneurs and managers must make decisions about where they are headed (strategic planning), how they expect to get there with the resources available to them (managerial planning), and, on a day-to-day basis, how best to use these resources (operational decisions). It is unlikely that these decisions will be made using formal models except in rare cases at the operational level for such activities as scheduling production, ordering inventory, and evaluating investments. Strategic and managerial decisions, however, are based on the same set of information used by larger firms even though it is less formal because the decision maker (owner or manager) is closer to market and competitive conditions. The role of the accountant (in many cases the organization's CPA) is to see that the entrepreneurial enterprise owner or manager has sufficient information to make these decisions. Outsiders such as CPAs render this advice as part of their service to their small business clients. Most large CPA firms have special divisions which are specifically designed to do this.

Too often, small enterprise management considers only transactions processing. Resource utilization is not planned. Realistic objectives are not formulated with plans to achieve these objectives based on the success factors. Goal setting is a decision-making process. The focal point of this process is usually the budget. Regardless of the accounting system used, a small entrepreneurial enterprise should have a budget or a plan for the future to serve as a framework for operating decisions and to force management and owners to make strategic and managerial decisions about the direction of business. A budget will go a long way toward coordinating the various decision-making activities and will help prevent the typical "seat-of-the-pants" reaction to economic and political events that constantly buffet the small business. An accounting system designed around the budget will give the small business needed direction. The lack of these plans is a major cause of small-business failure.

Information and Reporting Requirements

There are several levels of information required by a small entrepreneurial enterprise.[2] These levels include: (1) the basic legal requirements common to all organizations for reporting to third parties, tax authorities, and financial institutions; (2) basic control information for daily operations; (3) information for routine operational decisions; and (4) information for managing the enterprise.

The reporting requirements for small businesses tend to be simple. The information may be a set of operating and financial reports or an organized set of records for inventory, accounts receivable, cash balances, and accounts payable. Often only minimal records are required for management use in decision making.

This simplicity of information needs arises for two reasons. First, small-business transactions tend to be straightforward and very repetitive. Simple, easy-to-operate microcomputer accounting systems can be designed to capture this behavior. An example is provided in the appendix. Second, because the owner or manager is involved in ongoing operations much of the time, information on unusual events need not be reported in a formal system. Disclosure of

---

[2] This framework was proposed by Smith in "Information Systems for the Entrepreneurial Enterprise," p. 13.

unusual or complex events is best handled on a face-to-face basis between the manager, owner, coustomer, and creditors.

Many small-business owners and managers do not really want a complex accounting information system. They prefer the minimum records required to operate the business.[3] The absolute minimum is a record of *cash receipts* and *disbursements (a checkbook)*, a record of *accounts receivable,* and a record of *accounts payable.* The latter two records may consist of files of invoices for credit sales and credit puchases. From these minimum records and, if necessary, a physical inventory, a set of financial statements and tax returns can be prepared at any point in time for any period. Exceptions can be handled at the time of the statement preparation by a CPA if necessary. Most important, the small-business owner or manager can implement and operate this minimal system with little or no training. For really small enterprises, a *single-entry* accounting system is sufficient. Moreover, due to the simplicity of operation, a cash basis system often suffices. A discussion of these single-entry systems along with ledgerless accounting systems is presented in Appendix B. These systems can easily be converted by an accountant to an accrual basis at year-end.

Recently there have been several proposals for dual sets of accounting principles and disclosure requirements. The AICPA Committee on Generally Accepted Accounting Principles for Smaller and/or Closely Held Businesses concluded that there was strong support for consistent application of generally accepted accounting principles, but it recommended that disclosure (the extent of the detail of information) could vary based on the characteristics of the business. The FASB, in issuing *Financial Accounting Standard No. 21,* exempted closely held corporations from previously required disclosures of information about business segments and earnings per share. The basic philosophy underlying these differential disclosure requirements is that information not useful to the owners and creditors for small businesses does not warrant its preparation cost. More differential disclosure requirements may be issued in the future.

The second level of information is necessary for the enterprise to maintain a certain level of control over its operations. This would probably include various files or a database consisting of detailed customer, inventory, accounts receivable, and accounts payable records. Many benefits are found in these areas related to transaction processing and reporting. Transaction processing is simplified by using the microcomputer. Data are entered once, they are edited, and the files are updated. This streamlined data entry eliminates a considerable amount of paper work. In older manual systems this paper work often created errors, in spite of many controls. There is a large variety of these microcomputer systems. Even though most have a fairly standard set of reports, management can often find microcomputer software with the set of reports they need. A few of the more comprehensive packages have very flexible output. As an example, many have departmental statements, and provide comparisons and ratios. Good illustrations of these detailed records and reports are shown in Appendix A which describes a typical microcomputer system for a small business. Accounting systems such as these provide for the smooth running of the enterprise as

---

[3] See James B. Bower, Robert E. Schlosser, and Maurice Newman, *Computer Oriented Accounting Information Systems* (Cincinnati: South Western, 1985); and James B. Bower, Robert E. Schlosser and Charles T. Zlatkovich, *Financial Information Systems* (Boston: Allyn & Bacon, 1972) for a discussion of minimum records.

they record business transactions for decision making and for the preparation of reliable financial statements.

The third level of support that an accounting system can give the enterprise is a competitive edge in dealing with customers and vendors in the area of automatic decision making for routine decisions. Some examples are the decisions to reorder stock when inventories reach a low (reorder) point to ensure adequate stock to carry on business, the decision to pay vendors to take advantage of discounts to improve cash flows, and scheduling decisions to ensure that products reach their destination on time to satisfy customer demand. Many microcomputer programs are available to assist managers and employees in these routine decisions.

The fourth level in which the accounting information system can assist management of an entrepreneurial enterprise is in the area of management. The primary benefits of small microcomputer systems are not in the periodic processing of payroll checks, the printing of customer statements, and other standard periodic accounting procedures. It may well be that the entrepreneur's accountant or service bureau can do this periodic work at a more reasonable cost. The primary advantage of these microcomputer systems is found in the ability of management to interact with the files in an easy, self-taught way. This is the area in which microcomputer systems can really make a competitive difference in the success or failure of the small entrepreneurial enterprise. For example, this enhanced interaction allows the manager to:

1. Query a customer account to answer questions
2. Query the status of a particular inventory item to determine if it is on hand or when it will arrive
3. Determine how much cash will be needed to pay this week's payables
4. Assess the qualifications of a certain employee for a new job
5. Assess the tax effect of a new expenditure
6. Assess various construction plans for feasibility and cost
7. Aggregate and disaggregate financial statements to assess division performance

Many of these and other management questions tend to require immediate answers. The ability to obtain answers to these sometimes complex questions quickly and accurately can have an impact on the profitability of the firm.

Moreover, many microcomputer systems have the capability of helping entrepreneurs manage their operations and in some cases actually perform some of the operations. Budget systems are available for financial control. Even very small microcomputer systems have some provision for this and provide comparative statistics for the last year. The example in the appendix shows the minimum which can be expected from such systems. Many microcomputer systems have far more sophisticated budgeting systems than the one in the appendix. These cost more and are often more complex to operate too. Others are specialized for certain businesses, such as management and client billings.

Developing an Overall Information System Strategy and System Design

The overall accounting information system strategy should focus on the unique success factors of the entrepreneurial enterprise. Priorities need to be set by the owners and management for the selection of support applications and the software and hardware necessary to implement these applications. The applications should follow from the analysis indicated in the earlier section and specified in the chapters on structured design. A necessary balance will need to be struck between the need for information and the cost of obtaining this information. In other words, a cost-benefit analysis is important for small firms also. Fortunately, the cost of hardware and software for microcomputers has dropped dramatically over the last several years. A few hundred dollars will purchase some good accounting software and many microcomputer systems can be purchased for less than $1,000. These are not fancy, but they will provide a significant amount of information and, if used intelligently, can give the entrepreneur the competitive edge that is necessary for his or her success.

Good software is available for effective use by small businesses. There are excellent word processors for correspondence, file management, and mail merge functions. These packages assist in handling and maintaining large customer and prospect files. In the future, the interoffice communication ability of these systems will become increasingly important.

There are many reasonably priced integrated accounting packages such as the one illustrated in Appendix A. These generally have general ledger, accounts receivable, accounts payable, and inventory modules. Some have payroll modules and several integrate these into one package for on-line interactive accounting and management query.

Several database managers are available for managing various records, files, and entire databases. Some are organized around files such as customer, vendor, and inventory; others use relational databases and offer more flexible reporting and access. Some of the databases even provide graphic and analytical capabilities.

Many manufacturers and vendors provide word processing capabilities such as mailing list programs, tax planning packages, report writing, financial planning, material requirement planning, and statistical analysis packages. There are also numerous spreadsheet packages available to aid management in analysis of data and in supporting decisions, as illustrated in Chapter 17.

Finally there are many software packages for the microcomputer that integrate various subsets of these individual packages for easy use so that management of the entrepreneurial enterprise can readily concentrate on the business success factors in meaningful ways. Several vendors even specialize in various industries. For example, one vendor may offer an entire array of software as well as hardware to satisfy the information processing and accounting needs of a retail pharmacy or a law firm.

Selection Criteria

The procedure used to select a microcomputer system should be the same in concept as the procedure used to select a large mainframe system. Unfortunately entrepreneurs purchase systems that do not really satisfy their decision-making, transaction processing, and reporting needs in a cost-beneficial manner.

The structured system design steps should follow the outline given in Chapters 12 and 13. The selection of software must fit the decision-making needs of the business. The difference between the selection process in large businesses and that in small businesses is that in the latter, many of the steps outlined will be less formal. The accountant may be able to render this service. The key to the systems design process is the analysis of the needs of the small business and the subsequent specification of the hardware and software characteristics that will satisfy these requirements.

There are several key selection criteria that small-business managers and their accountants must consider. Several of these criteria are based on current limitations in the microcomputer environment. Many of these problem areas should subside with the passage of time as software becomes more flexible and computers access more storage resources.

First, the system must meet management needs in those areas critical to the success of the business. This is a problem with small-business systems because many software packages are so general in design that they do not match the needs of management. Management should avoid modifying these standard packages, for this will lead to many problems later when vendors offer software revisions. Moreover, installation and use are greatly enhanced when standard packages are used. Management should seek the software that meets most of the needs of the business at the beginning of the process.

Second, many systems are weak in internal control, though this is quickly improving as the storage capabilities and speed of the microcomputers increase. The system must have adequate control and data safeguards, or the firm's management and auditors will lose confidence in the information it provides.

Third, a reliable maintenance arrangement must be obtained through a good service network. A backup system at a nearby business may be necessary to allow continuing operations in case of machine failure.

Fourth, adequate documentation is often nonexistent. Many software systems are turnkey systems. Managers and auditors do not know how data are actually processed and what controls and safeguards are available. Moreover, with small systems, programs written by end users are often poorly documented. Management and auditors should insist on adequate documentation to give confidence in the information provided.

Fifth, great care must be taken to obtain audit trails. For example, in the system illustrated in Appendix A, options are available for transaction listings. These must be required, not optional. Effective numerical document control is necessary because it will enable managers and auditors to trace transactions.

Sixth, input routines should contain menus displaying all options and extensive error messages that can easily be understood.

Seventh, although data may be more free of input errors due to reasonableness controls, completeness controls, and data editing, once data have been entered, it can result in an erroneous update of the master file. Buffers with batch controls would help to increase accuracy at this point by allowing further data checking before the master file is updated.

Eighth, many systems are not expandable or compatible with larger systems. This may be a severe problem for growing companies. For example, many microcomputer systems are limited as to the number of customers, accounts, vendors, and inventory line items that can be handled.

Ninth, report generation ability must be present so that management can customize its output to obtain the necessary representation it needs for effective use of the information without writing special programs.

Tenth, the lack of trained personnel in information processing and accounting will require careful training of users. Training will make the system seem usable and give users more confidence in it. It is also helpful if the system is understandable (often called transparent) to the user so that he or she understands how it works. The user must be able to understand and follow the transaction flow or the generation of data for decision making. This will enhance the confidence in the system.

Finally, obsolescence may be a problem because of rapid changes in technology. Therefore, most vendors would rather sell than lease hardware and software. The user might end up with a considerable investment in the system. In some cases, had management waited a year or two, a much less expensive system would have provided even better information. From a competitive and economic perspective, it is critical that management and the accountant keep abreast of changes in hardware and software technology.

Implementation

Launching a new system for a small entrepreneurial enterprise can be a traumatic exercise for those who do not understand accounting or computer systems. The enterprise's accounting firm can render invaluable assistance here. As with larger systems, the maintenance of data integrity during the conversion process is critical if decisions are to be made on the analysis of this data in the future. Good procedures and controls are essential to ensure the continued integrity of the data and training is necessary to ensure that the system operates as designed.

Summary

A well-conceived small microcomputer system can be used effectively to give the entrepreneur the competitive edge. The information in these systems and the software available to access the information can easily help the owner or manager achieve success through an increased level of customer service; tighter inventory, receivable, payable, and cost control; and more informed promotional efforts and increased knowledge about the market. Most of these systems can generally be adapted to the informal style in most of these organizations.

INTERNAL CONTROL

Due to the environmental characteristics of the typical small business, effective internal control is both more difficult and easier to achieve. This is true even for microcomputer systems. Because of the limited resources available for control, the lack of interest in control, and the small number of employees, good internal control systems such as those described in Chapter 11 are rare. The primary problems encountered in small-business internal control were clarified by a field study of more than 120 small businesses.[4] The study used the small-business internal control questionnaire designed for manual systems. It highlights the need to use good microcomputer software for transaction processing. Many of the small-business systems analyzed did not have common accounting controls involving such transaction processing steps as the use of a chart of accounts; the listing and tracing of cash receipts; the use of imprest petty cash funds; and the use of purchase orders. Moreover, such common administrative controls as the use of budgets, cash projections, financial reports, and perpetual inventory records were not found in many of these firms. These shortcomings, as well as others, are indicative of the following fundamental problems in internal control for small businesses:

1. Little financial or systems expertise on the part of owners and management,
2. Little segregation of duties (often a part-time bookkeeper does everything),
3. Informal accounting and administrative procedures,
4. Informal styles of analysis, decision making, and reporting,
5. Limited personnel and financial resources, and, most important,
6. Limited funds for more comprehensive administrative and accounting controls.[5]

Even though many software packages lack many good control procedures, many of these problems can be compensated for by the use of good accounting software like that in Appendix A. The use of this type of software contributes positively to the control structure (in particular the accounting systems component) as discussed in Chapter 11. In addition to these problems, there is always the possibility that the owner or manager will influence the managerial and financial affairs of the business because of a closeness to operations and inevitable commingling of personal and business objectives.

Because of the closeness to operations, the owner's *supervisory control* (sometimes called *executive control*) over the business is much greater than that exerted by the owners and managers of larger businesses. This strength can compensate for many of the weaknesses in control procedures cited earlier. This control is especially effective when the owner or manager:

---

[4] This field study was conducted by graduate students in an accounting systems class over several quarters. See Robert A. Leitch, Gadis J. Dillon, and Sue H. McKinley, "Internal Control Weaknesses in Small Business," *Journal of Accountancy,* Copyright © (1981) by the American Institute of Certified Public Accountants, Inc., December 1981, pp. 97-101.

[5] William K. Grollman and Robert W. Colby, "Internal Control for Small Businesses," pp. 64-67, reprinted with permission.

1. Uses accounting information or a budget for planning and control and seeks explanations for variations from plans
2. Understands and is alert to unusual events and their potential impact on the business
3. Uses nonaccounting employees for some transaction processing functions
4. Personally observes the operation of the business
5. Plays a key role in each transaction processing cycle
6. Reviews and approves transactions that deviate from the norm and uses standard policies to handle the normal transactions
7. Has an accounting system (preferably a microcomputer system) that generates easy-to-understand, usable, and timely reports.[6]

Microcomputer systems, even though they can enhance the control structure when management uses good commercial software, present a different set of problems which expose the owner to various risks. Many of these are detailed in Appendix C for mini and microcomputer systems along with suggested controls. Earlier in the chapter, when reviewing selection criteria, we discussed several internal control deficiencies that are found in microcomputer systems. Several practical steps can be taken by the small entrepreneur to achieve greater control over the system and thereby obtain much greater confidence in the information provided by the system for his or her use.

First, the active participation of management in key transactions and decisions is important.

Second, even though the separation of duties is not economically practical with a small number of employees, better control can be achieved by (1) using a transaction log or listing (sometimes called a journal as in a manual system); (2) specifying a password to restrict use of the designated operator; and (3) using operators who are not trained in programming.

Third, access can be controlled by simply locking up the computer and diskettes in a closet or safe.

Fourth, passwords should be used for access to key files, even on network systems.

Fifth, control totals should be used for the number of transactions, dollar amounts, and debits and credits in accounting ledger entries.

Sixth, exception procedures should be added to flag unauthorized system use, unusual transactions, nonexistent accounts, extraordinary amounts, and other errors. An exception listing prcedure would bring any unusual activity to management's attention. In the typical microsystem this is not provided. It should be added for critical activities.

Seventh, data entry errors, transcription errors, and completeness errors are generally reduced due to the interactive menu mode of input which instructs the operator as to exactly what the options are and what to do. This is one of the

---

[6] Adapted with permission from Grollman and Colby. See the illustrative internal control questions for small business in section AAM 4300.020. Adapted with permission from AICPA, "Audit and Accounting Guides", published and copyrighted by Commerce Clearing House, Inc., 4025 W. Peterson Avenue, Chicago, Ill., 1986.

greatest control strengths of interactive minicomputer or microcomputer systems.

As far as small business is concerned, the mere fact that all transactions are processed in a consistent manner using application programs is an immeasurable strength because this is seldom the case with informal manual systems. This discipline should give management and the auditor added confidence in the information provided by the system. Other controls for microcomputer software, such as spreadsheets and local area networks, were discussed in Chapter 11. In summary, the small business presents a particular challenge to the systems designer or accountant because of special control problems which impact the control risk of the enterprise. An effective control system can be built around the microcomputer system and close supervision of the business's operations by the owner or manager.

SMALL SYSTEMS FOR CPA FIRMS

As in any small entrepreneurial enterprise, the smaller accounting firm can make excellent use of microcomputer systems in its decision making, transaction processing, and reporting. Moreover, the access to interactive software, processing speed, growth potential and flexibility, and excellent microcomputer software like that described earlier and illustrated in Appendix A may enable the firm to extend client services and enlarge its practice.

The format flexibility offered by systems such as the one illustrated in Appendix A and many other more sophisticated accounting packages allows the practitioner to better satisfy client requirements for write-up work and tax service. The professional accountant or a service bureau can provide year-end write-up work and prepare financial statements. Accountants and attorneys can offer assistance in tax planning. Both the professional accountant and the service bureau can assist in reporting to governmental agencies such as the IRA and FCC. Finally, many accounting firms and service bureaus will perform the day-to-day transaction processing activities and routine report preparation needed by really small businesses.

Additional types of services that were previously not feasible for smaller accounting firms can also be offered. A firm can undertake many more tax and financial planning activities with the aid of an interactive computer system and the excellent software which is commercially available. Most accounting firms, many consulting firms, and the Small Business Administration of the U.S. government offer management advisory services to help the small business with administrative control systems such as budgeting, inventory control, and cash management. The practitioner can evaluate the client's financial status by using spreadsheet programs and can ask many "what if" questions on behalf of the client to help with the client's strategic and managerial planning. Many small entrepreneurial enterprises will have difficulty designing and implementing these microcomputer systems. The accounting profession, service bureaus, and vendors of microcomputers with their expertise and software offer small businesses a wide variety of services that can assist in providing or designing an effective and efficient information system. Thus, the professional accountant can assist in designing an effective microcomputer accounting information system.

For example, the microcomputer system that one accounting firm uses has five microcomputers linked through a simple network. One is primarily a file server and serves as the host for the network. It has a modem. They also have four compatible portables for use at the client's office. The total investment in the system is in the neighborhood of $20,000. The firm consists of four partners, four professional staff members, a bookkeeper, two secretaries, and one part-time programmer for client work. The partners and the professional staff share the networked microcomputers and take the portables to client offices for fieldwork. The secretaries use the system for word processing and the bookkeeper uses one for processing routine transactions. One partner is totally in charge of computer operations. The firm is constantly seeking new applications to run on the computer. The firm plans to open an office in another town and link the offices via telecommunications. The following are some of the many applications that are run using the firm's microcomputer:

1. Payroll, W-2 and 941 forms, and check printing for several clients.
2. General ledger for several clients.
3. Integrated processing (general ledger, accounts receivable, accounts payable, inventory, and payroll) of transactions for several clients.
4. Time and billing using a commercially available software package.
5. Accounts receivable using a commercially available software.
6. Worksheet analysis using spreadsheet programs for tax planning, project control (cash flow), consolidations, summarizing information, and survey results.
7. Depreciation schedules and fixed asset reports.
8. Audit software for larger audit engagements.
9. Spreadsheet analysis of clients' financial affairs.
10. Developing management accounting software for several clients.
11. Statistical sampling and evaluations.
12. Database for their use and client use.
13. Tax preparation using tax software and communication with one of the tax services.
14. Telecommunications: In addition to communications to and from the staff portables, many microcomputers located in the clients' offices can communicate with the firm's system, and information (data files and programs) can be transferred by telephone lines. Clients also may use the firm's computer via time-sharing on evenings when it is not being used internally to access the integrated accounting package and data files stored by the firm.
15. Word processing using letter-quality and laser printers for reports, repetitive letters, confirmations, and accounting manuals for clients.[7]

---

[7] Robert C. Wyune and Alan Frotman, "Microcomputer: Helping Make Practice Perfect," *Journal of Accountancy,* Copyright © (1981) by the American Institute of Certified Public Accountants, Inc., December 1981, p. 39.

In general, the microcomputer system used by the small firm is used to effectively provide quick reliable service to the client for management purposes and to assist the auditor in the audit and related consulting and tax services.

IMPACT OF CLIENT MICROCOMPUTER SYSTEMS ON THE ACCOUNTING PROFESSION

Because of their simplicity, manual systems will continue to be used in many small businesses. Accounting services will continue to be used for tax planning and financial statement preparation. Whenever feasible and economically possible, however, microcomputer systems will increasingly be used in the future. They are inexpensive, effective, fast, precise and consistent, and flexible in providing decision-making information. The entrepreneur can command a wealth of information to better plan and manage the business's activities.

This movement toward micro systems is a major challenge to the accounting profession. When relatively few large organizations had large mainframe computers, the organization could hire experts to run the computer systems. Auditors could call upon experts within their respective firms to assist in the audit of these computer systems. Moreover, the accounting practitioner could also use experts to assist clients in the effective and efficient design of information systems. With the explosion of the number of organizations now purchasing or leasing mini or micro systems, the practitioner will no longer be able to call on the expert for help with system design or audit problems. The accountant must therefore become well trained in information systems design to be able to deal with the problems that will arise. Moreover, accounting professionals employed as controllers and staff accountants by large and small organizations will be expected to function effectively in this new computer environment. This burden of training must be shouldered by the profession. Management will lose confidence in the information provided by these new systems if the accountant is not involved in their design and operation. The lack of an accountant's influence can lead to insufficient controls, poor design, and unmet informational needs. The challenge facing the profession is enormous. Accountants are adapting to this new and rapidly changing technology.

SUMMARY

In this chapter, we reviewed the unique characteristics of the small entrepreneurial environment. We discussed several types of systems designed to meet the decision-making, transaction processing, and reporting needs of the small business. These small systems range from very simple manual bookkeeping to microcomputer systems. We outlined the internal control strengths and weaknesses involved in each of these systems. The focus and nature of many of these controls differ significantly from those found in large businesses. We also reviewed the importance of good system design, along with key aspects of the hardware and software selection process. In summary, the transaction processing needs, as well as the operational, managerial, and strategic decision-making needs, must be supported by the information system of the small business in a cost-effective way.

APPENDIX A

MICROCOMPUTER ILLUSTRATION

In this section, we present typical integrated microcomputer software for a small business. Although a specific package is illustrated here, it is similar to many others in the industry. During the design phases it is important that the analyst, accountant, or manager find that system with the characteristics which best meets their requirements, given their various constraints. This is an integrated system, as shown in Figure A19-1 which means that the posting of transactions in one of the modules will automatically update the accounts which are affected in other modules. Not all microcomputer systems work this way. Many are not integrated and consist of self-contained modules which are used to update a general ledger system on a periodic basis, like once a month. This system can be used as a batch-oriented system where a clerk could enter all similar transactions, print a listing (daily journal), review the transactions, and then post the transactions after corrections (reversing entries) are made. All of the modules work this way. In addition, this system can be used as an on-line system where each transaction is posted as it is entered by skipping the step for printing the transaction listings (journals). Moreover, some of the modules can be operated in batch and others in an on-line mode. For example, the sales system could be on line so that salespersons would know if items are in inventory and not already sold; all other modules could be batch processed for better internal control.

Data Files

This typical illustration actually contains five main files. Some more advanced microcomputer systems are organized as database systems; this one is not. It is a file-oriented system. The basic files[8] are:

> Chart of Accounts
> Financial Statement
> Vendor File
> Customer File
> Product File

---

[8] The actual files are: Accounts File, G/L Transaction File, G/L Report File, Customer File, Customer Open Invoice File, Customer Transaction File, Vendor File, Vendor Open Invoice File, Vendor Transaction File, Products File, Physical Inventory File, Bill/P.O. File, General File, Sort File. Actually for the first 12 there are two files; one for input and one data file. Refer to a DAC Easy Manual, DAC Software, Inc., Dallas, Texas, 1985 for details.

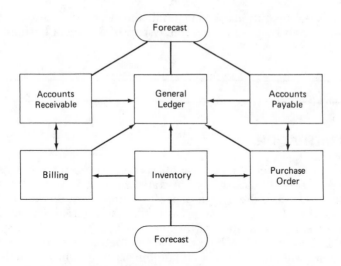

FIGURE A19-1   Integrated accounting system module.
Source: DAC Easy, DAC Software, Inc., Dallas, Texas. Adapted with permission.

The chart of accounts file has maintenance provisions for tailoring charts of account for a variety of organizations. General and detailed accounts can be included. General accounts are those summary accounts which receive transactions from other accounts. Detailed accounts are those which receive direct debit and credit entries and whose transactions are ultimately discharged to general accounts. Up to five levels are possible for easy summary of account classifications. For example, level 1 may be asset, level 2 may be current or fixed, level 3 may be the specific type of asset (e.g. inventory), and level 4 may be the product classification for the inventory item, for example. Each account contains the following information:

> Account Number
> Account Name
> Debit/Credit Code (1 or -1)
> Account Level (1 to 5)
> General Account (account to which data are sent)
> Clear to Account Number (for year-end closing)
> Previous Balance (as of the beginning of month)
> This Period (net debits and credits this period)
> Current Balance
> Historical Information (Balance, Variance, and %)
> > Year before Last
> > Last Year
> > Current YTD
> > Forecast at End of Year (entered using forecast procedure
> > > or entered manually)

The financial statements file enables management to customize the financial statement to emphasize the various aspects of the business for owners', managers', creditors' or auditors' use. This ability to format financial statements is very important because each small business will have different reporting needs and each must use software which either meets its needs or can be tailored to its needs. Some software packages even contain graphic capabilities[9] to enhance the presentation of the accounting information.

The customer file can be used to provide a great deal of information for transaction processing, reporting, and decision making. The file contains the following information which is typical of such systems for small businesses:

Customer Code (logical for sorting purposes)
Name
Contact
Address
City
State
Zip
Area Code and Phone Number
Salesperson Code
Customer Type
Discount
Days (for discount)
Days (due)
Account Type (balance forward or open invoice)
Credit Limit

Balance (posted by system automatically)
Credit Available (calculated automatically)
Last Sales Date
Last Payment Date
Financial Charge %
Sales Tax Rate
Statistical Information (year before last, last year, this year, forecast, variance, %)
Invoices
$ Sales
$ Cost
$ Profit
Variance $ & % (difference between FORECAST and THIS YEAR)

It should be noticed that this file contains a great deal of information for management purposes. Most any criteria, such as industry, location or credit association, for example, can be used to prepare marketing reports by customer type. The salesperson classification is useful for sales budgets and quotas for marketing effort analysis. Customer type classification is useful for sales statistics on the number of sales, the value of these sales, the cost of these sales, and their profit margin. These statistics are all potentially useful for small business marketing and promotion strategy. Prior to the microcomputer, this type of information was not available to the small business to manage their marketing efforts.

The vendor file also contains a variety of information for processing transactions and issuing reports for managerial use. The file, which is typical of such accounting systems, contains:

---

[9] Insight from Peachtree, Inc. for the Macintosh which was illustrated in chapter 15 is an excellent example of packages which have good graphic capabilities.

Vendor Code (logical)
Name
Address
City
State
Zip
Area Code and Phone Number
Territory
Vendor Type
Discount %
Days (for discount)
Days Due

Account Type (balance forward or open invoice)
Credit limit
Balance
Credit Available (calculated by system)
Last Purchase Date
Sales Tax Rate
Statistical information (year before last, last year, this year, forecast, variance, %)
Invoices
$ Purchased
Variances

Again, a variety of information is available for management to manage its purchasing and cash disbursement activities.

The inventory system uses a product file which contains a variety of characteristics found in many similar software packages for inventory management as well as for financial reporting purposes. The Product File contains the following information:

Inventory Number
Description
Measure (type of units)
Fraction (breakdown of measure)
Type (type of inventory or product)
Bin (location)
Vendor (primary)
Sales Price
Taxable? Y/N
Last Sales Date

Minimum (reorder point)
Reorder (optimum reorder quantity)
Last Purchase Date
Last Purchase Price
Standard Cost (if applicable)
Average Cost
On Hand/Committed
On Order, Units
On Order, Dollars
Statistical Information (see Table A19-1)

Much of this information is automatically calculated by the software over time as data are entered and transactions are entered in the other modules, as will be shown in the discussion of the modules which follows.

There is also a file for company information and a file for describing the general ledger interface. This last file enables management to assign account numbers which direct the automatic posting to the general ledger from the individual posting process for each module. In addition, codes may be entered into the system for purchase order information and invoice information such as freight, insurance, packaging, and the like. Invoice numbers and purchase order numbers can be generated automatically by this system and most other similar microcomputer systems for small businesses. Moreover, options are available for inventory costing; these are: last purchase price, standard cost, and average cost.

TABLE A19-1　Statistical information.[10]

	YEAR BEFORE	LAST YEAR	THIS YEAR	FORECAST	VARIANCE	%
Units purchased	395	473	525	595	−70	−11.8
# Purchases	3985	4783	5250	6000	−750	−12.5
Units sold	388	466	518	587	−69	−11.8
$ Sales	$7950	$9510	$10125	$11000	−$875	−8.0
$ Cost	$3950	$4715	$4985	$5124	−$139	−2.7
$ Profit	$4000	$4795	$5140	$5876	−$736	−12.5

Transaction Processing Routines

This illustrative system actually consists of a number of daily routines which use these files and interface with each other and the general ledger. The system is fully integrated as will be shown. A systems flowchart is presented to describe each of these procedures.

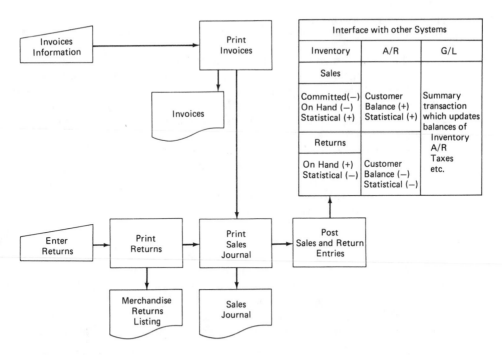

FIGURE A19-2　Integrated sales (invoices) and returns.
Source: DAC Easy, DAC Software, Inc., Dallas, Texas, 1985. Adapted with permission.

---

[10] Reprinted with permission from DAC Easy, DAC Software, Inc., Dallas, Texas, 1985.

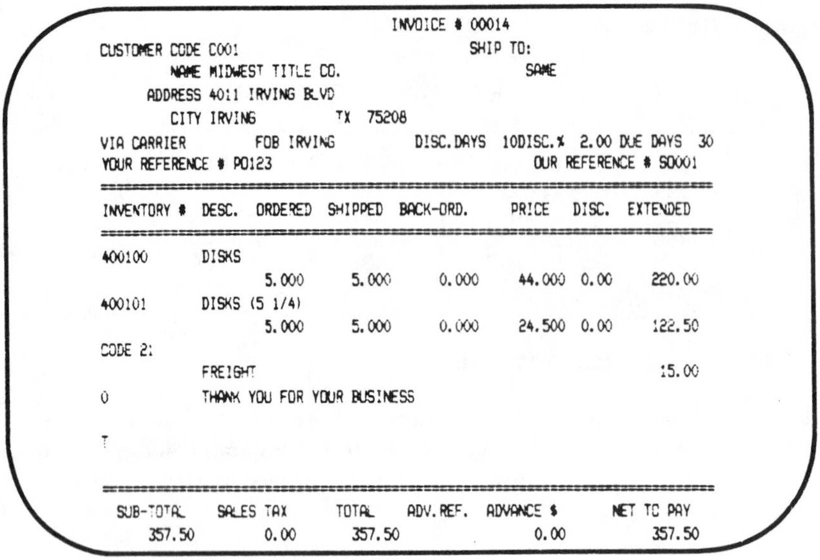

```
                              INVOICE # 00014
   CUSTOMER CODE C001                     SHIP TO:
             NAME MIDWEST TITLE CO.          SAME
             ADDRESS 4011 IRVING BLVD
             CITY IRVING        TX 75208
   VIA CARRIER        FOB IRVING       DISC.DAYS 10DISC.% 2.00 DUE DAYS 30
   YOUR REFERENCE # PO123                    OUR REFERENCE # SO001
   ==============================================================================
   INVENTORY # DESC.  ORDERED SHIPPED BACK-ORD.   PRICE  DISC.  EXTENDED
   ==============================================================================
   400100     DISKS
                        5.000   5.000    0.000   44.000  0.00    220.00
   400101     DISKS (5 1/4)
                        5.000   5.000    0.000   24.500  0.00    122.50
   CODE 2:
              FREIGHT                                            15.00
   0          THANK YOU FOR YOUR BUSINESS

   T


   ==============================================================================
   SUB-TOTAL  SALES TAX   TOTAL  ADV.REF.  ADVANCE $      NET TO PAY
     357.50     0.00     357.50               0.00          357.50
```

FIGURE A19-3 Billing menu.
Source: DAC Easy, DAC Software, Inc., Dallas Texas, 1985. Reprinted with permission.

The sales, return, and billing routine is shown in Figure A19-2. This rou tine will easily allow a small business to prepare sales invoices, sales returns, print the forms associated with these transactions, print a sales journal and post all these transactions to the general ledger, inventory system, and accounts receivable system, as shown in the figure. A billing menu will appear like the one completed in Figure A19-3 when users enter a sales transaction. A similar menu is presented for returns and prenumbered invoices, and credit memos may be printed for each for the customer. The sales journal is a summary journal with details and totals for sales and returns as well as miscellaneous transactions.

The purchase order system shown in Figure A19-4 will easily permit a small business to prepare purchase orders for its vendors, enter merchandise as it is received, control merchandise returned to vendors, print all the documents necessary for an audit or review of the system and post transaction information to the general ledger, inventory and accounts receivable system. These interfaces with other systems are shown in Figure A19-4. Figure A19-5 on page 658 illustrates the menu used for entering purchase order information. Similar menus are available for merchandise receipt and returns. The system will accommodate the printing of purchase orders and return memos on preprinted numbered forms for good control. Details and summary information can then be printed on a purchase journal.

The accounts receivable system will allow a small business to control its accounts receivable. Both routine cash receipts from customers as well as miscellaneous transactions can be entered into the system. They are posted after an automatic generation of any monthly finance charges to the accounts receivable customer file as shown in Figure A19-6 on page 658 and subsequently posted to

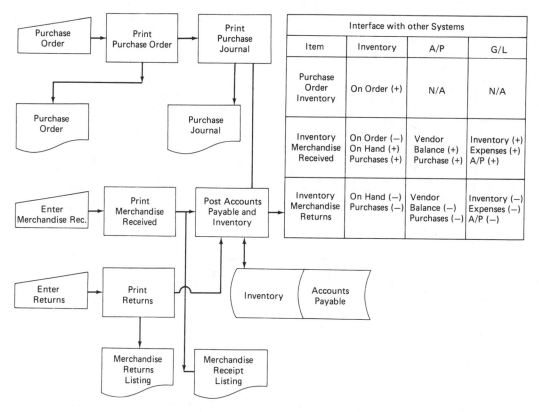

Interface with other Systems			
Item	Inventory	A/P	G/L
Purchase Order Inventory	On Order (+)	N/A	N/A
Inventory Merchandise Received	On Order (−) On Hand (+) Purchases (+)	Vendor Balance (+) Purchase (+)	Inventory (+) Expenses (+) A/P (+)
Inventory Merchandise Returns	On Hand (−) Purchases (−)	Vendor Balance (−) Purchases (−)	Inventory (−) Expenses (−) A/P (−)

FIGURE A19-4   Integrated purchase order system.
Source: DAC Easy, DAC Software, Dallas, Texas, 1985. Adapted with permission.

the general ledger control account for accounts receivable. Most of the transactions for most small business would probably originate in the billing system during the processing of sales and return transactions. Again, transaction journals can be printed for good control.

The accounts payable system will enable the small business to enter its non-inventory payables. It uses a menu system to enter the necessary payable information. It is used to indicate which vendor to pay and which checks to print. Once this decision is made it will automatically print the checks. It interfaces with other systems as shown in Figure A19-7 on page 659. For most small business most of the activity for payables related to inventory will originate during purchasing transactions as shown in Figure A19-4.

Finally, there is a general ledger system which is automatically posted during the previously described transaction processing systems. This system will also enable the small business to post miscellaneous transactions directly to the general ledger as shown in Figure A19-8 on page 660. There is a provision for listing these transactions through the printing of the general journal. Moreover,

```
                            PURCHASE ORDER # 00012
        VENDOR CODE K001                    REMARKS
              NAME KELLY PAPER                    DELIVERY BEFORE
           ADDRESS 108 GASTON                     MONDAY 3rd
              CITY DALLAS        TX  75242
        VIA CARRIER       FOB DALLAS      DISC.DAYS 10DISC.% 2.00 DUE DAYS 30
        YOUR REFERENCE # 123456                   OUR REFERENCE # P00012
        ===================================================================
        INVENTORY # DESC.                  ORDERED    PRICE   DISC.  EXTENDED
        ===================================================================
        200100      STATIONARY
                                            50.000   12.000  3.00    582.00

        CODE  1
        REF.123456   FREIGHT UNITED PARCEL SERVICE               50.00
        0            THANK YOU FOR YOUR PROMPT DELIVERY

        T

        ===================================================================
        SUB-TOTAL   SALES TAX    TOTAL   ADV.REF.  ADVANCE $    NET TO PAY
         632.00      0.00       632.00               0.00        632.00
```

FIGURE A19-5 Purchase order menu.
Source: DAC Easy, DAC Software, Inc., Dallas, Texas, 1985. Reprinted with permission.

there is a provision for the listing of account activity information, much of which originates in other systems.

All good microcomputer accounting systems for small business provide the user with simple ways to close the books periodically at the end of the month and annually.

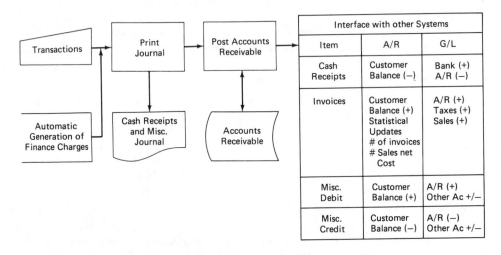

FIGURE A19-6 Integrated accounts receivable daily routine.
Source: DAC Easy, DAC Software, Inc., Dallas, Texas, 1985. Adapted with permission.

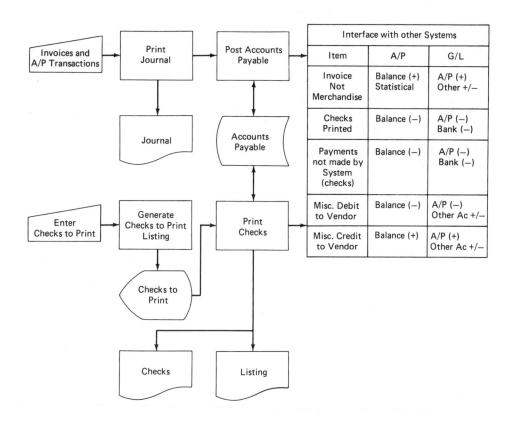

FIGURE A19-7 General accounts payable daily routine (not for merchandise invoices and cash disbursements).
Source: DAC Easy, DAC Software, Dallas, Texas, 1985. Adapted with permission.

Reports

Most small business accounting systems provide management with a large variety of reports to help manage their business. Many can be printed and most can simply be shown on the screen of the microcomputer for management decision making. The ones shown in this illustration will be the printed version and will be typical of small systems which are simple. There are many more sophisticated systems which offer specialized information for various industries and present information to management in more flexible ways such as graphs and charts.

In this example, financial statements can either be prepared for the period which contain only the information for the period or, as shown in Figure A19-9 on page 661 for the period with year to date, last year and variance information from last year information for management's use. A provision is also provided in this illustration as in most general ledger systems for budget information and a

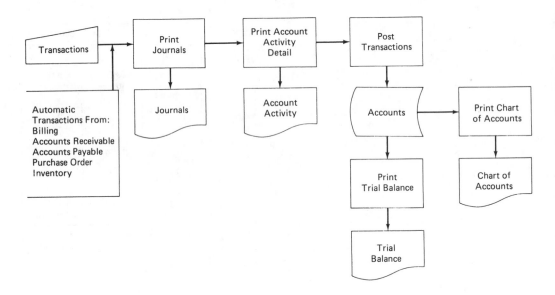

FIGURE A19-8 Integrated general ledger.
Source: DAC Easy, DAC Software, Dallas, Texas, 1985. Adapted with permission.

comparison of financial statements for a period with budget information for the period.

In the typical accounts receivable system, periodic statements, as shown in Figure A19-10 on page 662, can be printed with text information, as shown, or statements such as "If you don't remit the balance in your account immediately we will turn your file over to a human for collection". Moreover, aging reports, such as the one in Figure A19-11 on page 663, can be prepared for management of receivables and credit granting decisions. In most accounts receivable systems customer lists and provisions for labels are also provided for sales management and promotional efforts, for example.

In the typical accounts payable system, vendor information and lists are available to purchasing personnel to assist in making purchasing decisions. Aging reports, such as the one illustrated in Figure A19-12 on page 664, are also provided in most systems to help management to decide who to pay and when and to help manage cash flow.

Inventory systems for most small-business microcomputer accounting systems usually have provisions for sorting inventory many different ways for inventory management. The example here, as shown in Figure A19-9, provides for five different sorts and eleven different rankings so that management can extract as much information as possible from its product listings. A typical listing is shown in Figure A19-13 on page 665. Many inventory systems provide price listings for sales personnel, such as the one shown in Figure A19-14 on page 666. And many systems provide activity reports, like the one shown in Figure A19-15 on page 667, for each inventory item, which contain a wealth of information to

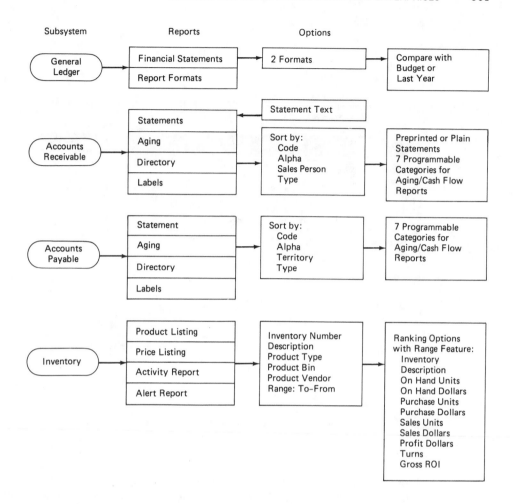

FIGURE A19-9 Integrated reporting structure.
Source: DAC Easy, DAC Software, Inc., Dallas, Texas, 1985. Reprinted with permission.

help management make informed decisions based on costs, prices, profits, inventory turns, and dollars sold for various products. For example, they may want to discontinue a low margin product with low turnover and high carrying costs. Moreover, most systems provide information on inventory on hand, on order, optimal order quantity, and price for purchasing to decide what and when to order.

In addition, all good systems such as this, provide transaction listings for effective audit trails, as illustrated in the flowcharts depicting the system; and other listings to aid in the audit process such as inventory count sheets with a reconciliation procedure.

```
J100
JACKS AUTO SUPPLY
ROBERT JOHNSON          STATEMENT          CLOSING DATE 08/29/85
2500 W. MOCKINGBIRD LN.
DALLAS      TX  75243                          PAGE   1/ 1
```

DATE	INVOICE #	DUE DATE	CD	DESCRIPTION	REF #	DEBITS	CREDITS	AMOUNT DUE	PAST DUE AMOUNT	PAST DUE DAYS
02/28/84	00002	03/29/84	1	I N V O I C E	PO 254	17.58				
04/15/84			2	MISC. DEBIT	F.C.	0.14				
08/16/85			3	P A Y M E N T	100			17.72	0.00	
01/01/80	00018	01/31/80	4	MISC. CREDIT				17.70	17.70–	
03/10/84	00019	04/09/84	1	I N V O I C E	7784	1592.67				
04/15/84			2	MISC. DEBIT	F.C.	4.77			1597.44	1597.44	507
07/12/85	00026	07/12/85	1	I N V O I C E		0.29			0.29	48
07/20/85	00027	08/19/85	1	I N V O I C E		77.89			77.89	10
01/01/80	1111	01/31/80	4	MISC. CREDIT	1111			2.96	2.96–	

	TOTAL BALANCE	PAST DUE BALANCE	DAYS
	1654.96	1675.62	507

FIGURE A19-10 Accounts receivable periodic statement.
Source: DAC Easy, DAC Software, Inc., Dallas, Texas, 1985. Reprinted with permission.

Management Information

As indicated earlier, one of the most important reasons for a small business to use such a system is the wealth of information which can be obtained from the files which contain transaction information. The reports above provide much of this for periodic and routine decisions. Many systems such as this provide look-up capabilities for management. For example, sales personnel can query a customer record to make a decision to grant credit by simply accessing the computer for information on that customer. As another example purchasing can call up a vendor record to view vendor history to settle payment disputes. As a further example, sales personnel can query the inventory file to see if out-of-stock items have been ordered and when the shipment is expected to arrive.

In addition, most systems have provisions for budget and planning information. This particular package, for example, actually has forecasting capability for management's use; this is probably not typical of very small systems, but typical of systems which are a little larger. Most, however, provide comparative statistics with financial and sales budget data.

```
DATE : 03-31                        DAC EASY ACCOUNTING                              PAGE No.   1
TIME : 14:48                         DAC SOFTWARE, INC.
                              4801 SPRING VALLEY ROAD    SUITE 110 B
                              DALLAS, TX.  75244     (214) 458-0038

CLOSING DATE : 03/31/85 RECEIVABLE:         A G I N G   R E P O R T
Sorted by : CODE
```

INVOICE	DATE	DUE	CD	AMOUNT	999 / 61	60 / 31	30 / 1	0 / -30	-31 / -60	-61 / -90	-91 / -999
A001	WEST SIDE OFFICE										
00001	013185	850302	1	88.88							
	020185		4	24.75-							
	031585		4	9.90-			54.23				
00010	031885	850417	1	1834.00				1834.00			
TOTAL CODE A001				1888.23	0.00	0.00	54.23	1834.00	0.00	0.00	0.00
A002	KELLY DISCOUNT OFFICE SP										
00002	013185	850302	1	623.65							
	033185		2	9.04			632.69				
00005	020185	850303	1	168.75							
	033185		2	2.36			171.11				
00006	020185	850303	1	1399.25							
	033185		2	19.58			1418.83				
00011	031885	850417	1	710.65				710.65			
TOTAL CODE A002				2933.28	0.00	0.00	2222.63	710.65	0.00	0.00	0.00
A003	OFFICE ANNEX										
00003	013185	850302	1	274.60							
	033185		2	3.98			278.58				
00013	032185	850420	1	4314.30				4314.30			
TOTAL CODE A003				4592.88	0.00	0.00	278.58	4314.30	0.00	0.00	0.00
A004	OFFICE OUTFITTERS										
12801	121084	850109	1	1517.00							
	013185		2	16.68							
	022885		2	23.00							
	033185		2	23.35	1580.03						
12830	121784	850116	1	842.00							
	013185		2	6.31							
	022885		2	12.72							
	033185		2	12.91	873.94						
TOTAL CODE A004				2453.97	2453.97	0.00	0.00	0.00	0.00	0.00	0.00

FIGURE A19-11   Aging report.

Source: DAC Easy, DAC Software, Inc., Dallas, Texas, 1985. Reprinted with permission.

APPENDIX B

SMALL BUSINESS MANUAL SYSTEMS

General

At the present time many small-business systems are still manual. Many use a cash register as the only mechanical or electronic device. This is rapidly changing, however, and more and more small businesses are beginning to use the

FIGURE A19-12 Accounts payable aging report.

Source: DAC Easy, DAC Software, Inc., Dallas, Texas, 1985. Reprinted with permission.

power of the microcomputer as previously described. The manual accounting system in a small business can be on either a cash or an accrual basis, involving either a single-entry or a double-entry system. The system may also include services provided by individuals outside the small business for a fee.

Cash basis accounting systems recognize revenue when cash is received and expenses when cash is paid. Accrual basis accounting systems recognize revenue in the period earned and expenses in the period in which they are incurred. In some cases the modified cash basis with capitalization of assets (depreciation) may suffice for reporting and tax needs in a small business. In other cases an accountant can easily convert cash basis statements to accrual based financial statements by making a series of adjusting entries at the end of the period.

DATE : 03-31
TIME : 13:36

DAC EASY ACCOUNTING
DAC SOFTWARE, INC.
4801 SPRING VALLEY ROAD   SUITE 110 B
DALLAS, TX. 75244   (214) 458-0038

PAGE NO.   1

TOTALS BY: INVENTORY #

INVENTORY PRODUCT LISTING Ranked by: INVENTORY #

INVENTORY#	DESCRIPTION	UNIT TYPE	BIN VENDOR	PRICE	MINIMUM REORDER	LAST SALE LAST PURCH.	LAST PURCH. PRICE	STANDARD COST	AVERAGE COST
100100	LETTER TRAY (BLACK)	UNIT	WH01	5.350	50.000	850318	2.668	0.000	2.704
		D1	W002			850318			
100101	TRASH CAN (BLACK)	UNIT	WH01	13.300	10.000	850318	6.650	0.000	6.650
		D1	W002			850318			
100102	PEN SET (BLACK)	UNIT	WH01	38.000	5.000	850318	19.000	0.000	19.000
		D1	W002			850315			
100103	PEN SET (WHITE)	UNIT	WH01	32.950	5.000	850318	18.050	0.000	18.406
		D1	W002			850315			
100200	LETTER TRAY (WHITE)	UNIT	WH01	4.950	25.000	850315	2.475	0.000	2.561
		D2	W002			850318			
100201	TRASH CAN (WHITE)	UNIT	WH01	12.950	10.000	850321	7.000	0.000	7.000
		D2	W002			850103			
200100	STATIONARY	CASE	WH09	19.950	300.000	850321	10.000	0.000	10.000
		S1	K001			850315			
300100	TAPE (1/2 ROLL)	CASE	WH06	36.950	5.000	850318	20.000	0.000	20.000
		T1	M002			850201			
300101	TAPE (1" ROLL)	CASE	WH06	46.000	5.000	850318	23.000	0.000	23.000
		T2	M002			850201			
400100	DISKS	CASE	WH07	44.000	50.000	850318	22.000	0.000	22.000
		D1	R001			850201			
400101	DISKS (5 1/4)	CASE	WH07	24.500	50.000	850318	12.250	0.000	12.249
		D2	R001			850201			
500100	PAPER (COMPUTER)	BOX	WH05	44.950	200.000	850321	21.600	0.000	22.135
		P1	M001			850318			
500101	PAPER (COMPUTER)	BOX	WH06	36.950	50.000	850321	20.000	0.000	20.000
		P2	K001			850103			
600100	RIBBONS (PRINTER)	CASE	WH01	24.950	50.000	850321	12.500	0.000	12.500
		R1	J001			850103			
600101	RIBBONS (PRINTER DK)	CASE	WH02	49.950	10.000	850318	25.000	0.000	25.000
		R1	J001			850103			

GRAND TOTAL   15

FIGURE A19-13 Inventory product listing.
Source: DAC Easy, DAC Software, Inc., Dallas, Texas, 1985. Reprinted with permission.

A double-entry accounting system with corresponding debits and credits, detailed records, and control accounts is effective in helping to ensure transaction recording accuracy. The double-entry system is self-checking because debits and credits must balance and the detailed records must add to the control totals in each account. A single-entry system, on the other hand, consists of only one entry for each transaction, either on an original document or on a classified listing of transactions such as daily sales, cash receipts, or purchases. These listings are often transcribed from the cash register tape.

```
DATE : 03-23 .                          DAC EASY ACCOUNTING              PAGE No.    1
TIME : 13:03                            DAC SOFTWARE, INC.
                                   4801 SPRING VALLEY ROAD      SUITE 110 B
                                   DALLAS, TX.  75244      (214) 458-0038

TOTALS BY: DESCRIPTION                   INVENTORY PRICE LISTING  Ranked by: DESCRIPTION
                                 UNIT  BIN
   INVENTORY#      DESCRIPTION    TYPE VENDOR    TAX     SALES PRICE   CODE LINE
  -----------    -------------   ----  ------   -----   -----------   ---- ----

   400100        DISKS            CASE  WH07      Y        44.000 BB
                                  D1    R001
   400101        DISKS (5 1/4)    CASE  WH07      Y        24.500 AB.BE
                                  D2    R001
   100200        LETTER TRAY (WHITE)  UNIT WH01   Y         4.950 B.DGE
                                  D2    W002
   100100        LETTER TRAY (BLACK)  UNIT WH01   Y         4.950 B.FFH
                                  D1    W002
   500100        PAPER (COMPUTER) BOX   WH05      Y        44.950 BA.F
                                  P1    K001
   500101        PAPER (COMPUTER) BOX   WH06      Y        36.950 BJ
                                  P2    K001
   100102        PEN SET (BLACK)  UNIT  WH01      Y        37.950 AI
                                  D1    W002
   100103        PEN SET (WHITE)  UNIT  WH01      Y        34.490 AH.JE
                                  D1    W002
   600101        RIBBONS (PRINTER OK)  CASE WH02  Y        49.950 BE
                                  R1    J001
   600100        RIBBONS (PRINTER)  CASE WH01     Y        24.950 AB.E
                                  R1    J001
   200100        STATIONARY       CASE  WH09      Y        19.950 AJ
                                  S1    K001
   300101        TAPE (1" ROLL)   CASE  WH06      Y        46.000 BC
                                  T2    W002
   300100        TAPE (1/2 ROLL)  CASE  WH06      Y        36.950 BJ
                                  T1    W002
   100101        TRASH CAN (BLACK)  UNIT WH01     Y        12.950 F.FE
                                  D1    W002
   100201        TRASH CAN (WHITE)  UNIT WH01     Y        12.950 G
                                  D2    W002

       GRAND TOTAL    15
```

FIGURE A19-14 Inventory price listing.
Source: DAC Easy, DAC Software, Inc., Dallas, Texas, 1985. Reprinted by permission.

Ledgerless Bookkeeping

If the file of source documents, such as sales invoices, is used as the accounting record rather than as a basis for posting to a ledger or listing, the system is a *ledgerless bookkeeping system.* The extreme case of a ledgerless system would be a drawer full of unpaid credit sales invoices, purchase invoices, and a checkbook. There are several disadvantages to such a single-entry ledgerless system:

1. There is no double-entry control (no way to balance the books).
2. There are no control accounts to compare with the detailed records or source documents.

```
DATE : 03-31                          DAC EASY ACCOUNTING                        PAGE No.   1
TIME : 13:38                          DAC SOFTWARE, INC.
                              4801 SPRING VALLEY ROAD     SUITE 110 B
                              DALLAS, TX. 75244      (214) 458-0038

TOTALS BY: INVENTORY #                INVENTORY ACTIVITY REPORT  Ranked by: PROFIT
                       UNIT BIN   UNIT PRICE                                              TURNS
INVENTORY#  DESCRIPTION  TYPE VENDOR UNIT COST  ON-HAND  PURCH. YTD SALES YTD COST YTD PROFIT YTD G.R.O.I.
```

INVENTORY#	DESCRIPTION	UNIT TYPE	BIN VENDOR	UNIT PRICE / UNIT COST	ON-HAND	PURCH. YTD	SALES YTD	COST YTD	PROFIT YTD	TURNS G.R.O.I.
200100	STATIONARY	CASE	WH09	19.950	119.000	400.000	275.000			2.310
		S1	K001	10.000	1190.000	4000.000	5480.000	2750.000	2730.000	2728.906
500100	PAPER (COMPUTER)	BOX	WH05	44.950	463.000	525.000	60.000			0.131
		P1	K001	22.135	10248.980	11640.000	2693.000	1346.000	1347.000	1361.659
500101	PAPER (COMPUTER)	BOX	WH06	36.950	241.000	300.000	57.000			0.236
		P2	K001	20.000	4820.000	6000.000	2103.000	1140.000	963.000	960.904
300101	TAPE (1" ROLL)	CASE	WH06	46.000	1.000	37.000	37.000			37.000
		T2	M002	21.000	23.000	851.000	1702.000	851.000	851.000	851.000
600100	RIBBONS (PRINTER)	CASE	WH01	24.950	24.000	80.000	57.000			2.370
		R1	J001	12.500	300.000	1000.000	1417.000	711.000	706.000	704.513
600101	RIBBONS (PRINTER DK)	CASE	WH02	49.950	10.000	35.000	25.000			2.500
		R1	J001	25.000	250.000	875.000	1243.000	625.000	618.000	618.000
300100	TAPE (1/2 ROLL)	CASE	WH06	36.950	5.000	38.000	32.000			6.400
		T1	M002	20.000	100.000	760.000	1176.000	640.000	536.000	536.000
400100	DISKS	CASE	WH07	44.000	88.000	112.000	23.000			0.261
		D1	R001	22.300	1936.000	2464.000	1005.000	506.000	499.000	498.305
400101	DISKS (5 1/4)	CASE	WH07	24.500	66.005	88.000	20.000			0.298
		D2	R001	12.249	813.610	1077.000	489.000	243.000	246.000	241.934
100102	PEN SET (BLACK)	UNIT	WH01	38.000	0.000	11.000	11.000			0.000
		D1	W002	19.000	0.000	209.000	415.000	209.000	206.000	0.000
100100	LETTER TRAY (BLACK)	UNIT	WH01	5.350	71.000	137.000	61.000			0.859
		D1	W002	2.704	192.000	373.000	295.000	165.000	130.000	129.976
100101	TRASH CAN (BLACK)	UNIT	WH01	13.300	5.000	25.000	20.000			4.150
		D1	W002	6.650	33.250	171.000	254.000	138.000	116.000	120.350
100103	PEN SET (WHITE)	UNIT	WH01	32.950	3.000	8.000	5.000			1.666
		D1	W002	18.406	55.220	147.000	172.000	92.000	80.000	79.968
100200	LETTER TRAY (WHITE)	UNIT	WH01	4.950	72.000	105.000	30.000			0.433
		D2	W002	2.561	184.440	273.000	144.000	80.000	64.000	66.508
100201	TRASH CAN (WHITE)	UNIT	WH01	12.950	10.000	18.000	8.000			0.800
		D2	W002	7.000	70.000	126.000	101.000	56.000	45.000	45.000
GRAND TOTAL					20216.500	29966.000	18689.000	9552.000	9137.000	

FIGURE A19-15 Inventory activity report.
Source: DAC Easy, DAC Software, Inc., Dallas, Texas, 1985. Reprinted with permission.

3. Great potential exists for lost transactions because of disadvantages 1 and 2 above.

4. Partial payments, receipt of part of an order, and other partial transactions play havoc with a ledgerless system because there is no effective way to record partial transactions on a source document.

5. Audit trails are poor. Entire files must be searched to trace transactions.

A single-entry ledgerless system has the following advantages:

a. It is economical.

b. It is simple to use.

c. It can provide sufficient information in a cost-effective way for many small firms.

d. It is relatively simple to use when complete payments on orders are made and received and few exceptions to the transaction are noted on the face of the invoice or other source document.[11]

Some control may be established by using batches for groups of transactions, prelisting the transactions, and, above all, prenumbering the source documents for numerical control and reference. Perhaps the most important disadvantage of either form of manual system is that neither can provide the management information that a microcomputer system can provide.

Cash Registers and Other Manual Processing Devices

The cash register can serve as an effective focal point for the sales and cash receipt transaction processing cycle. These cash registers can either be manual or small microcomputers which are designed for the express purpose of serving as a point-of-sale system. It can be used to record sales at the time of transaction; issue a customer receipt; total various sales statistics by department, type of merchandise, type of sale, and salesperson; generate machine-readable output such as a diskette or tape for further processing; communicate via modems or data transmission lines to a central microcomputer; compute taxes; calculate and issue change; and calculate the transaction totals. The cash register can also provide control over assets. Cash is controlled because a protected record is produced on a tape or disk locked inside the machine. The salesperson must be able to reconcile the cash balance in the cash drawer with this transaction record when the register is cleared by management personnel. As we noted in Chapter 15, some cash registers are quite sophisticated. In practice, the effective use of a cash register gives the small-business owner or manager the much-needed assurance that sales transactions are recorded properly and that sales personnel are accountable for the cash assets at their disposal.

Other Manual Procedures

There are many other manual procedures used by small business for control of their sales, assets, and operations. Some small businesses may use locked boxes of invoices and cash drawers in lieu of cash registers. One copy of the sales invoice is given to the customer and the other is retained in the locked box. At the end of the day the sales invoices must all reconcile with the beginning and ending balances in the cash drawer. Generally these invoices are prenumbered for numerical control, reference, and an audit trail.

Peg boards also are often used to record transactions in many small businesses. Peg boards consist of checks or cash disbursement vouchers overlaying a journal, such as a payroll register. As the bookkeeper prepares the checks, voucher, or invoice, a carbon copy is recorded on the journal. This system has the advantage of being simple and cheap, and of reducing transcription errors.

---

[11] Adapted with permission from James B. Bower, Robert E. Schlosser, and Charles T. Zlatkovich, *Financial Information Systems.*

Peg boards are quite useful in summarizing transactions for subsequent posting to the general ledger.

Illustration of Manual Sales Processing System for a Small Business

Many illustrations of manual applications were given in earlier chapters. Figure A19-16 illustrates a very simple system of cash sales designed around a cash register. The register has two drawers, one for each employee. Each employee has the key to that drawer. The register is designed to give the customer a receipt, and to record sales in detail by type of merchandise and by salesperson.

In this simple system each cashier rings up the sale, computes the tax, gives the customer the appropriate change computed by the register, and gives the customer a receipt. While this transaction is taking place, the cash register accumulates summary information on the type of sale, salesperson, merchandise sold, amount of sale, and tax information. At the close of the business day, the owner, in the presence of the cashiers, clears the register. The owner then reconciles the beginning cash balance and ending cash balance with the summary of transactions for each cashier. The owner then prepares the deposit slip and makes the bank deposit. The owner also posts the sales journal, the cash receipts journal, and the sales analysis by cashier and merchandise category for future reference. The cash register detail and summary tapes are filed by date, for reference and to create an audit trail. The key features in this simple system are the focal point of the cash register, the role of the owner, and the recording of data for future planning.

APPENDIX C

RISKS AND CONTROLS FOR MINI AND MICROCOMPUTER SYSTEMS[12]

Risks associated with *lack of segregation of duties* between the IS department and users (the individuals who initiate transactions, enter data, operate the computer, and prepare reports), include the following:

1. Perpetration and concealment of errors and irregularities
2. Unauthorized changes to master files
3. Inaccurate and incomplete processing of data
4. Processing errors
5. Incomplete and erroneous data
6. Uncorrected errors
7. Lost, added or altered data

---

[12] Adapted and reprinted with permission of Commerce Clearing House from The AICPA Audit and Accounting Guide, June 1, 1986, AAM 4250.030. Published and copyrighted by Commerce Clearing House, Inc., 4025 W. Peterson Ave., Chicago, Illinois, 60646.

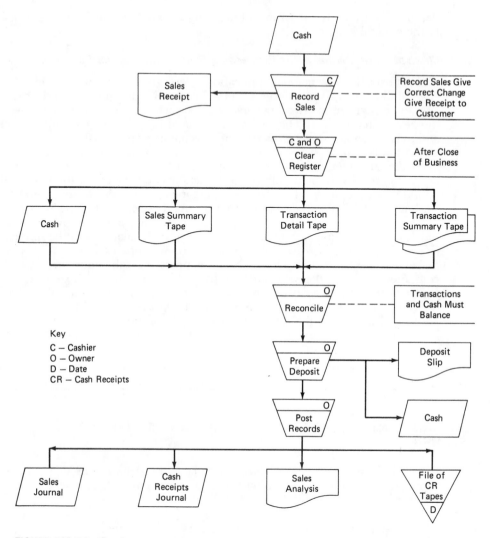

FIGURE A19-16 Simple manual system for a small business.

Appropriate controls include:

1. Maintenance of transaction logs and batch controls by user department
2. Independent review of transaction logs, processing logs, and batch control information
3. Management supervision
4. Passwords to control access to files and database
5. Required vacations and rotation of duties
6. Reconciliation of record counts and hash totals
7. Use of application programs to make changes in master files

8. Independent reconciliation of transaction totals recorded in batch control logs with input and output controls
9. Comparison of system manufacturer's utility program with authorized application version

Risks associated with the *location of the computer* in the same area as the user are:

1. Improper manipulation of data files
2. Unauthorized use or modification of computer files
3. Improper use of computer resources

Appropriate controls include:

1. Menus and procedures to control processing access
2. Management review of usage reports and logs
3. Periodic comparison of usage reports with processing schedule
4. Physical control over data-entry devices

Risks associated with *lack of segregation of functions within the IS department* (often programmers and operators are the same and many times are the actual end user), include:

1. Unauthorized access to information and programs
2. Perpetration and concealment of errors or irregularities
3. Errors caused by improper use or manipulation of data files or unauthorized or incorrect use of computer programs
4. Application programs that do not meet management's objectives

Appropriate controls include:

1. Use of a compiler to convert source code into object code
2. Comparison of library directories with manual records
3. Comparison of program in use with an authorized version
4. Use of interpretive language programs
5. Passwords to control access to libraries and files
6. Software controls to limit system access capabilities according to employee function
7. Test libraries
8. Management review of usage reports (history logs)
9. Systems of transaction logs, batch controls, processing logs, and run-to-run controls

Risks associated with *limited knowledge of computing* by the supervisor of IS operations:

1. Failure of systems to meet management objectives or operate according to management specifications
2. Lack of adequate application controls
3. Inadequate testing and review of systems

Appropriate controls include:

1. Operations documentation
2. Program documentation
3. System documentation
4. Use of third party to review new and modified programs and systems

Risks associated with *utility programs* used to enter and to modify data:

1. Unauthorized access and changes to data
2. Undetected errors in file manipulation
3. Lack of adequate application controls
4. Processing of unauthorized transactions and omitting of authorized transactions
5. Perpetration and concealment of errors or irregularities

Appropriate controls include:

1. Use of passwords to control access to data files
2. Use of application programs to update data
3. Independent control over transaction and master file changes, such as item count, control total and hash totals
4. Limited access to utilities
5. Removal of utilities from system when practical

Risks associated with the *use of diskettes for file storage:*

1. Processing the wrong file
2. Inability to detect errors in file changes
3. Inability to highlight operator errors

Appropriate controls include:

1. Control over access to diskettes
2. Storage of data in format not readable by key entry devices
3. Use of manual logs to control diskette library

Risks associated with *terminals* for data entry, inquiry, and other interactive functions:

1. Unauthorized input
2. Erroneous or fraudulent data
3. Errors caused by improper use or manipulation of data files or computer programs
4. Erroneous or incomplete data

Appropriate controls include:

1. Use of software that will allow only certain terminals to be used for specific functions
2. Use of physical controls to limit access to data files
3. Use of passwords to control access to data
4. Encryption of data and programs
5. On-line computer edit programs
6. Record counts, batch totals, run-to-run controls and verification
7. Error handling control procedures and error logs
8. Use of menus and procedures

Risks associated with the use of *commercially developed software packages:*

1. Failure of system to meet management and user objectives
2. Lack of adequate application controls
3. Inadequate testing of systems

Appropriate controls include:
1. Use of third party to review and evaluate proposed software

Risks associated with *inadequate documentation:*

1. Undetected errors during processing and system maintenance
2. Improperly trained personnel

Appropriate controls include:

1. Up-to-date user manuals

SELECTED REFERENCES

AMERICAN INSTITUTE OF CERTIFIED PUBLIC ACCOUNTANTS   *Audit and Accounting Manual,* Chicago, Ill.: Commerce Clearing House, 1986.
   "Guidelines for General System Specifications for a Computer System." New York: 1976.

BLANKENSHIP, RONALD C., and CAROL A. SCHOLLER, "The CPA, the Small Company and the Computer," *Journal of Accountancy*, August 1976, pp. 46–51.

BOER, GERMAIN B., and SAM W. BARCUS III, "How a Small Company Evaluates Acquisition of a Minicomputer, " *Management Accounting*, March 1981, pp. 13–23.

BOWER, JAMES B., ROBERT E. SCHLOSSER, and MAURICE NEWMAN, *Computer Oriented Accounting Information Systems*, Cincinnati, Ohio, South Western, 1985.

DAC Easy, DAC Software, Inc., Dallas, Texas, 1985.

GROLLMAN, WILLIAM K., and ROBERT W. CALLY, "Internal Control for Small Businesses," *Journal of Accountancy*, December 1978, pp. 64–67.

INSIGHT from Peachtree, Inc., Atlanta, Georgia, 1986.

LEITCH, ROBERT A., GADIS J. DILLON, and SUE H. MCKINLEY, "Internal Control Weaknesses in Small Businesses," *Journal of Accountancy*, December 1981, pp. 97–101.

MCDANIEL, LLOYD W., and HENRY WICHMANN, JR., Minicomputers: A Boom to Small Public Accounting Firms and Write-up Work," *National Public Accountants*, February 1979, pp. 22–26.

REA, R. C., "A Small Business Internal Control Questionnaire," *Journal of Accountancy*, July 1978, pp. 53–54.

SCHWARTZ, DONALD A., "Microcomputers Take Aim on Small Business Clients," *Journal of Accountancy*, December 1979, pp. 57–62.

SMITH, DONALD R., "Information Systems for the Entrepreneurial Enterprise," *Today's Executive* (Summer–Autumn 1986), Price Waterhouse, New York.

WYUNE ROBERT C., and ALAN FROTMAN, "Microcomputer: Helping Make Practice Perfect," *Journal of Accountancy*, December 1981, pp. 34–39.

ZIMMERMAN, HARRY, "Minicomputers: The Challenge for Controls," *Journal of Accountancy*, June 1980, pp. 28–35.

REVIEW QUESTIONS

1. What should be the focal point of an accounting system for a small business? Why?

2. What constitutes a set of minimum records for a small business?

3. What is a *ledgerless bookkeeping system*? What are its pros and cons?

4. List ten unique characteristics of the small business entrepreneurial environment that are important to consider in systems analysis, design, and implementation.

5. What breakthroughs made computer systems cost effective for small businesses? (See microcomputer chapter.)

6. What typical applications are offered by manufacturers and software vendors for small businesses?

7. How can word processing help small businesses?

8. Why is a business strategy important?

9. How can a small microsystem be useful to an accounting firm in expanding its practice?

10. Why are small entrepreneurial systems simpler than large systems?

11. What is the approximate cost of a very small system, and is this cost reasonable for a small-business owner?

12. Should a small-business owner purchase a software package and modify it to suit his or her needs? Or would this person be better off searching for one that is closer to his or her needs rather than modifying the system? If so, why? What if there is no software that fits?

13. How do small microcomputer systems and their associated business hardware pose a major challenge to the accounting profession?

14. How can small microsystems improve budgeting and planning activities for small businesses?

15. How can good accounting software for a microcomputer enhance the control environment of a small business?

16. How can good accounting software for microcomputers help owners or managers better manage their business?

17. What selection criteria should be considered in selecting small business accounting software?

18. List the internal control shortcomings typically found in small businesses. How can supervisory control strengthen or compensate for these weaknesses?

19. What categories of risk are associated with microcomputers? Cite at least two specific problems for each category and a control that can be used to reduce this risk.

CASES

19-1 List the major characteristics of the small-business environment and describe how each of these characteristics can influence information systems design.

19-2 Explain what is meant by a single-entry accounting system and how a single-entry accounting system on a cash basis can be converted to an accrual basis system at year-end.

19-3 The Orville Slick Oil Company* is a petroleum product distributorship located in Broken Bow, Nebraska. The company distributes the products of the Buffalo Oil Company of Texas as a jobber. All property, plant, and equipment are owned by Mr. Slick. Property used in the business includes two delivery trucks, a service truck, office space, a warehouse for storage of oil and grease, and a plant facility from which gas, fuel, and kerosene are distributed. Gas tanks, gas pumps, and air compressors are kept for use by regular customers. Detailed records are made of customers using this equipment.

The business is run by Mr. Slick. His wife, Gracie, keeps the books. One product delivery man is employed on a full-time basis. Various independent contractors and laborers are hired as needed to help with installation and repair of equipment.

Accounting is done on an accrual basis. A chart of accounts is used. At the end of the year, a local CPA prepares financial statements and tax returns. Mrs. Slick posts the books and reconciles the monthly bank statements. Mr. Slick prepares the monthly sales and excise tax returns.

Revenues are provided by the sale of gas, fuel, kerosene, oil, grease, and related products. Mr. Slick prices all products. The cost of these products from Buffalo Oil fluctuates considerably. Gas, fuel, and kerosene margins are reviewed monthly for this reason, and oil and grease margins are reviewed two or three times a year. Jobbers such as Mr. Slick have had considerable difficulty in evaluating selling prices to keep a reasonable margin and still be competitive.

Sales and Accounts Receivable

A delivery man delivers the product and prepares four copies of the sales ticket. Along with the blue original copy, the green copy is the customer receipt, the white copy is for cash or credit-card sales, and the yellow copy is for the credit sales. All credit sales are approved by the owner prior to delivery. Since Broken Bow is a small town, this is a simple matter for Mr. Slick because he knows everyone.

Both the white copy along with credit card receipt and the yellow copy along with the original are forwarded to the bookkeeper, Mrs. Slick. The bookkeeper checks the pricing and accuracy of each type of sale and places the cash in the vault. She then posts cash sales to the daily cash summary report and credit sales to the customer accounts receivable record, which is kept on a 3-x-5-inch card. Both cash and credit sales are posted to a daily sales summary, and the perpetual inventory records are updated. Mrs. Slick then files all original copies

---

* This case was originally prepared by Dr. Sue McKinley. The adapted version is used here with permission.

by number, all white copies by date, and yellow copies alphabetically by customer name.

Monthly the accounts receivable customer cards are pulled by the bookkeeper along with the alphabetical file of yellow invoices, and statements are prepared and mailed by the bookkeeper. The yellow copies of the invoice are mailed along with the statement. Part of the statement is supposed to be torn off and returned with the remittance.

For accounts that are more than one month past due, service charges are added by the bookkeeper at the same time that the statement is prepared. These charges are posted to the receivables card at that time also.

Cash Receipts

Along with cash sales just noted, the owner opens the mail, compares the cash receipts and/or credit card receipts with the remittance stubs (if the remittance stub is missing, he prepares a new one), and places all cash in the vault. The remittance stubs are forwarded to the bookkeeper, who posts the daily cash summary. Deposit slips are prepared and deposits are made whenever the owner goes to the bank, which is two or three times per week. Credit card receipts are mailed to Buffalo Oil Company as partial payment for petroleum products. The bookkeeper then posts the accounts receivable cards for the amount of the receipt noted on the remittance stub and files the remittance stub by date.

Cash Disbursements

Incoming mail is opened by the owner. Invoices are compared with receiving reports and are attached to purchase orders by the bookkeeper. They are then filed as they are received. A record of employee time is also kept by the bookkeeper. Periodically the owner reviews the unpaid invoice file and writes the necessary checks to pay the vendors. Employees are paid monthly. Buffalo Oil is also paid monthly for the difference between the invoice amount and the credit card receipts that have been remitted to Orville Slick Oil Company and forwarded to Buffalo Oil (as noted in the cash receipts discussion). All invoices and attached receiving reports are filed by vendor. Cash disbursement information, such as name, date, account number, and invoice number, is noted on a check stub.

Upon payment of the payroll, payroll records are posted by the bookkeeper. The bank account is reconciled monthly by the bookkeeper.

Inventory, Purchasing, and Receipt of Merchandise

A perpetual inventory card file is maintained. On each card, the product name, vendor, amount on hand, and amount on order are recorded. This file is arranged according to product name. As noted earlier as part of the sales procedure, the amount on hand is credited as sales are made.

The delivery man makes a casual assessment of items that are in short supply and gives the owner a note. The owner then prepares a purchase order for a reasonable quantity based on his fifteen years of experience as a jobber and sends the original to the vendor. Most products are ordered from the Buffalo Oil Company. A copy is given to the bookkeeper, who pulls the inventory card and updates the on-order amount. She then files the copy by vendor, pending delivery of the product.

Upon delivery, the delivery man who works for Orville Slick Oil Company pulls the purchase order copy, compares it with the products received, notes any exception on purchase order copy, prepares a receiving report, and pulls the inventory cards and updates the on-order and on-hand details for each item received. It is known when delivery will take place because all vendors have scheduled routes and the delivery man who works for Orville Slick Oil Company can be on hand to help the vendor's driver with difficult and often dirty work.

The delivery man then gives the purchase order copy, receiving reports, and inventory cards back to the bookkeeper. The bookkeeper follows up on the exceptions. Receiving reports and purchase orders are filed by vendor, awaiting a copy of the vendor's invoice.

General Comments

All buildings and inventory items are fenced and locked. Keys are kept in a locked vault (safe), and only the owner and his wife, the bookkeeper, know the combination. All documents are prenumbered. The check stubs, the daily cash summary, the daily sales summary, the accounts receivable file, the inventory file, and all other miscellaneous records are gathered by Mrs. Slick and posted to the general ledger once a month.

REQUIRED: From the notes gathered on the Orville Slick Oil Company:
1. Prepare a system flowchart for
   a. Sales and accounts receivable
   b. Cash receipts
   c. Cash disbursements
   d. Inventory, purchasing, and receipt of merchandise
2. Comment on the strengths and weaknesses of the control structure.
3. Suggest and flowchart a new system that will relieve the major accounting system and control procedure problems by using a microcomputer with (1) accounting applications and reporting packages; and (2) capability to generate special reports based on the transactions gathered in a normal course of business as described above.

Assume that there is no formal system where none is noted, and where a conflict occurs, assume that the system is confusing and not effective even for those who use it on a daily basis.

19-4 ABC LEASING.† ABC Leasing is a licensee for a major auto rental company; its location, in a resort city near the ocean, brings it both business and vacation customers. Annual sales volume is approximately $6 million, and the company has 60 full-time employees. Sales are expected to increase to $9 million over the next three years. The company has rental offices at the local airport, in several downtown locations, and in two neighboring towns. A local service bureau has been satisfying all its data processing needs, but this operation recently increased its charges to ABC to $2,000 per month. At this price the company decided it might pay to purchase its own computer.

To get some idea of how to approach the problem, ABC managers attended a seminar on small business minicomputer systems, where they talked to some managers from small businesses who recently had acquired computers. They learned two important things from these conversations: (1) approximately one half the total costs of the system would cover the hardware, and the remaining half would pay for the necessary software, supplies, consulting help, and assorted start-up costs; (2) they needed help in gathering the right information, asking the right questions of vendors, presenting the appropriate information to the vendors, and specifying the exact output they wanted from the system. ABC management approached its accounting firm for help in gathering and evaluating information for the computer purchase decision. The firm's consultant suggested ABC should:
1. Study the present data flow within the company.
2. Compile and classify information requirements.
3. Get computer system proposals from vendors.
4. Analyze the proposals and then select the best proposal from those submitted.

Data Flow Within the Company

After several weeks of data gathering by the clerical staff at ABC, the company was able to compile the relevant information necessary for specifying the parameters of the system the company needed (Figure C19-1). The data were important not only to ABC but also to the companies that would write the programs for the system because company management wanted all software developed by outside software vendors. The company president felt strongly that ABC should not create an IS department; therefore, the company would have to buy all its software from outside suppliers. This decision also meant that programs and machines acquired by the company would have to be readily usable by the existing clerical staff.

Finding out what information company managers need is no easy task, but ABC was able to identify some obvious needs by looking at existing problems. For example, monthly accounting reports, useful for controlling oper-

---

† Reprinted with permission from Boer and Barcus, "How a Small Company Evaluates Acquisition of a Minicomputer," *Management Accounting*, copyright © Institute of Management Accountants (formally National Association of Accountants), March, 1981, pp. 13–23.

General ledger accounts	133
Digits per account number	6
Entries per month to all accounts	900
Contract outstanding on any day	1,600
Payments received each month	1,400
Number of contracts processed monthly	7,900
Number of contracts in rental revenue master file	50,000
Payment vouchers per month	240
Number of entries per voucher	8
Number of vendors serving ABC Leasing	200
Journal entries per month for all disbursements	1
Automobiles bought and sold each month	250
Automobiles on hand	1,200
Number of digits in automobile number	6
Number of digits in automobile serial number	6
Unidentified payments per month	250
Outstanding billable items	900
Unapplied cash items at any time	1,500
Payroll checks per week	100
Full time employees	60

FIGURE C19-1   ABC leasing: system statistics.

ations and for projecting cash flows, arrived from the service bureau two or three weeks after the close of the month. The clerical staff was gradually getting behind in its preparation of operational analyses, with each sales increase putting them further behind. Given that sales would increase about 50% over the next three years, it was clear the company had to automate existing procedures just to enable the staff to continue performing its present activities.

At the beginning of the output definition process, company managers were convinced that automation of accounting procedures was the most important reason for buying a computer, but as they worked with defining system outputs they began to realize the profit potential of a computerized rental revenue file. Their current system showed a single number for sales revenue; however, the computerized rental revenue application could show rental revenue at a level as detailed as a specific automobile.

Such revenue detail would enable managers to evaluate the profitability of alternative mixes of corporation versus individual renters and small versus large automobiles. It also would allow them to evaluate the relative profitability of their rental locations and to assess the profit impact of various pricing strategies, strategies that involve alternative prices for mileage and day charges. Finally, managers realized that information about the most popular cars would enable them to alter the mix of automobiles they owned by selling less popular cars and replacing them with the more popular ones. In this case, then, output definition activities caused managers to shift their attention from the automation of clerical tasks to consideration of the profit potential of rental revenue information.

After their detailed review of management requirements, the company managers decided to implement the six applications listed below. They decided to start with the general ledger application because doing so would allow company personnel to get acquainted with the system using familiar data before they tried using the new information from the rental revenue system:

1. General ledger and financial reporting
2. Rental revenue
3. Cash payments and bank reconciliation
4. Fleet fixed assets
5. Unapplied cash and items billable
6. Payroll

These applications formed what management considered the basic components of the system the company needed. The information required by each application and the information flows among these applications were illustrated in a visual overview of the system which was most helpful in enhancing communication between managers and technical personnel. It also forced technical personnel to constantly be aware that no system component stands alone. The general ledger application served as the unifying element in the total system.

Not only did ABC managers have to specify the overall information flows, they also had to select those computer systems features compatible with their policy of using the present clerical staff to operate the new system.

Working again with its consultant, the company prepared the following list of computer techniques that would satisfy company needs:

1. On-line interactive processing

2. Menu selection and program prompting for data entry, inquiry, file update, and report generation

3. Multiprogramming

4. Printer spooling concurrent with other functions

5. Program prompting for such functions as paper changing and file mounting

6. Preparation of special reports by users through report writing software

7. Multiple security levels to limit file access to authorized individuals

On-line interactive processing with program prompting fits the company requirements well, because input station operators need little experience in computer operations. They simply respond to the questions appearing on the screen, and the system accepts only answers that fit a rigid set of constraints. The third requirement, which allows the machine to perform several activities simultaneously, was included at the suggestion of the consultant who felt the feature would be important for the company. Printer spooling allows operators to continue using terminals while the system prints reports, i.e., running the printer does not tie up the entire system so nobody can enter data during printing operations.

Requirements five and six are important because of the limited data processing knowledge of the personnel operating the machines. Prompting for paper and file changes requires less sophisticated personnel than a nonprompting system. Likewise, report writing software generally can be quickly mastered by nonprogramming personnel who can then create nonstandard reports from the data files whenever the company needs them.

The final requirement arose out of management concern about system controls. Large data processing operations employ enough people so that various duties can be segregated to maintain adequate internal control. ABC, however, simply planned to put the machine in a room where present clerical personnel would operate it. This room would be open to all employees, and data entry personnel would also print reports; in short, segregation of duties would be nonexistent. To compensate for this lack of separation, the company wanted to use machine controls to the extent technologically feasible. Purchasing software from an outside vendor helped remove one severe control problem usually present in small companies: program preparation and data entry by the same individuals. Use of a hierarchy of security levels, each higher level giving access to larger portions of the system, allowed the company to carefully control which personnel have access to specific portions of the computer system.

To assure that accurate data entered the system, ABC decided it wanted editing procedures on data input that included both field and multiple field tests. Specifically, the company wanted the system to edit for format, perform range tests on data items, compare values to master file elements, and verify logical relationships between and among fields. Field tests in an interactive system catch data errors while the operator enters data, a feature that increased accuracy and allows inexperienced personnel to correct mistakes before the input data become part of the data files. Both these features were important to ABC because it wanted to use its present clerical staff to operate the system. In addition to these input data editing tests, ABC wanted input data, transaction files, and master files processed under system control with each batch of data processed generating control or audit trail reports for user review.

One other feature the company considered that fits roughly under the heading of information requirements is that of documentation. System documentation refers to the procedure manuals, program listings, flow charts, listings of test data used to debug programs, and so on. ABC management especially was concerned about this feature because it planned to operate the system with no specialized data processing employees. This meant the instructions for using the programs and hardware would have to be written in clear, precise terms understandable to the present clerical staff; it meant ABC management would have to carefully scrutinize the material provided by the vendors before accepting it, and it meant that ABC would have to specify to the vendors in blunt terms that programs and hardware would be accepted only upon the receipt of documentation suitable for ABC personnel. Documentation is important in companies that have a fully staffed data processing department, but for ABC it wasn't just important–it was absolutely essential. Those factors for which the company decided it needed clear documentation were systems, programs, equipment and systems operation, user procedures and data control and error correction procedures.

Solicitation of Vendor Proposals

After it completed the study of data flow and management information requirements, the company moved to the next step in the computer acquisition process: solicitation of vendor proposals with a request for proposal (RFP). A request for proposal tells hardware vendors, and in the case of ABC Leasing, software vendors what the company wants from its system. The document describes in detail the specific company requirements for output, performance, and control procedures. In addition, it provides information such as company size, number of employees, and geographic location which helps vendors match their products with the company's needs.

Evaluating Vendor Proposals

The final step in the computer acquisition process deals with choosing a system from those proposed by the vendors. ABC management began this final phase by carefully reviewing the proposals for completeness and for responsiveness to the RFP. A list of questions was prepared for vendors submitting proposals with deficiencies such as missing data or incomplete responses to specific points in the RFP. Vendors were asked to answer these questions to clarify the ambiguities in their proposal. Unsatisfactory responses to these questions provided grounds for dropping a vendor because company management felt such unresponsiveness was a good indication of the service it could expect from this vendor in the future. After clarifying these points the company summarized the vendor proposal data in a format that facilitated vendor comparisons. To do this summary, ABC management simply created a large spread sheet that assigned columns to each vendor and rows to the specific elements related to each vendor.

All Factors Are Relevant.

Cost, of course, doesn't give the full picture. For instance, ABC Leasing looked at factors such as current user satisfaction with a vendor, the number of systems sold to date, the total years the software vendors had been in business, and the number of companies using the software produced by the software vendor. Company managers also asked these questions: Is a terminal "locked up" while the printer is running? Are data items protected from erroneous update when two or more programs request that item simultaneously? How much does response time slow down when one additional terminal is added to the system? They looked, too, at the expandability of the system to make sure the system could grow with the business. More importantly, they looked at whether the system could produce reports on time, i.e., regardless of the amount of main memory or the access speed of the disks, management wanted a system that delivered information on time.

Finally, the managers considered how fast the vendors could fix a machine if it broke down; that is, they evaluated the location of maintenance personnel, their hours of availability, the number available, and the comments of present customers on vendor maintenance service. ABC managers visited user installations and attended company demonstrations. They actually used the equipment to see how easily errors could be corrected, screens could be read, and paper could be loaded into a printer.

REQUIRED: Based on this case study, comment on the following:

1. The degree to which this small business followed the systems analysis, design, and implementation procedures outlined in Chapters 12 and 13.

2. The internal control considerations

3. The interaction between the accounting firm and management in the preparation of request for a proposal (RFP)

4. The point at which the vendor bids were solicited

5. The feasibility of using a microcomputer system to provide ABC Leasing with this needed information

6. The need for an interactive system

7. The profitability prospects of a new system

8. The criteria used for selection

19-5 The Kelly Home Building Company is a small building contractor located in the Piedmont area of the Carolinas. The company specializes in custom-built houses and is generally busy enough to retain most of its subcontractors on a regular basis. It has an excellent reputation and is generally asked to bid on many jobs for individuals as well as developers. Its business has grown and it is having a difficult time handling payrolls, billings, bank drawings, accounts payable to vendors and subcontractors, costs distributions, inventories, and scheduling of workers, subcontractors, and material. At the present time it employs a full-time bookkeeper to do the bookkeeping and cost distribution, and Mr. Kelly's son handles all the bid calculations. The company always seems to be two to three months behind and has often lost contracts because of excessive bids and because it has billed some customers for less than it should have due to delays in cost allocations. Quite simply, its financial affairs have been a mess, and Mr. Kelly doesn't even know at the end of the year how profitable the business has really been. He approaches you, as his accountant, for help. He has read and heard and talked to vendor salesmen about the new microcomputers and how they can help managers in his predicament.

REQUIRED:

1. Outline the approach you would advise Mr. Kelly to take to solve his problem.

2. Suggest how microcomputers may be able to help Mr. Kelly with decision making, transaction processing, and reporting.

3. Suggest some key specifications that Mr. Kelly should spell out when dealing with software and hardware vendors.

4. Design a job-cost system including internal control features using micro interactive computer software. This should include data file structure and the flow of documents.

19-6 The Wood Products Lumber Company is a building supply company located in the suburbs of a large metropolitan area. The company has been using a service bureau for sales analysis, inventory control, accounts payable, billings, payroll, and financial statement preparation.

The company has been experiencing two problems. First, when a sale is made, it really does not know if the item is in stock until it has actually checked the warehouse because the inventory listing is often a week old. The service bureau updates the listing once a week.

The second problem, common to many small businesses, is that Wood Products has had considerable difficulty planning future purchases, capital improvements, and new lines of merchandise. As a first step, the company believes that a comparison of monthly and departmental financial statements with "some" plan would be helpful in determining how well it is progressing. For example, is the company making any contribution to profit and general overhead from its lawn care line of products?

REQUIRED:

1. Using microcomputer software, similar to that illustrated in Appendix A of this chapter for small businesses, suggest an inventory system for Wood Products to solve the first problem. Your suggestion should include flowcharts and controls. Why would such a system be preferable to the current system of accumulating sales invoices and receiving reports and sending them to the service bureau for keypunching and processing?

2. How could a microsystem similar to the one suggested in Appendix A of this chapter help with the second problem? Would such a system enable management to engage in "what if" planning? If not, what could be done using other widely available microcomputer software?

3. Finally, would you suggest that Wood Products use a microcomputer system for preparing payroll, processing monthly statements, paying vendors, and preparing financial statements? In your answer to this, indicate the circumstances under which you would make your positive or

negative recommendation for these later applications.

19-7 REQUIRED:

1. Compare the internal control strengths and weaknesses of a small-business microcomputer system with those of a large mainframe system. Be sure to consider the following issues:

   a. Segregation of duties

   b. Physical control over assets (files and records)

   c. Security of records

   d. Compromise of programs for fraudulent purposes

   e. Integrity of data input

   f. Documentation

   g. Control totals

   h. Error correction procedures

   i. Audit trails

   j. Systems design

   k. Confidence of management and auditors in information output

   l. Backup systems

   m. Supervision and review

2. Compare the internal control strengths and weaknesses of a manual (one bookkeeper) system with those of a microcomputer system by considering the same issues just listed.

19-8

The heart of Duff's Mail Order Seed Company is its mailing list of potential customers and its inventory system. Assume that Duff's specializes in garden seeds and fruit and nut trees for the Southeast. It purchases potential names from such magazines as *Southern Life, Organic Gardeners,* and from the better known seed companies. It pays particular attention to its own repeat customers, whom it believes are keys to its success.

Mr. Duff currently sends promotional material and catalogs free to old customers and to those who respond to letters sent to potential customers whose names are obtained from the list just described. He also solicits names from advertisements in many regional and national gardening and do-it-yourself magazines. Merging all these names, keeping up with address changes, and keeping sales statistics on sources of promotion and purchased mailing lists has been a nightmare for Mr. Duff.

He has heard of some data management microcomputer systems that have mailing list, sales analysis, and inventory software.

REQUIRED: He has asked you, as his accountant, to prepare system specifications for his consideration. Your discussion with him leads you to believe that he is not really sure that such a system would be beneficial, and thus you also want to include in your report a review of the main benefits of such a system as well as its side benefits as they are related to other accounting data processing.

19-9

Lexington County News is a small newspaper with a weekly circulation of several thousand. They carry local news and advertisements and need to maintain a subscription list and bill subscribers on a monthly basis. They also need to charge customers for their advertisements and they need to manage their subscriptions and advertisement receivables to ensure a cash flow to sustain their operations. Moreover, they need to be able to access this receivable information in order to drop subscribers if they get too far behind in their payments and refuse to carry business ads for businesses that are delinquent.

REQUIRED: As their CPA, suggest how a small business accounting software package would assist Lexington County News in:

1. The management of their business (in particular their accounts receivable),

2. The control of their operations, and

3. Their cash management.

19-10

Ms. Marie Dobbs DMD has been in dental practice in suburban Denver for several years. Her practice has expanded and she needs to consider automating her patient records and her billing operations. After some careful consideration of her needs she has concluded that her basic patient record and billing processes are:

1. Diagnosis and treatment,

2. Generating charges for her services,

3. Preparation of patient invoices,

4. Preparation of insurance invoices to recover insured charges from insurance carriers,

5. Mailing these invoices,

6. Receipt of payment,

7. Generating recall notices to remind patients of their next appointments or needed routine dental care, and

8. Updating the general ledger.

This, she concludes with the assistance of her accountant, will require data on patients (history, care rendered, charges, recall requirements), invoices outstanding (accounts receivable and service charges), and insurance carrier information.

The sources of this information will be from patients, insurance carriers, and employees as they render patient care. The major data flows will be: patient input, recall notices, dental treatment information, invoice (patient and insurance carrier billing) data, patient and insurance payments, and general ledger updates.

REQUIRED: Prepare a systems flow chart of an automated online patient records and billing system that may be used in a request for vendor proposals.

19-11 Southwest Electronics is a small business that buys and sells electronic components for local businesses in the Houston area. It has been experiencing difficulties in managing its cash flow lately. It has trouble managing its receivables and determining which vendors to pay to take advantage of the various discounts vendors offer. Moreover, it would like to hold sales persons more responsible for checking the credit of customers who may be more than 60 days past due prior to completing a sale. Furthermore, it would like to determine which products are more profitable and which ones are not, so that it can make some decisions on continuing or discontinuing certain product lines.

REQUIRED: Explain how a microcomputer software package similar to the one outlined in Appendix A can be used to assist Southwest Electronics in the management of its cash flow and how such software might be able to aid in the determination of product profitability.

20

COMPUTER AUDITING

INTRODUCTION AND AUDIT RISK

Both external and internal auditors are vitally concerned about effective procedures for auditing computer systems. The ultimate objective of the external auditor is to render his or her opinion on the overall fairness of the financial statements. The auditor must do this in conformity with generally accepted set of auditing standards. The internal auditor's objective tends to be more concerned with the quality and relevance of management information, data integrity, the system effectiveness, the efficiency of combined management information systems, and the quality of managerial performance.

The external auditor needs to consider both materiality and audit risk in the planning of the audit and in evaluating whether the financial statements taken as a whole are presented fairly in conformity with generally accepted accounting principles.[1]

Materiality is defined as the magnitude of an omission or misstatement of accounting information that, in light of surrounding circumstances, makes it likely that a reasonable person relying on the information would have had their

---

[1] Auditing Standards Board, AU 312.08.

judgment changed or influenced by the omission or misstatement.[2]

External auditors are mainly concerned with audit risk and how it relates to financial statement assertions about account balances, classes of transactions, and disclosure. *Audit risk* is the risk that the auditor may unknowingly fail to appropriately modify his opinion on financial statements that are materially misstated.[3] There are three components of audit risk. They are: inherent risk, control risk, and detection risk.[4]

Inherent risk is the susceptibility of an account balance to material error assuming the client does not have any related internal controls. This is related to economic conditions, the general business environment, the susceptibility of certain accounts to fraud and errors, and complexity of certain types of transactions.

Control risk is the risk that misstatements that could occur in an account balance or class of transactions and that could be material, when aggregated with misstatements in other balances or classes, will not be prevented or detected and corrected on a timely basis by an entity's control structure.

Detection risk is the risk that the auditor's examination will not detect a material error in an account balance. This is influenced by the nature, timing, and extent of audit procedures.

In general, audit risk is the product of all three of these; inherent risk times control risk times detection risk, or, for example: .80 × .95 × .90 = .684. Internal auditors are mainly concerned about *business risk*. This can manifest itself in terms of invalid, irrelevant, and inaccurate data upon which transactions are based or decisions are made. It can also stem from inefficient and ineffective operations. Bad irrelevant data as well as inefficient and ineffective operations can follow from a poor accounting system, insufficient control procedures, and a control environment that is not conducive to good controls.

An entity's *control structure* [5] consists of three elements: (1) the control environment, (2) the accounting system, and (3) control procedures. The control environment as shown in Chapter 11 embodies management style, organization structure, audit committee, assignment of authority and responsibility, management control methods, personnel management, and external controls over an entity. "The accounting system consists of methods and records established to identify, assemble, classify, analyze, record and report an entity's transactions and to maintain accountability for related assets."[6] "Control procedures are

---

[2] "Qualitative Characteristics of Accounting," *Statement of Financial Accounting Concepts No. 2.,* Stamford, Conn., copyright by Financial Accounting Standards Board, Norwalk, Connecticut, 1980, p xv. Reprinted by permission.

[3] SAS No. 3, paragraph 25.

[4] "Audit Risk and Materiality in Conducting an Audit," *Statement on Auditing Standards No. 47,* Auditing Standards Board, American Institute of Certified Public Accountants, New York, N.Y., 1983. See Section 312.

[5] For a discussion and definition of each of these elements see *Statement on Auditing Standards No. 55 Consideration of the Internal Control Structure in a Financial Statement Audit.* American Institute of Certified Public Accountants, New York, N.Y. 1988; and its initial exposure draft "The Auditor's Responsibility for Assessing Control Risk," *Proposed Statement on Auditing Standards—Exposure Draft,* Auditing Standards Board, American Institute of Certified Public Accountants, New York, N.Y., January, 1987. See also *Internal Control—Integrated Framework: Exposure Draft, Committee of Sponsoring Organizations of the Treadway Commission,* 1991, for a discussion of internal control.

[6] SAS No. 55 and "The Auditor's Responsibility for Assessing Control Risk."

those policies and procedures in addition to the control environment and accounting system that management has established to provide reasonable assurance that an entity's established objectives are achieved."[7]

The advent of the computer has caused several problems for the auditor in determining the control structure, assessing control risk and detection risks associated with the assertions in the financial statements. First, audit trails, once highly visible, are often an unseen part of the computer system. Second, records, such as tape and disk files are readable only by machine. Third, the computer control structure is not readily apparent because it is generally founded on structured system analysis, design, and implementation procedures and based on programmed functions, operating and database systems, and hardware and software characteristics.

In general, the major steps in a computer audit parallel those in the audit of a traditional system. They are shown in Figure 20-1. The procedures and techniques, however, are very different and must be designed to cope with a computer system's control environment, system, and procedures and their complexity.

EDP AUDIT PROCESS

Preliminary Review

According to SAS No. 3 the "Preliminary phase of the auditor's review should be designed to provide an understanding of (a) the flow of transactions through the accounting system, (b) the extent to which EDP is used in each significant accounting transaction, and (c) the basic structure of accounting control"[8] The auditor should obtain an understanding of each of the three elements of the entity's control structure. This is needed to plan an effective and efficient examination of the entity's financial statements. The entity's control structure affects the auditability of the entity's financial statements, the potential areas of material misstatements, the risk that material misstatements may occur, and the subsequent design of compliance and substantive tests.[9]

First, the auditor should obtain an understanding of the control environment by examining the policies, procedures, organization, and other components of the control environment noted above and discussed in detail in Chapter 11.

Second, he or she must learn how the computer system operates by reviewing system documentation and interviewing accounting and system personnel. In general, "the auditor's understanding of the accounting system should include:

1. The major classes of transactions in the entity's operations,
2. How those transactions are initiated,

---

[7] Ibid.

[8] SAS No. 3.

[9] See W. Thomas Porter and William E. Perry, *EDP: Controls and Auditing* (Boston: Kent Publishing Co., 1987), or Ron Weber; *EDP Auditing: Conceptual Foundations and Practice*, McGraw Hill. 2nd ed. (New York: McGraw-Hill, 1988).

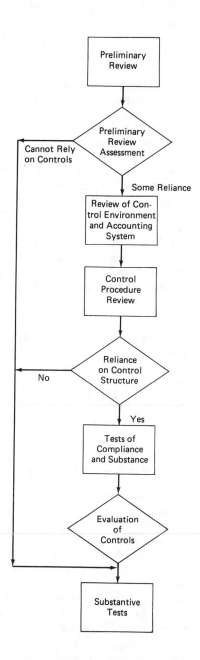

FIGURE 20-1   Computer audit process.
Source: Adapted from *Auditor's Study and Evaluation of Internal Control in EDP Systems,* AICPA, New York, 1977.

3. The accounting records, supporting documents, machine-readable information, and specific accounts in the financial statements involved in the processing and reporting of transactions.

4. The accounting processing involved from the initiation of a transaction to its inclusion in the financial statements, including how the computer is used to process the data, and

5. The financial reporting process used to prepare the entity's financial statements, including the preparation of significant accruals, deferrals and disclosures.[10]

Third, an understanding of the entity's control procedures is essential to the auditor's understanding of the control structure.

Thus for each significant computer application the auditor must ascertain in general its purpose, software, and hardware that are utilized in the processing steps, the nature of the processing steps (batch or on-line, for example), the database or file structure, and the personnel responsible for processing the information or running the system. A document flowchart or system flowchart may be helpful in this respect for it shows the source, destination, processing steps, and controls present in each transaction, decision, inquiry or reporting process. For database systems the data dictionary described in Chapter 10 will be invaluable in determining the flow of information and its impact on data elements.

Assessment of Preliminary Review

For each significant accounting application, the accounting controls must be evaluated in light of the overall control structure of the organization. The results of the procedures the auditor performs in understanding of an entity's control structure provide a basis for a preliminary assessment of the level of control risk. This preliminary assessment may be that control risk is limited or that control risk is not limited. For those where the risk is limited the auditor can or should rely on the control structure given the objective of the audit.

The purpose of this assessment is to reduce reliance on substantive audit tests, to determine the amount of control and detection risk, where effective control structure exists, where the cost of evaluating these controls is less than the cost of conducting substantive tests on compensating (duplicate) controls, and where these controls can be relied upon to assess the organizations accounting system and its resulting financial statement assertions.

The auditor may proceed in three ways from this assessment. First, perform a detailed review with a reasonably high expectation that reliance can be placed on internal control to further reduce control risk. Second, conduct extensive substantive tests of the application being considered to reduce control risk and detection risk. And, third, in some cases withdraw from the audit due to an independence conflict or lack of sufficient technical competence when complex computer systems are being used by the client. At this juncture an audit strategy should be planned to determine what would be the best approach in auditing

---

[10] "The Auditor's Responsibility for Assessing Control Risk," *Proposed Statement on Auditing Standards—Exposure Draft*, Auditing Standards Board, American Institute of Certified Public Accountants, New York, N.Y., January, 1987, p. 11.

the system, what technique to apply, and the overall scope of the investigation to best reduce the audit risk associated with the entity's audit.

Detailed Review

Next, given a decision that some reliance on the control structure seems likely and seems cost effective to pursue, the auditor begins a detailed assessment of the control structure of the organization's system and applications. It is important that the auditor first consider the potential causes of loss in an organization and then establish that there is a network of controls present that would protect the organization against the likelihood of those potential losses. In other words, the expected loss should be reduced to an acceptable level. These controls should be reviewed initially for pervasive weaknesses; because the discovery of such gaps would indicate any future reliance unwarranted. During this review process it is assumed that the existing controls function effectively. The auditor must determine if the system of controls will prevent, detect, and correct irregularities and fraudulent activities on a timely basis so that the financial statements are founded upon good set of financial records (database).

First, control environment issues like those noted in Chapter 11 need to be reviewed because they set the stage for a good control structure. These include general controls such as an appropriate organization structure, assignment of responsibility, employment and training policies, and the use of an audit committee. Next, it is important the accounting system match the information requirements of management. From an external audit perspective it must also meet the generally accepted accounting standards. A well-designed accounting system will help ensure the accurate processing of data on a day in and day out basis in accordance with managements policies. It will be the basis upon which management will make decisions and publish its reports including the financial statements. The nature of these controls are explained in detail in Chapter 11. Often a firm may use a questionaire[11] to be sure key components of the control structure are not overlooked. It is important to assess all the components of the control structure to assess the overall effectiveness of the system.

Following the review of control, environment and the accounting system, the auditor must evaluate the *control procedures* of significant applications. The significance of each application comes from the auditor's review of the organization and its accounting system. It will differ from organization to organization. A good place to begin would be the client's documentation which contains the systems flowchart for each application. For a database system, the overall schema of the system is also a good place to begin. Control procedures such as those mentioned in Chapter 11 for input, processing, output, and file (data) control should be reviewed.

A questionaire can be used to accomplish this review. Another method used to document the accounting system and application control procedures is called transaction flow accounting. This method requires the auditor identify: (1) the business cycles (e.g., sales and revenue collection); (2) the types of transactions which flow through each cycle (e.g., customer invoice); (3) the functions performed within each cycle (e.g., post accounts receivable record); and (4) the

---

[11] See for example, Peat, Marwick, Mitchell & Co. EDP Controls Questionaire shown in Porter and Perry, *EDP Controls and Auditing.*

internal control procedures in each cycle. Flowcharts are developed showing the transaction flow, functions performed, control objectives at each control point and control procedure.

Reliance on EDP Controls

Upon completion of this review process the auditor must determine that the necessary control structure is in place and that he or she can rely on the control structure; or that due to weakness in the system of controls, that reliance on the controls in certain applications or throughout the entire system is not warranted and that the tentative decision made earlier to rely on the control structure was wrong given the detailed evidence collected during the review. If the latter is the case, the auditor must then rely on substantive tests for the audit. Moreover, given the results of the detailed review, the auditor may still elect to use substantive tests for an application or for the entire system if such tests are more effective or economical than compliance tests for the controls being tested. Throughout this process the auditor must continually assess the control risk. This assessment is linked to the significance of the account or transaction and the possible presence of compensating (duplicate or redundant) controls.

Tests of Compliance

Once it has been determined that the necessary control procedures were designed into the accounting system, the next step is to test whether the actual system operates in compliance with these controls. The control risk is again assessed in terms of the need to subsequently depend on procedures to lower detection risk. A wide variety of procedures and techniques are available to help the auditor cope with the challenges of the computer environment. They each have their advantages and disadvantages, which are very much a function of the nature of the accounting and information system. For example, one procedure will be fine for a batch-oriented production system, but will fail to provide the auditor with useful audit evidence for an on-line order-entry system. These control procedures and techniques are outlined in Chapter 11.

The auditor may *audit around the computer.* Output is traced to input and vice versa on a test basis, and the computer is treated as a "black box." This approach was common practice twenty years ago. It is still a valid approach today for batch systems that are simple extensions of manual systems. To be effective, these batch systems should have: (1) clear audit trails where transactions can easily be traced through the various processing steps by using transaction logs, detailed ledgers, and a good system of referencing; (2) straightforward system logic; and (3) well-defined, tested, and widely accepted software. The major advantage of this procedure is its simplicity. To perform this type of audit, very little specialized training is necessary. The major disadvantage is that it completely ignores the very heart of the accounting and information system, which is the actual data processing and its associated controls.

To assess the actual processing of the information and its associated control procedures, the auditor needs to audit *through the system* to understand how the "black box" works. This is the only way the auditor can test compliance with specified accounting and control and procedures when the processing logic is complex, large volumes of data are processed, key elements of the control structure are computerized, and significant on-line random access activity is present.

The auditor can verify system logic by using flowcharts and can assess programming steps by examining the code to ensure that processing is to be performed in accordance with management guidelines and generally accepted accounting principles. Expert knowledge is required to do this. Computer packages may be used to generate a flowchart of the application program logic to graphically portray the flow of data through the system. These control flowcharting packages may even pinpoint control strengths and weaknesses. These control flowcharting packages aid in the review and evaluation of control procedures. These two desk checks are limited, for they do not test compliance.

Several *nonconcurrent* (cannot be implemented concurrently with other computer processing) processing procedures can be used to help the auditor assess system controls. To test the adequacy of the system of control procedures to prevent fraudulent activities or processing errors, test data (deck) can be used. A data set that includes both good and erroneous transactions is prepared. A sample listing of the types of data would include the following:

Valid transactions
Transactions not in sequence
Transactions exceeding control limits
Batch totals and other analytical steps
Incomplete, invalid, and missing transaction information
Using the wrong files
Field characteristics such as alphanumeric data in numeric field
Overflow of fields (data too long for field length)
Illogical conditions between fields and within records
Account numbers, part numbers, or transaction codes that do not match
    proper account numbers, part numbers, and transaction codes

Control procedures related to these transactions should be present and be operating to ensure the integrity of transactions and their resulting records or database. The test data may be processed using the system to test this premise. The results are then compared with a known solution of good and bogus transactions. This method is excellent if the variety of transactions is limited.

For larger complex systems, however, the variety of transactions and the number of potential problems that could be encountered become too large to manage by hand. The auditor must also not have the expertise required to test the complex logic of more advanced on-line random access systems. To handle this problem, *test data generators* have been devised which mechanically produce a wide spectrum of good and bad data.

The major advantages of the test data approach are simplicity and a good test of application program controls. The major disadvantages are: (1) keeping up with system modifications; (2) the complexity of some systems; and (3) the commingling of test data with actual data in on-line files for a system that cannot be shut down for an audit.

Master records and programs must be obtained to implement this compliance test. These must be used so as not to disrupt the client's operations. For simple sequential batch processing systems this is easy to accomplish. The auditor merely obtains a copy of the master file and program after the client processes the batch or random transaction. Then the auditor processes the test data using the copy of the file and the program. This should be controlled by the auditor and done on a surprise basis to be sure the files and programs tested are those actually uses and are the most current in use. In more complex systems, a simulated master record may be used that contains the essential characteristics of the client's master record. This is effective for complex and for some random access systems and will not interrupt the operations of the client.

To deal with *concurrency* and increasingly complex problems, several additional *advanced techniques* have been developed. The *integrated test facility,* or "minicompany," is one such technique. Its purpose is to test both input and data collection controls as well as processing controls. The auditor establishes a dummy entity, such as a division or cost center, in the database against which data, both good and bad, can be entered and processed along with live transactions. To monitor the system, this technique can be performed without the firm's knowledge. The major advantage is the regular programs are used under ordinary operating circumstances to test the effectiveness of the operating system and to test the adequacy of input and processing control procedures. This concurrent approach is a must for many on-line systems. Another significant advantage is that the flow of data can be tested as transactions are ultimately posted to the dummy entity accounts. The major disadvantages are that, as the auditor reviews these test transactions, he or she runs the risk of reversing real data.

In many complex systems actual data may also be *tagged* and *traced* through the system with the auditor taking *snapshots* of the database before and after each data processing procedure. The major advantage of this latter technique is that the auditor can follow the flow of the information through the system. Rather than use the actual database, a *parallel test facility* enables the auditor to test the operating system and its various general and application controls for compliance against a representation of the firm's database, application program, and operating system. *Parallel simulation* of representative programs can also be used on actual data. This representation uses a different program logic and database than that of the client. Results of the simulation would be compared with actual results to test the computer system. The purpose of parallel simulation is to check compliance with technical standards, organizational objectives, and program modification authorization procedures. *Reprocessing* is a version of this where the firm's actual processing is duplicated.

Evaluation of Controls

Upon reviewing the results of the compliance tests, the auditor needs to carefully evaluate the potential impact the weaknesses in the control structure may have on the financial statements or, in the case of the internal auditor, the managerial reports. To do this, the nature of the potential problems and irregularities should be considered (where the client is at risk) as well as the presence of compensating controls in the overall system. For example, extensive reconciliation procedures may compensate for the lack of an effective system of processing controls in a particular transaction.

Substantive Testing Phase

Based on this analysis of control risk coupled with an assessment of overall inherent risk, the auditor should plan a series of substantive audit procedures to obtain sufficient evidence to reduce detection risk. This must be done to render a conclusion on the likelihood of a material error existing in the computer system and on the financial statements. These tests should cover those areas where there was an absence of control procedures or the lack of effective compliance with control procedures. These tests are generally performed on account balances and the transaction details which comprise the balances. Substantive tests are performed to reduce the level of detection risk for financial statement assertions to an acceptable level. These requirements follow from the process just outlined. Moreover, in some instances substantive detection tests were considered more cost effective than review and compliance test procedures. They need to be performed in these applications. The results of these tests will then be used to help the auditor render a final opinion on the financial statements. Some of these substantive tests for detection of risk can be performed within the computer installation. These include:

Tests to identify erroneous logic
Test the accuracy of data
Tests to identify data inconsistency
Tests to reconcile data with physical counts
Confirmation of data with outside sources, and
Analytical review of account transaction statistics and account balances.

GENERALIZED AUDIT SOFTWARE

Computer programs can be written to handle many of the tests indicated, or to assist the auditor in performing many review, compliance, and substantive tests. These programs can be written by the client. If they are, they must be controlled and tested by the external auditor. They may also be written by an organization for internal audit purposes. Inventory listings, accounts receivable aging and payroll registers are examples of reports which can be prepared to assist in the audit process. Moreover, the auditor can write specialized audit software for certain clients or applications. These are applications and should follow the structured development phases notes in earlier chapters. The problem with this approach is that it may cost too much and less costly alternatives are likely to exist to perform the audit.

Many audit functions, however, are common for many clients and applications. For these, generalized audit software can be developed and utilized effectively to assist in the audit.[12] These programs can assist in many ways:

---

[12] See Porter and Perry, *EDP: Controls and Auditing;* or Weber, *EDP Auditing*, 2nd ed.

Access and retrieve data—Programs can read files that are simple, like sequential files, as well as complex random access files to extract data necessary to perform other audit steps. Several files may be accessed at the same time; for example, to extract data on all receivables over 90 days old for positive confirmations.

File reorganization—Some programs compare, sort, and merge retrieved files to facilitate the audit process. Comparisons of key statistics such as ratios can be made.

Statistical—Several packages provide routines to help the auditor draw a sample and perform statistical sampling procedures. Others support regression analysis and ratio analysis for analytical review.

Arithmetic calculation—Programs can perform calculations such as ratios, counts, footings, extensions, summary information such as control totals, and comparisons such as those between physical and recorded inventory.

Descriptive statistics—Software can be used for comparative analysis with industry standards and prior periods—that is, trend analysis.

Reporting—Programs can report the results of the analysis represented above in ways useful to the auditor and print the confirmation, for example.

In general, these audit software packages enable the auditor to be more efficient, spend more time doing analysis rather than clerical tasks, examine many more records, generate professional looking reports, and improve audit sampling.

To use the generalized software, the auditor must prepare a set of specification instructions such as data formats to link the generalized audit software with the characteristics of the system to be audited. The auditor must make sure that final reports are generated from files being tested. Not all generalized audit software packages will operate on all systems. Most are limited because they cannot be used in concurrent auditing and, as a result, cannot effectively be used to audit the processing logic in on-line database systems. On the other hand, most are very effective in auditing large-batch file-oriented systems. Most of the larger public accounting firms make good use of these packages to simplify the audit process and to reduce the training needed for their auditors to perform computer audits. In addition, internal auditors of many large organizations can use these effectively to audit a wide range of applications for numerous segments of the organization.

ADVANCED COMPUTER SYSTEMS

Auditing Procedures

Today many systems are very complex. Even small microcomputer systems use complex integrated logic and database schema. The computer has become even more integrated into the actual operations of the business. It is no longer just used for accounting records, it is used to decide which products to manufacture and when, whom to sell the products to, when to ship them, and when and how much inventory to order, for example. All of this activity impacts the accounting system. In this example, the cost accounting system, the order-entry and receivable system, and the various inventory systems are affected by the transactions processed by these systems. Moreover, these transactions may be generated from remote sales offices and inventory may be distributed from remote warehouses all automatically by the computer. The system, for example, may have an integrated system architecture like that described in Chapters 5 and 7 and use a common integrated database like that described in Chapter 10 to support its various applications as well as management inquiry on the status of various orders. Such advanced EDP systems are becoming more commonplace. They generally have the following characteristics which makes them difficult to audit using conventional methods including generalized audit software: (1) complex communication networks; (2) common databases which link many applications; and (3) complex integrated systems architecture where transactions affect many operational areas within the organization. This complexity makes the generation of an effective audit trail difficult and hard to follow.

In these cases the concurrent approaches[13] mentioned earlier can be used effectively. Moreover, the auditor can actually embed audit software in the operating or database system. This technique is called *system control audit review file* (SCARF)[14] or *concurrent processing*. Files are placed at certain key points within the system to monitor the flow of information and to gather data for the audit. Finally, a *simulated attack* may be used to test the computer system's security and access system.[15]

Audit Trails in Advanced Systems

Effective audit trails are essential to the audit whether the auditor audits around the computer by tracing transactions or uses a complex method to trace and tag transactions as they are processed in a concurrent auditing scheme. Even good microcomputer accounting software packages have good audit trails with capabilities that enable the auditor to trace and to retrieve information about transactions.

An audit trail must have three function:[16] creation of the audit trail or deletion when it is no longer necessary to retain the information, retrieval of information for managerial as well as for audit purposes, and modification when irregularities are detected. An example of a modification is the correction (or reversal) of the posting of a transaction to the wrong account. There are several ways to correct for an erroneous audit trail. The most common is to simply post another transaction to reverse and correct the erroneous transaction. This may be acceptable for simple batch processing systems which use data files, but it can create problems for complex database systems because the original data element which is used by many applications is never corrected. Thus a system must be

---

[13] See Porter and Perry, *EDP: Controls and Auditing; EDP Auditing*, 2nd ed. for a complete dicussion of these issues.

[14] See Weber, *EDP Auditing*, 2nd ed. for a complete discussion of SCARF.

[15] See Tom Alexander, "Waiting for the Great Computer Ripoff," *Fortune*, July 1978, pp. 143–52, for a discussion of simulated attacks and the results.

[16] Ron Weber, "Audit Trail System Support in Advanced Computer-Based Accounting Systems," *The Accounting Review*, April 1982, pp. 311–325.

used that corrects the original transaction which led to the erroneous data element. One must design an audit trail to correct the original transaction and the resulting data element and keep a record of these corrections. In other words, a more basic modification scheme is required for the modification function of the audit trail in complex database systems.

PLANNING AND TIMING THE AUDIT FOR ADVANCED COMPUTER SYSTEMS

All computer systems experience degradation over time. The components which experience this will most likely have weaknesses in control procedures. Thus these are the ones the auditor should concentrate on, given that they are significant and controls are not compensated for elsewhere as discussed earlier. In designing an audit program, the auditor should look for the subsystems where degradation is most likely to occur. These will be those systems which have been subject to the most frequent changes. There are two reasons for this. First, the need to make modifications ought to be a signal that the system did not meet the needs of management or it did not work well to start with. Second, any time a system is modified there is added potential for problems even though it was thoroughly tested subsequent to the change. According to the theory of system change,[17] these are the systems which are most likely to experience problems and potentially impact the integrity of the organization's data and financial statements.

The timing of the audit function is very important. When the life cycle of an EDP system is considered along with the complexity of system, it is important that the auditor be involved not only with the periodic audit of the financial statements if the auditor is external, or the operational review if he or she is internal, but with the actual design of the system. As discussed above many of the audit procedures require advanced preparation during the design stages to be sure the data files can be read by the generalized software and programs are written and imbedded to provide concurrent audit information on transactions processed through the system, for example. Moreover, the auditor can assist the client in the establishment of a effective control system so that more reliance can be placed on it to minimize the cost and extent of substantive testing during the annual financial audit. This too is done during the design stage for internal control purposes and audit efficiency.

USE OF MICROCOMPUTERS IN THE AUDIT PROCESS

Microcomputers and their associated communication software enable the auditor to use many powerful analysis, modeling, reporting, and communication functions to improve the efficiency and the effectiveness of the audit.[18] First, most large and many small accounting firms now have software available to assist the auditor in many of the mundane working paper and reporting tasks, like

---

[17] Gordon B. Davis, and Ron Weber, *Auditing Advanced EDP Systems: A Survey of Practice and Development of a Theory*, The Management Information Systems Research Center, The University of Minnesota, Minneapolis, Minn., 1983.
[18] See Porter and Perry, *EDP: Controls and Auditing*, Ch. 2.

the preparation of the trial balance and making and posting adjusting entries to generating a set of financial statements. Moreover, many of these programs can perform most of the functions mentioned earlier under the section of generalized software, such as statistical sampling and analytical review. In addition, auditors have at their disposal powerful spreadsheet, graphics, and word processing packages for their analysis of the client's records, presentation of their results to management and to the firm's partners. Moreover, with communication packages and database software, auditors in the field can convert client files into their own format for analysis and they can do it from remote locations. Then they can communicate all these results via electronic mail to the firm's office for their superior's review and guidance.

In the future it is anticipated that expert systems based on new artificial intelligence concepts will enhance the audit process even more as the auditor in the field can draw upon the expert knowledge of others to make judgmental decisions. The end result is that the auditor has a powerful decision support system to make his or her audit more effective and efficient. The auditor can then concentrate more on policy issues and assist clients more with their tough accounting decisions.

REPORTING ON THE CONTROL STRUCTURE

As an outgrowth of Watergate and overseas payments by several large corporations, the Foreign Corrupt Practices Act was passed in 1977. This act, along with actions of the Securities and Exchange Commission (SEC), the American Institute of Certified Public Accountants (AICPA), and the Financial Executives Institute's (FEI) Committee on Corporate Reporting, will have a profound impact on internal control and public disclosure of internal control.

The Foreign Corrupt Practices Act, among other things, amends the Securities and Exchange Act of 1934 to require that:

> (2) Every issuer which has a class of securities registered to section 12 of this title and every issuer which is required to file reports pursuant to section 25(d) of this title shall (A) make and keep books, records and accounts, which in reasonable detail, accurately and fairly reflect the transactions and dispositions of the assets of the user; and (B) devise and maintain a system of internal accounting controls sufficient to provide reasonable assurances that:
>
> > (i) transactions are executed in accordance with management's general or specific authorization;
> >
> > (ii) transactions are recorded as necessary (1) to permit preparation of financial statements in conformity with generally accepted accounting principles or any other criteria applicable to such statements, and (2) to maintain accountability for assets;
> >
> > (iii) access to assets is permitted only in accordance with management's general or specific authorization; and

(iv) the recorded accountability for assets is compared with the existing assets at reasonable intervals and appropriate action is taken with respect to any differences.[19]

These requirements are nothing more than a restatement of the definition of accounting control originally codified in Section 320.28 of the *Statement of Auditing Standards No. 1* and superseded by *Proposed Statement of Auditing Standards* on "The Auditor's Responsibility for Assessing Control Risk." The difference is that the former standards are now required.

The AICPA broadened the Foreign Corrupt Practices Act requirement, with the recommendation that management's assessment of the company's accounting system (and the controls over it) accompany the financial statements. This recommendation was endorsed by the FEI.[20]

The SEC proposed a rule and later withdrew this proposal to require that reports filed with the commission contain a statement that the issuer is in compliance with the Foreign Corrupt Practices Act. Upon withdrawal, the commission said it would look to the private sector to develop methods for voluntary disclosure and monitoring of internal records. The AICPA then issued the *Statement on Auditing Standards No. 30*, "Reporting on Internal Control," describing the procedures for different types of engagements for reporting on an entity's system of internal control. It further describes the form of the auditor report for such engagements.[21]

The Auditing Standards Board of the AICPA has subsequently released a discussion draft of a statement on auditing standards entitled "The Communication of Control Structure-Related Matters Noted in an Audit."[22] It provides guidance for reporting to the organizations audit committee or others charged with the same level of responsibility in the organization, such as the board or the owners. It defines reportable conditions and suggests various formats for reporting deficiencies or absence of deficiencies in the control structure involving the control environment, the accounting system, or the control procedures. It should be clear that the reporting of management's and the auditor's assessment of the control structure and its deficiencies is evolving into a well-defined practice.

SUMMARY

In general, the audit of computer systems is a challenge to the accounting profession, but procedures and techniques such as those just reviewed are being developed through continued research to meet this challenge. Regardless of the

---

[19] Securities Exchange Commission, *Foreign Corrupt Practices Act;* and Arthur Young & Co., *Foreign Corrupt Practices Act, 1977* (New York: Arthur Young & Co., 1978), p. 24.

[20] Deloitte, Haskins & Sells, *Internal Accounting Control* (New York: Deloitte Haskins & Sells, 1978).

[21] This sequence of events is outlined in Deloitte, Haskins & Sells, *The Week in Review,* August 15, 1980.

[22] "The Communication of Control Structure-Related Matters Noted in an Audit," *Proposed Statement on Auditing Standards—Draft for Discussion Purposes,* Auditing Standards Board, American Institute of Certified Public Accountants, New York, N.Y., December 1986.

set of techniques and procedures, the auditor must maintain control over their use and the output generated for the audit. Finally, both internal and external auditors should follow traditional practices to verify the results of processing. In the EDP audit, these are characterized by compensating procedures such as third-party confirmation of records, comparisons with other records, and review of procedures for reasonableness.

SELECTED REFERENCES

ABDEL-KHALIK, A. RASHAD, DOUG SNOWBALL and JOHN H. WRAGGE, The effects of Certain Internal Audit Variables on the Planning of External Audit Programs, *The Accounting Review*, April 1983, 215–227.

ALEXANDER, TOM, "Waiting for the Great Computer Rip-Off," *Fortune*, July 1978, pp. 143–52.

ALLEN, BRANDT, "The Biggest Computer Fraud: Lessons for CPAs," *Journal of Accountancy*, May 1977, pp. 52–62.

AMERICAN INSTITUTE OF CERTIFIED PUBLIC ACCOUNTANTS, *Audit Risk and Materiality in Conducting an Audit, Statement on Auditing Standards No. 47*, New York: Auditing Standards Board, 1983.

———*Reporting on Internal Control Statement on Auditing Standards No. 30*, New York: AICPA, Inc., 1980.

———*Statement on Auditing Standards No. 55 Consideration of the Internal Control structure in a Financial Statement Audit*, New York: AICPA, 1988.

———*The Auditor's Responsibility for Assessing Control Risk, Proposed Statement on Auditing Standards—Exposure Draft*, New York: Auditing Standards Board, January 1987.

AMERICAN INSTITUTE OF CERTIFIED PUBLIC ACCOUNTANTS, AUDITING STANDARDS EXECUTIVE COMMITTEE, *Codification of Auditing Standards and Procedures*, Statement on Auditing Standards No. 1, New York: AICPA, Inc., 1972.

CASH, JAMES I., JR., ANDREW D. BAILEY, JR., and ANDREW B. WHINSTON, "A Survey of Techniques for Auditing EDP-Based Accounting Information Systems," *The Accounting Review*, October 1977.

COMMITTEE OF SPONSORING ORGANIZATIONS OF THE TREADWAY COMMISSION, *Internal Control-Integrated Framework-Exposure Draft*, Committee of Sponsoring Organizations, N.Y., N.Y., 1991.

DAVIS, GORDON B., and RON WEBER, *Auditing Advanced EDP Systems: A Survey of Practice and Development of a Theory*, The Management Information Systems Research Center, The University of Minnesota, Minneapolis, Minn., 1983.

GALLEGOS, FREDRICK, DANA R. RICHARDSON, and A. FAY BORTHICK, *Audit and Control of Information Systems*, Cincinnati, Ohio: South-Western Publishing Co., 1987.

MANN, STEVE, "Mac on the Audit Trail," *Macworld*, February 1985, pp. 150–60.

PORTER, W. THOMAS, and WILLIAM E. PERRY, *EDP Controls and Auditing*, Boston, Mass.: Kent Publishing Co., 1987.

RENEAU, J. HAL, "Auditing in the Data Base Environment," *The Journal of Accountancy*, December 1977, pp. 59–65.

WATNE, DONALD A., and PETER B. B. TURNEY, *Auditing EDP Systems*, Englewood Cliffs, N.J.: Prentice Hall, 1984.

WEBER, RON, *EDP Auditing: Conceptual Foundations and Practice*, 2nd ed. New York: McGraw-Hill, 1988.

WEBER, RON, "Audit Trail System Support in Advanced Computer-Based Accounting Systems," *The Accounting Review*, April 1982, pp. 311–25.

REVIEW QUESTIONS

1. How does an integrated test facility (ITF) work? Would you prefer to use or not to use actual data and why? What are some of the problems associated with the use of an ITF? Contrast an ITF with tagging and tracing.

2. What is the questionnaire used for in the audit process? Prepare an internal control questionnaire for general controls related to systems development.

3. What environmental factors would create stress on an accounts receivable system and lead management to convert to: (a) an on-line system; and (b) a database system? What is the theory of systems change? Specifically how can it be used to perform a more effective audit of the (a) on-line system; and (b) database accounts receivable system?

4. Which subsystems are likely to change the most in the implementation of a distributed processing system? What impact will this have on the audit?

5. How can an effective audit trail be established in an on-line distributed processing database system for a corporation which sells tickets to sporting events through terminals located throughout the metropolitan area? What would management use this audit trail for and what features would be of interest to you as the external auditor?

6. The auditor must render a judgment at various stages in the computer audit. What are these stages? Are there any analytical techniques available to assist the auditor in rendering this judgment and what are they? What problems must the auditor overcome, if any, in rendering an unbiased judgment?

7. How can the microcomputer be effectively used to conduct the audit?

8. What is the difference between auditing around the computer and auditing through the computer?

9. What types of test transactions should an auditor include in test data and why?

10. What are the features of generalized audit software? What can it do to expedite an audit?

CASES

20-1 Boos & Baumkirchner, Inc., is a medium-sized manufacturer of products for the leisure-time-activities market. The company has been quite successful and operates three shifts, twenty-four hours a day, seven days a week. During the past year a computer system was installed, and inventory records of finished goods and parts were converted to computer processing. Each record of the inventory master file, which is stored on a magnetic disk, contains the following information:

Item or part number

Description

Size

Unit-of-measure code

Quantity on hand

Cost per unit

Total cost of inventory on hand

Date of last sale or usage

Quantity used or sold this year

Economic order quantity

Vendor code

In preparation for the year-end physical inventory, the client prepares two identical sets of preprinted and prepunched inventory-count cards. One set is for the inventory counts, and the other is to be used by the CPA in test counts. Basic information about the part/item number, description, size, and unit of measure is shown on the card.

In taking the year-end inventory, the firm's personnel mark the actual counted quantity on the face of each card. When all counts are complete, the counted quantity will be along with the other data will be read optically.

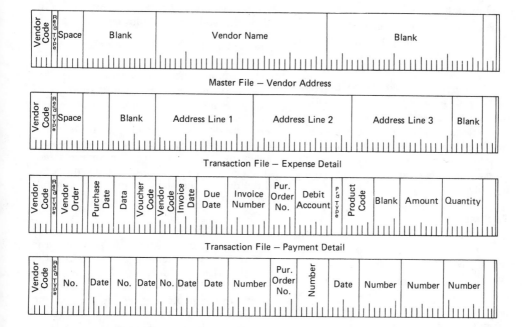

FIGURE C20-1   Tape format for audit of Solt Manufacturing Company.
Source: AICPA adapted

The results of the optical scanning will be processed against the random access disk file, and quantity-on-hand figures will be adjusted to reflect the actual count. A computer listing will be prepared to show missing inventory-count cards and all quantity adjustments of more than $100 in value. These items will be investigated, and all required adjustments will be made. When adjustments have been completed, the final year-end balances will be computed and posted to the general ledger.

The CPA has available a general-purpose audit software package that will run on the client's computer and can process random access files.

REQUIRED: List and describe at least five ways a general-purpose computer audit software package can be used to assist in all aspects of the audit of the inventory of Boos & Baumkirchner, Inc. (For example, the package can be used to read the disk inventory master file and list items and parts with a high unit cost

or total value. Such items can be included in the test counts to increase the dollar coverage of the audit verification.)
(AICPA adapted.)

20-2   Roger Peters, CPA, has examined the financial statements of the Solt Manufacturing Company for several years and is making preliminary plans for the audit of the year ended June 30. During this examination, Mr. Peters plans to use a set of generalized computer audit programs. Solt's EDP manager has agreed to prepare special tapes of data from company records for the CPA's use with the generalized progams.

The following information is applicable to Mr. Peters' examination of Solt's accounts payable and related procedures:

1.   The formats of pertinent tapes are shown in Figure C20-1

2.   The following monthly runs are prepared:

     a.   Cash disbursements by check number

b. Outstanding payables

c. Purchase journals arranged (1) by account charged and (2) by vendor

3. Vouchers and supporting invoices, receiving reports, and purchase order copies are filled by vendor code. Purchase orders and checks are filed numerically.

4. Company records are maintained on magnetic tapes. All tapes are stored in a restricted area within the computer room. A grandfather-father-son policy is followed for retaining and safeguarding tape files.

REQUIRED:

1. Explain the grandfather-father-son policy. Describe how files can be reconstructed when this policy is used.

2. Discuss whether company policies for retaining and safeguarding the tape files provide adequate protection against losses of data.

3. Describe how the CPA could use a generalized computer audit program to audit Solt's accounts payable system.
(AICPA adapted.)

20-3   An auditor is conducting an examination of the financial statements of a wholesale cosmetics distributor with an inventory consisting of thousands of individual items. The distributor keeps its inventory in its own distribution center and in two public warehouses. An inventory computer file is maintained on a computer disk, and at the end of each business day, the file is updated. Each record of the inventory file contains the following data:

a. Item number
b. Location of item
c. Description of item
d. Quantity on hand
e. Cost per item
f. Date of last purchase
g. Date of last sale
h. Quantity sold during year

The auditor is planning to observe the distributor's physical count of inventories as of a given date. The auditor will have available a computer tape of the data on the inventory file on the date of the physical count and generalized audit software.

REQUIRED:

1. The auditor is planning to perform basic inventory auditing procedures. Identify the basic inventory auditing procedures, and describe how the use of the generalized audit software and the tape of the inventory file data might be helpful to the auditor in performing such auditing procedures. Organize your answer as shown in Table C20-1.

2. If this were a complex database system rather than a batch processing system, could the auditor still use generalized audit software? How? Could the auditor make good use of system software in this more complex environment? How?

20-4   You are the internal auditor for a company that is implementing a new on-line update order-entry system. Salespersons enter transactions at intelligent terminals, which validate the

Table C20-1

BASIC INVENTORY AUDITING PROCEDURE	HOW GENERALIZED AUDIT SOFTWARE AND TAPE OF THE INVENTORY FILE DATA MIGHT BE HELPFUL
Observe the physical count, making the recording test counts where applicable.	Determining which items are to be test counted by selecting a random sample of a representative number of items from the inventory file as of the date of the physical count.

input data, check credit, and update a centralized orders master file. The system also is to be integrated with other application systems: inventory, purchasing, billing, accounts payable, cash receipts and disbursements, general ledger.

REQUIRED: Identify three economic events that you might monitor using concurrent auditing techniques. Explain what control objectives you hope to achieve by monitoring the events and why you have chosen these events for monitoring purposes. Why may it be necessary to use concurrent auditing techniques in this example?

20-5   The input transaction for a payroll program contains the following fields:

Employee number

Regular hours

Overtime hours

Expenses

Commissions

Vacation time

Sick time

REQUIRED:

1. Describe what techniques you can use to design a test for this program.
2. List five tests you might carry out to determine whether the input validation program processes the input data correctly.

20-6   At a weekly meeting of your business club, one of your clients excitedly told you of his recent acquisition of a microcomputer for general ledger accounting. Your client was particularly pleased with the hiring of a young man to handle all the processing on the system. This young man not only knows how to program in BASIC, PASCAL, and some other languages but has been a home computer hobbyist for years. During the hiring interview he had proudly displayed several computer circuit boards which he had constructed at home. Your client is convinced that this young man will be able to resolve every problem that could possibly develop with the new system.

REQUIRED:

1. Discuss the control and audit problems you are likely to encounter with your client's system.
2. What controls should you recommend that your client implement for the system?
3. What compliance tests are you going to perform on the controls you have recommended?

20-7   You are completing the Internal Control Questionnaire for systems development and documentation control. In reply to a question on the use of systems development standards, the manager of EDP replies: "We are a fairly small EDP department. We can't afford to maintain a large staff of systems analysts and programmers. Accordingly we purchase our application software from a software vendor and make modifications ourselves to make the programs work for us. Consequently systems development standards and documentation are irrelevant for our organization."

REQUIRED: Comment on the manager's statement from an internal control perspective.

20-8   The records in Table C20-2 are used to update the master file for a job costing system using microcomputer database program. N indicates a numeric field and C indicates a character (Alpha Numeric) field. The master file contains accounts that are the responsibility of each manager of a job:

REQUIRED: Suggest   any   validation checks you think appropriate. Make up any parameter values you need for your tests but make sure they are reasonable. All fields are fixed lengths.

20-9   The First National Bank of Townsend is in the process of installing on-line teller terminals. As an important part of their control system, they are considering backup and recovery methods. They would like to restore the system to the prior state if the system crashes—that is, they need a sysem which would undo the damage caused by the crash.

Table C20-2

CONTROL RECORD STRUCTURE	
Field	*Name, Type, Width, Decimal Places*
001	Record: type,C,1
002	Batch: number,N,4
003	Trans: type,C,4
004	Number: records,N,2
005	Dollar: total,N,9.2
006	Date,N,6

DETAILED RECORD STRUCTURE	
Field	*Name, Type, Width, Decimal Places*
001	Record: type,C,1
002	Trans: type,C,4
003	Account: No,N,12
004	Amount,N,10.2
005	Trans: date,N,6

REQUIRED:

1. How can they prevent the teller from entering the transactions which take place during the time of the crash twice or not at all?

2. Suggest how the First National Bank could establish an audit trail to trace transactions.

20-10 Microcomputer software has been developed to improve the efficiency and effectiveness of the audit. Electronic spreadsheets and other software packages are available to aid in the performance of audit procedures otherwise performed manually.

REQUIRED: Describe the potential benefits to an auditor of using microcomputer software in an audit as compared to performing an audit without the use of a computer.
(AICPA adapted.)

20-11 The Internal Audit Department of Sachem Manufacturing Company is considering the purchase of computer software that will aid the auditing process. Sachem's financial and manufacturing control systems are completely automated on a large mainframe computer. Melinda Robinson, the director of internal audit, believes that Sachem should acquire computer audit software to assist in the financial and procedural audits that her department conducts. The types of software packages that Robinson is considering are described below.

A *generalized audit software package* that assists in basic audit work such as the retrieval of live data from large computer files. The department would review this information using conventional audit investigation techniques. More specifically, the department could perform criteria selection, sampling, basic computations for quantitative analysis, record handling, graphical analysis, and the printing of output (i.e., confirmations).

An *integrated test facility package (ITF)* that uses, monitors, and controls "dummy" test data through existing programs and checks the existence and adequacy of program data entry controls and processing controls.

A *control flowcharting package* that provides a graphical presentation of the data flow of information through a system, pinpointing control strengths and weaknesses.

A *program (parallel) simulation and modeling package* that uses actual data to conduct the same systemized process by using a different computer-logic program developed by the auditor. The package can also be used to seek answers to difficult audit problems (involving many comparisons and computations) within statistically acceptable confidence limits.

REQUIRED:

1. Without regard to any specific computer audit software, identify the general advantages to the internal auditor of using computer audit software to assist with audits.

2. Describe the audit purpose facilitated and the procedural steps to be followed by the internal auditor to use a(n)

   a. generalized audit software package.

   b. integrated test facility package.

   c. control flowcharting package.

   d. program (parallel) simulation and modeling package. (Adapted from CMA exam.)

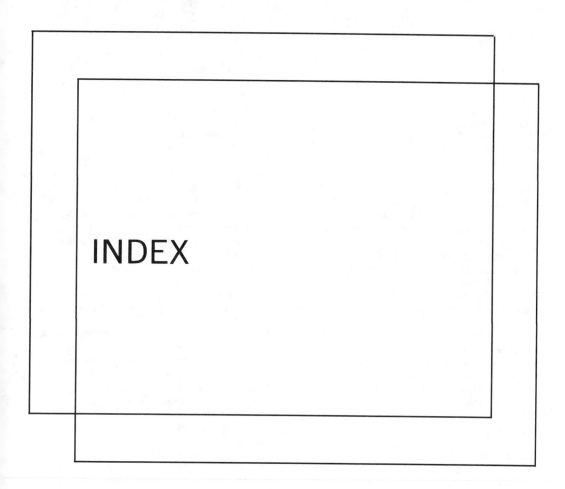

INDEX